HIRAGANA	KATAKANA	ROMAJI	HIRAGANA	KATAKANA	ROMAJI	HIRAGANA	KATAKANA	ROMAJI	HIRAGANA	KATAKANA	ROMAJI	HIRAGANA	KATAKANA	ROMAJI	HIRAGANA	KATAKANA	ROMAJI
			ま	マ	ma	や	ヤ	ya	ら	ラ	ra	わ	ワ	wa	ん	ン	n
			み	ミ	mi				り	リ	ri						
			む	ム	mu	ゆ	ユ	yu	る	ル	ru						
			め	メ	me				れ	レ	re						
			も	モ	mo	よ	ヨ	yo	ろ	ロ	ro	を	ヲ	o			
			みゃ	ミャ	mya				りゃ	リャ	rya						
			みゅ	ミュ	myu				りゅ	リュ	ryu						
			みょ	ミョ	myo				りょ	リョ	ryo						

ぱ	パ	pa															
ぴ	ピ	pi															
ぷ	プ	pu															
ぺ	ペ	pe															
ぽ	ポ	po															
ぴゃ	ピャ	pya															
ぴゅ	ピュ	pyu															
ぴょ	ピョ	pyo															

4. Although ぢ(ヂ) and づ(ヅ) are pronounced the same as じ(ジ) and ず(ズ) their use is limited to the following situations:

   (a) The voicing of the initial consonant of the second part of a compound, as when はな "nose" and ち "bleed" join to make はなぢ "nosebleed".

   (a) Repetition of the same sound, as in つづく "to continue".

For further explanation refer to the introductory essay at the beginning of this text.

JAPANESE FOR EVERYONE

◉ジャパニーズ・フォー・エブリワン

A FUNCTIONAL APPROACH TO DAILY COMMUNICATION

Gakken

Authors

Susumu NAGARA — Ph. D. in Linguistics, Emeritus, University of Michigan, Professor of International Communication, Hijiyama College (Hiroshima)

Yaeko NAKANISHI — Associate Professor of Japanese, Dokkyo University
Atsuo IGUCHI — Lecturer of Japanese, Dokkyo University
Naoko CHINO — Lecturer of Japanese, Sophia University
Akiko SHIMOMURA — Lecturer of Japanese, Sophia University
Hisayo YOKOBAYASHI — Associate Professor of School of International Studies, Kagoshima Immaculate Heart University
Yoichi YAMAURA — Lecturer of Japanese, Sophia University
Shin'ichi HAYASHI — Associate Professor of Japanese, Yamaguchi University
Nobuko HAYASHI — Instructor of Japanese, ORBIS
Akira SAITO — Educational Adviser of Japanese Language Division, Japan College of Foreign Languages

Foreword : Edward SEIDENSTICKER Professor Emeritus of Japanese, University of Columbia
Pronunciation Section Adviser : Junko HIBIYA Assistant Professor of Japanese, Keio University
English Editorial Adviser : Dave TELKE
Translation Adviser : Gaynor SEKIMORI (LOGOSTIKS)
Illustrations : Andy BOERGER
Mayumi TAKANO (E.D. sha Co., Ltd.)
Book Design : Hiroto KUMAGAI
Editorial Staff : Toshio ICHIKAWA
Sayomi NISHI
Publishing Manager (Planning) : Yukio TACHIBANA
Photographs (Jacket) : COLOR BOX
SEKAI BUNKA PHOTO

JAPANESE FOR EVERYONE

Published by GAKKEN Co., Ltd.
4-40-5 Kami-ikedai, Ohta-ku, Tokyo 145, Japan

Overseas distributors : Japan Publications Trading Co., Ltd.
P.O.Box 5030 Tokyo International, Tokyo 100-31, Japan

Distributors :
UNITED STATES: Kodansha America, Inc., through Oxford University Press
198 Madison Avenue, New York, NY 10016.
CANADA : Fitzhenry & Whiteside Ltd., 195 Allstate Parkway, Markham, Ontario L3R 4T8.
BRITISH ISLES AND EUROPEAN CONTINENT : Premier Book Marketing Ltd., 1 Gower Street, London WC1E 6HA
AUSTRALIA AND NEW ZEALAND : Bookwise International, 54 Crittenden Road, Findon, South Australia 5023.
THE FAR EAST AND JAPAN : Japan Publications Trading Co., Ltd., 1-2-1 Sarugaku-cho, Chiyoda-ku, Tokyo 101, Japan.

First edition 1990
Eighteenth printing 1997

ISBN: 0-87040-853-4
ISBN: 4-05-150723-8 (in Japan)
Printed in Japan

FOREWORD

A text which does not pretend that Japanese is an easy language, to be mastered in thirty hours or so, as some of the titles have it, but which offers all the advice and guidance possible is most welcome. Many texts make things seem easy by shunning the written language. This one does not. It quietly introduces the kana syllabary from the outset, and shortly begins introducing Chinese characters, and so the student is nudged into getting to work. All languages are difficult, but they are difficult in different ways. With Japanese the most stubborn problem is the complex system of writing. To pretend that it does not exist is dishonest. Not to make a huge thing of it but to confront it by carefully chosen and defined stages is realistically honest.

I think that my own early pains might have been lessened if I had had such a text. We who studied Japanese during the war, almost a half century ago, were thrown into the water and told to swim. In the years since, it has become evident that the student is less troubled if he or she has someone to explain a few things. This text explains things in an unobtrusive and friendly manner, all the while leading the way gently from problem to problem.

Professor Nagara is an old friend and someone who seems eminently qualified to do the work. We were together for some years at the University of Michigan. I found him unfailingly helpful when I had problems with the language —— and after all these years I go on having them. It is, I believe, the common lot. Several of the other contributors are old friends as well. I am happy to make this tiny contribution to the book both because it is a good book and because it is like a reunion.

Edward Seidensticker

PREFACE

There has been a steady increase in the number of elementary Japanese textbooks since a sudden surge of interest in the study of the language became apparent in the late seventies. Our justifications in adding one more to this constantly expanding reservoir of materials for beginning learners are numerous. For example, this text aims exclusively at the development of communicative skills in Japanese by following a notional-functional approach. Each lesson centers around the experience of a young American couple, Michael and Barbara Webb, who arrive at Narita Airport in Lesson 1. Your Japanese language learning progresses as they gain experience in dealing with various situations in subsequent lessons.

The vocabulary for each lesson was carefully selected so that it would provide the knowledge of Japanese essential for the newly arrived foreign businessman as well as the beginning learner. The functional assignments and accompanying grammatical practices selected for each lesson are all pertinent to the situation the two people are placed in. Special care was taken to make this textbook fill the needs of self-teaching learners, as well as those of the classroom. In order to free itself from the persistent accusation that Japanese language textbooks are skimpy in both the amount and variety of exercises, we have tried to supply an abundance of such material covering a full range of applications and usage. Taped exercises are also provided.

Susumu Nagara

CONTENTS

INTRODUCTION

Ⅰ. General Structure of This Textbook

This textbook contains 27 lessons. Lesson 1～26 consist of ① Dialogues in Japanese, ② Vocabulary, ③ Dialogue Comprehension Exercises, ④ Dialogues in English, ⑤ Functional Explanations, and ⑥ Grammatical Notes, when necessary. Functional and grammatical exercises are incorporated into ⑤ and ⑥, and are followed by ⑦ Reading Comprehension Exercises and ⑧ Listening Comprehension Exercises.

① All dialogues are conducted in natural, everyday spoken Japanese. They are somewhat longer and more substantial in content than what is found in most introductory texts. Their purpose is to familiarize you with genuine communication in context. Rather than memorize entire dialogues as such, concentrate on mastering those expressions most useful to your communication needs.

② Approximately 2,500 words and expressions are introduced in this text. New items appearing in the dialogues are explained in the vocabulary, with accent indicated for nouns, adjectives, adverbs, and verbs. New words appearing in other sections of each lesson are explained in additional vocabulary insertions. A listing of all vocabulary items is also provided in the index at the back of the book.

③ In order to test your understanding of the dialogues, complete the comprehension exercises before consulting the English translations.

④ The English translations of the dialogues attempt to preserve as much of the structure and flavor of the original Japanese as possible, without becoming excessively unnatural as English.

⑤, ⑥ Functional and grammatical explanations are detailed enough so that self-learners can benefit from them. Functions for each lesson are selected in relation to the specific context. Since the emphasis is on human relationships and levels of formality rather than on formal grammar, various expressions for specific communication functions are studied whenever they are considerd to be appropriate for your progress in learning. For example, in Lesson 1, Function Ⅴ (p. 27), various expressions for requests and responses are introduced. You are advised to select the ones most suited to your purposes and learn them well. In most cases, suitable forms will be in polite speech.

⑦ In contrast to the spoken language of the dialogues reading comprehension passages are intended to give you exposure to Japanese written style of speech. As with the dialogues, you are encouraged to grasp the general meaning of the passage, even though you may not be sure of the meaning of some of the words. Various types of writing including diaries, sales slips, signs and personal memos are presented so as to prepare you for what you are likely to encounter on a trip to Japan.

⑧ It is important to gain exposure to the sound and natural flow of the language from the beginning of your foreign language learning experience. The more you listen, the easier it will be to grasp what is being said. For persons unable to listen to the tapes, the scripts for all recorded materials are provided at the back of the book. Either have a native speaker read them for you, or practice reading them with a friend.

Ⅱ. Suggested Procedure for Using This Text:

First of all listen to the tape without looking at the text. When you have listened to the tape several times and feel you can hear the sounds distinctly, read the text while following the recorded tapes. When you feel confident that you recognize the sounds of the dialogue, try to imitate the Japanese pronunciation by following the recorded tapes. Next try to grasp the general meaning of the dialogue by looking up the meaning of the words in the vocabulary section. When you feel you understand the overall meaning of the dialogues, check it by attempting the Dialogue Comprehension Exercise. You may rely on the Dialogues in English in the early stages, however after Lesson 8 you should try to guess the meaning of the dialogues from the beginning, relying on the context for clues, rather than consulting the English translations.

Ⅲ. Special Features of This Text:

1. Minimal Use of *Romaji*

Anyone who has visited Japan after acquiring only a knowledge of the Romanized writing system will attest to the minimal use of *romaji* in real life. In addition, there have been too many instances in which an initial knowledge of '*romaji*' turned out to be a hindrance toward the acquisition of good Japanese speech habits. To be successful in using this text you must master the use of *Hiragana* and *Katakana* from the start. Begin by reading the explanation of the Japanese writing system on pp. 14-15. All example sentences are written in *Kana* beginning with Lesson 1. *Romaji* is supplied only through Lesson 3. To help you master *Hiragana* and *Katakana* more rapidly, *romaji* is printed in red, which becomes invisible when applying a red transparency if available. *Kana* syllabary charts are also found attached to the inside of the front cover for easy reference.

2. Communicative Goals

In this text we tried to take advantage of the various good points of both the functional syllabus and the structural syllabus. Accordingly explanations are made in as far as possible from the standpoint of function, with inflections and other grammatical features which cannot be classified as functions treated as grammar notes.

3. Unlike the textbooks published so far, we tried as much as possible to stay away from formal grammatical exercises. Instead, we have included numerous exercises to be completed in consideration of inter-personal relationships and situations shown by illustrations. Levels of formality and sentence styles are emphasized in these exercises.

Abbreviations and Notations

u-verb	verb ending in a consonant	「　」	Japanese quotation marks
ru-verb	verb ending in a vowel	～する	indicates nouns which form verbs by adding「する」"to do".
vi	intransitive verb		ex.　べんきょうする →べんきょう (noun) "study" →べんきょうする (verb) "to study"
vt	transitive verb		
adj.	adjective		
(な)	な-adjective		
[*romaji*]	pronunciation		
─┐	accent marker		

STRUCTURE OF THE JAPANESE LANGUAGE

The following explanations of Japanese pronunciation, writing and grammar should be read before beginning actual study of the lessons. They are intended as an introduction to help start you off on the right foot, and are by no means exhaustive or complete. You might have questions, or certain things might seem unclear. Certainly you will find that the order in which we present things differs from that followed by other texts. We have chosen this order with the conviction that it is the most meaningful way to present the material to English speakers studying the Japanese language. We are certain that all your questions will be answered as you progress in the study of the lessons.

I. Pronunciation of Japanese

A. Rhythm

For speakers of English, the greatest difficulty in learning to speak Japanese so that it really sounds like Japanese is not individual sounds so much as rhythm. English is accent timed. Accented syllables tend to be spaced evenly throughout a spoken utterance, each one receiving one beat, with any number of unaccented syllables crammed in on the upbeat. Individual sounds, of varying lengths to begin with, are further lengthened if accented or shortened if unaccented, resulting in a flow of sound that resembles a melody composed of whole, half, quarter, eighth and sixteenth notes.

In contrast, Japanese is syllable timed. The basic rule for speaking Japanese is to pronounce each and every syllable exactly the same length, and never lengthen or shorten a sound due to accent. In musical terms, we might say that Japanese is like a melody composed entirely of quarter notes, with each quarter note receiving one beat. This is why Japanese tends to sound monotonous or "machine gun-like" to the English ear. On the other hand, spoken with English rhythm, Japanese sounds turbulent or sloppy to the Japanese ear.

The following shows the phrase 「*watakushi wa*」 "as for me" pronounced with English and Japanese style rhythms:

English rhythm: *wa ta kushi wa* (the second and final syllables are accented and lengthened. ku and shi are crammed together into a single syllable.)
Japanese rhythm: *wa ta ku shi wa* (no accent, all syllables the same length)

B. Sounds and Syllables

1. Sounds

a. Vowels — Japanese has five vowels, pronounced as follows:

[*a*] as in "father" [*i*] as in "beet" or "bit" [*u*] as in "boot"
[*e*] as in "bait" or "bet" [*o*] as in "boat"

Caution ; (1) Always pronounce vowel sounds clearly and the same length. Never let them sound like "uh" as in "mother". (2) Do not round your lips when pronouncing [u] and [o] as you do in English. Practice saying these sounds, holding your lips apart with your fingers. (3) When [i] and [u] come between any pair of the voiceless sounds [p, t, ts, ch, k, s, sh, h] or [f] they tend to be whispered. Practice whispering [i̊] and [ů] in the following:

wa ta ků shi "I" / *shi̊ chi* "seven" / *sů ki ya ki* "*sukiyaki*" / *e n pi̊ tsu* "pencil"

b. Consonants —— Most consonant sounds are pronounced pretty much as they are in English and should present no problems, as seen by the sample words on the *Hiragana* chart in the following section. The following sounds however sometimes cause problems and require a word of explanation:

[*ts*] as in "cats". [ts] is common at the end of words in English, but there are only two examples where it comes at the beginning or middle: "tsunami" and "tsetse fly". In Japanese, [ts] usually appears only before the vowel [u].

[*g*] as in "get" or "go". Some speakers pronounce [g] so that it sounds like [ng] in the middle of a word. Either pronunciation is fine.

[*w*] as in "want". Practice saying [wa] without rounding your lips, as with [u] and [o].

[*h/f*] **f** is written before [u], **h** is written before [a, i, e, o] and [y]. [f] is pronounced with only a slight amount of friction between the upper and lower lips. Avoid pronouncing it like English [f], with a large amount of friction between the upper teeth and lower lip.

[*r*] Japanese [r] is nothing like the [r] in American English. It is made by lightly tapping the tip of the tongue just behind the teeth, in approximately the same position you place your tongue to say [l]. In the case of [l], the tongue is held in place momentarily while air is pushed out at the sides of the tongue. With Japanese [r], the tapping movement is so quick that air pressure has no time to build up, and is much like the technique of tonguing in brass and woodwind instruments.

2. Syllables

a. Syllables consist of a single vowel alone, or a vowel preceeded by either a consonant or a consonant + [y] sequence. See the *Hiragana* and *Katakana* charts in the following section for a complete listing of all Japanese syllables.

Often two or more vowels come together in series. Remember to pronounce each vowel with its proper sound and length. When two or more of the same vowels come together, simply hold the sound for the proper number of beats.

いえ	*i e*	"house"	おかあさん	*o ka a sa n*	"mother"
はい	*ha i*	"yes"	いいえ	*i i e*	"no"
あおい	*a o i*	"blue"	おおい	*o o i*	"many, much"
じゅうがつ	*ju u ga tsu*	"October"	おじいさん	*o ji i sa n*	"grandfather"

There are two exceptions to the above. When pronouncing the vowel sequences [ei] and [ou], modern speakers of Japanese often don't bother to give the second sound its proper value. Instead [ei] sounds like [ee], and [ou] sounds like [oo]. Consequently, we have romanized all such sequences as [ee] and [oo] in this book.

けいざい [*keezai*] "economy"　　おとうさん [*otoosan*] "father"

Practice reading and pronouncing the following sequences:

えい [*ee*]　せい [*see*]　てい [*tee*]　ねい [*nee*]　へい [*hee*]　めい [*mee*]　れい [*ree*]

おう [*oo*]　こう [*koo*]　そう [*soo*]　のう [*noo*]　ほう [*hoo*]　もう [*moo*]　ろう [*roo*]

b. Syllabic consonants —— In certain situations consonants themselves appear as syllables and are held for one beat. Syllabic consonants are indicated by a small「っ」in *Hiragana* (「ッ」in *Katakana*), and are spelled as double consonants (pp, tt, tts, tch, kk, ss, ssh, dd, gg). Practice distinguishing between ordinary consonants and syllabic consonants in the following pairs:

いた	*i ta*	"was here"	いった	*i t ta*	"went"
いち	*i chi*	"one"	いっち	*i t chi*	"match, coincide"
えど	*e do*	"Edo" (the old name for Tokyo)	ベッド	*be d do*	"bed"
にさい	*ni sa i*	"two years old"	いっさい	*i s sa i*	"one year old"
いこう	*i ko o*	"let's go"	にっこう	*ni k ko o*	"sunshine"

c. Syllabic nasal —— *Hiragana*「ん」(*Katakana*「ン」) represents a nasal sound held for one beat. In this book it is spelled **n**, but actual pronunciation is determined by whatever sound follows it.「ん」is pronounced:

[*m*]　before p, b, m (ex; えんぴつ enpitsu, pronounced *e m pi tsu*)
[*n*]　before t, ts, ch, s, d, j, z, n, r (ex; のんだ nonda, pronounced *no n da*)
[*ng*]　before k, g, ng (ex; にほんご nihongo, pronounced *ni ho ng go*)

Before vowels, [y] or [w], or when it comes at the end of a word,「ん」is pronounced similar to [ng], except that the top of the tongue does not touch the roof of the mouth and block the flow of air. While [ng] is pronounced with air flowing out of the nose only,「ん」before vowels, [y] or [w], or at the end of a word is pronounced with air flowing out of both the nose and mouth. (After you become proficient at making this sound, you might try using it before s, z, and r as well.)

In *romaji*, syllabic nasal「ん」coming before a vowel is written **n'** so as to distinguish it from the ordinary consonant **n**. Practice pronouncing the following words, remembering to give「ん」one beat:

きねん	*ki ne n*	"commemoration"	きんえん	*ki n' e n*	"no smoking"
さんねん	*sa n ne n*	"three years"	さんえん	*sa n' e n*	"three yen"

C. Word Accent

Different languages have different systems of accenting. In English, accented syllables are pronounced louder, longer and more clearly than unaccented syllables. In Japanese, accent has nothing to do with loudness, length or clarity of enunciation. Rather it involves changes in voice pitch.

Japanese words are pronounced on two levels of pitch, low and high. The first syllable of a word is pronounced low, with the second and subsequent syllables pronounced high, until an accented syllable is reached. An accented syllable is the last syllable of the word to be pronounced high, and in this book is marked with a ⏋. All syllables after the accent are pronounced low until the end of the word.

Different words have accents falling on different syllables. In words where the accent falls on the first syllable, the first syllable is pronounced high and subsequent syllables are pronounced low. In words where the accent falls on the final syllable, the first syllable of the following word is low. Some words have no accent. In such cases there is no fall from high to low, and the initial syllable of the following word continues at high pitch.

The following chart illustrates these various accent patterns for words of one, two, three and four syllables. ◯ represents the first syllable of the following word.

Word Accent Patterns

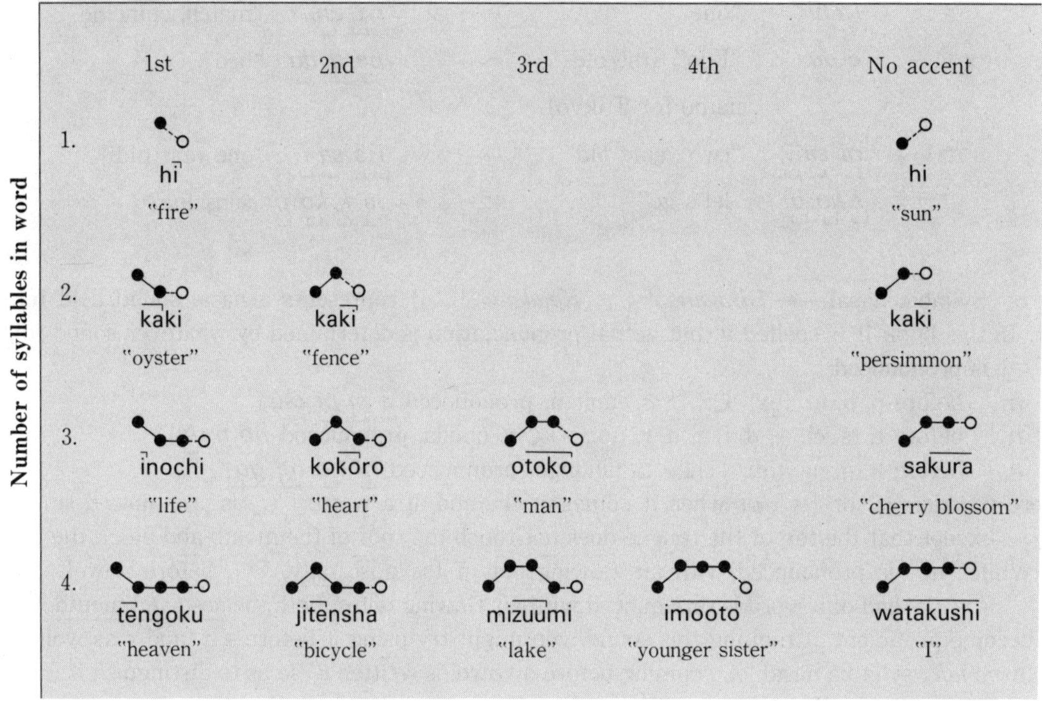

D. Sentence Intonation and Stress

Intonation and stress operate in Japanese is much the same way as in English. The best way to learn is to listen carefully to sentences on the tape and imitate as closely as possible.

II. The Japanese Writing System

Ordinary written Japanese employs a mixture of *'Kanji'*, or Chinese characters, together with two syllabic alphabets known as *'Hiragana'* and *'Katakana'*. *Kanji* are used for representing concrete concepts expressed as nouns, verbs, and adjectives and adverbs. *Hiragana* is used to write various grammatical markers, inflectional endings and other words not written in *Kanji*, while *Katakana* is generally reserved for words and names borrowed from other languages, excepting Chinese. You will be gradually introduced to some of the more essential *Kanji* beginning in Lesson 1, with a more detailed description found on pages 94 and 95. *Hiragana* and *Katakana* syllabary charts are shown below, including romanized representation and sample English words to serve as pronunciation helps. These charts should be memorized as quickly as possible.

HIRAGANA

1. **Vowels** あ [a] father い [i] ink う [u] two え [e] egg お [o] open

2. **Consonant + vowel**

(k)	か	[ka]	comic	き	[ki]	key	く	[ku]	coop	け	[ke]	kettle	こ	[ko]	coat
(s)	さ	[sa]	socks	し	[shi]	sheep	す	[su]	soup	せ	[se]	settle	そ	[so]	sew
(t)	た	[ta]	top	ち	[chi]	cheese	つ	[tsu]	tsunami	て	[te]	tent	と	[to]	tone
(n)	な	[na]	not	に	[ni]	knee	ぬ	[nu]	noodle	ね	[ne]	neck	の	[no]	know
(h)	は	[ha]	hocky	ひ	[hi]	heat	ふ	[fu]	food	へ	[he]	hem	ほ	[ho]	hope
(m)	ま	[ma]	mom	み	[mi]	me	む	[mu]	moon	め	[me]	menu	も	[mo]	moan
(y)	や	[ya]	yarn				ゆ	[yu]	uniform				よ	[yo]	yoyo
(r)	ら	[ra]	lock	り	[ri]	leak	る	[ru]	loon	れ	[re]	led	ろ	[ro]	loan
(w)	わ	[wa]	wand										を	[o]	open

3. **Syllabics** っ [tsu] ん [n] (see Sounds and Syllables for pronunciation)

4. **Consonant + y + vowel**

きゃ	[kya]	きゅ	[kyu]	きょ	[kyo]	しゃ	[sha]	しゅ	[shu]	しょ	[sho]
ちゃ	[cha]	ちゅ	[chu]	ちょ	[cho]	にゃ	[nya]	にゅ	[nyu]	にょ	[nyo]
ひゃ	[hya]	ひゅ	[hyu]	ひょ	[hyo]	みゃ	[mya]	みゅ	[myu]	みょ	[myo]
りゃ	[rya]	りゅ	[ryu]	りょ	[ryo]	ぎゃ	[gya]	ぎゅ	[gyu]	ぎょ	[gyo]
じゃ	[ja]	じゅ	[ju]	じょ	[jo]	びゃ	[bya]	びゅ	[byu]	びょ	[byo]
ぴゃ	[pya]	ぴゅ	[pyu]	ぴょ	[pyo]						

Note: The direct object particle [o] is written「を」, the direction particle [e] is written「へ」, and the topic marker [wa] is written「は」

KATAKANA

ア	[a]	イ	[i]	ウ	[u]	エ	[e]	オ	[o]
カ	[ka]	キ	[ki]	ク	[ku]	ケ	[ke]	コ	[ko]
サ	[sa]	シ	[shi]	ス	[su]	セ	[se]	ソ	[so]
タ	[ta]	チ	[chi]	ツ	[tsu]	テ	[te]	ト	[to]
ナ	[na]	ニ	[ni]	ヌ	[nu]	ネ	[ne]	ノ	[no]
ハ	[ha]	ヒ	[hi]	フ	[fu]	ヘ	[he]	ホ	[ho]
マ	[ma]	ミ	[mi]	ム	[mu]	メ	[me]	モ	[mo]
ヤ	[ya]			ユ	[yu]			ヨ	[yo]
ラ	[ra]	リ	[ri]	ル	[ru]	レ	[re]	ロ	[ro]
ワ	[wa]	ヲ	[o]	ン	[n]				

III. Outline of Japanese Grammar

A. Sentence Structure

English sentences are generally arranged SUBJECT－VERB－OBJECT. In Japanese the basic structure is SUBJECT－OBJECT－VERBAL, with the verbal (including verbs, be-verb, adjectives and な-adjectives) coming at the end. Thus, such English sentences as "Today is Friday." and "Johnny ran to school.", appear in Japanese as, "Today Friday is." and "Johnny to school ran".

The order in which information is presented in the sentence is also different. In English important information tends to be given first, with less important items tacked on the end. In Japanese less important items are gotten out of the way first, setting the stage for the important information which comes at the end. Hence the impression that Japanese sentences are somehow 'backward'.

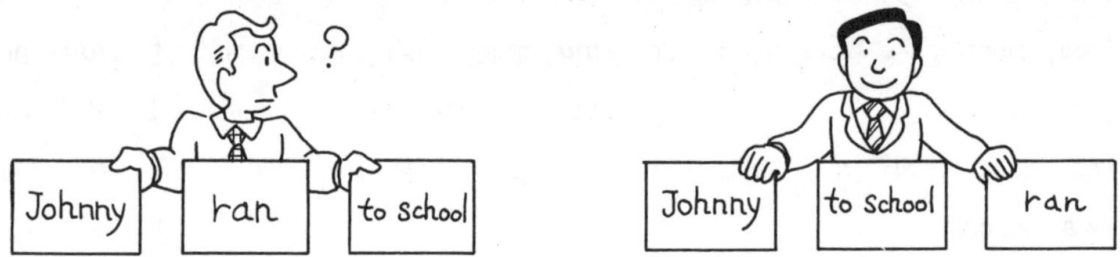

In English items obvious from the situation or context are commonly referred to by pronoun. In Japanese pronouns are less often used. Rather, known items are simply deleted from the sentence, resulting in sentences with no subject, transitive verbs with no direct object, indeed sentences consisting of verbs alone.

B. Grammatical Function within the Sentence

Subject, direct object, indirect object, location, time, etc. are determined in English by position before or after the verb, or by means of prepositions (to, in, at, etc.). In Japanese, function within the sentence is indicated by a series of markers attached after the word or phrase they mark, and known as "particles" or "postpositions". Some typical particles include が[ga] subject, を[o] direct object, に[ni] indirect object, location, time, etc., へ[e] direction. A list of particles and their use is given inside the back cover.

C. Sentence Topic: は [wa]

The particle は[wa] functions to introduce the topic of the sentence, i.e. the thing the sentence makes a statement about. Although not often used in English, sentences with topics can be made using such expressions as, "as for __", "regarding __", "about __", etc. The normal English sentence, "Johnny ran to school.", where Johnny appears as the subject, becomes, "As for Johnny, (he) ran to school." where Johnny is the topic, and "ran to school" is a statement about Johnny.

Most sentences in Japanese have topics, whether stated explicitly or assumed from context. Learning to handle such sentences properly is one of the greatest problems facing the beginning student.

D. Verbals and Verbal Inflection

In English, verb tense, aspect, voice, etc. are expressed by means of inflectional endings (-ed, -ing) and various auxiliary verb forms (is, am, be, should, etc.). Japanese verbals operate in essentially the same manner, with inflectional endings and auxiliaries added to the end of the various verbals. The discussion below is illustrated on the following Verbal Inflection Charts.

1. Verbs

(a) The root contains the meaning of the verb. There are two types of verb roots, those ending in consonants (known as "u-verbs"), and those ending in vowels (known as "ru-verbs"). Inflection patterns and the shape of certain endings differ between these two types. Also there are three irregular verbs whose various forms have to be memorized individually.

(b) The plain non-past form corresponds to present and future tense in English, and is the form in which verbs appear in the dictionary.

(c) The negative form is made by adding the negative auxiliary 「*nai*」. Note the addition of the vowel [a] to the end of u-verb roots. 「*Nai*」 is further inflected as shown in chart 3.

(d) The polite form is made by adding the polite auxiliary 「～*masu*」, which is further inflected as shown in chart 4. Note that u-verb roots have an [i] added, while ru-verb roots remain the same. This form is known as the "i-stem" (also called "continuative stem", or simply "stem"), and may be used alone with certain verbs to function as a noun.

(e) The て-form means "__ and", and is employed in a variety of grammatical constructions.

All other inflections and auxiliaries attach to the verb root following one of the above four patterns. A listing is given in Appendix 1. (p.334)

2. Be-verb

The be-verb (introduced in Lesson 1) is inflected much like verbs, but with fewer forms. The plain non-past 「*da*」 has two varient forms (「*na*」 and 「*no*」) used in certain grammatical constructions. In the negative form, the syllables [*dewa*] are often contracted to [*ja*] in both speaking and writing. Inflection of the polite be-verb 「*desu*」 is shown in Chart 4.

3. I (い) -adjectives, Na (な) -adjectives and Negative 「*nai*」

い-adjectives appear in the dictionary in their plain non-past forms, while な-adjectives are listed in their root forms and marked with (な). な-adjectives inflection parallels that of the be-verb, and there is an alternate plain non-past form 「*na*」 important in certain grammatical constructions.

Negative 「*nai*」 is inflected much like い-adjectives, except note the two て-forms used in different grammatical constructions.

E. Styles of Speech

Different styles of speech are used in Japanese depending on who is speaking to whom, what is being talked about, and the context in which the conversation takes place. In this text we learn to handle polite and plain styles, and become familiar with commonly used respect language terms and expressions.

1. Polite speech— is used in formal situations where participants interact rather like "representatives" engaging in "official business". Polite speech is used in business, in the class room, when addressing an audience, when speaking to a superior, shopping, or when speaking to a stranger on the street. Polite speech is characterized by use of the polite verbal forms 「*desu*」 and 「～*masu*」.

2. Plain speech— is used in informal, everyday situations between family, friends, equals, or when addressing inferiors such as children. Most thinking is done in plain speech, and plain speech forms the basis for most grammatical constructions. Plain speech is characterized by use of plain verbal forms.

3. Respect language—Besides the use of polite speech, further respect may be shown by the use of honorific terms when referring to others, and humble terms when referring to oneself.

VERBAL INFLECTION CHARTS

1. Verbs

	(a) Root	(b) Plain non-past	(c) Negative	(d) Polite (stem＋masu)
Verbs ending in consonants (u-verbs)	kak- (write) kog- (row) kas- (lend) shin- (die) yob- (call) nom- (drink) mat- (wait) kir- (cut) kaw- (buy)	kak-u kog-u kas-u shin-u yob-u nom-u mats-u kir-u ka-u	kaka-nai koga-nai kasa-nai shina-nai yoba-nai noma-nai mata-nai kira-nai kawa-nai	kaki-masu kogi-masu kashi-masu shini-masu yobi-masu nomi-masu machi-masu kiri-masu kai-masu
Verbs ending in vowels (ru-verbs)	mi- (see) tabe- (eat)	mi-ru tabe-ru	mi-nai tabe-nai	mi-masu tabe-masu
Irregular verbs	ik- (go) ku- (come) su- (do)	ik-u ku-ru su-ru	ika-nai ko-nai shi-nai	iki-masu ki-masu shi-masu

2. Be-verb

	Plain non-past	Negative	Polite
	da (is) (na, no)	dewa-nai (ja)	desu

3. Adjectives and Negative「nai」

	Root	Plain non-past	Adverbial	Negative
Adjectives (i-adj.)	taka- (high) yo/i- (good)	taka -i yo/i -i	taka-ku yo-ku	taka-ku-(wa)nai yo-ku-(wa)nai
Negative「nai」	na-	na-i	na-ku	na-ku-(wa)nai
Na-adjectives	shizuka-	shizuka-da (-na)	shizuka-ni	shizuka-dewa-nai (ja)

4. Polite「desu」and「〜masu」

	Polite negative	Probability / Let's form	て-form	Polite past	Polite negative past
desu	dewa nai desu dewa arimasen (ja)	deshoo	de	deshi-ta	dewa nakatta desu dewa arimasen (ja) deshita
〜masu	〜masen	〜mashoo	〜mashite	〜mashita	〜masen deshita

Imperative	Let's form	(e) て-form	Past
kak-e kog-e kas-e shin-e yob-e nom-e mat-e kir-e ka-e	kak-oo kog-oo kas-oo shin-oo yob-oo nom-oo mat-oo kir-oo ka-oo	kai-te koi-de kashi-te shin-de yon-de non-de mat-te kit-te kat-te	kai-ta koi-da kashi-ta shin-da yon-da non-da mat-ta kit-ta kat-ta
mi-ro tabe-ro	mi-yoo tabe-yoo	mi-te tabe-te	mi-ta tabe-ta
ik-e ko-i shi-ro	ik-oo ko-yoo shi-yoo	it-te ki-te shi-te	it-ta ki-ta shi-ta

	Probability	て-form	Past
	daroo	de	datta

Polite	Probability	て-form	Past
taka-i desu i-i desu	taka-i daroo i-i daroo	taka-ku-te yo-ku-te	taka-katta yo-katta
na-i desu	na-i daroo	na-ku-te na-i -de	na-katta
shizuka-desu	shizuka daroo	shizuka-de	shizuka-datta

CHARACTERIZATION

Michael Webb (32) is a business school graduate who has just found a job with Abe Sangyo, a medium-sized producer of industrial equipment with headquarters in Tokyo. With previous experience working in a bank, Michael is a quiet, serious young man who puts work before pleasure. He comes to Japan with his wife, Barbara.

Barbara Webb (30), originally from Canada, is active, adventurous and outgoing. She wants to try anything and everything.

The Webbs expect to stay in Tokyo for one year, and then transfer to the Osaka branch to help prepare for the opening of the company's new office in San Francisco.

パスポートを　みせてください

Show Me Your Passport Please

Dialogue I

Immigrations

1 Imm. Officer: パスポートを　みせてください。
pasupooto o misete kudasai.

2 マイケル（まいける）: はい。
hai.

3 Imm. Officer: マイケル・ウエッブさんですね。
Maikeru Uebbu-san desu ne.

4 マイケル: ええ、そうです。
ee, soo desu.

5 Imm. officer: かんこうですか、しごとですか。
kankoo desu ka, shigoto desu ka?

6 マイケル: かんこうじゃありません。しごとです。
kankoo ja arimasen. shigoto desu.

Dialogue II

Customs declaration

7 Cus. Officer: スーツケースを　あけてください。
suutsukeesu o akete kudasai.

8 マイケル（まいける）: はい、どうぞ。
hai, doozo.

9 Cus. Officer: これは、なんですか。くすりですか。
kore wa, nan desu ka? kusuri desu ka?

10 マイケル: いいえ、くすりじゃありません。
iie, kusuri ja arimasen.

11 Cus. Officer: じゃ、なんですか。
ja, nan desu ka?

12 マイケル: はちみつです。
hachimitsu desu.

13 Cus. Officer: みせてください。どうも。はい、いいですよ。
misete kudasai. doomo. hai, ii desu yo.

14 ああ、それは、なんですか。
aa, sore wa, nan desu ka?

15 バーバラ（ばーばら）: どれですか。
dore desu ka?

16 Cus. Officer: それです。なんですか。あけてください。
sore desu. nan desu ka? akete kudasai.

17 バーバラ: これは……。あの、じつは……、ハムです。
kore wa.... ano, jitsu wa...., hamu desu.

18 Cus. Officer: ハムですか。ハムは、だめですよ。
hamu desu ka. hamu wa, dame desu yo.

Vocabulary

Nouns:

1パスポート [pasupooto] passport
5しごと [shigoto] business, job, work
9くすり [kusuri] medicine
17ハム [hamu] ham
5かんこう [kankoo] sightseeing
7スーツケース [suutsukeesu] suitcase
12はちみつ [hachimitsu] honey

Adjectives:

13いい [ii] good, all right, no problem
18だめ（な）[dame(na)] not good, not be allowed

Verbs:

1みせて [misete] て-form of ru-verb「みせる」"to show"
7あけて [akete] て-form of ru-verb「あける」"to open"

Grammatical words:

1を [o] direct object marker
1ください [kudasai] used after the て-form of a verb to form a polite request: Please do such and such. ☞Function V
3さん [san] added to names, professions, etc., to indicate respect and a certain degree of familiarity: Mr., Mrs., Miss, Ms.
3です [desu] is, am, are (polite form of be-verb「だ」)
3ね [ne] tag question marker: huh? right? aren't you? doesn't he? etc.
5か [ka] question marker, added to end of statement to form a question
9は [wa] topic marker
9なに（なん）[nani (nan)] question word: what? ☞Function II
9これ [kore] this one, these ones
14それ [sore] that one, those ones
13よ [yo] marker functioning to emphasize what the person is saying
15どれ [dore] question word, used to ask "which one" or "which ones" out of a group of three or more items. ☞Function III

Expressions:

2はい [hai] yes, that's right, all right, here you are
4ええ [ee] yeah, that's right, (more casual than「はい」)
10いいえ [iie] no
4そうです [soo desu] that's right, that's so
8どうぞ [doozo] here you are, please go ahead, do as you wish
10〜じゃありません [ja arimasen] it is not__, I am not__, etc.
11じゃ（では）[ja (dewa)] well then, if that's the case
13どうも [doomo] thank you (shortened form of「どうもありがとう [doomo arigatoo]」)
14ああ [aa] expression of mild surprise: ah! oh!
17あの [ano] well, let me see
17じつは [jitsu wa] to tell the truth, the fact is

 すみません

When speaking with Japanese you often encounter the word「すみません [sumimasen]」. It is used in a variety of situations, and the basic intent is to excuse oneself.

Pardon me.

Thank you.

Excuse me, but…

I'm sorry, but…

Additional vocabulary for Exercise 1:

ラジオ [rajio] radio
バッグ [baggu] handbag, purse
本（ほん）[hon] book
テレビ [terebi] television
メニュー [menyuu] menu

Function I　Identifying things : A is B ; AはBです

The be-verb「です」is equivalent to English "is" in the sense of "equals", "is a member of the class" or "has the property of". Negative "is not" is expressed by the form「では　ありません」.

Statement	これは、くすりです。	This is medicine.
Question	これは、くすりです　か。	Is this medicine?
Answer	はい、くすりです。	Yes, it's medicine.
	はい、そう　です。	Yes, that's right.
	いいえ、くすり　では　ありません。	No, it's not medicine.
	（いいえ、くすり　じゃ　ありません。）	
	いいえ、そう　では　ありません。	No, that's not right.
	（いいえ、そう　じゃ　ありません。）	
	いいえ、ちがいます。	No, wrong.

Note: In informal speech,「では」is often pronounced and written「じゃ」.

Exercise 1: Answer "yes" or "no" to the following questions using「〜です」,「そうです」,「〜では／じゃ　ありません」and「ちがいます」.

1) A: バーバラ(ばーばら)さんですか。
   B: ＿＿＿＿＿＿。

2) A: パスポート(ぱすぽーと)ですか。
   B: ＿＿＿＿＿＿。

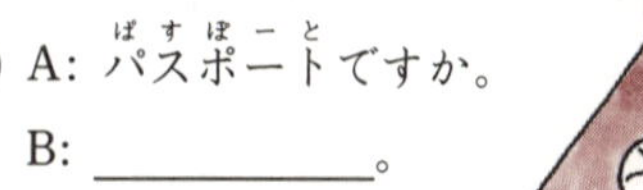

3) A: 本(ほん)ですか。
   B: ＿＿＿＿＿＿。

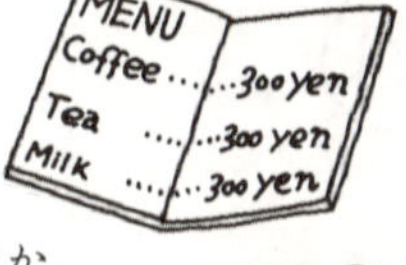

4) A: ラジオ(らじお)ですか。
   B: ＿＿＿＿＿＿。

5) A: スーツケース(すーつけーす)ですか。
   B: ＿＿＿＿＿＿。

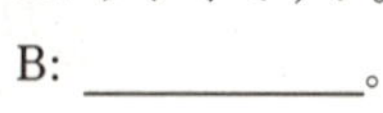

Dialogues in English

Dialogue I

Imm. Officer : Show me your passport, please.
Michael : Here you are.
Imm. Officer : You are Mr. Michael Webb, is that right?
Michael : Yes, that's right.
Imm. Officer : Sightseeing or business?
Michael : Not sightseeing. Business.

Dialogue II

Cus. Officer : Open your suitcase, please.
Michael : All right.
Cus. Officer : What is this? Is it medicine?
Michael : No, it's not medicine.
Cus. Officer : Well then, what is it?
Michael : It's honey.
Cus. Officer : Could I see it? Thank you. OK, fine. Ah, what is that there?
Barbara : Which do you mean?
Cus. Officer : That one there. What is it? Open it, please.
Barbara : This is...uhh..., to tell the truth, it's a ham.
Cus. Officer : Ham? Ham is not allowed.

Function II "What is this?"; これは、なん ですか

「なに」(in certain situations pronounced「なん」) is a question word meaning "what?".

Question	これは、なん ですか。	What is this?
Answer	くすり です。	It's medicine.
	くすり。	Medicine.
	わかりません。	I don't know.

Pronouns:

Pronouns corresponding to English I, you, he, him, etc. are used less frequently in Japanese. Note in the following examples that there is no explicit Japanese equivalent to English "it".

ex. Cus. Officer: それは、くすり ですか。 — Is that medicine?
マイケル：いいえ、くすり では ありません。 — No, (it) is not medicine.
Cus. Officer: なん ですか。 — What is (it)?
マイケル：はちみつ です。 — (It) is honey.
Cus. Officer: みせてください。 — Show (it) (to me) please.

Exercise 2: Answer the question「これは なんですか」using the pictures below. (new words appear in the vocabulary at the bottom of the next page.)

1)

2)

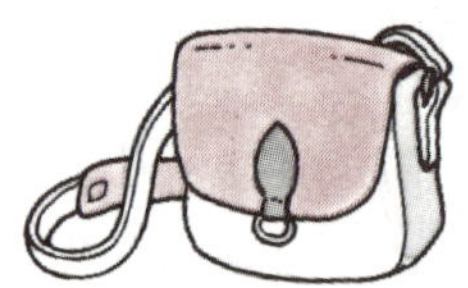

3)

4)

5)

6)

Exercise 3: Practice the following dialogue, substituting the underlined portions as shown.

ex. A: これは、<u>くすり</u>ですか。　B: いいえ、<u>くすり</u>じゃ ありません。
A: じゃ、なんですか。　B: <u>ジュース</u>(じゅーす)です。

1) ビール [biiru]
ウイスキー [uisukii]

2) ちず [chizu]
え [e]

3) ラジオ [rajio]
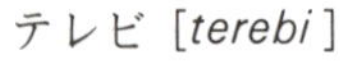
テレビ [terebi]

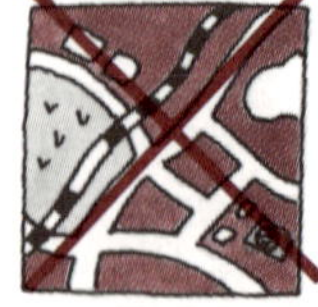

4) ペン [pen]
えんぴつ [enpitsu]

5) しんぶん [shinbun]
ざっし [zasshi]

6) びょういん [byooin]
ゆうびんきょく [yuubinkyoku]

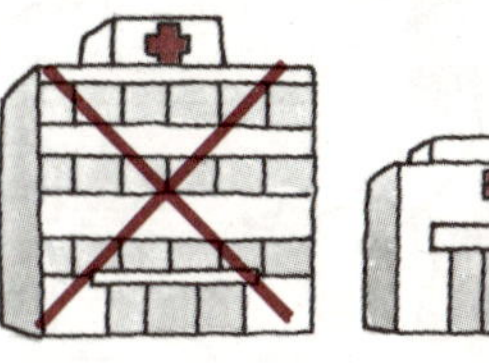

signs:  hospital  post office

Function III Identifying things by pointing them out;「これ」「それ」「あれ」「どれ」

これ (this one here), それ (that one there), あれ (that one over there), どれ (which one where?)

「これ, それ, あれ」help direct the listener's attention to objects according to their relative location. Use「これ」when indicating things near yourself, use「それ」when indicating things near the person you are speaking to, use「あれ」when indicating things distant from both.「どれ」= "to which should I direct my attention?"

ex.1. a: これは、ちずです。
b: それは、ゆうびんきょくです。
c: あれは、びょういんです。

ex.2. a: これを　みせてください。
b: それを　みせてください。
c: あれを　みせてください。

Vocabulary

かさ [kasa] umbrella
ジュース [juusu] soft drink
え [e] picture
えんぴつ [enpitsu] pencil
びょういん [byooin] hospital
でんわ [denwa] telephone
ウイスキー [uisukii] whisky
ペン [pen] pen, fountain pen
しんぶん [shinbun] newspaper
ゆうびんきょく [yuubinkyoku] post office
ビール [biiru] beer
ちず [chizu] map
ざっし [zasshi] magazine

ex.3. A: それを　みせてください。
B: どれですか。

ex.4. A: くすりは、どれですか。
B: これです。

Exercise 4: Fill in each of the blanks with the most appropriate word from「これ，それ，あれ，どれ」.

1)

(①)は
なんですか。
(②)
ですか。
あれです。
ああ、(③)
は、ちかて
つです。

2)

3)

Mitsukoshi
デパー
トは(⑥)
ですか。
デパート
は (⑦)
です。

4)

(⑧)を
みせて
ください。
(⑨)
ですか。
(⑩)
ですか。
いいえ。
じゃ、
(⑪)
ですか。
ええ、
(⑫)
です。

Function IV　Alternative questions : Is it A, or is it B?;　Aですか、Bですか

ex. Cus. Officer: それは、くすり　ですか、はちみつ　ですか。
Is that medicine, or honey?
バーバラ（ばーばら）: はちみつ　です。　It's honey.

Exercise 5: Look at the pictures and complete the following dialogues.

1) 

2) 

3) 

4)

1) A: バーバラ(ばーばら)さんですか、マイケル(まいける)さんですか。
   B: ＿＿＿＿＿＿＿。

2) A: かんこうですか、しごとですか。
   B: ＿＿＿＿＿＿＿。

3) A: ＿＿＿＿＿、ウイスキー(ういすきー)ですか。
   B: ＿＿＿＿＿＿＿。

4) A: ＿＿＿＿＿、＿＿＿＿＿＿＿。
   B: びょういんです。

Exercise 6: Practice the following conversation changing the underlined portions. Use the double underlined words as answers.

ex. A: すみません。それは、ペン(ぺん)ですか、えんぴつですか。
　　B: これですか。これは、えんぴつです。
　　A: そうですか。どうも……。

1) しんぶん，ざっし　2) ラジオ(らじお)，テレビ(てれび)　3) ちず，え　4) ビール(びーる)，ジュース(じゅーす)

Function V　Asking someone to do something (1)；みせてください

1 **Requests using the verb て-form**

本を　みせて。[*hon o misete*] Show me the book.

本を　みせて　ください。[*hon o misete kudasai*] Show me the book, please.

本を　みせて　くださいませんか。[*hon o misete kudasai masenka*] Won't you show me the book, please?

2 **Complying**

はい。(ええ。)(うん。) [*hai (ee) (un)*] Certainly.

ええ、いいですよ。[*ee, ii desu yo*] Yeah. OK.

いいですよ。はい、どうぞ。[*ii desu yo. hai, doozo*] Certainly. Here you are.

はい、わかりました。[*hai, wakarimashita*] Certainly. I understand (I'll do it).

3 **Outright refusal**

いいえ、だめです。[*iie, dame desu*] No way. No, I can't.

いいえ、いやです。[*iie, iya desu*] No, I refuse.

4 **Stalling**

あの、ちょっと… [*ano, chotto*] Well, you see ....

わるいけど… [*waruikedo*] Sorry, but ....

すみません。[*sumimasen*] I'm sorry.

もうしわけないんですが… [*mooshiwake nain desu ga*] I am awfully sorry, but ....

Vocabulary

ちかてつ [*chikatetsu*] subway
すみません [*sumimasen*] Excuse me. I'm sorry.
デパート [*depaato*] department store
ワイン [*wain*] wine

5 **Expressing appreciation**

どうも。[*doomo*] Thanks.

ありがとう。[*arigatoo*] Thank you.

どうも　ありがとう。[*doomo arigatoo*] Thanks a lot.

ありがとうございました。[*arigatoo gozaimashita*] Thank you very much.

6 **Response to the above**

いいえ。[*iie*] Don't mention it.

どういたしまして。[*doo itashimashite*] You're welcome.

ex. 1. Dialogue between friends

A: ちょっと　みせて。

B: うん。

A: ありがとう。

ex. 2. Formal dialogue I

Imm. Officer: パスポートを　みせてください。

マイケル: はい。

Imm. Officer: どうも。

ex. 3. Formal dialogue Ⅱ

Sales clerk: すみませんが、もういちど、なまえを　かいてくださいませんか。
Excuse me, but won't you write your name once again, please?

Customer: ええ、いいですよ。　OK. Here you are.

Sales clerk: どうも　ありがとうございました。　Thank you very much.

Customer: いいえ、どういたしまして。　You're welcome.

List of て-forms and polite requests for memorization

て-forms	polite requests
まって [*matte*] wait	ちょっと　まってください。
のんで [*nonde*] drink, take (medicine)	くすりを　のんでください。
よんで [*yonde*] read	ほんを　よんでください。
かいて [*kaite*] write, draw	なまえを　かいてください。
あけて [*akete*] open	スーツケースを　あけてください。
みせて [*misete*] show, let me see	パスポートを　みせてください。
とって [*totte*] pass, take	はちみつを　とってください。
かして [*kashite*] lend	ペンを　かしてください。
たべて [*tabete*] eat	すしを　たべてください。

Exercise 7: Practice the following conversation, substituting different requests. Comply or refuse as you wish.

ex. A: すみません。

B: はい。なんですか。

A: <u>てがみを　よんで</u>ください。

B: ________________。

1) なまえ，かいて　2) ちょっと，まって　3) しんぶん，とって　4) 本，よんで

5) かさ，かして　6) パスポート，みせて　7) スーツケース，あけて　8) おかね，かして

Exercise 8: Make up a dialogue asking someone to do something. Choose the request form most appropriate to each situation.

①

②

③

④

Listening Comprehension Exercise

Listen to the dialogues on the tape and choose the number of the picture which depicts the situation most appropriately.

A

B

C

D

E

F

①______ ②______ ③______ ④______ ⑤______ ⑥______

Vocabulary

ちょっと [*chotto*] a bit, a little
てがみ [*tegami*] letter
すし [*sushi*] *sushi*, raw fish and rice
おかね [*o-kane*] money

第2課 ぎんこうは、どこに　ありますか

Where Is There A Bank?

Dialogue I

Mr. Tsuchida is waiting for Mr. & Mrs. Webb at Narita Airport.

1 土田(つちだ)　：あのう、しつれいですが、ウエッブさんですか。
anoo, shitsuree desu ga, Uebbu-san desu ka?

2 マイケル(まいける)：はい、そうです。どなたですか。
hai, soo desu. donata desu ka?

3 土田　：あべさんぎょうの　土田です。
Abe sangyoo no Tsuchida desu.

4 マイケル：ああ、あべさんぎょうの　土田さんですか。
aa, Abe sangyoo no Tsuchida-san desu ka.

5 はじめまして。どうぞ　よろしく。
hajimemashite. doozo yoroshiku.

6 土田　：こちらこそ、どうぞ　よろしく。こちらは、おくさんですか。
kochira koso, doozo yoroshiku. kochira wa, okusan desu ka?

7 マイケル：はい、かないの　バーバラです。
hai, kanai no Baabara desu.

8 バーバラ(ばーばら)：はじめまして、バーバラです。どうぞ　よろしく　おねがいします。
hajimemashite, Baabara desu. doozo yoroshiku o-negai shimasu.

Dialogue II

Michael asks the location of a bank.

9 マイケル(まいける)：土田(つちだ)さん、ぎんこうは、どこに　ありますか。
Tsuchida-san, ginkoo wa, doko ni arimasu ka?

10 土田　：ぎんこうですね。ええと、このとおりの　むこうに、本(ほん)やが、あります。
ginkoo desu ne. eeto, kono toori no mukoo ni, hon-ya ga arimasu.

11 　ぎんこうは、その　本やの　となりです。
ginkoo wa, sono hon-ya no tonari desu.

12 マイケル：本やの　となりですね。その　本やは、大(おお)きいですか。
hon-ya no tonari desu ne. sono hon-ya wa, ookii desu ka?

13 土田　：いいえ、大(おお)きくありませんが、すぐ　わかりますよ。
iie, ookiku arimasen ga, sugu wakarimasu yo.

14 マイケル：そうですか。どうも　ありがとう。じゃ、いってきます。
soo desu ka. doomo arigatoo. ja, ittekimasu.

Dialogue III

Michael comes back and finds Barbara not there.

15 マイケル：おまたせしました。あれ、かないが　いませんね。どこですか。
o-matase shimashita. are! kanai ga imasen ne. doko desu ka?

16 土田　：バーバラさんは、あそこの　ほうせきやに　いますよ。
Baabara-san wa, asoko no hooseki-ya ni imasu yo.

17 マイケル：えっ、それは　たいへん。どの　みせですか。あそこの　小(ちい)さいみせですか。
e! sore wa taihen! dono mise desu ka? asoko no chiisai mise desu ka?

18 土田　：いいえ、あの　小さいみせじゃ　ありません。あれは、レストランです。
iie, ano chiisai mise ja arimasen. are wa, resutoran desu.

19 　そのまえの、きれいな　みせです。
sono mae no, kireena mise desu.

20 マイケル：じゃ、すぐ　よんできます。
ja, sugu yondekimasu.

Vocabulary

Nouns:

3さんぎょう [sangyoo] industry
6おくさん [okusan] your wife, someone else's wife
7かない [kanai] my wife
9ぎんこう [ginkoo] bank
10とおり [toori] street, road
10むこう [mukoo] over there, across the way
10本や（ほんや）[hon-ya] bookstore
11となり [tonari] next to, next door
16ほうせきや [hooseki-ya] jewelry store
17みせ [mise] shop, store
18レストラン [resutoran] restaurant
19まえ [mae] before, in front of

Adjectives:

12大きい（おおきい）[ookii] big, large
17小さい（ちいさい）[chiisai] small, little
17たいへん（な）[taihen(na)] terrible, awful, difficult
19きれい（な）[kiree(na)] beautiful, nice looking

Adverbs: 13すぐ [sugu] right away, soon

Verbs:

9あります [arimasu] polite form of u-verb「ある」"to exist" (used for inanimate objects)
16います [imasu] polite form of ru-verb「いる」"to exist" (used for animate objects)
15いません [imasen] negative polite form of ru-verb「いる」

Grammatical words:

が [ga] 1① softening marker 10② subject marker 13③ qualifying clause marker: but
2どなた [donata] who? (In plain speech use だれ [dare])
3の [no] possessive marker
9どこ [doko] where? (see Appendix)
9に [ni] location marker: in, on, etc.
10この [kono] +noun: this, these
11その [sono] +noun: that, those
16あそこ [asoko] over there (see Appendix)
17どの [dono] +noun: which

Expressions:

1あのう[anoo] Uhh... (used to get someone's attention)
1しつれいですが [shitsuree desu ga] Excuse me, but...
5はじめまして [hajimemashite] Nice to meet you.
5どうぞ　よろしく [doozo yoroshiku] May our future relationship be a pleasant one.
8よろしく　おねがいします [yoroshiku o-negai shimasu] same as「どうぞ よろしく」; also "Please, I beg of you."
6こちらこそ [kochira koso] The pleasure is all mine.
10ええと[eeto] Uhh... (used when pausing to think)
14いってきます [ittekimasu] lit. I'll go and come back.
15おまたせしました [o-matase shimashita] Sorry to have kept you waiting.
15あれ [are!] exclamation of mild surprise : Oh! Hey!
17えっ [e!] exclamation of mild surprise or when you missed what was said
20よんできます [yondekimasu] I'll go and call her.

Function I　Describing things(1): Uses of「の」

Function I-1　"Possessive"「の」; AのB

Two nouns may be joined by the so-called possessive marker「の」, where the first noun functions to modify the second.

ex.			
マイケル(まいける)	の	おくさん	Michael's wife
わたし	の	パスポート(ぱすぽーと)	my passport
日本(にほん)	の	カメラ(かめら)	Japanese camera, camera made in Japan
かない	の	バーバラ(ばーばら)	my wife, Barbara
東京(とうきょう)	の	人(ひと)	a person from Tokyo, people in Tokyo
レストラン(れすとらん)	の	まえ	front of the restaurant

Note: Longer phrases of three or more nouns are also possible.

ex. わたしの　日本の　ともだち　　my friend in (or from) Japan.

東京の　かいしゃの　人　　person from a company in Tokyo

Function I-2　Question word ＋の

だれ [*dare*] / どなた [*donata*]	who?	だれの/ どなたの	whose?
なに [*nani*]	what?	なんの	of what? what sort of?
どこ [*doko*]	where?	どこの	from where? existing where?

ex.1. A: だれの　パスポートですか。　Whose passport is it?

B: ウエッブさんの　パスポートです。　It's Mr. Webb's passport.

2. A: なんの　本ですか。　What sort of book is it?

B: えい語の　本です。　It's an English book.

3. A: どこの　ワインですか。　Where is the wine from? (lit. It's a wine from where?)

B: フランスの　ワインです。　It's a wine from France.　It's a French wine.

Exercise 1: Answer the following questions using the information given in the pictures.

① 
② 

③ 
④ 

① A: これは、なんですか。

B: ＿＿＿＿＿＿＿＿。

② A: だれの　パスポートですか。

B: ＿＿＿＿＿＿＿＿。

③ A: これは、どこの　ワインですか。

B: ＿＿＿＿＿＿＿＿。

④ A: これは、だれの　スーツケースですか。

B: ＿＿＿＿＿＿＿＿。

◆*Additional vocabulary*◆

日本語（にほんご）[*nihon-go*] Japanese (language)

スペイン [*supein*] Spain

Dialogues in English

Dialogue I

T: Uhh.... Excuse me, but are you Mr. Webb?

M: Yes, that's right. Who are you?

T: I'm Tsuchida of Abe Industries.

M: Ah, Mr. Tsuchida of Abe Industries. How do you do? Pleased to meet you.

T: The pleasure's all mine. And this is Mrs. Webb?

M: Yes, this is my wife, Barbara.

B: How do you do? I'm Barbara. Pleased to meet you.

Dialogue II

M: Mr. Tsuchida, where is there a bank?

T: A bank, right? Uhh, down this road a way there's a bookstore. The bank is next door to it.

M: A bookstore. Is the bookstore big?

T: No, it's not big, but you will find it right away.

M: OK. Thank you. Well then, I'll be back.

Dialogue III

M: Sorry to have kept you waiting. Hey, my wife's not here! Where is she?

T: Barbara's in that jewelry store over there.

M: What? That's terrible! Which store is it? Is it that small store over there?

T: No, it's not that small store. That's a restaurant. It's the nice looking store in front of that.

M: Well then, I'll go and call her right away.

Exercise 2: Ask questions concerning the pictures below using「だれの」,「なんの」or「どこの」. Several questions may be asked for each picture.

ex. 1. A: これは、<u>だれの</u>　ペンですか。　　B: それは、わたしの　ペンです。

2. A: それは、<u>なんの</u>　本ですか。　　B: 日本語の　本です。

3. A: これは、<u>どこの</u>　ワインですか。　　B: フランスの　ワインです。

①

②

③

④

⑤

⑥

⑦

⑧

<suggestions>

① かさ，イタリア，バーバラ　　② コンピューター，日本，マイケル
③ ビール，ドイツ，土田　　④ スーツケース，アメリカ，マイケル
⑤ テレビ，ソニー，土田　　⑥ 本，えい語，せんせい
⑦ カメラ，日本，マイケル　　⑧ ラジオ，東芝 [*tooshiba*]，土田

Function I-3　　**This + noun, that + noun;** この本，その本，あの本

「これ，それ，あれ，どれ」assume a slightly different form when used directly before a noun. This new form incorporates the possessive marker「の」. (see Appendix)

これ	this one here	この	本	this book here
それ	that one there	その	本	that book there
あれ	that one over there	あの	本	that book over there
どれ	which one where?	どの	本	which book where?

ex.1. A: この　本は、だれの　本ですか。　　Whose book is <u>this book</u>?

B: ああ、それは、わたしの　本ですよ。　　Oh, that's my book.

2. A: その　ラジオは、どこの　ラジオ？　(plain)　　Where was <u>that radio</u> made?

B: これ？　日本の　ラジオ。(plain)　　This? It's a Japanese radio.

3. A: あの　人(ひと)は、マイケル(まいける)さんの　おくさんですか。

Is that person over there Michael's wife?

B: いいえ、あの　人は、マイケルさんの　おくさんじゃ　ありません。

No, that person is not Michael's wife.

4. A: どの　本が、マイケルさんの　本ですか。　Which book is Michael's book?

B: この　本が、マイケルさんの　本です。　This book here is Michael's book.

B: この　本です。　It's this book here.

Grammar Note

Topic marker「は」and subject marker「が」

A word or a phrase marked by「は」is the topic of the sentence.「は」is roughly equivalent to the English expression "as for" or "speaking of". The rest of the sentence following「は」, perhaps including「が」, forms a statement about the topic.

Topic	Subject	Location	Verbal	
きょうは、	てんきが		いいです。	As for today, the weather is nice.
ぎんこうは、		あそこに	あります。	Speaking of the bank, it is over there.

Practical rules for using「は」and「が」in sentences like「A ＿ Bです。」:

1. Use「は」when **B** describes or tells the identity of **A**.

ex.1. わたしの　かないは、バーバラ(ばーばら)です。　My wife is Barbara.

2. あの　人は、めが　大(おお)きいです。　As for that person, his eyes are big.

2. Use「は」when **B** is a question word asking for a description or the identity of **A**. When **A** is included in the answer「は」is used.

ex.1. 本(ほん)やは、どこですか。　（本やは）あそこです。

2. これは、だれの　スーツケース(すーつけーす)ですか。　（それは）わたしの　スーツケースです。

3. Use「が」when **A** is a question word asking who or which object fits the description or identity **B**. Note the two possible answers for this type of question.

ex.1. X: どれが、マイケルさんの　パスポート(ぱすぽーと)ですか。

Y: これが、マイケルさんの　パスポートです。

（マイケルさんの　パスポートは）これです。

2. X: どの　人(ひと)が、バーバラさんですか。

Y: あの　人が、バーバラさんです。

（バーバラさんは）あの人です。

4.「は」is often used in negative sentences.

ex.1. あの人は、バーバラさんじゃ　ありません。　That person is not Barbara.

ぎんこうの　となりは、レストラン(れすとらん)じゃ　ありません。

Next door to the bank is not a restaurant.

Vocabulary

イタリア [itaria] Italy
アメリカ [amerika] America
コンピューター [konpyuutaa] computer
せんせい [sensee] teacher
ドイツ [doitsu] Germany

Exercise 3: Practice the following dialogue with a partner, substituting the underlined parts according to the pictures below. Be careful to use the most appropriate word from among「この, その, あの」.

ex. A: どれが、バーバラさんの　スーツケースですか。

B: この　スーツケースです。

Function II　Describing things (2): Adjectives; 小さい　みせ

Adjectives are generally used in two ways to describe nouns:

(1) As the verbal of sentence, with the noun appearing as the topic or subject.

「X　は、 (adj.) 」　　"X is (adj.)."

(2) Before the noun, modifying it directly.

「 (adj.) 　X」　　"(adj.) X"　"X which is (adj.)."

In (1), adjectives may be plain or polite depending on the situation, but in (2), adjectives are used in their plain form only (see pp.17～19 for explanation of adjective inflection).

ex. い-adj.　小さい [*chiisai*] "small"　　negative: 小さ［い］く＋ありません

あのみせは、小さい（です）。	That store is small.
このみせは、小さくありません。	This store is not small.
このみせは、小さくない（です）。	This store is not small.
あれは、小さいみせです。	That is a small store.

Japanese also has what are known as "な-adjectives", which function the same as "い-adjectives".

ex. な-adj.　しずか [*shizuka*] "quiet"　　negative: しずか＋じゃ（では）ありません

あのみせは、しずかです。	That store is quiet.
このみせは、しずかじゃありません。	This store is not quiet.
このみせは、しずかじゃないです。	This store is not quiet.
あれは、しずかなみせです。	That is a quiet store.

Adjectival opposites

小さい	[*chiisai*] small, little	↔	大きい	[*ookii*] big, large
やすい	[*yasui*] cheap, reasonable		たかい	[*takai*] expensive
ひくい	[*hikui*] low		たかい	[*takai*] high, tall
あたらしい	[*atarashii*] new		ふるい	[*furui*] old (used for things)
むずかしい	[*muzukashii*] difficult		やさしい	[*yasashii*] easy
ひろい	[*hiroi*] wide, spacious, big		せまい	[*semai*] narrow, small
いい	[*ii*] good, well, nice		わるい	[*warui*] bad
べんり(な)	[*benri(na)*] convenient, trouble saving, useful		ふべん(な)	[*fuben(na)*] inconvenient, out of the way
しずか(な)	[*shizuka(na)*] quiet, peaceful		うるさい	[*urusai*] noisy, disturbing
きれい(な)	[*kiree(na)*] clean, beautiful		きたない	[*kitanai*] dirty
おいしい	[*oishii*] good, delicious		まずい	[*mazui*] unappetizing
ちかい	[*chikai*] near		とおい	[*tooi*] far

Note 1: The words「べんり」and「ふべん」are not used to mean "suited (not suited) to one's schedule". Thus, sentences such as "Would such and such a time and place be convenient (or inconvenient) for you?" are expressed in Japanese using the phrases「つごう　が　いい」"is suitable" and「つごう　が　わるい」"is not suitable".

ex.1. このコンピューター(こんぴゅーたー)は、とても　べんりです。　This computer is very convenient.

2. きょうは、つごうが　いいですか。　Is it convenient for you today?

Note 2: The negative form of「いいです」is「よくありません」.

Exercise 4: Using the adjectives above describe the items below, as in the example sentences.

ex. (picture A)　1) この本(ほん)は、あたらしいです。　2) これは、あたらしい本です。

3) この本は、ふるくありません。

A

B

C

りんご [ringo] apple

D

へや [heya] room

E

くつ [kutsu] shoes

F

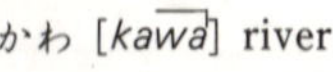

かわ [kawa] river

G

H

テープレコーダー [teepu rekoodaa] tape recorder

I

テスト [tesuto] examination

J

Exercise 5: Practice the following dialogue substituting the underlined parts. Be careful to use the most appropriate word from among「この，その，あの」.

ex. A: どれが、マイケル(まいける)さんの　くつですか。　　B: この　あたらしい　くつです。

1)

2)

3)

4)

5)

6)

Exercise 6: Practice the following type of dialogue with a partner.

ex. A: 東京(とうきょう)の　ちかてつは、ふべんですか。

B: ①はい、ふべんです。

②いいえ、ふべんじゃありません。べんりですよ。

1) あなたのへやは、ひろいですか。
2) あなたのへやは、しずかですか。
3) 日本語(にほんご)は、やさしいですか。
4) 日本のぶっかは、やすいですか。
5) かんじは、むずかしいですか。
6) あなたの　日本語の本(ほん)は、あたらしいですか。

Exercise 7: Practice the following conversation between a real estate broker and customer. Replace the underlined parts with the new words below, and change the ~~~~ part in an appropriate manner.

ex. Broker　: このへやは、どうですか。　　How do you like this room?

Customer: そうですね。ちょっと　せまいですね。

Broker　: そうですか。じゃ、これは　どうですか。

これは、せまくありませんよ。

Customer: そうですね。ひろいですが、ちょっと　たかいですね。

ex.	1)	2)	3)
せまい たかい	ふるい せまい	たかい うるさい	とおい たかい

4)	5)	6)
きたない ふべん	うるさい とおい	ふべん たかい

Exercise 8: Ask what someone thinks about the items below. Supply an answer as well.

1) アメリカ(あめりか)の　ワイン(わいん)	2) 東京(とうきょう)の　みち	3) かんじ
4) 日本のぶっか	5) あたらしい　コンピューター(こんぴゅーたー)	6) 日本語(にほんご)の　べんきょう
7) やすい　ウイスキー(ういすきー)	8) あなたの　へや	9) きょうの　てんき

Function III　Meeting someone for the first time: How do you do? ; はじめまして

People meeting for the first time might exchange greetings in the following manner:

polite ↑

ex.1. A: はじめまして、(name) です。どうぞ　よろしく　おねがいします。

B: はじめまして、(name) です。こちらこそ、どうぞ　よろしく　おねがいします。

2. A: はじめまして。どうぞ　よろしく　おねがいします。

B: こちらこそ、どうぞ　よろしく　おねがいします。

3. A: はじめまして。どうぞ　よろしく。(name) です。

B: はじめまして。どうぞ　よろしく。(name) です。

Exercise 9: Practice meeting and greeting other persons using the dialogue below.

A: (your name) です。
B: わたしは（ ① ）です。はじめまして。
A: どうぞ　よろしく。
B: こちらこそ（ ② ）。
A: あの、こちらは、ともだちの（ ③ ）さんです。
C: （ ④ ）です。（ ⑤ ）。どうぞ　よろしく。
B: どうぞ　よろしく　おねがいします。

Exercise 10: Practice making introductions as in the example of Exercise 9. Try to choose expressions taking social status and personal relations into consideration.
(Person A introduces himself to person C. Then A introduces B to C.)

	person A	person B	person C
1	Joe Atkinson	Michael: Joe's friend	たけうち : Joe's boss
2	〃	Steven: Joe's friend	まつだ : Joe's employee
3	〃	Elise: Joe's wife	やまだ : Joe's teacher
4	〃	Barbara: Mr. Webb's wife	いしかわ : father of Joe's friend

Vocabulary

たてもの [tatemono] building
ぶっか [bukka] prices
みち [michi] way, road
コート [kooto] overcoat
かんじ [kanji] Chinese characters
べんきょう [benkyoo] する study (to study)
あなた [anata] you

Function IV　Existence: there is, there are;「あります」「います」

The verb「ある (plain) /あります (polite)」means "to be", or "to exist". "Negation" or "non-existence" is indicated by「ない (plain) /ありません (polite)」. For people, animals and other animate things however, the verb「いる (plain) /います (polite)」is used. The negative form of「いる」is「いない (plain) /いません (polite)」. The place or position in which something exists is marked by the postposition「に」.

ex.1. A: ぎんこうは、どこに　ありますか。	Where is the bank?
B: 本(ほん)やの　となりに　あります。	It's next to the bookstore.
2. A: 日本語(にほんご)の本は、どこに　ありますか。	Where is the Japanese book?
B: そこの　つくえの　うえに　あります。	It's on that desk there.
3. A: ペン(ぺん)は、ここに　ありますか。	Is the pen here?
B: いいえ、ペンは、ここに　ありません。	No, the pen isn't here.
あそこの　つくえの　なかに　あります。	It's inside that desk over there.
4. A: マイケル(まいける)さんは、いま、どこに　いますか。	Where is Michael now?
がっこうに　いますか。	Is he at school?
B: いいえ、くうこうに　います。	No, he's at the airport.

Note: The be-verb「です」is also used to indicate existence. With「です」however, location is not marked with「に」as it is with「ある」.

ex.1. A: ぎんこうは、どこ　ですか。	Where is the bank?
B: そこ　です。	It is over there.
2. A: バーバラさんは、どこ　ですか。	Where is Barbara?
B: バーバラさんは、ほうせきや　です。	She's in the jewelry store.

Exercise 11: Fill the blanks with「います」or「あります」.

1) 本やの　まえに、ぎんこうが（　　　）。
2) バーバラ(ばーばら)さんは、ほうせきやに（　　　）。
3) ゆうびんきょくの　むこうに、びょういんが（　　　）。
4) がっこうの　となりの　ぎんこうに、マイケルさんが（　　　）。
5) つくえの　うえに、バーバラさんの　ペンが（　　　）。
6) 土田(つちだ)さんは、どこに（　　　）か。
7) バーバラさんの　バッグ(ばっぐ)は、どこに（　　　）か。

The following words are useful in specifying location or position with reference to some other object.

ⓐ つくえの　まえ [mae] front

ⓑ つくえの　うしろ [ushiro] behind, back

ⓒ つくえの うえ [ue] above, over
ⓓ つくえの うえ [ue] top, on
ⓔ つくえの した [shita] beneath, under, bottom

ⓕ つくえの まわり [mawari] around
つくえの そば [soba] next to, beside
つくえの ちかく [chikaku] near

ⓖ つくえの むこう [mukoo] past, beyond, far side
ⓗ つくえの よこ [yoko] side

ⓘ つくえの みぎ [migi] right
ⓙ つくえの ひだり [hidari] left

ⓚ 本やの となり [tonari] next to, next door

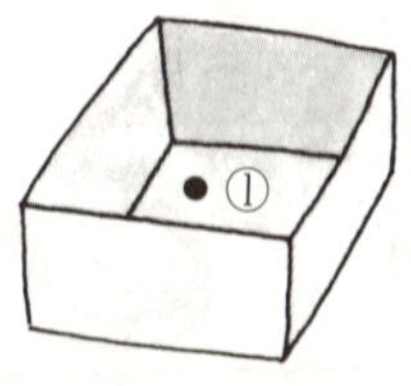

ⓛ はこの なか [naka] in, inside
はこの まんなか [man-naka] middle, very center

はこ [hako] box

Exercise 12: Tell the location of the items pictured below using「に　あります/います」and「です」.

ex. A: でんわは、どこに　ありますか。

B: でんわですか。でんわは、つくえの　よこに　ありますよ。

でんわですか。でんわは、つくえの　よこです。

ex.　でんわ

1)　ねこ cat

2)　いぬ dog

4)　めがね glasses

5)　ゆうびんきょく

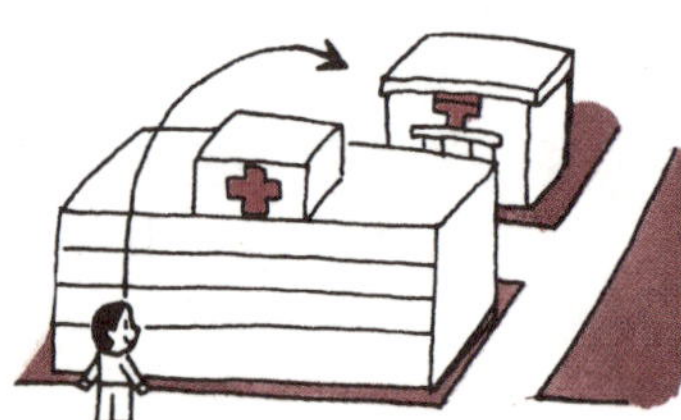

6)　ベンチ(べんち) bench

ふんすい fountain

Exercise 13: Answer the following questions referring to the map.

1) 東京(とうきょう)ぎんこうは、どこに　ありますか。
2) バーバラ(ばーばら)さんは、どこに　いますか。
3) 土田(つちだ)さんは、どこに　いますか。
4) 本(ほん)やの　なかに、だれが　いますか。
5) はなやの　ひだりに、なにが　ありますか。
6) びょういんの　ちかくに、なにが　ありますか。
7) バーバラさんの　そばに、なにが　いますか。

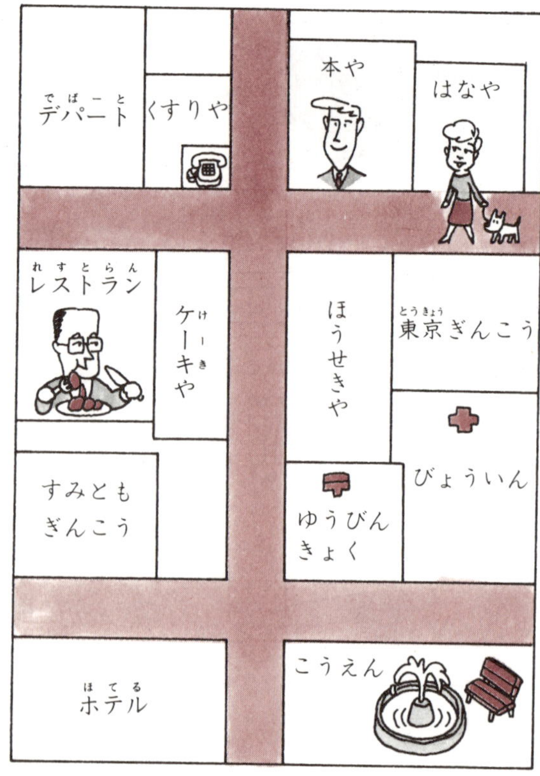

Exercise 14: Using the map, construct dialogues as in the example.

ex. A: あのう、すみませんが。

B: はい、なんですか。

A: はなやは、どこに　ありますか。

B: はなやですか。はなやは、本やの　となりに　ありますよ。

A: どうも　ありがとうございます。

B: どういたしまして。

Reading Comprehension Exercise

これは、こうえんです。こうえんのまわりに、大きいたてものが、たくさんあります。こうえんのなかは、しずかです。こうえんのまんなかに、ふんすいがあります。ふんすいのまわりに、ベンチがあります。ベンチのうしろに、大きい木があります。大きい木のしたのベンチに、バーバラさんがいます。

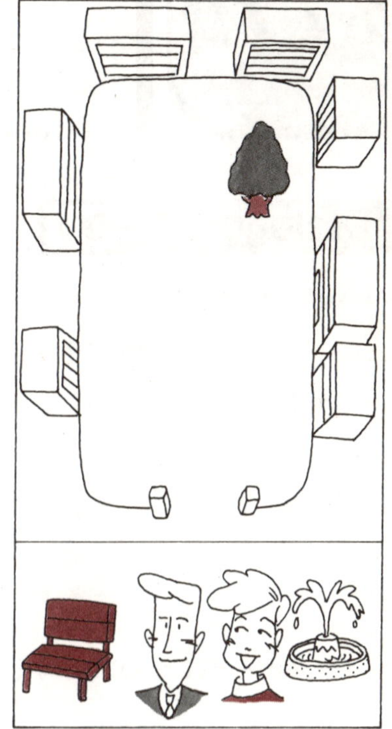

◆Vocabulary◆

たくさん [*takusan*] many, a lot
木（き）[*ki*] tree, wood

Exercise 15: Draw a picture of the park based on the information in the above passage. Compare your picture with those of your classmates and see if there are any differences. Speak only in Japanese.

Listening Comprehension Exercise

Listen to the statements on the tape and mark T (true) or F (false).

1. (　　)
2. (　　)
3. (　　)
4. (　　)
5. (　　)
6. (　　)
7. (　　)

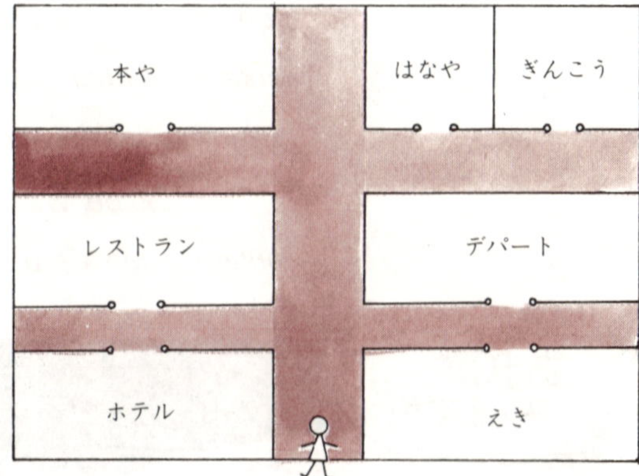

Vocabulary

ねこ [*neko*] cat	いぬ [*inu*] dog	めがね [*megane*] glasses
ふんすい [*funsui*] fountain	ベンチ [*benchi*] bench	
はなや [*hana-ya*] flower shop	くすりや [*kusuri-ya*] drugstore	ケーキや [*keeki-ya*] cake shop
えき [*eki*] station	ホテル [*hoteru*] hotel	こうえん [*kooen*] park

第3課　ここから　ホテルまで、どのくらい　かかりますか

How Long Does It Take From Here To The Hotel?

Dialogue I

At Narita Airport

土田(つちだ)　：いま、3時(じ)ですね。じゃ、いきましょうか。

マイケル(まいける)：ええ。ここから　ホテル(ほてる)まで、どのくらい　かかりますか。

土田　：そうですねえ。くるまで、2時間(じかん)ぐらい　かかります。

マイケル：ずいぶん　とおいですね。でんしゃは、ありますか。

土田　：でんしゃも　ありますが、あまり　べんりじゃ　ありません。

きょうは、タクシー(たくしー)で　いきましょう。

マイケル：そうですね。そうしましょう。

Tsuchida : *ima, san-ji desu ne. ja, ikimashoo ka.*

Maikeru : *ee. koko kara hoteru made, dono kurai kakarimasu ka?*

Tsuchida : *soo desu nee. kuruma de, ni-jikan gurai kakarimasu.*

Maikeru : *zuibun tooi desu ne. densha wa, arimasu ka?*

Tsuchida : *densha mo arimasu ga, amari benri ja arimasen.*

kyoo wa, takushiī de ikimashoo.

Maikeru : *soo desu ne. soo shimashoo.*

Dialogue II

On the way to the hotel

マイケル：みちが　すいていますね。
土田　　：ええ、あまり　こんでいませんね。
　　　　　あっ、あれが　みえますか。
バーバラ(ばーばら)：どれですか。あの　大(おお)きい　たてものですか。
土田　　：いいえ、あの　たてものじゃありません。
　　　　　その　となりです。
マイケル：なんですか。
土田　　：ディズニーランド(でぃずにーらんど)ですよ。
マイケル：ああ、あれが　東京(とうきょう)ディズニーランドですか。
バーバラ：大きいですね。
土田　　：ええ、とても　大きいですよ。バーバラさん、
　　　　　いつか、いっしょに　いきましょう。
　　　　　おもしろいですよ。
バーバラ：ええ、そうしましょう。

Maikeru : *michi ga suite imasu ne.*
Tsuchida : *ee, amari konde imasen ne.*
a! are ga miemasu ka?
Baabara : *dore desu ka? ano ookii tatemono desu ka?*
Tsuchida : *iie, ano tatemono ja arimasen.*
sono tonari desu.
Maikeru : *nan desu ka.*
Tsuchida : *Dizunii-Rando desu yo.*
Maikeru : *aa, are ga Tokyo Dizunii-Rando desu ka?*
Baabara : *ookii desu ne.*
Tsuchida : *ee, totemo ookii desu yo. Baabara-san,*
itsuka, isshoni ikimashoo.
omoshiroi desu yo.
Baabara : *ee, soo shimashoo.*

Vocabulary

Nouns :

3 くるま [*kuruma*] car 4 でんしゃ [*densha*] train 6 タクシー [*takushii*] taxi

19 いつか [*itsuka*] someday, sometime (also used as adv.)

Counters :

1 時 [*ji*] time, an hour, o'clock 3 時間 [*jikan*] time, number of hours

Parts of the day

きのう yesterday	きょう today		あした tomorrow
	ごぜん(ちゅう) before noon, a.m.	ごご afternoon, p.m.	
よる night	ひる day		よる night
0：00	12：00		24：00
ばん night	あさ morning / ひる noon	ゆうがた early evening	ばん
ゆうべ last night	けさ this morning		こんばん tonight

Adjectives :

20 おもしろい [*omoshiroi*] interesting, fun

Adverbs :

4 ずいぶん [*zuibun*] to a great degree, much more than expected (used for modifying adjectives and verbs)

5 あまり [*amari*] (not) so much, (not) so often (used for modifying adjectives and verbs) ☞ Grammar Note

18 とても [*totemo*] a lot, very (mainly used before adjectives) ☞ Grammar Note

19 いっしょに [*issho ni*] together

Verbs :

2 かかります [*kakarimasu*] polite form of u-verb「かかる」"to take" (as with time or money)

10 みえます [*miemasu*] polite form of ru-verb「みえる」"to be visible"

Grammatical words :

2 から [*kara*] from (used with time, place, people, etc.)

2 まで [*made*] up to and including, until, as far as

3 で [*de*] postposition marking the instrument or means by which an action is performed

3 〜ぐらい（くらい）[*gurai* (*kurai*)] about, approximately

5 も [*mo*] too, also, even (when used with topic, subject and direct object,「は」,「が」and「を」are dropped. ☞Lesson 4 for further discussion)

Expressions :

1 いきましょうか [*ikimashoo ka*] Shall we go?

2 どのくらい [*dono kurai*] About how much? (used with time, money, distance, weight, etc.)

3 そうですねえ [*soo desu nee*] Let me see. 7 そうしましょう [*soo shimashoo*] Yes, let's.

8 すいています [*suite imasu*] be uncrowded 9 こんでいません [*konde imasen*] not be crowded.

Dialogue Comprehension Exercise

Answer the following questions.

1) 成田(なりた)くうこうから　ホテル(ほてる)まで、どのくらい　かかりますか。
2) 成田くうこうから　東京(とうきょう)までは、ちかいですか。
3) ホテルまで、タクシー(たくしー)で　いきますか、でんしゃで　いきますか。
4) きょうは、みちが　こんでいますか。
5) 東京ディズニーランド(でぃずにーらんど)は、小(ちい)さいですか。

Function I Qualifying statements using "but" ; でんしゃも　ありますが、…

The conjunction「が」is used when a statement is to be qualified by adding a contrasting statement.

statement 1 が、statement 2　　statement 1, but statement 2

ex. 1. 成田(なりた)は、あたらしい　くうこうですが、すこし　ふべんです。

Narita is a new airport, but it is a bit inconvenient.

2. 東京(とうきょう)は、おもしろいですが、ぶっかが　たかいです。

Tokyo is interesting, but prices are expensive.

3. バス(ばす)も　ありますが、時間(じかん)が　かかります。

There's a bus as well, but it takes a lot of time.

Note 1:「…が」comes at the end of the statement being qualified, whereas English "but" comes at the beginning of the qualifying statement.「が」may be preceded by either plain or polite forms.

Note 2: Sometimes a statement ending in「…が」is left dangling, leaving the qualifying notion implied.

ex. 1. 東京は　おもしろいですが…

Tokyo is interesting, but ... (I wouldn't want to live there, etc.).

2. バスも　ありますが…　　There's a bus as well, but ... (it takes too long, etc.).

Exercise 1: Qualify the first sentence with the second using「…が」.

1) すしは　おいしいです。すしは　たかいです。
2) 日本(にほん)は　せまいです。日本は、人(ひと)が　たくさん　います。
3) 日本語(にほんご)は　むずかしいです。日本語は　おもしろいです。
4) このざっしは、ふるいです。あのざっしは、あたらしいです。
5) タクシー(たくしー)は　べんりです。タクシーは　たかいです。
6) ここは　しずかです。あそこは　うるさいです。
7) きょうは、つごうが　いいです。あしたは、だめです。
8) このレストラン(れすとらん)は、たかいです。あのレストランは、やすいです。

Dialogues in English

Dialogue I

T : It's now 3:00. Well then, shall we go?

M : OK. How long does it take about from here to the hotel?

T : Let me see, it takes about two hours by car.

M : That's sure a long way alright. Is there a train?

T : There's a train as well, but it isn't very convenient. Today let's go by taxi.

M : Yes, let's do that.

Dialogue II

M : The road is not crowded, is it!

T : You are right, it's not so crowded. Oh! Can you see that over there?

B : Which? Is it that big building?

T : No, not that building. Next to it.

M : What is it?

T : It's Disneyland!

M : Oh, so that's Tokyo Disneyland, is it?

B : It's big, isn't it!

T : Yes, it's very big. Let's go together sometime, Barbara. It's fun.

B : Yes, let's do that.

Exercise 2: Answer the questions in the affirmative, but add some qualifying or contrasting notion of your own.

ex. A：しごとは　おもしろいですか。
B：ええ、おもしろいですが、とても　いそがしいです。

1) すしは、おいしいですか。
2) あなたは、日本語(にほんご)の本(ほん)を　よみますか。
3) コンピューター(こんぴゅーたー)は、べんりですか。
4) あなたは、日本(にほん)のテレビ(てれび)を　みますか。

Grammar Note I

Modifying degree of qualification ;「とても」「あまり」

Both「とても」and「あまり」add the idea "very" or "extremely", but「あまり」is used in negative constructions：「あまり…ません」"not very…".

ex. 1. あの人(ひと)は、とても　きれいな人ですね。
That person over there is a very beautiful person.

2. きょうは、くるまが、とても　おおいですね。　There are certainly a lot of cars today.
3. てんきが、あまり　よくありません。　The weather is not very good.
4. このテレビは、あまり　たかくありません。　This television is not very expensive.

Exercise 3: Answer the questions below on your own using「とても」or「あまり」.

ex. A：日本語は、おもしろいですか。
B：はい。とても　おもしろいです。
orいいえ。あまり　おもしろくありません。

1) 東京(とうきょう)の　ぶっかは、たかいですか。
2) あなたの　日本語の本は、あたらしいですか。
3) 日本の　おさけは、おいしいですか。
4) ひらがなは　むずかしいですか。
5) 日本の　テレビは、おもしろいですか。
6) 東京の　みちは、きれいですか。
7) あなたの　いえから　がっこうまで、とおいですか。
8) きょうの　てんきは、いいですか。

Grammar Note II

Verb : present & future ;「いきます」「いきません」

Telling what one "does" or "is going to do" : **Verb stem**＋ます
Telling what one "does not do" or "is not going to do" : **Verb stem**＋ません

	affirmative	negative
to drink	のみ　ます	のみ　ません
to wake up	おき　ます	おき　ません
to read	よみ　ます	よみ　ません
to write	かき　ます	かき　ません
to buy	かい　ます	かい　ません
to wait	まち　ます	まち　ません
to go back	かえります	かえりません

	affirmative	negative
to go	いき　ます	いき　ません
to open	あけ　ます	あけ　ません
to eat	たべ　ます	たべ　ません
to sleep	ね　ます	ね　ません
to see, watch	み　ます	み　ません
to show	みせ　ます	みせ　ません
to do	し　ます	し　ません

ex. 1. まいにち、東京(とうきょう)へ いきます。 I go to Tokyo every day.
2. あした、東京へ いきます。 I am going to go to Tokyo tomorrow.
3. あしたは、東京へ いきません。 I am not going to go to Tokyo tomorrow.
4. いつも、本(ほん)を よみます。 I read books all the time.
5. なまえを かきます。 I write my name. / I am going to write my name.
6. くすりを のみます。 I take madicine. / I am going to take medicine.

Note:「へ」is used with verbs of motion (「いく」,「くる」, etc.) to indicate the direction or destination: to, toward, into.

Exercise 4: Construct sentences as in the example. Be sure to choose a verb which fits.

ex. こうえん → まいにち、こうえんへ いきますが、きょうは、いきません。

1) ビール(びーる) 2) てがみ 3) テニス(てにす) 4) りんご 5) しごと
6) テレビ(てれび) 7) しんぶん 8) かいしゃ

Exercise 5: Construct questions using the words listed below and answer them.

1) よく，日本(にほん)，えいが，みます 2) あなた，となり，だれ，います
3) いつも，なに，べんきょうします 4) きょう，どこ，いきます
5) いつも，なんの 本，かいます 6) きょう，なに，たべます

Exercise 6: Particle Exercise; Fill in the blanks with the most appropriate particle chosen from the list. The same particle may be used several times.

〔が (subject) から まで で に が (but) の〕

1) 東京(とうきょう)えき（ ） 日光(にっこう)（ ）、でんしゃ（ ）、2時間(じかん)ぐらい かかります。
2) くうこうは こんでいます（ ）、みちは すいています。
3) A: つくえ（ ）した（ ）、なに（ ） いますか。 B: ねこ（ ） います。
4) タクシー（ ）、マイケルさん（ ）いえへ いきます。

Function II Numerals

Cardinal numbers

a. 0 ぜろ／れい *zero／rei*

b. 1–10

1	2	3	4	5	6	7	8	9	10
一	二	三	四	五	六	七	八	九	十
いち	に	さん	よん/し	ご	ろく	なな/しち	はち	く/きゅう	じゅう
ichi	*ni*	*san*	*yon/shi*	*go*	*roku*	*nana/ shichi*	*hachi*	*ku/kyuu*	*juu*

Vocabulary

いそがしい [*isogashii*] busy
おさけ [*o-sake*] liquor
ひらがな [*hiragana*] the cursive syllabary
いえ [*ie*] house, home
テニス [*tenisu*] tennis
よく [*yoku*] often, much
えいが [*eega*] movie

c. Counting beyond 10

11（十一）*juu-ichi*	100（百）*hyaku (-byaku, -pyaku)*
12（十二）*juu-ni*	1,000（千）*sen, (-zen)*
⋮	10,000（一万）*ichi-man*
19（十九）*juu-ku, juu-kyuu*	100,000（十万）*juu-man*
20（二十）*ni-juu*	1,000,000（百万）*hyaku-man*
30（三十）*san-juu*	10,000,000（千万）*sen-man*
40（四十）*yon-juu*	100,000,000（一億）*ichi-oku*
50（五十）*go-juu*	1,000,000,000（十億）*juu-oku*
60（六十）*roku-juu*	10,000,000,000（百億）*hyaku-oku*
70（七十）*shichi-juu, nana-juu*	
80（八十）*hachi-juu*	
90（九十）*kyuu-juu*	

Note: Both Arabic numerals (1,2,3 ...) and Chinese numerals（一，二，三 ...）are used in written Japanese. When writing horizontally Arabic numerals are usually employed, but when writing vertically top to bottom traditional Chinese numerals are often used.

d.

101	*hyaku ichi*	200	*ni-hyaku*
111	*hyaku juu-ichi*	300	*san-byaku*
1,001	*sen ichi*	400	*yon-hyaku*
1,111	*sen hyaku juu-ichi*	500	*go-hyaku*
2,000	*ni-sen*	600	*rop-pyaku*
2,222	*ni-sen ni-hyaku nijuu-ni*	700	*nana-hyaku*
3,000	*san-zen*	800	*hap-pyaku*
33,333	*san-man san-zen san-byaku sanjuu-san*	900	*kyuu-hyaku*
444,444	*yonjuu-yon-man yon-sen yon-hyaku yonjuu-yon*	8000	*has-sen*

Caution: Whereas Western style counting changes units (ones, thousands, millions, billions, etc.) every three digits, Chinese style counting changes every four digits（いち，まん，おく，etc.）.

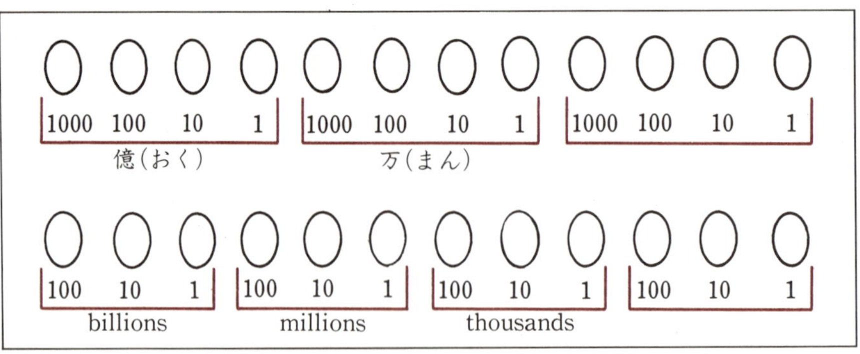

Exercise 7: Read the numbers below.

1) 15 2) 8 3) 25 4) 150 5) 473 6) 63 7) 2600
8) 1989 9) 13320 10) 100,000 11) 174,789 12) 1,000,000

For further practice, open your textbook at random and read the page numbers.

Function III　Telling time; hours「時」, minutes「分」

Hours are given as「**number**＋時（じ）」

Minutes are given as「**number**＋分（ふん／ぷん）」

	hour, o'clock 時 [*ji*]		minute (number of minutes) 分 [*fun, pun*]		number of hours 時間 [*jikan*]	
1	一時	*ichi-ji*	一分（間）	*ip-pun (kan)*	一時間	*ichi-jikan*
2	二時	*ni-ji*	二分	*ni-fun*	二時間	*ni-jikan*
3	三時	*san-ji*	三分	*san-pun*	三時間	*san-jikan*
4	四時	*yo-ji*	四分	*yon-fun*	四時間	*yo-jikan*
5	五時	*go-ji*	五分	*go-fun*	五時間	*go-jikan*
6	六時	*roku-ji*	六分	*rop-pun*	六時間	*roku-jikan*
7	七時	*shichi-ji*	七分	*nana-fun*	七時間	*shichi-jikan* *nana-jikan*
8	八時	*hachi-ji*	八分	*hap-pun*	八時間	*hachi-jikan*
9	九時	*ku-ji*	九分	*kyuu-fun*	九時間	*ku-jikan*
10	十時	*juu-ji*	十分	*jip-pun*	十時間	*juu-jikan*
11	十一時	*juuichi-ji*		*jup-pun*		
12	十二時	*juuni-ji*	三十分	*sanjip-pun* *sanjup-pun*	三十時間	*sanjuu-jikan*

ex.1. A:　いま、なん時ですか。　　What time is it now?

B:　10時42分です。　　10:42.

2. 3時ごろ、成田くうこうへ　いきます。　　I am going to go to Narita Airport around 3:00.

3. あしたの　ごご4時に、マイケルさんに　あいます。

I am going to meet Michael tomorrow at 4:00 p.m.

Other expressions:

1:00	1時 (one o'clock) *or* ちょうど1時 (exactly one o'clock)
3:15	3時15分 (three fifteen) *or* 3時15分すぎ (15 minutes past three)
5:27	5時27分 *or* ごぜん5時27分 (five twenty-seven a.m.)
8:30	8時30分 (eight thirty) *or* 8時はん (half past eight)
15:45	15時45分 *or* ごご3時45分 (three forty-five p.m.) *or* ごご4時15分まえ (15 minutes to four)
21:50	21時50分 *or* ごご9時50分 *or* ごご10時10分まえ

ex.4. いま、9時はんですね。10時15分まえに、ぎんこうのまえで、あいましょう。

It's now 9:30. Let's meet in front of the bank at 15 minutes to ten.

Note 1: When speaking of approximate times the suffix「ごろ [*goro*]」is added after the time as shown in example 2. Recently younger Japanese have begun to use「ぐらい [*gurai*]」in place of「ごろ」.

Note 2: When speaking of some event, etc. happening "at" such and such a time use the postposition「に」.

ex. 3時<u>に</u>、バーバラさんに　あいます。　　I am going to meet Barbara at 3 o'clock.

Exercise 8: Ask your partner the time. Answer as indicated below.

ex. A：すみません。いま、なん時(じ)ですか。

B：ちょうど２時(じ)です。

A：どうも。

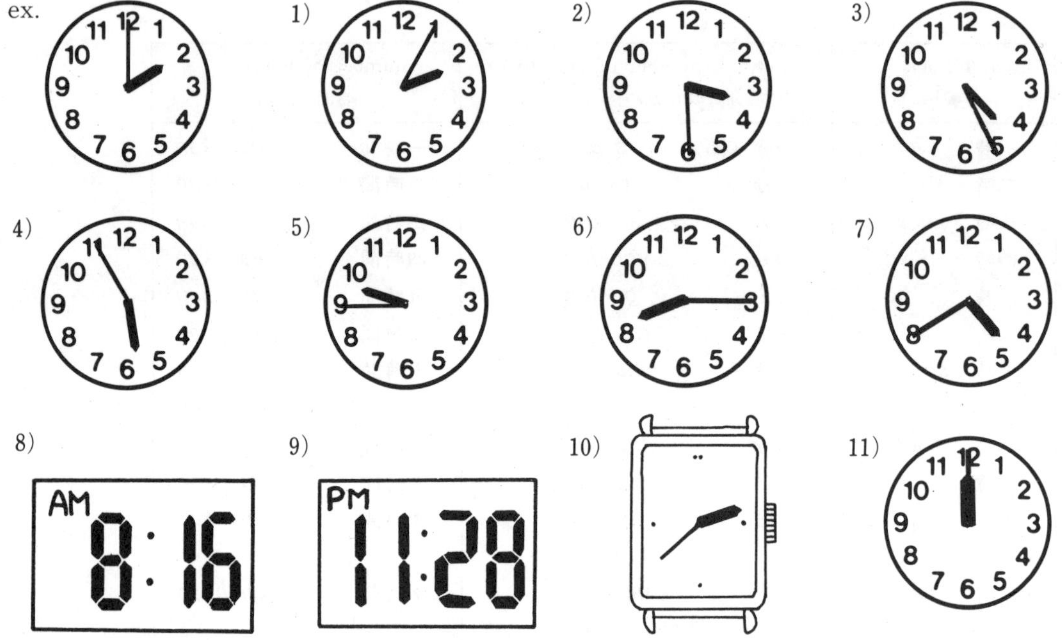

Function IV　Counting hours and minutes;「時間」「分(間)」

Units of measure (time, distance, weight, volume, etc.) are counted by giving the number + unit. The unit for hours is「時間（じかん）」, the unit for minutes is「分（ふん／ぷん）」or「分間（ふんかん／ぷんかん）」. (☞ Chart, Function Ⅲ)

ex.1. A: 東京(とうきょう)えきから　ディズニーランド(でぃずにーらんど)まで、どのくらい　かかりますか。

About how long does it take from Tokyo station to Disneyland?

B: バスで、35分(ふん)　かかります。　It takes 35 minutes by bus.

2. A: まいにち、なん時間(じかん)、しごとを　しますか。　How many hours do you work every day?

B: ８時間、しごとを　します。　I work 8 hours.

3. A: 東京から静岡(しずおか)まで、しんかんせんで、どのくらいですか。

About how long does it take by bullet train from Tokyo to Shizuoka?

B: １時間はんぐらいです。　It takes about one hour and a half.

B: さあ、ちょっと　わかりません。　Well, I'm not sure exactly.

Note 1:「ぐらい」"approximately" may be added after the number of minutes or hours.

Note 2:「どのくらい」itself means "about how much", and「かかります」means "take (time)" or "cost (money)". Sometimes it may be necessary to clarify by adding the word「時間」or「おかね」as topic.

ex. 時間は、どのくらい　かかりますか。　About how much time does it take?

おかねは、どのくらい　かかりますか。　About how much will it cost?

Exercise 9: Look at the chart and answer the questions.

1) 田中さんは、まいにち、なん時に　ねますか。
2) 田中さんは、まいにち、なん時に　おきますか。
3) 田中さんは、まいにち、なん時間、ねますか。
4) 田中さんは、まいにち、なん時間、しごとを　しますか。
5) ひるやすみは、なん時から　なん時までですか。
6) ひるやすみは、なん時間ですか。
7) 田中さんは、なん時に、うちを　でますか。
8) 田中さんは、なん時に、うちに　かえりますか。
9) 田中さんは、まいにち、なん時間、テレビを　みますか。
10) 田中さんは、まいにち、なん時間、えい語の　べんきょうを　しますか。

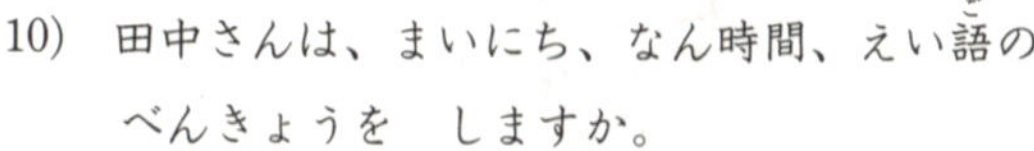

11) 田中さんのうちから　かいしゃまで、どのくらい　かかりますか。

12) 田中さんは、なん時ごろ、あさごはんを　たべますか。

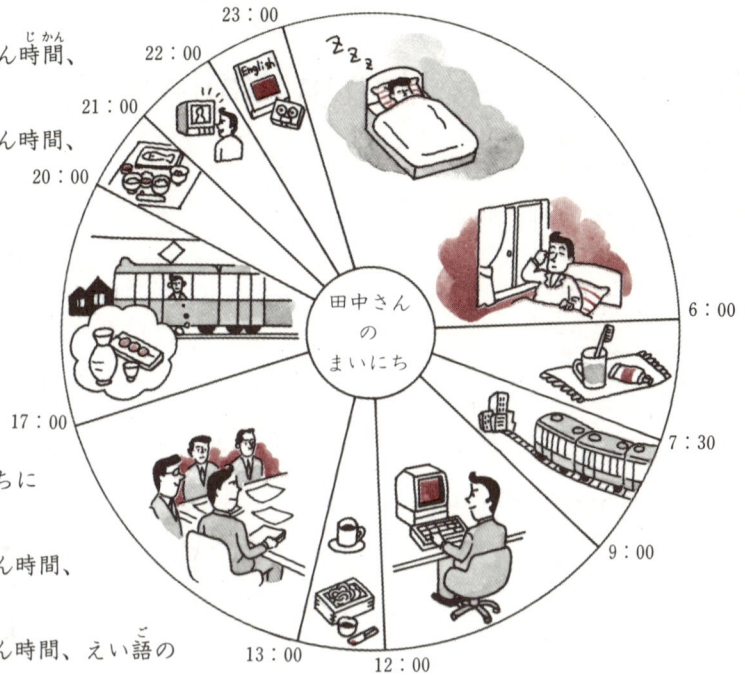

Exercise 10: Construct questions following the pattern below and answer them.

ex. 成田→ホテル，くるま ⇨ 成田から　ホテルまで，くるまで，どのくらい　かかりますか。

1) あなたのいえ→がっこう，でんしゃ
2) あなたのいえ→かいしゃ，でんしゃ
3) 成田→あなたのくに，ひこうき
4) 東京→京都　しんかんせん（2時間40分）
5) 東京えき→ディズニーランド，バス（30分）

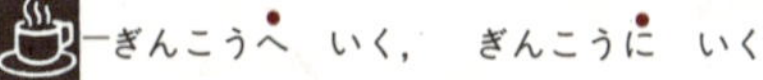

ぎんこうへ　いく，　ぎんこうに　いく

「へ」indicates the direction in which, or the person, place or object toward which, movement occurs, while「に」indicates the end point of such movement. In actual use, this difference is not always so important. Note however,「に」encompasses a much broader range of meanings, including its use as the indirect object marker, location marker with「ある」and「いる」, and marker for various time words.

ex. 1.何時に、うち へ／に　かえりますか。 What time do you return home?
2.田中さん へ／に　てがみを　だしました。 I sent a letter to Mr. Tanaka.
3.バーバラさんは、どこに　いますか。 Where is Barbara?
4.9時に、マイケルさんに　あいます。 I'm going to meet Michael at 9:00.

Vocabulary

ひるやすみ [hiruyasumi] noon recess, lunch hour
うち [uchi] home, house
でます [demasu] polite form of ru-verb「でる」"to go out, come out, leave"
くに [kuni] country, place grew up in
ひこうき [hikooki] airplane
あさごはん [asagohan] breakfast (lit. morning meal)

Exercise 11: Using the Japan Railway time table, ask and answer as in the example.

ex. A：すみません。東京（とうきょう）から　新大阪（しんおおさか）まで、しんかんせんで、どのくらい　かかりますか。
　　B：３時間（じかん）ぐらいです。

しんかんせん（ひかり）	
東京	9:07
なごや	10:58
京都（きょうと）	11:42
新大阪（しんおおさか）	12:00
おかやま	12:52
ひろしま	13:38
はかた	15:04

1)　東京　→おかやま

2)　なごや　→　はかた

3)　東京　→ひろしま

4)　東京　→　はかた

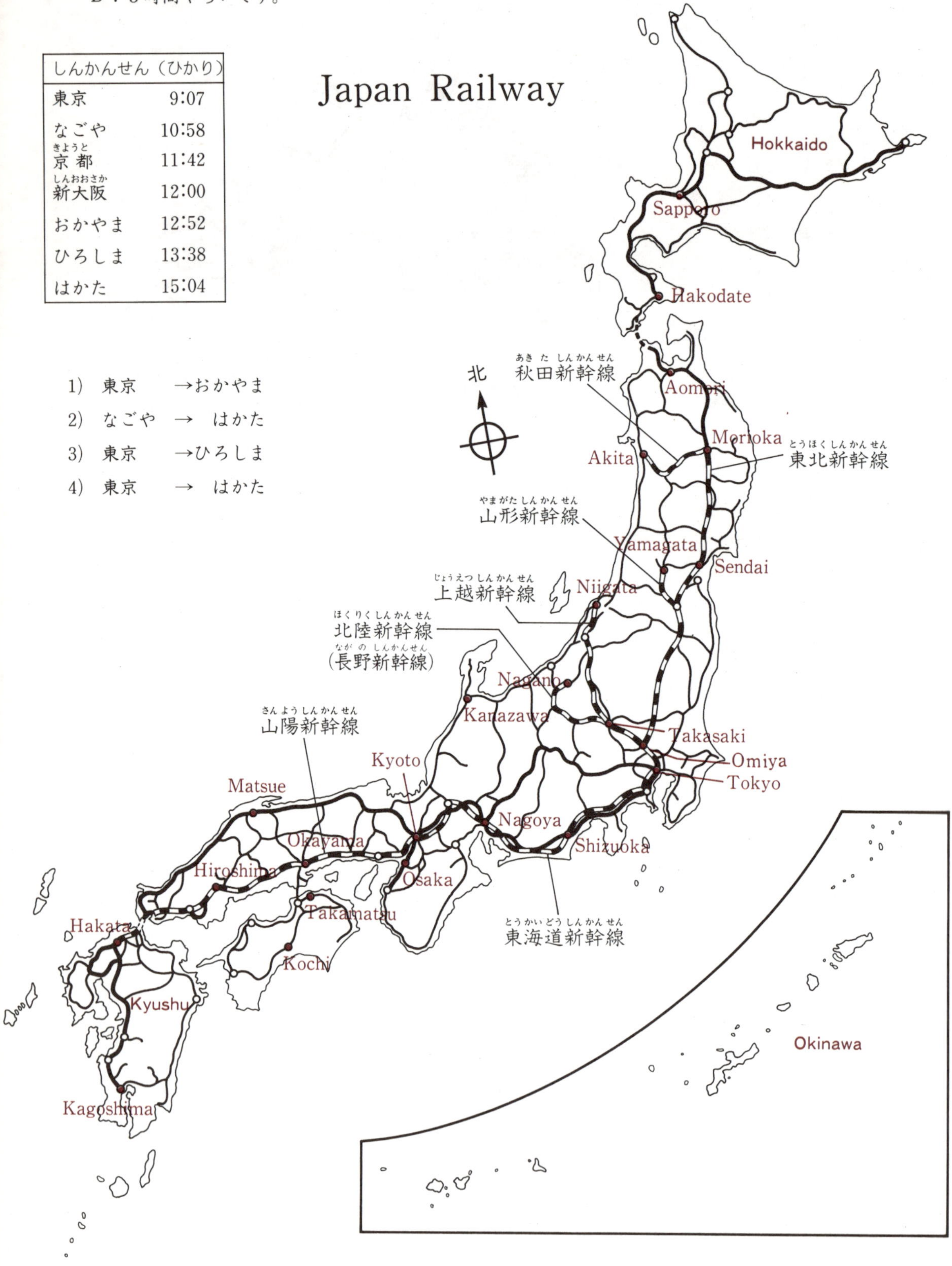

Japan Railway

北

Hokkaido
Sapporo
Hakodate
秋田新幹線（あきたしんかんせん）
Aomori
Morioka
東北新幹線（とうほくしんかんせん）
Akita
山形新幹線（やまがたしんかんせん）
Yamagata
Sendai
上越新幹線（じょうえつしんかんせん）
Niigata
北陸新幹線（ほくりくしんかんせん）
（長野新幹線（ながのしんかんせん））
Nagano
Kanazawa
Takasaki
Omiya
Tokyo
山陽新幹線（さんようしんかんせん）
Kyoto
Matsue
Nagoya
Okayama
Shizuoka
Hiroshima
Osaka
Takamatsu
Hakata
東海道新幹線（とうかいどうしんかんせん）
Kochi
Kyushu
Okinawa
Kagoshima

Function V Suggesting doing something; いきましょう

The verb let's form (see p.18) is used to propose or suggest doing that action. The let's form of polite「〜ます」is「〜ましょう」.

ex.1. A: でんしゃで　いきましょうか、タクシーで　いきましょうか。
Shall we take the train or a taxi?
B: でんしゃは、ちょっと　ふべんです。タクシーで　いきましょう。
The train is a bit inconvenient. Let's take a taxi.
A: (Accepting) じゃ、そうしましょう。　In that case, let's do so.

2. A: ビールを　のみましょうか。　Shall we have some beer?
B: (Accepting) ええ、いいですね。　Yes, that would be great.
(Refusing) いいですね。でも、ちょっと、いまは…。
That sounds good. But at the moment I'm afraid, uh....

A negative question is also commonly used to suggest or invite some sort of action.

ex.3. A: ビールを　のみませんか。　Why don't we have some beer?
B: ええ、のみましょう。　Yes, let's.

4. A: テニスを　しませんか。　Why don't we play tennis?
B: (Accepting) ええ、しましょう。　Yes, let's.
(Refusing) ざんねんですが、ちょっと、ようが　あって…。
Too bad, but I'm busy and so, uh ....

Exercise 12: Look at the pictures and act the dialogues as shown in the examples.

ex.1. A: すきやきを　たべましょうか。
B: ええ、たべましょう。
2. A: いっしょに　いきませんか。
B: ざんねんですが、ちょっと　ようが　あって……。

1)ビール，のみます　2) テニス，します　3) えいが，みます　4) ワイン，かいます

Vocabulary

すきやき [sukiyaki] *sukiyaki*

Exercise 13: Practice the conversation below changing the underlined parts as shown.

ex. 5時(じ)／うちへ　かえります⇨ A:　5時ですね。うちへ　かえりましょうか。

B:　①ええ、かえりましょう。

②ええ、でも　ちょっと…。

1) 12時／　ごはんを　たべます
2) むずかしい／　せんせいに　ききます
3) 雨(あめ)／　タクシー(たくしー)で　いきます
4) 田中(たなか)さんの　たんじょう日(び)／　パーティー(ぱーてぃー)を　します
5) あしたは　テスト(てすと)／　いっしょに　べんきょうします

Exercise 14: Take turns with your partner in suggesting or inviting courses of action, as in the example below.

ex. A：　みち子(こ)さん、あした、テニス(てにす)を　しましょう。

B：　いいですね。しましょう。　(Accepting)

B：ざんねんですが、あしたは、ちょっと…。　(Refusing)

Reading Comprehension Exercise

東京(とうきょう)のちかくには、成田(なりた)くうこう があります。羽田(はねだ)くうこう もあります。羽田くうこうは、こくないせんの くうこうですが、成田くうこうは、こくさいせんの くうこうです。羽田は、東京のみなみにあります。東京から、モノレール(ものれーる)で、30分(ぷん)ぐらいかかります。とてもちかいです。べんりです。成田くうこうは、東京のひがしにあります。とても大(おお)きい くうこうですが、すこしとおいです。東京から成田まで、くるまで、2時間(じかん)ぐらいかかります。でんしゃもありますが、すこしふべんです。

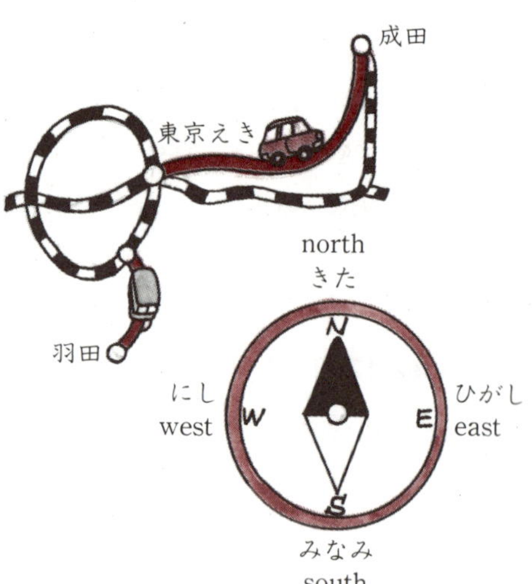

◆**Vocabulary**◆

こくないせん [kokunai-sen] domestic airlines
こくさいせん [kokusai-sen] international airlines
モノレール [monoreeru] monorail
みなみ [minami] south
ひがし [higashi] east
きた [kita] north
にし [nishi] west

Exercise 15: Fill the blanks on the chart comparing Narita Airport and Haneda Airport.

羽田	こくないせん		東京のみなみ	モノレールで30分	べんり
成田		とおい			

Listening Comprehension Exercise

Listen to the tape and answer the following questions.

◆Vocabulary◆
もういちど　いいます [moo ichido iimasu] I'll say once again.

1) Listen to the dialogue and do the following.

① Choose what you consider to be the most important message for Mr. Tsuchida.

a. (　) みちが　こんでいます。

b. (　) いま、11時(じ)です。

c. (　) 東京から　成田まで、1時間(じかん)はんぐらい　かかります。

② Mark T or F.

a. (　) 東京から　成田までのみちは、すいています。

b. (　) 東京から　成田までのみちは、とても　こんでいます。

c. (　) 東京から　成田まで、でんしゃで、1時間30分(ぷん)　かかります。

d. (　) いま、成田まで、くるまで、5時間はんぐらい　かかります。

2) Listen to the statements, and draw in the hands of the clock.

①

②

③

④

⑤

⑥

Vocabulary

ごはん [gohan] boiled rice, meal; breakfast (あさごはん), lunch (ひるごはん), dinner (ばんごはん)
ききます [kikimasu] polite form of u-verb「きく」"to hear, listen to, ask"
雨 (あめ) [ame] rain
たんじょう日 [tanjoobi] birthday
パーティー [paatii] party

すこし　やすんだほうが　いいですね

It Would Be Better To Rest A Bit

Dialogue I

In the lobby of the hotel

土田(つちだ)　：さあ、つきました。ここが、東京(とうきょう)インターナショナル・ホテルです。
バーバラ：土田さん、わたしは、ちょっと　つかれました。
土田　：じゃ、すこし　やすんだほうが　いいですね。
ウエッブさんも？
マイケル：わたしは、だいじょうぶです。
ひこうきのなかで、よく　ねました。
バーバラ：ええ、マイケルは、どこでも、よく　ねます。
このあいだは、おきゃくさんのまえで、ねていましたよ。
土田　：へえ、それは　すごいですね。　ええと、マイケルさん、
すぐ、チェック・インを　したほうが、いいんじゃないですか。
マイケル：ええ、そうしましょう。
土田：じゃ、わたしは、ここで　まっています。

Dialogue II

Back in the lobby one hour later.

マイケル：おまたせしました。バーバラは、シャワーを　あびていますが、
すぐ、きます。
土田　：そうですか。じゃ、バーで　まちましょう。
ところで、ひこうきのしょくじは、なんでしたか。
にくでしたか、さかなでしたか。
マイケル：さかなじゃありませんでした。にくと　やさいでした。

土田（つちだ）　：それじゃ、ゆうしょくは、さかなが　いいですね。
　　　　　マイケルさんは、おすしが　すきですか。

マイケル：ええ、すきです。

土田　　：バーバラさんは?

マイケル：かないも　すきですよ。
　　　　　まえは、あまりすきじゃありませんでしたが、
　　　　　いまは、なんでも　たべます。

土田　　：そうですか。じゃ、すしやへ　いきましょうか。

マイケル：いいですね。

Vocabulary

Nouns:

8おきゃくさん [*o-kyaku-san*] guest (polite form of「きゃく」)

10チェック・インする [*chekku-in* (*suru*)] check in (to check into)

13シャワー [*shawaa*] shower

15バー [*baa*] barroom, bar

16しょくじ [*shokuji*] meal

17にく [*niku*] meat

17さかな [*sakana*] fish

18やさい [*yasai*] vegetables

19ゆうしょく [*yuushoku*] supper

26すしや [*sushi-ya*] *sushi*-bar

Adjectives:

9すごい [*sugoi*] wonderful, terrific, magnificent

20すき（な）[*suki*(*na*)] is liked (「わたしは、すしが　すき」lit. As for me, *sushi* is liked.)

Adverbs:

5だいじょうぶ [*daijoobu*] fine, no problem, OK

Verbs:

1つきました [*tsukimashita*] polite past tense of u-verb「つく」"to arrive"

2つかれました [*tsukaremashita*] polite past tense of ru-verb「つかれる」"to get tired, worn out"

3やすんだ [*yasunda*] plain past tense of u-verb「やすむ」"to rest"

7ねます [*nemasu*] polite form of ru-verb「ねる」"to sleep"

10します [*shimasu*] polite form of irregular verb「する」"to do"

12まっています [*matteimasu*] polite progressive form of u-verb「まつ」"to wait"

13あびています [*abiteimasu*] polite progressive form of ru-verb「あびる」"to take a shower or bath"

14きます [*kimasu*] polite form of irregular verb「くる」"to come"

Grammatical words:

6で [*de*] location marker "in, at, on". Indicates location where action takes place, as opposed to「に」, which indicates where something exists.

ex.　すしや<u>で</u>　たべる。　We eat <u>at</u> the *sushi* bar.

　　 すしや<u>に</u>　いる。　We are <u>at</u> the *sushi* bar.

8お [*o*] prefix added to various words to make them polite.

ex.「きゃく」"customer, guest" →「おきゃく」

18と [*to*] and (used to join nouns only)

26へ [*e*] direction marker, used with verbs of motion (「いく」「くる」etc.) to indicate direction or destination
25 Question word ＋「でも [*demo*]」 means "any __" when used with affirmative predicate (see Lesson13, p.170 for further explanation)

ex. どこでも [*doko demo*] anywhere　なんでも [*nan demo*] anything, everything

Expressions:

3やすんだほうがいい [*yasunda hoo ga ii*] It would be better to rest. ☞Function Ⅵ
8このあいだ [*konoaida*] the other day　9へえ [*hee*] Wow! Gee!
16ところで [*tokorode*] by the way (used to introduce a new theme for discussion)
19それじゃ [*soreja*] well then, in that case
24まえは [*mae wa*] formerly, before (suggesting "but not now")
25いまは [*ima wa*] at present, now (suggesting "but not before" or "but not much longer")

Dialogue Comprehension Exercise

Answer the following questions.

Dialogue Ⅰ

1) だれが、つかれましたか。
2) だれが、ひこうきのなかで　ねましたか。

Dialogue Ⅱ

3) バーバラさんは、なにを　していますか。
4) 土田(つちだ)さんと　マイケルさんは、どこで、バーバラさんを　まっていますか。
5) ひこうきのしょくじは、なんでしたか。
6) ゆうしょくは、なにを　たべますか。
7) マイケルさんは、おすしが　すきですか。
8) バーバラさんは、おすしが　すきですか。

Dialogues in English

Dialogue Ⅰ

T: Alright, here we are. This is the Tokyo International Hotel.
B: I'm a bit tired out, Mr. Tsuchida.
T: Well then, it would be better to rest up a bit, I suppose. You too, Mr. Webb?
M: Me, I'm fine. I slept well on the plane.
B: Yes, Michael sleeps well anywhere. The other day he was sleeping in front of guests.
T: Wow. That's an accomplishment, alright! Well then, wouldn't it better to check in right away, Michael?
M: Yes, I believe so.
T: I'll be waiting for you here then.

Dialogue Ⅱ

M: Sorry to have kept you waiting. Barbara is taking a shower, but she'll be here shortly.
T: Is that so? Well then, let's wait at the bar. By the way, what did you have to eat on the plane? Did you have meat or fish?
M: We didn't have fish. We had meat and vegetables.
T: In that case, fish would be good for dinner. Do you like *sushi*, Michael?
M: Yes, I do.
T: What about Barbara?
M: My wife likes it too. She didn't like it much before, but now she eats anything.
T: Really? Well then, shall we go to a *sushi* bar?
M: That would be great!

Function I

Describing past states and conditions; にくでした。

		affirmative	negative
non-past	Noun＋だ	ここは、ホテルです。	ここは、ホテルじゃ　ありません。
	な-adj.	ここは、しずかです。	ここは、しずかじゃ　ありません。
	い-adj.	ここは、せまいです。	ここは、せまく　ありません。 ここは、せまく　ない　です。
past	Noun＋ だ	ここは、ホテルでした。	ここは、ホテルじゃ　ありませんでした。
	な-adj.	ここは、しずかでした。	ここは、しずかじゃ　ありませんでした。
	い-adj.	ここは、せまかったです。	ここは、せまく　ありませんでした。 ここは、せまく　なかった　です。

Note: The past tense of い-adjectives is formed by dropping the final「い」and adding「かった」.

〈other examples〉

さむ~~い~~ → かった

やすい→やすかった　　　たかい→たかかった
大きい→大きかった　　　小さい→小さかった
むずかしい→むずかしかった

ex.1. ひこうきのしょくじは、にくでした。さかなじゃ　ありませんでした。
The food on the airplane was meat. It was not fish.

2. わたしは、いま、阿部産業(あべさんぎょう)のしゃいんです。
I am presently an employee of Abe Industries.
まえは、田中産業(たなかさんぎょう)のしゃいんでした。
Previously I was an employee of Tanaka Industries.

3. ここは、まえは、こうえんでした。とても　しずかでした。
In the past this was a park. It was very quiet.
こんなに　うるさく　ありませんでした。
It wasn't this noisy.

4. きのうの　パーティーは、とても　たのしかったです。
Yesterday's party was really fun.

Exercise 1: Look at the pictures on the next page and explain as in the example below.

ex. 大(おお)きい　　小(ちい)さい

まえは、大きかったですが、いまは、大きく ありません。 小さいです。

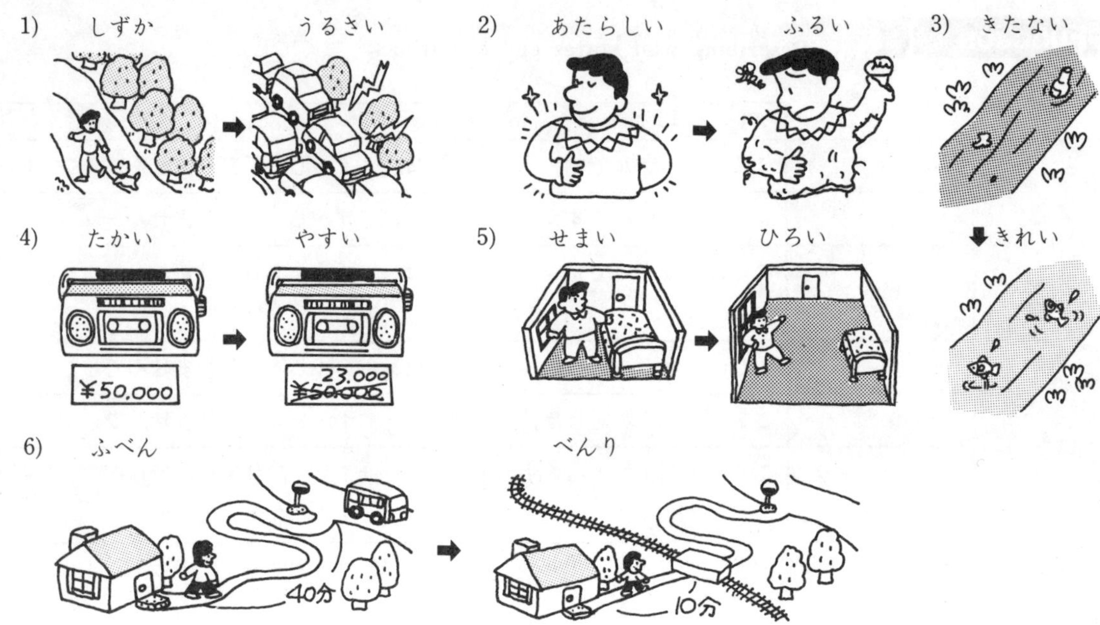

Exercise 2: Answer the following questions using「～でした」or「(じゃ) ありませんでした」.

1) きのうは、日(にち)よう日(び)でしたか。
2) きのうは、いそがしかったですか。
3) きのうは、いい天気(てんき)でしたか。
4) きのうは、雨(あめ)でしたか。
5) ゆうべのテレビは、おもしろかったですか。
6) ゆうべは、さむかったですか。

Function II

Describing past events: verb past tense; ねました

	affirmative	negative
non-past	いきます　go, am going to go	いきません　don't go, am not going to go
past	いきました went, have gone	いきませんでした didn't go, have not gone

Japanese verb forms have two main tenses, the non-past and past. The non-past corresponds to both present and future tenses in English, while past tense denotes an action or state completed in the past, or completed in the past but result of which is still in effect in the present.

ex.1. わたしは、まいにち、べんきょうします。　I study every day.
2. わたしは、いつも、でんしゃのなかで、本(ほん)を　よみます。　I always read books on the train.
3. わたしは、あした、テニスを　します。　I am going to play tennis tomorrow.
4. わたしは、けさ、パンを　たべました。　I ate some bread this morning.
5. わたしは、きのう、えいがを　みました。　I saw a movie yesterday.
6. マイケルは、よく　ねますが、タクシーのなかでは　ねませんでした。　Michael sleeps all the time, but he didn't sleep in the taxi.
7. わたしは、ちょっと　つかれました。　I (got and now) am a bit worn-out.
8. さあ、つきましたよ。　OK, (we arrived and) here we are.
9. 電車(でんしゃ)が　きましたよ。　The train (arrived and) is here.

Exercise 3: Answer the following questions on your own.

ex. きのう、学校(がっこう)へ　いきましたか。→はい、いきました。

→いいえ、いきませんでした。

1) きのう、えいがを　みましたか。
2) きのう、日本語(にほんご)のべんきょうを　しましたか。
3) きのう、ビールを　のみましたか。
4) みちは、こんでいましたか。
5) ゆうべは、よく　ねましたか。
6) けさ、しんぶんを　よみましたか。

Exercise 4: Practice the following conversation changing the underlined part.

ex. A: きょうは、なにを　しましょうか。

B: <u>テニスを　しましょう</u>。

A: <u>テニス</u>ですか。きのう　<u>しましたよ</u>。　きょうは、<u>えいがに　いきましょうよ</u>。

1) B: こうえんへ　いきます。
A: うちで、本(ほん)を　よみます。

2) B: えいがを　みます。
A: ドライブを　します。

3) B: レコードを　ききます。
A: プールで　およぎます。

Exercise 5: Look at the pictures and answer the question:

土田(つちだ)さんは、きのう、なにを　しましたか。

1) 
2) 
3) 

4) 
5) 

Exercise 6: Michael talks about his life. Complete the following narrative using the words given in the list below. Change the form of the words as necessary.

わたしは、ニュージャージーの　小(ち)さいまちで（①）。　10さいまで、そこに（②）。
11さいのとき、ニューヨークへ（③）。そして、ニューヨークの　学校へ（④）。
わたしは、学校が　とても（⑤）。ともだちが　たくさん（⑥）。
だいがくで、けいざいと　日本語(にほんご)を（⑦）。

a.うまれます　b.すきです　c.います　d.はいります　e.いきます　f.べんきょうします

Vocabulary

日よう日 [nichiyoobi] Sunday
ドライブする [doraibu(suru)] drive (to drive)
およぎます [oyogimasu] polite form of u-verb「およぐ」"to swim"
花 [hana] flower
11さいのとき [juuissai no toki] when I was 11 years old
だいがく [daigaku] university, college
うまれます [umaremasu] polite form of ru-verb「うまれる」"to be born"
はいります [hairimasu] polite form of u-verb「はいる」"to enter"
レコード [rekoodo] record, phonograph
プール [puuru] swimming pool
－さい [sai] (counter for age) years old
そして [soshite] and then, next
けいざい [keezai] economy, economics
まち [machi] town

Function III On-going action: progressive form; シャワーを　あびています。

The idea of an action in progress or repeated over a period of time is expressed by the て-form of the verb followed by「いる」"to be, exist".

	affirmative	negative
non-past	本を　よんで　います。	本を　よんで　いません。
past	本を　よんで　いました。	本を　よんで　いませんでした。

ex.1. バーバラは、へやで　シャワーを　あびていますが、すぐ　きます。

Barbara is taking a shower in the room, but will be here shortly.

バーで　まっていましょう。

Let's (be) wait(ing) for her in the bar.

2. マイケルは、ひこうきのなかで、本を　よんでいませんでした。ねていました。

Michael was not reading a book on the plane. He was sleeping.

Note: In speaking「～ています」is often shortened to「～てます」.
ex. 本を　よんでいます。→　本を　よんでます。／本を　よんでません。

Exercise 7: Look at the picture and tell what each person is doing.

Exercise 8: Practice the following conversation, replacing the underlined part with the expressions below.

person A

①もしもし、わたしです。
③山田さんを　おねがいします。
⑤そうですか。じゃ、また　あとで　でんわします。

person B

②ああ、中村さん、こんにちは。
④山田さんは、いま、
ex.（タイプを　うちます）
→タイプを　うっています。

1) てがみを　かきます。
2) おきゃくさんと　はなします。
3) でんわを　します。
4) コーヒーを　いれます。
5) かいぎを　します。
6) (whatever you like)

Function IV Listing more than one object (1)

Function IV-1 Also, too, as well as; かないも すきです。

ex.1. これは、わたしのペンです。 This is my pen.
それも、わたしのペンです。 That is my pen too.
あれも、わたしのペンです。 That over there is also my pen.
ぜんぶ、わたしのペンです。 All of them are my pens.

2. Mr. Smith: わたしは、アメリカ人です。 I'm an American.
Mr. Webb: わたしも、アメリカ人です。 I'm an American too.

3. わたしは、えい語も、スペイン語も、日本語も わかります。
I can understand English, Spanish, and Japanese as well.

Note:「も」replaces topic「は」, subject「が」and direct object「を」, but follows other particles「へ」,「に」,「で」, etc. to form double particle constructions.

ex.1. わたしは、京都へ いきます。大阪へも いきます。
I'll go to Kyoto. Also to Osaka.

2. はなやは、そこにも、あそこにも あります。
There is a flower shop just over there, and way over there as well.

Exercise 9: Look at the pictures and complete the sentences using「も」.

1) でんわは、たばこやのまえに あります。
それから、ex. ぎんこうのまえにも あります。

2) これは、日本語のじしょです。
それから、____________。

3) 女の人が、でんわのよこに います。
それから、____________。

4) はなは、つくえのうえに あります。
それから、____________。

Vocabulary

コーヒー [koohii] coffee
もしもし [moshimoshi] Hello!
こんにちは [konnichiwa] Good morning. Good afternoon.
タイプ [taipu] typewriter
うつ [utsu] (u-verb) to strike, hit, beat, knock
タイプを うつ to operate a typewriter
また [mata] again, once more
あとで [atode] later
はなします [hanashimasu] polite form of u-verb「はなす」"to talk, speak"
かいぎ [kaigi] meeting
たばこや [tabako-ya] tobacco shop
それから [sorekara] and then, after that, next, in addition
おんな [onna] woman
本だな [hon-dana] bookshelf
じしょ [jisho] dictionary

5) わたしは、よく　テニスをします。
それから、＿＿＿＿＿＿＿＿＿＿。

6) きのうは、すきやきを　たべました。
それから、＿＿＿＿＿＿＿＿＿＿

Function Ⅳ-2　A and B；AとB

「と」is used to combine two or more nouns, and is equivalent to English "and".

ex. A: つくえのしたに、なにが　ありますか。
B: はこと　バッグが　あります。
A: つくえのうえに、なにが　ありますか。
B: 本と、ノートと、ペンと、えんぴつが　あります。

Exercise 10: Look at the picture and answer the questions using「と」. Then change the sentence using「も」.

ex. 田中(たなか)さんは、どこに　いきましたか。
→京都(きょうと)と　大阪(おおさか)に　いきました。
→京都に　いきました。それから、
大阪にも　いきました。

1) へやのなかに、だれが　いますか。
2) 土田(つちだ)さんは、だれに　でんわを
かけましたか。
3) バッグは、どこに　ありますか。
4) どこの　ワインが　おいしいですか。

Function Ⅴ　Expressing likes and dislikes；すき，きらい

The な-adjective「すき」expresses the notion "I like such and such". "I dislike such and such" is expressed by the な-adjective「きらい」.

ex.1. わたしは、すしが　すきです。　I like *sushi*. (lit. As for me, *sushi* is liked.)
マリアさんは、すしが　きらいです。
Maria dislikes *sushi*. (lit. As for Maria, *sushi* is disliked.)
マリアさんは、すしは　すきじゃありません。　Maria doesn't like *sushi*.

2. わたしは、テニスは　すきですが、マラソンは　すきじゃありません。
I like tennis, but don't like long-distance running.

3. マイケルさん、てんぷらは　すきですか。　　Michael, do you like *tempura*?
　まあ、きらいじゃありませんが…。　　Well, I don't dislike it, but....

4. ウィルソンさんは、すしが　すきですが、スミスさんは、すきじゃありません。
　Wilson likes *sushi*, but Smith doesn't.

Exercise 11: Look at the pictures and tell what Barbara and Michael like and do not like.

ex.1. マイケルさんは、ジャズが　すきですが、バーバラさんは、ジャズは　すきじゃありません。
　2. マイケルさんは、ジャズが　すきです。　バーバラさんは、ジャズが　きらいです。

	ex. ジャズ	①てんぷら	② ゴルフ	③ えいが	④ かぶき	⑤ テニス
マイケル						
バーバラ						

Exercise 12: How about you? Tell if you like the things mentioned in Exercise 11.

Function VI　Offering advice ; やすんだほうが　いいですよ

The idea "it would be better to do such and such" is expressed using the plain past tense of the verb (see p.18) followed by the phrase「～ほうが　いい」.

〔1〕**Advice**

strong encouragement

Verb-た　ほうがいいですよ。　　You had better __.
Verb-た　ほうがいいでしょう。　　I think it would be better to __.
Verb-た　ほうがいいんじゃありませんか。　　Wouldn't it better to __?

mild suggestion

〔2〕**Accepting**

そうですね。　　Oh, yes. I see.
ええ、そうします。　　Yes, I will.

〔3〕**Refusing**

そうですね。でも…。
　That may be so. But....
ええ、でも、ちょっと…。
　Yeah, but. You see....

まどを
あけたほうが
いいんじゃ
ありませんか。
そうですね。
(そうしましょ
う。)

Vocabulary

ジョギングする [jogingu(suru)] jogging (to jog)　やきゅう [yakyuu] baseball
すいえい [suiee] swimming　アイスクリーム [aisukuriimu] ice cream
サラダ [sarada] salad　メロン [meron] melon　うどん [udon] Japanese noodles
ノート [nooto] notebook, note　でんわを かける [denwa o kakeru] to call, telephone
ジャズ [jazu] jazz　ゴルフ [gorufu] golf　かぶき [kabuki] *Kabuki*, Japanese traditional drama

ex.1. A: どうしましたか。 What's wrong?
B: ちょっと、おなかが…。 My stomach is a little, uh ....
A: じゃ、びょういんに いったほうが いいですよ。
Well, in that case, you had better go to the hospital.
B: ええ、そうします。 Yeah, I will.

ex.2. A: 1時間(じかん)ぐらい、まったほうが いいんじゃありませんか。
Wouldn't it be better if you waited about an hour?
B: ええ。でも、いま いきます。 Yes, well perhaps so, but I'm going to go now.

Exercise 13: Respond to the following statements with the appropriate advice.

1) 本(ほん)を わすれました。 ( )
2) みちが わかりません。 ( )
3) おなかが いたいです。 ( )
4) おかねを なくしました。 ( )
5) 日本語(にほんご)が わかりません。 ( )

a. 学校(がっこう)で、べんきょうしたほうが いいですよ。
b. びょういんに いったほうが いいですよ。
c. けいさつへ いったほうが いいですよ。
d. ちずを みたほうが いいですよ。
e. ともだちに かりたほうが いいですよ。

Exercise 14: What advice would you give in each of the following situations? Use the responses in the box, or think of something appropriate on your own.

1) かないが びょうきです。 2) ちょっと つかれました。 3) みちが こんでいます。
4) かぜを ひきました。 5) あした、テストが あります。

a. 電車(でんしゃ)で いった b. すぐ、べんきょうした c. はやく うちへ かえった
d. くすりを のんだ e. はやく うちを でた f. すこし やすんだ
g. びょういんに いった h. はやく ねた

Answering yes or no

Consider the following:

1. Q:すしは、すきですか。 Do you like *sushi*?
A:はい、すきです。 Yes, I do.
いいえ、すきじゃありません。 No, I don't.
2. Q:すしは、すきじゃありませんか。 Don't you like *sushi*?
A:はい、すきじゃありません。 No, I don't.
A:いいえ、すきです。 Yes, I do.

Whereas English yes and no confirm or deny the reality itself (in this case liking or not liking *sushi*), Japanese「はい/ええ」and「いいえ」reply "true" or "false" to the question. "True. I do not like *sushi*." "False. I do like *sushi*."

Vocabulary

わすれました [*wasuremashita*] polite past tense of ru-verb「わすれる」"to forget"
なくしました [*nakushimashita*] polite past tense of u-verb「なくす」"to lose"
おなかが いたい [*onaka ga itai*] to have a stomach ache
けいさつ [*keesatsu*] police
かりた [*kari-ta*] past tense of ru-verb「かりる」"to borrow"
びょうき [*byooki*] illness, sickness
はやく [*hayaku*] soon, early
かぜ [*kaze*] cold; かぜを ひきました [*hikimashita*] I have a cold.
くすりを のんだ [*kusuri o nonda*] I took medicine.
ハンカチ [*hankachi*] handkerchief

Reading Comprehension Exercise

Number the following sentences in proper order so they form a coherent conversation.

Part 1

(1) ウエッブさん、日よう日は、いつも、なにをしますか。

( ) どんなばんぐみが　すきですか。

( ) ええ、しますよ。きのうは、テニスをしました。

( ) そうですね、ゆっくりねます。それから、テレビをみます。

( ) ニュースです。CNN のニュースをよくみます。

( ) スポーツは、しませんか。

Part 2

(1) テニスは、なん時間ぐらいしましたか。

( ) そうですか。なにをたべましたか。

( ) それから、なにをしましたか。

( ) 2時間ぐらいです。それから、六本木のレストランにいきました。

( ) ディスコへいきました。1時間はんぐらい、おどりました。

( ) それじゃ、すこしつかれましたね。

( ) イタリアりょうりです。

( ) ええ。でも、とても　たのしかったです。

◆Vocabulary◆

ゆっくり　ねます [*yukkuri nemasu*] to have a good sleep

ばんぐみ [*bangumi*] TV program

ニュース [*nyuusu*] news

スポーツ [*supootsu*] sports

ディスコ [*disuko*] disco

りょうり [*ryoori*] cooking

たのしい [*tanoshii*] pleasant, enjoyable

おどりました [*odorimashita*] polite past tense of u-verb「おどる」"to dance"

Listening Comprehension Exercise

Listen to the dialogue on the tape and answer the following questions.

1) What did Mr. Tanaka forget? Circle the correct items.

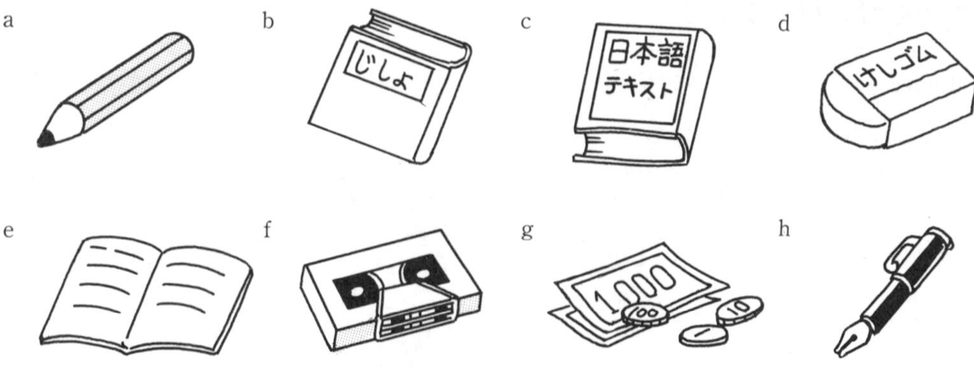

2) What is the one thing Mr. Nakamura did not lend?

3) How does Mr. Nakamura sound? Circle one.

① sympathetic　② worried　③ sarcastic　④ amused

第5課　ビールが　のみたいですね

I'd Like To Have Beer

Dialogue I

At the sushi bar

土田　　：のみものは、何が　いいですか。

マイケル：きょうは　あたたかいから、
　　　　　ビールが　のみたいですね。

バーバラ：わたしも、ビールが　いいです。

土田　　：すしは、何を　たべたいですか。

マイケル：そうですね。わたしは、トロ。

バーバラ：じゃあ、わたしは、えびが　いいわ。

土田　　：すみません。ビールを３本。
　　　　　それから、トロを　ふたつと、
　　　　　えびを　ひとつ、おねがいします。

Dialogue II

After dinner

マイケル&バーバラ：ごちそうさまでした。

土田　　：いいえ、どういたしまして。どうですか、東京のすしは。

バーバラ：ええ、とても　おいしかったわ。

マイケル：ずいぶん　人が　おおいですね。どうしてですか。

土田　　：きょうは、きゅうりょう日のあとの　金よう日だからですよ。
　　　　　すこし　あるきましょうか。

マイケル：いいですね。ところで、いま、何時ですか。

土田　　：ええと…、ああ、10時10分まえです。

マイケル：そうですか。ニューヨークは、いま、あさですね。

土田(つちだ)　：ええ、あさの８時ごろですね。

マイケル：それじゃ、りょうしんが　しんぱいしているから、ちょっと、ホテルで　でんわを　したいんですが。

土田　：じゃ、すぐ　ホテルに　かえりましょう。

Dialogue III

Making an international phone call

マイケル　：もしもし、ニューヨークへ　でんわを　かけたいんですが。

Tel. operator：でんわばんごうは、何(なん)ばんですか。

マイケル　：ニューヨークの　234-5978です。

Tel. operator：きょくばんは、何ばんですか。

マイケル　：ああ、すみません。マンハッタンですから、212です。

Tel. operator：はい。でんわを　きって、おまちください。

Vocabulary

Nouns:

1のみもの [nomimono] something to drink, drink
6トロ [toro] fatty part of the tuna
7えび [ebi] shrimp
15きゅうりょう日 [kyuuryoo-bi] payday
15あと [ato] after
15金よう日 [kin'yoobi] Friday
21りょうしん [ryooshin] parents
21しんぱいする [shinpai] worry, concern (to worry, to be concerned)
26でんわばんごう [denwa bangoo] telephone number
28きょくばん [kyokuban] area code

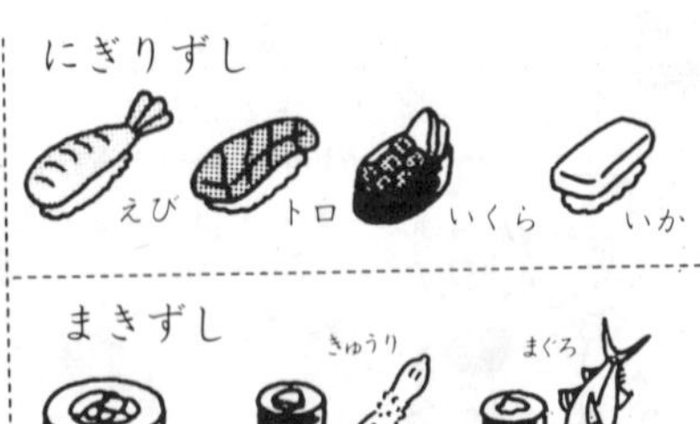

Counters:

8 －本 [hon, bon, pon] for counting long, thin objects, etc.
10ひとつ [hito-tsu] one (counting objects)
9ふたつ [futa-tsu] two
26 －ばん [ban] ① ordinal number marker.「いちばん，にばん，さんばん…」"number one (first), number two (second), number three (third) …, etc. ② counter for telephone numbers, etc.

Adjectives:

2あたたかい [atatakai] warm
13おいしかった [oishikatta] past tense of「おいしい」"delicious"

Verbs:

16あるきましょう [arukimashoo] "let's form" of u-verb「あるく」"to walk"
31きって [kitte] て-form of u-verb「きる」"to cut"

Grammatical words:

2 phrase＋から [kara] because __
3 verb＋たい [tai] to want to __

Expressions:

7わ [wa] sentence-final particle used by women for emphasis, etc.
10おねがいします [o-negai shimasu] Please. I request.
11ごちそうさまでした [gochisoosama deshita] Thank you for the food.
12どういたしまして [doo itashimashite] Not at all. Don't mention it.
12どうですか [doo desu ka] How is it? How are you?
14どうしてですか [dooshite desu ka] Why is that?
22でんわを する (かける) [denwa o suru (kakeru)] to make a telephone call, call
31でんわを きる [denwa o kiru] to hang up
31おまちください [o-machi kudasai] Please wait. (politer than「まってください」)

Dialogue Comprehension Exercise

Mark the following T or F.

Dialogue I

1) ( ) バーバラさんと マイケルさんは、ビールを のみました。
2) ( ) バーバラさんは、トロを たべました。
3) ( ) 土田さんは、すしを たべませんでした。

Dialogue II

4) ( ) いま、10時(じ)10分(ぷん)です。
5) ( ) マイケルさんは、ホテルで、でんわを かけます。
6) ( ) きょうは、きゅうりょう日(び)です。

Shorter answers with「です」

When asked「あなたは、どこから きましたか」"Where did you come from?", one replies「わたしは、東京から きました」"I came from Tokyo." But it is also possible to shorten your answer by replacing「から きました」with the be-verb.「わたしは、東京です」"As for me, Tokyo." In plain speech the be-verb may even be omitted altogether.

ex. 土田：すしは、何を たべますか。 What would you like in the way of *sushi*?
マイケル：わたしは、えびです。 Shrimp for me.
バーバラ：わたしは、トロ。 *Toro* for me!

Function I Telephone numbers

でんわばんごうは、何(なん)ばんですか。 What is the telephone number?

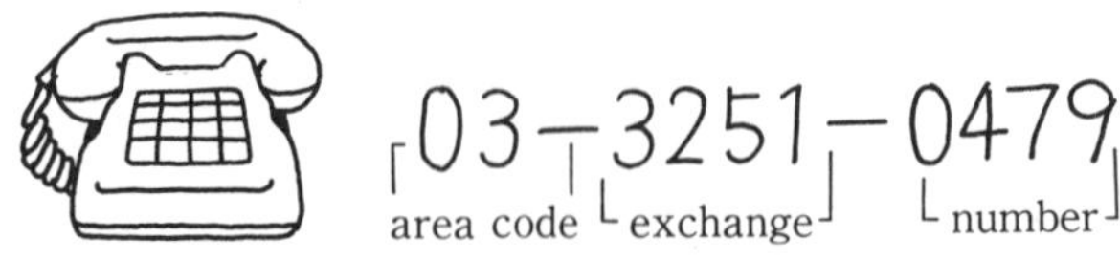

When giving telephone numbers, simply say each number individually, without worrying about tens, hundreds or thousands. Separate area code, exchange and number with「の」.「ばん」"number" at the end is optional.

0 3（の）3 2 5 1（の）0 4 7 9 （ばん）
ぜろ さん （の） さん にい ごう いち （の） ぜろ よん なな きゅう

Note: For the sake of clarity, 0 is pronounced [*zero*], 4 [*yon*], 7 [*nana*] and 9 [*kyuu*]. Single syllable numbers 2 [*ni*] and 5 [*go*] are usually pronunced long: 2 [*nii*], 5 [*goo*].

Exercise 1: Pronounce the following telephone numbers.

1） 03-3379-4911　　2） 03-3493-3150
3） 03-3726-8357　　4） 0742-34-6722
5） 0292-54-6141　　6） 045-582-5012

Exercise 2: Ask three of your classmates their telephone numbers and write them in your notebook.

ex. A：あのう、あなたのうちの　でんわばんごうを　おしえてください。
B：東京（とうきょう）　0 3　の　3 2 3 4　の　3 5 8 9　です。
A：0 3　の　3 2 3 4　の　3 5 8 9　ですね。
B：ええ、そうです。
A：ありがとう。

◆**Vocabulary**◆ おしえてください [*oshiete kudasai*] please tell me

Dialogues in English

Dialogue I

T : What would you like to drink? (lit. What would be good in the way of drinks?)

M : It's warm today, so I guess I'd like to have beer.

B : I'd like beer too.

T : What would you like to eat in the way of *sushi*?

M : Well, let's see. "*Toro*" for me.

B : In that case, I would like shrimp.

T : Excuse me! Three bottles of beer. Also two orders of *toro* and one order of shrimp, please.

Dialogue II

M & B : Thank you very much! The food was delicious.

T : Not at all. Don't mention it. How do you like Tokyo *sushi?*

B : Yes, it was very good.

M : There certainly are a lot of people. Why is that?

T : It's because today is the Friday after payday. Should we walk for a bit?.

M : That sounds good. What time is it now, by the way?

T : Just a moment. It's, uh.... Oh, yes! It's ten minutes to ten.

M : Really? It's morning in New York now, isn't it?

T : Yes, it's around eight in the morning, I believe.

M : In that case then, I'd sort of like to make a telephone call at the hotel, because my parents are worried.

T : OK, then. Let's return right away to the hotel.

Dialogue III

M : Hello. I'd like to make a call to New York.

Op.:What is the number, please?

M : New york, 234–5978.

Op.:What is the area code, please?

M : Oh, yes. I'm sorry. It's Manhattan, so it's 212.

Op.:OK. Would you hang up and wait, please.

Function II　Counting objects;　1本(ぽん), ひとつ

	～本（ほん，ぼん，ぽん）	～つ
1　いち	一本　いっぽん	一つ　ひとつ
2　に	二本　に　ほん	二つ　ふたつ
3　さん	三本　さんぼん	三つ　みっつ
4　し	四本　よんほん	四つ　よっつ
5　ご	五本　ご　ほん	五つ　いつつ
6　ろく	六本　ろっぽん	六つ　むっつ
7　なな	七本　ななほん／しちほん	七つ　ななつ
8　はち	八本　はっぽん／はちほん	八つ　やっつ
9　く／きゅう	九本　きゅうほん	九つ　ここのつ
10　じゅう	十本　じゅっぽん／じっぽん	十　とお
How many?	何本　なんぼん	いくつ

1. Long slender objects such as pencils, bottles, cans, fingers, rolls of film, cassette tapes, etc. are counted by giving the number plus the counter「本」(ほん，ぼん，ぽん).
2.「つ [*tsu*]」is a general purpose counter for objects. It is used only with "Japanese" numerals (underlined parts in the list above) however, and not with the "Chinese" numerals we have learned thus far. For all practical purpose, Japanese numerals are used to count only as far as 10.

ex. 1. A：きのう、ビールを、何本　のみましたか。　How many bottles of beer did you drink yesterday?
　　B：3本　のみました。　I drank three bottles.

2. A：きのう、すしを、いくつ　たべましたか。　How many *sushi* did you eat yesterday?
　　B：トロを　3つと、えびを　5つ　たべました。　I ate three *toro* and five shrimp.
　　バーバラは、十(とお)ぐらい　たべました。　Barbara ate about ten.

Note: Numbers themselves are generally not followed by the particles「を」or「が」.

ex. 1. ○ビールを　3本　ください。　Give me three bottles of beer.
　　×ビールを　3本を　ください。
　　×ビール　3本を　ください。
2. ○ビールが　3本　あります。　Here are three bottles of beer.
　　×ビールが　3本が　あります。
　　×ビール　3本が　あります。

Exercise 3: Try ordering the items below using「～本」or「～つ」.

ex.

ビールを　1本、
おねがいします。

1)

2)

3) 

4) 

5) 

6) 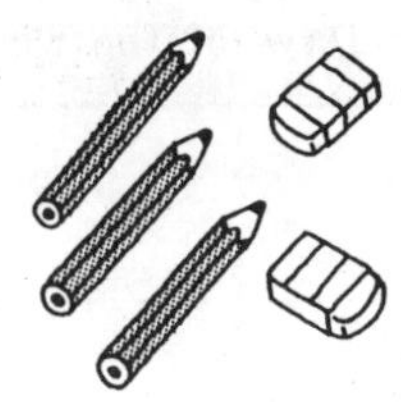

Exercise 4: For the following items, mark, those counted by「～本」with ○, and those counted by「～つ」with △.

1) (　) りんご　2) (　) ペン　3) (　) けしゴム　4) (　) ハンバーガー　5) (　) すし
6) (　) えんぴつ　7) (　) かさ　8) (　) バナナ　9) (　) バッグ　10) (　) ネクタイ

Function III　Indicating specific times

1 **Dates:** Years months and days are all numbered and given in the order:

____年 [*nen*]"year" ____月 [*gatsu*]"month" ____日 [*ka, nichi*] "day"

Years are read using Chinese numerals.

ex. 1990年（せん　きゅうひゃく　きゅうじゅう　ねん）
平成２年（へいせい　に　ねん）
昭和39年（しょうわ　さんじゅうきゅう　ねん）

Readings for months and days are shown below. Note that days 2～10 are read as Japanese numerals, with「日」pronounced [*ka*]. Other days are read as Chinese numerals, with「日」pronounced [*nichi*]. １日, 14日, 20日, 24日 simply memorize.

１月	いちがつ	January	１日	ついたち	1st
２月	にがつ	February	２日	ふつか	2nd
３月	さんがつ	March	３日	みっか	3rd
４月	しがつ	April	４日	よっか	4th
５月	ごがつ	May	５日	いつか	5th
６月	ろくがつ	June	６日	むいか	6th
７月	しちがつ	July	７日	なのか	7th
８月	はちがつ	August	８日	ようか	8th
９月	くがつ	September	９日	ここのか	9th
10月	じゅうがつ	October	10日	とおか	10th
11月	じゅういちがつ	November	11日	じゅういちにち	11th
12月	じゅうにがつ	December	12日	じゅうににち	12th
何年	（なんねん）	What year?	14日	じゅうよっか	14th
何月	（なんがつ）	What month?	20日	はつか	20th
何日	（なんにち）	What day?	24日	にじゅうよっか	24th

ex. A：あなたの　たんじょう日(び)は、いつですか。　When is your birthday?
B：８月６日(がつむいか)です。　August 6th.

Vocabulary

ハンバーガー [*hanbaagaa*] hamburger
ネクタイ [*nekutai*] necktie, tie
バナナ [*banana*] banana
ケーキ [*keeki*] cake

2 **Days of the week:** The marker for "day of the week" is「ようび日」.

日(にち)よう日(び) Sunday	月(げつ)よう日(び) Monday	火(か)よう日(び) Tuesday	水(すい)よう日(び) Wednesday
木(もく)よう日(び) Thursday	金(きん)よう日(び) Friday	土(ど)よう日(び) Saturday	

ex. A：3月10日(とおか)は　何(なん)よう日(び)ですか。 What day of the week is the March 10th?
B：土よう日です。 Saturday.

3 **Today, yesterday, tomorrow:**

Day:	おととい the day before yesterday	きのう yesterday	きょう today	あした tomorrow	あさって the day after tomorrow
Week:		先週(せんしゅう) last week	今週(こんしゅう) this week	来週(らいしゅう) next week	さ来週(らいしゅう) the week after next
Month:		先月(せんげつ) last month	今月(こんげつ) this month	来月(らいげつ) next month	さ来月(らいげつ) the month after next
Year:	おととし the year before last	きょねん last year	今年(ことし) this year	来年(らいねん) next year	さ来年(らいねん) the year after next

Note 1: The words above are usually not followed by the particle「に」.
Note 2: Also useful are「こんどの__」"next __, this coming __" and「このまえの__」"last __".

ex. 1. おととい、すしやに　いきました。 We went to a *sushi* bar the day before yesterday.
2. こんどの　土よう日も、また　いきます。 We are going again this coming Saturday as well.
3. このまえの　日よう日に、ディズニーランドに　いきました。来月の　14日に、また　いきます。
We went to Disneyland last Sunday. We are going to go again on the 14th of next month.

Exercise 5: Look at the calendar below and answer the following questions.

1) きょうは、何月何日(なんがつなんにち)、何(なん)よう日(び)ですか。
2) ひなまつりは、何よう日でしたか。
3) いつ、テニスを　しましたか。
4) こんどの　日(にち)よう日(び)に、何(なに)をしますか。
5) いつ、ゴルフに　いきますか。
こんどの　土(ど)よう日(び)ですか。
6) 春分(しゅんぶん)の日(ひ)は、来週(らいしゅう)の　火(か)よう日(び)ですか。
7) 来週の　土よう日は、何日(なんにち)ですか。
8) いつ、えいがに　いきましょうか。
(Answer on your own)

3月

日	月	火	水	木	金	土
				1	2	3 ひなまつり
4	5	6 きょう	7	8	9	10
やまのぼり 11	12	13	14	15	16	17 ゴルフ
18	19	20 春分の日	21	22	23	24
25	26	27	28	29	30	31

Exercise 6: Answer the following questions.

1) きょうは、何月何日(なんがつなんにち)、何(なん)よう日(び)ですか。
2) きのうは、何月何日、何よう日でしたか。
3) あさっては、何月何日、何よう日ですか。
4) おとといは、何月何日、何よう日でしたか。
5) 今年(ことし)のクリスマスは、何よう日ですか。
6) あなたの　たんじょう日(び)は、いつですか。

Function IV　Telling what you want to do; すしを　たべたいです。

「〜たい」is used when telling what you yourself want to do, or when asking what someone else wants to do.「たい」is added to the verb stem, and is further inflected like adjectives.

かく →	かきたい	かきたくない	かきたかった
to write →	I want to write	I do not want to write	I wanted to write

The object of verb-たい may be indicated with either「を」or「が」, or may appear as the sentence topic.

ex. 1. すしを　たべます。I eat *sushi*.　　すし　を／が　たべたいです。I want to eat *sushi*.

ex. 2. 土田：バーバラさん、マイケルさん、何(なに)を　のみたいですか。
Barbara and Michael, what do you want to drink?
マイケル：わたしは、ビールが　のみたいです。　I want to drink beer.
バーバラ：わたしは、ビールは　のみたくありません。ジュースが　のみたいです。
I don't want to drink beer. I want to drink juice.

Note 1:「〜たい」can also be used as a means of asking to be allowed to do something. You might want to soften the effect however, by adding「＿んですが」.
ex. 1. でんわを　かけたいんですが…。　I would like to make a phone call please.
2. あした、やすみたいんですが…。　I would like to take off tomorrow please.

Note 2:「〜たい」is generally not used to suggest some sort of action, in the way that English "Would you like to ＿?" is used. Instead use「〜ませんか」(Lesson 3, p. 55).
ex. 1. A：ひろこさん、やまに　いきたいですか。　Are you wanting to go to the mountains, Hiroko?
B：いいえ、いきたくありません。　No, I am not.
2. A：ひろこさん、やまに　いきませんか。　Would you like to go to the mountains, Hiroko?
B：ええ、でも、ちょっと　つごうが　わるいんです。　Yes, but I'm tied up at the moment.

Note 3: When stating what someone else wants to do it is more proper to use the form「〜たがる」"to appear to want to ＿".
ex. 田中(たなか)さんが、あなたに　あいたがっていますよ。
Apparently Mr. Tanaka wants to meet you.

Exercise 7: Answer what you want to do as in the picture.

1) あなたは、どこへ
いきたいですか。
A：＿＿＿＿＿へ
＿＿＿＿＿。

2) 何(なに)が　たべたいですか。
A：＿＿＿が＿＿＿＿＿。
3) 何(なに)が　のみたいですか。
A：＿＿＿が＿＿＿＿＿。

Vocabulary

ひなまつり [hinamatsuri] Doll's or Girl's Festival (see p.119)
春分の日（しゅんぶんのひ）[shunbun no hi] the Vernal Equinox
サンドイッチ [sandoitchi] sandwich
クリスマス [kurisumasu] Christmas
コーラ [koora] Coke, cola

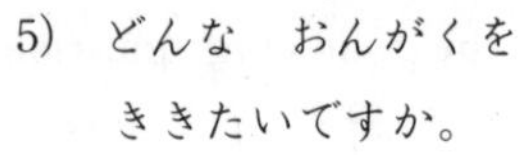

4) こんばん、何(なに)が したいですか。

A：＿＿＿＿＿＿

＿＿＿＿＿＿。

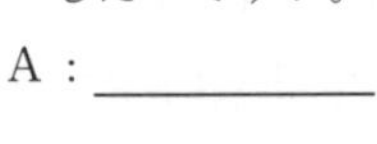

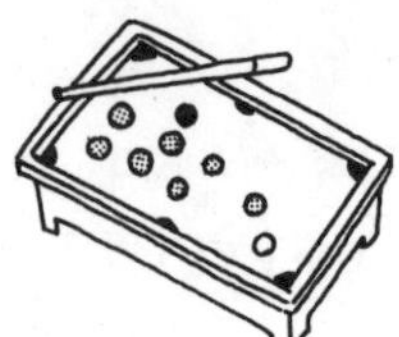

5) どんな おんがくを ききたいですか。

A：＿＿＿＿＿＿＿＿。

6) 来週(らいしゅう)の 日(にち)よう日(び)には、どんなことを したいですか。

A：＿＿＿＿＿＿＿＿に

＿＿＿＿＿＿＿＿。

7) だれに あいたいですか。

A：＿＿＿＿＿＿に

＿＿＿＿＿。

Exercise 8: Answer the following questions on your own.

1) 今年(ことし)のなつに、どんな ことを したいですか。 2) こんばん、何(なに)を たべたいですか。

3) どんな スポーツを したいですか。 4) どこに りょこうしたいですか。

5) どんな 本(ほん)が よみたいですか。

Exercise 9: Tell what Michael is saying in each of the following situations.

1)

2)

3)

Grammar Note　Plain form of verbs and adjectives

The use of plain and polite speech forms is described in the Outline of Japanese Grammar(p.17).

ex. plain form: あした、がっこうへ いく？ (informal style)

polite form: あした、がっこうへ いきますか。 (formal style)

Verb		polite (ます-form)		plain	
		non-past	past	non-past	past
u-verb	affirmative	kak-i-masu	kak-i-mashita	kak-u	kai-ta
	negative	kak-i-masen	kak-i-masen deshita	kak-a-nai	kak-a-nakatta
ru-verb	affirmative	tabe-masu	tabe-mashita	tabe-ru	tabe-ta
	negative	tabe-masen	tabe-masen deshita	tabe-nai	tabe-nakatta

Vocabulary

ビリヤード [biriyaado] billiards　おんがく [ongaku] music　ロック [rokku] rock music

どんな [donna]+noun "what sort of __?"　なつ [natsu] summer

こと [koto] matter, affair, fact, question;　どんな こと [donna koto] what sort of thing?

りょこうする [ryokoo (suru)] travel, trip (to travel, make a trip)　水（みず）[mizu] water

きっぷ [kippu] ticket　シャツ [shatsu] shirt　やまのぼり [yama nobori] mountain climbing

Note 1: See p.18 for the inflection patterns of other verbs ending in consonant. Pay particular attention to the root ending in w (ex. かう [*Kau*]).

Note 2: Irregular

くる (to-come)	ku-ru	ki-masu	ko-nai	ki-ta	ko-nakatta
する (to do)	su-ru	shi-masu	shi-nai	shi-ta	shi-nakatta
いく (to go)	ik-u	iki-masu	ika-nai	it-ta	ika-nakatta

い-adj.

わかい "young"

		non-past	past
affirmative	plain	waka-i	waka-katta
	polite	waka-i desu	waka-katta desu
negative	plain	waka-ku-nai	waka-ku-nakatta
	polite	waka-ku-nai desu waka-ku arimasen	waka-ku-nakatta desu waka-ku arimasen deshita

な-adj. & Copular (だ／です)

		affirmative		negative	
		non-past	past	non-past	past
な-adj. (げんきな)	plain	genki-da	genki-datta	genki-ja-nai	genki-ja-nakatta
	polite	genki-desu	genki-deshita	genki-ja-arimasen	genki-ja -arimasen deshita
Noun＋Copular (男(おとこ) だ)	plain	otoko da	otoko datta	otoko ja nai	otoko ja nakatta
	polite	otoko desu	otoko deshita	otoko ja arimasen	otoko ja arimasen deshita

Exercise 10: Practice making plain non-past and past verb forms, in both the affirmative and negative.

ex. かきます (to write)　かく，かかない，かいた，かかなかった

1) u-verb: ① はなします (to talk) ② いいます (to say) ③ まちます (to wait)
④ のみます (to drink) ⑤ うたいます (to sing) ⑥ わかります (to understand)

2) ru-verb: ① たべます (to eat) ② いれます (to put in) ③ うまれます (to be born)

3) irregular: ① します (to do) ② いきます (to go) ③ きます (to come)

Function V　Stating reasons ; あたたかいから

Various plain or polite verbals and verbal constructions may be followed by「から」to form expressions of the type "because such and such".

1 reason から、result

ex. 1. いい天気(てんき)だから、こうえんへ　いきましょう。

The weather's nice, so let's go to the park!

2. けしきが　きれいだったから、しゃしんを　とりました。

We took a picture because the scenery was lovely.

3. ここの　すしは　おいしいから、ここで　たべましょう。

Let's eat here because their *sushi* is good.

4. つかれたから、もう　ねます。　I'm going to bed now because I am tired.

Note 1: It is possible to reverse the order.

ex. ここで　たべましょう。ここの　すしは、おいしいから。

Note 2: Another form「ので」is also used in a similar manner as「から」, except that when「ので」comes after the be-verb「だ」,「だ」appears in its alternate form「な」.「から」is often used for making threats, excuses or justifications, while「ので」is generally reserved for more formal situations to objectively state the reasons for such and such.

ex. 1. あついので、まどを　あけてください。　It's hot so please open the window.
2. がくせいなので、あまり　お金(かね)が　ありません。　I'm a student so I don't have much money.
3. みちが　こんでいたので、おくれました。　I'm late because the streets were crowded.

2 Answering the question "why?"

ex. 1. A：どうして、そのさかなを　たべませんでしたか。　Why didn't you eat that fish?
B：あまり　おいしくなかったからです。　Because it wasn't very good.
2. A：きのう、かいしゃに　きませんでしたね。なぜですか。
You didn't come to the office yesterday. Why not?
B：かぜを　ひいたからです。　Because I had a cold.

Note 3: To ask the reason for something, use「なぜ」or「どうして」.

Note 4:「ので」may be used in place of「から」above, except that the sequence「のでです」is never used.

ex. A：どうして　おくれましたか。　Why were you late?
B：すみません。みちが　こんでいたので。　I'm sorry, the street was crowded, and so....
×みちが　こんでいたのでです。

Exercise 11: Give the first sentence as a reason for the second.

ex. つかれました。もう　ねます。⇨つかれた　から／ので、もう　ねます。

1) あした、はやく　おきます。きょうは、はやく　かえります。
2) チェックインを　します。ちょっと　まってください。
3) ゆうべ、あまり　ねませんでした。きょうは、ねむいです。
4) テレビを　かいたいです。秋葉原(あきはばら)へ　いきます。
5) いい天気(てんき)です。銀座(ぎんざ)まで　あるきましょう。
6) 日本人(にほんじん)じゃ　ありません。かんじは、あまり　しりません。
7) あのセーターは、たかかったです。かいませんでした。

Exercise 12: Complete the following sentences any way you wish.

ex. あついから、(ビールが　のみたいです／ビールを　のみましょう)。

1) つかれたから、(　　)。
2) りょうしんが　しんぱいしているから、(　　)。
3) きょくばんは、東京(とうきょう)だから(　　)。
4) (　　)、たくさん　かいました。
5) お金(かね)が　ないから、(　　)。
6) へやが　きたないから、(　　)。
7) (　　)、はやく　うちに　かえりたいです。
8) (　　)、土(ど)よう日(び)に、わたしのうちに　きてください。

Vocabulary

ねむい [nemui] sleepy, drowsy　日本人 [Nihonjin] Japanese (people)　セーター [seetaa] sweater
しりません [shirimasen] polite negative form of u-verb「しる」"to find out";「しっている」"to know"

Reading Comprehension Exercise

〈土田(つちだ)さんの日記(にっき)〉

きょうは、マイケルさんたちと、すしやへいった。マイケルさんも、バーバラさんも、すしがすきだからだ。トロと、えびと、いかを、たくさんたべた。ビールものんだ。とてもおいしかった。マイケルさんたちは、りょうしんがしんぱいしているので、ホテルから、ニューヨークへ、でんわをかけた。10時ごろだった。わたしは、りょうしゅうしょをわすれたので、もういちど、すしやへいった。よるなので、こんどは、すいていた。おなかがすいたので、もうすこし、そこでたべた。たかかった。

◆Vocabulary◆

りょうしゅうしょ [*ryooshuusho*] receipt
おなかが　すいた [*onaka ga suita*] I am hungry, I was hungry
〜たち [*tachi*] added to personal pronouns and names to make them plural
　　わたしたち [*watashi-tachi*] we
と [*to*] with　　いか [*ika*] squid
もうすこし [*moo sukoshi*] a little more

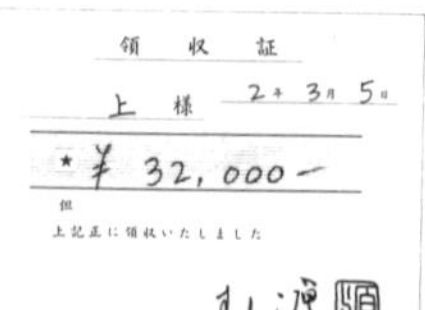
領　収　証
上　様　2年3月5日
★¥32,000−
但
上記正に領収いたしました
すし源

Exercise 13: Answer the following questions.

1) マイケルさんたちは、何時(なんじ)ごろ、どこへ、でんわをかけましたか。
2) マイケルさんたちは、だれに、でんわを　しましたか。
3) 土田さんは、どうして、すしやへもどりましたか。

Listening Comprehension Exercise

Listen to the tape and do as directed.

1) Write in Michael's schedule on the calendar.

a　b　c　d　e

4月						
日	月	火	水	木	金	土
			1	2	3	4
5	6	7	8	9	10	11
12	13	14	15	16	17	18
19	20	21	22	23	24	25
26	27	28	29 みどりの日	30		

2) Which is the correct telephone number?

① a. 03-238-5060　b. 03-328-0560
　c. 03-238-5006
② a. 0471-59-8252　b. 0741-59-8252
　c. 0471-59-8262
③ a. 0478-52-1489　b. 0478-22-1894
　c. 0748-52-1489

3) Listen and write down the telephone number.

＊ The telephone exchange for Tokyo was changed from a three-digit to a four-digit number as of January 1, 1991.

Vocabulary

日記（にっき）[*nikki*] diary
みどりの日 [*midori no hi*] Greenery Day (national holiday)

第6課　それは　いくらですか

How Much Is It?

Dialogue I

Mr. Tsuchida meets Mr. Webb on his way to the station and asks him about his first day at the office.

土田（つちだ）　：ウエッブさん、しごとは　どうでしたか。
マイケル：さいしょの日（ひ）だから、ちょっと　つかれました。
でも、おもしろかったですよ。
土田　：オフィスの人（ひと）は　どうですか。
マイケル：ええ、みんな　しんせつで、あかるい人たちでした。
土田　：それは　よかったですね。
マイケル：それに、わかくて　きれいな　女の人（おんなのひと）が、
たくさん　いますね。
土田　：そうでしょう。
マイケル：でも、バーバラには、ひみつですよ。
土田　：ところで、あしたは　休み（やすみ）ですね。ウエッブさんは、
何（なに）をしますか。
マイケル：ええ、銀座（ぎんざ）のデパートへ　いきます。アパートへ
ひっこすので、いろいろなものが　いるんですよ。
土田　：ああ、アメリカから　もってこなかったんですね。
マイケル：いえ、……その、もってきたんですが、バーバラが、
あたらしいのを　ほしがっているものですから。

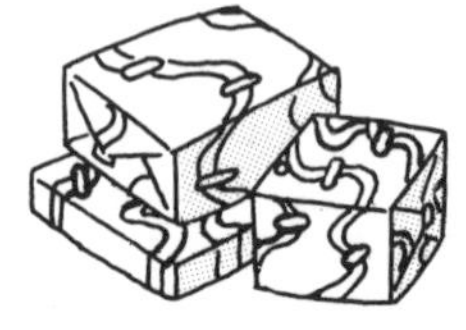

Dialogue II

At the department store

てんいんA：いらっしゃいませ。

バーバラ　：この白(しろ)いシーツが　ほしいんですが、もっと　大(おお)きい　サイズのは、ありませんか。

てんいんA：大きいのですね。ちょっと、おまちください。

(a few minutes later)

すみません。これが、いちばん　大きい　サイズなんです。

バーバラ　：そうですか。じゃ、けっこうです。どうも　ありがとう。

てんいんB：いらっしゃいませ。

バーバラ　：アイロンが　ほしいんですが、どんな　ものが　ありますか。

てんいんB：はい、いろいろ　あります。どうぞ　ごらんください。

バーバラ　：そのアイロンは、いくらですか。

てんいんB：15,000円(えん)です。

バーバラ　：ちょっと　高(たか)いですね。

もうすこし、安(やす)くて　かるいのは　ありませんか。

てんいんB：そうですね。それでは、こんなのは　いかがですか。

11,000円ですが、これは、かるくて　じょうぶです。

おねだんも、あまり　高(たか)くありません。

バーバラ　：ああ、そうですか。じゃ、これで　けっこうです。これを　ください。

てんいんB：はい、ありがとうございます。

Vocabulary

Nouns:

2さいしょ the very first
4オフィス office
5みんな（みな）all, everyone, everything
7女の人（おんなのひと）woman
10ひみつ secret
13アパート apartment
14もの things, articles, goods
18てんいん sales clerk
19シーツ sheets
20サイズ size
25アイロン iron

Counters:

28円（えん）yen

Adjectives:

5しんせつ（な）kind
5あかるい cheerful, bright, well-lighted
14いろいろ（な）various (often used as adverb without「に」. See adverb use of な-adj. in Lesson 12, p.163)
19ほしい（I）want (something); ex. アイロンがほしい "I want an iron." lit. An iron is wanted.
30かるい light ↔ おもい heavy
32じょうぶ（な）sturdy, strong, well made, durable

Adverbs:

19もっと more
22いちばん number one; used as superlative marker, "the most"

Verbs:

14ひっこす (u-verb) to move to another residence
14いる (u-verb) to be needed, necessary
17ほしがる (u-verb) to appear to want, desire (used when telling what someone else wants)

Grammatical words:

5－たち suffix indicating plural: 人たち（ひとたち）people
27いくら question word: how much?
31こんな such, like this (cf. そんな, あんな see Appendix)

Expressions:

18いらっしゃいませ Welcome!
けっこうです 23① That's alright then. (No thank you.)
34② Fine. (I'll take it.)
31いかがですか How about it? How is it? How are you?

〈Colors〉

白（しろ），白（しろ）い	white
赤（あか），赤（あか）い	red
青（あお），青（あお）い	blue
黒（くろ），黒（くろ）い	black
きいろ，きいろい	yellow
ちゃいろ，ちゃいろい	brown
オレンジ	orange
ピンク	pink

Dialogue Comprehension Exercise

Answer the following questions.

Dialogue Ⅰ

1) マイケルさんの、さいしょの日（ひ）の　しごとは、どうでしたか。
2) オフィスの人（ひと）は、どうでしたか。
3) オフィスには、どんな　女（おんな）の人（ひと）が　いましたか。
4) あした、マイケルさんは、どこに　いきますか。
5) マイケルさんは、だれと　かいものに　いきますか。

Dialogue Ⅱ

1) バーバラさんは、白（しろ）いシーツを　かいましたか。
2) バーバラさんは、いくらの　アイロンを　かいましたか。
3) バーバラさんは、どんな　アイロンを　かいましたか。

◆Vocabulary◆　かいもの shopping

Function I Offering explanation or justification "you see"; 「＿のです」「＿んです」

Structure

	Explanation clause	
Noun +だ	Noun +な Noun +だった	+のだ (plain) +のです (polite) +んだ +んです (colloquial)
な-adj.	-な -だった	
い-adj.	plain form	
Verb	plain form	

「＿のだ」,「＿のです」or「＿んだ」,「＿んです」suggests that the speaker is offering an explanation or justification for whatever he is talking about, rather than simply stating it is a fact. Equivalent to "you see" in English.

When used as a question, it suggests that the speaker wants the listener to give an explanation or justification.

ex.1. A: どうして、きのう、会社(かいしゃ)を 休(やす)んだんですか。

Why did you take off from work yesterday?

B: かないが、びょうきだったんです。 My wife was sick, you see.

2. A: ゆうべ、パーティーに 来(き)ませんでしたね。なぜですか。

Hey, you didn't come to the party last night! Why not?

B: しごとが、おわらなかったんです。 I didn't finish work, you see.

Dialogues in English

Dialogue I

T : How did work go, Mr. Webb?
M : It was my first day, so I'm a bit tired. It was interesting though.
T : How are the people in the office?
M : All of them were kind and cheerful.
T : Which is nice for you, huh?
M : Besides, there were lots of young, pretty girls.
T : So you thought so too!
M : It's a secret from Barbara though.
T : By the way, tomorrow is a day off, right? What are you going to do, Mr. Webb?
M : Oh, we're going to go to a department store in Ginza. We're going to be moving into an apartment, so there are lots of things we need.
T : Oh, so you didn't bring things from America?
M : No. Well, we did bring some things, but since Barbara is wanting everything new ….

Dialogue II

A : Welcome.
Ba: I would like these white sheets, but don't you have them in a larger size?
A : Large ones, right? Just a moment, please. I'm sorry, but this is the largest size.
Ba: I see. That's all right then. Thank you.
B : Welcome.
Ba: I would like to buy an iron. What sort of ones do you have?
B : We have various kinds. Please have a look.
Ba: How much is that iron?
B : It's 15,000 yen.
Ba: That's a bit expensive. Don't you have something that's a bit cheaper and lighter?
B : Let me see. Well then, what about one like this? It's 11,000 yen, but it's lightweight and durable. The price is not so high either.
Ba: You don't say? Well then, this will be fine. I'll take it.
B : Alright. Thank you very much.

3. A: なんで、そんなに　べんきょうするんですか。　How come you study so much?
   B: あした、テストが　あるからです。　Because there's a test tomorrow.
   あした、テストなんです。　There's a test tomorrow, you see.

Note 1: In expressions using「__のです」or「__んです」the notion of "reason for" is not so explicit as in expressions using「から」or「ので」, so often times it is not necessary to worry about what the equivalent would be in English. This is especially true in the case of negative「ないんです」and「なかったんです」, which frequently appear simply as alternatives to polite「ありません」and「ありませんでした」.

ex. これは、あなたの　ぼうしじゃ　ないんですか。　Isn't this your hat?
＝これは、あなたの　ぼうしじゃ　ありませんか。

Note 2:「なんで」is used in colloquial speech instead of「なぜ」.

Exercise 1: Reply to the following, implying an explanation or justification in your response.

ex. 「どうしたんですか。」「(あたまが　いたい)」⇨「あたまが　いたいんです。」
What's the matter?　Well you see, I have a headache.

1) 「よく　べんきょうしますね。」「(あした、テストが　あります)」
2) 「むずかしい　かんじを　しっているんですね。」「(じしょを　ひきました)」
3) 「どうして　おくれたんですか。」「(みちが　こんでいました)」
4) 「なぜ、あした、学校(がっこう)に来(こ)ないんですか。」「(くにから、ちちが　来(き)ます)」
5) 「どうして　かわなかったんですか。」「(高(たか)かったです)」

Exercise 2: Look at the pictures below and tell what each person is doing, did or will do.

1)
コンタクトレンズ――。
どうしたんですか。
2)
コート______。
デパートに行(い)くんですか。
3)
ゆうべ、アメリカにでんわしたんですか。
______
______。
4)
ビールをたくさんかったんですね。
Beer
5)
どうして来なかったんですか。
6)
どうしてたべないんですか。
さかなは、______
______。

Vocabulary

よく well
ひく (u-verb) to draw, pull, catch (cold)
おくれる (ru-verb) to be late
コンタクトレンズ contact lens
しっている to know (progressive form of「しる」)
じしょを　ひく to consult a dictionary
ちち father
おとす (u-verb) to drop, lose
りょうきん fare

Function II

Qualifying statements using "however" ; でも，けれども，しかし

Sentence 1。	でも、 けれども、 しかし、	Sentence 2。

Another way to qualify a given statement is to add a contrasting or a contradicting statement beginning with「でも」"however, though" (see Lesson 3 p.47, for qualifying use of「が」).

ex.1. いまの　アパートは、せまいです。でも、安くありません。

The apartment we live in now is small. It is not cheap however.

2. 日本語のべんきょうは、むずかしいです。でも、とても　たのしいです。

Studying Japanese is difficult. But it's very interesting.

The words「けれども」,「けれど」,「けども」and「けど」are also used to make qualifying statements. Like「が」, they can come at the end of the statement to be qualified, or like「でも」they can be placed at the head of the qualifying statement.「しかし」"however" (bookish) is used at the head of the qualifying statement only.

ex.1. このアイロンは、安いけど、とても　じょうぶです。

This iron is cheap, but very durable.

2. 東京は、おもしろいです。けれども、ぶっかが　高いですね。

Tokyo is interesting. But prices are really expensive, aren't they.

3. 10時まで、まちました。しかし、田中さんは、来ませんでした。

I waited for Mr. Tanaka until 10 o'clock. But he didn't come.

Exercise 3: Answer the following questions using「が」,「けれども」,「でも」, etc.

ex. Q: えいがを　見ましたか。→(おもしろくなかった)

⇨ A: ええ、見ました　が/ けれど、おもしろくなかったです。

⇨ A: ええ。でも、おもしろくなかったです。

1) おすしを　たべましたか。→(おいしくなかった)

2) ニューヨークへ　でんわを　かけましたか。→(りょうきんが　高い)

3) 東京の　ちかてつは、べんりですか。→(あさは、こんでいる)

4) ここから、ふじ山が　見えますか。→(雨の日は、見えません)

5) しごとは、おもしろいですか。→(とても　いそがしい)

6) あなたは、日本の　しんぶんを　よみますか。→(むずかしい)

Grammar Note I

Contrastive use of「は」

The topic particle「は」is commonly used when contrasting statements are made about different items.

ex.1. すしは　すきですが、サンドイッチは　すきじゃありません。

Sushi I like, sandwiches I don't like.

2. わたしは、すしが　すきですが、スミスさんは、きらいです。

I like *sushi*, but Mr. Smith hates it.

Note 1: When subjects or direct objects appear as topics,「が」and「を」are replaced by「は」.

ex. へやが　ひろいです。 → へやは　ひろいですが…。

コーヒーを　のみます。→ コーヒーは　のみますが…。

Note 2: When other sentence elements appear as topics,「は」is simply added on, resulting in double particle constructions.

ex.1. フランスには　いきますが、ドイツには　いきません。

I'm going to go to France, but I am not going to go to Germany.

2. 日本(にほん)では　ゆうめいですが、アメリカでは　ゆうめいじゃありません。

In Japan he's famous, but in the U. S. he's not famous.

Exercise 4: Contrast the items below as in the example.

ex. すし / てんぷら（すき・きらい）→すしは　すきですが、てんぷらは　きらいです。

1) 日本語(にほんご) / スペイン語(ご)（わかる・わからない）　2) ステーキ / ハンバーグ（高(たか)い・安(やす)い）

3) なつ / ふゆ（あつい・さむい）　4) ハワイ / アラスカ（あたたかい・さむい）

5) アメリカ / 日本（ひろい・せまい）

Function III　Listing two or more actions, qualities, etc. ; ひろくて、あかるい

Two or more verbals may be juxtaposed in a single sentence by using the て-form to mean "and". The て-form of the be-verb is「で」; adjectives add「－くて」(see p.18).

ex.1. A: あなたの　オフィスは、どうですか。　How is your office?

B: ええ、ひろくて、あかるいです。　It's big and well lighted.

2. A: 東京(とうきょう)の　ちかてつは、どうですか。　How are the subways in Tokyo?

B: きれいで、とても　べんりです。　Clean and very convenient.

3. マイケルさんは、アメリカ人(じん)で、かいしゃいんです。

Michael is an American and a company employee.

4. 田中(たなか)さんのうちには、キャデラックと　ベンツがあって、おてつだいさんが、2人(ふたり)　います。

At Mr. Tanaka's house they have a Cadillac and a Bentz, and there are two maids.

「そして」"and then" and「それに」"in addition, moreover" may be used to connect sentences.

ex.5. きのうは、土田(つちだ)さんと　すしやに　いった。そして、おいしい　トロを　たべた。

Yesterday I went to a *sushi* shop with Mr. Tsuchida. We had good *toro*.

6. わたしの会社(かいしゃ)は、きゅうりょうが　いい。それに、休(やす)みも　たくさん　ある。

At the company where I work the pay is good. Moreover we get lots of vacation time.

Note : Combining favorable and unfavorable expressions with the て-form sounds a bit unusual. Contrasting notions should be joined with「が」,「でも」,「けれども」, etc.

ex. ×　ちかてつは、こんでいて、べんりです。

○　ちかてつは、こんでいるけれど、べんりです。

Vocabulary

スペイン語（スペインご）Spanish (language)　ステーキ steak　ハンバーグ hamburger

ふゆ winter　にぎやか（な）lively, bustling

つめたい cold to the touch　にわ garden

Counting persons:

Japanese numerals are used for one and two persons. Three or more people are counted by Chinese numerals.

1人	2人	～人	3人 さんにん	4人 よにん	10人 じゅうにん
ひとり	ふたり	～にん	1000人 せんにん		何人 なんにん?

Exercise 5: Choose two adjectives from the box below and use them to make a single sentence.

ex. このシーツは、(白(しろ)い)(大(おお)きい)⇨このシーツは、白(しろ)くて、大きいです。

1) 土田(つちだ)さんのいえは、＿＿＿＿。 2) このみせは、＿＿＿＿。
3) このジュースは、＿＿＿＿。 4) このアイロンは、＿＿＿＿。
5) このスーツケースは、＿＿＿＿。 6) フィリップさんは、＿＿＿＿。
7) この町(まち)は、＿＿＿＿。

大きい	小(ちい)さい	あたらしい	ふるい	高(たか)い	安(やす)い
ひろい	せまい	たのしい	やさしい	おもい	かるい
おいしい	しずか(な)	にぎやか(な)	しんせつ(な)	つめたい	白い

Exercise 6: Choose two expressions from the box below and use them to make a single sentence.

ex. マイケルさんは、(アメリカ人(じん))(かいしゃいん)

⇨マイケルさんは、アメリカ人で、かいしゃいんです。

1) バーバラさんは、＿＿＿＿。 2) 土田さんは、＿＿＿＿。 3) 京都(きょうと)は、＿＿＿＿。
4) オフィスの女(おんな)の人(ひと)は、＿＿＿＿。 5) 土田さんのいえには、＿＿＿＿。

・きれいだ	・マイケルさんの おくさんだ		・男(おとこ)の人(ひと)だ
・わかい	・ふるい町だ	・へやに いる	・ひろいにわが ある
・カナダ人(じん)だ	・阿部産業(あべさんぎょう)の しゃいんだ		・本(ほん)を よんでいる
・ゆうめいな てらが、たくさん ある			・犬(いぬ)が 2ひき いる

Grammar Note II

Pronominal use of「の」; 青いの

い-adj (-い)	＋の
な-adj (-な)	

" … one"

「の」may be used after adjectives to function as a pronoun equivalent to English "one".

ex.1. A: 白(しろ)いシーツを 見(み)せてください。

Show me some white sheets, please.

B: 青(あお)いのは ありますが、白いのは ありません。(青いシーツ→青いの)

We have blue ones, but we don't have white ones.

Vocabulary

てら Buddhist temple
かいしゃいん company employee
-ひき (びき, ぴき) counter for animals, fish, insects: 1ぴき, 2ひき, 3びき…

2. はい、おかしです。どうぞ、すきなのを　とってください。

Here's some sweets. Please go ahead and take whichever ones you like.

Noun Pronoun　＋　の

"mine, yours, his,..."

A noun followed by the possessive marker「の」may function as a possessive pronoun.

ex.1. A: これは、だれの　車(くるま)ですか。　　Whose car is this?

B: わたしのです。きのう、かったんです。　（わたしの　車　→　わたしの）

It's mine. I bought it yesterday.

2. バーバラさんの　スーツケースは　ありますが、マイケルさんのは　ありません。

Barbara's suitcase is here, but Michael's is not.

3. A: フランスの　ワインを　のみますか、ドイツの　ワインを　のみますか。

Will you have French wine or German wine?

B: フランスのを　のみます。　　I'll have the French one.

Exercise 7: Practice using「の」as a pronoun as in the example.

ex. この本(ほん)は、わたしの本です。⇨この本は、わたしのです。

1) このボールペンは、田中(たなか)さんのボールペンです。
2) このテレビは、ソニーのテレビですか。
3) このかばんは、バーバラさんのかばんですか。
4) このかさは、だれのかさですか。
5) 土田(つちだ)さんの車は、あの白(しろ)い車ですか。
6) このワインは、どこのワインですか。

Exercise 8: Further practice using「の」as a pronoun. Construct dialogues as in the example.

ex. A: すみません、くつを　見(み)せてください。 B: はい、どうぞ。

A: 白いのは　ありませんか。 B: 黒(くろ)いのは　ありますが、白いのは　ありません。

1) セーター　・赤(あか)い　・黒い
2) じしょ　・小さい　・大きい
3) カメラ　・ドイツ　・日本(にほん)
4) かさ　・安(やす)い　・高(たか)い
5) へや　・ひろい　・せまい
6) マフラー　・じみ(な)　・はで(な)

Function IV　"That will be fine"; それで　いいです

Statement	Noun X　で　いいです。	X is all right. X will do.
	Noun X　で　けっこうです。	(polite)
Question	Noun X　で　いいですか。	Is X all right?
	Noun X　で　よろしいですか。	(polite)

ex.1. A: すみません。いま、このサイズだけなんですが。

I'm sorry. This is the only size we have right now.

B: そうですか。じゃ、それで　いいです。

Is that so? In that case, that will do.

2. A:かいぎを、いつ、しましょうか。木よう日で　よろしいですか。

When should we have the meeting? Will Thursday be alright?

B: ええ。それで、けっこうです。　　Yes, that will be fine.

Exercise 9: How would you reply? Make up some response to the following.

1) A salesclerk tells you:

いま、ネクタイは、赤いのと　青いのは　ありますが、ほかのは　ないんです。

2) Your colleague asks you: かいぎを　したいんですが、10日で　いいですか。

3) The host asks you:

① のみものは、何が　いいですか。　② すきやきで　いいですか。

Exercise 10: Particle exercise : Fill in the parentheses with either「が」or「で」.

1) A:みかんが　2つ　ありますから、1つ　どうぞ。

B:わたしは、小さいの（　）いいから、あなたが、大きいのを　たべてください。

2) A:こんどの土よう日に、ゴルフを　しませんか。

B:すみません。日よう日（　）、つごうがいいんですが。土よう日は、しごとなんです。

3) A:すもうのきっぷが　あるんですが、わたしは、あまり　すきじゃないので、どうぞ。17日のと　18日のが　あります。

B:わたしは、17日に　大阪に　いくから、18日の（　）いいな。

C:じゃ、わたしは、17日の（　）いいです。

Function V　Shopping

1 Asking and telling prices

Asking prices : これ　いくら？(plain)　/　これ　いくらですか。(polite)

これは　おいくらですか。(formal)　　How much is this?

ぜんぶで、いくらですか。　　How much is it altogether?

Telling prices : 1,000円です。(polite)　/　1,000円で　ございます。(formal)　　It's 1,000 yen.

このえんぴつは、4本で　200円です。These pencils are four for 200 yen.

ぜんぶで、1,200円です。　　Altogether, that's 1,200 yen.

2 Asking to see something else

もっと　大きいのは、ありませんか。 Don't you have something larger?

もうすこし　安いのが、いいんですけど…。

Uh, something a little cheaper would be better.

もうすこし　かるいのが、ほしいんですけど…。

Uh, I was looking for something a bit lighter.

Vocabulary

ボールペン ballpoint pen

じみ（な）plain, quiet, subdued, unpretentious

ほかの another, something else, the rest

かばん bag, briefcase

はで（な）flashy, loud

みかん tangerine

マフラー muffler, scarf

すもう *sumo* wrestling

3 Buying

Deciding on something: これを　ください。　I'll take this. Give me this please.

これで　いいです。(polite) ／これで　けっこうです。(formal)
This will be fine. This one will do. I'll settle for this.

これが　いいです。　I want this one. (lit. This one is good.)

じゃ、これに　します。　Well, I'll take this. (lit. I choose this.)

Deciding not to buy: いいえ、けっこうです。(polite)　No thank you. That's fine.

じゃあ、いりません。　No, I don't need it.

じゃ、また　こんどに　します。　Well, I'll get it next time.

[Japanese currency]

Exercise 11: Look at the pictures and practice the following dialogue with a partner, changing the underlined parts.

A : customer　　B: salesclerk

A : このりんごは、いくらですか。

B : ひとつ　150円(えん)です。

A : ちょっと　高(たか)いですね。こっちのは？

B : それは、ひとつ　100円です。

A : じゃあ、それを　いつつ　ください。それから、みかんを　ひと山(やま)　ください。

B : ありがとうございます。ぜんぶで、1,000円です。

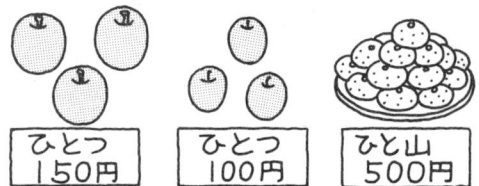

ひとつ 150円　ひとつ 100円　ひと山 500円

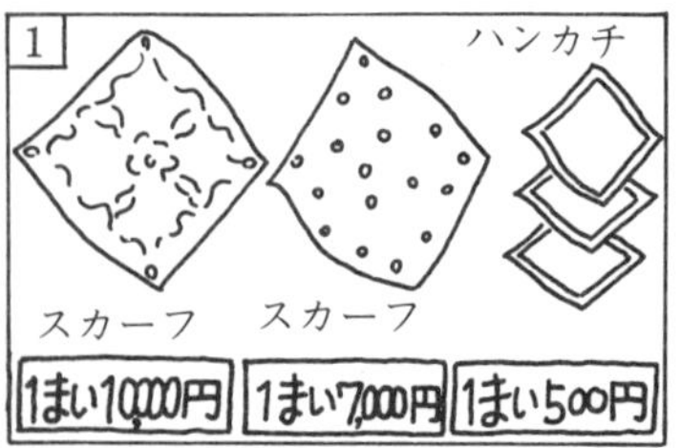

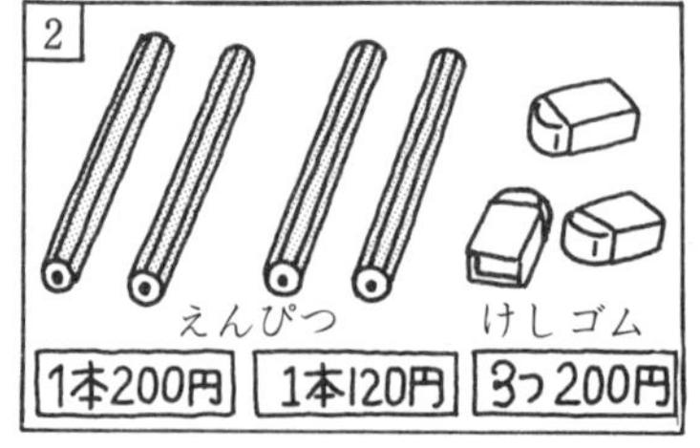

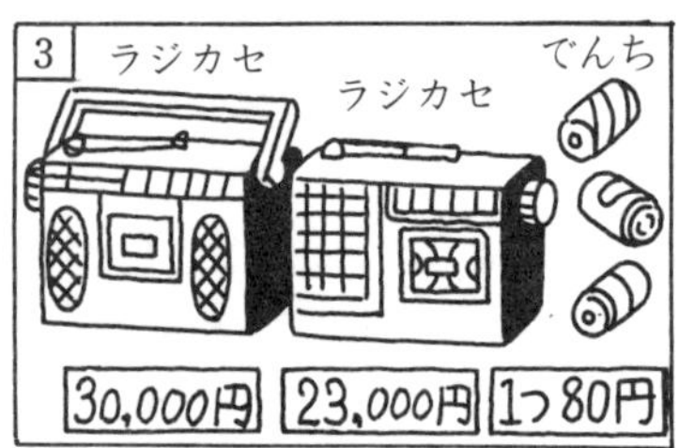

Vocabulary

こっち this way, this one
スカーフ scarf
ハンカチ handkerchief
－山（やま）counter for a pile or heap (use Japanese numerals)
ラジカセ radio cassette
－まい counter for thin, flat objects
でんち battery
おつり change

Reading Comprehension Exercise

〈マイケルの日記〉

きょうは、バーバラといっしょに、銀座のデパートにいった。大きくて、きれいなデパートだった。それに、てんいんも、しんせつだった。けれども、ねだんは高かった。バーバラは、11,000円の、日本製のアイロンをかった。アイロンは、かるくてじょうぶだが、すこし小さい。もうすこし大きいのがよかったが、バーバラが、きにいったのだから、しかたがない。

かえりに、小さいみせがあったので、ぼくも、はいった。せまいところに、人がたくさんいたので、こんでいた。てんいんは、あまりしんせつではなかったが、すごく安かった。

◆Vocabulary◆

ねだん price
きにいる It pleases me. It's to my liking.
しかたがない cannot be helped, have no choice, be inevitable
かえりに on the way home
ところ place
日本製（にほんせい） made in Japan
ぼく I (used by men and boys)
すごく terribly, bitterly

Exercise 12: List the good and the bad points of a department store and a small shop.

	good points	bad points
デパート	①：	②：
小さいみせ	③：	④：

Listening Comprehension Exercise

Listen to the tape and do as directed.

1) You will hear five sums of money spoken on the tape. Write the letter of the correct pictured amount of currency in the parentheses. If no pictured sum is equivalent to the amount you hear, write ×.

① (　　)
② (　　)
③ (　　)
④ (　　)
⑤ (　　)

a.
1000円 500 50 100 10 10 10

b.
5000円 500 500 500 50 10 100 100 100 100 10 10

c.
1000円 1000円 500 100 100 100 10 10 100 100 100 100 10 10

2) Answer the following questions.

① おきゃくさんは、青いネクタイを　見ましたか、赤いのを　見ましたか。
② おきゃくさんは、日本のネクタイを　見ましたか。
③ フランスのネクタイは、いくらでしたか。
④ おきゃくさんは、どんなネクタイを　かいましたか。
⑤ おつりは、いくらでしたか。

KANJI

As Professor Seidensticker mentioned in the foreward to this text, the *Kanji* writing system offers persistent difficulty for students of Japanese. The word *Kanji* itself literally means Chinese characters of the Han Dynasty, but Japanese imported Chinese characters and their pronunciations from the Wu, Tang, Sung, Ming and Ching periods as well. These Chinese pronunciations are collectively called the "*on*" readings in Japanese. Chinese characters were also borrowed for indigenous Japanese words of similar meaning but which retain their native Japanese pronunciations. These pronunciations are called the "*kun*" readings.

Unfortunately, most frequently used *Kanji* have both "*on*" and "*kun*" pronunciations, and occasionally they have several of each, while in contemporary Chinese each character has but one pronunciation. In the initial stage of your Japanese language studies it is not necessary to be concerned about the "*on*" and "*kun*" distinction, which will naturally become more recognizable to you as you progress.

You have already been exposed to some *Kanji* in this book. Most of them are numerals, time expressions, or place names. Of course the use of *Kanji* is not necessarily limited to these categories. As has already been pointed out, Japanese speakers use *Kanji* to represent concepts which are usually expressed by nouns, verbs and adjectives, etc. It shouldn't be too difficult to figure out the meanings of some of the *Kanji*. For example, the character「人」, which appeared in Lesson 2, represents a person because it looks like a standing person. The character for tree is「木」because it is the result of the simplification of a tree shape. In Lesson 5 the character「木」is used to represent Thursday, because the Japanese decided to use what the ancient Chinese considered to be the elements of this world to represent the days of the week, i.e.「日」(sun),「月」(moon),「火」(fire),「水」(water),「木」(wood),「金」(metal),「土」(earth), when they borrowed the concept of the week from the Western world.

The meaning of many more *Kanji* become easier to figure out when some rudimentary rules are explained. You can understand the shape of「日」if you imagine the existence of a black dot in the middle of the sun, while the character for the moon becomes easier to understand if you imagine「月」representing a crescent shaped moon. The meaning of the character「明」, which appears in Lesson 19, is "bright" because it is bright when you have both the sun and the moon simultaneously in the sky. The character for fair weather is「晴」which consists of "sun"「日」and "blue"「青」, as shown in Lesson 14.

The character「休」, which appears in Lesson 6, consists of a modified version of「人」plus「木」, and it means "to rest". If you understand that「人」appears as「亻」when it is used as a component part of another character, the meaning of「休」becomes clearer. The character「休」depicts a person leaning against a tree resting. As another example, when a horizontal bar is added at the foot of the character「木」it becomes「本」meaning "foundation or basis".「本」is also used to mean "book" because books are the foundation of learning. 「本」is also used for counting the number of stick-like objects, as seen in Lesson 5. In Lesson 20 we see「体」which is made up of person and「本」.「体」means "body" because body is the foundation on which human beings exist. Can you guess the meanings of the characters「林」consisting of 2 trees, and「森」consisting of 3 trees? The answers are found at the bottom of this page.

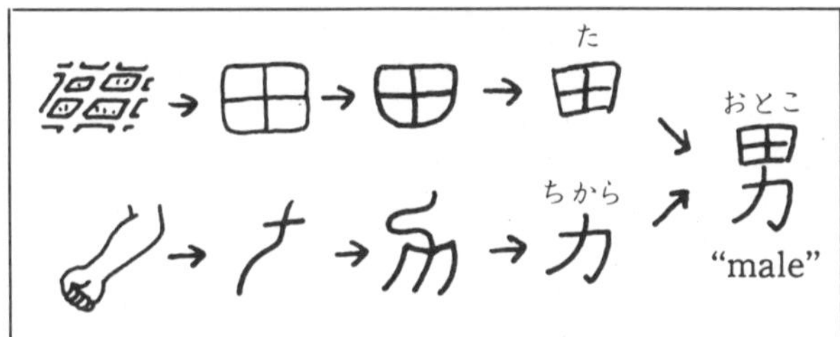

「田」represents "rice field" because it is supposed to symbolize the way land is sectioned for rice cultivation.「田」alone can be used to mean "rice field", but it also can be used for various other related meanings in combination with some other characters.「力」means "strength" because it is said that「力」reminded the Chinese of the shape of flexed bicep muscles. The character for "male" is formed by adding「力」underneath「田」, because in the ancient agrarian society, men were supposed to be strong enough to do chores in the rice fields.

You probably have realized by now that the *Kanji* system is not as incoherent as it may have looked to you when it was first introduced. You probably have also realized that these basic building-block characters which posses their own semantic identities can be clues to understanding the meanings of many of the *Kanji* characters. The characters「一, 人（亻）, 木, 日, 月, 青, 田 and 力」are examples of basic building-block *Kanji* known as radicals in *Kanji* dictionaries. The Chinese decided on 214 radicals, giving each one a number of its own. For example,「亻」is the ninth radical, and is usually designated as the "person" radical.

Besides making use of radicals to look up new characters in the dictionary, it is also possible to locate new characters by counting the number of strokes used in writing them, or they can be found listed according to their "*on*" and "*kun*" pronunciations.

The Japanese Ministry of Education has stipulated that Japanese elementary school children must be taught to read and write 1,006 characters, known as the "*Kyoiku Kanji*" (Educational *Kanji*). Also they decided that by the end of the twelfth grade children should be exposed to 1,945 characters known as the "*Joyo Kanji*" (Everyday Use *Kanji*), which include the *Kyoiku Kanji*. The additional 939 characters are for recognition only, children are not required to be able to write them. We do not pretend that you can gain even a rudimentary knowledge of *Kanji* by completing this textbook, since the study of *Kanji* is not its primary goal. However we have used about 450 of the most frequently occurring *Kyoiku Kanji*, and these are accompanied by pronunciation written in *Hiragana* for their first several occurrences, so that you can use the "*on*" or "*kun*" for the pronunciation index which is attached to any *Kanji* dictionary available.

※「林」means "grove" and「森」means "forest".

区役所に行ったことがありますか

Have You Ever Been To The Ward Office?

Dialogue I

Michael tells Mr. Tsuchida that he is going to register as an alien.

マイケル：あしたは、外国人とうろくに行くつもりなんですが…。

土田　：ああ、そうですか。とうろくのばしょを、しっていますか。

マイケル：ええ、港区の区役所ですね。

土田　：行ったことがありますか。

マイケル：いいえ、ないんです。

土田　：そうですか。あしたは土よう日だから、12時までですよ。
こんでいるかもしれませんよ。

マイケル：だいぶ、まつでしょうか。

土田　：ええ、まつでしょうから、はやく、うちを出たほうがいいですね。

マイケル：ところで、のりものは、地下鉄がいいでしょうか、それとも、
バスがいいでしょうか。

土田　：地下鉄では行かないほうがいいでしょう。地下鉄は、すこしふべん
なんですよ。駅を出てから、あるいて10分ぐらいかかります。

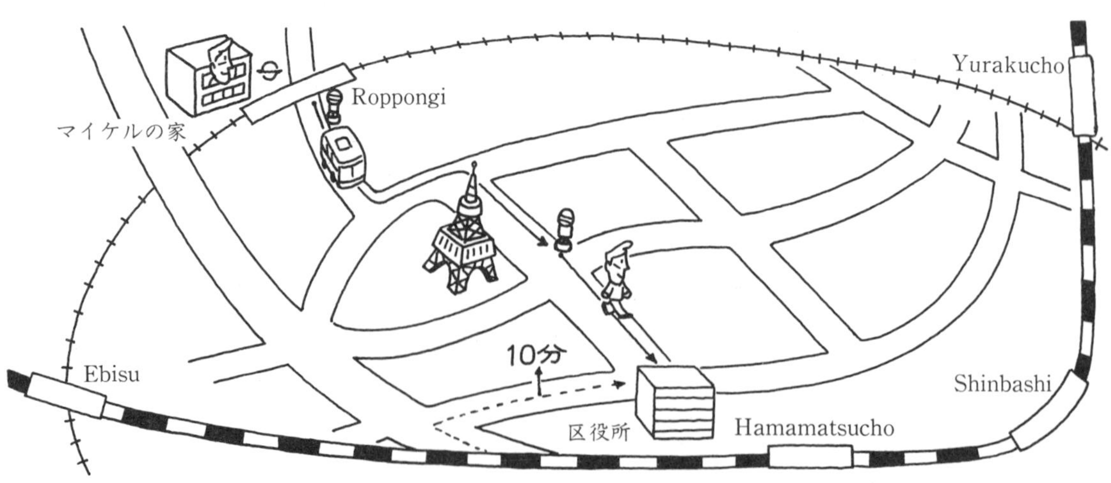

Dialogue II

Next Monday at the office.

土田　：ウエッブさん、外国人とうろくは、おわりましたか。

マイケル：それが……じつは、まだなんです。

土田　：え、どうかしたんですか。

マイケル：行ったんですが、とてもこんでいたので、できなかったんです。

土田　：家を、何時に出たんですか。

マイケル：それが、9時に出るつもりだったんですが、雨がふっていたので、やむまでまって、10時ごろ、出たんです。

土田　：それで、区役所には、何時につきましたか。

マイケル：11時すぎだったんです。ですから、さ来週の土よう日に、もういちど、行くつもりです。

土田　：さ来週の土よう日は、しゅくじつですよ。

マイケル：ああ、そうですか。しりませんでした。こまったなあ。

土田　：あしたの朝、会社を休んで行ったほうがいいですよ。きっと、すいているでしょう。

マイケル：そうですね。それじゃあ、朝、区役所に行ってから、会社に来ます。

＊ Government and municipal offices are now closed Saturdays as of May 1, 1992.

Vocabulary

Nouns:

1外国人（がいこくじん）foreigner, alien
2ばしょ place, site, location
10のりもの vehicle, means of transportation
1とうろくする registration (to register)
3区役所（くやくしょ）ward office
24しゅくじつ national holiday (see p.119)

Adverbs:

8だいぶ（だいぶん）a lot, quite a bit
15まだ yet
27きっと for sure, for certain

Verbs:

17できる (ru-verb) ①to be possible, can be done（わたしは、日本語ができる。lit. "As for me, Japanese can be done", "For me Japanese is possible" i. e. "I can speak Japanese") ②to be finished, to be ready ③to be made (from, of)
19ふる (u-verb) to fall, come down: 雨がふる。 It rains.
20やむ (u-verb) to stop
25こまる (u-verb) to be in a fix, to be perplexed

Grammatical words:

1＿つもり plan to ＿, intend to ＿ ☞Function Ⅲ
8＿でしょう probably is (plain: だろう) ☞Function Ⅴ
10それとも or else
22ですから and therefore (plain: だから)

Expressions:

4 __ことがある I have the experience of doing __ ☞Function Ⅱ

7 __かもしれない It may be __, perhaps __ ☞Function Ⅴ

15 それが… The truth of the matter is... What happened was...

13 あるいて10分 10 minutes on foot

16 どうかしたんですか What happened?

Dialogue Comprehension Exercise

Answer the following questions.

Dialogue Ⅰ

1) マイケルさんは、あした、どこへ行くつもりですか。
2) マイケルさんは、港区の区役所に行ったことがありますか。
3) どうして、地下鉄で行かないほうがいいのですか。

Dialogue Ⅱ

4) マイケルさんは、外国人とうろくをしましたか。
5) マイケルさんは、区役所に、何時につきましたか。
6) どうして、マイケルさんは、外国人とうろくができなかったんですか。
7) マイケルさんは、もういちど、区役所に行きます。それは、いつですか。

Function Ⅰ

Situation continuing until such a time; 雨がやむまで

「まで」used after a plain non-past verb means "until such and such a time", "until such a time as __", etc. (see Lesson 3 for「…から…まで」)

ex.1. 何時まで、会社にいますか。 Until what time will you be at the office?

このしごとがおわるまで います。 I'll be there until this work is finished.

2. 雨がやむまで まちましょう。 Let's wait until it stops raining.

3. ニューヨークのりょうしんは、わたしが電話をかけるまで、しんぱいしていました。

My parents in New York were worried until I telephoned them.

Exercise 1: Make a response as in the example, using the expressions in parentheses.

ex. いつまで まちますか。(ともだちが 来る) →ともだちが来るまで まちます。

1) いつまで、会社を休みますか。 (びょうきが なおる)
2) 雨は、いつまでふりますか。 (あしたの朝)
3) いつまで、日本にいますか。 (大学を そつぎょうする)
4) いつまで、はたらきますか。 (こどもが うまれる)
5) いつまで、日本語をべんきょうしますか。 (漢字を たくさんおぼえる)

Exercise 2: Describe the pictures below telling what the people do until such time as indicated.

ex.
2時間
ちょうじょうにつくまで、
2時間あるきます。
1)
ともだちが
来る。
2)
3)
しょくじが
できましたよ。

4) 

5) 

6) 

7) 

Function II

Telling a past experience; 行ったことがあります

Plain past verb +「ことがある」is used to form expressions like "I have done such and such", "I once did such and such", etc. Note the difference in meaning between this and the simple past tense.

ex.1. A: すしを、たべたことがありますか。 — Have you ever eaten *sushi*?

B: はい、あります。 — Yes, I have.

いいえ、ありません。 — No, I haven't.

いいえ、まだ、たべたことはありません。 — No, I haven't eaten it yet.

Dialogues in English

Dialogue I

M: Tomorrow I'm planning to go in for alien registration.

T: Ah, really? Do you know where the place to register is?

M: Yeah, the Minato ward office, isn't it?

T: Have you ever been there?

M: No, I haven't.

T: I see. Tomorrow is Saturday, so it's open only until 12:00, you know. It might be crowded!

M: Will there be a long wait, do you think?

T: Yeah, you probably will have to wait, so you'd better leave home early.

M: Which would be better to take, by the way? The subway, or the bus?
(lit: As for means of transportation, by the way, would the subway be good? Or else, would the bus be good?)

T: I don't think you should take the subway. The subway is a bit inconvenient. It takes about 10 minutes on foot after leaving the station.

Dialogue II

T: Did you finish with your alien registration, Mr. Webb?

M: Well, you see, as a matter of fact, not yet.

T: What! What happened?

M: I went alright, but it was very crowded and I wasn't able to do it.

T: What time did you leave home?

M: Well, it's like this. I intended to leave at 9:00 sure enough, but it was raining, and so I waited until it stopped, and left around 10:00.

T: So anyway, what time did you arrive at the ward office?

M: It was after 11:00. Therefore I plan to go again on Saturday the week after next.

T: Saturday the week after next is a national holiday.

M: Oh, is that so? I didn't know that. That presents a problem.

T: I suggest you take off work tomorrow morning and go. I'm sure it won't be so crowded.

M: That's for sure. Alright then, I'll come to work after going to the ward office in the morning.

Vocabulary

なおる (u-verb) to get well, mend
そつぎょうする graduation (to graduate from, finish)
こども child, children
おぼえる (ru-verb) to learn, remember
ちょうじょう top, summit
キャッチボール play catch
ただいま Hi, I'm back!
おまちどうさま Sorry to have kept you waiting!
ゴルフ用品（ゴルフようひん）golfing equipment

2. A: 先週(せんしゅう)、京都(きょうと)に行(い)きました。　I went to Kyoto last week.

   B: わたしも、まえに、京都に行(い)ったことがあります。　I have been to Kyoto before too.

3. ドイツ語(ご)は、べんきょうしたことがありますが、フランス語(ご)は、ありません。

   I have studied German, but I haven't studied French.

4. 田中(たなか)さんに、あったことある？　(colloquial)　Have you ever met Mr. Tanaka?

Note: In this and many grammatical constructions,「こと」coming after a verb functions to make the verb into a noun.

〔日本語(にほんご)を話(はな)すこと〕が　できる。＝　日本語ができる。　I can speak Japanese.

〔このえいがを見(み)たこと〕が　ある。　I've seen this film before. (lit. The seeing of this film exists.)

Exercise 3: Make up questions, "Have you ever done such and such?", for the following. Answer using both affirmative「はい」and negative「いいえ」.

ex.

1) 日本のおさけ

2)

3) きゅうしゅう

A: ハワイに行ったことがありますか。

B: はい、行ったことがあります。

B: はい、きょねん、行きました。

B: いいえ、まだです。

4)

5) やきとり

6)

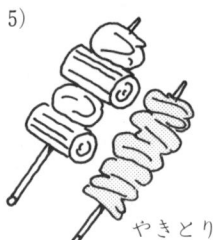

Exercise 4: Complete the following dialogues using「〜たことがある」.

1) A: この本(ほん)を________________。

   B: ええ、おもしろかったですよ。

2) A: 京都に________________。

   B: ええ、ふるいおてらが、たくさんありましたよ。

3) A: 日本(にほん)のおまつりを見(み)たことがありますか。

   B: いいえ、____________。はじめてです。

4) A: なっとうを______________。

   B: ____________。どんなあじが、するんですか。

5) A: はじめまして。山田(やまだ)です。

   B: あ、どうも。でも、山田さんには__________________。

   A: え、そうですか。これは、しつれいしました。

Exercise 5: Talk about something you have done (in Japan) using「〜たことがある」.

Vocabulary

かぶき *Kabuki,* a traditional form of drama
まんが cartoon, comic book
なっとう fermented soybeans
じゅぎょう class, classroom lesson
はたらく (u-verb) to work, labor
そうじする cleaning (to clean)
アルバイト part-time job, side job
（お）まつり festival
あじ taste, flavor
のぼる (u-verb) to go up, climb
コンサート concert
夏休み（なつやすみ） summer vacation
つづける (ru-verb) to continue
やきとり barbecued chicken
はじめて for the first time
しつれいしました Pardon me!

Function III　Stating a plan or intention; かいものに行くつもりです

The plain non-past verb followed by「つもり」is used to form expressions like "I plan to do such and such", "I intend to do such and such", and indicates a greater degree of intention than「〜たい」"I want to __", "I would like to __".

Question: あした、秋葉原に行きますか。　Are you going to go to Akihabara tomorrow?
Answer: (affirmative)　ええ、行くつもりです。　Yes, it is my intention to go.
(negative)　いいえ、行かないつもりです。　No, I'm not planning to go.
(negative)　いいえ、行くつもりはありません。　(much stronger than the above)
No, I have no intention of going.

ex.1. A: 来月から、フランス語を べんきょうするつもりですが、あなたも、いっしょに しませんか。
I intend to study French beginning next month. Why don't you study it too along with me?
B: いいえ、わたしは、フランス語は、べんきょうしたくありません。
No, I don't want to study French.

2. A: きのうは、どうして、来なかったんですか。　Why didn't you come yesterday?
B: 行くつもりでしたが、かぜを ひいたので、うちに いました。
I planned to go, but I caught a cold, and so I stayed home.
A: そうですか。それは、ざんねんでしたね。　Really? That was too bad, wasn't it.

Note: If you have no special plans you might answer as follows.
ex. A: 日よう日は、何を しますか。　What are you doing on Sunday?
B: べつに、何も しません。　Nothing in particular.
とくに、よていは、ありません。　I have no plans in particular.
まだ、わかりません。　I don't know yet.

Exercise 6: Reply to the following questions using「〜つもり」.

1) 日本語のじゅぎょうのあと、何をしますか。　A: ともだちと＿＿＿＿＿＿＿＿。
2) こんばん、何をするつもりですか。　A: えいがを＿＿＿＿＿＿＿＿。
3) こんどの日よう日は、どうするつもりですか。　A: 山に＿＿＿＿＿＿＿＿。(のぼる)
4) きょうのごご、銀座に行きますか。　A: いいえ、＿＿＿＿＿＿＿＿。
5) 日本で、何をするつもりですか。　A: 日本の会社で＿＿＿＿＿＿＿＿。(はたらく)

Exercise 7: Practice the following dialogue with a partner, first using the suggestions below, and then using your own ideas.

A: (　①　) は、どうするつもりですか。
A: わたしは、(　③　) つもりです。

B: (　②　) つもりですが、あなたは？
B: それは、いいですね。

1) こんばん,　ひとりで、テレビを見る,　ともだちとコンサートに行く
2) 来週の日よう日,　家を、そうじする,　テニスをする
3) 夏休み,　デパートで、アルバイトをする, ハワイに行く
4) 来年,　日本語のべんきょうを、つづける,　国にかえる

Function IV Ordering events in time; 区役所に行ってから、会社に来ます。

1 **Verb 1 -て、Verb 2** Verb 1 and Verb 2

The て-form alone is simply a general means for joining two or more actions in a single statement. The actions are often relevant to each other and occur within a short time span. In most cases the actions are understood as occuring in the order stated.

ex.1. うちにかえって、電話をします。 I'm going to go home and make a telephone call.

2. すしやに行って、トロをたべました。 I went to a *sushi* bar and ate *toro*.

2 **Verb 1 -て+から、Verb 2** Verb 2, after Verb 1／Verb 1, and then Verb 2

When you want to specify that action 2 takes place "after" action 1, use the て-form+「から」.

ex.1. べんきょうを してから、あそびます。 I'll enjoy myself after I study.

2. ホテルに かえってから、ニューヨークのりょうしんに、電話を かけます。

I'm going to call my parents in New York after returning to the hotel.

3 **それから／そして**

Conjunctive expressions like「それから」"after that" and「そして」"and then" may also be used to order events in time.

ex.1. きのう、あたらしいアパートを見ました。それから、かいものに行きました。

We looked at the new apartment yesterday. After that we went shopping.

2. A: きょうは、朝、おきてから、何をしましたか。

What did you do today after getting up in the morning?

B: シャワーをあびて、コーヒーをのんで、しんぶんをよんで、それから、うちを出ました。

I took a shower, drank coffee, read the newspaper, and then went out.

3. 花やで、花をかいました。そして、ウエッブさんのうちに行きました。

I bought some flowers at the flower shop. And then I went to Mr. Webb's home.

Exercise 8: Practice the following sentences as shown in the example.

ex. うちに かえる……シャワーをあびる → うちに かえって、シャワーをあびます。

1) とこやに行く……かみを切る
2) 学校に行く……日本語をべんきょうする
3) ホテルにかえる……すこし休む
4) 銀行に行く……ドルをかえる

Exercise 9: Practice the following sentences as shown in the example.

ex. しゅくだいをする ，ねる → しゅくだいをしてから、ねます。

1) えいがを見る ，しょくじをする
2) まどをあける ，そうじをする
3) 駅を出る ，10分あるく
4) 大学にはいる ，アルバイトをする
5) にくをたべる ，やさいをたべる
6) チェックインする，へやに はいる

Vocabulary

とこや barbershop　かみ hair　ドル dollar ; ドルを かえる to exchange dollars for yen
かえる (ru-verb) to exchange, change　は teeth　みがく (u-verb) to polish, brush (teeth)
いってらっしゃい Goodby. See you later. (use to someone leaving the house or office on an errand, etc.)
おはよう（ございます）Good morning!　あさごはん breakfast

Exercise 10: Look at the pictures below and tell what Michael does every morning. Use「〜て」,「〜てから」or「それから」as indicated.

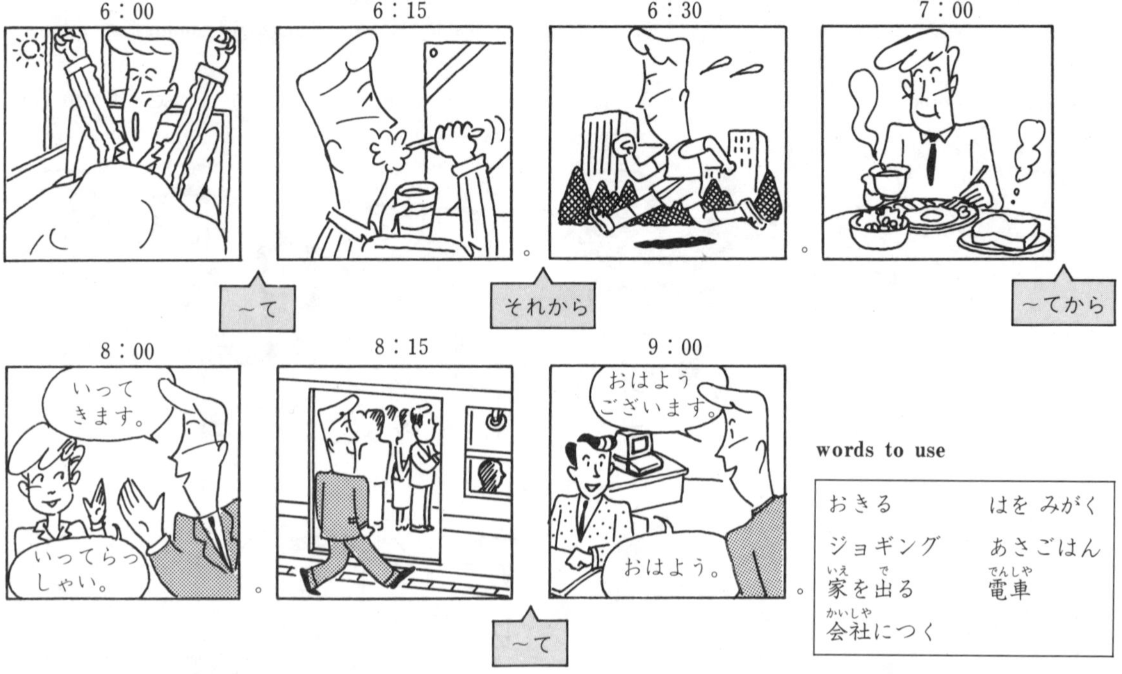

Function V

Indicating the degree of certainty; こんでいるかもしれません

The following are some of the methods used for expressing various of certainty.

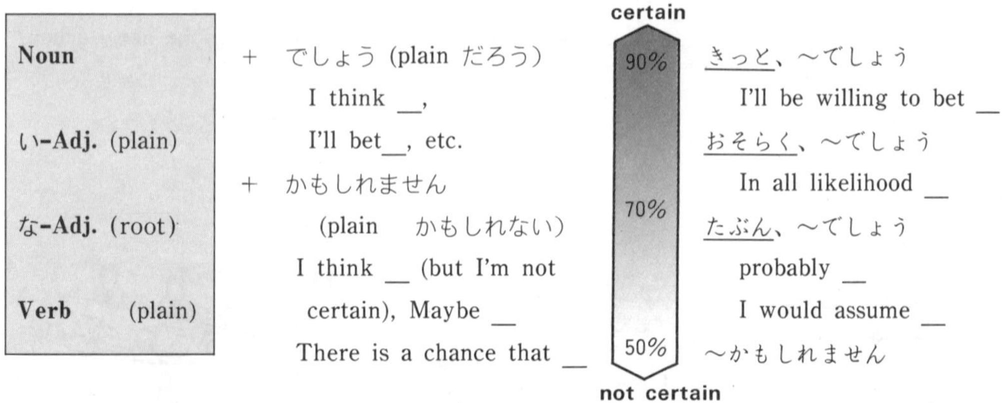

		certainty	
Noun	＋ でしょう (plain だろう) I think __, I'll bet__, etc.	90%	きっと、〜でしょう I'll be willing to bet __
い**-Adj.** (plain)			おそらく、〜でしょう In all likelihood __
な**-Adj.** (root)	＋ かもしれません (plain かもしれない) I think __ (but I'm not certain), Maybe __ There is a chance that __	70%	たぶん、〜でしょう probably __ I would assume __
Verb (plain)		50%	〜かもしれません
		not certain	

ex.1. ごぜんちゅう、雨(あめ)がふりますが、ごごは、はれるでしょう。

It will rain in the morning, but there's a good chance it will clear in the afternoon.

2. あれは、きっと、日本(にほん)の車(くるま)でしょう。　I'll bet that's a Japanese car.
3. あしたは、おそらく、あついでしょう。　In all likelihood tomorrow will be hot.
4. 田中(たなか)さんは、たぶん、来(く)るでしょう。　Mr. Tanaka will probably come.
5. 土田(つちだ)さんは、ハンバーグが、すきじゃないかもしれません。

   Maybe Mr. Tsuchida doesn't like hamburgers.
6. マイケルさんは、きのう、区役所(くやくしょ)に行(い)ったかもしれません。

   It might be that Michael went to the ward office yesterday.

Note 1: When referring to yourself use the form「かもしれない」rather than the form「でしょう」.

Note 2: The expression「〜んじゃないでしょうか」is more polite.

ex. 田中さんは、来るでしょう。　I think Mr. Tanaka will come.

田中さんは、来るんじゃないでしょうか。　Isn't it probable that Mr. Tanaka is coming?

Exercise 11: Look at the pictures and tell what person A is thinking. Give the reason if you can.

1) あしたの天気は、どうですか。

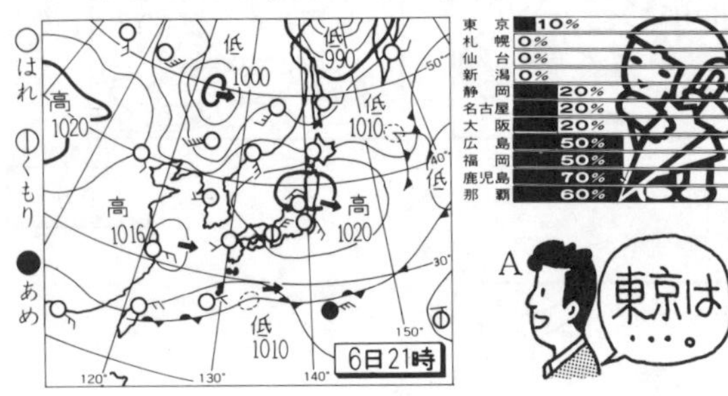

2) 土田さんは、きのう、何をしたでしょうか。

3) あの人は、日本人でしょうか。

4) あのみせのりょうりは、どうでしょうか。

Exercise 12: Look at the pictures below and answer the questions supplying ① the likely action, ② a reason.

ex. 港区の区役所は、わかりますか。→行ったことがあるから、きっと、わかるでしょう。

1) キャサリンさんは、きょう、来ますか。

2) ひるから、雨がふるでしょうか。

3) 区役所は、こむでしょうか。

4) 市川さんは、テニスをするでしょうか。

5) 田中さんは、パーティーに行くでしょうか。

Reading Comprehension Exercise

マイケルさんは、火よう日に、港区の区役所に行って、外国人とうろくをしました。マイケルさんは、まえに、区役所に行ったことがあります。そのときは、こんでいたので、とうろくができませんでした。また、こんでいるかもしれないので、火よう日は、はやく、うちを出ました。地下鉄は、ふべんなので、バスで行きました。

区役所で、じゅうしょと、なまえと、パスポートのばんごうを、紙にかいて出しました。パスポートを見せて、すこし、まちました。10時までまって、外国人とうろくしょをもらって、かえりました。外国人は、いつも、このとうろくしょをもっています。

◆**Vocabulary**◆

じゅうしょ address
紙（かみ）paper
出す（だす）(u-verb) to present, send in
とうろくしょ registration papers
もらう (u-verb) to get, to be given

Exercise 13: Read the passage above and answer the following questions.

1) マイケルさんは、まえに、区役所に行ったことがありますか。
2) マイケルさんは、なぜ、火よう日に、区役所に行ったのですか。
3) マイケルさんは、なぜ、うちを、はやく出たのですか。
4) マイケルさんは、区役所に、何で行きましたか。それは、なぜですか。
5) 区役所で、何時まで、まちましたか。

Listening Comprehension Exercise

1) Listen to the tape and indicate the weather for each city using the symbols given.

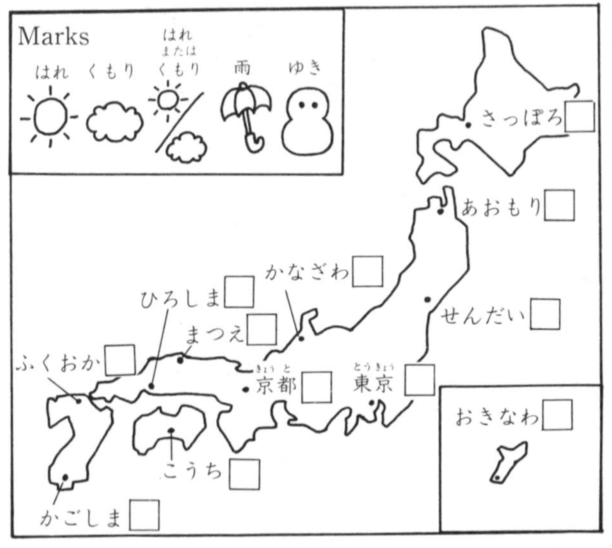

2) Listen to the tape, and indicate who has done what using "○" or "×".

○……したことがある
×……したことがない

	テニス	ゴルフ	つり
田中			
土田			

つり fishing

Vocabulary

ラーメン Chinese noodles
スポーツマン sportsman
くも cloud
くもる (u-verb) to become cloudy
くもり cloudy
ときどき sometimes
日にやける to get suntan
つれる (ru-verb) to be able to catch (fish)

第8課　車(くるま)と電車(でんしゃ)と、どちらが　はやいですか

Which Is Quicker, Car Or Train?

Dialogue I

Michael leaves the office with Mr. Nomura.

マイケル：じゃ、おさきに、しつれいします。

土田(つちだ)　：おつかれさまでした。さよなら。

野村(のむら)　：ウエッブさんは、何(なに)でかえりますか。

マイケル：わたしは、地下鉄(ちかてつ)です。

野村　：じゃ、いっしょに行(い)きましょう。ところで、六本木(ろっぽんぎ)のおたくは、どうですか。

マイケル：べんりですが、あのへんは、夜(よる)も車(くるま)がおおくて、うるさいんですよ。

野村　：そうでしょうね。それに、つうきんの電車(でんしゃ)は、こんで、たいへんでしょう？

マイケル：ええ、ほんとうに。なんとかならないでしょうか。

Dialogue II

Waiting for the train.

マイケル：おたくは、どちらですか。

野村　：うちですか。4か月(げつ)まえに、浦和(うらわ)へひっこしたんですよ。

マイケル：まえより、遠(とお)いんですか。

野村　：ええ、だいぶ遠いです。3度(ど)ものりかえるから、2時間(じかん)ちかくかかります。

マイケル：えっ、2時間も。そんなにかかるんですか。たいへんですね。車と電車と、どちらが、はやいですか。

野村　：やっぱり、電車のほうが、はやいでしょう。みちが、こみますから。

マイケル：行きとかえりと、どちらが、こみますか。

野村　　：行きのほうが、ひどいと思いますよ。

Dialogue III

On the train

マイケル：へえ。日本では、電車の中で、大学生やサラリーマンが、まんがを読んでいるとききましたが、ほんとなんですねえ。

野村　　：びっくりしたでしょう。イヤホンで、音楽をききながら、しんぶんを読んでいる人もいますね。

マイケル：それから、ねている人もいますね。わたしは、こうこくを見ながら、漢字や、カタカナのことばを、べんきょうしていますけど…。

野村　　：ああ、ウエッブさんは、べんきょう家ですね。でも、しゅうかんしの こうこくは、むずかしいでしょうね。

マイケル：ええ、しらないことばが、たくさんあって、むずかしいですね。でも、日本語のきょうかしょほどじゃありませんよ。

Vocabulary

Nouns:

6おたく　① your home (polite) ② you
7あのへん that area, around there (also このへん，そのへん，どのへん)
9つうきんする commuting (to commute)
19行き（いき）going, the way there (stem of irregular verb「行く」)
19かえり returning, the way home (stem of u-verb「かえる」)
21大学生（だいがくせい）university student, college student
21サラリーマン "salary man", white collar worker, business man
22ほんと shortened form of「ほんとう」"really"
23イヤホン earphone
26カタカナ *katakana*, square phonetic syllabary

いえ，うち，おたく

「いえ」,「うち」and「おたく」all mean "house".「いえ」usually refers only to the house itself, whereas「うち」means the "home where a family lives".「おたく」is used to indicate someone else's residence, and is never used in speaking of one's own home.

26ことば word, language　　25こうこく advertisement
27べんきょう家（べんきょうか）diligent student, person who studies all the time
28しゅうかんし weekly magazine　　30きょうかしょ textbook

Counters:

13-か月（かげつ）number of months　　15-度（ど）number of times

Adjectives:

17はやい quick, fast, early　　20ひどい awful, terrible, severe

Verbs:

15のりかえる (ru-verb) to change (trains, planes, etc.); from「のる」"to ride" and「かえる」"to change"
20思う（おもう）(u-verb) to think, consider　　23びっくりする (irregular) to become surprised

Grammatical words:

どちら 19① which one? ② which way?　12③ where? (see Appendix)
14__より than __　　20と quotation marker　　21や and …etc.
15も as much as, as long as, as far as (used after counted units of time or amount)
23～ながら while __ ☞Function III　　30__ほど as much as __, as many as __ (used after nouns)

Expressions:

1おさきに、しつれいします I'm leaving before you. Goodbye.
2おつかれさまでした Thanks for your hard work and effort.　　2さよなら（さようなら）Goodbye.
11なんとかならないでしょうか Can't something be done (about the situation)?
15 2時間ちかく nearly two hours (adverbial form of「ちかい」"near")
18やっぱり I guess __, after all __, when you think about it __ (「やっぱり」is more colloquial than「やはり」)
18__（の）ほう direction (indicates a thing singled out from two or more alternatives)

Dialogue Comprehension Exercise

Answer the following questions.

1) ウエッブさんのうちは、どこにありますか。
2) ウエッブさんのうちのまわりは、しずかですか。
3) 野村(のむら)さんのうちは、会社(かいしゃ)から近(ちか)いですか。
4) 野村さんのうちから会社まで、どのくらい、かかりますか。
5) ウエッブさんは、電車(でんしゃ)の中(なか)で、どうして、びっくりしましたか。
6) ウエッブさんは、いつも、電車の中(なか)で、何(なに)をしていますか。

Function I

Describing qualities or conditions:
Modifying nouns with entire clauses; しんぶんを読(よ)んでいる人(ひと)

Not only verbals alone but entire sentences may function as clauses modifying nouns. This is done by ① putting the verbal in plain (non-past, past, negative, etc.) form, and ② placing the entire modifying clause in front of the noun being modified.

	Verb　読(よ)む		い-adj.　ながい "long"	
non-past	しんぶんを　読む	人	かみが　ながい	人
past	しんぶんを　読んだ		かみが　ながかった	
negative	しんぶんを　読まない		かみが　ながくない	
negative past	しんぶんを　読まなかった		かみが　ながくなかった	

	Noun 休み		な-adj. すき（な）	
non-past	日曜日が　休みの（だ→の）	人	すしが　すきな	人
past	日曜日が　休みだった		すしが　すきだった	
negative	日曜日が　休みじゃない		すしが　すきじゃない	
negative past	日曜日が　休みじゃなかった		すしが　すきじゃなかった	

ex.1. 電車の中で、本を読んでいる人　　a person who is reading a book on the train

2. 田中さんが、きのう、かった本　　a book which Mr. Tanaka bought yesterday

3. アイスクリームをうっているところ　　a place where they sell ice cream. (=a place ice cream is sold)

4. 日本語が、あまりじょうずじゃない人　　a person whose Japanese is not so good

5. 目が大きくて、はなが高い人　　a person with big eyes and a high bridged nose

Note: Oftentimes the subject particle「が」is replaced by the possessive particle「の」without change in meaning.

ex.1. マイケルがかった本　→　マイケルのかった本　　a book which Michael bought

2. 足がながい人　→　足のながい人　　a person with long legs

3. 車がない人　→　車のない人　　a person without a car

Dialogues in English

Dialogue Ⅰ

M: Well, I'll be going then.

T: You put in a hard day. Goodbye.

N: How do you get home (=What method of transportation do you use in getting home), Mr. Webb?

M: Me, I take the subway.

N: Let's go together then. How is your place in Roppongi, by the way?

M: It's convenient, but there's a lot of traffic around there even at night, so it's noisy.

N: I bet it is. Moreover it's rough with the crowded commuter trains, right?

M: That's for sure. Can't something possibly be done?

Dialogue Ⅱ

M: Where is your home?

N: My home? Well you see, four months ago we moved to Urawa.

M: Is that farther away than before?

M: Yeah, quite a bit farther. I change trains all of three times, so it takes me nearly two hours.

M: What? Two whole hours! It takes that long? That's terrible! Which is quicker, car or train?

N: I suppose the train is quicker, when it comes right down to it. The roads get so crowded and all.

M: Which is more crowded, coming in to work or going home?

N: Coming in is much worse, I think.

Dialogue Ⅲ

M: Well I'll be! I'd heard that in Japan university students and even businessmen read comics on the train. And what do you know, it's true!

N: I bet you're surprised. There are also people reading the newspaper while listening to music by earphone.

M: Also people sleeping, right? As for me though, I look at the advertisements and study words written in Chinese characters and *katakana*.

N: You're one for studying, alright! I'll bet that advertisements for weekly magazines are difficult though!

M: Right! They're difficult with all the words I don't know. Not as difficult as my Japanese textbook however.

Exercise 1: Look at the picture and fill in the blanks as in the example.

ex. A: <u>ハンバーガーを食べている</u>人は、だれですか。
B: 山田さんです。

1) ベンチで、ともだちと＿＿＿＿人は、花田さんです。
2) ふんすいのそばで＿＿＿＿人は、林さんです。
3) ＿＿＿＿男の子は、＿＿＿＿です。
4) A: ＿＿＿＿人は、だれですか。
B: あれは、みち子さんです。
5) プールで＿＿＿＿人は、浜田さんです。
6) プールのよこで＿＿＿＿女の子は、
花子ちゃんです。
7) A: マイケルさんとバーバラさんが、＿＿＿＿
ところは、どこですか。
B: プールのむこうです。

◆**Vocabulary**◆

～ちゃん a diminutive form of「～さん」(used between friends or when speaking to children)
しゃしんを とる to take a picture, photo
なわとび skipping rope　スケートボード skateboard
男の子（おとこのこ）boy　女の子（おんなのこ）girl

Exercise 2: For the following pairs of sentences, use the first sentence as a clause modifying the noun in the second sentence.

ex. バーバラさんは、アイロンをかいました。そのアイロンは、11,000円でした。
Barbara bought an iron.　　The iron was 11,000 yen.
⇨バーバラさん が／の かったアイロンは、11,000円でした。
The iron Barbara bought was 11,000 yen.

Note: Barbara is no longer the topic of the new combined sentence (the sentence is now about the iron, telling how much it cost), but rather the subject (in this case the buyer) of the modifying clause, and therefore must be marked with「が」or「の」.

1) わたしは、会社につとめています。その会社は、日比谷にあります。
2) ともだちが、じしょをかいました。そのじしょは、小さくてべんりです。
3) 紙に、じゅうしょと、電話ばんごうを書きました。その紙は、つくえの上にあります。
4) みちがわかりません。そんな人は、こうばんに行って、たずねます。
5) 野村さんは、きのう、レストランへ行きました。そのレストランは、安くておいしかったです。

行く，来る

Hurry up, Barbara!

The usage of「行く」「来る」does not always correspond to the English words "go" and "come".「行く」is used when the speaker, someone or something moves from the speaker's position or moves in a direction away from the speaker's viewpoint.「来る」is commonly used when the speaker, someone or something moves towards speaker's position or towards the direction where the speaker has placed his viewpoint.

I'm coming!
I'm coming!

Function II　Reason or explanation: use of て-form; 電車がこんで、たいへんです。

Oftentimes a clause ending in a て-form gives a reason or explanation for the clause that follows.

ex.1. 電車がこんで、たいへんです。(＝電車がこむから、たいへんです。)

The trains being so crowded, it's terrible.

2. 車がおおくて、うるさいんです。　It's noisy, there being so much traffic.
3. へやが広くて、きもちがいいですね。　It's a big room, so it feels good.
4. すしがすきで、よく、すしやへ行きます。　I like *sushi*, so I often go to a *sushi* bar.
5. びょうきで、学校を休みました。　I was ill and missed school.

Note: The above examples might also be expressed using「から」or「ので」. (see Lesson 5, p.79)

Exercise 3: Fill in the blanks using the most appropriate words from the list below.

1) まわりが＿＿＿＿＿＿、べんきょうができません。
2) 日本の夏は、＿＿＿＿＿＿たいへんです。
3) わたしは、ビールが＿＿＿＿＿＿、よくのみます。
4) 漢字が＿＿＿＿＿＿、こまります。
5) 区役所が＿＿＿＿＿＿、外国人とうろくが、できませんでした。
6) 東京のぶっかが＿＿＿＿＿＿、びっくりしました。

しずか	うるさい	さむい	あつい	わからない
すき	こんでいる	おもい	きらい	高い

Exercise 4: Answer the following questions using the て-form as in the example.

ex. おたくのまわりは、しずかですか。

(しずか・いいところ)　⇨ええ、しずかで、いいところですよ。

(車がおおい・うるさい)　⇨いいえ、車がおおくて、うるさいです。

1) みせは、近いですか。(遠い・ふべん)
2) 日本のおかしは、どうですか。(あまい・おいしい)
3) 新宿は、すきですか。(にぎやか・すき)
4) 日本の6月は、すきですか。(雨がおおい・きらい)
5) このきょうかしょは、いいですか。(絵がたくさんある・いい)
6) 電車の中のこうこくが、わかりますか。(漢字がおおい・わからない)

Function III　Doing something while doing something else; 音楽をききながら

Verb 1 (stem) ＋ ながら、　Verb 2

"Verb 2 while Verb 1"

Note: Verb 2 indicates the main action.

This construction indicates that the second action occurs concurrently with the first.

ex.1. わたしたちは、音楽をききながら、しょくじをしました。

We ate dinner while listening to music.

Vocabulary

つとめる (ru-verb) to be employed

たずねる (ru-verb) to inquire, call on someone

こうばん police box

あまい sweet

2. マイケルさんは、こうこくを見(み)ながら、漢字(かんじ)のべんきょうをします。
   Michael studies Chinese characters while looking at advertisements.

3. マイケルさんと野村(のむら)さんは、おしゃべりをしながら、あるきました。
   Michael and Mr. Nomura walked while talking.

Exercise 5: Tell what the person is doing in each of pictures using「〜ながら」.

1) 2) 3) 4)

<hints> ギターを ひく, うたを うたう, ちずを 見(み)る, さがす, じしょを ひく

Function IV Counting units of time: years, months, weeks, days

1 Units of time

	Years	Months	Weeks	Days
1	1年 いちねん	1か月 いっかげつ	1週間 いっしゅうかん	1日 いちにち
2	2年 にねん	2か月 にかげつ	2週間 にしゅうかん	2日 ふつか
3	3年 さんねん	3か月 さんかげつ	3週間 さんしゅうかん	3日 みっか
4	4年 よねん	4か月 よんかげつ	4週間 よんしゅうかん	4日 よっか
5	5年 ごねん	5か月 ごかげつ	5週間 ごしゅうかん	5日 いつか
6	6年 ろくねん	6か月 ろっかげつ	6週間 ろくしゅうかん	6日 むいか
7	7年 ななねん しちねん	7か月 なながげつ	7週間 ななしゅうかん	7日 なのか
8	8年 はちねん	8か月 はっかげつ はちかげつ	8週間 はっしゅうかん	8日 ようか
9	9年 きゅうねん	9か月 きゅうかげつ	9週間 きゅうしゅうかん	9日 ここのか
10	10年 じゅうねん	10か月 じっかげつ じゅっかげつ	10週間 じっしゅうかん じゅっしゅうかん	10日 とおか
14	14年 じゅうよねん	14か月 じゅうよんかげつ	14週間 じゅうよんしゅうかん	14日 じゅうよっか
20	20年 にじゅうねん	20か月 にじっかげつ にじゅっかげつ	20週間 にじっしゅうかん にじゅっしゅうかん	20日 はつか
How many 〜?				
	何年 なんねん	何か月 なんかげつ	何週間 なんしゅうかん	何日 なんにち

Note: Compare specific times and units of time on the chart below.「かん」means "period, duration". Note that it is required for weeks and hours, and is optional in the case of years, months, days and minutes.

Time Expressions	Years	Months	Weeks	Days	Hours	Minutes
specific	いちねん	いちがつ	(だい)いっしゅう(め)	ついたち	いちじ	いっぷん
unit	いちねん(かん) にねん(かん)	いっかげつ(かん) にかげつ(かん)	いっしゅうかん にしゅうかん	いちにち ふつか(かん)	いちじかん にじかん	いっぷん(かん) にふん(かん)

2 The following words are used to indicate a specific past or future time, measured in units from the present or some referent time.

unit of time＋ まえ	＋	に＋ Verb	"__ ago", "__ before", "previous __"
unit of time＋ あと/後		です	"in __", "__ later" "__ after"

ex.1. A: いつ、ひっこしましたか。 When did you move?
B: 4か月まえに、ひっこしました。 We moved 4 months ago.

ex.2. A: いつ、ひっこしますか。 When are you going to move?
B: 2週間 あとに/後に、ひっこします。 We are going to move in 2 weeks.

Note: The optional「かん」is not used before「まえに」and「あとに/後に」.
○ みっかかん の りょこうに行きます。
× みっかかん まえに、日本に来ました。
○ みっか まえに、日本に来ました。

Exercise 6: Answer the following questions using the information in parentheses.

1) どのくらい、日本にいますか。(3 years)
2) 京都に、どのくらい、いましたか。(4 days)
3) いつ、車をかいましたか。(5 months ago)
4) いつ、うちを出ましたか。(2 hours ago)
5) 夏休みは、何週間ですか。(8 weeks)
6) いつ、おきましたか。(30 minutes ago)
7) いつ、ヨーロッパに行きますか。(in 1 month)
8) いつ、日本語のべんきょうを、はじめましたか。(give your own answer)
9) あなたのりょうしんは、いつ、けっこんしましたか。(give your own answer)

Grammar Note Emphatic use of「も」

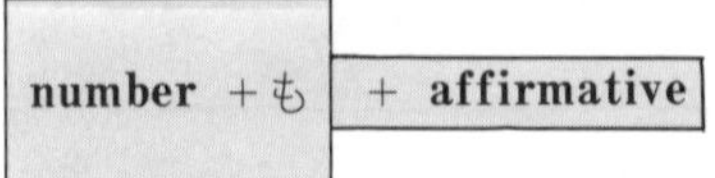

Using「も」after a number or quantity indicates that it is greater than what is expected.

ex.1. 3度も のりかえます。 I change (trains) all of 3 times!
2. 2時間も かかります。 It takes 2 whole hours!

Note: 〈**number** ＋も＋ **negative**〉 suggests the amount is smaller than would be expected.
ex. 10分もかかりません。 It doesn't take you even ten minutes.
あたらしいのは、1つもありません。 As for new ones, we don't have even one!

Exercise 7: Construct dialogues as follows.

ex. 成田→ホテル／3時間／ かかる ⇨ A: 成田からホテルまで、3時間かかります。
B: えっ、3時間も？そんなに、かかるんですか。

1) ビール／ 5本／ のむ
2) 日本のけっこんしき／ 300万円／ かかる
3) ざっし／ 4さつ／ かう
4) ヨーロッパ／ 2か月／ りょこうする
5) 車／ 3だい／ もっている
6) 石川さん／ こどもが6人／ いる

Vocabulary

ギター guitar
ひく (u-verb) to play a stringed instrument
うた song
うたう (u-verb) to sing
さがす (u-verb) to look for, search, seek
ヨーロッパ Europe
はじめる (ru-verb) to begin
けっこんする marriage (to marry)
けっこんしき wedding ceremony
－だい counter for relatively large manufactured items such as cars, bicycles, television sets, etc.
－さつ counter for books, magazines, etc.
もつ (u-verb) to hold, possess

Function V　Listing more than one object (2); AやB, AとかB

limited	AとB	A and B (see Lesson 4, p.66)
unlimited	AやB（など） AとかB（とか）（など）	A, B, etc. for example, A, B, etc.

ex.1. 音楽をきいている人や、まんがを読んでいる人がいます。
There are people listening to music, people reading comics, etc.

2. くうこうには、銀行や、レストランなどがあります。
At the airport there is a bank, restaurant, and other such facilities.

3. シーツとか、アイロンとか、いろいろなものを、かいました。
I bought various items, including sheets, an iron, etc.

Note 1:「など」used at the end of a series of nouns means "etc., and so forth".
Note 2: When giving examples, begin with「たとえば」"for example".

ex. A: どんなところへ行きたいですか。　What sort of place would you like to go?
B: そうですねえ。おんせんがあって、あまり遠くないところ、たとえば、箱根や伊豆へ行きたいですね。
Well, I'd like to go some place with a hot spring that's not too far away, for example Hakone or Izu.

Exercise 8: Answer the following questions, using the additional vocabulary items given below if necessary. Use「や」,「とか」, etc.

1) スーパーには、何が、ありますか。
2) やおやで、どんなものを、かいましたか。
3) どんなスポーツが、すきですか。
4) あなたのへやには、どんなものが、ありますか。
5) しょくじのあと、どんなのみものを、のみますか。

additional vocabulary

せんざい laundry soap　トイレットペーパー toilet paper　けしょうひん cosmetics
にんじん carrot　キャベツ cabbage　じゃがいも potato　レタス lettuce
なす（び）eggplant　たまねぎ onion　サッカー soccer　やきゅう baseball
たっきゅう pingpong　ラグビー rugby　つくえ desk　本だな bookshelf
ラジカセ radio-cassette player　CD（シーディー）compact disk

Function VI　Comparison (1); 電車のほうが　はやい

Statement	Bは、Aより＿です。	B is more ＿ than A.
Question	AとBと、どちらが＿ですか。 AとBと、どちらのほうが＿ですか。	Which is more ＿, A or B? 〃
Answer	Aより、Bのほうが＿です。 Aは、Bほど (negative) ＿。 AもBも、＿です。	B is more ＿ than A. A is not as ＿ as B. A and B are both ＿.

ex.1. (statement) 電車は、車より　はやいです。　It's quicker by train than by car.

2. Q: 電車と車と、どちらのほうが、はやいですか。 Which is faster, train or car?
   A: 車より、電車のほうが、はやいです。 It's quicker by train than by car.
   A: 車は、電車ほど、はやくありません。 By car is not as fast as by train.
3. Q: すしと天(てん)ぷらと、どっちがすき？ (plain)
   Which do you like better, *sushi* or *tempura?*
   A: 天ぷらのほうが、すき。 I like *tempura* better.
   A: すしも天ぷらも、すき。(＝どちらもすき。) I like both *sushi* and *tempura*. (I like both of them).

Note:「__ほど」mainly occurs in negative comparisons.
ex. Q: 横浜(よこはま)は、大(おお)きいですか。 Is Yokohama big?
A: ええ。でも、東京(とうきょう)や大阪(おおさか)ほど、大きくありません。 Yes, but not as big as Tokyo, Osaka, etc.
A: ええ、大きいですが、東京ほどじゃありません。 Yes, it is big, but not as big as Tokyo.

Expressions of degree

Adverbs like「ずっと」"great amount (time, distance, etc.)",「ちょっと／すこし」"a little",「もっと」"more" or numbers may be used to indicate the extent of the difference between two items.

ex.1. きゅうりょうは、部長(ぶちょう)より社長(しゃちょう)のほうが、ずっとおおいです。
As far as salary goes, the president of a company gets far more than a division manager.

2. みちは、月曜日(げつようび)より日曜日(にちようび)のほうが、もっとこんでいます。
The roads are much more crowded on Sundays than on Mondays.

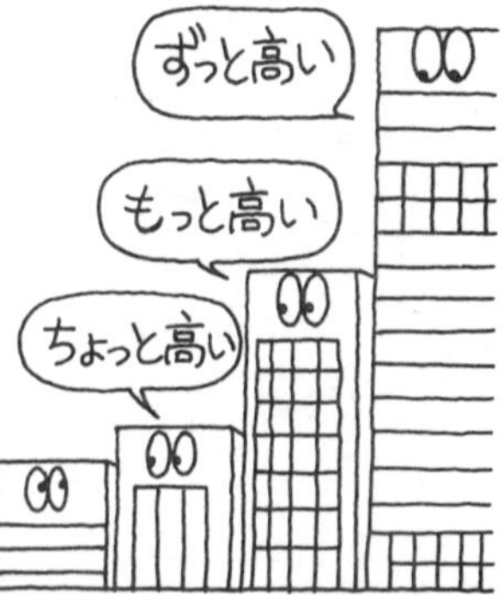

3. バスで行(い)くより、車(くるま)で行くほうが、ちょっとはやいです。
It's a little bit quicker going by car than by bus.

4. 大阪へは、しんかんせんより、ひこうきのほうが、2時間(じかん)はやいです。
For getting to Osaka, the plane is 2 hours quicker than bullet train.

5. こづかいは、ぼくより、あにのほうが、1,000円(えん)おおいです。
My brother gets 1,000 yen more for his allowance than I do.

Exercise 9: Compare the items given as in the example, answering in both affirmative and negative. For affirmative answers, use「ずっと」,「ちょっと」,「すこし」.

ex. エベレスト／ふじ山(さん)／高(たか)い
⇨ Q: エベレストとふじ山と、どちらのほうが高いですか。
A: エベレストのほうが、ずっと高いです。(affirmative)
or ふじ山は、エベレストほど、高くありません。(negative)

1) 日本(にほん)／ アメリカ／ 広(ひろ)い
2) 6月(がつ)／ 8月／あつい
3) 月曜日(げつようび)／ 金曜日(きんようび)／ つかれる。
4) レコード／ CD／ 高(たか)い
5) 行(い)きの電車(でんしゃ)／ かえりの電車／ こんでいる
6) 日本のワイン／フランスのワイン／おいしい
7) 和食(わしょく)／ 洋食(ようしょく)／ すき
8) しんかんせん／ ひこうき／ はやい

◆**Vocabulary**◆
スーパー supermarket
やおや vegetable market, grocery
和食（わしょく）Japanese cuisine
洋食（ようしょく）Western cuisine

Exercise 10: Answer the following questions using the statistics given.

1) 和食がすきな人と、洋食がすきな人と、どちらが おおいですか。
2) 夏のりょこうは、うみへ行った人より、山へ行った人のほうが、おおいですか。
3) たばこを、ぜんぜんすわない人と、すう人と、どちらが、何人おおいですか。
4) たばこをすう女の人は、たばこをすわない女の人より、何人すくないですか。

		男	女
どちらがすきですか	和食	22人	31人
	洋食	28人	19人
夏のりょこうは、どこへ行きましたか	うみ	27人	30人
	山	23人	20人
たばこをすいますか	まいにち	20人	4人
	ときどき	15人	10人
	すわない	15人	36人

Exercise 11: Compare the various features of these two part-time positions.

(A)
しごと：モデル
お金：10,000円/hour
時間：5時間/week
ばしょ：六本木

(B)
しごと：えい語の先生
お金：6,000円/hour
時間：10時間/week
ばしょ：千葉

<hints> 近い↔遠い　　むずかしい↔やさしい
おもしろい↔つまらない　　おおい↔すくない

ex. 1時間のお金は、えい語の先生より、モデルのほうがおおいです。
Regarding hourly pay, the model receives more than the English teacher.

1) しごとの時間は、＿＿＿＿＿＿。　2) 1週間のお金は、＿＿＿＿＿＿。
3) はたらくところは、＿＿＿＿＿＿。　4) しごとは、＿＿＿＿＿＿。
5) あなたは、AとBと、どちらのほうがいいですか。それはなぜですか。

Function VII　Stating an opinion; …と思います

Plain statement ＋と思います

The quotation marker「と」, followed by the verb「思う」"to think" may be used to state an opinion: "I think such and such", "I believe such and such".

		statement	opinion
definite	polite	とてもいい本です。	とてもいい本だと思います。
	plain	とてもいい本（だ）よ。	とてもいい本だと思う(わ)よ。
not so certain	polite	これがいいでしょう。 これがいいんじゃありませんか。	これがいいだろうと思います(けど/が)。 これがいいんじゃないかと思います(けど/が)。
	plain	これがいいだろう。 これがいいんじゃない。	これがいいだろうと思うけど。 これがいいんじゃないかと思うけど。

Vocabulary

うみ sea
モデル model
ワープロ word processor
ぜんぜん entirely, wholly, not at all
つまらない uninteresting
マナー manners
はがき postcard
ときどき sometimes
すくない few in number, small amount
すう (u-verb) to breathe in, smoke

There are two possible negative forms; 「negative statement＋と思う」 and 「affirmative statement＋と（は）思わない」. Note the slightly different connotations.

ex.1. Q: この本を、どう思いますか。　What do you think of this book?
　A: とてもいいと思います。　I think it is very good.
　あまりよくないと思います。　I don't think it is very good.

2. Q: 日本のぶっかは、高いと思いますか。　Do you think prices in Japan are high?
　A: ええ、高いと思います。　Yes, I think they are high.
　ええ、そう思います。　Yes, I think so.
　いいえ、高いとは思いません。　No, I don't think they are high.

Note 1: Sometimes「と」may be followed by「は」particularly in negative sentences.

Note 2: Use「と思います」for telling what you yourself think. Use「と思っている」when stating someone else's opinion.

ex. バーバラさんは、日本のぶっかは高いと思っています。　Barbara thinks that Japanese prices are high.

Note 3:「と」is used for both direct and indirect quotation of thoughts and ideas (…と思う), spoken utterances (…という), written messages (…と書く), and things heard (…ときく), etc. The quoted statement is generally given in plain style speech.

ex.1. かれは、あした行くといいました。　He said he'd go tomorrow.
2. てがみに、とてもげんきだと書きました。　I wrote in my letter that we were all quite healthy.
3. 田中さんは、先週、ホンコンへ行ったとききましたが…。
　I heard Mr. Tanaka went to Hong Kong last week, but ….

Exercise 12: Restate the following sentences as an opinion using「…と思います」.

1) 日本の車のほうが安いでしょう。
2) はやく、びょういんへ行ったほうがいいですよ。
3) ワープロは、べんりです。
4) マイケルさんは、べんきょう家です。
5) あのレストランは、安いけれど、あまりおいしくありません。

Exercise 13: Give your opinion in answer to the following questions.

1) スポーツを、たくさんしたほうがいいですか。
2) 電車の中の日本人のマナーは、いいですか。
3) 日本語は、むずかしいと思いますか。
4) 電車の中のこうこくを、どう思いますか。
5) 日曜日に、ディズニーランドへ行きたいんですが、電車と車と、どちらがいいでしょうか。
6) まいにち、たばこをすう人が、たくさんいますが、どう思いますか。

Exercise 14: Look at the pictures and fill in the blanks with appropriate words.

◀1)山田さんは、きのう、＿＿＿＿＿といいました。

2)はがきに、＿＿＿＿＿と＿＿＿＿＿。▶

◀3)わたしは、車より＿＿＿＿＿と＿＿＿＿＿。

じこ　accident

4)成田への道で、＿＿＿＿＿と＿＿＿＿＿。▶

Reading Comprehension Exercise

〈みち子さんのはなし〉

わたしのクラスには、りょこうのすきな人がおおいです。外国へ行ったことがある人も、たくさんいます。ことしの夏、ヨーロッパに行った人もいますが、ハワイや韓国へ行った人ほど、おおくはありません。日本の のりものやホテルは高いから、外国へ行ったほうが安いと、次郎くんがいっていましたが、ほんとうでしょうか。わたしも、来年の春休みに、3週間ぐらい、ヨーロッパへ行きたいと思って、アルバイトをはじめました。

◆**Vocabulary**◆　クラス class　外国（がいこく）foreign country　韓国（かんこく）Korea
～くん suffix added to names of boys and younger men　春休み（はるやすみ）spring vacation

Exercise 15: Make questions for the following answers asking the underlined part.

ex. Q: みち子さんのクラスには、(何がすきな人が、おおいですか)。
A: りょこうがすきな人が、おおいです。

1) Q: ことしの夏、(　　　　　　　)。
A: ハワイや韓国へ行った人が、おおいです。

2) Q: 次郎くんは、日本のりょこうと、外国のりょこうと、(　　　　　　　)と思っていますか。
A: 外国のりょこうのほうが、安いと思っています。

3) Q: みち子さんは、(　　　　　　　)。
A: 来年の春休みに行きたいと思っています。

4) Q: (　　　　　　　)。
A: 3週間ぐらい、行きたいと思っています。

Listening Comprehension Exercise

Listen to the tape and answer the following questions.

1) True or false?

① (　　) マイケルさんは、クラシックより、ジャズがすきだ。
② (　　) 土田さんは、ジャズがきらいだ。
③ (　　) 土田さんは、クラシックがすきじゃない。
④ (　　) バーバラさんは、クラシックがすきだ。

2) 土田さんは、今週と来週と、どちらがいそがしいですか。

◆**Vocabulary**◆　クラシック classical music

■Culture Note■

国民の祝日
National Holidays

Japan has 13 nationally proclaimed holidays in the year. On these days schools, banks and most businesses are closed.

1月1日	元旦	**New Year's Day** — celebrating the beginning of the new year.
1月15日	成人の日	**Coming-of-Age Day** — on which boys and girls reaching the age of 20 are ceremonially recognized as adults.
2月11日	建国記念の日	**National Foundation Day** — devoted to fostering a sense of national pride.
3月21日ごろ	春分の日	**Vernal Equinox** — a time for renewing a sense of one's closeness to nature.
4月29日	緑の日	**Greenery Day** — formerly Emperor Hirohito's birthday, the new name symbolizes a love and regard for nature.
5月3日	憲法記念日	**Constitution Day** — commemorating the adoption of the present constitution.
5月5日	こどもの日	**Children's Day** — a day for expressing devotion to one's children and a concern for their future happiness.
9月15日	敬老の日	**Respect-for-the-Aged Day** — a day for showing respect to the elderly and a concern for their welfare.
9月23日ごろ	秋分の日	**Autumnal Equinox** — a time for venerating one's ancestors and those who have passed away.
10月10日	体育の日	**Health-Sports Day** — proclaimed a national holiday at the time of the Tokyo Olympics, a day for active participation in some sort of sports activity.
11月3日	文化の日	**Culture Day** — paying tribute to the ideals of freedom, peace and cultural advancement.
11月23日	勤労感謝の日	**Labor Thanksgiving Day** — paying tribute to the ideals of hard work and labor.
12月23日	天皇誕生日	**Emperor's Birthday** — a day for paying respect to the emperor.

＊**Golden Week** — three national holidays are bunched together at the end of April and the first week in May. This, plus a two-day weekend, makes it more convenient for many businesses to simply shut down for the entire period. Golden Week has become a time for leisure activity, with many people going on trips, either in Japan or abroad.

Festivals (1)

Festivals are traditional events celebrated annually. Two such festivals celebrate children as they grow, and one of these has been set aside as the national holiday, Children's Day.

3月3日 ひなまつり Doll's or Girl's Festival — celebrated by setting out dolls in scenes representing ancient court life.

5月5日 たんごのせっく Boy's Festival — celebrated by flying "Koinobori" or carp streamers and displaying models of armor used by warriors long ago.

第9課 切手を　あげましょう

Let Me Give You A Stamp

Dialogue I

Barbara is looking through her stamp collection when her neighbor, Mrs. Yamada, drops by.

Mrs. 山田：きれいな切手ですねえ。コアラだから、オーストラリアの切手ですか。

バーバラ　：ええ、ともだちに　もらったんです。

3まいあるから、1まい、あげましょう。

Mrs. 山田：えっ、くださるんですか。うれしいわ。

むすこが、切手をあつめているんですよ。

めずらしい外国の切手を見るのは、

たのしいですね。

バーバラ　：ほかにも、いろいろありますよ。パンダの切手や、

めずらしい魚の切手もありますから、

これもあげましょう。どうぞ。

Mrs. 山田：まあ、こんなにたくさん？どうもありがとう。

きっと、むすこが、よろこびますわ。

バーバラ　：主人は、こんばん、おそいと言ってましたから、

どうぞ、ごゆっくり。

Dialogue II

Mrs. Yamada sees a picture of Barbara's folks back home.

Mrs. 山田：そこにあるのは、ごかぞくの　しゃしんですか。

バーバラ　：ええ、アメリカにいる、かぞくのしゃしんです。

まん中が母で、そのうしろに　たっているのが、妹です。

Mrs. 山田：きれいな方ですねえ。妹さんのとなりにいるのが、ご主人ですか。

バーバラ　：ええ、そうです。市役所に　つとめているんですよ。

Mrs. 山田：そうですか。お子さんは、3人ですね。
いちばん下のお子さんは、おいくつですか。

バーバラ　：来月、6つになると言ってました。

Mrs. 山田：じゃ、もうすぐ、学校ですね。

バーバラ　：ええ。ことし、小学校に はいります。

Dialogue III

Mr. Yamada drops by a few days later.

Mr. 山田：こんばんは。これ、すこしですけど……どうぞ。

マイケル：何ですか。わあ、大きないちごですね。どうもありがとう。
かないも、わたしも、だいすきなんです。

Mr. 山田：いなかの兄が、りょうしんといっしょに、つくっているんですよ。

マイケル：お兄さんが、ごりょうしんと いっしょにねえ。そうですか。
山田さんは、いなかは、どちらですか。

Mr. 山田：静岡です。

マイケル：ああ、静岡は、いちごで、ゆうめいですね。テレビで見ました。
ごかぞくは、みんな静岡ですか。

Mr. 山田：いいえ、姉はけっこんして、大阪に住んでいます。
弟 は、商社員で、4年前から、ドイツに行っています。

Vocabulary

Nouns:

1切手（きって）postage stamp
1コアラ koala bear
1オーストラリア Australia
8パンダ panda
19市役所（しやくしょ）municipal office
26いちご strawberry
28いなか country, place grew up in, back home
35商社員（しょうしゃいん）trading company employee
15（ご）かぞく family, folks
5むすこ son
13主人（しゅじん）my husband: ご主人 someone else's husband
17母（はは）mother
17妹（いもうと）younger sister
29お兄さん（おにいさん）elder brother (honorific)
34姉（あね）elder sister
35弟（おとうと）younger brother
20お子さん（おこさん）someone else's child (honorific)

school		student
小学校（しょうがっこう）	primary school	小学生（しょうがくせい）
中学校（ちゅうがっこう）	junior high school	中学生（ちゅうがくせい）
高等学校（こうとうがっこう）	high school	高校生（こうこうせい）
大学（だいがく）	university, college	大学生（だいがくせい）

Note: The words「中学校」and「高等学校」are often shortened to「中学（ちゅうがく）」and「高校（こうこう）」respectively.

22 6つ（むっつ）six, six years old

Adjectives:
4うれしい happy, glad, pleased
6めずらしい out of the ordinary, not often encountered
13おそい slow, late
27だいすき（な） favorite
Adverbs:
23もうすぐ soon, very shortly, anytime now
Verbs:
3あげる (ru-verb) to give ☞Function V
4くださる (u-verb) to give (me) ☞Function V
5あつめる (ru-verb) to gather, collect, bring together
12よろこぶ (u-verb) to be happy, pleased
17たつ (u-verb) to stand
28つくる (u-verb) to make, grow
34住む（すむ） (u-verb) to live, dwell
Grammatical words:
22＿（に）なる to turn into ＿, become ＿ ☞Function I
Expressions:
14どうぞ、ごゆっくり Please stay awhile longer.
18きれいな方(かた) pretty person (「方(かた)」is a polite word for「人(ひと)」"person")
21いちばん下(した)のお子(こ)さん the youngest child
21おいくつですか How old (is he)?
24小学校(しょうがっこう)にはいる to start elementary school
25こんばんは [*konbanwa*] Good evening.
25すこしですけど、どうぞ It isn't much, but please accept it.
26わあ Wow! Oh!

Counting age:

1さい / 一つ(ひとつ)	9さい / 九つ(ここのつ)
2さい / 二つ(ふたつ)	10さい / 十(とお)
3さい / 三つ(みっつ)	11さい
4さい / 四つ(よっつ)	12さい
5さい / 五つ(いつつ)	
6さい / 六つ(むっつ)	20さい / 二十(はたち)
7さい / 七つ(ななつ)	
8さい / 八つ(やっつ)	何さい？ / いくつ

Dialogue Comprehension Exercise

1) Answer the following questions.

① バーバラさんは、山田(やまだ)さんに、何(なに)をあげましたか。
② バーバラさんは、コアラの切手(きって)を買(か)いましたか。
③ 山田さんは、なぜ、切手をもらって、よろこびましたか。
④ 市役所(しやくしょ)につとめている人(ひと)は、だれですか。
⑤ しゃしんの、妹(いもうと)さんのよこにたっている人は、バーバラさんのお母(かあ)さん "mother" ですか。
⑥ マイケルさんは、こんばん、はやくかえるでしょうか。

2) Where do Mr. Yamada's parents live? Where do his brothers and sisters live?

① りょうしん〔　　〕 ② 兄(あに)〔　　〕 ③ 姉(あね)〔　　〕 ④ 弟(おとうと)〔　　〕

Function I

Describing a change in state (1): A turns into B, A becomes B ; 来月(らいげつ)、6つになります

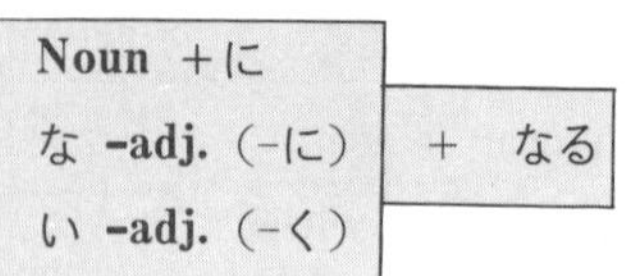

Noun ＋に	
な -adj. (−に)	＋ なる
い -adj. (−く)	

ex.1. むすこは、大学生(だいがくせい)になります。
My son will become a college student.
2. へやが、きれいになりました。 My room became clean.
My room is clean.
3. こどもは、大きくなります。 The children will grow up.

The verb「なる」means "to turn into, become". In many cases the non-past form indicates future "will become", while past tense generally means "became and is now".

ex. 4. いま、5つです。来月、6つになります。 He's five now. He will be six next month.

5. 日本語のべんきょうが、おもしろくなりました。

The study of Japanese has become interesting.

6. 1つ50円ですから、ぜんぶで、250円になります。

That's 50 yen for one, so altogether it comes to 250 yen.

7. 弟は、スーパーマンになりたいと思っています。

My little brother thinks he wants to become Superman.

8. 日本語がじょうずになったから、日本に行きたくなりました。

My Japanese has gotten good, so now I want to go to Japan.

Remember:「～たい」"I want __" is inflected like an adjective.

Exercise 1: Practice the following conversation, choosing appropriate answers from the list of words on the next page.

ex. A: まいにち、よく、れんしゅうしました。 I practiced hard every day.

B: じょうずになりましたね。 You have become very good at it, haven't you.

1) A: 来月、駅の前に、大きいスーパーができるんですよ。

B: じゃ、＿＿＿＿＿＿＿＿＿＿。

2) A: せっけんで、手をあらったよ。

B: ＿＿＿＿＿＿＿＿＿＿。

◆**Vocabulary**◆ せっけん soap 手（て） hand あらう (u-verb) to wash

Dialogues in English

Dialogue Ⅰ

Y: My, such beautiful stamps! That's a koala bear, so is it an Australian stamp?

B: Yes, I got it from a friend. I have three of them, let me give you one.

Y: What, give me one? I'm thrilled!
My boy collects stamps. It's fun to see exotic stamps from foreign countries.

B: I have various other ones besides. There's some panda stamps and stamps with exotic fish, so let me give you these as well. Here.

Y: Gosh! So many? Thank you very much.
I know my boy will be pleased.

B: My husband said he would be late this evening, so please stay awhile longer.

Dialogue Ⅱ

Y: Is that a picture of your family there?

B: Yes, It's a picture of my folks back home in America. The one in the center is my mother, and the one standing behind her is my younger sister.

Y: My, but she's a pretty person! Is the one standing next to your sister her husband?

B: Yes, that's right. He works at the municipal office building.

Y: Is that so? They have three children, right? How old is the youngest child?

B: They said he would be six next month.

Y: Well then he should be starting school soon.

B: Yes, he starts elementary school this year.

Dialogue Ⅲ

Y: Good evening. Here you are. It isn't much, but, uh ...

M: What is it? Wow! What big strawberries!
Thank you very much. My wife and I both love them.

Y: My brother and my parents in the country grow them.

M: Your brother along with your parents. I see.
Where did you grow up, Mr. Yamada?

Y: In Shizuoka.

M: Ah, Shizuoka is famous for strawberries.
I saw it on television. Are all your folks back in Shizuoka?

Y: No, my elder sister is married and living in Osaka. My younger brother works for a trading company and has been in Germany now for four years.

3) A: あなたは、さしみがきらいでしたね。
   B: ええ。でも、このごろ、________________。

4) A: 4月に、もう1人、子どもがうまれます。
   B: じゃ、太郎ちゃんは、________________。

5) A: おしごとは、このごろ、どうですか。
   B: ええ、とても________________。

6) A: ひっこしたんですか。
   B: ええ、前より、すこし________________。

お兄さん	きれい（な）	べんり（な）	いそがしい	すき（な）
遠い	高い	じょうず（な）	へた（な）	

Exercise 2: Tell what each person would like to become. You may choose appropriate answers from the list below.

Q: 何になりたいですか。

① 太郎は、まんががじょうずだから、________________と思っています。
② みち子は、いろいろな国へ行きたいから、________________と思っています。
③ はる子は、子どもがすきだから、小学校の________________と思っています。
④ あなたは？ ________________。

しょくぎょう occupation

会社員 company employee	いしゃ doctor	まんが家 cartoonist	先生 teacher
銀行員 bank employee	えいがスター film star	スチュワーデス stewardess	
ファッションモデル fashion model	けんちく家 architect	デザイナー designer	

Function II　Describing the present state (1); ドイツに行っています。

As described in Lesson 4, the progressive form of the verb「て-form＋いる」is used to report an action in progress at the time indicated, and equivalent to English "is doing".

ex.1 A: いま、何をしていますか。　What are you doing now?
　　 B: 本を読んでいます。　I'm reading a book.

2. ごぜんちゅう、ずっと、日本語をべんきょうしていました。
   I was studying Japanese all morning.

Vocabulary

さしみ *sashimi*, raw fish
もう1人（もうひとり）one more person
とまる (u-verb) to stop, park
でかける (ru-verb) to go out, leave for somewhere
このごろ these days, lately
へた（な）poor, bad, unskillful
しゅみ hobby
テニスクラブ tennis club

「～ている」may also indicate a currently on going process, where the action itself is not necessarily being performed at the moment.

ex. 1. いま、とてもおもしろい本を読んでいます。

I'm currently (in the process of) reading an extremely interesting book.

2. 4月から、学校で、ドイツ語をべんきょうしています。

I'm studying German at school starting last April.

「～ている」form also refers to an existing state resulting from a completed action.

ex. 1. わたしは、けっこんしています。　　I'm married.

2. 弟は、いま、ドイツに行っています。

My younger brother (went to and) is in Germany now.

3. マイケルさんは、日本に来ています。　　Michael (came to and) is in Japan.

4. りょうしんは、静岡に住んでいます。　　My parents live in Shizuoka.

5. かれは、市役所につとめています。　　He works at the municipal office.

Note: In rapid speech, the initial い of「いる」is regularly dropped in this construction.

Thus: つとめています → つとめてます,　　しっていますか → しってますか

Exercise 3: Complete the following sentences about Mr. Tanaka using the progressive form.

1) 田中さんは、世田谷に__________います。
2) 東京銀行に__________います。
3) しゅみで、切手を__________います。
4) かぞくは、りょうしんだけです。
まだ、__________いません。
5) ホンダの車を__________います。
6) けいおう大学を__________います。

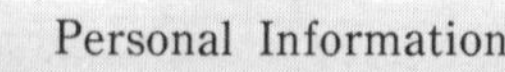
Personal Information

田中　一男

(1)住所：東京　世田谷
(2)しょくぎょう：銀行員（東京銀行）
(3)しゅみ：切手をあつめる
(4)かぞく：父と母
(5)車　：　ホンダ
(6)大学：　けいおう大学そつぎょう

Exercise 4: The following sentences tell actions. Rewrite them so they describe states.

ex. 黒い車が、3時にとまりました。 ⇨ 黒い車が、3時から、とまっています。

1) 先週、りょうりの本をかりました。
2) 3年前、大阪にひっこしました。(use「住む」)
3) よし子さんは、2時にでかけました。
4) 5年前に、テニスクラブにはいりました。

Grammar Note　Further uses of「の」

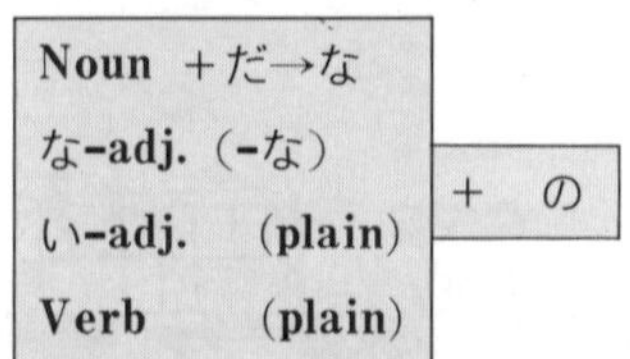
Noun　＋だ→な
な-adj.（-な）
い-adj.　(plain)
Verb　(plain)
＋　の

[1] Pronoun「の」"one" or "one's" (introduced in Lesson 6) used after adjectives and verbs may refer to a person, thing, place, time, etc., depending on the context.

ex. 1. いちごをくれたのは、だれ？

Who was the person that gave us strawberries?

ex. 2. きのう、バーバラさんが買ったのは、何？ What is the thing that Barbara bought yesterday?

[2] Another use of「の」is to turn the preceding phrase into a noun.

ex.1. 漢字(かんじ)をおぼえるのは、たいへんです。 The learning of Chinese characters is difficult.

2. さむいのはいいけど、あついのはいやです。 The cold is all right, but I hate the heat.

3. あしたが休(やす)みなのは、うれしいです。 I'm happy that tomorrow is a holiday.

In this use,「の」is roughly equivalent to「こと」(see Lesson 7, p.100), and the two might be interchanged, with「こと」sounding somewhat formal or bookish.

ex.4. むすこは、切手(きって)を あつめる の／こと が、だいすきです。 My boy loves to collect stamps.

5. 田中(たなか)さんが、きのう、うちに 来(き)た の／こと をしっていますか。

Do you know that Mr. Tanaka came to our house yesterday?

6. このへんが、こんなに しずかな の／こと は、めずらしいんじゃありませんか。

Isn't it strange for this area to be so quiet?

When the sentence involves something perceived directly by the senses however,「の」is preferred.

ex.1. つめたいかぜがふくのを、かんじました。 I felt a cold wind blow.

2. 田中さんがへやを出(で)るのを、見(み)ました。 I saw Mr. Tanaka leave the room.

Note:「こと」cannot be replaced by「の」in certain fixed expressions.

ex.1. あの人は、メキシコに住(す)んだことがあります。(×の) That person has lived in Mexico.

2. マイケルは、日本語を話(はな)すことができます。(×の) Michael can speak Japanese.

Exercise 5: Complete the following sentences.

田中さんが、新宿で買(か)いました。8,000円でした。

黒田さんが、土曜日につくりました。

1) 田辺(たなべ)さんが________のは、8000円(えん)のネクタイです。

2) 田辺さんがネクタイを_______のは、新宿(しんじゅく)です。

3) 「ケーキを_____のは、だれですか。」「黒田(くろだ)さんです。」

4) 黒田さんが土曜日(どようび)に_____のは、ケーキです。

Exercise 6: Tell what each person likes to do using「の」.

1) 山本(やまもと)さんは、__________が、すきです。それから、

__________もすきです。

2) 田中(たなか)さんは、__________が、すきです。

3) 黒田(くろだ)さんは、__________が、じょうずです。

4) 山田(やまだ)さんは、__________はたのしい と言(い)っています。

しゅみ

山本：えいがを見(み)る，音楽(おんがく)をきく。

田中：テレビで，すもうを見る。

黒田：おかしをつくる。

山田：切手をあつめる。

Exercise 7: Tell about each person using the words given as in the example.

ex. 中村(なかむら)さん（京都(きょうと)に住(す)む） → 京都に住んでいるのは、中村さんです。

1) 山田さん（車(くるま)で来(き)た）

2) 田中さん（銀行(ぎんこう)につとめる）

3) マイケルさん（テニスがすき）

4) 土田さん（電車(でんしゃ)にのる）

5) バーバラさん（買(か)いものをする）

山田さん

田中さん

Function III　Listing more than one object(3): "both A and B"; かないも　わたしも

AもBも	→ A and B both, A and B as well (affirmative sentence)
	→ Neither A nor B　　(negative sentence)

ex. 1. ウエッブさんもおくさんも、切手(きって)をあつめるのがすきです。

Mr. and Mrs. Webb are both fond of collecting stamps.

2. ウエッブさんは、鎌倉(かまくら)へも日光(にっこう)へも、行(い)きました。

Mr. Webb went both to Kamakura and to Nikko as well.

3. くだものが、たくさんありますね。いちごもみかんも、すきですか。

There certainly are all kinds of fruits. Do you like both strawberries and tangerines?

はい、いちごもみかんも、だいすきです。

Yes, I'm very fond of both strawberries and tangerines.

いいえ、いちごもみかんも、すきじゃありません。

No, I don't care for either strawberries or tangerines.

いいえ、いちごはすきですが、みかんはきらいです。

No, I like strawberries, but I don't care for tangerines.

Note 1: Any number of items may be joined in this manner.

ex. わたしは、はしるのも、およぐのも、ダンスをするのもすきです。

I enjoy running, swimming, and dancing as well.

Note 2: Compare the difference between「も」and「と」.

ex. はしるのも、およぐのも、すきです。　I like running and I like swimming too.

はしるのと、およぐのが、すきです。　I like running and swimming.

Exercise 8: Answer the following question as in example 3 above.

テニスもゴルフも、しますか。

1) マイケルさんは、＿＿＿＿＿＿＿＿。

2) 山田(やまだ)さんは、＿＿＿＿＿＿＿＿。

3) バーバラさんは、＿＿＿＿＿＿＿＿。

Exercise 9: Look at the picture and complete the following dialogues.

1) A: ナイフとフォークは、どこですか。

B: ＿＿＿＿＿＿＿＿テーブルの上(うえ)にあります。

2) A: バナナとりんごが、ありますか。

B: いいえ、＿＿＿＿＿＿＿＿＿＿＿＿。

3) A: プレゼントのはこが、ありますか。

B: ええ、テーブルの＿＿＿＿＿＿＿＿ありますけど。

4) A: ビールもワインも、ありますね。

B: いいえ、＿＿＿＿＿＿が、＿＿＿＿＿＿。

5) A: じゃ、テーブルのみぎにあるのも、＿＿＿＿、ワインですか。

B: ええ、そうですよ。

◆Vocabulary◆

ナイフ knife　フォーク fork　テーブル table

プレゼントする present, gift (to give)

Function IV Speaking of family members; Honorific and humble terms

Two sets of terms are used in referring to family members. Humble terms are used when referring to members of one's own family, and honorific terms are used for members of someone else's family. In actual fact, many different words are used for "father", "mother", etc., but only the most common are listed below.

Humble (my-)	Honorific (your-)	
かぞく	ごかぞく	family, folks
りょうしん	ごりょうしん	parents
父(ちち)	お父(とう)さん	father
母(はは)	お母(かあ)さん	mother
きょうだい	ごきょうだい	brothers and sisters
兄(あに)	お兄(にい)さん	elder brother
姉(あね)	お姉(ねえ)さん	elder sister
弟(おとうと)	弟(おとうと)さん	younger brother
妹(いもうと)	妹(いもうと)さん	younger sister
主人(しゅじん)	ご主人(しゅじん)	husband
かない	おくさん	wife

Humble (my-)	Honorific (your-)	
子ども	お子(こ)さん	child
むすこ	むすこさん／ぼっちゃん	son
むすめ	むすめさん／おじょうさん	daughter
そふ	おじいさん	grandfather
そぼ	おばあさん	grandmother
まご	おまごさん	grandchild
おじ	おじさん	uncle
おば	おばさん	aunt
いとこ	おいとこさん	cousin
おい	おいごさん	nephew
めい	めいごさん	niece

Note: Personal names are less frequently used in Japan. When addressing family members younger than oneself, use name or nickname, with「－くん」attached to boys' names and「－ちゃん」attached to girls'. When addressing persons older however, it is more common to use their honorific title, as indicated by the enclosures in the list above.

Exercise 10:

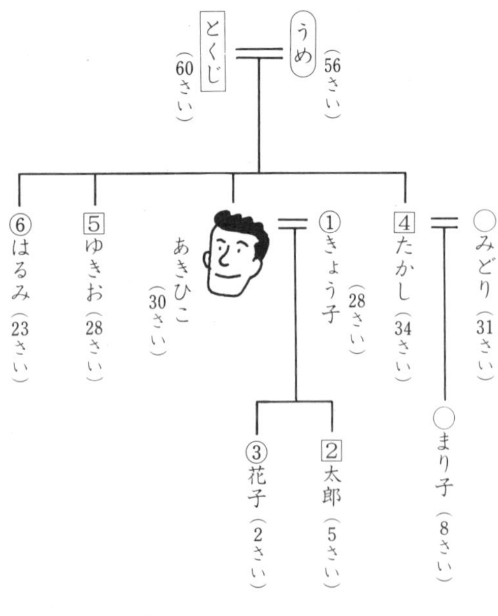

○：女の人　□：男の人

1) Pretend you are Akihiko and introduce the members of your family as numbered. Also reply as in the example.

ex. ① A: かないのきょう子(こ)です。
　　B: おくさんですか。はじめまして。

2 A: ＿＿＿の＿＿＿です。
　B: ＿＿＿ですか。こんにちは。

③ A: ＿＿＿の＿＿＿です。
　B: ＿＿＿ですか。こんにちは。

4 A: ＿＿＿の＿＿＿です。
　B: ＿＿＿ですか。はじめまして。

5 A: ＿＿＿の＿＿＿です。
　B: ＿＿＿ですか。はじめまして。

⑥ A: ＿＿＿の＿＿＿です。
　B: ＿＿＿ですか。どうぞよろしく。

2) Answer the following questions.

① ゆきおさんには、弟さんがいますか。 ② はるみさんは、ゆきおさんのお姉さんですか。

③ ゆきおさんには、お兄さんが、何人いますか。 ④ ゆきおさんは、けっこんしていますか。

⑤ 太郎くんは、ゆきおさんのお兄さんですか。

Function V　Giving and receiving (1);　あげる，くれる，もらう

1 Giving to someone

「あげる」expresses giving to an equal or superior.「さしあげる」is an honorific form of「あげる」.「やる」"to give" to an equal (in informal speech) or inferior, including giving food or water to animals and plants, etc.

Giverが　Thing givenを　Receiverに

ex. 1. 先生に、花をさしあげました。
I gave flowers to the teacher.

2. きのう、ともだちに、花をあげました。
I gave flowers to my friend yesterday.

3. 父：子どものたんじょう日に、何をやろうか。
What should we give our child for his birthday?
母：そうねえ。英語の絵本をあげましょうか。
Humm. Shall we give him a picture book in English?

4. わたしは、まいあさ、花に、水をやります。
I water the flowers every morning.

Note:「やる」"to do, to give" is a rough sounding word not usually used by women. For ex. 3, a woman would say; 子どものたんじょう日に、何をあげましょうか。

2 Someone gives to me

「くれる」means "to give to me (or you or him, etc.)", and generally implies that the giver is an equal or inferior.「くださる」means the giver is an equal or superior.

Giverが　Receiverに

ex. 1. 先生が、田中さんに、本をくださいました。
The teacher gave a book to Mr. Tanaka.

2. A：その切手は、だれがくれたんですか。
Who gave you that stamp?
B：弟がくれました。
My younger brother gave it to me.

③ **Receiving from someone**

「もらう」"to receive" implies the person giving is an equal or inferior.「いただく」is used in polite speech when the giver is an equal or superior.

Receiverが　　**Giver**に／から

ex. 1. (わたしは) 先生に、本をいただきました。
I received a book from the teacher.

2. A: その切手は、だれからもらったんですか。
Who did you get that stamp from?
B: 弟に、もらいました。
I got it from my younger brother.

3. A: だれが、あのチョコレートをもらったんですか。
Who received that chocolate?
B: 田中くんが、もらったんです。
Tanaka received it.

Exercise 11:

1) Look at the picture and tell what each person gave you.
ex. 黒田さんは、花をくれました。
① 山田先生は、________________。
② 母に、________________。
③ 黒田さんに、________________。
④ 太郎は、________________。

2) Describe each item as in the example.
ex. これは、黒田さんにもらった花です。
①これは、________________本です。
②これは、________________チョコレートです。
③これは、________________マフラーです。

Exercise 12: Answer the following questions.

1) あなたの国では、けっこんする人に、どんなものをあげますか。
2) 去年のクリスマスに、お母さんから、どんなものをもらいましたか。
3) お父さんのたんじょう日に、何をあげたいですか。
4) ともだちは、びょうきで、びょういんにいます。おみまいに、何をあげますか。

Reading Comprehension Exercise

きょうは、田中さんのたんじょう日です。36さいになりました。おくさんからのプレゼントは、白いエプロンでした。むすこのひろしくんは、お父さんのかおを、じょうずにかいて、プレゼントしました。田中さんは、ひろしくんのかいた絵を見て、とてもよろこびました。田中さんのうちの前に、1時間ぐらい前から、赤いスポーツカーがとまっています。あれは、弟の次郎さんの車です。次郎さんが、かぞくといっしょに来ているんでしょう。田中さんのおくさんは、だいどころで、りょうりをしています。こんやは、きっと、にぎやかなしょくじになるでしょう。

◆Vocabulary◆

かお face　じょうずに neatly, skillfully　スポーツカー sports car　だいどころ kitchen
次郎さんが、来ているんでしょう Jiro has probably come.　こんや this evening

Exercise 13: Answer the following questions.

1) 田中さんは、きょう、いくつになりましたか。
2) ひろしくんから、どんなものをもらいましたか。
3) 白いエプロンは、だれに、もらいましたか。
4) 赤い車は、いつから、とまっていますか。
5) 次郎さんは、1人で来ていますか。
6) 次郎さんは、田中さんのお兄さんですか。
7) だいどころで、りょうりをしているのは、だれですか。

Listening Comprehension Exercise

Listen to the tape and do as instructed.

1) Dialogue I: Fill in the blanks with the correct words.
   ① 早川さんは、______に _______を _______ました。
   ② バーバラさんは、______に _______を _______ました。
   ③ クッキーは、_______の_______が つくりました。
2) Dialogue Ⅱ: Fill in the blanks with the letter of the correct word from the list. Show the direction of giving or receiving by adding arrowheads.

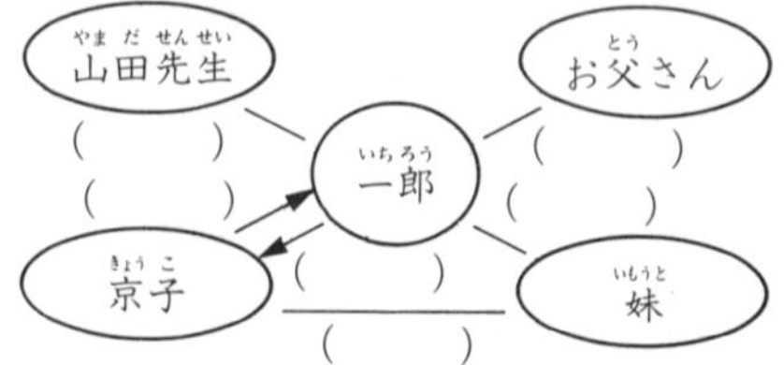

a.イギリスの切手	b.ハンカチ
c.英語のじしょ	d.花
e.ボールペン	f.ブローチ
g.チョコレート	

3) Fill in the required information about Mrs. Yamada's children.

	1st	2nd	3rd
男 or 女			
とし			
しごと・学校			

Vocabulary

おみまい(する) visiting a sick person (to visit a sick person)　イギリス England
ブローチ brooch　とし age　クッキー cookie

よく　いらっしゃいました

Welcome!

Dialogue I

The Yoshidas are preparing for a party with the help of Mrs. Ishikawa.

Mrs. 吉田(よしだ)：もう、4時(じ)になりましたか。

Mrs. 石川(いしかわ)：いいえ、まだですよ。

Mrs. 吉田：ちょっと、さむくなりましたね。そのまどをしめてくださいませんか。

Mrs. 石川：はい。ストーブをつけて、あたたかくしましょうか。

Mrs. 吉田：ええ、おねがいします。あ、ざぶとんが、まだ出(で)ていませんね。
すみませんが、おしいれから出(だ)してください。

Mrs. 石川：はい、わかりました。

Mr. 吉田：ねえ、きのうもらったおかしは…。どこ？

Mrs. 吉田：ああ、あれは、子(こ)どもたちが食(た)べてしまったけれど、
カステラが買(か)ってあります。そこのとだなに、入(はい)っていますよ。

Dialogue II

Michael and Barbara arrive.

Mr. 吉田：やあ、ウエッブさん、よくいらっしゃいました。
どうぞ、おあがりください。

マイケル：しつれいします。りっぱなおたくですね。

Mrs. 吉田：おそれいります。こちらへどうぞ。
どうぞ。(offering a cushion)
お茶(ちゃ)でもいかがですか。それとも、コーヒーがよろしいでしょうか。

バーバラ：ありがとうございます。お茶をいただきます。

Mrs. 吉田：おかしもどうぞ。

マイケル：いただきます。あまくて、おいしいですね。

Mrs. 吉田：もう１ぱい、お茶をいれましょうか。

マイケル：いいえ、もう、けっこうです。ごちそうさまでした。

バーバラ：ごちそうさまでした。とてもおいしかったです。

Dialogue III

Mr. and Mrs. Yoshida show Michael and Barbara their house.

バーバラ：この家(いえ)は、いつごろ、できたんですか。

Mr. 吉田(よしだ)：もう、10年(ねん)になりますね。家の中(なか)を、ごあんないしましょうか。

バーバラ：あら、どうも。日本の家を見(み)るのは、はじめてなんですよ。

Mrs. 吉田：ちらかっていますけど……どうぞ。ここが居間(いま)で、となりが食堂(しょくどう)です。

マイケル：きれいな絵(え)が、かかっていますね。

Mr. 吉田：はずかしいんですが、ぼくがかいたんですよ。

マイケル：え、ほんとうですか。おじょうずですね。

Mr. 吉田：いやあ、おそれいります。さあ、２かいへ行(い)きましょうか。

ここが、むすこのへやです。……あれ、また、電気(でんき)がつけてある。

だめだなあ。

マイケル：おや、ギターがおいてありますね。ＣＤも、たくさんならんでいますね。

Mr. 吉田：ええ。むすこは、音楽(おんがく)がだいすきなんですよ。

Mrs. 吉田：(calling from downstairs) あなた、北村(きたむら)さんたちが、いらっしゃいましたよ。

Vocabulary

Nouns:

4ストーブ space heater
5ざぶとん cushions for sitting on
6おしいれ closet for bedding, cushions, etc.
10カステラ sponge cake
10とだな cupboard
16お茶（おちゃ）green tea
24あんないする guidance
26居間（いま）living room
26食堂（しょくどう）dining room
30 2かい（にかい）2nd floor
31電気（でんき）electricity, electric light
35あなた ① you ② darling (wife calling her husband)

Counters:

20-はい／ばい／ぱい counter for cups, glasses, or spoonfuls of something
30-かい／がい ① lst floor, 2nd floor, etc. ② one floor, two floors, etc.

Adjectives:

13りっぱ（な）fine, great
28はずかしい embarrassing, ashamed

Adverbs:

もう／もう 1① already 20② another, more, again

Verbs:

3しめる (ru-vt) to close
4つける (ru-vt) to turn on, fix, attach
6出す（だす）(u-vt) to take or put out
26ちらかる (ru-vi) to be messy
27かかる (u-vi) to be hanging
33おく (u-vt) to set, place
33ならぶ (u-vi) to line up, be in a row
35いらっしゃる honorific verb meaning "to exist, go, come"

Grammatical words:

16でも postposition meaning "at least", "if nothing more" (used when suggesting or offering something)
23いつごろ when? about what time?

Expressions:

11よくいらっしゃいました Welcome. Glad to have you come.
12おあがりください Do come in. (politer than「あがってください」)
13しつれいします Excuse me (for the action I am about to perform).
14おそれいります So nice of you to say so. Excuse me. I'm sorry. etc.
20お茶をいれる to make tea
21もう、けっこうです I'm fine, I've had enough
25あら Oh! Why? My goodness! (used by women)
29え Oh! What?
30さあ well

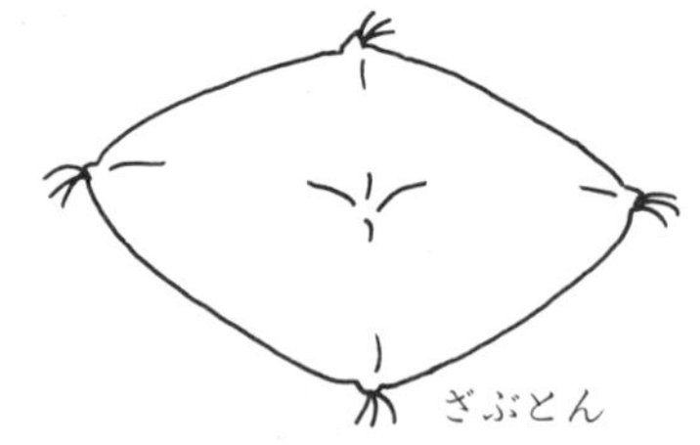

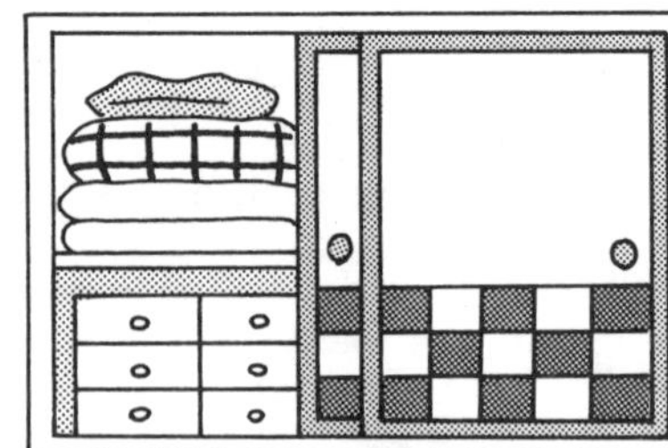

Dialogue Comprehension Exercise

Mark T or F.

1) (　　) ストーブをつけたのは、吉田さんのおくさんです。
2) (　　) とだなの中には、カステラがあります。
3) (　　) マイケルさんは、コーヒーをのんで、おかしを食べました。
4) (　　) バーバラさんは、まえに、日本の家を見たことがあります。
5) (　　) 吉田さんは、居間にかけてある絵を買いました。
6) (　　) 吉田さんのむすこさんは、音楽がだいすきです。

Grammar Note I **Transitive and intransitive verb pairs**

Transitive verbs (vt) take subjects (doer of the action marked by「が」), and direct objects (receiver of the action marked by「を」). Intransitive verbs (vi) take subjects only, and in this case the subject is the thing or person experiencing or undergoing the action of the verb.

ex. 1. マイケルさんが、まどを あけました。	Michael opened the window.	あける (ru–vt)
（かぜで）まどが あきました。	The window opened (by the wind).	あく (u–vi)
2. 母(はは)が、電気(でんき)を つけました。	Mother switched on the light.	つける (ru–vt)
電気が つきました。	The light came on.	つく (u–vi)
3. 吉田(よしだ)さんが、絵(え)を かべに かけました。	Mr. Yoshida hung the picture on the wall.	かける (ru–vt)
かべに、絵が かかっています。	The picture is hanging on the wall.	かかる (u–vi)
4. 車(くるま)を とめる。	I'll stop the car.	とめる (ru–vt)
車が とまる。	The car stops.	とまる (u–vi)

Dialogues in English

Dialogue I

Mrs.Y: Is it 4:00 already?
Mrs. I: No, not yet.
Mrs.Y: It's gotten a bit chilly. Won't you close that window please?
Mrs. I: Sure. Should I light the space heater and warm up the room?
Mrs.Y: Yes. Please do. Oh my, the cushions are not out yet. I'm very sorry, but would you take them out of the closet for me please?
Mrs. I: Yes, certainly.
Mr. Y: Hey, what about the sweets someone gave us yesterday? Where are they?
Mrs.Y: Oh, those. The kids ate them up. But we do have some sponge cake. It's in the cupboard there.

Dialogue II

Mr. Y: Ah, Mr. and Mrs. Webb! Welcome! Do come in!
M: Excuse us. My, you have a nice house!
Mrs.Y: You're so kind to say so. Right this way, if you please. There you are.
How would you like some tea at least? Or perhaps you'd prefer coffee instead?
B: Thank you. I'll have tea.
Mrs.Y: Won't you have some cake as well?
M: Thank you. I will. It's sweet, very nice.
Mrs.Y: Shall I fix you another cup of tea?
M: No, I'm fine. It was very good.
B: Thank you very much. It was very delicious.

Dialogue III

B: How long ago was this house built?
Mr. Y: 10 years now, I believe. Shall I show you around?
B: Why, thank you. This is the first time I've seen a Japanese home.
Mrs.Y: It's a bit messy, but come along.
This here is the living room, and next to it is the dining room.
M: What a lovely picture hanging on the wall!
Mr. Y: I'm ashamed to admit it, but it was me who painted it.
M: Oh, really? You're very talented.
Mr. Y: Not at all. It's good of you to say so. Shall we go upstairs then?
This is our son's room. Oh oh, the light's on again. When will he ever learn?
M: Hey! A guitar! And a whole bunch of compact disks as well.
Mr. Y: Yeah, our son is very fond of music.
Mrs.Y: Hey! Mr. and Mrs. Kitamura have arrived!

In Japanese there is a long list of transitive-intransitive verb pairs, where the verb roots are obviously related.

vt		vi	
あける	open	あく	open
しめる	close	しまる	close
かける	hang	かかる	hang
つける	attach, turn on	つく	attach, go on
けす	put out, extinguish	きえる	go out, extinguish
出す(だす)	put out, take out	出る(でる)	go out, leave, exit
入れる(いれる)	put in, take in	入る(はいる)	go in, enter
ならべる	line up	ならぶ	line up
ちらかす	mess up	ちらかる	be messy
おとす	drop, knock down	おちる	fall down

vt		vi	
かえる	change	かわる	change
とめる	stop	とまる	stop
うごかす	move	うごく	move
あげる	raise up	あがる	rise up, enter (house)
さげる	hang down, carry	さがる	hang down
のせる	put aboard (car, plane, etc.)	のる	get in (vehi- cle), ride
ねかす	put to sleep	ねる	go to sleep
はじめる	begin, start	はじまる	begin, start
なくす	lose	なくなる	be missing
こわす	break	こわれる	be broken
なおす	cure, heal	なおる	recover, get well

Note: The transitive form of intransitive「なる」"to become" is「なす」"to make, do". In modern Japanese however「なす」is replaced by「する」.

Exercise 1: Explain the following pictures using transitive or intransitive verbs as in the example.

ex. かきを（おとす）
Knock down a persimmon from the tree.

りんごが（おちる）
An apple dropped from the tree.

1) ドアが(　　　)。　ドアを(　　　)。

2) ドアが(　　　)。　ドアを(　　　)。

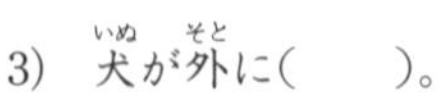

3) 犬(いぬ)が外(そと)に(　　)。　犬を外に(　　)。

4) ろうそくが(　　)。　ろうそくを(　　)。

Vocabulary

ドア door　　外（そと）outside　　ろうそく candle

Function I　Describing the present state (2); "Vt ＋てある", "Vi ＋ている"

The て-form of transitive verbs followed by「ある」"to exist" forms expressions meaning "has been done", "someone has done", etc. Whereas「～ている」(see Lesson 9) implies that the state has been brought about by an unidentified person or natural force,「～てある」implies that someone brought about the state for a reason.

ex.1. A: ストーブをつけてください。　Turn on the space heater please.
B: もう、つけてあります。　It has already been turned on. / Someone has already turned it on.
cf. もう、ついています。　It's already on.

ex.2. A: まどが、あいていますね。　The window is open, isn't it.
B: ええ、あついから、あけてあるんです。
Yeah, it's been opened because it's warm, you see.

Note: In「～てある」constructions, the direct object of the transitive verb may be indicated by either「を」or「が」.

ex.　ドアをしめた。 I closed the door.　→　ドアをしめてある。／ドアがしめてある。　The door has been closed.

Exercise 2: Describe the series of pictures using「vi て-form ＋いる」,「vt て-form ＋いる」and「vt て-form ＋ある」, as in the example.

ex.

電気(でんき)がついています。　⇨
The light is on.

男(おとこ)の人(ひと)が、電気をけしています　⇨
The man is turning off the light.
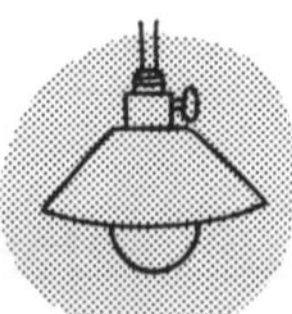
電気が、けしてあります。
The light has been turned off.

1) 電気が、＿＿＿＿＿。
女(おんな)の人(ひと)が、電気を＿＿＿＿＿。
電気が、＿＿＿＿＿＿。

2) まどが、＿＿＿＿＿。
男の人が、まどを＿＿＿＿＿。
まどが、＿＿＿＿＿＿。

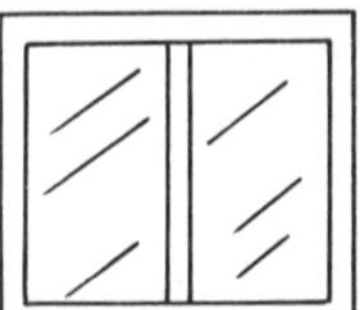

3) まどが、＿＿＿＿＿。
女の人が、まどを＿＿＿＿＿。
まどが、＿＿＿＿＿＿。

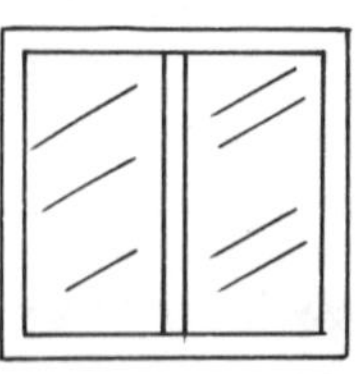

Exercise 3: Look at the picture and complete the dialogues below using「～ている」or「～てある」as in the example.

ex.（出る・出す）　「コップとおさらは、もう<u>出ていますか</u>。」
「ええ、<u>出してあります</u>よ。」

1)　（つく・つける）
「ストーブが＿＿＿＿＿ね。けしましょうか。」
「いいえ、けさないでください。へやがさむいから、
＿＿＿＿＿＿んです。」
「電気も＿＿＿＿＿＿よ。」「ああ、電気は、けしてください。」

2)　（あく・あける）
「まどが、＿＿＿＿＿＿＿ね。しめますか。」
「すこし　空気がわるいから、＿＿＿＿＿んです。」

3)　（ならぶ・ならべる）
「テーブルの上に、コップとおさらをならべて。」
「もう、＿＿＿＿＿わよ。」
「かわいい　にんぎょうが＿＿＿＿＿＿わね。」
「わたしが、あつめているのよ。」

4)　（入る・入れる）
「ビールは、れいぞうこに入れましたか。」
「はい、もう＿＿＿＿＿＿ます。」

Grammar Note II　「もう」"already, yet",「まだ」"not yet"

もう＋ **Affirmative**	**"already, yet"**
まだ＋ **Negative**	**"not yet"**

ex.1.	A: もう４時になりましたか。	(polite)	Is it 4 o'clock yet?
	もう４時になった？	(colloquial)	
	B: いいえ、まだ４時になりません。	(polite)	No, it is not 4 o'clock yet.
	まだ４時になっていません。		
	まだです。／ううん、まだ。	(colloquial)	No, not yet.
2.	A: ひるごはんは、もう食べましたか。	(polite)	Did you already eat lunch?
	ひるごはんは、もう食べた？	(colloquial)	
	B: いいえ、まだ食べていません。	(polite)	No,I haven't eaten yet.
	ううん、まだ食べてない。	(colloquial)	
	いいえ、まだです。		No, not yet.

Vocabulary

空気（くうき）air　　コップ cup, glass　　（お）さら dish, plate
かわいい pretty, cute　　にんぎょう doll　　れいぞうこ refrigerator

Exercise 4: Make up questions and answers relating to the scene below using the cue words.

ex. Q: Aさんは、もうアイスクリームを買いましたか。
A: いいえ、まだ買っていません。

<cue words>
買う　食べる　のむ　およぐ
シャワーをあびる　コーヒー
アイスクリーム　ケーキ
2時

Exercise 5: Construct dialogues between the persons listed below using the words in parentheses.

ex.　persons: 日本人と外国人　　　words: (京都・すし)
⇨もう京都へ行きましたか。→はい、もう行きました。／いいえ、まだ行っていません。
⇨もうすしを食べましたか。→はい、もう食べました。／いいえ、まだ食べていません。

1) 日本人と外国人　(かぶき・しんかんせん)　　2) 先生と学生　(しゅくだい・本)
3) ともだちと、ともだち (あのえいが・この新聞)　　4) 母と子ども　(かお・手)

Function II　"To do thoroughly and completely"; 食べてしまいました

Verb て-form ＋ しまう

The verb「しまう」"to finish up, put away" added to the て-form of a verb suggests that the action is done thoroughly and completely.

ex.1. 子どもが、おかしを食べてしまいました。　The child ate up the sweets.
2. もう、そうじもせんたくも、してしまいました。
I'm all done with both the cleaning and the laundry already.
3. いま、この本を読んでしまうから、ちょっと、まっていてください。
I'll finish reading this book in a moment, so please wait a second.

Note: In less formal speech「～てしまう」is shortened to「～ちゃう」and「～でしまう」is shortened to「～じゃう」.

ex.1. 手紙は、もう書いちゃいました。　I'm all done writing the letter.
2. この本は、もう読んじゃった。　I've already read this book.

Exercise 6: Practice the following type of dialogue with a partner.

ex. ひらがなを　おぼえる⇨ Q: もう、ひらがなを　おぼえてしまいましたか。
もう、ひらがなを　おぼえちゃった？
A: はい、おぼえてしまいました。／うん、おぼえちゃった。
or A: いいえ、まだです。／ううん、まだ。

1) ケーキを食べる　2) 本を読む　3) ビールをのむ
4) 手紙を書く　5) しごとをする　6) しゅくだいをする

Exercise 7: Look at the pictures and complete the dialogues as in the example.

ex. A：ゆうびんきょくに行(い)くけど、出(だ)す手紙(てがみ)、ある？

B：じゃ、ちょっとまってて。<u>この手紙、すぐ書(か)いてしまうから。</u>

まってて＝まっていて "lit. please be waiting"

◁1) A: としょかんに行くんだけど、かえす本、ある？

B: じゃ、ちょっとまってて。＿＿＿＿＿＿＿＿。

2) at the coffee shop: A: もう出(で)ましょうか。 ▷

B: ちょっとまってて。＿＿＿＿＿＿＿＿。

◁3) A: もう、かいぎをはじめますよ。 (コピーをとる。)

B: ちょっとまってて。＿＿＿＿＿＿＿＿。

4) A: さんぽに行かない？ ▷

B: ちょっとまってて。おさらを＿＿＿＿＿＿＿＿。

Function III　Describing a change in state (2): "to turn A into B"; あたたかくする

Noun ＋ に な-adj. (－に) い-adj. (－く)	＋	する します	"to make into (noun)" "to make (adj.)"

Note: In many cases the subject of this construction is a person.

ex.1. この魚(さかな)は、新(あたら)しいから、さしみにしましょう。

This fish is fresh so I'll make *sashimi* out of it.

2. へやを あたたかくします。　I will make the room warm.

3. こおりを入(い)れて、ジュースを つめたくしましょう。　Let me add ice and make the juice cold.

4. そうじをして、へやを きれいにしました。　I vacuumed and cleaned up the room.

Exercise 8: Complete the following dialogues using「〜く/に　する」. Choose an appropriate word from the list below.

ex. A：このスーツケースは、おもいですね。　B：じゃ、本を出して、<u>かるくしましょう。</u>

1) A：すみません。いま、べんきょうしているんです。ラジオの音(おと)を＿＿＿＿＿ください。

B：あ、ごめんなさい。

2) A：少(すこ)し、スカートがながいですね。

B：そうですね。少し、＿＿＿＿＿＿ましょうか。

3) このバッグは、高(たか)いですね。もう少(すこ)し＿＿＿＿＿＿くださいませんか。

4) A：スープがつめたくなりましたね。

B：じゃ、少し＿＿＿＿＿＿ましょう。

5) おきゃくさんが来(く)るから、へやをそうじして、＿＿＿＿＿＿ください。

6) A：よく、かぜをひくんですよ。B：じゃ、スポーツをして、からだを＿＿＿＿＿ほうがいいですね。

7) このへやは、くらいですね。そこのスタンドをつけて、＿＿＿＿＿ほうがいいですね。

8) A：みかんを、たくさんもらいました。　B：じゃ、＿＿＿＿＿のみましょう。

安(やす)い　じょうぶ(な)　あたたかい　ジュース　小さい　みじかい　きれい(な)　あかるい

Function IV　Offering to do something; ストーブをつけましょうか

「**Let's form** ＋か」"Shall I __?" can be used when offering to do something for someone.

ex.1. A: あついですね。まどを あけましょうか。 It's very hot. Shall I open the window?
B: ええ、おねがいします。 Yes. Please do.
いえ、けっこうです。 No, that's alright.

2. A: そのバッグを もちましょうか。 Shall I hold the bag?
B: あ、どうも すみません。 Ah, thank you very much.

Exercise 9: Offer to do such and such using the appropriate verb in the list below.

ex. A：駅(えき)まで、車(くるま)でおくりましょうか。　B：いえ、けっこうです。あるきますから…。

1) A：英語(えいご)で＿＿＿＿＿＿。　B：はい、おねがいします。日本語はあまりわかりませんので…。
2) A：フォークを＿＿＿＿＿＿。　B：いえ、けっこうです。はしで、だいじょうぶです。
3) A：リボンを＿＿＿＿＿＿。　B：はい、おねがいします。プレゼントですから。
4) A：＿＿＿＿＿＿。　B：すみません。ひとりでは、できないんです。
5) A：ゆうしょくを＿＿＿＿＿＿。　B：わあ、ありがとうございます。ごちそうさま。

つける　もってくる　せつめいする　てつだう　ごちそうする

Function V　Paying a visit

Answering the door

host: （はい）どなたですか。 (Yes) Who is it?
guest: (name) です。 It's (name).
host: いらっしゃい。 Welcome.
おまちしていました。 We've been expecting you.
guest: こんにちは。/こんばんは。 Hello! / Good evening.
host : どうぞ おあがりください。/お入(はい)りください。 Please come in.
どうぞ こちらへ。 This way, if you will.
guest: では、しつれいします。/おじゃまします。
Well then, pardon me./ I'll inconvenience you.
きょうは、ここで、しつれいします。いそいでいますので。
I am in a hurry today, so I'll have to be going.
(lit. I will excuse myself.)

Vocabulary

としょかん library
音（おと）sound
スープ soup
スタンド desk or floor lamp
はし chopsticks
てつだう (u-vt) to help
かえす (u-vt) to give back, return
ごめんなさい Excuse me. Pardon me.
からだ body
みじかい short
リボン ribbon
ひとり alone
ごちそうする treat someone to something to eat or drink
さんぽする walk, stroll
スカート skirt
くらい dark
おくる (u-vt) to see someone off
せつめいする explanation

Giving a gift

guest: これ、(つまらないものですが) どうぞ。

Here you are, (it's nothing really), if you will (accept it please).

host: ありがとうございます。/どうも、おそれいります。

Thank you very much. / How kind of you, thanks.

Making a guest feel at home

host : どうぞおかけください。/おすわりください。

Sit down please, if you will (in a chair or sofa / on a cushion).

guest: しつれいします。 Excuse me then, I will.

Entertaining

host : 何もありませんが、どうぞ。 We don't have anything, but help yourself.

guest: いただきます。 Thank you I will. (lit. I will receive.)

host : もう いっぱい/ひとつ いかがですか。 How about another cup / piece?

guest: ありがとうございます。いただきます。 Thank you. I will.

いいえ、もうけっこうです。ごちそうさまでした。 No, I'm fine. It was very good, thank you.

Leave taking

guest: そろそろ、しつれいします。 It's getting to be that time. I'll be excusing myself.

host : まだ いい/よろしい じゃありませんか。 Can't you stay a little longer?

guest: きょうは、どうもありがとうございました。 Thank you very much for today.

host : いいえ、こちらこそ。 No, the pleasure was all mine.

Saying goodbye

host : また、ぜひどうぞ (いらしてください)。 Be sure to come again please, if you will.

guest: しつれいします。/ さようなら。/おやすみなさい。Excuse me. / Goodbye. / Good night.

Exercise 10: Complete the following dialogue.

Situation: You visit an acquaintance bringing some cookies you baked.

host: どなたですか。

you: ____①____。こんにちわ。

host: ああ、いらっしゃい。どうぞ、おあがりください。

you: ____②____。これ、わたしが作(つく)ったクッキーですが、____③____。

host: あなたが作ったんですか。どうもありがとうございます。

host: どうぞ おかけください。

you: では、____④____。

host: コーヒーがよろしいですか。それとも、お茶(ちゃ)がよろしいですか。

you: コーヒーを____⑤____。

host: もういっぱい、いかがですか。

you: ____⑥____。

you: もう、くらくなりましたから、____⑦____。

host: そうですか。じゃ、またいらしてください。

Reading Comprehension Exercise

もう４時はんになりますが、むすこは、まだ学校からかえりません。むすこのへやを見てください。くつしたや、ざっしや、ボールなどが、ちらかっています。それに、ベッドの上には、ぬいだパジャマと、ギターがおいてあります。へやの電気は、けしてありますが、つくえの上の電気は、けしてありません。それに、ドアもまども、しめてありません。ＣＤはきれいにならべてありますが、つくえの上の本は、きれいにならべてありません。かべに紙がはってあります。その紙に、「ちらかさない」と書いてあります。

◆Vocabulary◆

くつした socks	ボール ball	ベッド bed
ぬぐ (u-vt) to take off	パジャマ pajamas	はる (u-vt) to put up, paste

Exercise 11: Complete the picture of the room based on the information in the above paragraph.

〈**hints**〉

1. とけい watch, clock
2. ベッド
3. 電気
4. ドア
5. まど
6. ＣＤ
7. 本
8. 紙

Listening Comprehension Exercise

Listen to the dialogues and answer the questions, choosing the correct letter.

1) おきゃくさんは、なぜ、かえると言いましたか。
   - a. もう、10時ですから。
   - b. もう、おそくなりましたから。
   - c. バスが、なくなりましたから。

2) いま、れいぞうこに、りんごが
   - a. ３つ、入っています。
   - b. ２つ、入っています。
   - c. １つ、入っています。
   - d. １つも、入っていません。

3) 日本語の手紙は、
   - a. まだ書いたことがありません。
   - b. まだ読んだことがありません。
   - c. まだもらったことがありません。

つまらないものですが…

It's a worthless thing really, but here you are.

When giving a gift, offering food or drink to a guest, etc., Japanese consider it good manners to speak of the thing being given in a deprecatory fashion, even if it is in fact quite valuable.

I have nothing good enough to offer you, but please go ahead.

第11課　もしもし、北村さん、いらっしゃいますか

Hello! Is Mr. Kitamura There, Please

Dialogue I

Michael answers a call at the office.

月野　　：もしもし。

マイケル：はい、安部産業、営業1課です。

月野　　：山川貿易の月野ともうしますが、

　　　　　課長の北村さん、いらっしゃいますか。

マイケル：はい。「すきの」さんですね。

月野　　：いいえ、「つきの」です。

マイケル：は？　おそれいりますが、もういちど、おねがいします。

月野　　：「つきの」。「た・ち・つ・て・と」の、「つ」です。

Dialogue II

Copying material

北村：黒田さん、その電話の よこの しりょうを、3部ずつ、いそいで

　　　コピーしておいて。山川貿易の月野さんが、いらっしゃるから。

黒田：この青いのですか。

北村：いや、その白いの。それから、大阪支社のほうこくは？

黒田：あ、そこのキャビネットの、2ばんめのひきだしに、入っていますよ。

北村：(opening the drawer) あ、あった、あった。

　　　じゃ、これもたのむよ。

　　　コピーは、ぼくのつくえの上に、おいておいて。

　　　2時までに、できる？

黒田：はい。いそいでします。

Dialogue III

Mr. Tsukino comes to the office. Mr. Kitamura introduces Michael.

北村（きたむら）：ごしょうかいします。こちらは、マイケル・ウエッブともうしまして、こんどできる、うちのアメリカ支社（ししゃ）のたんとうです。日本語、だいじょうぶですから。

月野（つきの）：あ、これはどうも。わたくし、山川貿易（やまかわぼうえき）の月野ともうします。どうぞよろしく。(presents calling card)

マイケル：マイケル・ウエッブです。はじめまして。さっきは、電話（でんわ）で、しつれいしました。

(presenting his calling card and looking at the calling card he received)

「つきの・よう」と読（よ）むんですか。

月野：いや、「洋（よう）」と書（か）いて、「ひろし」と読むんです。

マイケル：なるほど。日本人の名前（なまえ）は、むずかしいですね。

めいし Calling card

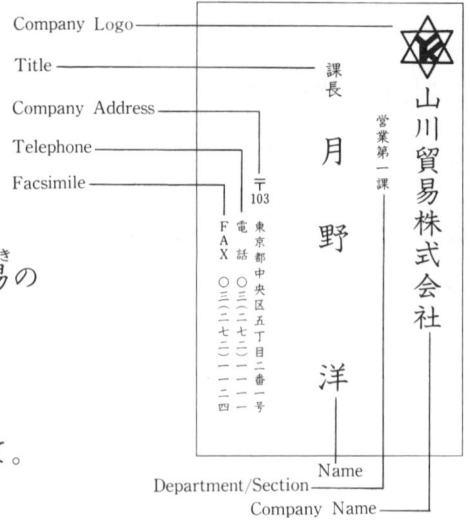

Company Logo
Title: 課長
Company Address: 〒103 東京都中央区五丁目二番一号
Telephone: 電話 〇三（二七二）一一一一
Facsimile: FAX 〇三（二七二）一一二四
Name: 月野 洋
Department/Section: 営業第一課
Company Name: 山川貿易株式会社

Vocabulary

Nouns:

2営業（えいぎょう）business, operation
21課（いっか）the first section
3貿易（ぼうえき）trade
9しりょう material, literature
10コピーする copy
12支社（ししゃ）branch office
12ほうこくする report
13キャビネット cabinet
13ひきだし drawer
19しょうかいする introduction
22たんとうする manager, person in charge

Counters:

9 -部（ぶ）counter for magazines, brochures and other documents, also parts of a novel, etc.
13 -ばんめ counter for ordinal numbers: 1ばんめ "first", 2ばんめ "second", 3ばんめ "third"

Adverbs:

28さっき before, earlier, previous, awhile ago

Verbs:

15たのむ (u-vt) to request, ask someone to do something

Positions within a Japanese company

会長（かいちょう）	chairman of the board
社長（しゃちょう）	company president
専務（せんむ）	senior managing director
常務（じょうむ）	managing director
部長（ぶちょう）	division manager
課長（かちょう）	section manager
係長（かかりちょう）	assistant manager
主任（しゅにん）	foreman

20 もうす (u-vt) humble verb meaning "to say, call"

Grammatical words:

9 ずつ a piece, each ☞ Function Ⅰ

10 ～ておく to do such and such in preparation ☞ Function Ⅱ

17 までに by __ ☞ Function Ⅳ

Expressions:

12 いや no

14 あった、あった Here it is! Here it is!

24 これはどうも Well, how nice. What a surprise. Pleased to meet you.

28 しつれいしました Pardon me (for something I have done).

31 なるほど I see what you mean.

Dialogue Comprehension Exercise

Answer the following questions.

1) だれが、だれに、電話(でんわ)をかけましたか。
2) 北村(きたむら)さんは、黒田(くろだ)さんに、何(なに)をたのみましたか。
3) 白(しろ)いしりょうは、どこに、おいてありましたか。
4) 黒田さんは、コピーした しりょうを、どうしておきますか。
5) 月野(つきの)さんとウエッブさんは、前(まえ)に、あったことがありますか。
6) 月野さんの名前(なまえ)は、「よう」ですか、「ひろし」ですか。

Dialogues in English

Dialogue Ⅰ

T: Hello!

M: Hello, this is Abe Industries, First Operations Section.

T: This is Tsukino of Yamakawa Trading. Is the section manager, Mr. Kitamura, there please?

M: Yes. Did you say your name was Mr. Sukino?

T: No. It's Tsukino.

M: What? I'm sorry. Would you say that once again please?

T: Tsukino. "Tsu", as in "ta·chi·tsu·te·to".

Dialogue Ⅱ

Ki: Kuroda, hurry up and make three copies each of the material there beside the phone. Mr. Tsukino of Yamakawa Trading is coming.

Ku: You mean the blue ones?

Ki: No, the white ones. Also, what about the report from the Osaka branch office?

Ku: Oh, it's in the second drawer of that cabinet there.

Ki: Oh yes. Here it is. I want you to do this too then. Leave the copies on top of my desk. Can you have them ready by 2:00?

Ku: Sure, I'll do them right away.

Dialogue Ⅲ

Ki: Let me introduce you. This is Michael Webb, who will be in charge of our soon to be completed American branch office. He understands Japanese, (so you won't have any problems communicating with him.)

T: Well, pleased to meet you. My name is Tsukino, of Yamakawa Trading. A pleasure to meet you.

M: Michael Webb. How do you do? I'm sorry about the telephone call earlier. Do you read your name "Yoo Tsukino"?

T: No, you write "Yoo", but pronounce it "Hiroshi".

M: I see. Japanese names are difficult alright.

Function I　So many "of each"; しりょうを3部ずつ

「ずつ」used after a counter or indefinite quantity adds the meaning "of each", "a piece" or "at a time".

ex. 1. むすめとむすこが、3人ずついます。
　　I have three daughters and three sons.
　　(lit. I have three of each, daughters and sons.)

2. 新しい漢字を、10かいずつ書いて、れんしゅうする。
　　I practice new *kanji* by writing them ten times each.

3. A: 62円の切手と、200円の切手を、5まいずつください。
　　Give me five each of the 62 and 200 yen stamps.
　B: ぜんぶで、1310円になります。
　　The total comes to 1310 yen.

4. 少しずつ、入れてください。
　　Please add a little at a time.

Exercise 1: Look at the pictures and answer the questions as in the example.

ex. 何をもらいましたか。

A: りんごとみかんを、
1つずつもらいました。
ぜんぶで、2つもらいました。

1) お子さんは、何人ですか。

A: ________と________が
________います。

2) おすしは、何を食べましたか。

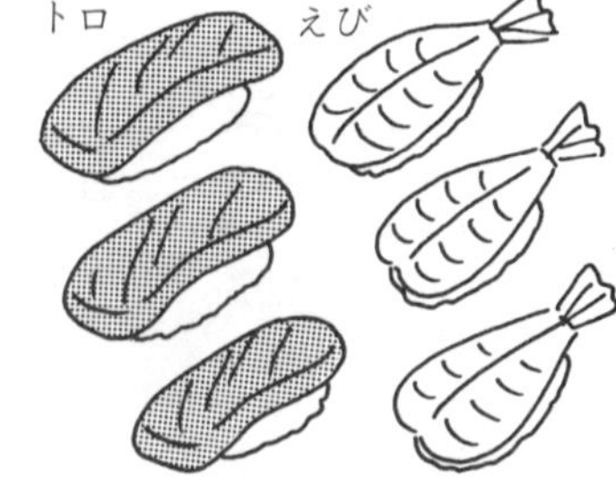

A: ________と________を
________食べました。
ぜんぶで______食べました。

3) のみものは、何にしますか。

A: ________と________を
______おねがいします。
ぜんぶで、__________。

4) コピーしましょうか。

しりょう
material

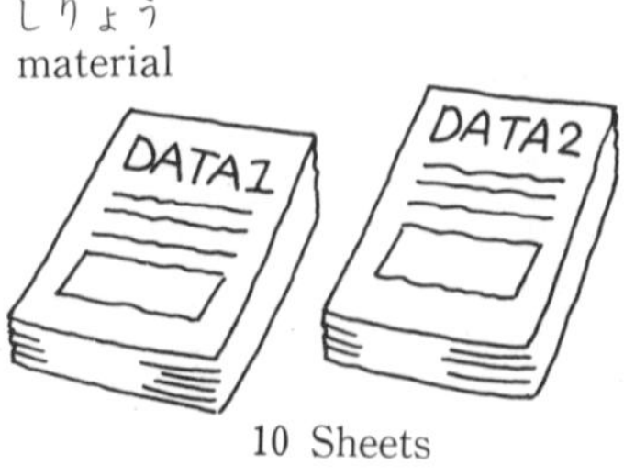

10 Sheets

A: ええ、________を________
コピーしてください。
ぜんぶで、__________。

5) 切手をもらったんですか。

A: ええ、____________
____________。

Function II Doing something as advance preparation; コピーしておく

The て-form followed by「おく」"to place" means to do the action in preparation for future use.

ex. 1. 会議(かいぎ)があるから、しりょうを、コピーしておきましょう。

I have a meeting, so let me copy the material and have it ready.

2. あしたは、しけんがあるから、よく、ふくしゅうしておいてください。

There's an examination tomorrow, so review thoroughly in preparation.

3. ひこうきは、こむから、3か月前(げつまえ)に、よやくしておいたほうがいいですよ。

The planes will be crowded, so it's better to make reservations 3 months in advance.

Exercise 2: Look at the picture and answer the following question.

Q: お客(きゃく)さんが来(き)ます。何(なに)をしておきますか。

ex. a. ひろしは、へやをかたづけておきます。　　b. ＿＿＿＿＿＿＿＿。

c. ＿＿＿＿＿＿＿＿。　　d. ＿＿＿＿＿＿＿＿。

e. ＿＿＿＿＿＿＿＿。

〈**Hints**〉 りょうり　れいぞうこ　げんかん　テーブル

Exercise 3: Reply to the following questions using the key words given. Add further items on your own.

1) りょこうをします。その前(まえ)に、どんなことをしておきますか。

ex. スーツケース・にもつ・入(い)れる ⇨ スーツケースに、にもつを入れておきます。

① ホテル・よやくする　② きっぷ・買(か)う　③ ちず・見(み)る

2) けっこんします。その前に、どんなことをしておきますか。

① へや・かりる　② 家具(かぐ)・買う　③ けっこん式(しき)のしょうたいじょう・出(だ)す

3) 日本語のテストがあります。その前に、どんなことをしておきますか。

① テキスト・ふくしゅうする　② テープ・きく　③ 漢字(かんじ)・べんきょうする

Vocabulary

かたづける (ru-vt) to put in order, straighten up　ふく (u-vt) to wipe　げんかん front door, entry way

家具（かぐ）furniture　しょうたいじょう invitation card　テキスト textbook

Function III

The manner in which an action is done (1): adverbial use of the て-form ; いそいでコピーします

A verb in the て-form sometimes functions adverbially, to describe the manner or means in which the following action is performed.

ex. 1 電車にのって行きましょう。 Let's go by train
(lit. Let's ride the train and go.)

2. えきまで、はしって行きました。 We ran to the station.
(lit. We ran and went to the station.)

3. いそいでコピーします。 I'll hurry up and copy it.

4. よろこんでうかがいます。 I'll visit you with pleasure.

5. ねぼうしたので、あわててうちを出ました。
I left home in a frenzy because I overslept.

Exercise 4: Describe the manner in which the following actions are done using an appropriate verb て-form.

1) えいがかんが　こんでいたので、えいがを（　　　）見ました。
2) そばは、はしを（　　　）食べます。
3) 時間がないから、タクシーに（　　　）行きましょう。
4) 駅は近いから、（　　　）行きましょう。
5) 小さい字は、めがねを（　　　）見ます。
6) ともだちがまっているので、（　　　）行きました。

かける	いそぐ	つかう
はしる	あるく	たつ
のる		

Exercise 5: Answer the questions referring to the pictures, using a verb in the て-form. Next tell what you yourself do!

1) 学校から家まで、あるいてかえりますか。

2) 日本語は、どうやっておぼえますか。

3) ウエッブさんは、どうやってカタカナをべんきょうしますか。

A: いいえ、＿＿＿＿＿＿。　A: テープを＿＿＿＿＿＿。　A: 電車の中のこうこくを＿＿＿。

Vocabulary

そば buckwheat noodles　字（じ） character, letter　えいがかん movie theater
めがねを かける to put on or wear glasses　つかう (u-vt) to use
どうやって How? In what manner?:「やって」is the て-form of「やる」"to do" used adverbially.

Function IV Action completed by such a time ; 2時までに

「までに」used after a plain non-past form of a verb or various time words indicates the time "by" or "before" which an action is completed. **Caution:** do not confuse 「までに」 with 「まで」, which indicates the time "until" which an action or state continues (see Lesson 7, p.98).

ex. 1. コピーは、10時までにできる？ Will the copies be ready by 10 o'clock?

cf. 10時まで残業(ざんぎょう)できる？ Can you work over time until 10 o'clock?

ex. 2. 来週(らいしゅう)、テストがありますから、それまでに、この漢字(かんじ)をおぼえたいんです。

Next week there's an exam, and so I want to memorize these characters before then.

cf. 来週、テストがありますから、それまで、いっしょに、べんきょうしましょう。

Next week there's an exam, so let's study together until then.

ex. 3. お客(きゃく)さんが来(く)るまでには、おわるでしょう。

We'll probably finish by the time the guests arrive.

Exercise 6: Construct a dialogue between A and B using「までに」as in the example below. Use a proper speech style depending on the situation and the relationship between the two people.

ex. person A: 客(きゃく)／ person B: せんたく屋(や)／ thing: シャツ／ time due: あさって／ action: できる

⇨A: (すみません。いそいでいるんですが、) このシャツ、あさってまでに、できますか。

B: あさってですね。はい、できますよ。 or あさってまでには、ちょっと…。

	person A	person B	things	time due	action
①	課長(かちょう)	ウエッブさん	ほうこくしょ	あした	できる
②	母(はは)	子(こ)ども	そうじ	ゆうがた	おわる
③	客(きゃく)	ウェーター	りょうり	11時	できる
④	ウエッブさん	黒田(くろだ)さん	しごと	4時	おわる
⑤	こいびと	こいびと	セーター	たんじょう日(び)	できる

Exercise 7: Fill in the blanks with「までに」or「まで」.

1) 6時40分(①)、上野駅(うえのえき)に来(き)てください。 2) 去年(きょねん)(②)、六本木(ろっぽんぎ)に住(す)んでいました。

3) あさってから夏休(なつやす)みですから、しごとを、あした(③)おわりたいと思(おも)います。

4) お客さんが来る(④)、へやをそうじしておきます。

5) A: ほうこくしょは、3時(⑤)できますか。 B: ほかのしごとを2時(⑥)しますから…。

6) わたしが行(い)く(⑦)まっていてくださいね。いそいで、2時(⑧)行きますから。

7) A: 日曜日(にちようび)は、昼(ひる)ごはんができる(⑨)ねているんですよ。

B: 10時ごろ(⑩)は、おきたほうがいいですよ。

◆Vocabulary◆

せんたく屋 (せんたくや) laundry
ウェーター waiter
ほうこくしょ report
こいびと lover

Function V　Talking on the telephone

Person X calls person Y, but person Z answers.

(**The phone rings**)

Z: はい、～でございます。
Hello, this is __.

X: Xですが、Yさんをおねがいします。
This is X calling. Can I speak to Mr. Y?

Z: はい、しょうしょう、おまちください。
Yes. One moment please.

Y: はい、Yですが…。
Hello, Y speaking ....

おまたせしました。Yです。
Sorry to have kept you waiting. This is Y.

At the office:

Z: Yは、せきを、はずしておりますが…。
Y is not here at the moment ....

Yは、外出中（がいしゅつちゅう）ですが…。
Y is out at the moment ....

Yは、会議中（かいぎちゅう）ですが…。
Y is in conference at the moment ....

At home:

Z: Yは、でかけておりますが…。
Y is out ....

Yは、るすですが…。
Y is not here ....

Yは、まだ、かえりませんが…。
Y is not back yet ....

Z: 何（なに）か、おことづけがありますか。
Is there some message?

Note:「中（ちゅう）」stuck on the end of nouns denoting actions means "during", "while doing" or "in the middle of doing" such and such an action.

X: いいえ、けっこうです。
No, that's alright.

では、また、のちほど、お電話（でんわ）します。
I'll call later then.

X: はい。では、Xから電話があったと、おつたえください。Yes, please tell him/her there was a call from X.

Z: そちらさまの電話番号（ばんごう）は？
What is your telephone number please?

X: 03-238-4567　です。

Z: 03-238-4567、Xさまですね。おつたえします。
03-238-4567, Mr. X, right? I'll relay the information.

X: では、よろしくおねがいします。
Please do. Thank you.

(**Wrong number**)

A: ～さんのおたくですか。
Is this the __ residence?

B: いいえ、ちがいますけど。
No, it isn't.

A: あ、どうもしつれいしました。
Oh, I'm terribly sorry.

B: いいえ。　Not at all.

Exercise 8: Practice speaking on the phone using the information below.

1) Mr. Webb calls Mr. Tsuchida. Mrs. Tsuchida answers the phone. She says her husband is out and asks Mr. Webb if he wants to leave a message. Mr. Webb says he'll call again after six.

ウエッブ：もしもし、＿＿①＿＿、ご主人を＿＿②＿＿。
Mrs.土田：主人は、いま、＿＿③＿＿。
ウエッブ：いつごろ、おかえりになりますか。　About what time will he be home?
Mrs.土田：＿④＿までにはかえると思いますが。何か、＿＿⑤＿＿。
ウエッブ：いえ、＿＿⑥＿＿。また、そのころ＿＿⑦＿＿。では、しつれいします。
Mrs.土田：ごめんください。

2) Mr. Webb calls Mr. Hayashi, a car salesman. Another salesman answers and says Mr. Hayashi is out, so Mr. Webb leaves a message for Mr. Hayashi to call him. The salesman asks Mr. Webb his telephone number.

ウエッブ：もしもし。　Salesman: はい、東西自動車です。
ウエッブ：おそれいりますが、＿＿①＿＿。　Salesman: 林は、ただいま、＿＿②＿＿。
ウエッブ：じゃ、かえったら＿＿③＿＿とおつたえください。
Salesman: はい。お客さまの＿④＿は？
ウエッブ：567-8910です。　Salesman: はい。＿⑤＿、ウエッブさまですね。
ウエッブ：ええ。じゃ、よろしくおねがいします。

3) You phone your friend's home, his mother answers and says he's out. You say you'll phone again later. Your friend's mother asks your name.

4) A phones C at the office. B answers and says that C is out at the moment. A asks B to tell C that the time of the appointment has been changed. B repeats the message.

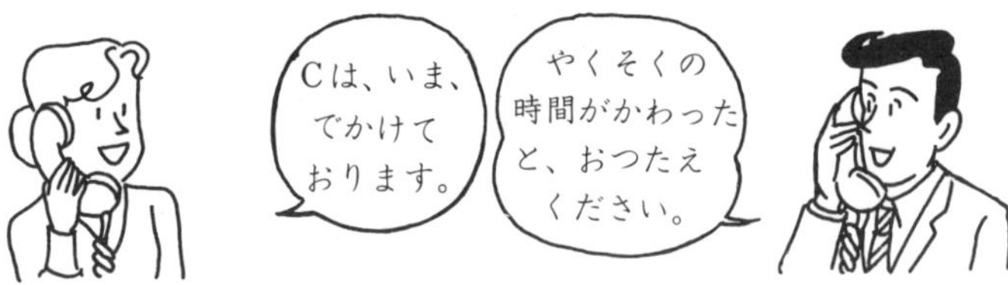

Cは、いま、でかけております。
やくそくの時間がかわったと、おつたえください。

はい…はい…

In Japanese it is extremely important for the listener to constantly assure the person speaking that he is following the conversation by nodding his head and interjecting「はい」,「ええ」,「うん」,「そうです」at regular intervals. This behavior is so ingrained and automatic, that it is common to see a person on the telephone nodding his head and going「はい…はい…、うん…うん…」to the speaker on the other end of the line.

Vocabulary

そのころ about that time
自動車（じどうしゃ）car, automobile
ごめんください ① Goodbye ② Is anyone home?, Is anyone there?
ただいま just now, just this moment

Reading Comprehension Exercise

Which sign might occasion the following sentences? Write the letter of the sign in the parentheses.

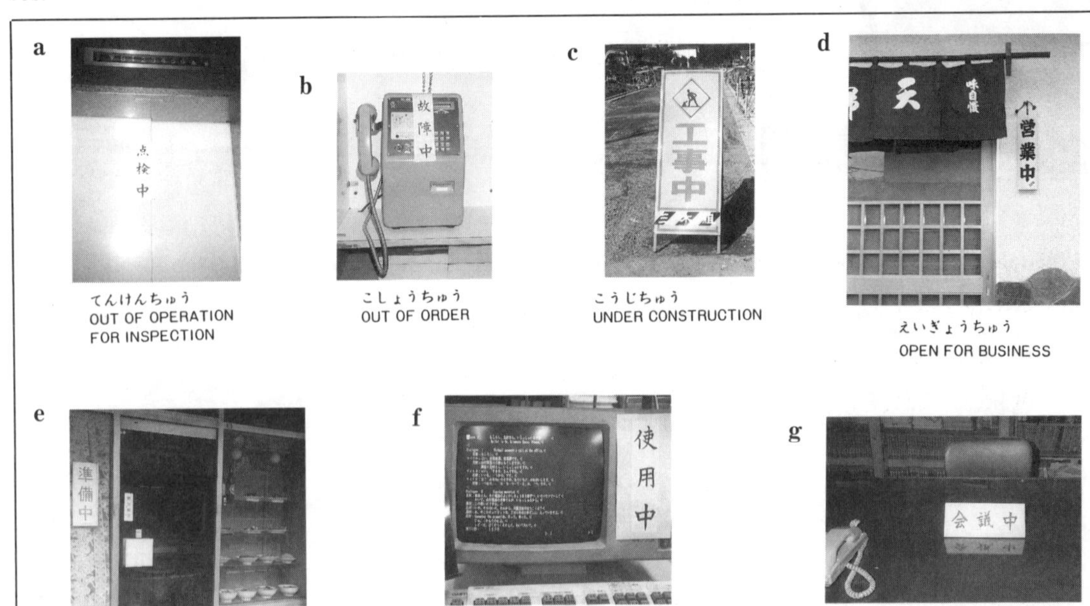

a てんけんちゅう OUT OF OPERATION FOR INSPECTION

b こしょうちゅう OUT OF ORDER

c こうじちゅう UNDER CONSTRUCTION

d えいぎょうちゅう OPEN FOR BUSINESS

e じゅんびちゅう CLOSED (IN PREPARATION)

f しようちゅう IN USE

g かいぎちゅう MEETING IN PROGRESS

ex. このエレベーターは、いま、うごいていませんね。かいだんをのぼりましょう。（a）

1) まだ、あいていないですね。ほかの店に行きましょう。（　）

2) こわれているんですね。電話が1つだけだから、ふべんですね。（　）

3) ああ、よかった。ここは、あいている。ここで食事をしましょう。（　）

4) この道はだめだ。ほかの道をとおりましょう。（　）

5) ほかの人がつかっています。少しまちましょう。（　）

6) いま、会議をしているんですね。また、あとで来ましょう。（　）

◆Vocabulary◆

エレベーター elevator　　かいだん stairs　　のぼる (u-vi) to go up, climb

とおる (u-vi) to pass, go by

Listening Comprehension Exercise

Listen to the dialogues on the tape and circle the correct word in the parentheses.

1) ただしいのは、どちらですか。　Which word in parentheses is correct?

① 電話をかけた人は、（島田さん　田中さん）です。

② 田中さんは、いま、会社に（います　いません）。

③ 田中さんは、（1　7）時にかえります。

④ 安田産業の電話番号は、（03-762-8111　03-726-8111）です。

2) ぜんぶで、何時間、べんきょうしますか。　（1時間　2時間　3時間）

3) ウエッブさんのともだちは、何人いますか。　（5人　10人　15人）

4) ぜんぶで、何円になりますか。　（500円　850円　1000円）

第12課 わたしは、マイケル・ウエッブともうします

My Name Is Michael Webb

Dialogue I

The people at work hold a welcome party for Michael under the cherry blossoms. Mr. Tanabe comes late.

森(もり)　：田辺(たなべ)さんは、おそいですね。
山下(やました)：場所(ばしょ)が、わからないのかもしれませんねえ。
森　：ちゃんとつたえたから、知(し)ってるはずですがねえ。
　　メモといっしょに、ちずも、わたしたし…。
田辺：いやあ、すみません。おそくなりました。
　　日比谷(ひびや)から、タクシーにのったんだけど、
　　道(みち)がひどくこんでねえ。
森　：きょうは、金曜日(きんようび)ですからねえ。じゃあ、そろそろはじめましょうか。
田辺：あれ、花田(はなだ)さんは来(こ)ないの？
森　：少(すこ)しおそくなるけど、来(く)るはずです。
　　それから、広報課(こうほうか)の浜野(はまの)さんも、仕事(しごと)が早(はや)くおわったら来ると言(い)ってました。

Dialogue II

Michael introduces himself.

マイケル：みなさん、こんばんは。わたしは、マイケル・ウエッブともうします。こんど、みなさんといっしょに、はたらくことになりました。１か月前(げつまえ)に、ニューヨークから来ました。アメリカでは、銀行(ぎんこう)につとめていましたが、大学(だいがく)で、日本語を少しならったし、それに、日本にきょうみがあるので、

この会社（かいしゃ）に入（はい）りました。しゅみは、音楽（おんがく）とテニスです。時間（じかん）があったら、りょこうもしたいと思（おも）っています。家族（かぞく）は、つまと２人です。どうぞ、よろしくおねがいします。

(everyone claps)

田辺（たなべ）　：では、ウエッブさんをかんげいして、かんぱいしましょう。

みんな　：かんぱい！

マイケル：やあ！　ぼくのコップに、さくらの花（はな）びらが入りましたよ！

Dialogue III

After the welcome party

野村（のむら）　：きょうは、ずいぶん、にぎやかでしたねえ。ウエッブさん、みんなで、もう１けん、行（い）きませんか。この近（ちか）くに、いい店（みせ）があるんです。

マイケル：そうですねえ。せっかくですが、きょうは、ビールも飲（の）んだし、おさけも飲んだから、きぶんが少（すこ）し…。

野村　：そうですか。少し飲みすぎたんですね。二日（ふつか）よいになったら、こまりますね。

マイケル：ええ。きょうは、早（はや）く帰（かえ）ることにします。またこんど、さそってください。

野村　：そうですね。ざんねんですが、そうしましょう。

Vocabulary

Nouns:

4メモ memo
14みなさん ladies and gentlemen, everyone
21かんげいする welcome
23さくら cherry blossoms
12広報課（こうほうか） public relations section
19つま my wife
21かんぱいする toast
23花びら（はなびら） flower petal
28きぶん feeling, how a person feels: いいきぶん "I feel good", きぶんがわるい "I feel ill"
30二日よい（ふつかよい） hangover

Counters:

25－けん counter for shops, houses, etc.

Adverbs:

3ちゃんと exactly, properly, explicitly, the way it should be done
8そろそろ eventually, about time (to do such and such)

Verbs:

4わたす (u–vt) to hand, give, pass

17ならう (u-vt) to learn, study
31さそう (u-vt) to invite along

Grammatical words:

3はず ought, should, is supposed to do ☞ Function I
4〜し used with verbals to mean "be or do such and such as well"; often intended as an explanation or excuse for some behavior or circumstance ☞ Function V
13〜たら when, if ☞ Function Ⅳ

Expressions:

5いやあ、すみません Hey guys! Sorry!
15〜ことになりました it has been decided that __, some course of action has come about ☞ Function Ⅱ
17〜にきょうみがある I am interested in __
23やあ！ Hey!
25もう１けん one more place, another bar or restaurant
27せっかくですが that would be nice, but..., the conditions for that are ideal, but....
29飲みすぎた I drank too much.
31〜ことにします I will decide to __, I choose such and such course of action ☞ Function Ⅱ

Dialogue Comprehension Exercise

Mark T or F.

Dialogue I

1) (　) 田辺さんは、ちずとメモをもっていました。
2) (　) 花田さんは、パーティーに来ません。
3) (　) 田辺さんは、電車がこんで、おくれました。

Dialogue II

4) (　) ウエッブさんは、ニューヨークから、２か月前に来ました。
5) (　) ウエッブさんは、日本の会社で、日本語をべんきょうしました。
6) (　) ウエッブさんには、子どもはいません。

Dialogue III

7) (　) ウエッブさんは、ビールとおさけを飲みました。
8) (　) ウエッブさんは、いま、いいきぶんです。
9) (　) ウエッブさんは、これから、みんなと、近くの店に行きます。

Function I　Telling what ought to be; 来るはずです。

「〜はずです」expresses an expectation concerning what "ought to", "should" or "is supposed to" be.

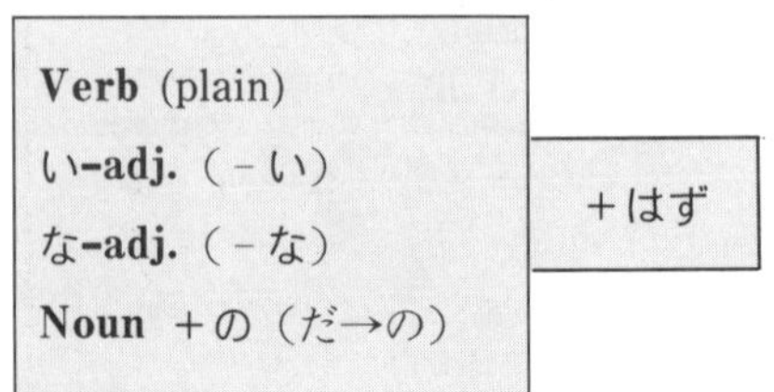

ex.1. 田中さんは、６時までに来るはずでしたが、なかなか来ませんでした。
Mr. Tanaka was supposed to come by 6:00, but he didn't arrive until long after that.

2. この店のコーヒーは、おいしいはずです。
The coffee at this shop ought to be good.

3. そうじをしたから、へやは、きれいなはずです。　I cleaned, so the room should be tidy.

4. これは、バーバラさんのハンドバッグのはずです。　I expect this is Barbara's handbag.

There are two negative constructions using「はず」. In the first, the verbal before「はず」is negative, and the meaning is simply "not supposed to", "not expected to", etc. In the second,「はず」is followed by「～がない」or「～はない」(not「～では／じゃ　ない」) and the meaning is stronger, "no way", "it's impossible", etc.

ex.1. 田中(たなか)さんは、まだ仕事(しごと)をしているから、来ないはずです。

I wouldn't expect Mr. Tanaka to come because he's still working.

2. 田中さんは、いま、りょこうしているから、来るはずがありません。

There is no way Mr. Tanaka will come because he's on a trip right now.

3. これは、インスタントコーヒーだから、あまりおいしくないはずです。

This is instant coffee, so I expect it won't be very good.

4. A：もう、12時になりましたね。　It's 12:00 already, isn't it.

B：いや、そんなはずはありません。　No. That's impossible!

Note:「はず」is never used in stating what you intend to, or what you are scheduled to do. Such expressions use「つもり」(see Lesson 7, p.101) or「ことになっている」(see Function Ⅱ).

ex. わたしは、あす、会議(かいぎ)に出(で)るつもりです。　I plan to attend the meeting tomorrow.

わたしは、あす、会議に出ることになっています。　I am supposed to attend the meeting tomorrow.

Dialogues in English

Dialogue I

Mori : Mr. Tanabe's late.

Y : Maybe he doesn't know the place.

Mori : He ought to know. I passed on the information explicitly. I even gave him a map along with the memo.

T : Hey guys! Forgive me, I'm late! I took a cab from Hibiya, but the streets were terribly crowded, and uh....

Mori : Because it's Friday today, huh! OK, then. It's about that time, shall we begin?

T : Hey? Isn't Miss Hanada coming?

Mori : She'll be a bit late, but she's supposed to be coming. Also Hamano of Advertising said he'd come if he finishes work early.

Dialogue II

M : Good evening, everyone. My name is Michael Webb. I will be working with you from now on. I came from New York one month ago. In the States I worked at a bank, but I took a bit of Japanese at the university. Also I have an interest in Japan, and so I joined this company. My hobbies are music and tennis. I'd also like to travel if I have the time. There are two of us, my wife and myself. We would appreciate your support.

T : Alright then, let's give a toast of welcome to Mr. Webb!

Everyone : Cheers!

M : Hey! There's a cherry blossom petal in my cup!

Dialogue III

N : It was quite lively today, don't you think? What say we all head for another place, Mr. Webb? There's a nice bar close by.

M : Yes, uh.... That sounds nice, but today I had beer and *sake* both, and I'm feeling a little, uh ....

N : Is that so? Had a bit too much to drink, huh? It would be rough if you got a hangover, I guess.

M : Yeah. Today I think I'll go home early. Please invite me again next time.

N : Really? That's too bad, but let's do it that way.

Exercise 1: Complete the following sentences using「～はずです」.

ex. A: 田中(たなか)さんは、おそいですねえ。

B: 3時に来ると言(い)っていたから、もうすぐ（来るはずです）。

1) A: 田辺(たなべ)さんは、もうでかけましたか。　B: 田辺さんの車があるから、まだ__________。
2) A: 浜野(はまの)さんは、ドイツ語がわかると思(おも)いますか。　B: ドイツの大学(だいがく)を出(で)たんだから、________。
3) A: このはしは、きれいですか。　B: まだ、だれもつかっていないから、__________。
4) A: チンさんは、なに人(じん)でしょうか。　B: 北京(ペキン)から来たと言っていたから、__________。
5) A: 田辺さんは、バスで来ますか。　B: いや、地下鉄(ちかてつ)の駅(えき)から、タクシーで________よ。

Exercise 2: Look at the pictures below, then supply an explanation for each of the「はず」expressions.

1) ________から、場所(ばしょ)を知(し)っているはずです。

2) ________から、きょうは、来ないはずです。

3) ________から、銀行(ぎんこう)は、休みのはずです。

4) ________から、だれか、いるはずです。

5) ________から、50さいのはずです。

6) ________から、安(やす)いはずです。

Exercise 3: Answer the following questions using「～だろうと思います」,「～かもしれません」or「～はずです」as in the example. (see「～だろう」「～かもしれません」Lesson 7, p.103)

ex. 田中さんは、パーティーに来るでしょうか。⇨　来るはずです。
たぶん、来るだろうと思います。
来るかもしれません。

1) あなたのお母(かあ)さんは、日本にきょうみがありますか。
2) あなたのお母さんは、来年(らいねん)の夏(なつ)、外国(がいこく)にりょこうしますか。
3) 来年の1月までに、このきょうかしょの　べんきょうが、ぜんぶおわりますか。
4) いま、あなたのお父(とう)さんは、どこにいますか。
5) 円高(えんだか)（円安(えんやす)）は、つづくでしょうか。
6) あなたのともだちは、あなたに、たんじょう日(び)のプレゼントをくれるでしょうか。

Function II "To decide on"「〜ことにする」, "to be decided on"「〜ことになる」

1 Personal decisions; "To decide on"

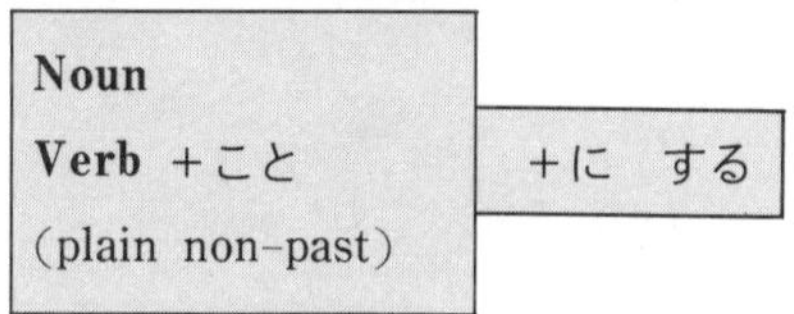

「にする」used after a noun or verb ＋「こと」(see Lesson 9, p.126) means that the person himself "decides upon" or "chooses" that particular thing or action.

ex.1. 飲みものは、何にしますか。 What will you choose to drink?

2. あついから、ビールにしましょうか。 It's hot, so perhaps I'll choose beer.

3. 来年から、フランス語をべんきょうすることにしました。

I decided to study French beginning next year.

4. 会議は、10時にはじめることにします。 My decision is to begin the meeting at 10:00.

Using「にしている」for「にする」indicates the thing or course of action one "has decided upon or set" for himself. It also might indicate an action one performs routinely.

ex.1. ニューヨークの両親に、毎月、電話をかけることにしています。

The routine I follow is to call my parents in New York every month.

2. 電車にのるときは、こうこくを見ながら、漢字のべんきょうをすることにしています。

When I ride the train, what I do is study Chinese characters while looking at advertisements.

2 Impersonal decisions; "To be decided on"

Verb (plain non-past) ＋こと ＋ に なる

As explained in Lesson 9 (p.122), a noun followed by「になる」means "to become" that particular noun. When verb ＋「こと」is used as the noun, the expression means "to become such and such an action", i.e. that particular action has been "decided upon, arranged, worked out", etc.

ex. 来年から、フランス語をべんきょうすることになりました。

1. It has been decided that I study French beginning next year.

2. 会議は、10時からはじめることになりました。

It has been arranged to begin the meeting at 10:00.

「になっている」is used when stating the way one's schedule stands, or "the way things are", i.e. rules, customs, social conventions, etc.

ex. 来週、ヨーロッパに、しゅっぱつすることになっています。

1. I am scheduled to leave for Europe next week.

2. 日本では、家の中では、くつをはかないことになっています。

In Japan, shoes are never worn inside the home.

Vocabulary

なに人（なにじん）what nationality
円高（えんだか）strong yen (dollar down)
つづく (u-vi) to continue, keep on
中国人（ちゅうごくじん）Chinese
あかり light
円安（えんやす）yen decline (strong dollar)
バーゲン／バーゲンセール bargain sale

Exercise 4: Complete the following sentences using「～にする」or「～にしている」.

1) A：デパートは、きょうは、休みですよ。　B：じゃ、あした____①____。
2) 昼ごはんは、いつも、サンドイッチを____②____。
3) つかれたので、きょうは、もう、うちに____③____。
4) では、話のつづきは、あした____④____。
5) 日曜日は、かないと、デパートに買いものに____⑤____ので、つごうがわるいんですが…。
6) A：ちょっと、ビールを飲んで帰りませんか。
   B：きょうは、うちに早く帰る____⑥____ので…。
   A：そうですか。あなたに、ぜひ話しておきたいことがあったんですけど…。
   B：じゃあ、いっしょに____⑦____。ちょっと、うちに電話をして来ますから…。

Exercise 5: Describe how Mr. Tanaka's and Michael's schedules are arranged as in the example.

ex. 田中さんは、朝9時に、会議に出ることになっています。

田中さん

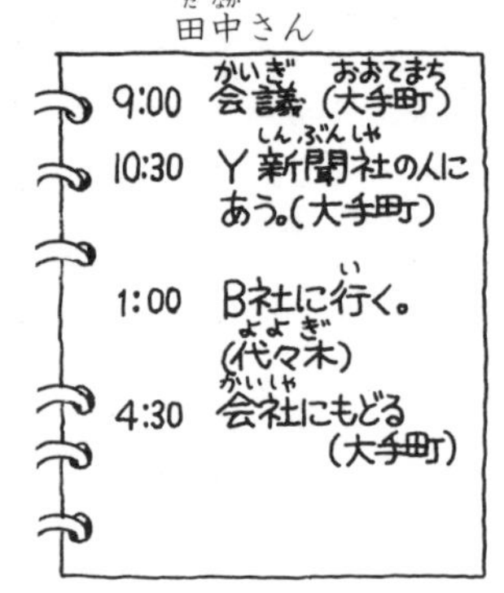

9:00 会議（大手町）
10:30 Y新聞社の人にあう。（大手町）
1:00 B社に行く。（代々木）
4:30 会社にもどる（大手町）

ウエッブさん

1:00 課長と銀行に行く。（大手町）
3:00 会議（恵比寿）
7:00 A社のカークさんとあう。

Exercise 6: Look at the menu and order whatever you like. Fill in the blanks with suitable items and practice the dialogue.

A：飲みものは、何がいいですか。（①）がいいですか、（②）がいいですか。
B：きょうはあついから、（③）がいいですね。
A：ああ、いいですね。わたしも、それにしましょう。食事は、何がいいですか。
B：そうですね、わたしは（④）にします。
A：じゃ、わたしは、（⑤）にしましょう。
　　すみません、（⑥）2つ、（⑦）と（⑧）を1つずつおねがいします。
Clerk：はい、ありがとうございます。
　　では、（⑨）円いただきます。

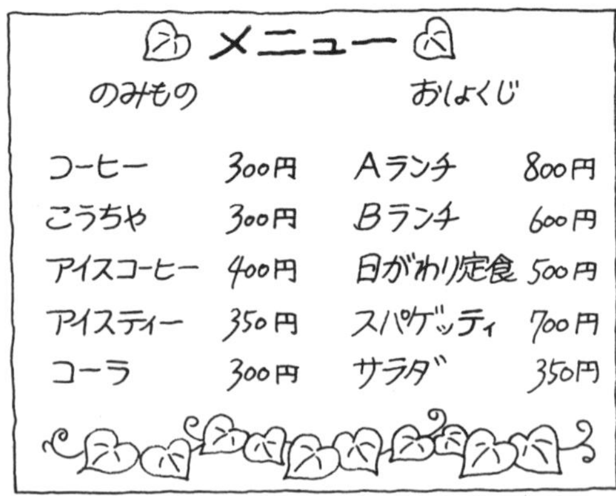

メニュー
のみもの
コーヒー 300円
こうちゃ 300円
アイスコーヒー 400円
アイスティー 350円
コーラ 300円
おしょくじ
Aランチ 800円
Bランチ 600円
日がわり定食 500円
スパゲッティ 700円
サラダ 350円

Vocabulary

話（はなし）a talk or story (stem of「はなす」)
つづき continuation, sequel (stem of「つづく」)
新聞社（しんぶんしゃ）newspaper company
～社（しゃ）_company
ランチ lunch
アイスコーヒー iced coffee
アイスティー iced tea
こうちゃ tea, black tea
定食（ていしょく）a full course meal which includes bread or rice, soup, salad and a beverage besides the main dish
日がわり定食（ひがわりていしょく）full course meal which differs each day
スパゲッティ spaghetti
和定食（わていしょく）a full course of Japanese meal

Function III　To be in excess; 飲みすぎる

The verb「すぎる」"to pass by, exceed" added to the stem of verbs, adjective roots and to certain な-adjectives means "too much".

ex.1. ビールを飲みすぎて、少し、きぶんがわるい。　I drank too much beer and feel a little ill.
　2. このセーターは、わたしには、大きすぎます。　This sweater is too big for me.
　3. この店は、にぎやかすぎますね。もっと、しずかなところへ行きましょう。
　　This shop is too noisy. Let's go someplace quieter.

Exercise 7: Describe the following situations using「〜すぎる」.

1) このふろは、＿＿＿＿＿。
2) ダイヤのネックレスは、わたしには、＿＿＿＿。
3) このケーキは、わたしには、＿＿＿＿＿。
4) このシャツは、＿＿＿＿＿。
5) 山田さんは、＿＿＿＿＿＿。
6) ゆうべは、おさけを＿＿＿＿＿＿。

Exercise 8: Complete the following dialogues using「〜すぎる」.

1) A: 土曜日は、朝6時にでかけましょうか。　B: ＿＿＿＿＿。7時にしませんか。
2) A: 朝8時から、夜10時まで、仕事をしています。　B: ＿＿＿＿＿て、つかれませんか？
3) A: このテストの問題は、ぜんぶ、すぐわかりましたよ。　B: そうですか。あなたには＿＿＿。
4) A: 家族は2人ですが、へやが9つあります。　B: それじゃ、＿＿＿でしょう？
5) A: ちょっと、あじをみてください。　B: しょっぱい！　しおを＿＿＿んじゃありませんか。
6) A: あしたは、10時に行きましょうか。　B: いえ、それでは＿＿＿。9時までに来てください。
7) A: きょうは、あついですね。　B: わたしは、北海道から来たので、東京の夏は、＿＿＿＿。
8) A: 日本の新聞を読んでいるんですか。　B: ええ。でも、漢字が＿＿＿、わからないんですよ。

Function IV　Conditional (1): "if" or "when"; 時間があったら

The conditional form of verbals is made by adding the inflection「〜たら」, which follows the same pattern as past「〜た」, and is equivalent to English "if" or "when". In the structure「**verbal 1**＋〜たら、**verbal 2**」, verbal 1 represents the condition which triggers verbal 2. Hypothetical conditions are often introduced by「もし」or「もしも」, which may be interpreted as "supposing" or "in the event that".

Vocabulary

ふろ bath	ダイヤ diamond	ネックレス necklace
しょっぱい salty	問題（もんだい）question, problem	しお salt

	past tense	～たら (positive)	～たら (negative)
Verb	来た	田中さんが来たら、会議をはじめましょう。 Let's begin the meeting when Mr. Tanaka gets here.	来なかったら
い-adj.	あつかった	あつかったら、まどをあけてください。 If you are hot, please open the window.	あつくなかったら
な-adj.	きれいだった	そのへやがきれいだったら、かります。 I'll rent it if it's a nice room.	きれいじゃなかったら きれいでなかったら
Noun + be-verb	すしだった	おいしいすしだったら、食べます。 If it's good *sushi*, I'll have some.	すしじゃなかったら すしでなかったら

ex.1. もし、ふろがあつすぎたら、水を入れてください。

If the bath is too hot, please add cold water.

2. もしも、雨がふったら、お花見はやめます。

Cherry blossom viewing will be canceled in the event of rain.

Note 1: The expression「～たらいい」"it would be nice if __" has a variety of uses:

ex.1. あした、はれたらいいですね。　It would be nice if it's clear tomorrow.

2. 田中さんも、いっしょに来たらよかったですね。

It would be nice if Mr. Tanaka had come with us too, wouldn't it?

Note 2: Sometimes a plain non-past verbal followed by「～といい」is used in place of「～たらいい」. The meaning is the same, but「～といい」sounds a bit old fashioned or bookish. (see Lesson 15, p.195)

Exercise 9: Construct sentences using the following as conditions, as in the example.

ex. かぜをひく。⇨（もし／もしも）かぜをひいたら、くすりを飲みます。

1) 道がこんでいる。
2) 100万円ある。
3) あした、雨がふる。
4) へやが、さむい。
5) 12時になる。
6) 日本語が、じょうずになる。
7) 安くて、いいアパートです。

Function V　Enumerating facts; ビールも飲んだし、おさけも飲んだ

「し」coming after plain form verbals means something similar to "and ... etc.". Used when enumerating facts,「し」often suggests that such facts explain or justify one's actions, feelings, opinions, etc.

ex.1. 電車の中には、新聞を読んでいる人もいるし、ねている人もいます。

On the train there are people reading newspapers, and people sleeping as well.

Vocabulary

いやになる to become disgusted　　ガイド guide

けいやくしょ contract (the document itself)

2. A：あした、テニスをしませんか。　　Why don't we play some tennis tomorrow?
   B：そうですねえ。でも、あしたは、えいがも見たいし…。

   Well, yeah, but tomorrow I want to see a movie, and so forth (and so therefore ...).
3. このナイフは、かるいし、よく切れます。　This knife is light weight and cuts well, etc. (which is why I bought it, or like to use it, or recommend it, etc.).
4. 田中さんは、ハンサムだし、あたまがいいし、とても人気があります。

   Mr. Tanaka is handsome, intelligent and a very popular person.
5. そのアパートは、駅から遠いし、せまいから、あまり よくありません。

   The apartment is far from the station, small, etc., and therefore not very good.

Note 1: Only items leading to the same conclusion may be joined by「し」. Items leading to different conclusions would be better joined with「が」"but".

ex. ×このアイスクリームは、おいしいし、高いし…。

This ice cream is delicious, and it's expensive, etc... (and so therefore what conclusion are you supposed to draw?).

⇨ ○このアイスクリームは、おいしいが、高い。　This ice cream is delicious, but expensive.

Note 2: Such connectives as「それに」"besides that",「そのうえ」"moreover" are commonly used in conjunction with「し」.

ex. このナイフは、かるいし、よく切れるし、それに安いんです。

This knife is light weight and cuts well. Besides that, it's cheap.

Exercise 10: Fill in the blanks with suitable words from the list below.

1) 地下鉄は、〔　〕し、〔　〕から、よくのります。
2) あのレストランは、〔　〕し、〔　〕から、いつもこんでいます。
3) 東京のアパートは、〔　〕し、〔　〕から、いやになります。
4) 日光は、〔　〕し、〔　〕から、1度、行ったらどうですか。
5) このバッグは、〔　〕し、〔　〕から、べんりです。

広い　せまい　おそい　はやい　きれい　きたない　おもい
かるい　べんり（な）　ふべん（な）　安い　高い　おいしい　まずい
大きい　小さい　遠い　近い　ゆうめい（な）　ゆうめいじゃない

Function VI　The manner in which an action is done (2): adverbial uses of adjectives; 仕事が、早くおわる。

The adverbial forms of い-adjectives and な-adjectives (see p.18) may be used to describe the manner in which an action is performed. (For the adverbial use of the て-form see Lesson 11, p.149)

ex.1. あしたは、早く　おきます。　Tomorrow I'm going to get up early.
2. おかしを、小さく　切ってください。　Please cut the cake into small pieces.
3. 元気に　あいさつをします。　We greet one another in a cheerful manner.
4. へやを、きれいに　そうじしましょう。　Let's clean the room spotlessly.
cf. いそいで　行きましょう。　Let's go in a hurry.

Exercise 11: Describe the actions pictured below using the adverbial form of the words listed in the box.

1) おさらを、
＿＿＿＿＿あらいます。

2) 字は、＿＿＿書いて
ください。

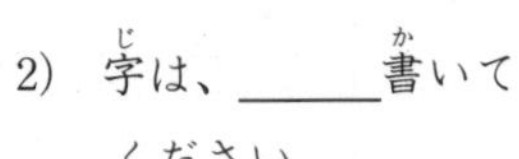

3) びょういんでは、
＿＿＿あるきましょう。

4) かみを、＿＿＿切って
ください。

5) ゆうべは、
＿＿＿帰りました。

6) 夕食は、みんなで
＿＿＿食べます。

早い	しずか（な）	うるさい	にぎやか（な）	ながい	みじかい
きれい（な）	大きい	小さい	安い	おそい	たのしい
きたない	ていねい（な）“polite, careful, conscientious”				

Function VII Introducing yourself; わたしは、マイケル・ウエッブともうします

Useful expressions

1. **Your name** わたしは、……です。／わたしは、……といいます。(polite)
   わたしは、……ともうします。(more polite)
2. **Where from** ……から来ました。／国は、……です。
   ……しゅっしんです。／しゅっしんは、……です。
   ……大学をそつぎょうしました。
3. **Age** いま、……さいです。
4. **Family** どくしんです。I'm single.
   つまと、子どもが2人います。
   I have a wife and two children.
5. **School, place of employment, job, etc.**
   いま、……です。 I'm now a ＿＿.
   せんこうは、……です。 My major is ＿＿.
   (job) をしています。／仕事は、(job) です。
6. **Hobbies, sports, etc.**
   しゅみは……です。／……がすきです。

Additional occupations
商社員（しょうしゃいん） employee of a trading company
公務員（こうむいん） public employee, civil servant
弁護士（べんごし） lawyer
写真家（しゃしんか） photographer
大学教授（だいがくきょうじゅ） university professor
店員（てんいん） salesclerk
主婦（しゅふ） housewife

7. **Purpose in coming to Japan**

1. **Verb (plain non-past)** ＋ために、日本に来ました。
   ex.1. 日本の文化をべんきょうするために、日本に来ました。
   I came to Japan in order to study Japanese culture.
2. **Noun** (ex. 仕事、かんこう) ＋で、日本に来ました。
   ex. 仕事で、日本に来ました。I've come to Japan on business.

Exercise 12: Introduce yourself using the above expressions and Michael's self-introduction in Dialogue II as reference.

Reading Comprehension Exercise

〈マイケルが、帰りの電車の中で思ったこと〉

今夜は、わたしのかんげい会だった。こうえんで、さくらの花を見ながら、おさけを飲むのは、はじめてだった。「『夜ざくらけんぶつ』というんですよ」と、山下さんが言っていた。夜だから、さむいだろうと思っていたが、そうでもなかった。ほかの人たちも、たくさん来ていたし、わたしたちも、ずいぶん飲んだから、とてもにぎやかだった。わたしは、ちょっと飲みすぎた。青いかおで、うちに帰ったら、バーバラは、しんぱいするだろう。でも、赤いかおで帰ったら、おこるかもしれないし…。そうだ、とちゅうで、コーヒーを飲んで帰ることにしよう。

◆Vocabulary◆

かんげい会（かんげいかい）welcome party
夜ざくらけんぶつ（よざくらけんぶつ）viewing cherry blossoms at night
とちゅう（で）on the way
そうでもなかった It wasn't so at all
おこる (u-vi) to get angry

Exercise 13: Mark T or F.

1)（　）レストランで、マイケルさんのかんげい会をした。
2)（　）こうえんは、とてもさむかった。
3)（　）マイケルさんは、いま、とてもきぶんがいい。
4)（　）マイケルさんは、コーヒーを飲んで帰ることにした。

Listening Comprehension Exercise

Listen to the dialogues on the tape and do as directed.

1) Listen to dialogues A and B, and mark ○ if you think Mr. Hayashi says he is going, × if you think he says he is not.

   Dialogue A : ________　　Dialogue B : ________

2) Listen to the self-introduction and mark T or F.

   ①（　）わたしは、ウエスト・テキサス大学のしゅっしんです。
   ②（　）いま、新聞社につとめています。
   ③（　）子どもの名前は、ジムです。
   ④（　）日本に来るのは、はじめてです。
   ⑤（　）仕事で、日本に来ました。

第13課 小包(こづつみ)を出(だ)しに　行って来ます

I'm Going To Go Mail A Parcel

Dialogue I

Michael is going to the post office and Mr. Tanabe asks him to buy some stamps and post-cards.

マイケル：田辺(たなべ)さん、ゆうびんきょくは、昼休(ひるやす)みもあいていますか。

田辺　　：ああ、もちろん、あいていますよ。

マイケル：じゃあ、ちょっと、小包(こづつみ)を出(だ)しに行って来ます。

田辺　　：すみませんけど、ついでに、切手(きって)とはがきを買(か)って来てくれませんか。

マイケル：はい、いいですよ。どのくらい買って来ましょうか。

田辺　　：62円の切手を300まいと、はがきを100まい、おねがいします。

マイケル：わかりました。じゃあ、行って来ます。
なるべく早(はや)く帰(かえ)って来ます。

田辺　　：りょうしゅうしょを　わすれないでください。

Dialogue II

At the post office

マイケル　　：この小包、おねがいします。

postal clerk：こうくうびんですか、ふなびんですか。

マイケル　　：ふなびんでは、アメリカまで、どのくらい
かかりますか。3週間(しゅうかん)ぐらいで、とどきますか。

postal clerk：ふつうは、とどきますが、今(いま)、こんでいるから、
3週間でとどくかどうか、わかりませんよ。

マイケル　　：そうですか。じゃあ、こうくうびんにします。
10日(とおか)までに、とどきますね。

postal clerk：だいじょうぶですよ。この用紙に、お名前とご住所、あて先となかみなどを、書いてください。

マイケル　：それから、お金をおくりたいんですが、何ばんのまどぐちへ行ったらいいんでしょうか。

postal clerk：げんきんかきとめですね。3ばんと4ばんです。

マイケル　：どうも。

Dialogue III

Back at the office

マイケル：ただいま。はい、切手と、はがきと、りょうしゅうしょです。

田辺　：あ、すみませんでした。ところで、ウエッブさん、こんどの週末は、何かよていがありますか。

マイケル：土曜日は、テニスをするつもりですが、日曜日は、べつに何もありませんが。

田辺　：ああ、よかった。じつは、日曜日のすもうのきっぷを2まい、もらったんですけど、ぼくは、きゅうに、つごうがわるくなったんです。よかったら、おくさんといっしょに、いかがですか。

マイケル：わあ、それはどうも。いちど、すもうを見てみたいと思っていたんですよ。

Vocabulary

Nouns:

3小包（こづつみ）parcel, package

11ふなびん surface mail, sea mail

18あて先（あてさき）receiver's name and address

20まどぐち service window

22げんきんかきとめ registered mail for sending cash

11こうくうびん air mail

18用紙（ようし）form

18なかみ contents

27週末（しゅうまつ）weekend

Adverbs:

2もちろん of course, certainly

8なるべく as ＿ as possible

27何か（なにか）something

34いちど once, one time

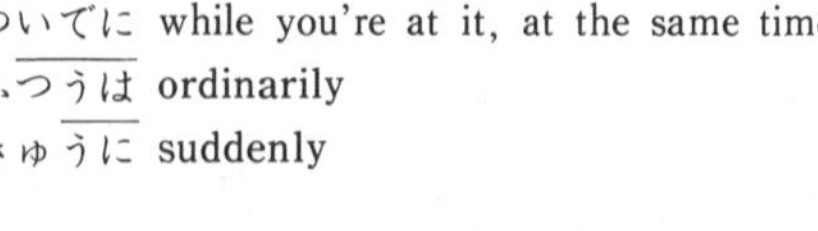

4ついでに while you're at it, at the same time

14ふつうは ordinarily

32きゅうに suddenly

Verbs:

13とどく (u-vi) to arrive

Grammatical words:

34～てみる to try and do ☞Function Ⅲ

Expressions:

3小包を出す to send a parcel

4～てくれませんか Won't you please do __?

8なるべく早く as quickly as possible

15とどくかどうか、わかりません I don't know if it will arrive or not.

30べつに…ない not … in particular

33よかったら if you don't mind, if it's alright with you, if you like

Dialogue Comprehension Exercise

Mark T or F.

Dialogue I

1) (　) ゆうびんきょくは、昼は、休みです。

2) (　) マイケルさんは、小包を出したいので、ゆうびんきょくに行きます。

3) (　) マイケルさんは、小包のりょうしゅうしょを、もらって来ます。

Dialogue II

4) (　) マイケルさんは、ふなびんで、小包を出します。

5) (　) こうくうびんで出したら、アメリカに、3週間でとどきます。

Dialogue III

6) (　) マイケルさんは、土曜日に、テニスをしたいと思っています。

7) (　) マイケルさんは、日曜日に、田辺さんと、すもうを見ることにしました。

8) (　) マイケルさんは、すもうを見たことがありません。

Function Ⅰ　Go, come, etc. for the purpose of __; 小包を出しに行きます

Verb stem＋に　行く／来る etc.

The particle「に」coming after the stem of a verb means "in order to" or "for the purpose of" doing the action of the verb.

Follow this by「行く」and you form the expression "to go to do such and such". Other verbs which may replace「行く」in this construction include「来る」,「もどる」"to return",「かえる」and「でかける」.

ex. 1. いっしょに、えいがを見に行きませんか。　Won't you go with me to see a movie?

2. 日本へは、何をしに来たのですか。　What did you come to Japan for?

3. 日本語を勉強しに来ました。　I came to study Japanese.

4. うちにかぎをわすれたので、とりに帰りたいんですが。

I forgot my key at home, so I want to go back to get it.

Note: With certain activities such as「買いもの」,「テニス」,「ダンス」, etc., the verb「する」may be omitted.

ex. 1. 買いものをしに行く。→買いものに行く。　"to go shopping"

2. ゴルフをしに行く。→ゴルフに行く。　"to go golfing"

Vocabulary

お金をおろす to withdraw money from the bank　　書店（しょてん）bookstore

Exercise 1: Answer the question「何をしに行きますか」for each of the pictures below.

3 すし勝

ex. お金(かね)をおろしに行きます。

1) 本を__________。

2) 東京のまちを______________。

3) すしを_________。

4) 海(うみ)に__________。

5) テレビを________。

Function II **Go and do an errand; ゆうびんきょくに行(い)って来(き)ます**

One use of the て-form of a verb followed by「来る」is to indicate a situation where the actor will go and do something and then return again. In English such a situation is often expressed as "go and do" such and such, with the returning taken for granted.

ex. 1. 魚(さかな)を買(か)って来ます。	I'm going to go buy some fish.
2. はがきを出(だ)しに行って来ます。	I am going to go mail a letter.

▶Dialogues in English◀

Dialogue I

M : Mr. Tanabe, is the post office open at lunch time as well?

T : Yes, of course it's open!

M : In that case, I'm going to go mail a parcel.

T : Pardon me, but won't you get me some stamps and postcards while you're at it?

M : Sure, that would be fine. How many do you want me to get?

T : Three hundred 62 yen stamps and one hundred post cards, please.

M : Right. Well, I'm off then. I'll be back as quickly as I can.

T : Please don't forget the receipt.

Dialogue II

M : I'd like to send this parcel.

P : Is that air mail or surface?

M : Approximately how long will it take to America by surface mail? Will it arrive in about three weeks?

P : Ordinarily it would arrive, but it's busy now and so I'm not sure if it will arrive in three weeks or not.

M : Is that so? Well in that case, I think I'll send it air mail. It will arrive by the 10th, right?

P : No problem. Please fill out this form with your name and address, the name and address of the receiver, contents, etc.

M : Also I'd like to send money. Which window should I go to?

P : That's registered mail for cash, right? Windows three and four.

M : Thanks.

Dialogue III

M : I'm back! Here you go. Stamps, postcards and the receipt.

T : Ah, sorry to have put you to the trouble. By the way, Mr. Webb, have you got something planned for this weekend?

M : I intend to play tennis on Saturday, but Sunday I don't have anything in particular.

T : Oh, good! You see, I received two tickets for Sunday's *sumo* match, but something else came up. If you'd like, how about going with your wife?

M : Hey, thanks! I was thinking I'd like to see *sumo* once.

3. ちょっと、テニスに行って来ました。　I went and played a bit of tennis (and returned).

Note 1: Other uses of the て-form were dealt with in Lesson 7, p.102, and Lesson 11, p.149.

Note 2: Notice how the different expressions function in the situations pictured below.

魚を買いに行く。
魚　まさ
"I'm going to go buy some fish."
"I'll go get some fish!"
魚を買って来ますね。
魚　まさ
魚を買って来ました。
"I bought some fish!"
"I bought some fish!"
魚を買って行くから…
魚　まさ
魚を買って来たよ。
"I'll buy some fish and bring it with..."

Exercise 2: Ask someone to go and do the following errands as in the example.

ex. 小包を出す（ゆうびんきょく）⇨ゆうびんきょくに行って、小包を出して来てください。

1) ざっしを買う（本屋）　2) くすりをもらう（びょういん）　3) お金をおろす（銀行）

4) 本をかえす（としょかん）　5) 外国人とうろくをする（区役所）

Exercise 3: Construct「～て来る」or「～に来る」sentences using the verbs in parentheses.

ex. あした、成田くうこうに（行く）⇨あした、成田くうこうに行って来ます。

1) きのう，どうぶつえんで，パンダの赤ちゃんを（見る）

2) さっき、新聞屋さんが、お金を（とる）。　3) きのう、ともだちが、わたしに（会う）

4) きのう、わたしは、ともだちに（会う）　5) あした、としょかんで、本を（かりる）

6) あさって、駅で、しんかんせんのざせきを（よやくする）

7) 来週、いなかの両親が、わたしの新しい家を（見る）

Grammar Note

Some __, all __, no __, any __; いつか，いつも，いつでも

A question word followed by the question particle「か」means "some __". Followed by「も」it means "all __" or "every __" in affirmative constructions, and "no __" in negative constructions. A question word followed by「でも」means "any __". The following chart gives possible translation for various question words.

	—か	—も affirmative	—も negative	—でも
いつ	いつか sometime	いつも all the time, always	いつも……ない never	いつでも anytime, whenever
どこ	どこか somewhere	どこも everywhere	どこも……ない nowhere	どこでも anywhere, wherever
だれ（どなた）	だれか someone	みんな，みな，すべて everyone	だれも……ない no one	だれでも anyone, whoever
何	何か something	みんな，みな，すべて everything	何も……ない nothing	何でも anything, whatever
どれ	どれか one of them	どれも everyone, all of them	どれも……ない none of them	どれでも any of them, whichever one

ex. 1. A：いつか、おたくに行きたいんですが。　I'd like to go to your home sometime.

B：火曜日でなかったら、いつでもいいですよ。

Anytime is OK, as long as it's not a Tuesday.

火曜日は、いつも、ダンスをならいに行っているんです。

Tuesday I always go to learn dancing.

A：ああ、それで、火曜日は、いつもうちにいないんですね。

I see. That means Tuesdays you are never at home.

ex. 2. A：XとYとZのうちの、どれかをあげますが、どれがいいですか。

I will give you one, either X, Y or Z. Which would you like?

B：うーん、どれもいいですねえ。　Yes, well, they're all nice, aren't they.

C：わたしは、どれでもいいですよ。　Anyone is all right with me.

ex. 3. A：きょう、だれか、あなたのうちに来ますか。　Is someone coming to your house today?

B：いいえ、だれも来ません。　No, no one is coming.

Note 1: Notice the difference between「そのはこに、何が入っていますか」"What's inside the box?" and「そのはこに、何か入っていますか」"Is there something inside that box?".

Note 2: Particles「へ」,「に」,「から」,「まで」can be followed by「も」or「でも」.

だれに　会いましたか。　だれにも　会いませんでした。　I didn't meet anyone.

どこへ　行きましたか。　どこへも　行きませんでした。　I didn't go anywhere.

どこから　見えますか。　どこからでも　見えますよ。　It can be seen from anywhere.

cf. 何を　買いましたか。　何も　買いませんでした。

Note 3: Words such as「みんな」、「みな」and「すべて」are used in place of「だれも」and「何も」in affirmative sentences.

Exercise 4: Fill in the blanks with some —, all —, no —, or any — expressions.

1) A：となりのへやに（　）いますか。ちょっと見て来てください。　B：（　）いませんでしたよ。
2) A：地下鉄は、（　）こんなに、こんでいるんですか。　B：いいえ、朝と夕方だけです。
3) A：さしみや、すしや、てんぷらは、食べますか。　B：ええ、（　）すきだから、よく食べますよ。
4) A：こんどの旅行は、どこに行きましょうか。　B：わたしは、（　）いいですよ。
5) A：北海道に行ったことがありますか。　B：いいえ。でも、（　）行きたいと思っています。
6) A：いつ、あなたのうちに行きましょうか？　B：（　）いいですよ。
7) A：あまいものが（　）ないから、（　）買って来ましょう。何がいいですか。
   B：（　）いいですよ。
8) A：ここにある3つのものの中から、（　）1つをえらんでください。　B：（　）いいんですか。
9) あの人に、（　）で、会ったはずなんですが…。
10) A：読みたい本があったら、（　）1さつ、えらんでください。
   B：うーん。（　）あまり読みたくありませんねえ。
11) A：この前の日曜日は、（　）へ行きましたか。
   B：いいえ、（　）行きませんでした。日曜日は、（　）こんでいますから。

Vocabulary

どうぶつえん zoo　赤ちゃん（あかちゃん）baby　とる (u-vt) to take

ざせき seat　新聞屋（しんぶんや）local office in charge of newspaper delivery

あまいもの sweet things　えらぶ (u-vt) to choose, select　中（なか）among

Function III "Try doing ＿", "do ＿ and see"; すもうを見てみる

The verb「みる」"to see" used after the て-form of a verb means to do something and "see what happens", or "to try doing" such and such.

ex. 1. これは、何のジュースでしょう。ちょっと、飲んでみてください。

I wonder what sort of juice this is? Please drink it and see.

2. あの人に、道をきいてみましょう。 Let's try asking that person directions.

3. 日本人に、日本語で話してみたら、つうじました。

When I tried speaking Japanese to a Japanese, he understood!

Exercise 5: Practice the following dialogue, substituting the underlined portions with the words and phrases indicated.

A：うめぼしを食べたことがありますか。 B：いいえ、まだありません。

A：おいしいですよ。ぜひ、いちど食べてみてください。

1) 日本のしょうせつを読む， おもしろい
2) 伊豆に行く，きれいなところ
3) 日本のきものを着る， きれい
4) ファクシミリをつかう， べんり

Exercise 6: Complete the dialogues using「〜てみる」,「〜てみます」,「〜てみたい」, etc.

1)A：奈良に行ったことがありますか。 B：いいえ、まだです。いちど、＿＿＿＿＿。

2)A：あれ、道をまちがえたのかな。 B：ちょっと、ちずを＿＿＿＿＿＿。

3)A：駅の前に、新しいレストランができましたよ。

B：こんど、いっしょに、＿＿＿＿＿＿。

4)A：このワンピースは、いかがですか。 B：じゃ、ちょっと＿＿＿＿＿。

5)A：ともだちをさそって来ませんか。 B：ええ。じゃ、電話して＿＿＿＿＿。

Function IV "Whether or not"; 3週間で とどくかどうか

The expression「かどうか」used after nouns, verbs, adjectives, etc. adds the meaning "whether or not". Plain forms of verbs and い-adjectives, and the roots of な-adjectives are used.

ex. 1. あした、天気がよくなるかどうか、わかりません。

I don't know if the weather's going to be clear tomorrow or not.

2. このスープ、おいしいかどうか、ちょっと飲んでみて。

Try a bit of this soup and see whether it's alright or not.

Exercise 7: Answer the following questions as shown in the example.

ex. Q：山田さんは、来ますか。(電話できく)

⇨A：来るかどうか、わからないから、電話できいてみます。

1) そのはこの中に、何か入っていますか。(あける)

2) 土田さんは、こんどの木曜日は、つごうがいいですか。(きく)

3) 田中さんは、へやにいますか。(見る)

4) ペンギンは、アフリカにすんでいますか。(本でしらべる)
5) そのアパートは、新(あたら)しいですか。(不動産屋(ふどうさんや)にきく)

Exercise 8: Reply to the following questions as shown in the example.

ex. Q：その仕事(しごと)は、4時までにおわりますか。(やる)
A：おわるかどうか、わからないけれど、やってみます。

1) その本は、むずかしいですか。(読(よ)む)
2) 日本語で、せつめいができますか。(する)
3) 区役所(くやくしょ)は、まだあいていますか。(行く)
4) その魚(さかな)は、おいしいですか。(食(た)べる)
5) 山田(やまだ)さんは、あのバラの花(はな)をくれるでしょうか。(たのむ)

Function V

Asking someone not to do something; わすれないでください。

The following methods may be used to get someone to stop or refrain from doing some action:

1 **Negative request:**
"Please do not"

	くださいませんか	**(polite)**
negative て-form + (〜ないで)	ください	**(neutral)**
	ちょうだい／ね	**(colloquial)**

ex. 1. 門(もん)の前(まえ)に、車(くるま)をとめないでくださいませんか。
Would you please not park your car in front of the gate?
2. 夜(よる)おそく、電話をしないでください。　Please do not call late at night.
3. あした、テニスに行くとき、お金(かね)をわすれないでね。
Don't forget your money when we go to play tennis tomorrow.
4. うそを言(い)わないでちょうだい。　Don't tell lies!

Note 1: In colloquial speech「ちょうだい」is often used by women and children in place of「ください」.

2 **Admonishment:**
"You must not"

	いけません／いけない
て-form + は +	だめです
	こまります

ex. 1. ここに、ごみをすててはいけません。
You mustn't throw your rubbish here!
2. ろうかを走(はし)っちゃだめよ。　You mustn't run in the halls!
3. A：あした、会社を休みたいんですが…。　Uh, I'd like to take off tomorrow.
B：いや、休んじゃこまりますよ。　No, that wouldn't be convenient for us.

Note 2: In colloquial speech「ては」→「ちゃ」,「では」→「じゃ」.
Note 3:「〜てはいけません」is often used for stating general rules or social taboos.
ex. しばふの中(なか)に入(はい)ってはいけません。　Keep off the grass!

Vocabulary

うめぼし pickled *ume*, salted plum
ファクシミリ facsimile
しょうせつ novel
〜かな I wonder ...
ペンギン penguin
アフリカ Africa
不動産屋（ふどうさんや）real estate agent
きもの *kimono*, traditional Japanese wear
まちがえる (ru-vt) to make a mistake
ワンピース dress, frock
しらべる (ru-vt) to inquire, investigate
バラ rose

3 **Negative command:** "Do not!"

plain non-past ＋ な

ex. 1. ごみをすてるな。 Don't litter!

2. あまりおそく帰って来るなよ。 Don't get home too late!

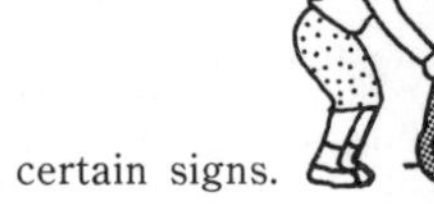

Note 4: A negative command sounds very harsh, and is used by men or on certain signs.

4 **Reasons why not:** Wherever it seems a bit awkward or impolite to come right out and say "do not do", it is common to list reasons why such an action should not be done.

ex. 1.

ここはせまいし、
小さい子どもが
いるので…
こうえん

There's not much room here, besides there are small children.

ex. 2.

あの、ここは
ちゅうしゃ
きんしになって
いますから…

Uh, excuse me, this is a no parking zone.

ex. 3. A：たばこをすいたいんですが…。 I would like to smoke, but ...

B：ええと、ここは禁煙だし、子どももいますので、ちょっと…。

Well, there's no smoking here, besides there are children around, and so uh ....

Exercise 9: For each of the situations pictured below, have the person request or command the other person not to do what they are doing.

Exercise 10: Look at the pictures on the next page and write the letter of the sign to which each of the following statements refers.

1) 今、たばこをすってはいけないことになっているんですね。(　　)
2) もしもし、きょうは火曜日だから、ごみを出しちゃいけませんよ。(　　)
3) 工事中です。中に入ってはいけません。(　　)
4) ここに、車をとめてはいけません。(　　)
5) あら、このセーター、水であらっちゃだめなんだわ。(　　)

a. たちいりきんし

No Admittance
No Trespassing
Keep Out

b.

禁煙
7-10

No Smoking

c.

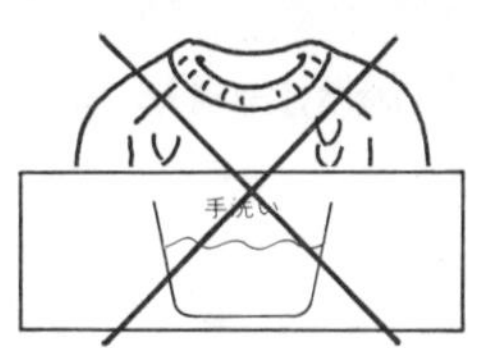

Do not hand wash

d.

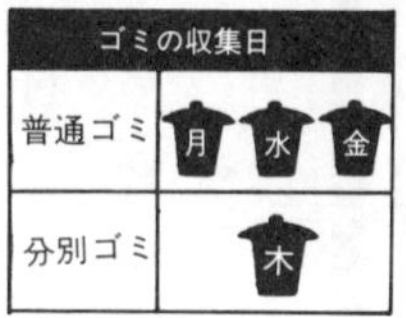

Garbage collection days

e. ちゅうしゃきんし

No Parking

Reading Comprehension Exercise

〈マイケルの日記（にっき）〉

日曜日（にちようび）に、バーバラと、すもうを見に行った。ぶじに、国技館（こくぎかん）についたのだが、おなかが、ぺこぺこだった。じつは、とちゅうで、食事（しょくじ）をするつもりだったのだが、てきとうな店（みせ）が、みつからなかったのだ。それで、そばを歩（ある）いている人（ひと）に、国技館の中（なか）で食事ができるかどうか、きいてみた。

「ええ、できますよ。レストランもありますし、おべんとうも売（う）っています。でも、中で売っているビールは高いから、どこかで、かんビールを買（か）って行ったほうがいいですね。」

これは、しんせつなアドバイスだった。バーバラは、おすもうさんを見て、言った。「まあ。あの人たちは、毎日（まいにち）、ここで、高いビールを飲（の）んでいるんだわ。」

◆Vocabulary◆

国技館（こくぎかん）National Sports Arena
てきとう（な）adequate, suitable
それで therefore, for that reason
かんビール beer in a can
アドバイス advice
ぶじに safely, without incident
おなかがぺこぺこ to be hungry, starving
みつかる (u-vi) to be found
（お）べんとう box lunch
おすもうさん *sumo* wrestler

Exercise 11: Answer the following questions.

1) マイケルさんたちが、国技館についたとき、おなかがぺこぺこだったのは、どうしてですか。
2) 国技館の中では、何を売っていますか。
3) バーバラさんが、おすもうさんを見て、「毎日、高いビールを飲んでいるんだわ。」と言ったのは、どうしてだと思（おも）いますか。

Listening Comprehension Exercise

Person A wants to smoke. Indicate whether person B's response is positive (P), or negative (N).

① ( )　② ( )　③ ( )　④ ( )　⑤ ( )

◆Vocabulary◆

わ sentence-final particle used by women for emphasis, etc.
さる monkey
おる (u-vt) to bend, break
ふとる (u-vi) to grow fat

第14課 ホンコンで買ったそうです

She Said She Bought Them In Hong Kong

Dialogue I

Michael and Miss Kuroda discuss different people at the party.

マイケル：あの赤いワンピースを着ている方は、どなたですか。

黒田　　：ああ、あれは、土田さんのおくさんです。

マイケル：あちらの、着物の方は？

黒田　　：事務の鈴木さんじゃありませんか。
パーティーのときは、いつも和服だから。

マイケル：あ、ほんとうだ、ちっともわからなかった。
いつもと、感じが、ぜんぜんちがいますね。
花田さんのはいているくつ、すてきですねえ。

黒田　　：ホンコンに行ったとき、買ったそうですよ。

マイケル：なかなか、にあいますね。
おや、山下さんがいませんねえ。
どうしたんでしょう。

黒田　　：きっと、まだ会社でしょう。今日中に、
大阪支社に送るほうこくしょが
あるって言ってましたから。

マイケル：ああ、きのうも、一日中、ずっと、
やっていましたねえ。

黒田　　：あれは、ウエッブさんのおくさんでしょう。
しゃれたぼうしを、かぶっているわね。

マイケル：ああ、まだ、しょうかいしていませんでしたか。
それは、しつれいしました。

Dialogue II

At the *sushi* counter

花田　：日本料理では、何が、いちばんすきですか。

バーバラ：わたしは、おすしが、いちばんすきです。

花田　：このごろは、アメリカでも、おすしを
よく食べるそうですね。
むこうのおすしは、日本のとおなじですか。

バーバラ：ええ。あじは、ほとんどおなじですけど、ねだんは、もっと安いですよ。
でも、しゅるいは、日本ほど多くありません。

花田　：うちの近くに、とても安くて、おいしいおすし屋さんがありますから、
こんど行くとき、おさそいしますね。

バーバラ：ええ。ぜひ、おねがいします。

Vocabulary

Nouns:

4事務（じむ）office or clerical work, office
5和服（わふく）*kimono*, Japanese style dress
7感じ（かんじ）feeling, looks, appearance
19ぼうし hat, cap
22日本料理（にほんりょうり）Japanese cuisine
28しゅるい kind, type, variety
29近く（ちかく）near, close by

Adjectives:

8すてき（な）lovely, cute

Adverbs:

6ちっとも (not) at all, one bit (neg. constructions)
7ぜんぜん not at all (neg. constructions)
10なかなか ① considerably, quite ② not easily, not readily
13今日中に（きょうじゅうに）by the end of today
16一日中（いちにちじゅう）all day, the entire day
27ほとんど almost (all), nearly (all)

Verbs:

1着る（きる）(ru-vt) to wear, put on
10にあう (u-vi) to fit, go well with, suit
19かぶる (u-vt) to put on, wear (hat, etc.)
19しゃれる (ru-vi) to dress fancy; しゃれた fancy, stylish

Examples using「なかなか」

1) マイケルさん、日本語が、なかなかじょうずですね。
Your Japanese is quite good, Michael.

2) ２時のやくそくだったが、ともだちは、なかなか来なかった。
We agreed to meet at 2:00, but my friend didn't arrive until long past the scheduled time.

3) 日本語が、なかなかじょうずにならない。
My Japanese just doesn't seem to improve.

Grammatical words:

9〜そうです someone said that ＿
16〜じゅう throughout ☞Function Ⅱ
26おなじ same

Expressions:

6ほんとうだ You're right. It's true.
11おや Oh! Hey! Why? Wait! (used to express surprise, doubt, etc.)
12どうしたんでしょう What do you suppose happened?
30おさそいします honorific form of「さそう」"to invite" (see Lesson 21, p.264)

Dialogue Comprehension Exercise

1) Mark T or F.

① (　　) 土田さんのおくさんは、着物を着ている。

② (　　) 花田さんは、ホンコンで買ったくつを はいている。

③ (　　) 会社の人は、みんな、パーティーに来ている。

④ (　　) 黒田さんは、パーティーの前に、バーバラさんに会ったことがある。

⑤ (　　) アメリカのすしより、日本のすしのほうが、しゅるいが多い。

2) Answer the following questions.

① 赤いワンピースを着ているのは、だれですか。

② 着物を着ているのは、だれですか。

③ 山下さんは、どうして、パーティーに来ていないのですか。

④ バーバラさんは、日本料理では、何が、いちばんすきですか。

⑤ バーバラさんは、パーティーが終わったら、花田さんと、すし屋へ行きますか。

Function I

Indicating specific times: "when __"; ホンコンに<u>行ったとき</u>

Specific times may be indicated by using「とき」"time" modified by various clauses. Such expressions are equivalent to "when such and such" clauses in English.

Verb +とき (plain non-past)	ex. 1. こんど、すし屋へ行くとき、おさそいします。 Next time we go to a *sushi* shop I'll invite you along. 2. ハワイに行くとき、水着を買いました。 I bought a swimsuit when going to Hawaii. (before going)
Verb +とき (plain past)	3. ハワイに行ったとき、水着を買いました。 I bought a swimsuit when I went to Hawaii. (while there)
い**-adj** (plain) +とき	4. 小さいとき、ピアノをならっていました。 I took piano lessons when I was little.
な**-adj** (－な) +とき	5. へやが、もっとしずかなときに、話をしましょう。 Let's talk when the room is quieter.
Noun +の+とき (だ→の)	6. 学生のとき、フランス語を勉強しました。 I studied French when I was a student.

Note 1: The tense of the verbal modifying「とき」often presents a problem. Adjectives and the be-verb usually appear in the non-past form, even though the time they indicate in the principal clause is past, and are translated as past in English.

ex. 1. 小さいとき、……た。　　When I was little....

2. 学生のとき、……た。　　When I was a student....

Note 2: With verbs, it helps to keep in mind that non-past form indicates an action that happens "all the time" or is "not yet completed", while past form is used when the action is "over and finished", or else over, but with the resultant state "still in effect". The following examples show how this affects the interpretation.

ex. 1. お客(きゃく)さんが来るときには、へやを、きれいにしておきます。
I clean the room and have it ready when guests come. (whenever guests come, or before their arrival)
2. わからないときは、先生(せんせい)に聞(き)いてください。
When you don't understand, please ask the teacher.

Note 3: 「とき」may be interpreted as "before", "when" or "after" depending on the context and the tense of the verb.

食(た)べるとき，いただきますと言う。You say "itadakimasu" before eating.

食(た)べるとき，はしをつかう。You use chopsticks when eating.

食(た)べたとき，ごちそうさまと言う。You say "gochisoo-sama" when you have eaten.

Exercise 1: Mark the letter of the expression appropriate to each of the following situations.

A
- ex. 夜(よる)、ねるとき　(a)
- 1. 家に帰(かえ)ったとき　(　)
- 2. へやに入(はい)るとき　(　)
- 3. ごはんが終(お)わったとき　(　)
- 4. お客さんが来たとき　(　)
- 5. 昼(ひる)、人に会(あ)ったとき　(　)
- 6. 朝(あさ)、人に会ったとき　(　)
- 7. 夜、人に会ったとき　(　)
- 8. ごはんを食べるとき　(　)

B
- a. おやすみなさい
- b. ごちそうさま（でした）
- c. おはよう（ございます）
- d. こんにちは
- e. いただきます
- f. よくいらっしゃいました
- g. しつれいします
- h. ただいま（帰りました）
- i. こんばんは

Dialogues in English

Dialogue Ⅰ

M: Who is that person in the red dress?
K: Oh, that's Mr. Tsuchida's wife.
M: What about that person over there in the *kimono*?
K: Isn't it Miss Suzuki who works in the office? She always wears Japanese dress when we have parties.
M: Yes, you're right. I didn't recognize her at all. She looks completely different from usual. Those are nice shoes Miss Hanada has on.
K: She said she bought them when she went to Hong Kong.
M: They suit her rather well, don't you think? Hey! Mr. Yamashita isn't here, is he! What do you suppose happened to him?
K: He's probably still at the office. He said there was a report he had to send off to the Osaka branch sometime today.
M: Oh yes, I believe he was working on it all day yesterday as well.
K: That's your wife, isn't it? My but that's a fancy hat she's wearing!
M: Oh, you mean I haven't introduced you yet? Sorry about that.

Dialogue Ⅱ

H: Of all Japanese foods, which do you like best?
B: I like *sushi* best.
H: I hear that nowadays people eat a lot of *sushi* in America as well. Is the *sushi* there the same as the *sushi* in Japan?
B: Yes, the flavor is nearly the same, but the price is less expensive. There is not as much variety as in Japan, however.
H: Near our home there's a *sushi* shop that's good and inexpensive. The next time we go I'll invite you.
B: Yes. please do so by all means.

Exercise 2: When do you do the following? Answer using「〜とき」.

ex. あいさつをします ⇨ 人に会ったとき、あいさつをします。

1) 会社に電話をします。 2) じしょで、しらべます。 3) ごちそうを作っておきます。
4) さとうを入れます。 5) まどをしめます。 6) くすりを飲みます。

Function II "Throughout such and such a period"; 一日中

Added to certain time words,「中」, pronounced「じゅう」, means "throughout" or "all through" the entire period of time.

一日中	all day long
一晩中	all night long
一年中	all year long
夏じゅう	all summer long

ex. 1. きのうは、一日中、雨がふっていました。
Yesterday it rained the entire day.
2. テストがあるので、一晩中、勉強しました。
There's a test, so I studied all night.
3. 京都には、一年中、おおぜいの人が来ます。
Many people come to Kyoto throughout the entire year.
4. 今年は、夏じゅう、海ではたらきました。 I worked at the beach all summer long this year.

Exercise 3: Fill in the blanks with an appropriate time word plus「中（じゅう）」.

1) A: ハワイは、いつも、あたたかくていいですねえ。 B: ええ、（ ）、夏とおなじですよ。
2) A: もう、ごご8時だから、スーパーは、しまっていますね。
B: ええ。でも、コンビニエンス・ストアは、（ ）ひらいていますよ。
3) かぜをひいて、きのうは、（ ）ねていました。
4) ゆうべは、むしあつかったから、（ ）クーラーをつけていました。
5) いやあ、つかれました。今日は、（ ）いそがしかったんです。
6) A: 夏休みは、どうするんですか。 B:（ ）、ビアガーデンで、アルバイトをするつもりです。
7) A: トマトは、夏のやさいですよね。 B: ええ。でも、（ ）、店で売っていますよ。

Function III Time limit: "before the end of"; 今日中に

「中に」added to certain time words, etc. means "sometime during" or "anytime during", or "before the end of". In this construction「中」is pronounced「ちゅう」, with a few instances where it is pronounced「じゅう」.

今日中に	sometime today
今年中に	sometime this year
今週中に	sometime this week
今月中に	sometime this month
10月中に	sometime in October
夏休み中に	sometime during summer vacation

ex. 1. そくたつで送ったから、今日中につきますよ。
I sent it express, so it should arrive sometime today.
2. 今年中に、ぜひ、けっこんしたいですね。
I definitely want to get married sometime this year. (before the end of this year)
3. 10月中に、アメリカに行くことになりました。
It's been decided that I go to America sometime in October.

Note: Another use of「〜中」"during, in the middle of" was explained in Lesson 11, p.151.

Exercise 4: Complete the following sentences as in the example.

ex. 宿題は、あしたまでだから、(今日中に) しておきます。

The homework is due tomorrow, so I'll get it ready sometime today.

1) あしたは、銀行が休みだから、(　　　　) 行っておきます。

2) 来週はいそがしいから、(　　　　) にやっておきましょう。

3) 来年はオーストラリアに帰るから、(　　　　) 京都に行っておきます。

4) 来月、ひっこすから、(　　　　) ひっこしのしたくを しておきます。

Function IV　"Same as __"「__とおなじ」, "different from"「__とちがう」

__とおなじ "same as __"	__とちがう "different from __"
Xは、Yとおなじです。X is the same as Y. XとYは、おなじです。X and Y are the same. XとYは、おなじ物です。 X and Y are the same thing.	Xは、Yとちがいます。X is different from Y. XとYは、ちがいます。X and Y are different. XとYは、ちがう物です。 X and Y are different things.

ex.1. A: アメリカのおすしは、日本のとおなじですか。

Is American *sushi* the same as Japanese *sushi*?

B: ええ、あじや、ねだんは、ほとんどおなじです。

Yes, the flavor and price are nearly the same.

2. A: 日本の車と、アメリカの車は、おなじですか、ちがいますか。

Are Japanese and American cars the same, or different?

B: かたちは、ほとんどおなじですが、ハンドルのいちが、ちがいます。

The shape is nearly the same, but the position of the steering wheel is different.

3. 花田さんと黒田さんは、おなじバッグを持っています。

Miss Hanada and Miss Kuroda have the same handbags.

Note:「おなじ」comes directly before the noun it modifies.

Exercise 5: Which items of apparel are the same and which are different?

ex. ① AとBは、とけいと、くつと、ハンドバッグが、おなじです。

② AとBは、ぼうしと、洋服と、くつしたが、ちがいます。

1) BとCは、____。　2) CとDは、____。

3) DとAは、____。　4) AとCは、____。

5) BとDは、____。

Vocabulary

さとう sugar
むしあつい hot and muggy
ビアガーデン beer garden
したくする preparations
コンビニエンス・ストア convenience store
クーラー air conditioner
トマト tomato
洋服（ようふく）western clothing, suit, dress
ひらく (u-vi, vt) to open, begin
どうするんですか What are you going to do?
ひっこしする moving to another residence

Exercise 6: Tell what are the same and what are different in the pictures of Exercise 5. Use appropriate verbs from the list.

ex. ① Aは、Bとおなじくつをはいています。

② Aは、Bとちがう洋服(ようふく)を着(き)ています。

1) Aは、Cと________________。

2) Bは、Cと________________。

3) Cは、Dと________________。

4) Dは、Aと________________。

5) Bは、Dと________________。

apparel	put on	take off
ワンピース dress せびろ business suit セーター sweater シャツ shirt うわぎ coat, jacket	きる	ぬぐ
スカート skirt ズボン pants, slacks くつした socks くつ shoes	はく	
ぼうし hat, cap	かぶる	ぬぐ，とる
ネクタイ necktie ベルト belt とけい watch ネックレス necklace	する	とる はずす
めがね glasses	かける	

Grammar Note

"No longer"「もう」, **"still"**「まだ」

「まだ」and「もう」are used to express completion or non-completion.

まだ＋ **affirmative**	"still do"
もう＋ **negative**	"no longer do" "do no more"

Note: See Lesson 10, p.138 for previous explanation of「まだ」and「もう」.

ex. 1. 土田さんは、まだ、会社で仕事(しごと)をしています。

Mr. Tsuchida is still working at the office.

2. A: これは、もう、つかいませんか。 Won't you be using this anymore?

B: いいえ、まだ、つかいますよ。すてないでください。

No, I'm still using it. Don't throw it away, please.

Exercise 7: Construct a conversation as shown in the example.

ex. さむい

A: まだ、さむいですか。

B: いいえ、もう、さむくありません。

1) （銀行が）あいている

A:________________。

B:________________。

しまっていますよ。

2) （雨が）ふっている

A:________________。

B:________________。

3) いたい

A:＿＿＿＿＿＿＿＿。

B:＿＿＿＿＿＿＿＿。

4)（ケーキが）ある

A:＿＿＿＿＿＿＿＿。

B:＿＿＿＿＿＿＿＿。

5) 食べたい

A:＿＿＿＿＿＿＿＿。

B:＿＿＿＿＿＿＿＿。

Function V　Reporting information second hand; ホンコンで買(か)ったそうです

There are several methods for passing on information which you yourself received from sources other than first hand experience. The source of the information might be indicated using such expressions as「～によると」"according to so and so" or「～の話(はなし)では」"according to what so and so says".

1 (～によると)　～そうです。
(～の話(はなし)では)　～のだそうです。
～んだそうです。

ex. 1. 天気よほうによると、今年(ことし)の冬(ふゆ)は、さむいそうです。　According to the weather report, this winter will be cold.

2. 今年の冬は、さむいんだそうです。
We're supposed to have a cold winter this year.

～んですって。
～ですって。
～んだって。
～って。

3. （女）田中(たなか)さん、休み(なん)ですって。
(He said that) Mr. Tanaka isn't coming.

4. （男・女）田中さん、来ない(んだ)って。
(He said that) Mr. Tanaka won't be coming.

Note:「～ですって」「～（だ）って」are used in casual informal conversation.「～ですって」is used mainly by women.

2 (～が) (～で)　～と言(い)っていました
～って言ってました

ex. 5. 兄(あに)が、このじしょは いいと言っていましたよ。
My elder brother said this dictionary is good.

6. 天気よほうで、あしたは、晴(は)れると言っていました。　On the weather report they said tomorrow will be fine.

(～に)　～と書いてありました
～って書いてありました

7. 新聞(しんぶん)に、きのう、じしんがあったって書いてありました。　It said in the newspaper there was an earthquake yesterday.

(～から)　～と聞(き)きました
～って聞きました

8. 田中さんから、けっこん式(しき)は、来月の5日(いつか)だと聞きました。　I heard from Mr. Tanaka the wedding is on the 5th of next month.

Exercise 8: Make up a dialogue using the words given as in the example below. Take note of the relationship between the two people in the conversation.

ex. けっこんする，会社をやめる（OL—OL）

⇨ A: 田中さん、けっこんするんですって。

B: ええ。わたしも聞いたわ。それで、会社をやめるんですって。

1) てんきんする，ニューヨークへ行く（会社員：男—男）
2) びょうき，にゅういんする（先生—学生）
3) アルバイトがいそがしい，勉強をする時間がない（大学生：男—女）
4) 仕事が終わらない，パーティーに行かない（OL—OL）

Exercise 9: Add an appropriate phrase and complete the following.

1) A：もしもし、野村さんですか。マイケルですが、かぜをひいたので、今日は休みます。

B：課長、マイケルさんは＿＿＿＿＿＿。

2) A：もしもし、今日は、会議でおそくなるから、ばんごはんは、うちで食べないからね。

B：お母さん。お父さん、今日は、＿＿＿＿＿＿。

3) A：今日は、かさは、いらないでしょうか。

B：持って行ったほうがいいですよ。天気よほうで、＿＿＿＿＿＿。

4) A：日本語の勉強は、どうですか。

B：Aさんは、＿＿＿＿＿＿けど、わたしは、たいへんです。

Function VI Comparison (2): superlative expressions; おすしが、いちばんすきです

Use the following patterns when comparing three or more items.

1 **A**と**B**と**C**では / **X**（**A**＋**B**＋**C**）の中で / **X** のうちで ｝ **A**が、いちばん〜です。 — Of A, B and C, A is the most __. / Of X, A is the most __.

2 **X**で、いちばん〜のは、**A**です。 — Of X, the most __ is A.

3 **X**のうちで、**A**ほど〜（の）はありません／いません。 — Among X, there's nothing as __ as A.

◆**Vocabulary**◆ OL（オー・エル）female office worker (abbreviated from "office lady")

やめる (ru-vt) to resign, stop, give up

てんきんする a change in job site (to be transferred)

にゅういんする hospital admission

ex.1. A: 日本料理(にほんりょうり)では、何が、いちばんすきですか。 Of all Japanese foods which do you like most?

B: すきやきが、いちばんすきです。 I like *sukiyaki* the most.

C: 日本料理は、みんな／ぜんぶ　すきです。 I like all Japanese food.

2. A: お茶(ちゃ)と、コーヒーと、紅茶(こうちゃ)では、どれが、いちばんすきですか。

Which do you like most, green tea, coffee or tea?

B: どれも、すきです。 I like all of them.

C: どれも、すきではありません。 I don't like any of them.

3. 家族(かぞく)の中で、いちばん、せが高いのは、ぼくです。 I am the tallest in my family.

4. あなたほど、すてきな人は、いません。 No other person is as pretty/handsome as you.

Exercise 10: Look at the graph and answer the following questions.

1) 東京では、何月が、いちばんあついですか。
2) 東京では、何月が、いちばんさむいですか。
3) 東京で、いちばん雨が多(おお)いのは、何月ですか。
4) 東京で、いちばん雨が少(すく)ないのは、何月ですか。
5) 1月と5月と10月では、何月が、いちばん雨が多いですか。

Annual temperature and rainfall in Tokyo

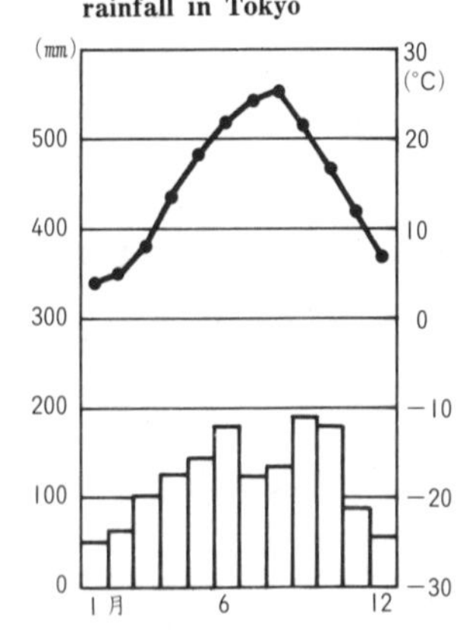

Exercise 11: Make an expression using「ほど～（は）ない」as in the example.

ex.A: かがみよ、かがみ。せかいで、いちばんきれいなのはだれ？わたし？

B: いいえ、しらゆきひめです。（しらゆきひめ，きれい，人)。

⇨ いいえ、しらゆきひめです。しらゆきひめほど、きれいな人は、いません。

1) A: その本、そんなにおもしろいの？
B: ええ、（これ，おもしろい本，読(よ)んだこと）

2) A: けっこん、おめでとう。
B: ありがとう。（今日(きょう)，うれしい，日)。

3) A: あじは、どうですか。
B: ええ、（これ，おいしい物(もの)，食べたこと)。

4) A: エベレストは、そんなに高い山なんですか。
B: ええ、（エベレスト，高い，山)。

5) A: あついですねえ。
B: ほんとうに。一年中(いちねんじゅう)で（8月，あつい，月)。

6) A: おてつだいしましょうか。
B: ありがとう。（あなた，しんせつ，人)。

Exercise 12: The graph on the right shows the results of a survey investigating the number of comic books Japanese children read each month.
Look at the graph and comment on it.

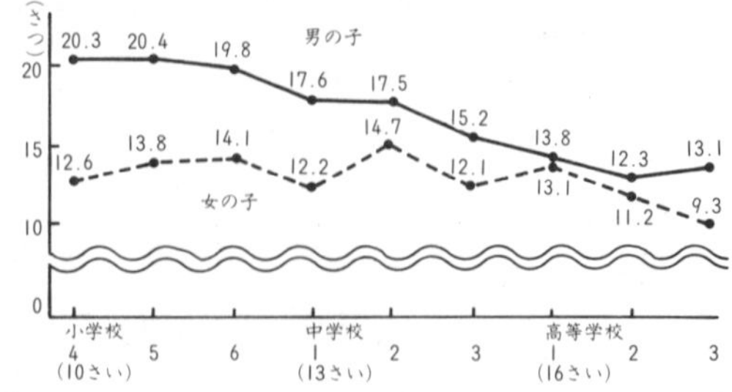

Vocabulary

かがみ mirror, looking glass
日（ひ）day, sun
晩ごはん（ばんごはん）supper
せかい world
おてつだいする honorific form of「てつだう」"to help"
しらゆきひめ Snow White

Reading Comprehension Exercise

Arrange the following story in the proper order.

1 → (　) → (　) → (　) → (　) → (　) → 7

1　ねずみのお父さんが、むすめのチュー子に聞きました。

「チュー子は、だれと、けっこんしたい？」

「せかいで、いちばん強い人と、けっこんしたいわ。」

2「風さん、あなたは、せかいで、いちばん強い方です。どうぞ、むすめとけっこんしてください。」

「わたしは、かべに、まけてしまいます。かべは、わたしより強いですよ。」と、風は、こたえました。

3「太陽さん、あなたほど強い方は、せかいに いません。どうぞ、むすめとけっこんしてください。」

「わたしより、雲のほうが強いです。」と、太陽は、こたえました。

4「かべさん、あなたは、せかいで、いちばん強い方です。どうぞ、むすめとけっこんしてください。」

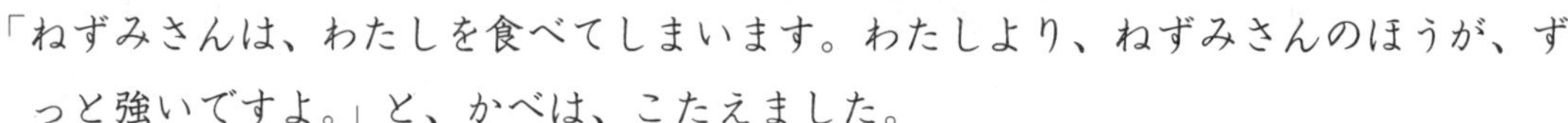

「ねずみさんは、わたしを食べてしまいます。わたしより、ねずみさんのほうが、ずっと強いですよ。」と、かべは、こたえました。

5　そこで、お父さんは、太陽のところへ行きました。

6「雲さん、あなたほど強い方は、せかいに いません。どうぞ、むすめと、けっこんしてください。」

「わたしは、風ほど強くありません。」と、雲は、言いました。

7　チュー子は、となりのチュー太郎とけっこんしました。

◆**Vocabulary**◆

ねずみ mouse
強い（つよい）strong
太陽（たいよう）sun
まける (ru-vi) to lose, be defeated
こたえる (ru-vi) to answer
ソフトボール softball
チュー squeek (the sound a mouse makes)
のうぎょう agriculture, farming

Listening Comprehension Exercise

Listen to the tape and fill in the blanks.

Dialogue 1: (Refer to the map on the following page.)

1)________に行きたい人は、「えびす」で、________にのりかえます。

Dialogue 2:

2)日本で、いちばん おおぜいの人がするスポーツは、________とソフトボールです。

テニスをする人は、________や________ほど多くありません。

Dialogue 3:

3)日本人のすきな仕事は、

1ばんめ ____。　2ばんめ ____。　3ばんめ ____。　4ばんめ ____。　5ばんめ ____。

Culture Note

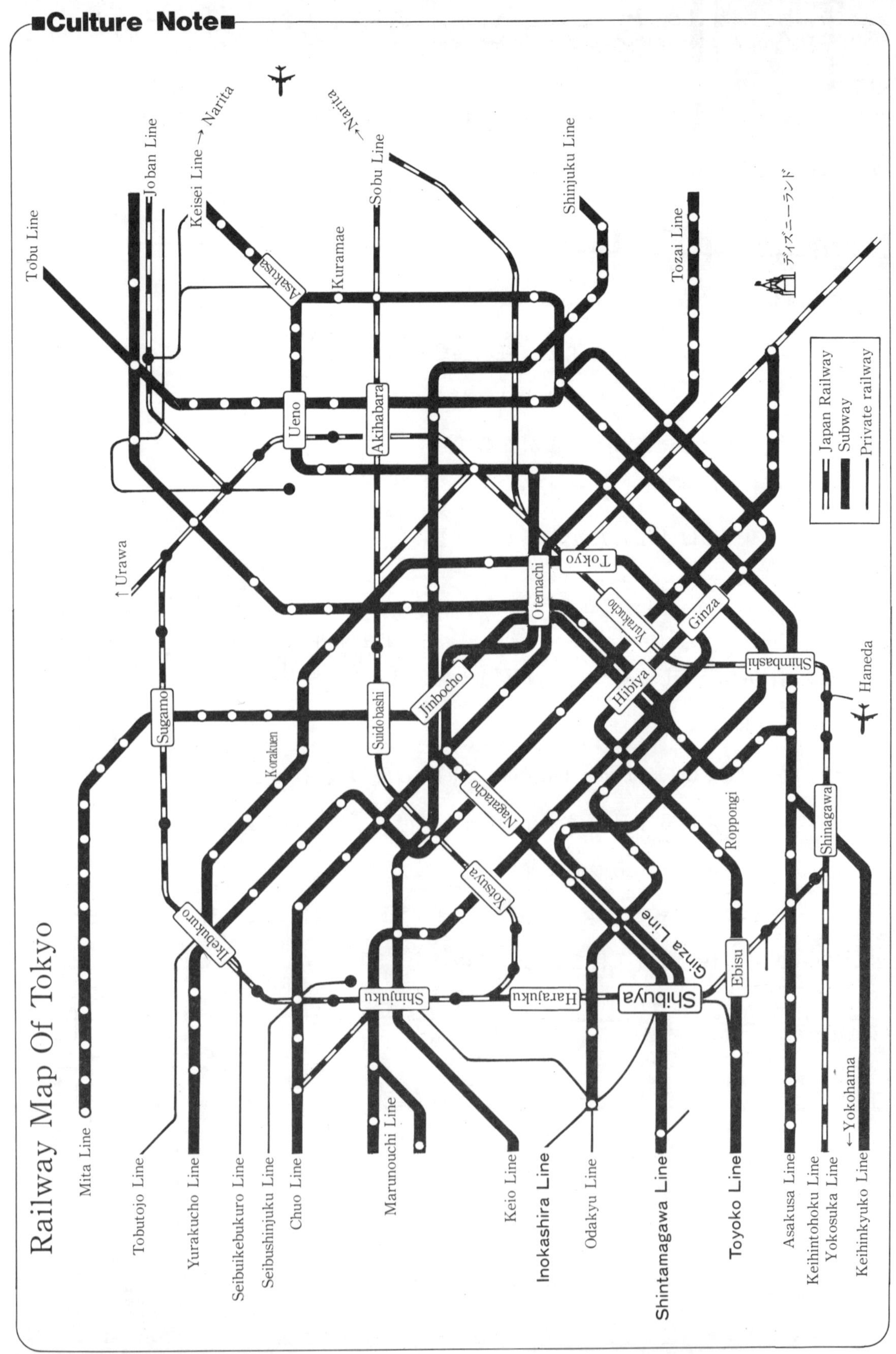
Railway Map Of Tokyo
Japan Railway
Subway
Private railway
Mita Line
Tobutojo Line
Yurakucho Line
Seibuikebukuro Line
Seibushinjuku Line
Chuo Line
Marunouchi Line
Keio Line
Inokashira Line
Odakyu Line
Shintamagawa Line
Toyoko Line
Asakusa Line
Keihintohoku Line
Yokosuka Line
Keihinkyuko Line
Tobu Line
Joban Line
Keisei Line → Narita
←Narita
Sobu Line
Shinjuku Line
Tozai Line
ディズニーランド
Asakusa
Kuramae
Ueno
Akihabara
↑Urawa
Otemachi
Tokyo
Yurakucho
Ginza
Shimbashi
Haneda
Hibiya
Jinbocho
Suidobashi
Sugamo
Korakuen
Nagatacho
Roppongi
Shinagawa
Yotsuya
Ikebukuro
Shinjuku
Harajuku
Shibuya
Ebisu
Ginza Line
←Yokohama

第15課 ちょっと、うかがいますが…

Excuse Me A Moment, I'd Like To Ask You…

Dialogue I

Michael needs help finding an address.

マイケル：ちょっとうかがいますが、桜(さくら)が丘(おか)3丁目(ちようめ)5番地(ばんち)は、このへんですか。

女の人　：さあ、ちょっと、わかりませんが。

マイケル：すみません。あのう、桜が丘3丁目5番地に行きたいんですが。

男の人　：このへんは4丁目だから、もう少(すこ)し先(さき)じゃないですか。
いっしょに行きましょうか。

マイケル：どうも、ごしんせつに。すみません。

(a few minutes later)

男の人　：(checking the sign on a telephone pole) あれ、おかしいなあ。
このへんが3丁目のはずなのに、「松(まつ)が丘(おか)」と書いてある。
しょうがない。あの店(みせ)で聞(き)いてみましょう。
（店で）ちょっとうかがいますが、桜が丘3丁目は、どう行くんでしょうか。

店の人　：ああ、桜が丘3丁目ですね。この道(みち)を、300メートルぐらい行くと、左(ひだり)がわに、ガソリンスタンドがあります。

男の人　：はい、ガソリンスタンドですね。

店の人　：そのかどを、左にまがって、しばらく行くと、広(ひろ)い通(とお)りに出ます。
そのむこうが、3丁目です。

男の人　：ガソリンスタンドのかどを、左にまがって、広い通りのむこうですね。ありがとうございました。

マイケル：どうも。

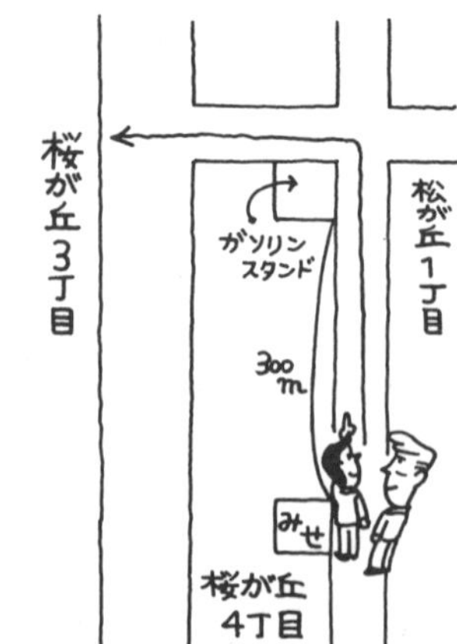

Dialogue II

Michael arrives at last.

マイケル：おそくなりまして。

Mr. 中村：あ、いらっしゃい。おまちしていましたよ。

うちは、すぐ、わかりましたか。

マイケル：いやあ、それが、道にまよってしまって…。

男の人に聞いてみたら、かえって、わからなくなってしまったんですよ。

Mr. 中村：それは、たいへんでしたねえ。あ、雨ですよ。ぬれないでよかったですね。

どうぞ、あがって、ゆっくりしてください。

マイケル：さいきん、よくふりますねえ。

Mr. 中村：まったくですねえ。まるで、つゆのようです。

毎日、雨ばかりで、いやになりますねえ。

マイケル：ところで、むすこさんが、留学生のしけんに、うかったそうですね。

おめでとうございます。すごいですねえ。むずかしかったんでしょうね。

Mrs. 中村：さあ、遊んでばかりいたけど…。まぐれじゃないかしら。

でも、アメリカの大学は、入ってから、たいへんだそうですね。

ちょっと、しんぱいなんですよ。

Vocabulary

Nouns:

6先（さき）ahead, further along, before, previous

14ガソリンスタンド gas station

14左がわ（ひだりがわ）left side ↔右がわ（みぎがわ）right side

16かど corner

30つゆ rainy season

34まぐれ luck, accident, twist of fate

32留学生（りゅうがくせい）student studying abroad

> **3丁目5番地**
>
> Streets are not always named or numbered in Japan. Rather, addresses are based on the principle of designating smaller and smaller areas. Tokyo and other large cities for instance are divided in to several 区 (wards), with each 区 containing a number of 町 (towns). 町 are usually divided into between 2～8 丁目 (districts), each 丁目 encompassing maybe 10～60番地 (blocks). The houses in each 番地 are numbered in order —1号, 2号, 3号, etc.–running around the entire block. The address Michael is looking for in this lesson is written:
>
> | 東京都 | 世田谷区 | 桜が丘 | 3丁目 | 5番地 | 23号 |
> |---|---|---|---|---|---|
> | city, | ward, | town, | district, | block, | house number |

Counters:

13メートル meter

Adjectives:

9おかしい strange, funny

31いや（な）disagreeable, unpleasant, distasteful

Adverbs:

16 しばらく for a while
29 さいきん recently
26 かえって just the opposite, contrary to one's expectation
30 まるで completely, no matter how you look at it

Verbs :

1 うかがう (u-vt) to ask (information, etc.) ; humble word meaning「聞く」
16 まがる (u-vt) to turn (a corner), to be bent
27 ぬれる (ru-vi) to get wet
25 まよう (u-vi) to get mixed up, lost
32 うかる (ru-vi) to pass (an examination)

Grammatical words:

10 (verbal plain)＋のに in spite of ☞ Function II
13 (verb plain non-past)＋と if, when ☞ Function IV, V
30 (の) よう like ☞ Function III
31 ばかり nothing but, only ☞ Function I

Expressions:

2 さあ well ... (I don't really know, I can't say for sure, etc.)
11 しょうがない It can't be helped. There's nothing else to do. (＝しかたがない)
17 広い通りに出る You come out onto a wide street.
30 まったくですねえ That's for sure. You can say that again.
30 まるでつゆのよう just like the rainy season
31 いやになります I'm getting sick and tired of it.
34 まぐれじゃないかしら I wonder if it wasn't an accident.

Dialogue Comprehension Exercise

Mark T or F.

Dialogue I : 1) (　) 中村さんの家は、すぐわかりました。
2) (　) 男の人は、桜が丘で、道を聞きました。
3) (　) 桜が丘は、ガソリンスタンドの かどにあります。

Dialogue II : 4) (　) マイケルさんは、雨にぬれました。
5) (　) 中村さんのむすこさんは、アメリカの高校に、留学することになりました。
6) (　) 中村さんのむすこさんは、よく勉強していたそうです。

Function I "Only, just";「だけ」「ばかり」

1 Two forms「だけ」and「ばかり」may be used after nouns in the sentence to add the idea of "only" or "just". For example, given two items, A and B,「Aだけ」is a simple statement of fact concerning the situation at hand: "Only A (not B)".「Aばかり」on the other hand means that A and B have been placed on a scale and the scale tips unevenly to A, producing a situation that is "abnormal" or "out of balance". Rather than simply report the situation at hand,「ばかり」often talks about "all the time", "everytime", "all over", "everywhere", etc. Moreover「ばかり」often expresses the speaker's attitude toward the imbalance: "not right", "unfair", "I wish it were me instead!".

Aだけ

Aばかり

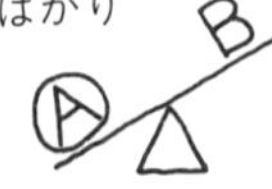

ex. 1. 太郎が 休んでいる。 Taro is absent.
太郎だけが 休んでいる。 Only Taro is absent. (Everyone else is present.)
太郎ばかり 休んでいる。 It's always Taro that's absent. (Not fair to the rest of us! I wish I could skip out like that!)

2. この前の日曜日、ディズニー・ランドに行ったが、人ばっかりで、おもしろくなかった。

We went to Disneyland last Sunday, but it was no fun, nothing but people, people. (everywhere you look, people!) In this sentence「人だけ」would mean, "people only, no dogs or cats, no cartoon characters, etc".

Note 1:「ばっかり」is a more emphatic form of「ばかり」.
Note 2:「だけ」and「ばかり」tend to be inserted between the noun and the following postposition.「は」,「が」and「を」are often deleted when these forms are used.

ex. 花子(はなこ)は、サラダを　食べている。→花子は、サラダばかり　食べている。

2「だけ」used after plain form verbs means "just do such and such".

ex. 1. ブラジルに行くじゅんびができて、あとは、ひこうきにのるだけです。

Preparations for my trip to Brazil are complete, all that remains is just to board the plane.

ex. 2. Clerk: いい くつですよ。はいてみませんか。

They're lovely shoes. Would you like to try them on?

Customer: いいえ、ちょっと、見ているだけなんです。　No, I'm just looking.

Dialogues in English

Dialogue I

M : Just a moment. I'd like to ask you if I may. Is Sakuragaoka, 3 chome, 5 banchi in this vicinity?
Woman : Well, I don't really know.
M : Excuse me. Uh, I'd like to get to Sakuragaoka, 3 chome, 5 banchi.
Man : This area here is 4 chome, so isn't it a bit further on? Should I go with you?
M : Thank you. That's very kind of you.
Man : Gee, that's strange. This area ought to be 3 chome, but instead it says "Matsugaoka". There's nothing else to do. Let's ask at that shop over there. Excuse me, I'd like to ask if I may. How does one get to Sakuragaoka 3 chome?
Clerk : Oh, Sakuragaoka 3 chome? Go along this street 300 meters or so and there will be a gas station on the left hand side.
Man : A gas station, I see.
Clerk : Turn left at that corner and go straight for a ways and you will come to a wide street. The other side will be 3 chome.
Man : Turn left at the corner with the gas station, and it's the other side of the wide street. Thank you very much.
M : Thanks.

Dialogue II

M : I'm late.
Mr. N : Ah, welcome. I've been expecting you. Did you find the house right away?
M : No. You see, well. I got a bit lost. When I asked a man directions, I got even more mixed up.
Mr. N : You had a rough time then. Oh oh! It's raining. It's a good thing you didn't get wet. Come in, if you will, and make yourself at home.
M : We've been having a lot of rain recently, haven't we?
Mr. N : You can say that again. It's just like the rainy season. Every day nothing but rain. It gets a person down, doesn't it.
M : Hey. I heard your boy passed the exam for study abroad. Congratulations. That's terrific. I'll bet it was difficult.
Mrs. N : Humph! All he did was fool around. I'm not sure but it wasn't just an accident. But they say American universities are difficult after one gets in. I'm a bit concerned.

[3]「ばかり」is often used after a verb て-form, and followed by the be-verb or「いる」"to exist". The meaning expressed is similar to that described for nouns.

ex. 1. 太郎(たろう)は、食べてばかりいて、花子(はなこ)をてつだいません。

All Taro does is eat. He doesn't help Hanako.

2. 子(こ)どもたちは、遊(あそ)んでばかりで、ちっとも勉強(べんきょう)しないんですよ。

All the children do is fool around, they don't study at all!

Exercise 1:

1) Construct sentences using「ばかり」as in the example.

ex. ジャズを聞(き)いている。⇨ ジャズばかり　聞いている。　He listens only to jazz.

⇨ ジャズを　聞いてばかりいる。　All he does is listen to jazz.

① テレビを見ている。　③ まんがを読んでいる。　④ ひらがなで書いている。

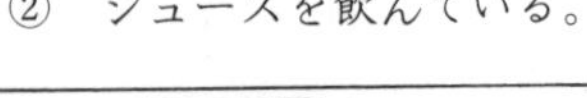

② ジュースを飲(の)んでいる。

⑤ お酒(さけ)を飲んでいる。　⑥ 遊んでいる。　⑦ ねている。　⑧ 食べている。

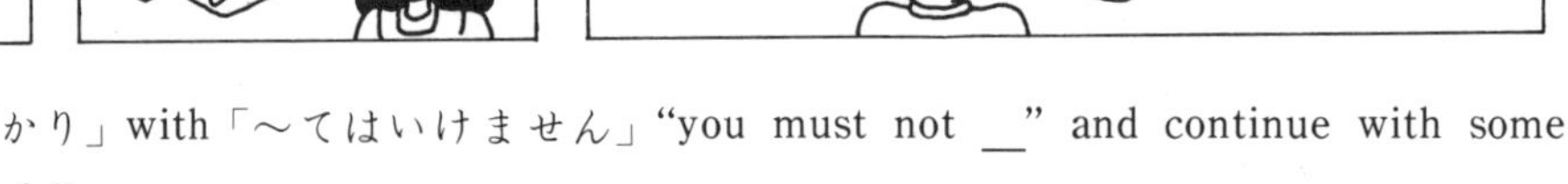

2) This time use「ばかり」with「〜てはいけません」"you must not __" and continue with some other suggestion as follows.

ex. ジャズを聞いている。　⇨ ジャズばかり聞いていてはいけません。

クラシックも聞いてください。

Exercise 2: Fill in the blanks with「だけ」or「ばかり」.

1) A：山田(やまだ)さん、きのうのお昼(ひる)は、何を食べました？

B：カレーライスです。いつも、お昼は、カレーにしてるんです。

A：えっ！カレー（①）食べてて、あきませんか。カレーといっしょに、何か、ほかの物(もの)も食べているんですか。

B：いいえ、カレー（②）ですよ。

A：それじゃ、からだによくないですね。サラダも食べたほうがいいですよ。

2) A：何人か、まだ会社に残(のこ)って、仕事(しごと)をしていますか。

B：いいえ、田中(たなか)さん（③）です。ほかの人たちは、もう帰(かえ)ったはずです。

A：田中さんは、いつも残業(ざんぎょう)（④）していますねえ。そんなに、いそがしいんでしょうか。

3) A：べっそうに行くんですって？　何をしてすごすんですか。
B：いや、ゆっくりねる（⑤）ですよ。ふだん、いそがしいものですから…。
A：でも、ねて（⑥）いるのは、もったいないですねえ。
何か、スポーツは、しないんですか。
B：そうですねえ。じゃ、ねて（⑦）いないで、テニスをしようかな。

Function II　"In spite of the fact that __"; 3丁目のはずなのに

Verb	plain (non-past／past)	＋　のに
い-adj.	plain (non-past／past)	
な-adj.	plain non-past（－な） plain past（－だった）	
Noun	Noun ＋な（だ→な） Noun ＋だった	

「のに」is used to complain, protest, lament or express surprise, disbelief, etc. that things are different than one normally would expect, and is equivalent to English "even though__" or "in spite of the fact that __", etc.

Note: Before「のに」use the be-verb form「な」instead of「だ」.

ex.1. かれは、来週、旅行に行くのに、まだ よういをしていません。
He hasn't made preparations yet in spite of the fact that he's going on a trip next week.

2. お金をはらったのに、しなものをくれません。
They won't give me the merchandise, even though I paid for it.

3. あの人は、わかいのに、いろいろなことを知っています。
Although he is young, that person knows many things.

4. 朝から寒かったのに、セーターを持って来ませんでした。
Even though it's been chilly all day, I didn't bring a sweater.

5. 花子さんは、絵がじょうずなのに、あまりかきません。
Hanako doesn't draw much, even though she is very good at drawing.

6. あの人は、学生なのに、ちっとも勉強をしません。
That person doesn't study at all, even though he's a student.

Note 1：「それなのに」"in spite of that" functions as a sentence connective.
ex. 来週、旅行に行きます。それなのに、まだよういをしていません。
He's going on a trip next week. In spite of that however, he hasn't made any preparations yet.

Note 2：「のに」is usually not followed by volitional expressions such as "let's __", "I will __", etc.
ex. ×　雨がふっているのに、テニスに行きましょう。
→○　雨がふっているけれど、テニスに行きましょう。

Vocabulary

カレーライス curried rice
のこる (u-vi) to remain, stay behind
すごす (u-vt) to spend time, live from day to day
もったいない wasteful, such a waste!
あきる (ru-vi) to get tired of
べっそう villa, country house
ふだん usually, always

Exercise 3: Indicate by letter an appropriate ending to each of the sentences below.

1) 春なのに、( )
2) ねだんが高いのに、( )
3) 手紙がとどいているはずなのに、( )
4) 病気なのに、( )
5) お花見に行ったのに、( )
6) 日曜日なのに、( )

a. 会社を休みません。
b. さくらの花は、もう、ちっていました。
c. あたたかくなりません。
d. おいしくありません。
e. 電車がこんでいます。
f. へんじが来ません。

Exercise 4: Construct a sentence using「のに」to explain the following pairs of pictures.

1) 2) 3) 4)

Function III **Describing appearances: "looks like, seems like"; まるで、つゆのようです。**

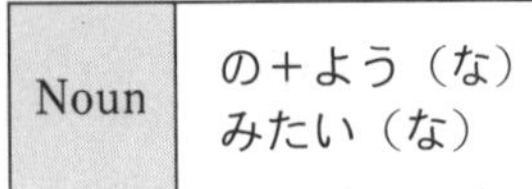

Noun	の＋よう（な） みたい（な）

The two な-adj. forms「よう(な)」and「みたい(な)」both mean "is like, similar to, same as", and may be used to describe how something appears, the manner in which it behaves, etc. by comparing it to some other noun.

ex.1. 毎日、雨がふって、まるでつゆのようです。(つゆみたい)
It's just like the rainy season, raining every day.

2. そばは、スパゲッティのような食べ物です。(スパゲッティみたいな)
"Soba" is a food like spaghetti.

3. まり子さんは、女なのに、男のように話します。(男みたいに)
Mariko speaks like a boy even though she's a girl.

4. くみ子さんの手は、雪のように白い。
Kumiko's hands are white like snow.

5. きのう会った人は、サンタクロースみたいな かおをしていました。
The person I met yesterday had a face like Santa Claus.

6. ウエッブさんは、カール・ルイスのように、速く走ります。
Mr. Webb runs fast like Carl Lewis.

Note 1:「よう(な)」can be used in any style of speech, while「みたい(な)」is more colloquial.
Note 2:「まるで」"completely" is optional, and serves to strengthen the comparison.

Exercise 5: Fill the blanks with suitable words from the list below.

1) 外は、とても寒かったから、手が（　）のようになりました。
2) 広くて、りっぱな　にわですね。（　）みたいですね。
3) ホワイトさん、日本語が、じょうずですね。まるで（　）のようです。
4) ぬいぐるみが、すきなんですか。まるで（　）みたい……。
5) 11月なのに、今日は、（　）のようにあたたかいです。
6) ぞうりは、（　）のような物です。着物を着たときに、はきます。
7) 小さい子どもが、8人もいます。まるで（　）みたいですね。
8) きゅうに、そらが、（　）のようにくらくなって、雨がふってきた。

〔子ども，　ようちえん，　こおり，　日本人，　春，　夜，　サンダル，　公園〕

Function IV　Conditional (2) "when, whenever"; 行くと

In addition to「〜たら」(Lesson 12, p.161) there is a second conditional form「と」, which is added after plain non-past verbals. Either「と」or「〜たら」may be used when speaking of actions, states, etc. that did or do come about when or whenever such and such conditions were or are met, with「と」sounding somewhat bookish.

ex.1. 朝、おきたら／おきると、雪がふっていました。
　When I got up in the morning it was snowing.
2. 家に　帰ったら／帰ると、小包がとどいていました。
　When I got home (I found) a parcel had arrived.
3. 秋になって、寒くなったら／寒くなると、コートを着ます。
　When autumn comes and it turns chill I wear a coat.

However if the relation expressed is inevitable (causal, etc.),「と」is preferred. Hence「と」is often used when stating instructions, natural laws, scientific principles, etc.

ex.4. あのかどを右にまがると、ガソリンスタンドがあります。
　When you turn right on that corner you will find a gas station.
5. 春になると、あたたかくなります。　When spring comes, it grows warm.
6. この白いボタンをおすと、きっぷが出てきます。
　When you push this white button a ticket comes out.

Note 1:「と」is never followed by commands, requests, suggestions, wishes.
ex. ×　雨がやむと、ハイキングに行きましょう。
→○　雨がやんだら、ハイキングに行きましょう。When the rain stops, let's go for a hike.

Note 2:「と」is also used in making suggestions or admonishments, however「といい」and「とだめ」sound less direct and more general than「〜たらいい」and「〜たらだめ」. (see Lesson 12, p.162)
ex. たばこをすったらだめですよ。　You mustn't smoke!
たばこをすうとだめですよ。　Smoking is no good.

Vocabulary

春（はる）spring
ぬいぐるみ stuffed toy animal
ようちえん kindergarten
ちる (u-vi) to fall (leaves), scatter
ぞうり Japanese sandals, thongs
サンダル sandals
へんじする answer, reply
そら sky

Exercise 6: Look at the pictures and complete the sentences.

1) このボタンを________と、________。
2) ここに立つと、ドアが________。
3) ここに____________________と、
電話ができます。
4) このキーを__________と、
字が、__________。
5) 50メートルぐらい行って、________と、
左(ひだり)がわに、病院(びょういん)が見えます。
6) 夏(なつ)になると、①__________。
② on your own。
7) 電車をおりると、田中(たなか)さんが
____________________。

Exercise 7: Draw lines connecting sentences in A with appropriate sentences in B, then combine the two into a single sentence using「〜たら」or「と」.

ex. 銀行に行ったら、もうしまっていました。／銀行に行くと、もうしまっていました。

A
ex. 銀行に行きました。
1) マイケルさんに電話しました。
2) げんかんのドアをあけました。
3) へやをかたづけました。
4) 夕方(ゆうがた)、魚屋(さかなや)へ行きました。
5) うちのそばまで来ました。
6) 山(やま)の上(うえ)まで、のぼりました。

B
・ピアノの音(おと)が聞(き)こえました。
・さんまを、安く売(う)っていました。
・るすでした。
・遠(とお)くの海(うみ)が見えました。
・もう、しまっていました。
・にもつを持(も)った男の人が、立(た)っていました。
・つくえの下に、1000円がおちていました。

Function V Giving directions how to get to somewhere

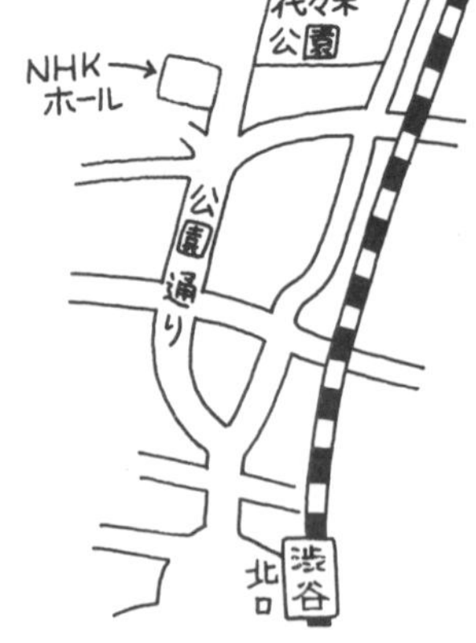

ex. A：ＮＨＫ(エヌエイチケー)ホールへは、どう行ったらいいですか。
How does one get to the NHK Hall?
B：渋谷駅(しぶやえき)で電車をおりて、北口(きたぐち)に出ます。そして、公園通(こうえんどお)りを代々木公園(よよぎこうえん)のほうへ、まっすぐ行くと、左(ひだり)がわに、ＮＨＫホールがあります。
Get off the train at Shibuya Station, and go out the north exit. Go straight along Kooen Doori in the direction of Yoyogi Park and the NHK Hall will be on the left.

Vocabulary

キー key
おりる (ru-vt) to get off, get down
テレホンカード telephone card
かたづける (ru-vt) to put __ in order, clear, put away
魚屋（さかなや）fish market
さんま Pacific saury
にもつ load, baggage

Useful expressions

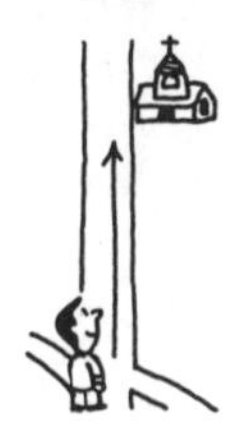

この道(みち)を
Follow this road

まっすぐ straight ahead
少(すこ)し a bit
2、3分 2 or 3 minutes
しばらく for a while
100メートルほど／ぐらい about 100 meters

行くと、教会(きょうかい)があります。
and you will come to a church.

Additional vocabulary

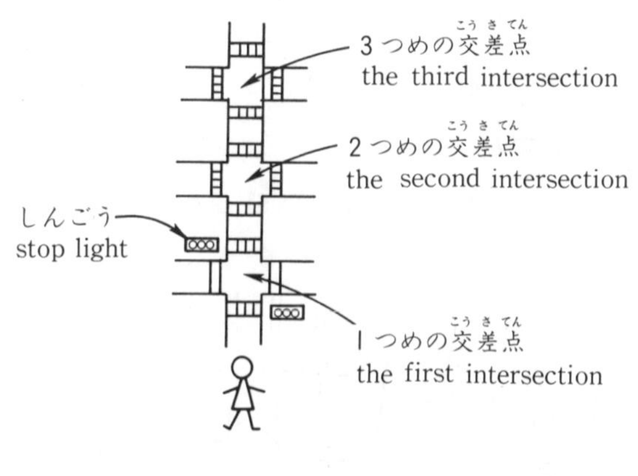

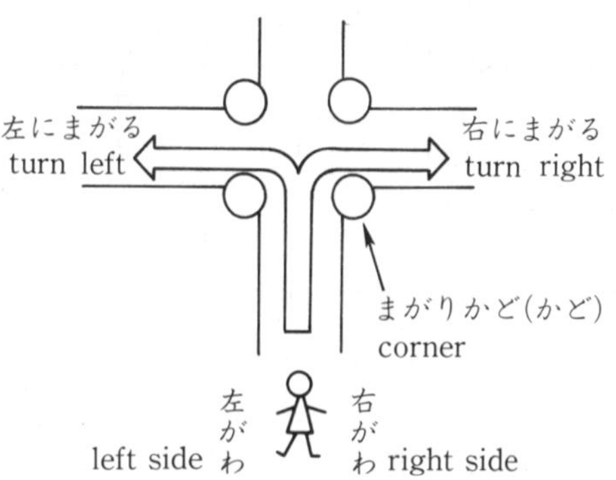

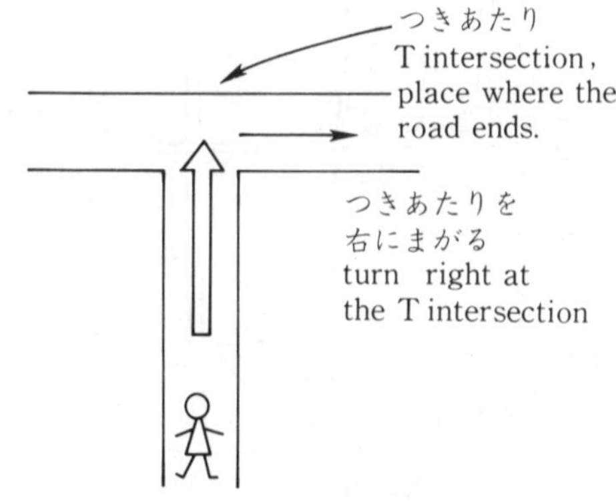

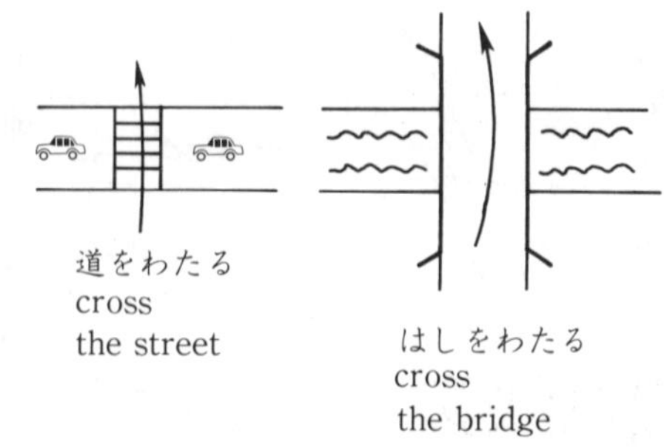

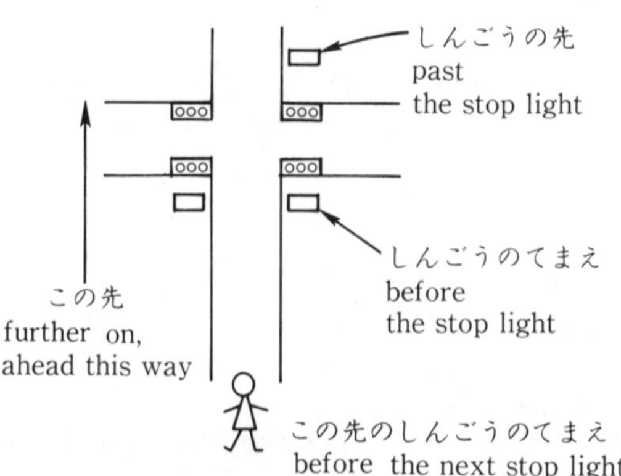

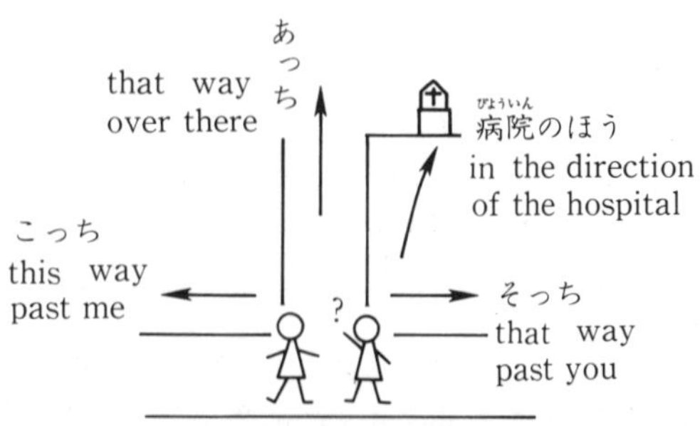

Exercise 8: Give directions for getting to the starred locations using the words in parentheses.

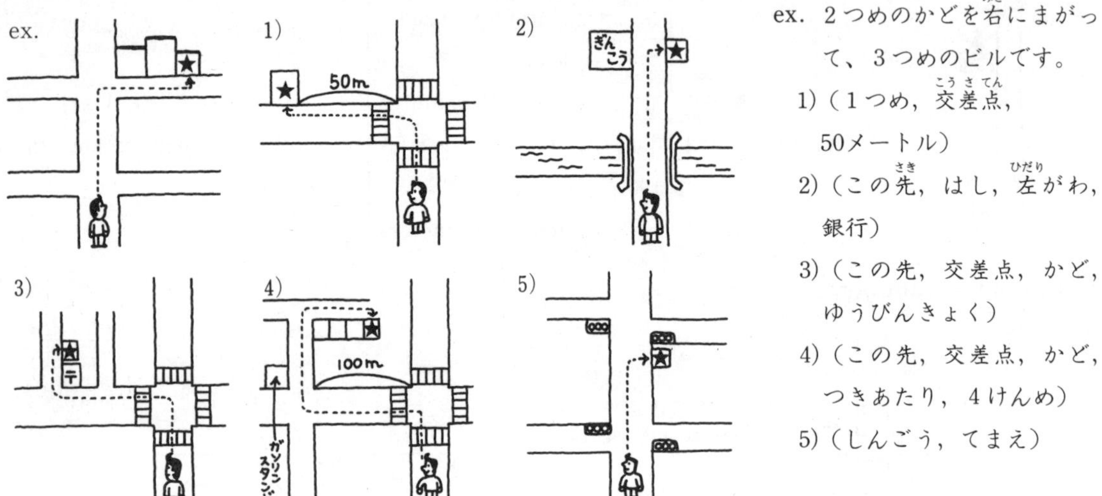

ex. 2つめのかどを右(みぎ)にまがって、3つめのビルです。

1)（1つめ，交差点(こうさてん)，50メートル）

2)（この先(さき)，はし，左(ひだり)がわ，銀行）

3)（この先，交差点，かど，ゆうびんきょく）

4)（この先，交差点，かど，つきあたり，4けんめ）

5)（しんごう，てまえ）

Exercise 9: You are walking around Ginza. At points A, B and C, different people ask you how to get to various places. Give directions.

1) at point A: すみません。「有楽町(ゆうらくちょう)マリオン」に行きたいんですが。 You : ＿＿＿＿＿＿。

2) at point B:

① あのう、「みつこしデパート」へは、どう行ったらいいですか。 You : ＿＿＿＿＿＿。

② この通(とお)りをわたって、5つめのかどを左ですね。それから、「わこう」へは、どう行ったらいいでしょうか。 You : ＿＿＿＿＿＿

3) at point C:

すきやきを食べたいんですが、「スエヒロ」へは、どう行ったらいいですか。 You : ＿＿＿＿＿＿

Vocabulary

スペース space
がめん screen, scene, view
倍角（ばいかく）double size font
数字（すうじ）number, numeral
もじ letter, character
ローマ字（ローマじ）Roman letters used to write Japanese
つぎに next, secondly
あみかけ "write" shading
アンダーライン underline
あみ shading (in printing)
りょうほう both

Reading Comprehension Exercise

The following is part of an operating manual for personal computer word processer software. Read and answer questions in the exercise that follows.

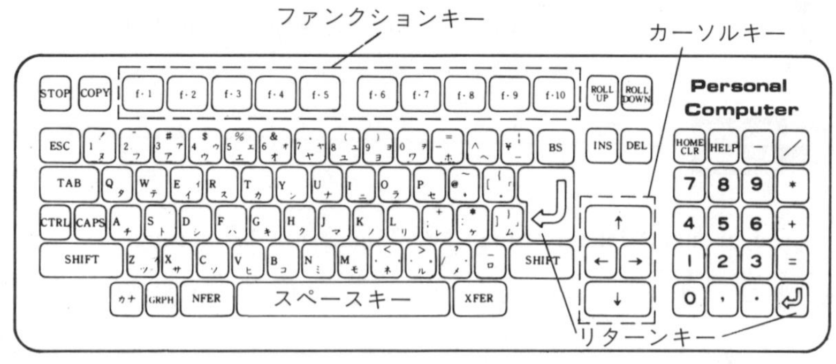

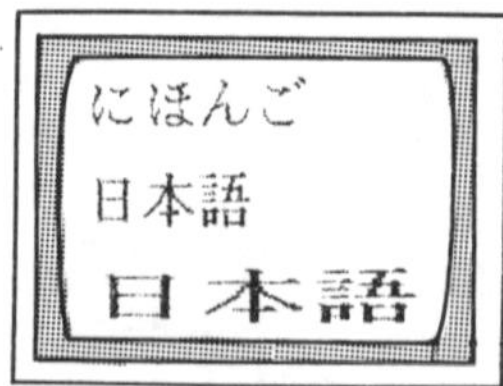

1. ローマ字で "nihongo" と入れると、がめんに、ひらがなが出ます。
2. つぎに、スペースキーをおすと、漢字になります。
3. Ｆ１キーをおすと、倍角(ばいかく)になります。
4. Ｆ２キーをおすと、"あみかけ"になります。
   "あみ"のしゅるいは、数字(すうじ)でえらびます。
   1—日本語　　2—日本語
5. Ｆ３キーをおすと、アンダーラインがつきます。
   アンダーラインのしゅるいは、数字でえらびます。
   1—日本語　　2—日本語

〔ちゅうい〕倍角と"あみかけ"のりょうほうをするときは、Ｆ１キーをおして、倍角にしてから、Ｆ２キーをおしてください。

〔ちゅうい〕倍角とアンダーラインのりょうほうをするときは、Ｆ１キーで倍角にしてから、Ｆ２キーをおしてください。

Exercise 10:

1) When the input appears on the screen, which configuration is produced by pushing the keys in the following sequence?
   Input：わたしの家族
   key：Ｆ１＋Ｆ２＋２

   ① わたしの家族　　② わたしの家族　　③ わたしの家族

2) The following input appears on the screen. What sequence of keys produces this configuration?

   わたしは、ウエップです。

   もじ：わたしは、ウエップです。
   キー：＿＿＿＋＿＿＿＋＿＿＿

Listening Comprehension Exercise

Referring to the map in Exercise 9, listen to the directions given and choose which location the person is heading for.

1) from point A（a．ソニービル　b．はんきゅうデパート　c．プランタン銀座(ぎんざ)デパート）
2) from point B（a．銀座とうきゅうホテル　b．銀座コア　c．わこう）
3) from point E（a．まつやデパート　b．さんわ銀行　c．すみとも銀行）

第16課 北村は、今、席をはずしております

Kitamura Is Not In At The Moment

Dialogue I

Miss Kuroda answers the phone. Michael thinks her Japanese a bit strange.

黒田　：はい、営業第１課でございます。はい、もうしわけございませんが、北村は、今、席をはずしております。はい、四谷商事の山下様ですね。はい、もどりましたら、こちらから、お電話をさしあげます。はい、しつれい いたしました。

マイケル：あのう、黒田さん、いま、課長さんを「北村」って言ったでしょう？どうして、「北村さん」って言わないんですか。ちょっと、教えてくれませんか。

黒田　：外の人に言うときには、自分の会社の人たちには「さん」をつけないのよ。

マイケル：でも、ふつうは、「黒田さん、お電話です」って言うでしょう？

黒田　：そうね、どうせつめいしたらいいか、ちょっとむずかしいんだけど…、会社の中にも、「内」と「外」があって…。

マイケル：うーん、どうもわからないな。そういうことを、どこかで教えてくれないかなあ。

黒田　：わたしも教えてあげるけど、東京には、日本語学校がたくさんあるから、仕事のあとで、かよってみたら？

Dialogue II

Miss Kuroda interrupts the conversation between Mr. Kitamura and Michael.

北村　：ウエッブ君、れいの件だけど、もうレポートをまとめてくれた？

マイケル：それが…　まだ…。

北村（きたむら）　：じゃ、野村君（のむらくん）にてつだってもらって、いそいでまとめてください。あしたの会議（かいぎ）で発表（はっぴょう）することになっているから、今日中（きょうじゅう）に、しあげてくれますか。

マイケル：はい、そうします。どうもすみません、おそくなって…。

黒田（くろだ）　：お話（はな）し中（ちゅう）、すみません。あの、課長（かちょう）、お客様（きゃくさま）がいらっしゃいました。

北村　：どなた？

黒田　：さきほど、お電話があった、四谷商事（よつやしょうじ）の山下（やました）さんです。

北村　：あ、そうだ、そうだ。で、どこに？

黒田　：あちらの応接室（おうせつしつ）にいらっしゃいます。

北村　：ん、すぐ行く。で、もうお茶、出（だ）してくれた？あっ、それから、ミーティング中（ちゅう）でも、住友商事（すみともしょうじ）の木村（きむら）さんから電話があったら、つないでくれる？　たいせつな用件（ようけん）があるんだ。

黒田　：はい、わかりました。

Dialogue III

At the Japanese language school

マイケル：あのう、すみませんが。

事務員（じむいん）　：はい、何でしょうか。

マイケル：日本語の会話（かいわ）のクラスについて、教（おし）えてもらいたいんですが。

事務員　：はい。えーと、プライベートのクラスと、グループのクラスがありますけど。

マイケル：そうですか。グループのクラスは、何人ですか。

事務員　：クラスによってちがいますが、だいたい10人ぐらいです。曜日（ようび）や、授業料（じゅぎょうりょう）については、こちらのパンフレットに書いてあります。

マイケル：（パンフレットを読みながら）なるほど。じゃあ、うちに帰（かえ）って、かんがえてみます。きまったら、もう一度（いちど）、来ます。

事務員　：はい。お待（ま）ちしています。

Vocabulary

Nouns:

1営業（えいぎょう） business, sales
1第1課（だいいっか） section one
2商事（しょうじ） commercial matters, commercial company
8自分（じぶん） oneself
13内（うち） inside, interior
3こちら this, this here, this way, here, oneself
16日本語学校（にほんごがっこう） Japanese language school
18れい example; れいの the thing in question
18件（けん） affair, subject, case
18レポートする report
21発表（はっぴょう）する announcement, presentation
30あちら that, that over there, that way, there, that person
30応接室（おうせつしつ） reception room
32ミーティング meeting
33用件（ようけん） business, matter or concern to be discussed
36事務員（じむいん） clerk, office worker
37会話（かいわ） conversation
38グループ group
42授業料（じゅぎょうりょう） tuition, school fee
42パンフレット pamphlet, brochure

Adjectives:

33たいせつ(な) important, precious, valuable
38プライベート(な) private

Adverbs:

14どうも by any means, however hard one may try
28さきほど a little while ago, earlier
41だいたい generally, on the whole

Verbs:

4いたします polite form of u-vt「いたす」, humble verb meaning「する」"to do"
7教える(おしえる) (ru-vt) to teach, show how, inform
17かよう (u-vi) to commute, go back and forth between two points
18まとめる (ru-vt) to bundle together, put in order
22しあげる (ru-vt) to finish, complete
33つなぐ (u-vt) to tie together, connect
44かんがえる (ru-vt) to think, consider
44きまる (u-vi) to be decided, settled, arranged

Grammatical words:

2～様（さま） Mr., Mrs., Miss, Ms.; honorific suffix added to names, occupations, etc.
5～って variant pronunciation of quotation marker「と」
7(verb て-form) ＋くれる do such and such (for me) ☞Function Ⅲ
16(verb て-form) ＋あげる do such and such for you ☞Function Ⅲ
20(verb て-form) ＋もらう have someone do such and such (for me) ☞Function Ⅲ

Expressions:

1もうしわけございません I'm terribly sorry.
2席(せき)をはずす to be out, to be not in his place
2～ております humble progressive form, means the same as「～ています」
15そういうこと that sort of thing
12そうね Perhaps. That's right. I'll think about it.
15～てくれないかなあ I wonder if you won't do such and such for me
18れいの件(けん) the matter you're working on, the business in question, the thing we've talked about before, etc.
29で shortened form of「それで」
31ん shortened form of「うん」Uh huh. OK.
33電話をつなぐ to put through a call
37について about, regarding, pertaining to, in regard to
41によって according to, depending on
45お待ちしています We'll be waiting for you. We'll be expecting you.

Dialogue Comprehension Exercise

Answer the following questions.

Dialogue Ⅰ:

1) 黒田(くろだ)さんは、電話で、だれと話(はな)しましたか。
2) 電話がかかってきたとき、北村(きたむら)さんは、いましたか。

3) 黒田さんは、電話で、北村課長(かちょう)のことを、なんと言いましたか。それは、どうしてですか。

4) 黒田さんは、マイケルさんに、どうしたらいいと言いましたか。

Dialogue Ⅱ:

5) 北村さんは、マイケルさんに、何をたのみましたか。

6) 会社に来たのは、だれですか。また、その人は、いま、どこにいますか。

Dialogue Ⅲ:

7) この日本語学校(がっこう)の、グループのクラスの人数(にんずう)は、だいたい何人ですか。

8) パンフレットには、どんなことが書いてありますか。

9) マイケルさんは、日本語学校に入(はい)ることにしましたか。

◆Vocabulary◆　人数（にんずう）the number of persons

Dialogues in English

Dialogue Ⅰ

Ku: Hello, Sales, Section one. Yes, I'm very sorry but Kitamura is not in at the moment. I see, that's Mr. Yamashita of Yotsuya Shoji, correct? Right. He'll call you when he gets back. Fine. Goodbye.

M: Uh, Miss Kuroda. I believe you just spoke of the section manager as "Kitamura". Why don't you call him "Kitamura-san"? Could you explain to me?

Ku: When speaking to outside persons, you don't add "san" to the names of person's within your own company.

M: Yes, but normally I'd say "Kuroda-san, telephone!", right?

Ku: That's true. How to explain? It's a bit difficult. But there's an "inside" and an "outside" within the company as well.

M: Hmm. I'm missing something I'm afraid. Isn't there some place where they teach such things?

Ku: I will teach you myself, but in Tokyo there are many Japanese language schools, so why don't you try attending one after work?

Dialogue Ⅱ

Ki: Michael, about that matter I asked you to take care of. Have you put together a report for me yet?

M: Uh, not yet.

Ki: In that case, have Nomura help you and get it together right away. I want you to finish it for me sometime today no matter what, because I'm supposed to present it at the meeting tomorrow.

M: Alright. I'll do it. I'm sorry to have taken so long.

Ku: Sorry to interrupt your conversation. Uh, you have a visitor, Mr. Kitamura.

Ki: Who?

Ku: Mr. Yamashita of Yotsuya Shoji, who called just a while ago.

Ki: Oh, yeah, that's right! And where is he?

Ku: He's in the meeting room over there.

Ki: OK. I'll be there shortly. And, uh, have you served him tea yet? Oh yes, and another thing. If there's a call from Kimura of Sumitomo Shoji, put him through, will you, even if I'm in conference? There's an important matter I want to discuss.

Ku: Yes. I understand.

Dialogue Ⅲ

M: Uh, excuse me please.

Cl: Yes. May I help you?

M: I'd like some information about Japanese language classes.

Cl: Certainly. Well, we have private classes and group classes.

M: I see. How many persons in group classes?

Cl: It differs with each class, but generally about ten persons. This pamphlet contains information regarding days and tuition.

M: (reading the pamphlet) Yes, I see. Well then, I'll go home and think about it, and come again when I've decided.

Cl: Good. We'll be expecting you.

Note on the Dialogue: Respectful speech

Oftentimes it is proper to indicate a certain amount of respect in your speech. This is done by using humble terms when speaking of yourself, and honorific terms when speaking of or addressing others. Some commonly used humble and honorific terms are listed below.

Humble	Neutral	Honorific	English equivalent
	名前	お名前	(honorific prefix) name
	しんぱい	ごしんぱい	(honorific prefix) worry
すし屋	すし屋	おすし屋さん	(honorific suffix) Mr., Mrs., Miss
部長	部長	部長さん	
だれ	だれ	どなた，どちらさま	who
家内	つま	おくさん，おくさま	wife
会社のもの	会社の人	会社の方	person from some company
父，父親	父，父親	お父さん／お父さま	father (see L.9, Family members)
おります	います（いる）	いらっしゃいます	to be, exist (animate)
まいります	来ます（来る）	いらっしゃいます	to go
まいります	行きます（行く）	いらっしゃいます	to come

No hard and fast rule can be given as to when humble and honorific terms should be used in place of neutral. It depends on how one views the situation and the nature of the person being spoken to. Women tend to use respectful speech more often. Also note that when speaking to a "respected outsider", "oneself" is extended to include members of one's family, employees of the same company, members of the same group, etc.

Function I　Interrupting, getting someone's attention; お話し中、すみませんが

Several expressions might be used to get someone's attention. Since the speaker is in a sense intruding upon that person, such expressions tend to be apologetic. Expression (1) is often used to introduce the other expressions, or any of the expressions might be used alone.

(1)あの…	(2)すみませんが	Pardon me, but ...
	(3)しつれいですが	Excuse my impoliteness, but ...
	(4)もうしわけありませんが	There is no way I can apologize, but ...
	(5)おそれいりますが	I'm terribly sorry, but ...
	(6)お仕事中、もうしわけありませんが I can't begin to apologize for interrupting your work, but ...	
	(7)お仕事中、まことに、もうしわけありませんが There is really and truly no way I can begin to apologize for interrupting your work, but ...	

Exercise 1: Practice getting a person's attention and responding in each of the situations below. Continue the conversation in an appropriate manner.

1) time of the next bus?

2) a woman dropped her purse.

3) the way to the station?

4) small change please.

5) this coming Sunday is what date?

6) how to buy a ticket?

〈**hints**〉 つぎの，　おとす，　おちる，　お金を小さくする，　こんどの，さいふ　purse

Function II　Making suggestions and giving advice;　仕事(しごと)のあとで、かよってみたら？

1	**Verb past tense**	+	ほうがいい	"it would be better to __"
2	**Conditional「たら」**	+	どう	"how about if you do __"
3	**Conditional「たら／と」**	+	いい	"it would be good if you did __"

The above constructions are commonly used when making suggestions. Note the progression in degree of forcefulness in the example sentences.

ex. 1. 部長(ぶちょう)に、そうだんしてみたら、いかがでしょうか。

How about if you tried discussing it with the division manager?

2. 部長に、そうだんしてみたら、どうですか。

Why don't you try discussing it with the division manager?

3. 部長に、そうだんしてみたら、いいですよ。／　部長に、そうだんすると、いいですよ。

You ought to try discussing it with the division manager.

4. 部長に、そうだんしたほうが、いいんじゃないんですか。

Wouldn't it be better if you tried discussing it with the division manager?

5. 部長に、そうだんしたほうが、いいと思いますよ。

I believe you should try discussing it with the division manager.

Note 1: In familiar speech「たら」is often left dangling (i.e. rising intonation) to give the equivalent of "why don't you __?".

ex. A: この書類(しょるい)、どうしたらいいかしら。　Whatever should I do about these papers?

B: そうね。部長に、そうだんしてみたら？

That's a good question. Why don't you try discussing it with the division manager?

B: そうね。部長に、そうだんしてみたら、どう？

That's a good question. How about if you try discussing it with the division manager?

The most common way to suggest that someone not do something is to follow the negative form of the verb with「ほうが いい」.

ex. 1. からだにわるいから、たばこをすわないほうが、いいですよ。

You ought not to smoke because it's bad for your health.

2. 夜おそくまで、おきていないほうが、いいと思うよ。

I think it would be better if you didn't stay awake until so late at night.

Exercise 2: Suggest doing, or not doing, the following actions.

ex. このアイロンを買う。→ このアイロンを買ったらどう（ですか）。
このアイロンを買ったほうが、いいですよ。
このアイロンを買わないほうが、いいですよ。

1) 先に、会社に帰る。　2) 山田さんに、この仕事をたのむ。　3) あの本を読む。
4) けいやくをキャンセルする。　5) マイケルさんに、会いに行く。　6) ホテルを予約しておく。

Exercise 3: Choose a suggestion appropriate to each of the following.

1) 山川貿易の電話番号が、わからないんですが。（ ）
2) 京都について、知りたいんですが。（ ）
3) あれ！　道がわからなくなりましたよ。（ ）
4) 日本の「すし」は、おいしいですか。（ ）
5) 今日はいそがしくて、この仕事は、とてもできません。（ ）
6) あしたは、雨がふるそうですよ。（ ）

＊104　number to call for telephone directory assistance

a. ええ、おいしいですよ。一度、食べてみたら、どうですか。
b. じゃあ、あした、することにしたら？
c. 104で聞いてみたら、いいですよ。
d. じゃ、あしたは、海に行かないほうが、いいんじゃない？
e. あの店で聞いてみたら、どうですか。
f. としょかんで、しらべたら、いいですよ。

Function III　Giving and receiving (2): giving and receiving actions

Words denoting the giving and receiving of things were explained in Lesson 9 (p.129). These same words can be used to denote the giving and receiving of actions by simply putting the action to be given or received in the て-form.

1. Doing for someone.　**2. Someone does for me.**　**3. Receiving an action from someone or having someone do some action.**

ex. 1. 社長のにもつを、持ってさしあげました。　I carried the boss's baggage for him.

2. 社長が、ほめてくださった。　The boss praised me.

3. 社長に、ほめていただきました。　I received praise from the boss.

4. 花田さんが、黒田さんに、サンドイッチを買って来てあげました。

Miss Hanada bought some sandwiches for Miss Kuroda.

5. 父が、わたしに、セーターを買ってくれました。　My father bought me a sweater.

6. 妹は、父に、セーターを買ってもらいます。

My younger sister is going to have father buy her a sweater.

7. お母さんが、子どもに、クッキーを作ってあげる。

Mother is going to make some cookies for her children.

8. 犬を、さんぽに、つれて行ってやる。　I'll take the dog for a walk.

Note: The polite request form「〜てください」is simply imperative form of「〜てくださる」. The imperative form of「〜てくれる」may also be used to make request.

ex.1. ちょっと、そこの本を、とってください。　Will you give me that book please?

2. ちょっと、そこの本を、とってくれ。　Hey, give me that book please!

Exercise 4: Substitute the underlined portions in the following dialogues with the words and phrases given below. Use appropriate forms to fill blanks (a), (b), (c) in each dialogue.

1)　黒田：ウエッブさん、(a) すてきなセーターですね。

マイケル：ありがとうございます。(b) 家内があんでくれたんですよ。　（家内が、あむ）

黒田：あら、いい (c) おくさんですね。　（家内→おくさん）

① a. いいかばん　b. アメリカの母が送る

② a. しゃれたネクタイ　b. 妹がプレゼントする

2)　土田：ウエッブさん、(a) とけいは、みつかりましたか。　（とけいが、みつかる）

マイケル：ええ、(b) 黒田さんがみつけてくれました。　（黒田さんが、みつける）

土田：それは、よかったですね。

Caution: みつかる (u-vi) to be found;　みつける (ru-vt) to look for, to find

① a. 新幹線に、まにあう　b. 友達が、車で送る

② a. 駅までの道が、わかる　b. おまわりさんが、教える

③ a. 仕事が、終わる　b. 田辺さんが、てつだう

3)　田辺：ウエッブさん、(a) このあいだのレポートは、どうなりましたか。

マイケル：ええ、(b) 部長に見ていただきました。　（部長が、見る）

田辺：ああ、そうですか。

① a. れいの書類　b. 部長が、サインをする

② a. 来週のきゅうか　b. 課長が、きょかする

③ a. このあいだの企画　b. 社長が、ほめる

Vocabulary

けいやくする contract (to sign a contract)
〜について about, concerning
まにあう to be in time
きゅうか vacation
おまわりさん policeman
きょかする permission
キャンセルする cancellation
あむ (u-vt) to knit
サインする signature (to sign)
企画（きかく）plan

4)　黒田(くろだ)：バーバラさん、元気(げんき)になってよかったですね。病気(びょうき)のとき、ご主人(しゅじん)は、何かしてくれましたか。

バーバラ：ええ、(a) そうじをしてくれました。　(そうじをする)

マイケル：それに、(b) せんたくもしてあげたよ。(せんたくをする)

① a. 買(か)い物(もの)をして来る　　b. 食事(しょくじ)を作(つく)る

② a. お医者(いしゃ)さんに電話をする　　b. くすりをもらって来る

③ a. こおりで、あたまをひやす　　b. ねつをはかる

5)　部長：北村課長(きたむらかちょう)は、書類(しょるい)をチェックしてくれましたか。

マイケル：はい、(a) サインもしてくださいました。　(サインをする)

①　漢字のまちがいをなおす

②　書類の書(か)き方(かた)を教(おし)える

Exercise 5: Compose statements appropriate to the situations pictured below. The first picture requires a request, the second picture requires a description of the resultant action. In both instances use expressions of giving and receiving.

1) 北村さん ↔ 北村さんのむすこ (太郎(たろう))

2) 太郎 ↔ 犬(いぬ)

太郎：お父さん、__________。

北村：むすこに________。

太郎：父(ちち)に________。

犬：太郎さん、__________。

太郎：犬を________。

犬：太郎さんに________。

3) 部長 ↔ 課長

課長：部長、でんぴょうに、__________。

部長：__________。

課長：部長に__________。

4) マイケル ↔ 花田(はなだ)

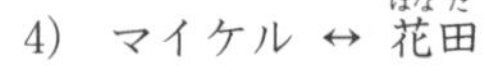

マイケル：花田さん、__________。

花田：ウエッブさんに__________。

マイケル：花田さんに__________。

Exercise 6: Complete the paragraph below telling who did what.

7月10日は、ぼくのたんじょう日(び)でした。たんじょう日には、みんなが、いろいろなプレゼントをしてくれました。

父は、______________。

母(はは)は、______________。

妹(いもうと)は、______________。

ガールフレンドは、______________。

Reading Comprehension Exercise

会議が終わって、席にもどると、つぎのようなメモが、おいてありました。

れんらくメモ

北村　様　6月　10日4:30AM (PM)

FROM四谷商事 山下様

※TEL有（もう一度TELします・TELください）

※その他

用件・商品カタログの件で，そうだんしたいとのこと。
・あす、午前中にTELしてください。
黒田(受)

◆**Vocabulary**◆

れんらくする contact, a communication
TEL 有（テルあり） there was a phone call
来訪（らいほう）する visit
その他（そのた） other
用件（ようけん） business, reason for phoning, etc.
商品（しょうひん）カタログ catalogue of merchandise
〜とのこと functions as direct quotation, "what the person said"
黒田受（くろだ　うけ） received by Kuroda

Note: In passing on information regarding official matters, such expressions as「〜ということです」and「〜とのこと（です）」are commonly used.

Exercise 7: What information is contained in the above memo? Indicate whether the following statements are T or F.

1. (　) 四谷商事の山下さんから、北村課長に電話がありました。
2. (　) 6月10日、午後4時半ごろ、北村課長が、四谷商事の山下さんに、会いに行きました。
3. (　) 四谷商事の山下さんが、6月10日午後4時半ごろ、北村課長に、会いに来ました。
4. (　) 四谷商事の山下さんは、商品カタログのことについて、北村課長と、そうだんしたいと思っています。
5. (　) 四谷商事の山下さんは、あしたの午後、北村課長に電話をするつもりです。
6. (　) 四谷商事の山下さんは、北村課長からの電話を、あしたの午前中、待っています。
7. (　) 四谷商事の山下さんからの電話をうけたのは、黒田さんです。

Listening Comprehension Exercise

Listen to the dialogue on the tape and choose the correct answer from the list below.

1) 佐藤さんがたずねて来たのは、
(北村　黒田　ウエッブ) さんに会うためです。
2) 佐藤さんが待っていたのは、
(A　B　C　D) の場所です。
3) 佐藤さんは、だいたい
(5分　15分　25分　35分) 待ちます。

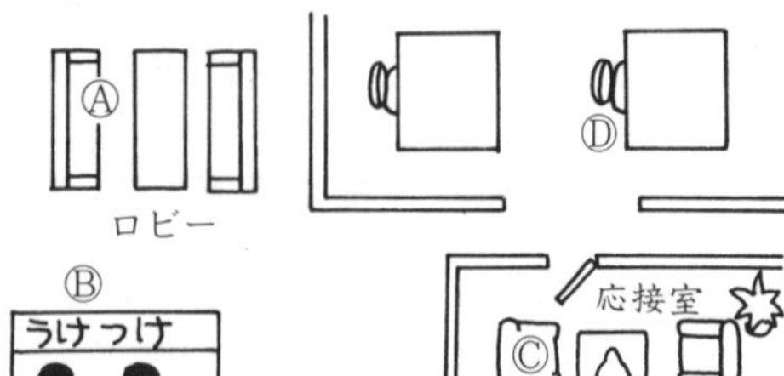

Vocabulary

ひやす (u-vt) to cool, chill
はかる (u-vt) to weigh, measure
書き方（かきかた） how to write, manner of writing
ガールフレンド girl friend
チェックする check
ねつ temperature
レジ register, check-out counter
まちがい mistake
ねつをはかる to take one's temperature
でんぴょう slip, chit
うける (ru-vt) to receive

第17課

大阪へ行ってほしいんだけど…

I'd Like You To Go To Osaka

Dialogue Ⅰ

At the office. Section manager, Kitamura, orders Michael to go to Osaka on business.

北村　：ウエッブ君、ちょっと。

マイケル：はい。

北村　：あのね、来週の金曜日に、大阪に行ってほしいんだけど。

マイケル：え、大阪ですか。

北村　：うん。大阪の、うちの子会社を知っているね。

マイケル：はい。第一貿易という会社ですね。

北村　：そう。そこの会議に出席してほしいんだ。

マイケル：はあ。何の会議でしょうか。

北村　：れいの、アメリカへ支社を出す件についての会議なんだ。

マイケル：はい、わかりました。何か、書類を持って行きますか。

北村　：いや、ファクシミリで送ったからいいよ。

マイケル：その日のうちに帰らなくてもいいですか。

北村　：うん、いいよ。ちょうど金曜日だから、土・日にかけて、京都と奈良でも見物して来たらいいよ。報告は、ファクシミリで送っておいて。

マイケル：あのう、家内をつれて行ってもいいですか。

北村　：もちろん。でも、おくさんの費用は、自分で、はらってくださいよ。

マイケル：わかりました。家内もわたしも、まだ日本国内を旅行していないので、ぜひ、いっしょに行きたいです。

Dialogue II

At the office

マイケル：あのう、課長、出張の計画書を見ていただきたいんですが。

北村：あ、わるいけど、客が来たので、あとにしてもらいたいんだ。

マイケル：はい。じゃ、またあとで来ます。

黒田：あのう、ウエッブさん、京都に行くんですって。

マイケル：ええ、大阪の出張の帰りに、よるつもりなんです。

黒田：ちょっと、おねがいしてもいいかしら。

マイケル：ええ、何ですか。

黒田：京都の「やつはし」というおかしを買って来てもらいたいの。うちの母がだいすきなのよ。

マイケル：ああ、いいですよ。

北村：ああ、ウエッブ君。さっきの、出張の計画書の件だけど、手があいたから、持って来て。今、見てしまうから。

マイケル：はい。

Vocabulary

Nouns:

5子会社（こがいしゃ）subsidiary company
15土・日（どにち）Saturday and Sunday
16見物（けんぶつ）する sightseeing
22出張（しゅっちょう）する business trip
22計画書（けいかくしょ）proposal, plan of action, itinerary
7出席（しゅっせき）する attendance
19費用（ひよう）expense
20国内（こくない）domestic, within the country

Adverbs:

32さっきの the aforementioned

Verbs:

26よる (u-vi) to drop in, stop by

Grammatical words:

16でも postposition meaning "at least", "something such as" or "something similar" ☞Function III

Expressions:

3あのね uh, well, excuse me
6第一貿易という会社 a company called "Daiichi Booeki" ☞Function II
8はあ what? ah, yes
14その日のうちに within that day, the same day
14〜てもいい alright even if one does ☞Function IV
15土・日にかけて take Saturday and Sunday, spend Saturday and Sunday
23あとにする I'll do it (take care of it, etc.) later.
33手があく to have time, be free

Dialogue Comprehension Exercise

1) Read Dialogue I and answer the following.

① 北村課長は、マイケルさんに、どこに行ってほしいと言っていますか。

② 会議は、どこでしますか。

③ マイケルさんは、何の会議に出ますか。

④ マイケルさんは、何か、書類を持って行きますか。

⑤ マイケルさんは、出張に、1人で行きますか。

2) Read Dialogue II and mark the following statements T or F.

①（　）マイケルさんは、出張の計画書を書きました。

②（　）北村課長は、今、いそがしいので、あとで、マイケルさんのところへ行きます。

③（　）北村課長は、お客さんに、わるいことをしました。

④（　）マイケルさんは、黒田さんに、大阪のおかしを買って帰ることになりました。

⑤（　）黒田さんは、「やつはし」が、だいすきです。

Function I　Asking someone to do something (2); 大阪へ行ってほしい

1 The following three expressions may also be used when asking someone to do something for you.

(person に)	Verb て-form +	ほしい もらいたい いただきたい

When the person you are asking the favor of is included in the sentence, mark with the particle「に」.

〈Between equals〉

ex.1. A：あの、ちょっと、テーブルの上の塩を、取ってほしいんだけど。

Uh, excuse me, but I want you to pass the salt that's on the table.

B：(man) ああ、いいよ。Sure thing! ／ (woman) ええ、いいわよ。Yes, of course.

B：ごめん。今、ちょっと…。

I'm sorry, but I'm unable to do at the moment.

ex.2. A：すみません。この荷物を、はこんでもらいたいんですけど。

Excuse me, but I'd like to have you carry these bags.

B：はい。／ええ、いいですよ。　Alright.／ Sure thing.

〈Superior to inferior〉

ex. 3. A：山田君、ちょっと、会議室に来てほしいんだけど。

Yamada, I'd like you to come to the conference room a moment.

B：はい、わかりました。／ はい、かしこまりました。(politer)

Yes, of course. ／ Yes, whatever you say.

B：もうしわけありませんが…。／もうしわけございませんが…。(politer)

I'm terribly sorry, but ...

〈Inferior to superior〉

ex. 4. A：部長、この書類に、サインをしていただきたいんですが。

Mr. Division Manager, I'd like to have you sign these papers for me please.

B：はい。／ああ、いいよ。／はい、いいですよ。 Sure. Alright.

B：わるいけど、今、ちょっと…。 Sorry, I'm busy at the moment.

[2] When you want someone not to do something;

(person に)	**negative て-form** (～ないで) + ほしい / もらいたい / いただきたい **"I want you not to do that."**
	Verb て-form + ほしくない / もらいたくない / いただきたくない **"I don't want you to do that."**

Dialogues in English

Dialogue Ⅰ

Ki : Just a moment, Michael!

M : Yes?

Ki : Uh, I'd like you to go to Osaka on Friday of next week.

M : What? Osaka?

Ki : Yes. You're acquainted with our subsidiary in Osaka, right?

M : Yes. A company called Daiichi Booeki.

Ki : That's right. I want you to attend a meeting there.

M : I see. What sort of meeting, I wonder?

Ki : It's a meeting about, you know, our proposal to expand to the U. S.

M : I understand. Do I take some documents or something?

Ki : No, that's alright. I sent them by FAX.

M : Is it alright if I don't return the same day?

Ki : Sure, that's alright. It just so happens the meeting is on Friday, so you ought to spend Saturday and Sunday looking around Kyoto and Nara at least. Send me a report of the meeting by FAX first.

M : Uh, would it be okay if I took my wife along?

Ki : Of course! But please pay for her expenses yourself, however.

M : I understand. Neither my wife nor I have traveled around Japan yet, so I'd like to take her with me by all means.

Dialogue Ⅱ

M : Mr. Section Manager, uh, I'd like to have you look at my itinerary for the business trip.

Ki : Ah, I'm sorry, but I have a visitor. So I want you to talk to me later.

M : OK. I'll come again later then.

Ku : Oh, Mr. Webb! I hear you're going to Kyoto?

M : That's right. We plan to stop there on the way back from the business trip to Osaka.

Ku : Would it be alright to ask a little favor, I wonder?

M : Sure. What is it?

Ku : I'd like to have you bring me back some sweets from Kyoto called "Yatsuhashi". My mother just loves them.

M : Sure. That would be fine.

Ki : Oh, Michael. About the itinerary you mentioned earlier for the business trip. I'm free now, so bring it to me. I'll finish looking at it now.

M : Alright.

ex.5. 母が病気でねているので、大きい音を出さないでほしいんですが。

My mother's sick in bed, so I'd, uh, like you not to make any loud noises.

6. 人のわるくちは、言ってもらいたくないですね。

I don't want you to speak ill of others!

Note:「～んだけど」or「～んですけど」, etc. may be added at the end to soften the impact of such expressions.

Exercise 1: The following is a new employee complaining about his boss. Pretend you are the boss and tell the employee what you want him to do or not do.

うちの課長、ちこくをすると、すごくうるさいんです。たった1分おくれただけで、15分ぐらい、もんくを言うんですよ。それだけじゃなくて、えんぴつを使いすぎないで、紙をたいせつにして、もっと残業をして、字をきれいに書いてとか、もう、いやになるくらいなんです。

毎日、くたくたにつかれて、週末は、ねるだけなんですよ。だから、ガールフレンドと、デートをする時間もなくて…。

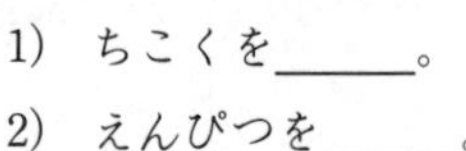

1) ちこくを＿＿＿。
2) えんぴつを＿＿＿。
3) 紙を＿＿＿＿＿＿。
4) もっと残業を＿＿＿。
5) 字を＿＿＿＿。

Exercise 2: Choose the more appropriate of the phrases in the brackets to complete the sentences below.

1) To someone you don't know in the park.

A：すみません、カメラのシャッターを、おして {ほしいんだけど　いただきたいんですが}。

B：ええ、いいですよ。

2) Division manager to subordinate

A：うちあわせをしたいので、あす、8時半までに、会社に来て {ほしいんだけど　いただきたいんですが}。

B：すみません。あしたは、9時に、山川貿易で、月野さんに会うことになっていますので…。

3) Between fellow workers at lunch time.

A：黒田さん、ぼくにもハンバーガーを買って来て {ほしいんだけど　いただきたいんですけど}。

B：ええ、いいですよ。野村さんもいかが？

C：そうだな。ぼくにも {買って来てよ　買って来ていただきたいな}。

Vocabulary

ちこくする to be late, tardy　たった only　もんく complaint; もんくを言う to complain
くたくたにつかれる to become dead tired　デートする date (to go on a date)
シャッター shutter　うちあわせする consultation, preliminary discussion, planning meeting
あす tomorrow　そうだな That's true, alright.　しんじゅ pearl

Exercise 3: How would you request the person to do the actions indicated below? Keep in mind the status of the speaker and listener.

1) Section manager, Kitamura, asks Miss Kuroda to copy some documents.

2) You ask a friend to meet you tomorrow morning at 8:00 in front of the station.

3) A customer asks the salesman to show her some samples.

4) Two employees ask their superior to attend their wedding.

出席(しゅっせき)する　to attend

5) An employee asks his boss to read his report.

6) You ask the store clerk for some change.

こまかくする　to make small, to change money.

Function II　Explaining about an item; XというY

Sometimes a name alone may not sufficiently identify the item you are speaking about for the listener. In such cases, the construction「XというY」is frequently employed, where X is the name of the item and Y is the class to which it belongs: "Y by the name of X", "X belonging to the class Y".

ex.1. カローラという車　an automobile called "Corolla"

2. マイケル・ウエッブというアメリカ人　an American by the name of Michael Webb

3. A：あそこの木のえだにとまっているのは、何(なん)という鳥(とり)ですか。

What is the name of the bird perched on that branch over there?

(lit. As for the one perched on the branch over there, it is a bird of what name?)

B：ああ、あれは、「すずめ」ですよ。　Oh, that's a sparrow!

Exercise 4: Ask someone if he is familiar with the following items. Use the information written underneath as explanation, followed by a statement of your own.

ニコン

日本のカメラ

ex. A：ニコンというカメラを知(し)っていますか。

B：いいえ。どんなカメラですか。

A：日本のカメラで、とてもいいカメラです。

1)

みきもと

しんじゅを売(う)っている店

2) バーバラさん

マイケルさんのおくさん

3) きんたろう

日本のむかし話(ばなし)に出てくる男の子

4) 

サンシャインビル

東京で2ばんめに高いビル

5) 

カーネーション

母(はは)の日(ひ)に、お母(かあ)さんにプレゼントする花(はな)

Function III Using「__でも」when offering something; 金閣寺(きんかくじ)でも見物(けんぶつ)して来(き)たら？

「でも」is frequently used when offering something, making a suggestion or giving advice. Rather than specify one and only one item, it suggests there are other possible choices as well, if the person spoken to so desires.「でも」also serves to express modesty and a desire not to seem imposing on the part of the speaker.

ex.1. お茶(ちゃ)でもいかがですか。How about some tea or something? How about some tea at least?

cf. お茶は、いかがですか。How about some tea?

2. せっかく京都(きょうと)に行くんだから、金閣寺でも見物して来たら？

As long as you are going to Kyoto, why don't you at least see Kinkakuji (or some other interesting place)?

3. 天気がいいから、散歩(さんぽ)でもして来(こ)ようかな。

Seeing it's nice weather, perhaps maybe I'll go for a walk or something.

4. そんなに、ぐあいがわるいんだったら、出張(しゅっちょう)は、野村(のむら)さんにでもかわってもらったら？

If you feel so bad as that, why not have Mr. Nomura or someone replace you on the business trip?

Note:「でも」replaces「は」,「が」and「を」, and is added after「に」, etc.

Exercise 5: Looking at the pictures, complete the following statements using「noun ＋でも」.

1) つかれたでしょう。

________。

2) たいくつですねえ。

________。

3) いい天気ですねえ。

________。

Vocabulary

むかしばなし old tale, fairy tale
母の日（ははのひ）Mother's Day
ビル building
カーネーション carnation
たいくつ（な）tedious, boring

4) おなかがすきましたね。 ＿＿＿＿＿＿＿＿。

5) マイケルさんが来るまで、 ＿＿＿＿＿＿＿＿。

6) こんどの日曜日は、車で、 ＿＿＿＿＿＿＿＿。

Function IV　Requesting permission; 〜てもいいですか

The verb て-form plus「も」"too, even" forms a construction meaning "even if one does" (see Lesson 25. p.306 for further discussion). Following this with such words as「いい」,「よろしい」"good" or「かまわない」"I don't mind" gives expressions like "alright even if one does", "not mind even if one does", which are commonly employed in asking or granting permission.

Different ways of asking for permission

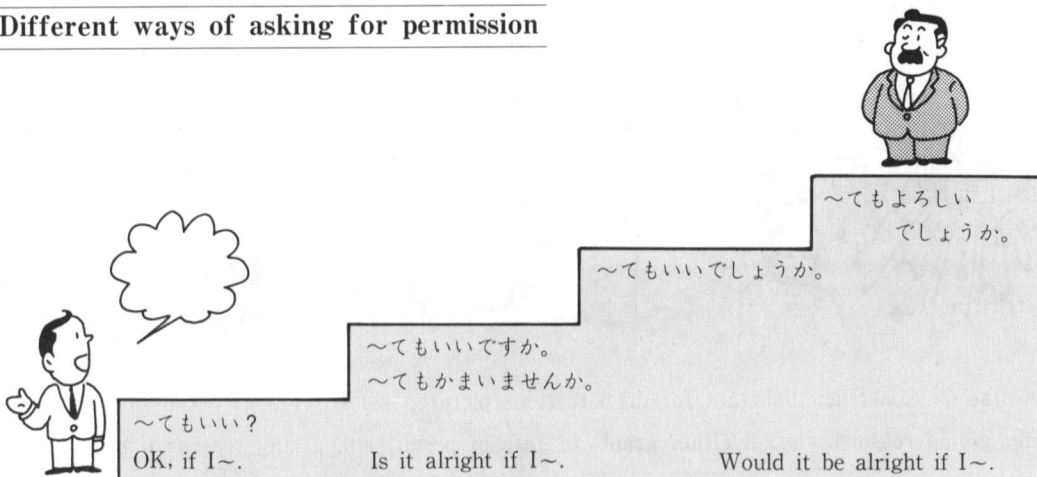

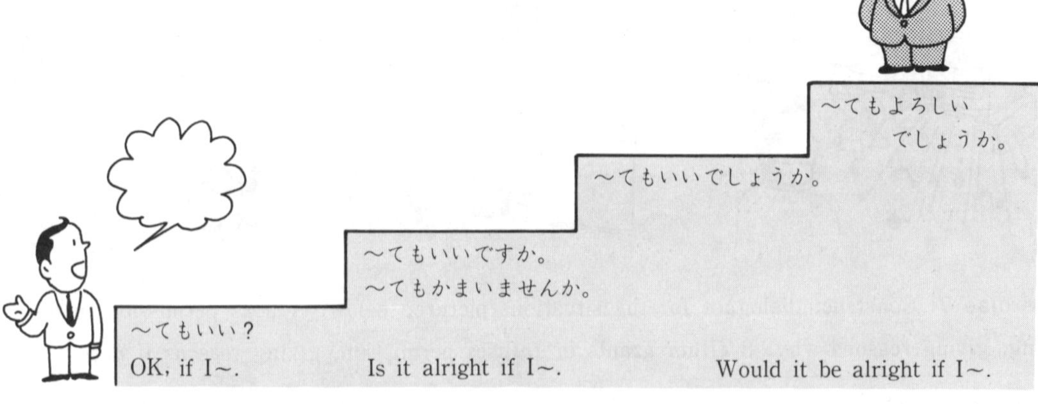

ex.1. A：お母(かあ)さん、このケーキ、食べてもいい？ Mommie, is it OK if I eat this cake?

B：ええ、いいわよ。 Yes, it's alright.

B：だめよ。お客様(きゃくさま)に出すんだから。 No, it's not. I'm going to serve it to guests.

2. A：今日(きょう)、お宅(たく)に行ってもよろしいでしょうか。

Would it be alright if I came to your house today?

B：ええ。どうぞ、いらっしゃい。 Yes, please do.

B：ちょっと、母(はは)が病気(びょうき)なので…。 Well you see. Mother is sick and so...

3. A：この辞書(じしょ)をかりてもいいでしょうか。

Would it be alright if I borrowed this dictionary?

B：ええ、もちろん。あしたまで、使(つか)っていてもかまいませんよ。

Sure, of course. I don't mind if you use it until tomorrow.

A：ありがとう。たすかります。 Thanks. That's a big help.

4. A：課長、この時刻表(じこくひょう)は、先月(せんげつ)のものですよ。もう、すててもよろしいですか。

Mr. Section Manager, this is last month's train schedule. Is it alright if I throw it away?

B：いや、すてないでください。ちょっと、調(しら)べたいことがあるから。

No, please don't throw it away. There's something I want to check.

Exercise 6: Ask permission to do something in each of the situations below. Reply yes or no.

1) コーヒーに、さとうを入れる。 to a guest

2) このかさを、かりたい。 to a station employee

3) いけんを言いたい。 to the teacher

4) テレビの音(おと)を小さくしたい。 to your brother

5) カードで、はらいたい。 to a salesclerk

6) 5時前に帰(かえ)りたい。 to your boss

Exercise 7: Construct dialogues for the situations pictured below. A asks permission to do something, giving reasons why. B either grants or refuses permission, giving reasons if necessary.

1) in the room
friends

2) in the room
friends

3) in the cafeteria at work
fellow employees

Vocabulary

おきがさ spare umbrella kept in one's office, etc.
カード card, credit card
ふとる (u-vi) to grow fat; ふとっている to be fat
やせる (ru-vi) to lose weight, become thin; やせている to be thin
いけん opinion, view
行き先（いきさき，ゆきさき）destination

Reading Comprehension Exercise

〈マイケルの日記〉

仕事が終わってから、京都見物をする予定だったので、バーバラと2人で、東京を出発した。わたしの仕事が終わるまで、1人で京都を見物すると言って、バーバラは、とちゅうの京都駅で、新幹線をおりた。バーバラは、仕事が終わったら、ホテルに電話してほしいと言った。

新大阪駅には、第一貿易の人が、2人、むかえに来てくれていた。会社は、駅から近かった。会社の人にあいさつをして、すぐに会議がはじまった。アメリカに支社を出す件についての話し合いが、早く終わったので、ほかのことについても話し合った。第一貿易の人たちは、これからも、ずっと、きょうりょくしてもらいたいと言った。そのあと、えんかいになった。

10時ごろ、大阪駅からバーバラに電話した。バーバラは、ちょっと、おこっていた。「もっと早く、電話してほしかった」と言った。それで、花を買って、急いでホテルへ行った。

◆Vocabulary◆

話し合う（はなしあう）(u-vt) to consult, discuss; 話し合い（はなしあい）consultation

きょうりょくする cooperation

急ぐ（いそぐ）(u-vt) to hurry, make haste

むかえる (ru-vt) to meet, receive

えんかい banquet, party

Exercise 8: Answer the following questions.

1) バーバラさんは、マイケルさんに、どんなことをたのみましたか。
2) 第一貿易の人は、マイケルさんに、何をたのみましたか。第一貿易の人のことばで、こたえなさい。
3) マイケルさんは、なぜ、花を買って、ホテルに行ったのですか。
4) マイケルさんが、バーバラさんに電話するのがおそくなったのは、どうしてですか。

Listening Comprehension Exercise

Listen to the tape and do as instructed.

1) Michael makes a note of what the section manager says. Fill in the spaces with the appropriate information.

Today: 6月5日
① （ ）月（ ）日（ ）時
② 行き先 （　　　　　）
③ 会う人 （　　　　　）
④ 用件 （　　　　　）

2) Circle the correct answer.

① 何を持って行きますか。

{a. サンプル　b. けいやく書　c. カタログ}

② ウエッブさんが会うのは、{a. 山本部長　b. 山田課長　c. 山田部長} で、{a. ふとっている　b. やせている} 人です。

第18課 テレビを見たり、ラジオを聞いたり

Watching TV, Listen To The Radio, And So Forth

Dialogue I

日本語学校で

マイケル：おくれて、すみません。

市川先生：かまいませんよ。お仕事が、なかなか、終わらなかったんでしょう。

マイケル：いえ、じつは、そうじゃないんです。電車の中で、日本語のテープを聞いているうちに、のりこしてしまったんです。

市川先生：ああ、そうだったんですか。のりこすぐらいはいいけど、テープを聞きながら道を歩くとあぶないから、気をつけてくださいね。

マイケル：はい、気をつけます。予習・復習の時間が、なかなか、取れないものですから…。今度から、おくれないようにします。

Dialogue II

授業のあとで

マイケル：先生、聞き取りが、なかなか、じょうずにならないんですが、どうしたらいいでしょうか。

市川先生：そうですね。ウエッブさんは、テレビかラジオを、持っていますか。

マイケル：はい、テレビもラジオも、持っています。でも、仕事がいそがしくて、なかなか、テレビも、ゆっくり見られません。

市川先生：でも、ラジオなら、通勤のとちゅうの、電車の中でも聞けるでしょう。

マイケル：聞けますが、ラジオを聞くだけで、日本語が、じょうずになりますか。

市川先生：ええ、もちろん。毎日、聞いているうちに、ニュースも、わかるようになりますよ。

マイケル：でも、ニュースや交通情報は速すぎて、とても聞き取ることができません。

市川先生：さいしょは、天気予報が、せいかくに聞き取れればいいですよ。そのうち、だんだん、耳がなれてくるでしょうから、しんぱいは、いりませんよ。

Dialogue III

（マイケルの家で）

マイケル：ただいま。

バーバラ：お帰りなさい。おそかったわね。10時には帰ると言ってたのに、もう11時よ。

マイケル：うん、とちゅうで、じこがあってね。電車が、おくれたんだよ。

バーバラ：そういえば、さっき、テレビのニュースで、じこのために、電車が止まっているって言ってたわ。

マイケル：バーバラは、毎日、ゆっくり、テレビを見る時間があっていいね。

バーバラ：あら、ひまだから見てるんじゃなくて、日本語の勉強をしているのよ。

マイケル：あ、そうか。日本語学校の先生も、テレビを見たり、ラジオを聞いたりするのは、聞き取りの勉強になるって言ってたよ。

バーバラ：先生が、「言ってた」じゃなくて、「おっしゃっていた」でしょう。

Vocabulary

Nouns:

3テープ　tape, cassette tape
8予習（よしゅう）する　preparation for new lessons
11聞き取り（ききとり）　hearing
20交通（こうつう）　traffic
20情報（じょうほう）　information
22耳（みみ）　ear
27じこ　accident

Adjectives:

7あぶない　dangerous
21せいかく(な)　correct, accurate
30ひま(な)　free, not busy, nothing to do

Adverbs:

21そのうち(に)　in time, before long, by and by, soon
22だんだん　gradually, step by step

Verbs:

1おくれる　(ru–vi) to be late
2終わる（おわる）　(u–vi) to end, finish
4のりこす　(u–vt) to ride past, miss one's stop
15見られる（みられる）　(ru–vi) can be seen, possible to see
16聞ける（きける）　(ru–vi) can be heard, possible to hear
20聞き取る（ききとる）　(u–vt) to hear what's being said
22なれる　(ru–vi) to get used to
22いる　(u–vi) to be needed, necessary
33おっしゃる　(u–vi) to say (honorific)

Grammatical words:

10〜ようにする　see to it that __ ☞Function V　　18〜ようになる　come to be, become ☞ Function Ⅳ

16なら　conditional marker: "in the case of", "in the event that" (used after nouns and plain form verbals)

20〜ことができる　such and such can be done ☞ Function Ⅲ

30〜のよ　plain form of 「〜のですよ」(used by women)

Expressions:

7気をつける　to be careful, use caution

8時間がとれる　to be able to take time

9〜ものですから　because __ ;「〜ものです」means the same as「〜のです」(see Lesson 6, p.85)

24お帰りなさい　Welcome home!

27そういえば　that reminds me, come to think of it

31テレビを見たり、ラジオを聞いたり　watching TV, listening to the radio ☞Function II

Dialogue Comprehension Exercise

Mark T or F.

Dialogue I

1) (　) マイケルさんは、仕事が、なかなか終わらなかったので、日本語の授業におくれました。

2) (　) マイケルさんには、復習をする時間が、あまりありません。

Dialogue II

3) (　) マイケルさんは、日本語の聞き取りが、じょうずです。

4) (　) マイケルさんは、まだ、日本語のニュースや、交通情報を聞き取ることができません。

Dialogue III

5) (　) バーバラさんは、毎日、ひまだから、テレビを見ています。

6) (　) バーバラさんは、テレビを見たら、日本語がじょうずになると思っています。

Function I　Apologizing, asking forgiveness

〈Useful expressions〉

1. ごめん。／しつれい。　Sorry! Excuse me!
2. ごめんなさい。　Pardon me. Forgive me.
3. すみません（でした）。　I'm sorry.
4. しつれいしました。　Excuse me please.
5. もうしわけありません（でした）。　I must apologize.
6. もうしわけございません（でした）。　I really must apologize.

Words such as「たいへん」"terribly",「ほんとうに」"truly",「まことに」"sincerely",「どうも」"more than can be expressed" are often added to the above.

ex.1. ほんとうに、もうしわけありません。　I really and truly must apologize.

2. どうも、すみませんでした。　I'm very sorry.

The action or reason for which you are apologizing can be stated using the て-form.

ex. 1. A：おくれてごめんなさい。待った？　Sorry I'm late! Did you wait long?

B：ううん、そんなに。どうしたの？　Uh uh. Not so long. What happened?

A：じこのために、道がこんでいたものだから。

The streets were crowded because of an accident, you see.

2. A：れんらくがおくれて、すみませんでした。会議が、なかなか、終わらなかったものですから。

I'm sorry I took so long in contacting you. The meeting just didn't end when it was supposed to.

B：ああ、そうですか。かまいませんよ。　Oh, is that so? No problem.

or ちゃんと、れんらくしてくれないと、こまるなあ。

It's hard for me if you don't get in touch like you were supposed to.

3. A：めんどうなことを おねがいして、たいへん、もうしわけございません。

It's unforgivable of me for asking you to do such a troublesome thing.

B：いいえ、どういたしまして。　Not at all. Think nothing of it.

Note: The form「ため（に）」"due to, because of" may also be used in stating reasons.

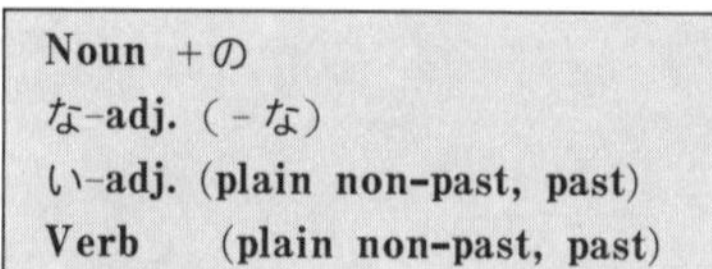
Noun ＋の
な-adj. (－な)
い-adj. (plain non-past, past)
Verb (plain non-past, past)

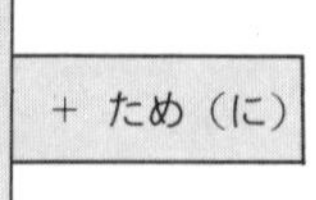
＋ ため（に）

ex. 1. バスがおくれたために、ちこくしました。

I was late because the bus was delayed.

2. 田中さんは、かぜのために、パーティーに来られないそうです。

Mr. Tanaka will not be able to come to the party because of a cold.

Dialogues in English

Dialogue I

M : Sorry I'm late!

I : No problem. Work just didn't finish up like it was supposed to, huh?

M : No. As a matter of fact, it wasn't like that. As I was listening to my Japanese tape on the train, I rode right past my stop.

I : Oh, is that what happened? Something like riding past your stop is alright, but walking along the street listening to your tape is dangerous, so please take care!

M : Yes. I'll be careful. You see, I'm just not able to take time for studying ahead or reviewing. I'll try not to come late in the future.

Dialogue II

M : Teacher, my hearing just doesn't seem to improve like it should. What do you think I should do?

I : Hm, let me see. Do you have a TV or radio, Mr. Webb?

M : Yes, we have both a TV and a radio. But I'm busy with work however, and am not really able to spend time watching TV.

I : Yes, but in the case of the radio you can also listen to it on the train going to and from work, can't you?

M : I can. But will my Japanese improve just by listening to the radio?

I : Yes, of course. As you listen every day, eventually you will be able to understand even the news.

M : Yes, but the news and traffic information are too fast. It's impossible for me to catch what they are saying.

I : At first it will be good if you can understand the weather report accurately. As time goes on, your ears will become accustomed I'm sure, and so there is no need to worry.

Dialogue III

M : I'm home!

B : Welcome back. You're late, aren't you. You said you'd be back at 10:00, and here it's already 11:00.

M : There was an accident on the way and the train was late.

B : Come to think of it, they said a while ago on the news on TV that the trains were stopped because of an accident.

M : You're lucky, Barbara. You've got time every day to spend watching TV.

B : What? I'm not watching it because I have nothing to do. You realize I'm studying Japanese.

M : Oh, I see. The teacher at the Japanese language school too was saying that watching TV, listening to the radio and so forth is good practice for hearing.

B : For "the teacher was saying", aren't you supposed to use "osshatte ita" instead of "itte ta"?

Exercise 1: Make an apology suitable to each of the situations below. Finish A's reply by choosing an expression from **a.** ～ **f.** below.

1) A　B

boy friend　girl friend

駅の近(ちか)くまで、車で行きましたが、道が、とてもこんでいました。やくそくした時間より、1時間もおくれました。

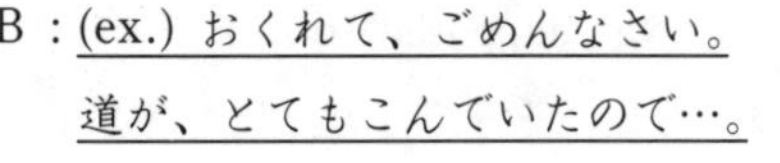

B：(ex.) おくれて、ごめんなさい。道が、とてもこんでいたので…。

A：そう、あまりおそいから、〔ex. **f**〕。

2) A　B

colleagues

火曜日に、Aさんのうちで、パーティーをします。Bさんも行くつもりでしたが、きゅうに、大阪(おおさか)に出張(しゅっちょう)することになりました。

B：＿＿＿＿＿＿＿＿＿＿＿＿＿＿＿＿。

A：いいえ。Bさんにも、ぜひ〔　　　　〕。

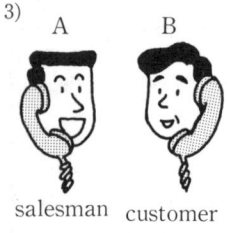

3) A　B

salesman　customer

Bさんは、Aさんと3時に会(あ)うやくそくをしていました。でも、会議がながくなって、3時には会えませんでした。Aさんは、帰(かえ)ってしまいました。

B：もしもし、Bですが…。さきほどは、もうしわけありませんでした。＿＿＿＿＿＿＿＿＿＿＿＿。

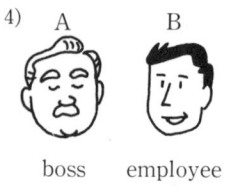

A：ああ、そうですか。では、〔　　　　〕。

4) A　B

boss　employee

Bさんは、Aさんからかりた書類(しょるい)に、コーヒーをこぼしました。

B：＿＿＿＿＿＿＿＿＿＿＿＿＿＿＿＿。

A：こまるねえ。もっと〔　　　　〕。

5) A　B

librarian　student

図書館(としょかん)から、本を3さつ、かりましたが、いそがしくて、読む時間がありませんでした。それで、かえすのがおそくなりました。

B：＿＿＿＿＿＿＿＿＿＿＿＿＿＿＿＿。

A：そうでしたか。じゃあ、〔　　　　〕。でも、これからは、気(き)をつけてくださいよ。

a. しんぱいしたよ。	**b.** また、今度(こんど)、よろしくおねがいします。
c. しかたがないですね。	**d.** 来ていただきたかったんですが、ざんねんですね。
e. 気をつけてくださいよ。	**f.** もう、来ないかと思ったよ。

Vocabulary

こぼす (u-vt) to spill
ゲーム game
ざんねん（な）disappointing, regrettable, too bad
こうかんする exchange

Function II "Doing this, that, and other" ; ～たり、～たり

Verb (past stem) +	たり、	Verb (past stem) +	たり
な／い-adj. (past stem) +	たり、	な／い-adj. (past stem) +	たり

The inflection「～たり」means do (be, is) such and such "among other things", "etc.". One or several items may be listed using「～たり」, the final「～たり」is followed by「する」(「～たり、～たりする」).

ex. 1. 夜は、テレビを見たり、レコードを聞いたりして、すごします。
My evenings I spend watching TV, listening to records, etc.

2. 日曜日は、せんたくをしたり、そうじをしたり、ときどき、買い物にでかけたりします。
Sundays I do the laundry, clean house, and sometimes go shopping.

3. 公園には、おおぜいの人がいて、散歩をしたり、絵をかいたり、話をしたりしています。
In the park there are lots of people strolling, drawing pictures, talking, and so forth.

4. 小さい子どもがいるので、ここで、野球をしたりしてはいけません。
You mustn't play baseball and the likes here because there are small children around!

The same item in the affirmative and negative joined by「～たり」means "sometimes yes, sometimes no, depending ...".

5. A：毎朝、ジョギングをしていますか。 Do you jog every morning?
B：いいえ。したり、しなかったりです。 No. Sometimes I do, sometimes I don't.

6. A：お仕事のほうは、どうですか？ いそがしいですか？ How is work? Are you busy?
B：ええ、いそがしかったり、ひまだったりです。
Yes, well, sometimes busy, sometimes not.

Note: Sometimes the final「する」is replaced by「です」.
ex. A：毎朝、日本の新聞を読んでいますか。 Do you read a Japanese newspaper every morning?
B：いいえ、読んだり、読まなかったりです。 Sometimes I do, sometimes I don't.

Exercise 2: どんなことをしますか。

1) パーティーでは？

2) 休みの日には？

Exercise 3: Supply appropriate words in the spaces below. There is no need to limit yourself to only two items.

1) ＿＿＿＿たり、＿＿＿＿たりするのは、けんこうにいいですね。
2) ＿＿＿＿たり、＿＿＿＿たりすると、病気(びょうき)になりますよ。
3) ＿＿＿＿たり、＿＿＿＿たりして、旅行(りょこう)のじゅんびをします。
4) ＿＿＿＿たり、＿＿＿＿たりして、日本語の勉強(べんきょう)をしています。
5) ガールフレンドのたんじょう日(び)には、＿＿＿＿たり、＿＿＿＿たりします。

Exercise 4: Answer the following questions as in the example. Next answer using some other expression.

ex. A：毎日(まいにち)、新聞(しんぶん)を読みますか。　B：いいえ、読んだり、読まなかったりです。

1) A：日曜日には、いつも、ゴルフに行きますか。
B：いいえ、＿＿＿＿＿＿＿＿。

2) A：毎晩(まいばん)、テレビを見るんですか。
B：いいえ、＿＿＿＿＿＿＿＿。

3) A：いつも、ぼうしをかぶっているんですか。
B：いいえ、＿＿＿＿＿＿＿＿。

4) A：日本では、やさいは、1年中(ねんじゅう)高いですか。
B：いいえ、＿＿＿＿＿＿＿＿。

◆**Vocabulary**◆
けんこう health ; けんこう(な) healthy, fit
毎晩（まいばん）every evening, every night
じゅんびする preparation

Function III　Telling if something is possible or not possible; できる，できない

There are various ways to say such and such an action is possible.

1 **Noun (showing action)** / **Verb (plain non-past)＋こと** ＋が　できる　"such and such an action is possible, can be done"

Remember:「Verb (plain non-past)＋こと」also functions as a noun. (see Lesson 7, p.100)

ex.1. スペイン語ができたら、一度(いちど)、メキシコへ行ってみたいですね。
If it were possible for me to speak Spanish, I'd like to go once to Mexico.

2. ごめんね。10円玉(えんだま)がなかったから、電話ができなかったよ。
Sorry! I couldn't phone because I didn't have a ten yen coin!

3. 子どものときは、ぜんぜん、泳(およ)ぐことができませんでした。
When I was a child I couldn't swim at all.

4. 先生がいそがしかったので、しつもんをすることができませんでした。
The teacher was busy so it was not possible for me to ask him any questions.

5. マイケルさんは、日本語で手紙(てがみ)を書くことができるんですよ。
Michael can write letters in Japanese!

2 **Potential auxiliary** (see Appendix)　**u-verb root＋eru** / **ru-verb root＋rareru**

手紙を書く	→	手紙　を／が　書ける	It is possible to write a letter.
電話を　かける	→	電話を／が　かけられる	It is possible to telephone.

ex.1. スペイン語が話せたら、スペインを旅行(りょこう)してみたいんですが…。

If I could speak Spanish, I'd like to try traveling around Spain.

2. バーバラは、何でも食べられますので、どうぞ、しんぱいしないでください。

Barbara is able to eat anything, so please don't worry.

Note 1: Although purists insist that the correct form of the potential after ru-verb is「られる」, there is a strong tendency in modern Japanese to shorten this to「れる」.

ex. 食べられる → 食べれる　　この木(き)のみは、食べれますか。 Is this nut edible?

Note 2: Potential forms of the irregular verbs are:

行く → 行かれる（行ける), 来る → 来られる（来れる), する → できる

Note 3: Intransitive verbs which express possibility:

見る "to see" — 見える "to be visible", 聞(き)く "to hear" — 聞こえる "to be audible"

ex.1. ここから、ふじ山(さん)が、よく見えますよ。 Mt. Fuji is clearly visible from here.

2. となりのへやの、ラジオの音(おと)が聞こえますか。 Can you hear the radio in the next room?

Exercise 5: While planning for a trip, Michael and Barbara look at the following brochures trying to decide which hotel to stay at.

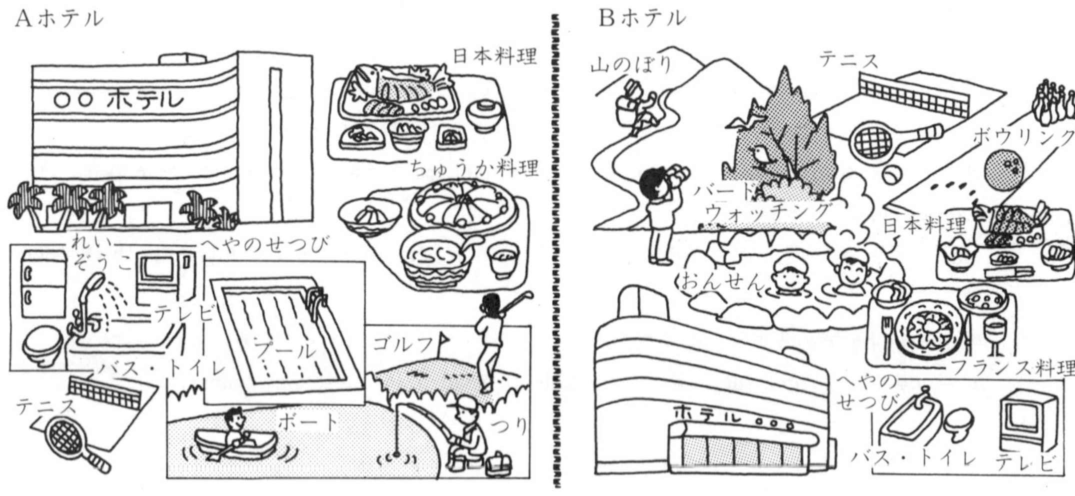

1) What sort of things are possible at hotel A and B? Complete the following list.

Aホテルで、できること：ex. プールで泳(およ)ぐことができます。(プールで泳げます。)

① (スポーツ) ＿＿＿＿＿。＿＿＿＿＿。

② (食事(しょくじ)) ＿＿＿＿＿。＿＿＿＿＿。

③ (へやで) ＿＿＿＿＿。＿＿＿＿＿。＿＿＿＿＿。

④ (others) ＿＿＿＿＿。＿＿＿＿＿。

Bホテルで、できること：ex. テニスをすることができます。(テニスができます。)

① (スポーツ) ＿＿＿＿＿。＿＿＿＿＿。＿＿＿＿＿。

② (食事) ＿＿＿＿＿。＿＿＿＿＿。

③ (へやで) ＿＿＿＿＿。＿＿＿＿＿。

④ (others) ＿＿＿＿＿。＿＿＿＿＿。

◆Vocabulary◆

ちゅうか料理(りょうり) Chinese cuisine　バス bath
トイレ toilet　ボート boat　ボウリング bowling
バードウォッチング bird watching　せつび facilities　いけ pond

2) Referring to the list completed on the previous page, make statements comparing the two hotels.

① Aホテルでは、プールで＿＿＿＿＿＿が、Bホテルでは、＿＿＿＿＿＿。
② Aホテルでも、Bホテルでもできるスポーツは、＿＿＿＿＿＿。
③ Aホテルでは、れいぞうこが＿＿＿＿＿が、Bホテルでは、＿＿＿＿＿＿。
④ 日本料理(りょうり)は、＿＿＿＿＿＿でも、＿＿＿＿＿＿。
⑤ Bホテルでは、フランス料理が＿＿＿＿＿し、Aホテルでは、＿＿＿＿＿。
⑥ Aホテルのいけでは、＿＿＿＿＿＿。
⑦ Bホテルでは、へやのおふろのほかに、＿＿＿＿＿＿。

Function IV

Describing a change in state (3): "to become such that __"; ～ようになる

「よう(な)」"is like, similar to, same as" (see Lesson 15, p.194) is used together with the verb 「なる」"to become" to form the construction「**Verb (plain non-past)** ＋ようになる」, which means "come to be such that __", "get to be such that __", etc.

ex. 1. 日本では、6月になると、よく雨がふるようになります。
　When it turns June in Japan, lots of rain comes to fall.
2. 店(みせ)がきれいになってから、たくさんのお客さんが来るようになりました。
　After the store was remodeled, it became such that many customers came (i.e. started having many customers).

The various forms expressing possibility (see Function III) are often employed in this construction.

ex. 3. 日本語の新聞(しんぶん)が読めるようになりたいです。
　I would like to get such that I am able to read a Japanese newspaper.
4. 練習(れんしゅう)しているうちに、スケートができるようになりました。
　As I practiced, I got so that I was able to skate.
5. おかげさまで、ワープロが使(つか)えるようになりました。
　Thanks to you, I got such that I am able to use my word processer.

Exercise 6: Using the pictures as a hint, tell what sort of things it has become possible to do in each of the following sentences.

1) 毎日(まいにち)、日本語のラジオほうそうを聞いたので、＿＿＿＿＿＿。
2) 夏休み中(ちゅう)、プールにかよったので、＿＿＿＿＿＿。
3) 何度(なんど)もころんで、やっと、自転車(じてんしゃ)に＿＿＿＿＿＿。
4) 毎日、練習したので、漢字がじょうずに＿＿＿＿＿＿。
5) 日本人の友達(ともだち)に教(おし)えてもらって、日本のうたが、＿＿＿＿＿＿。

Vocabulary

ほうそうする broadcast
ころぶ (u-vi) to fall down, tumble
自転車（じてんしゃ）bicycle
かならず certainly, without fail
何度も（なんども）any number of times
やっと with difficulty, at long last
せいせき results, record, marks
このつぎ next, next time

Function V "Make an effort to __", "see to it that __"; ～ようにする

The construction「**Verb (plain non-past)**＋ようにする」"to do such that __" is equivalent to such English expressions as "see to it that __", "make an effort to—", or "take care that __".

ex.1. もっと、漢字をおぼえるようにします。

I will make an effort to learn more Chinese characters.

2. A：食事に気をつけて、病気にならないようにしないといけませんよ。

You have to watch your diet and see to it that you don't become sick!

B：はい。ちゃんと、えいようをかんがえて、食事をするようにします。

Right! I'll take care to consider nourishment and eat properly.

Exercise 7: Complete the following dialogues using an appropriate expression with「ようにする」as in the example

ex. 先生：今日の漢字のテストは、せいせきが悪かったですね。

学生：すみません。もっと、勉強するようにします。

1) 先生　：きのう、日本語のテープを聞きましたか。

マイケル：いいえ。今晩は、かならず＿＿＿＿＿＿＿。

2) 医者　：かぜですから、たばこをすってはいけませんよ。

マイケル：はい、＿＿＿＿＿＿＿。

医者　：それから、お酒も、あまり飲まないでください。

マイケル：はい、＿＿＿＿＿＿＿。

3) バーバラ：帰りがおそいときは、電話をしてね。

マイケル：うん、＿＿＿＿＿＿＿。

4) 先生　：また、おくれましたね。

マイケル：すみません。あしたは、＿＿＿＿＿＿＿。

5) 先生　：宿題は、どうしましたか。

マイケル：すみません。わすれました。このつぎは、＿＿＿＿＿＿＿。

Grammar Note "while still"「うちに」, "while"「あいだに」

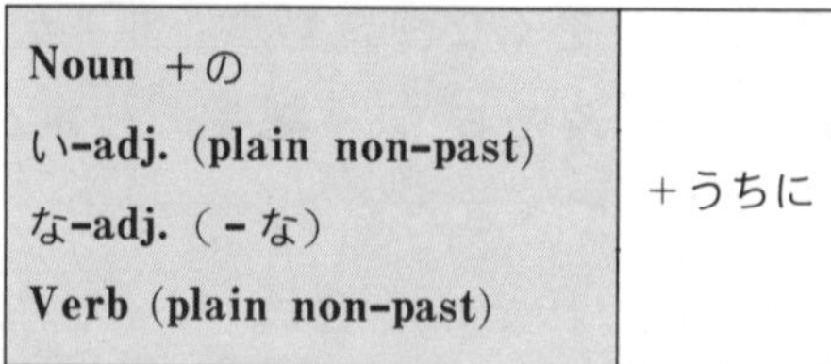

Noun ＋の い-**adj. (plain non-past)** な-**adj.** (－な) **Verb (plain non-past)**	＋うちに

Noun ＋の **Verb (plain non-past)**	＋あいだに

The location words「うち」"inside" and「あいだ」"between" may be used with qualifying phrases to define periods of time.「うちに」indicates a period within which an action occurs, and corresponds to English "while still" or, in negative constructions, "before".「あいだに」indicates a period during or throughout which an action occurs, and is equivalent to English "while".

ex.1. 学生のうちに、よく勉強しておきなさい。 Study hard while you are still a student.

学生のあいだに、いろんな所を、旅行するつもりです。

I plan to travel lots of places during the time I am a student.

2. どうぞ、あついうちに、食べてください。 Please go ahead and eat it while it's still hot.

スープがさめないうちに、飲んでください。 Please eat your soup before it gets cold.

×スープがさめないあいだに、飲んでください。

× Please eat your soup while it does not get cold.

3. 雨がふらないうちに帰ったほうがいいと思うから、これで、しつれいします。

I think it's best I go before it starts raining, so I'll be leaving now.

雨がやんでいるあいだに、買い物に行って来ましょう。

Let's go and do our shopping while the rain has stopped.

×雨がふらないあいだに、買い物に行って来ましょう。

× Let's go and do our shopping while it does not rain.

Note:「うちに」is also used to indicate an event building up or reaching a climax as some action is being done.

ex. 先生の話を聞いているうちに、ねむくなってきた。 I grew tired as I listened to the teacher speak.

Exercise 8: Are「うちに」and「あいだに」used properly in the following sentences? Mark T or F.

1) ( ) 来年から、ねだんがあがります。安いうちに、買っておいたほうがいいですよ。
2) ( ) 赤ちゃんがおきないあいだに、そうじをしてしまいましょう。
3) ( ) 紅茶がさめますよ。あついあいだに、飲んでください。
4) ( ) マイケルさんが会社に行っているうちに、アメリカの両親から、小包がとどきました。
5) ( ) レコードを聞いているうちに、おどりたくなってきました。
6) ( ) 暗くならないうちに、散歩に行って来ましょう。
7) ( ) 課長が席をはずしているうちに、お客さんが、たずねてきました。
8) ( ) へんじを出さないうちに、また、つぎの手紙が来てしまいました。

Reading Comprehension Exercise

〔Q〕今年の4月に、課長になりました。はじめは、とてもうれしかったのですが、このごろは、ちょっと…。課長になってから、前より残業が多くなりました。部下が仕事をしているのに、わたしだけ、先に帰れませんから。休みの日も、「課長の仕事が、ちゃんとできるだろうか？」「部下を、うまくコントロールできるだろうか」などと考えて、ちっとも、つかれが取れません。さいきん、夜もねむれないんです。ベッドに入ってから、2時間も3時間もねむれないことが、多いんです。それで、朝早く、おきられませんし、朝食も、あまり食べられません。新聞も、あまり読めないんです。読むと、頭がいたくなって…。会社に行くのが、つらくなりました。

（東京都・会社員・Y. T.）

〔A〕Yさんは、とてもまじめな方だと思います。たしかに、課長の仕事は、たいへんだろうと思います。でも、人間は、1人で、何もかもすることはできません。部下に、仕事をまかせることも、ひつようです。そして、休みの日には、スポーツをしたり、散歩をしたり、いい音楽を聞いたりしてください。そのうちに、リラックスできるようになります。それでも、つかれが取れなかったり、ねむれなかったりしたら、せんもんのお医者さんに、そうだんしてください。

◆Vocabulary◆

コントロールする control
朝食（ちょうしょく） breakfast
たしかに indeed, to be sure
何もかも（なにもかも） everything, all
ひつよう（な） necessary
せんもん field of study, speciality
そのために therefore, owing to that, because of that
はじめは at first
つかれ fatigue
つらい painful, hard
リラックスする to relax
部下（ぶか） subordinate
ねむる (u-vi) to sleep
まじめ（な） sincere
人間（にんげん） human being, man, mankind
まかせる (ru-vt) to leave up to someone else
それでも nevertheless, still
すすめる (ru-vt) to advise, suggest, urge

Exercise 9: Answer the following questions.

1) Regarding Y. T.'s question:

① Y. T. さんがつかれるのは、どうしてですか。

② Y. T. さんは、休みの日には、どんなことを、考えていますか。

③ そのために、Y. T. さんは、どうなりましたか。

2) Regarding the comment:

① 会社では、どのようにすることを、すすめていますか。

② 休みが取れたら、どうすることを、すすめていますか。

③ もし、つかれが取れなかったら、どうすることを、すすめていますか。

Listening Comprehension Exercise

A person from a travel agency interviews a job applicant. Listen carefully :

1) Mark the things Mary Smith can do with ○, can't do with ×.

①（ ）日本語を話す　②（ ）ひらがなを読む　③（ ）かたかなを読む

④（ ）漢字をじょうずに書く　⑤（ ）スペイン語を話す　⑥（ ）英文タイプをうつ

⑦（ ）コンピューターを使う　⑧（ ）朝早くから、はたらく

2) Choose the correct answer.

① マリー・スミスさんは、漢字が、どのくらい読めますか。（a. 100字　b. 800字　c. 1800字）

② マリー・スミスさんは、漢字が、どのくらい書けますか。（a. 100字　b. 400字　c. 800字）

③ 1時間はたらいて、どのくらいのお金がもらえますか。（a. 1200円　b. 3200円　c. 2000円）

④ しけんのけっかは、いつごろ、わかりますか。（a. 3日後　b. 1週間後　c. 10日後）

⑤ しけんのけっかは、何で、知らせてもらえますか。（a. 電話　b. 電報　c. 手紙）

◆Vocabulary◆

けっか result
英文（えいぶん） written English
知らせる（しらせる） (ru-vt) to inform
つかう (u-vt) to use, make use of
電報（でんぽう） telegram

第19課 お盆(ぼん)って、何ですか

What Is O-bon?

Dialogue I

Michael talks with Miss Hanada at the office.

花田(はなだ)　：ウエッブさん、もうすぐ、しょうよが出るわね。

マイケル：え？　しょうゆ？

花田　：「しょうゆ」じゃないわ。「しょうよ」よ。ボーナスのことよ。ボーナスって何か、知ってます？

マイケル：もちろん、知っていますよ。ぼくは、３週間ぐらい、休みがほしいなあ。

花田　：１週間だけよ、夏休みは。

マイケル：ボーナスを、休みでもらえないんですか。

花田　：ええ、日本では、ボーナスは、お金でもらうのよ。

マイケル：へえ、どのくらい？

花田　：ふつうは、給料(きゅうりょう)の２～３か月分(ぶん)ね。でも、ウエッブさんのばあいは、0.8か月分ぐらいかしら、新入社員だから。

マイケル：なんだ、0.8か月しか出ないのか。それに、１週間だけか、夏休みは。やっぱり、働(はたら)きすぎなんじゃない、日本人は。

花田　：そうね。わたしも、そう思うわ。アメリカでは、どのくらい休むの？

マイケル：人によるけど、だいたい１か月ぐらいかな。

花田　：え、１か月も！　いいわねえ。

Dialogue II

マイケル：花田(はなだ)さん、夏休みは、どうするんですか。

花田　：いなかに帰るの、お盆(ぼん)だから。でも、お盆には、おおぜいの人が、いなかに帰るから、電車や道路(どうろ)がこんで、たいへんなの。電車の指定席券(していせきけん)を買うために、駅で、長(なが)いあいだ、ならんだりするのよ。

マイケル：へえ、そうですか。それで、お盆というのは、何ですか。

花田　　：かんたんには，説明(せつめい)できないけど、仏教(ぶっきょう)のおまつりで、このときに、しんだ人のたましいが、帰って来るの。そのたましいをなぐさめるために、みんなで、「盆おどり」というダンスをするのよ。

マイケル：ふうん。ところで、花田さんのいなかって、どこですか。

花田　　：鹿児島(かごしま)よ。

マイケル：すみません。鹿児島って、どこですか。

花田　　：九州(きゅうしゅう)の、いちばん南(みなみ)にある県(けん)よ。桜島(さくらじま)という火山(かざん)があるわ。

マイケル：ああ、一度、テレビで見たことがあります。ほんものを見てみたいなあ。

花田　　：いつか、おくさんと遊(あそ)びに来(き)て。いい所(ところ)よ。

マイケル：ええ、ありがとう。ぜひ、行きたいですね。

そうだ！　こんどの夏休みに行ってもいいですか。

花田　　：えっ……。

Vocabulary

Nouns:

1しょうよ bonus　　2しょうゆ soy sauce　　3ボーナス bonus

10 2～3か月（にさんかげつ） 2 or 3 months　　11 0.8か月（れいてんはっかげつ） eight tenths of a month

11新入社員（しんにゅうしゃいん） new employee　　13働きすぎ（はたらきすぎ） overwork

18お盆（おぼん） *O-bon* ☞p.245　　19道路（どうろ） road

19指定席券（していせきけん）reserved seat ticket
22仏教（ぶっきょう）Buddhism
23たましい soul, spirit
24盆おどり（ぼんおどり）*Bon-odori*, *Bon* dance
28県（けん）prefecture
28火山（かざん）volcano
29ほんもの the real thing

Adjectives:

22かんたん(な) simple, easy

Verbs:

23しぬ (u-vi) to die
23なぐさめる (ru-vt) to console

Grammatical words:

10－分（ぶん）division, part, segment; 給料（きゅうりょう）の2～3か月分 2 or 3 months pay

11～かしら I wonder if

12～しか…ない no more than, only ☞Function Ⅱ

Expressions:

1わね same as「ね」(used by women)
10（の）ばあい in the case of
12なんだ、～のか Do you mean to say...? What do you mean...! (used to express disappointment or indignation)
15人による depending on the person
20長（なが）いあいだ for a long time
25ふうん Hmm.
32そうだ！ Hey, that's it! I've got it!

Dialogue Comprehension Exercise

Answer the following questions.

Dialogue Ⅰ

1) マイケルさんは、ボーナスを、何（なに）でもらいたいと言っていますか。
2) マイケルさんは、ボーナスを、どのくらい、もらえますか。
3) マイケルさんは、自分（じぶん）がもらうボーナスを、多（おお）いと言っていますか、少（すく）ないと言っていますか。
4) アメリカでは、夏休みは、だいたい、どのくらい取（と）れますか。

Dialogue Ⅱ

5) 花田さんのいなかは、どこですか。
6) 花田さんは、どうして、夏休みに、いなかへ帰るのですか。
7) 花田さんは、お盆（ぼん）には、みんなで、何をすると言っていますか。
8) マイケルさんは、何を見てみたいと言っていますか。

Function Ⅰ Talking about feelings and emotions

1 Expressing your own emotions

まあ、うれしい！
うらやましいなあ。
楽（たの）しいなあ。
とてもしあわせです。
きゃっ！こわい！
こわい frightening
電車がこんでいていやだなあ。

To express your own immediate emotional response to any situation, simply use the appropriate adjective or verb describing that emotion, preceded perhaps by such interjectives as「まあ」,「わあ」,「きゃっ」,「えっ」or「えーっ」.

ex. 1. この花をくださるんですか。まあ、うれしい！
You mean you'll give me these flowers? I'm thrilled!

2. 今日(きょう)は、楽(たの)しいなあ。テニスをするのは、ひさしぶりなんですよ。
Today I'm really enjoying myself! It's been such a long time since I've played tennis!

3. いい友達(ともだち)がたくさんできて、しあわせです。 I'm happy to have so many good friends!

4. だれにも、わたしの気持(きも)ちをわかってもらえないのが、かなしい。
It grieves me that no one understands my feelings!

5. だれも会(あ)いに来てくれないので、さびしい。 I'm sad because no one comes to see me!

6. こんだ電車にのるのは、いやです。 I hate riding on crowded trains!

7. 雨で、ピクニックに行けないなんて、つまらない。
How disappointing! Not being able to go on a picnic because of rain!

Dialogues in English

Dialogue I

H: We'll be getting our "*shooyo*" pretty soon, Mr. Webb.

M: What did you say? *Shooyu*?

H: Not *shooyu*. *Shooyo*. It means bonus. Do you know what a bonus is?

M: Of course I do! As for me, I think I'd like about three weeks vacation!

H: Summer vacation is only one week!

M: Can't we receive our bonus as vacation time?

H: No. In Japan bonuses are received in the form of money, you see.

M: Really? How much about?

H: Usually it's the equivalent of about two or three months pay. But in your case I would imagine about eight tenths of a month, seeing as you're a new employee.

M: Well of all things! You mean I only get eight tenths of a month? On top of that, only one week summer vacation? There's no two ways about it. Japanese work too much, don't you think?

H: Yes. I agree. In America about how much vacation do you have?

M: That depends on the person. But in general, a month or so, I believe.

H: What? One whole month! How nice! (I'm envious!)

Dialogue II

M: What are you going to do summer vacation, Miss Hanada?

H: I'll be going back home. It's *O-bon*, you know. Except at *O-bon* many people go back home and the trains and roads are so crowded, it's terrible. People wait in line for a long time at the train station in order to buy reserved seat train tickets and such.

M: Really? Is that so? And what then is *O-bon?*

H: It can't be explained simply, but it's a Buddhist festival, and at that time the souls of people who have died return. In order to console those souls, everyone dances what is known as "*Bon-odori*".

M: Hmm. Where do you come from, by the way?

H: From Kagoshima.

M: Pardon me, but where is Kagoshima?

H: It's the southernmost prefecture in Kyushu. There's a volcano called Sakurajima.

M: Ah! I saw it once on TV. Gosh, I'd like to see the real thing!

H: It's a lovely place. Please come for a visit sometime with your wife.

W: Why, thank you. I would like to go for sure. Hey, that's it! Would it be all right if we came this summer vacation?

H: What?!!

8. なんだ、5位か。いっしょうけんめい走ったのに、がっかりしちゃった。

   What? Fifth place? And I ran so hard and all. How disappointing!

9. 1たい0で、まけたなんて、くやしい！ It really burns me, losing one to nothing!

10. えっ！ 銀行は、3時までですか。こまったなあ。お金をおろしたいのに。

    What? The banks are only open until 3:00? How troublesome! Just when I want to withdraw some money.

11. ああ、びっくりした。きゅうに、犬がとび出してくるんだもの。

    Oh, what a fright I had! Suddenly this dog came jumping out, you see.

12. 斎藤さんと、結婚することになったんですって？ うらやましいわ。

    You say you're getting married to Mr. Saito? How I envy you!

13. うーん、もう、おこったぞ。 Ooh, now I really am angry!

Note: Many of the verbs describing emotions in Japanese view the emotion as an action, that is, a change to a new emotional state:「おどろく」"to become surprised",「おこる」"to become angry",「がっかりする」"to become disappointed", etc. Hence, a sentence such as「びっくりする」does not mean "I'm surprised" or "What a surprise!", but rather "One gets surprised.", "You will be surprised.", etc. To exclaim "I'm surprised!","What a surprise!", etc. requires use of the past tense「びっくりした」lit. "I (became and now) am surprised!" (see Lesson 4, p.62)

2 Describing and reporting emotions

The same words may be used to describe or report your own, or someone else's emotional state.

ex. 1. 彼女は、いつも、やくそくの時間におくれるので、こまります。

I get bothered because my girl friend is always late!

2. この大きいへびを見たら、田中さんは、きっと、おどろきますよ。

If Miss Tanaka sees this huge snake, she will surely become frightened.

3. 田中さんは、大きいへびを見て、おどろきました。

Miss Tanaka saw a huge snake and became frightened.

4. 田中さんは、大きいへびを見て、おどろいていました。

Miss Tanaka was frightened because she saw a huge snake.

When speaking of someone else's emotional state it might be appropriate to indicate that what you say is based on appearance, conjecture or hearsay. Some of the ways this can be done include:

1. **Adj. root** ＋がる "appears"

   ex. 太郎君は、野球の試合にまけて、くやしがっていました。

   Taro appeared to be really disappointed over losing the baseball game.

2. **Adj. root** ＋そう（な）

   ex. マイケルさん、テニスがすきなんですね。ずいぶん楽しそうでしたよ。

   You like tennis, don't you, Michael. You seemed to be really enjoying yourself.

3. 「〜だろう」「〜でしょう」 "probably, I bet"

   ex. 花田さんを映画にさそってあげたら、きっと、よろこぶでしょう。

   I bet Miss Hanada would really be delighted if you asked her to a movie.

4.　「～と思う」　"I believe, I think"

ex. 子どもたちをディズニーランドにつれて行ったら、よろこぶと思いますよ。

I think the children would be happy if you took them to Disneyland.

5.　「～と言う」　"He said"

ex. マイケルさんは、京都に行ったけど、雨がふって、つまらなかったと言っていました。

Michael went to Kyoto but it rained and he said it was no fun at all.

Exercise 1: Make an appropriate emotional response to the following.

1) A: すみません。これ、こわしてしまったんです。
   You: ＿＿＿＿＿。これ、1つしかないんですよ。
2) A: こんど、大阪に転勤することになったんですよ。
   You: じゃ、これからは、なかなか会えなくなりますね。＿＿＿＿＿なあ。
3) A: (approaching someone from behind) わっ！　　You: ＿＿＿＿＿。
4) A：すみません。きゅうに用事ができて、テニスができなくなったんですよ。
   You: 楽しみにしていたのに、＿＿＿＿＿。
5) 今年のベースアップは，0.7%だそうですよ。
   You: なんだ、＿＿＿＿＿。
6) A: よく勉強しましたね。テストは、100点でしたよ。
   You: ＿＿＿＿＿。90点しか取れないと思っていました。
7) A: 買い物に行って来てちょうだい。　You: ＿＿＿＿＿。今、友達と遊んでいんるだよ。

Exercise 2: Tell how the people below feel. Use appropriate words from the list on the next page.

1)

鈴木さんと
結婚するので、
1か月休みが
ほしいんですが。
斎藤

1か月も？
斎藤さんの仕事を
だれにたのんだら
いいかなあ。

おめでとう。
いいわねえ。
わたしも…

斎藤さん、
よかったわねえ。

ええ…

星

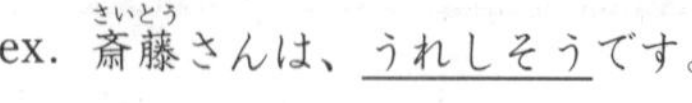

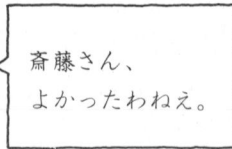

ex. 斎藤さんは、うれしそうです。
① 課長さんは、＿＿＿＿＿。
② 浜野さんは、＿＿＿＿＿。
③ 花田されは、＿＿＿＿＿。
④ 黒田さんは、＿＿＿＿＿。
⑤ 星さんは、＿＿＿＿＿。

Vocabulary

これから from now on, hereafter
楽しみにする to look forward to
ベースアップ raise of the wage base
おめでとう Congratulations!
用事（ようじ） business, something to do
(%)パーセント percent
わっ expression of surprise
ねえ same as「ね」

2) 花田さんは、＿＿＿＿＿＿。　　3) 星（ほし）さんは、＿＿＿＿＿＿。

3) 女の子は、＿＿＿＿＿＿。
男の子は、＿＿＿＿＿＿。　　4) お客さんは、＿＿＿＿＿＿。

うれしい	よろこぶ	いや（な）	がっかりする	おどろく
かなしい	こまる	くやしい	さびしい	うらやましい

Exercise 3: Use an appropriate word describing some emotion in the parentheses below.

A: 水野（みずの）さん、にこにこして、ずいぶん（　①　）ですねえ。何か、あったんですか。
B: ええ、ボーナスを、6か月分（ぶん）も、もらったんだそうですよ。
A: へえ、それは、すごい！（　②　）なあ。ぼくは、2か月分しか、もらえないんですよ。
そんなに、たくさんのお金を、何に使（つか）うんだろう。
B: おくさんに、おくさんが前から（　③　）ていた、ダイヤのネックレスをプレゼントするそうです。
C: まあ、いいご主人（しゅじん）を持（も）って、おくさん、（　④　）ですねえ。
B: そうそう、ぼくたちにも、ごちそうしてくれるそうですよ。
C: わあ、（　⑤　）！　いつ？
B: こんどの木曜日。
A: えーっ、（　⑥　）だなあ。ぼくは、その日、出張（しゅっちょう）なんですよ。

Grammar Note I　Inverted word order

Normally least important items come first in Japanese sentences, while more important items come toward the end nearest the verbal (see Sentence Structure, p.16). In some cases however, the speaker might be overly anxious and say the most important item first, and then, almost as an afterthought, tack less important items on after the verbal.

ex. 1. 1週間だけよ、夏休みは。(←夏休みは、1週間だけよ。) Only one week, summer vacation!

2. けんこうによくないよ、たばこをすっちゃ。(←たばこをすっちゃ、けんこうによくないよ。)
It's not good for your health, smoking cigarettes!

3. 花をあげたの？先生に。(←先生に、花をあげたの？)
Did you give the flowers to the teacher?

4. ああ、楽（たの）しかった、友達（ともだち）が来てくれて。(←友達が来てくれて、楽しかった。)
Oh, what a nice time we had, my friend came!

Function II "No more than __"; ～しか…ない

The construction「～しか…ない」means "no more than __", "only __, and no more", etc.「～しかない」used after verbs means "the only thing left to do is __".

ex. 1. この店は、お盆とお正月しか休みません。

This store closes only at *O-bon* and New Years.

2. あれ！　さいふの中に、1000円しか入ってない！

What? I've only got 1000 yen in my wallet, no more!

3. 5日間しか休めないなんて、がっかりしました。

We can only take five days vacation and no more? How disappointing!

4. もっと休みたかったら、会社をやめるしかありませんね。

If you want more time off, the only thing you can do is to quit your job.

Note: While「しか…ない」implies that the amount is unthinkably small,「だけ」(see Lesson 15, p.190) merely states such and such an amount, no more, no less. An even more powerful expression is formed by combining「だけ」and「しか…ない」.

ex. A: おそれいります。いま、店においてあるのは、これだけなんです。

I'm terribly sorry, but this is all we have in the store right now.

B: これだけしかないんですか。しかたがないですね。じゃあ、これで、けっこうです。

This is all you have? That's too bad! Alright then, I'll settle for this!

B: 店には、これしかなかったんですよ。 This was all they had in the store.

Exercise 4: Reply using「～しか…ない」, as in the example.

ex. A: 夏休みは、何日、取れるんですか。

B: それが、(1週間しか、取れないんですよ)。〈1週間〉

1) A: 東京から京都まで、新幹線で、どのくらいかかるんですか。ずいぶん、かかるんでしょう？

B: いいえ、＿＿＿＿＿＿＿＿＿＿。〈2時間45分〉

2) A: 東京に住んでいると、やちんが、ずいぶんかかるんでしょう？

B: ええ。でも、わたしは、社宅に住んでいますから、＿＿＿＿＿＿＿＿。〈2万円〉

3) A: 楽しいショーですねえ。終わりまで、あと何時間ありますか。

B: あと20分で、終わりですよ。

A: あと＿＿＿＿＿＿＿。ざんねんだなあ。

4) A: あなたの会社には、英語を話せる人が、たくさんいるんでしょう？

B: それが…、＿＿＿＿＿＿＿＿。〈2、3人〉

5) A: 食事をして行きたいんだけど、君、お金を持ってる？

B: いま、＿＿＿＿＿＿＿けど…。〈1000円〉

A: なんだ、それだけしかないのか。じゃ、食事をしないで、うちに帰ろう。

6) A: お母さん、友達が5人来るんだけど、おかし、買ってある？

B: えっ、5人も？　ケーキが＿＿＿＿＿＿＿よ。こまったわねえ。〈3つ〉

Vocabulary

にこにこする to smile
そうそう Oh yes, now I remember!
やちん rent (for house, apartment, etc.)
社宅（しゃたく）company housing for employees
ショー show
2、3人 2 or 3 persons
終わり（おわり）end
君（きみ）you (a men's word used among equals or to inferiors or children)

7) A: このバッグは、あの店しか売ってないそうですよ。

B: じゃ、ほしかったら、あの店に__________________。〈買いに行く〉

8) A: あの映画は、今日までだそうですよ。

B: そうですか。じゃ、雨がふっているけど、今日、______________。〈見に行く〉

Function III Asking information about something unfamiliar; お盆って何ですか。

～ というのは／とは／ って	＋ **Question word** ＋ですか。

The expression「～というのは」lit. "as for the one called __" is commonly used when asking or telling such things as identity, definition, description or explanation concerning items which are unfamiliar.「～というのは」is sometimes shortened to「～とは」(bookish) or「～って」(colloquial).

ex.1. A: ホンコンというのは、どんな所ですか。／ホンコンって、どんな所ですか。

What sort of place is Hong Kong? (lit. As for the one called Hong Kong, what sort of place is it?)

B: 店がたくさんあって、とてもにぎやかな所です。

It's a very busy place with many stores.

2. A: 「はらが立つ」って、どういうことですか。 What does it mean,「はらが立つ」?

B: 「おこりたくなる」ということですよ。 It means to get angry.

3. A: とうふって、何ですか。 What is *tofu*?

B: だいずで作った、白くてやわらかい食べ物ですよ。

It's a soft, white food made from soybeans.

4. A: あのたてものの中に、入っちゃだめだよ。

You mustn't go inside that building over there.

B: だめって、どうしてですか。 Why do you say, "mustn't"?

A: 工事中で、あぶないからだよ。 Because it's under construction and it's dangerous.

5. 「ひなまつり」というのは、3月3日に、ひなにんぎょうをかざって、女の子の成長をいわう、日本の行事です。 *Hinamatsuri* is a Japanese festival celebrating the growing up of little girls, and is celebrated on March 3rd by putting out "*Hina*" dolls.

6. ワープロとは、コンピューターを使った、タイプライターのようなものです。

A word processor is like a computerized typewriter.

Exercise 5: For the following pictures construct a dialogue between A and B, where A asks identity, definition, description, etc., and B replies. Use「～というのは」or「～って」.

1) 鹿児島／どこ

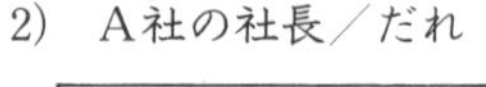
2) A社の社長／だれ

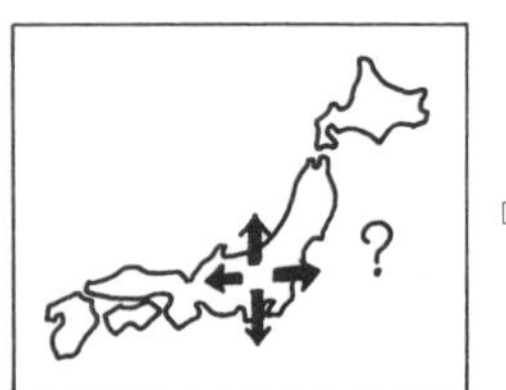

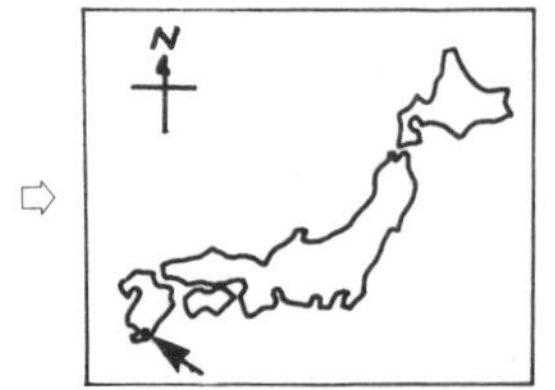

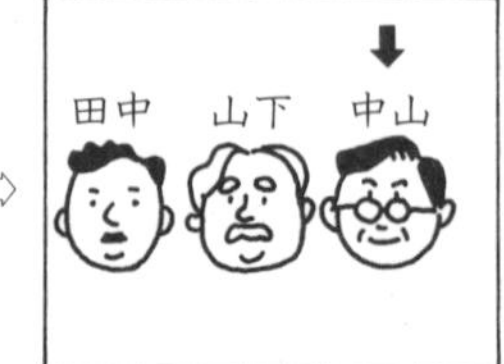

3) かき／何

4) 夏休み／いつ

7/20～9/5

5) 行けない／なぜ

6) 京都／どんな所

Exercise 6: Use「～というのは」,「～って」or topic「は」in the sentences below.

1) A: 日本では、夏に、よく「そうめん」を食べるんですよ。
   B: そうめん（　）、どんな物ですか。
   A: そうめん（　）、「うどん」のような食べ物で、うどんより、ほそいんですよ。

2) A: わたしは、山はすきですが、海（　）、あまりすきじゃないんですよ。
   B: すきじゃない（　）、どうしてですか。
   A: だって、泳げないんです。人が泳いでいるのを見ているだけじゃ、つまらないですから。

3) A: ウエッブさん、お中元（　）、もうおくりましたか。
   B: お中元（　）、何ですか。
   A: お中元というのは、お盆のころ、おせわになった人におくる、おくりもののことですよ。
   B: 「おせいぼ」というの（　）、聞いたことがありますけど。
   A: ああ、それは、12月におくる、おくりものですよ。

Grammar Note II　Embedded questions

When embedded in other sentences, questions appear in their plain form.

	Question	Embedded Question
ex. 1.	ボーナスって、何ですか。 What is a bonus?	ボーナスって何（だ）か、知っていますか。 Do you know what a bonus is?
2.	今、何時ですか。 What time is it now?	今、何時（だ）か、わかりますか。 Do you know what time it is now?
3.	だれに聞いたらいいでしょうか。 Who do you suppose I should ask?	だれに聞いたらいいか、教えてください。 Please tell me who I should ask.

Vocabulary

じんじゃ shrine　　そうめん thin wheat noodles　　ほそい thin, slender
だって well, because　　お中元（おちゅうげん）mid-year gift　　おせわになる to receive help or care
おせいぼ year-end gift　　おくりもの present, gift

4. 来週のパーティーには、何人来ますか。 How many people are coming to the party next week?

何人来るか、聞いていません。 I haven't heard how many people are coming.

5. 夏休みは、どこに行きますか。 Where are you going summer vacation?

どこに行くか、まだ決(き)めていません。 I haven't decided yet where I'm going.

Exercise 7: Embed the first question into the second sentence.

ex. どこへ行くつもりですか。花田さんに聞(き)きました。 →どこへ行くつもりか、花田さんに聞きました。
→花田さんに、どこへ行くつもりか、聞きました。

1) 斎藤(さいとう)さんの結婚式(けっこんしき)は、いつですか。聞いていますか。
2) 駅で、何時間ならびましたか。もう、わすれてしまいました。
3) だれが来ませんか。早く、調(しら)べておいたほうがいいですよ。
4) 大阪は、どこにありますか。この地図(ちず)で、教(おし)えてください。
5) あしたのパーティーに、だれが来ますか。知りません。
6) ホテルを予約(よやく)できましたか。黒田さんに聞いてみます。
7) 田中(たなか)さんは、何をしていますか。木村(きむら)さんだったら、知っているでしょう。
8) 会議を、いつしますか。マイケルさんと、そうだんしておいてください。

Exercise 8: Look back at the pictures for Exercise 5 and ask questions using an embedded question, as in the example.

ex. 鹿児島(かごしま)／どこ → 鹿児島はどこにあるか、知っていますか。

Function IV Telling why and for what purpose; 買うために

Noun ＋の Verb (Plain non-past)	＋ため（に）	"for __, for the sake of __" "for the purpose of __, in order to __"

ex. 1. マイケルさんは、黒田さんのために、京都のおみやげを買って来ました。
Michael brought back a gift from Kyoto for Miss Kuroda.

2. バーバラさんが、いつもテレビを見ているのは、何のためか、わかりますか。
Do you know why it is that Barbara is always watching TV?

3. 会議に出るために、来週、大阪へ出張(しゅっちょう)することになりました。
I'm supposed to go to Osaka next week in order to attend a meeting.

4. フランス語をおぼえるためには、やはり、フランスに留学(りゅうがく)したほうがいいでしょうね。
In order to learn French, I suppose it would be better after all to attend school in France, right?

Vocabulary

いみ meaning
家族旅行（かぞくりょこう） trip with one's family
声（こえ） voice
エンジン engine
てちょう notebook
ダイヤル dial
ガソリン gasoline, gas
はっきり clearly, distinctly
まわす (u-vt) to spin, turn, dial

Caution: In cases where you indeed want something to, or not to, come about, but where that thing itself is not necessarily the ultimate purpose you have in mind it may be more appropriate to use「ように」"such that __, so as to __, in such a way as to __" (see Lesson 18, p.228〜9).

ex.1. × かぜをひかないために、気をつけてください。

× Please take care for the purpose of not catching a cold.

○ かぜをひかないように、気をつけてください。

○ Please take care so as not to catch a cold.

2. × だれでも読めるために、字を、きれいに書いてください。

× Please write your letters clearly, in order that anyone can read them.

○ だれでも読めるように、字を、きれいに書いてください。

○ Please write your letters clearly, such that anyone can read them.

(Note, the person above is not writing for the purpose of having anyone and everyone read what he writes.)

3. わたしにもわかるように、もっとやさしく説明してください。

Please explain more simply so that it is understandable to me too.

Exercise 9: Join each expression in (**a**) with an appropriate expression in (**b**) using「ため（に）」.

(**a**)	(**b**)
1) ことばのいみを調べる	・レストランを予約する
2) 新幹線にのる	・ワープロを使う
3) マイケルさんのかんげい会をする	・東京駅に行く
4) わからないところを教えてもらう	・車のエンジンを止める
5) ガソリンを入れる	・休みを取る
6) 書類を、速くきれいに書く	・先生のへやに行く
7) 家族旅行に行く	・辞書をひく

Exercise 10: Complete the following sentences with an appropriate verb from the list below using「ため（に）」or「よう（に）」.

1) 明日中に________________、小包を、速達で出します。
2) みんなに、はっきり______________、大きな声で話してください。
3) アメリカから来た友達に___________、新宿のホテルに行きました。
4) 授業に______________、もう少し早く、家を出ることにします。
5) 電話番号を_____________、てちょうを見ながら、ダイヤルをまわしました。
6) このパンフレットは、外国人にも______________、英語やフランス語などで書いてあります。
7) 子どもが___________、おかしを、たくさん買っておきました。
8) 病気が早く_____________、薬を飲んでねます。
9) 病気を早く______________、薬を飲んでねます。

よろこぶ	会う	読める	とどく	おくれる	聞こえる	なおる	なおす	まちがえる

Reading Comprehension Exercise

日本の会社では、ふつう、夏と冬に、給料の２、３か月分ずつ、ボーナスが出ます。日本人は、このお金で、いなかに帰ったり、旅行をしたり、レジャーを楽しんだり、ちょきんをしたりします。

ウエッブさんは、新入社員なので、ボーナスは、0.8か月分しかもらえないから、がっかりしています。アメリカでは、ボーナスを、休みでもらうこともできますが、日本には、そういう しゅうかんがないことを知って、ウエッブさんは、おどろきました。

日本人も、さいきんは、だいぶ、夏休みを取るようになりました。しかし、ヨーロッパやアメリカにくらべると、まだ、夏休みは、みじかいです。

◆Vocabulary◆

しゅうかん custom, practice
レジャー leisure, recreation
ちょきんする savings, deposit
楽しむ（たのしむ）(u–vt) to enjoy
くらべる (ru–vt) to compare

Exercise 11: Write a short paragraph on the following themes:

1) わたしの国の夏休み　　2) わたしの国のボーナス

Listening Comprehension Exercise

Listen to the tape and answer the following questions.

1) 「さっぽろ」の「雪まつり」の写真は、どれですか。

a.

b.

c.

d.

2) 「さっぽろ」は、どこにありますか。

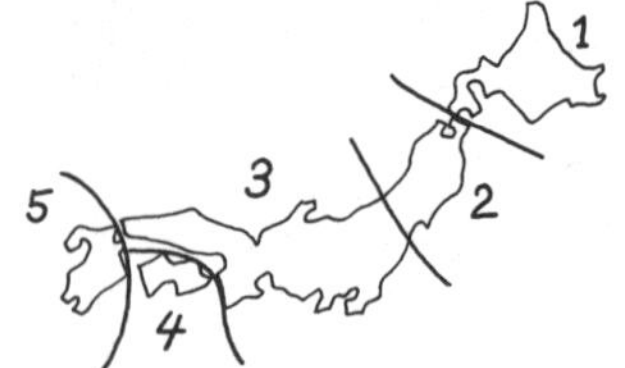

3) 「さっぽろ」の「雪まつり」は、いつですか。

a. FEB 2月 (← 12–18)

日	月	火	水	木	金	土
・	・	・	1	2	3	4
5	6	7	8	9	10	⑪
12	13	14	15	16	17	18
19	20	21	22	23	24	25
26	27	28	・	・	・	・

b. FEB 2月 (← 1–4)

日	月	火	水	木	金	土
・	・	・	1	2	3	4
5	6	7	8	9	10	⑪
12	13	14	15	16	17	18
19	20	21	22	23	24	25
26	27	28	・	・	・	・

4) ゆみ子さんは、なぜ、「さっぽろ」の「雪まつり」の写真を見ていますか。

a. ゆみ子さんが、旅行の予約をするため。

b. バーバラさんを旅行にさそうため。

c. 去年の「雪まつり」を思い出したから。

c. FEB 2月 (← 19–25)

日	月	火	水	木	金	土
・	・	・	1	2	3	4
5	6	7	8	9	10	⑪
12	13	14	15	16	17	18
19	20	21	22	23	24	25
26	27	28	・	・	・	・

Vocabulary

雪まつり（ゆきまつり）Snow Festival
思い出す（おもいだす）(u–vt) to remember, recollect

■Culture Note■

Festivals (2) **New Years and *O-bon***

The Japanese year is punctuated by two major festivals, New Years and *O-bon*. New Years celebrates the beginning of the new year, and *O-bon* is a Buddhist festival for the veneration of one's ancestors. At these times schools, factories and businesses close down for a week or so and most people return to their home towns to celebrate. Because of the masses of people on the move, transportation systems are terribly over-crowded.

In older times New Years and *O-bon* marked divisions in the bussiness year, and represented the two times a year when live-in employees were allowed vacation. It was customary for employers to hand out extra sums of cash to their workers so they could afford the trip home, and in modern times this has evolved into the practice of giving bonuses twice a year, once before *O-bon* and once before New Years. Also evolving from this division of the business year is the practice of giving out gifts to persons with whom one has had dealings as a token of appreciation and continuing good will. The mid-summer gift is known as「御中元 *O-chuugen*」, and the year end gift is called「御歳暮 *O-seebo*」. At such times department stores set up special gift corners and the weekend after bonuses are paid is especially packed with gift shoppers.

New Years — is celebrated by enjoying *o-sechi, o-zooni* and other special foods. *O-sechi* consists of an array of different foods packed into 3 or 5 stacked boxes and eaten over a three day period beginning January 1. Because it is prepared in advance, it helps free the housewife from the chore of preparing meals. Japanese nowadays have little occasion to wear traditional style dress, and so many people dress up in Japanese style clothing and make the traditional New Year's visit to a *Shinto* Shrine. Needless to say, popular shrines are virtually inundated with the flow of people.

O-bon — a Buddhist festival centering around July 15(or in some areas, August 15). This is the time when spirits of the dead return to this world and people visit the family grave to pay respect. Other activities include:

July 13 — The day on which the spirits return. They are welcomed by lighting a lantern in front of the house.

July 15, 16 — The time when the spirits go back to the other world. Candles are lighted and lanterns are put in small boats and floated on the river.

As a means of consoling the visiting spirits, people gather at temples or other open spaces and dance Bon odori. The tunes to which the people dance come from all over the country, and each has its own particular dance movements. In modern times the religious flavor has been lost and Bon odori is regarded as a form of recreation intended as relief from the summer heat.

▲New Year's visit to a *Shinto* Shrine.

▲Lanterns floating on the river.

ウエッブさん、がんばって！

Go, Michael! Go!

Dialogue I

At the office

田辺(たなべ)　：ウエッブさん、北村課長から、例(れい)の話(はなし)を聞きましたか。

マイケル：いえ、まだです。じつは、今(いま)、来たところなんです。

田辺　：そうですか。じゃ、課長から、ちょくせつ話を聞いてください。おや、どうしたんですか、そのけがは？

マイケル：ええ、天気(てんき)がいいから、自転車(じてんしゃ)で駅まで行こうと思ったんです。そして、うちの近くのかどをまがろうとしたとき、転(ころ)んだんです。

田辺　：ああ、そうですか。気をつけてくださいね。それに、もうすぐ社内運動会(しゃないうんどうかい)でしょう？　ウエッブさんにも、リレーに出てもらおうと思っていますから。

マイケル：ええ。ええっと…、運動会は、いつでしたっけ。

田辺　：今月の18日ですよ。

マイケル：ああ、もうすぐですね。ところで、雨がふったら、どうなるんですか。

田辺　：雨ですか。雨がふれば、運動会は、えんきですよ。

マイケル：そうですか。ふらなければいいですね。

Dialogue II

At the company sports tournament

北村　：花田君(はなだくん)、リレーは、もうはじまってる？

花田　：ええ。ちょうど今、田辺さんが走っているところです。ほら、あそこ…。

北村　：黒田君や、ウエッブ君はまだ？

花田　：黒田さんが、これから走るところです。
今、田辺さんが、黒田さんにバトンを
わたしていますよ。
黒田さん、がんばって！

北村　：黒田君、がんばれ！

花田　：つぎは、ウエッブさんですよ。

（黒田さんが、ウエッブさんにバトンをわたそうとしたとき、転ぶ）

花田　：あーっ、黒田さんが転んだ！　黒田さん、しっかり！

北村　：あ、ウエッブ君がたすけて、バトンを取った。　走れ！　走れ！
ウエッブ君、速いなあ……。ところで、黒田さんは、だいじょうぶかな。

花田　：ええ、ちょっと、見て来ます。

Dialogue III

After the relay

北村　：みんな、ごくろうさま。よくがんばったね。１位にはなれなかったけど、
３位に入賞したんだから、りっぱだよ。

みんな　：ありがとうございます。

北村　：それで、黒田さんのけがは、だいじょうぶ？

マイケル：今、あっちで、手あてをしています。
バトンをわたそうとしたとき、転んで、足を強くうったそうです。

北村　：そう、たいへんだったね。じゃ、３位入賞をいわって、帰りに、
ビールでかんぱいしようか。

みんな　：わーっ、いいですね。さんせい！

Vocabulary

Nouns:

4けが する injury　　8リレー する relay race (to relay)

10運動会（うんどうかい）sports tournament；社内運動会（しゃないうんどうかい）company sports tournament

16えんきする postponement
22バトン baton
33入賞（にゅうしょう）する win a prize
36手あて（てあて）する treatment
40さんせいする agree ("count me in", "that's a good idea")

Adverbs:

3ちょくせつ directly, nothing in between

Verbs:

24がんばる (u-vi) to try hard, do one's best
29たすける (ru-vt) to help, save, aid, lend a hand

Grammatical words:

19〜ところ just as, just about to, on the point of, in the process of, etc. ☞ Function Ⅲ

Expressions:

2いえ No.
5行こう I will go, let's go
10ええっと Uh ...
11いつでしたっけ？ When was it again? (I heard once, but I don't remember)
14どうなるんですか what's happening? what are you doing?
19ほら See! Look! There!
28あーっ Oh, no!
28しっかり！ Come on! Cheer up! Don't give up!
32ごくろうさま Thank you. Thank you for your trouble.

> ウエップ君（くん）　黒田君（くん）
>
> Usually「-君」is attached to the names of males equal or lower than oneself, but as seen in the dialogue, higher ranking men sometimes use it in addressing lower ranking females. Recently however there is a tendency to use「-さん」for both males and females.

Dialogue Comprehension Exercise

Answer the following questions.

Dialogue Ⅰ

1) ウエップさんは、いつ、けがをしましたか。
2) ウエップさんは、運動会（うんどうかい）で、何に出ますか。
3) 18日に雨がふったら、運動会は、どうなりますか。

Dialogue Ⅱ

4) 田辺さんのつぎに、だれが走りますか。
5) 転（ころ）んだのは、だれですか。
6) 転んだ人は、けがをしましたか。
7) ウエップさんたちは、何位（なんい）になりましたか。
8) ウエップさんたちは、運動会のあと、何をしますか。

Function Ⅰ　Expressing a decision to act: "I will __"; 〜ようと思う

The plain and polite let's forms may also be used to express a decision on the part of the speaker to do such and such an action, and are equivalent to "I will __" in English.

Plain let's form

u-verb root + oo	書こう
ru-verb root + yoo	食べよう
Irregular	行こう，来（こ）よう，しよう

ex. 1. さあ、さいごのきょうぎだ。よし、がんばろう。
Well, it's the final event. Alright then! I'll give it all I've got!

2. もう、6時だ。さあ、起（お）きようか。
It's 6 o'clock already. Shall I get up then? (speaking to oneself)

3. A: もう、おすしは、いいですか。　Have you had enough *sushi*?

B: ええ、おなかがいっぱいで、もう食べられませんわ。

Yes. I'm full and can't eat any more.

A: じゃ、残(のこ)りは、ぼくが食べることにしましょう。

In that case, I'll just eat up what's left.

4. あしたは、早く起(お)きようと思います。

I think I'll get up early tomorrow.

5. いっしょに映画(えいが)でも見ようと思って、バーバラさんに電話をしました。

I gave Barbara a call, thinking I'd see a movie or something with her.

6. 来年の夏(なつ)、イギリスに行こうと思っています。

I'm thinking of going to England next summer.

Note: The let's form +「と思う」or「と思っている」means roughly the same as「つもり」(see Lesson 7, p.101), except that with「つもり」the plan is much more definite.

ex. 来年の夏、イギリスに行くつもりです。

I'm planning to go to England next summer.

Dialogues in English

Dialogue Ⅰ

T: Mr. Webb. Did you hear about that matter, you know, from, section manager, Kitamura?

M: No, not yet. As a matter of fact, I just now got here.

T: Is that so? Well then, please hear about it directly from the section manager. Hey! What happened to you? That injury!

M: Well, you see, it's nice out, so I thought I'd take my bike to the station. And when I tried to turn the corner near our house, I fell over.

T: Gee, is that so? Please be careful, alright? Besides, the company sports tournament is pretty soon, right? I'm thinking of having you take part in the relay race as well.

M: Fine. Uh, when was the sports tournament again?

T: It's the eighteenth of this month!

M: Gosh, that's pretty soon, huh? What happens if it rains, by the way?

T: You're asking about rain? If it rains, the sports tournament will be postponed.

M: I see. Let's hope it doesn't rain, eh?

Dialogue Ⅱ

Ki: Has the relay race already begun, Miss Hanada?

Ha: Yes. Mr. Tanabe is just now running. See? Over there!

Ki: What about Miss Kuroda, Michael and the others? Not yet?

Ha: Miss Kuroda is just about to run now. Now Mr. Tanabe is handing Miss Kuroda the baton. Go, Kuroda! Go!

Ki: Give it all you've got, Kuroda!

Ha: Next it's Mr. Webb.

(Miss Kuroda stumbles just as she's handing the baton to Michael.)

Ha: Oh,no! Miss Kuroda fell down! Come on, Miss Kuroda!

Ki: Oh! Michael gave her a hand and took the baton! Run! Run! Gee, Michael is really fast! I wonder, is Miss Kuroda alright though?

Ha: Just a moment? I'll go see.

Dialogue Ⅲ

Ki: Thank you, everyone! You all did your best. Even though we didn't come in first, we did win third prize, so you were terrific!

All: Thank you very much!

Ki: And Miss Kuroda's injury? Is she alright?

M: They're treating her right now over there. She fell down as she tried to pass the baton, and it seems she banged her leg rather severely.

Ki: I see. That was really too bad. Well then, shall we celebrate winning third place and toast ourselves with some beer on the way home?

All: Wow! Great! Count me in!

Exercise 1: Express the following sentences as "I think I will __" or "I'm thinking I will __".

1) あしたは、学校に行く。　2) もっと、勉強する。　3) この本を、今日中に読む。
4) あのベンチにすわる。　5) 10時に、会議を始める。　6) あの店で、コーヒーを飲む。

Exercise 2: Do the same for the following sentences, and then use them at appropriate places in the conversations below.

1) ヨーロッパに旅行する。　2) 両親に電話をかける。　3) たばこをやめる。
4) おれいの手紙を書く。　5) 毎日、会社に歩いて行く。　6) 体重をへらす。

① A: さいきん、運動ぶそくなんですよ。
それで、(　　　)。
B: ああ、それは、けんこうにいいですね。

② A: 去年買った服が、着られなくなったんですよ。
B: へえ。そんなに太ったんですか。
A: ええ。それで、もう少し、(　　　)。

③ A: アメリカで、大雨がふったそうですね。
B: ええ、ちょっとしんぱいでね、(　　　)。

④ A: さいきん、禁煙の場所が多くなりましたね。
B: ええ。それで、(　　　)。

⑤ A: 夏休みは、どうするんですか。
B: (　　　)。
A: それは、うらやましいなあ。

⑥ A: きれいなテーブルクロスですね。
B: メキシコの友達が送ってくれたんですよ。
それで、(　　　)。

Function II　"To try to do __"; かどを まがろうとする

The construction 「**plain let's form** ＋とする」 means "to try to do such and such".

ex. 1. ほら、けがをした鳥が、飛ぼうとしている！
Look! The injured bird is trying to fly!

2. 父は、ワインのせんをぬこうとしたが、できなかった。
My father tried to pull out the wine cork, but he couldn't.

3. 電話をかけようとしたら、10円玉がなかったんです。
When I tried to phone, I didn't have a 10 yen coin, you see.

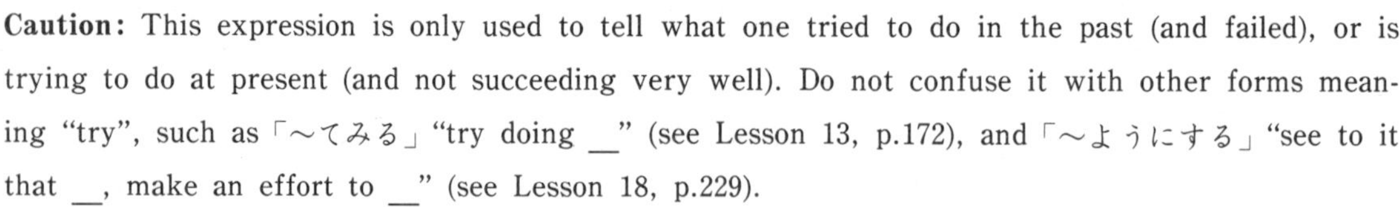

Caution: This expression is only used to tell what one tried to do in the past (and failed), or is trying to do at present (and not succeeding very well). Do not confuse it with other forms meaning "try", such as 「～てみる」 "try doing __" (see Lesson 13, p.172), and 「～ようにする」 "see to it that __, make an effort to __" (see Lesson 18, p.229).

ex. 1. ジュースを飲もうとして、こぼしてしまいました。
I tried to drink the juice, but I spilled it.

2. このジュースを飲んでみたら、おいしかった。(×　飲もうとしたら)
When I tried drinking this juice, it was good.

3. 毎日、ジュースを飲むようにしています。(×　飲もうとしています)
I'm trying to drink juice every day.

Vocabulary

おれい thanks
服 (ふく) clothes, dress
大雨 (おおあめ) heavy rain
体重 (たいじゅう) weight
運動ぶそく (うんどうぶそく) not enough exercise
テーブルクロス tablecloth
へらす (u-vt) to reduce, cut down

Exercise 3: What are the people below trying to do? Use「～oo (yoo) としている」.

Exercise 4: Complete the following sentences using「～oo (yoo) とする」,「～てみる」and「～ようにする」as appropriate.

1) すみません。あしたから、朝早く（起(お)きる）。
2) 毎朝(まいあさ)、早く（起きる）いるんですが、なかなか、起きられないんです。
3) 朝早く起きると、そんなに気持(きも)ちがいいんですか。じゃ、わたしも、一度(いちど)、朝早く（起きる）。
4) あ、あぶない！　子どもが、川(かわ)を泳(およ)いで（わたる）ています。
5) これからは、川を、泳いでわたったりしません。はしを（わたる）。
6) この川を、泳いでわたれるかどうか、今度(こんど)、（泳ぐ）。

Function III　Indicating at what point the action stands; 走っているところです。

「ところ」"place, location" modified by various tenses of the verb indicates at what point the action stands.

present: 走るところ　　progressive: 走っているところ　　past: 走ったところ

present	progressive	past
* is on the point of running * is on the verge of running * is just about to run * is ready to run	* is in the process of running * is in the middle of running	* has just run * has just finished running * is on the point of having just completed running

ex. 1. すみません。また、あとで来てください。これから、でかけるところなんです。
I'm sorry. Please come again later. You see, I'm just about to leave now.

2. あした、日本語の試験(しけん)があるので、今(いま)、その勉強(べんきょう)をしているところです。
There's a test in Japanese tomorrow, and right now I'm in the middle of studying for it.

3. 夏休みに、何をしようかと、今、考えているところです。

   I'm presently in the process of thinking about what I should do over summer vacation.

4. 父は、今、おふろに入ったところなんです。30分後に、また、電話をしていただけませんか。

   My father is just now gone into the bath. Could you call back again in 30 minutes please?

5. はい、今、おふろからあがったところです。少々、お待ちください。

   Yes, he's just now finished his bath. One moment please!

6. 買い物に行こうと思っているところに、木下さんが来ました。

   Mr. Kinoshita came just as I was thinking of going shopping.

Note: Similar to「past tense ＋ところ」is the expression「past tense ＋ばかり」. Although both mean "have just done __", 「ところ」means "just now", "at this instant", while「ばかり」means "a while ago".

ex. 1. 父は、今、帰ってきたところです。 My father just now came home.

2. 父は、帰ってきたばかりで、まだ、食事をしていません。
   My father just got home a while ago and he hasn't eaten dinner yet.

3. 日本語の勉強を始めたばかりで、まだ２か月しかたっていません。
   I've just begun studying Japanese, and only two months have gone by.

Exercise 5: Tell the point at which the action stands, using「ところ」.

Exercise 6: Michael goes mountain climbing with some friends from work. Tell what the people are about to do, in the process of doing, or have just finished doing, in each of the photos.

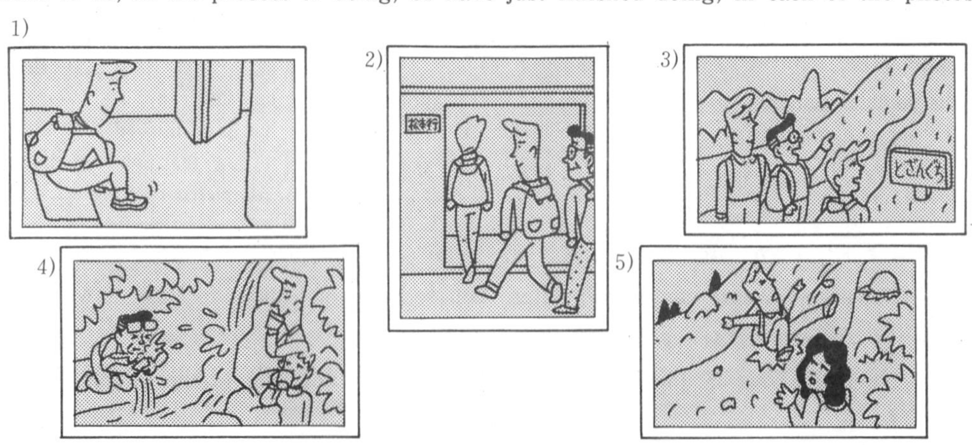

Function IV　Exclaiming what you see; あ、黒田さんが転(ころ)んだ。

When reporting what you see as an exclamation, the past tense form of the verb is used (see Lesson 19, p.236 for explanation).

ex. 1.　あ、来た、来た。　　2.　あーっ、黒田さんが転んだ。　　3.　打(う)った、取(と)った、投(な)げた。

4. A:　もうすぐ、富士山(ふじさん)が見えるはずなんですけどねえ。

We ought to be seeing Mt. Fuji very shortly now.

B:　あ、見えました、見えました。　Oh, I see it! I see it!

5. 書類(しょるい)を、このつくえの上に、おいたはずなんだけどなあ。あ、あった、あった。

I thought I left the papers on top of this desk. Oh, here they are! Here they are!

Exercise 7: Report what is happening in the following pictures as an exclamation using the past tense.

Function V　Conditional (3): "if __, then __"; 雨が ふれば

A third conditional form is made by adding the conditional inflection「-eba (reba)」, and is used in making conjectural or hypothetical "if __, then __" statements,

Conditional「〜えば（れば）」

Verbs	**u-root ＋ eba**	書けば
	ru-root ＋ reba	食べれば
	Irregular: 行けば, 来(く)れば, すれば	
い-adj.	**root**＋ければ	高ければ
な-adj.	**root**（－で）＋あれば	きれいであれば
Be-verb	であれば	
Negative	（で）なければ	

Vocabulary

火（ひ） fire: 火をつける to set fire, light
投げる（なげる） (ru-vt) to throw
とざんぐち start of a trail up a mountain
ホームラン home run
ランナー runner

ex. 1. 1時までに駅に行けば、山田さんに会えますよ。

If you get to the station by one o'clock, then you can meet Mr. Yamada.

2. もし、安ければ、そのつくえを買います。安くなければ、買いません。

I'm going to buy that desk if it's not expensive. If it is expensive, then I'm not going to buy it.

3. もし、あした、晴れれば、ディズニーランドに行きます。

If it's nice tomorrow, then we are going to go to Disneyland.

"If __, then __" statements can also be made using「～たら」(see Lesson 12, p.161), which may be substituted for「～えば」in the above examples.「～えば」is not used in conditional sentences meaning "when" or "whenever". Instead「～たら」and「と」(see Lesson 15, p.195) are used.

ex. 1. 京都駅に着いたら、田中さんが、むかえに来ていました。

When I arrived at Kyoto Station, Mr. Tanaka was there to meet me.

京都駅に着くと、田中さんが、むかえに来ていました。

When I arrived at Kyoto Station, Mr. Tanaka was there to meet me.

× 京都駅に着けば、田中さんが、むかえに来ていました。

2. 太郎が来たら、会議を始めましょう。

Let's begin the meeting when Taro gets here. (Taro is definitely coming)

太郎が来れば、会議がうまくいくでしょう。

The meeting will go well if Taro comes. (it is not known if he will come or not)

Note 1: Active verbs with「～えば」cannot be followed by commands, requests, suggestions, admonitions, etc.

ex. もし、京都に行ったら、おみやげを買って来てください。(×行けば)

If you go to Kyoto, please buy me a present.

Note 2:「～えば」is often used to state instructions, scientific principles, etc.

ex. お金を入れて、白いボタンをおせば、きっぷが出てきます。

Put in your money, press the white button, and out comes a ticket.

Exercise 8: Reply to the following by stipulating an appropriate condition.

1) A: お客さん、いちごは、どうですか。安くしますから、買ってくださいよ。

B: そうですね。＿＿＿＿ば、買ってもいいけど。

2) A: あした、いっしょに、ピクニックに行きませんか。

B: そうですね。天気が＿＿＿＿ば、行ってもいいですよ。

A: じゃ、ＮＴＴの177に電話して、たしかめてみましょう。

3) A: ここから駅まで、何分ぐらいですか。

B: 歩くと、遠いですが、＿＿＿＿ば、10分ぐらいです。

4) A: この漢字の意味を知っていますか。

B: さあ、わたしは、ちょっと…。辞書を＿＿＿＿ば、わかると思いますよ。

5) A: 子どものころ、何になりたいと思っていましたか。

B: バスケットボールの選手です。もう少し、せが＿＿＿＿ば、選手になれたんですけど…。

Vocabulary

たしかめる (ru-vt) to make sure, ascertain　～ごろ time, when　バスケットボール basketball
選手（せんしゅ）player　スキー skiing　スキー場（スキーじょう）ski area

6) A: いいカメラですねえ。ぼくも、そんなカメラがほしいなあ。

B: そうですか。わたしは、もう使(つか)わないから、＿＿＿＿ば、持(も)って行ってもいいですよ。

7) A: スキー場(じょう)では、もうスキーができますか。

B: ええ、もう少し雪(ゆき)が＿＿＿＿ば、スキーができるようになります。

8) A: あした、映画(えいが)を見に行きませんか。

B: ええ。でも、こんでるでしょう？　＿＿＿＿ば、行ってもいいけど…。

Exercise 9: Mark ○ or × if you think the following conditional forms are used correctly or not.

1) (　)　京都に着(つ)いたら、電話をしてください。
2) (　)　京都に着けば、電話をしてください。
3) (　)　９時に家を出れば、まにあいますよ。
4) (　)　田中さんが来れば、会議を始(はじ)めましょう。
5) (　)　あつければ、窓(まど)をあけてもいいですよ。
6) (　)　山田さんに会(あ)ったら、この手紙(てがみ)をわたしてください。

Function VI　Cheering on and cheering up

1 Cheering someone on

1) To someone about to take part in a sports competition or drama, someone about to take an examination or begin some big undertaking, etc.

Expressions:

がんばって（ください）。
しっかり　やってください。
ぜひ、～してください。
　ex. ゆうしょうしてください
　　　せいこうしてください。

ex. 1. リレーに出るんだって？　がんばってね。
I hear you're going to run in the relay. Good luck!

2. 今度(こんど)の仕事は、たいへんですね。しっかり、やってください。
This next job is going to be hard. Hope you do a good, thorough job!

3. 野球(やきゅう)の試合(しあい)では、ぜひ、ゆうしょうしてください。
Be sure to win the baseball game.

Response:

informal　（男）うん、がんばるよ。（女）ええ、がんばるわ。
formal　（男・女）はい、がんばります。　Yes, I'll do the best I can!

2) Shouting encouragement

Imperative inflection「～e, ～ro」

u-root + e	走(はし)れ (hashir-e)	
ru-root + ro	なげろ (nage-ro)	
Irregular:	行け, 来(こ)い, しろ	

The imperative form is very straightforward and direct and not generally used, except at sports events, etc. when everyone is excited.

2 Cheering someone up

1) To someone sick or injured

Expressions:

> 早く、よくなってください。
> おだいじに。

ex. 1. 交通じこで、けがをしたんですって？　早くよくなってくださいね。
I hear you were injured in a traffic accident. Hurry up and get well.

2. かぜをひいたんですか。どうぞ、おだいじに。
Have you caught a cold? Please take care of yourself.

Response:

informal　（男）うん、ありがとう。（女）ええ、ありがとう。

formal　（男・女）はい、ありがとうございます。　Yes. Thank you very much.

2) To someone who has lost, failed, had an accident, etc.

Expressions:

気にしないで（ください）。	Don't be concerned about it.
気をおとさないで（ください）。	Don't get down hearted.
がっかりしないでください。	Don't be disappointed.
元気を出して（ください）。	Chin up!
しんぱいしないで（ください）。	Don't worry about it!
くよくよしないで（ください）。	Stop moping!
だいじょうぶですよ。	Everything will be OK.

ex.1. A: すみません。おさらをわってしまったんです。　I'm sorry! I broke a plate!
B: いいんですよ。気にしないでください。　That's alright. Think nothing of it!

2. テストの点が、悪かったんですか。でも、そんなに、がっかりしないで。
Did you get a bad score on the exam? Even so, don't be so disappointed!

Response: うん、ありがとう。　ええ、ありがとう。　はい、ありがとうございます。

Note: Often in daily life cheering up and cheering on are done at the same time.
ex. テストの点が、悪かったんですか。気をおとさないで、がんばってくださいね。
Did you get a bad score on the exam? Don't let it get you down. Try harder.

3 Praise: To someone who has done well or succeeded, etc.

Expressions:

> おめでとう（ございます）。
> よかったですね。
> すばらしかったですね。etc.

ex.1. ゆうしょう、おめでとうございます。
Congratulations on your victory!

2. 試験にうかったんですって？　よかったですね。
I hear you passed the exam. That's really great!

3. スミスさん、この前の写真展、すばらしかったですね。
Mr. Smith, your photograph exhibition the other day was really something!

4. ウエッブさんのラストスパート、すごかったですね。
Mr. Webb, that final spurt you put on was really terrific.

Response: ありがとう。　ありがとうございます。

Exercise 10: Cheer on, cheer up or praise the people in the following pictures.

1) About to run a marathon

2) Sick in the hospital

3) Something spilled on the tablecloth

4) Won first place

5) Going abroad on business

6) Bad score on the exam

Reading Comprehension Exercise

Michael turns in the request form on the right to his section manager, Mr. Kitamura.

1) What sort of form is it? Fill in the parentheses with appropriate words or expressions.

　＊マイケルさんは、（　①　）ために、先週（せんしゅう）の（　②　）に、会社に出ました。それで、そのかわりに、来週の火曜日に、（　③　）と思っています。その日は、（　④　）にいるつもりです。

2) Mr. Kitamura wants to praise Michael for the good job he did in preparing for the sports tournament. What sort of things might he say?

諸届願　9月15日

所属 営業1課	氏名 マイケル・ウェッブ

1	2	3	④	5	6 (crossed out)	7	8
欠勤	有給休暇	特別休暇	代休	遅刻	早退	残業	休日出勤

9月19日 火曜日　時　分から
月　日　曜日　時　分まで

理由（くわしく書く）
先週の日曜日，運動会のじゅんびのために休日出勤したので，代休をとりたいと思います。

連絡先　自宅
☎ (401) 8901

◆**Vocabulary**◆
氏名（しめい） person's name
そのかわりに rather than that, instead of that, in place of that
所属（しょぞく） department or section one belongs to
代休（だいきゅう） vacation for extra time put in
休日出勤（きゅうじつしゅっきん）する working on a holiday
連絡先（れんらくさき） place where a person can be contacted
早退（そうたい）する leave work early
理由（りゆう） reason
自宅（じたく） home

Listening Comprehension Exercise

Listen to the description of the marathon race on the tape and choose the diagram which fits the description.

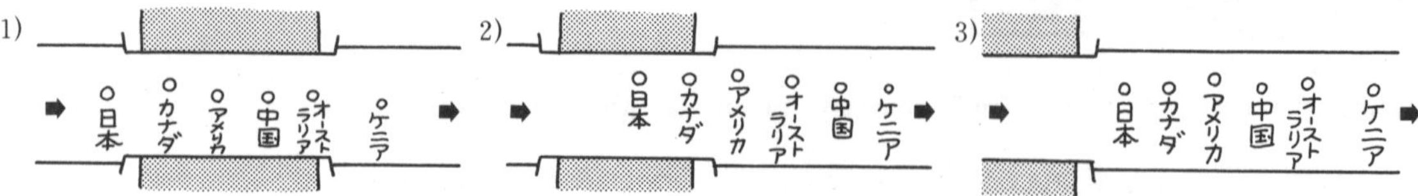

◆**Vocabulary**◆
大会（たいかい） tournament, competition, event
中国（ちゅうごく） China
カナダ Canada
ケニア Kenya

第21課 どこではらえば、いいんですか

Where Do I Pay It?

Dialogue I

Barbara calls on her neighbor, Mrs. Tanabe.

バーバラ：おくさん、ちょっと、お聞きしたいことがあるんですけど。

田辺夫人(たなべふじん)：はい、何でしょう。

バーバラ：こんなものが、ゆうびんで来たんですけど、これ、何でしょう。

田辺夫人：ああ、電気代(でんきだい)のせいきゅうですよ。

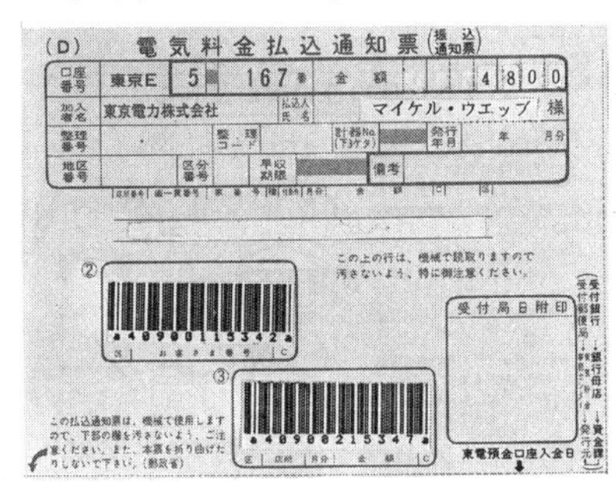

(D) 電気料金払込通知票（振込通知票）

口座番号 東京E 5 167 番　金額 4800

加入者名 東京電力株式会社　払込人氏名 マイケル・ウエッブ 様

整理番号　整理コード　計器No.(下3ケタ)　発行年月 年 月分

地区番号　区分番号　早収期限　備考

この上の行は、機械で読取りますので汚さないよう、特に御注意ください。

② 409001153342　お客さま番号

③ 409002153347

受付局日附印

東電預金口座入金日

この払込通知票は、機械で使用しますので、下部の欄を汚さないよう、ご注意ください。また、本票を折り曲げたりしないで下さい。（郵政省）

バーバラ：電気代？　ああ、電気の料金(りょうきん)ですか。あの、これ、どこではらえば、いいんですか。

田辺夫人：近(ちか)くの銀行ではらえば、いいんですよ。駅前(えきまえ)にある銀行なら、どこでもいいですよ。

バーバラ：そうですか。それで、銀行で、どうしたらいいんですか。

田辺夫人：銀行に行くと、あんないの人がいますから、その人に聞けば、わかりますよ。

バーバラ：そうですか。銀行は、3時までですよね。まにあうでしょうか。

田辺夫人：ええ、今(いま)行けば、まにあいますよ。でも、来月の8日(ようか)までに、はらえばいいんでしょう？あした、ゆっくり、いらっしゃれば？　あしたなら、わたしも行きますし。

バーバラ：ありがとうございます。でも、あしたは、ちょっと用(よう)があるものですから。

Dialogue II

Barbara goes to the bank, finds someone in charge and asks him.

バーバラ：あのう、電気代をはらいたいんですが、どうしたらいいんでしょう？

係員(かかりいん)：電気代(でんきだい)ですか。電気代の方(かた)は、こちらの窓口(まどぐち)です。このボックスのカードを、お取(と)りください。

カードの数字(すうじ)が、ここについたら、お客様(きゃくさま)の番(ばん)ですよ。

バーバラ：(comparing her number with the number on the board)

ずいぶん、待(ま)つんですね。

係員(かかりいん)：そうですね。月末(げつまつ)は、いつも、こむんですよ。

バーバラ：毎月(まいつき)こうだと、たいへんですね。

係員：ええ。あの、お客様は、こちらの銀行に、口座(こうざ)をお持(も)ちですか。

バーバラ：ええ、主人(しゅじん)のですけど。

係員：それなら、口座からの自動(じどう)ひきおとしにすると、べんりですよ。

バーバラ：自動ひきおとしって、何ですか。

係員：口座から、自動的(じどうてき)に、毎月(まいつき)の電気代(でんきだい)をはらうんです。

バーバラ：どうすれば、いいんですか。

係員：このもうしこみ用紙(ようし)に、お名前(なまえ)と、ご住所(じゅうしょ)をお書きになって、ここに、いんかんをおしてください。

バーバラ：あの、すみません。いんかんは、持ってないんですが、サインでいいですか。

係員：ええ、かまいませんよ。ご主人のサインを、もらって来てください。

Dialogue III

Barbara meets Mrs. Tanabe on the way home from the bank.

田辺夫人(たなべふじん)：あら、バーバラさん。銀行は、もう、おすみになりました？

バーバラ：ええ。

田辺夫人：どう？　かんたんだったでしょう？

バーバラ：ええ、銀行の人が、しんせつに教(おし)えてくれました。それで、来月から、自動ひきおとしにすることにしました。

田辺夫人：ああ、自動ひきおとしなら、べんりでいいですね。

バーバラ：田辺さん、荷物(にもつ)をたくさんお持ちですねえ。1つ、お持ちしましょう。

田辺夫人：あら、あら、どうも。

Vocabulary

Nouns:

2夫人（ふじん）housewife, Mrs.
3ゆうびん mail
4電気代（でんきだい）electricity bill
4せいきゅうする demand
8駅前（えきまえ）in front of the station

18係員（かかりいん）person in charge
19ボックス box
20番（ばん）one's turn, order
22月末（げつまつ）end of the month
24口座（こうざ）savings account
26自動ひきおとし（じどうひきおとし）automatic withdrawal
30もうしこみ用紙（もうしこみようし）application form
31いんかん personal seal, stamp

Adverbs: 28自動的に（じどうてきに）automatically

Verbs: 34すむ (u-vi) to be finished, end, be over

Grammatical words:

8なら conditional "if" ☞ Function Ⅱ
23こう like this, in this manner
19お＋ verb stem ＋ください honorific request construction
24お＋verb stem＋です honorific verb construction
30お＋ verb stem ＋になる honorific verb construction
40お＋verb stem＋する humble verb construction ☞ Function Ⅲ

Expressions: 31いんかんをおす to apply one's seal

Dialogue Comprehension Exercise

Dialogue Ⅰ

1) バーバラさんのうちに、ゆうびんで来たのは、何でしたか。
2) 田辺（たなべ）さんは、電気代（でんきだい）を、どこではらえばいいと言いましたか。
3) バーバラさんは、田辺さんといっしょに、銀行に行くことにしましたか。

Dialogue Ⅱ

4) 銀行の係員（かかりいん）は、バーバラさんに、どうすればべんりだと言いましたか。
5) バーバラさんは、これから、毎月（まいつき）、銀行に、電気代をはらいに行くつもりですか。

Dialogue Ⅲ

6) バーバラさんは、田辺さんに、何をしてあげましたか。

Function Ⅰ Giving instructions or directions; ～すればいい

The conditional forms「～たら」and「と」followed by「いい」(lit. "it would be good if __") are used in making suggestions and giving advice (see Lesson 16, p.205). Conditional「～えば（れば）」also forms an equivalent expression,「～えばいい」, which is generally used to give instructions or directions rather than opinion, and is equivalent to English "you can do __", "you just do __", "what you do is __", "all you do is __", etc.

ex.1. A: すみません。この書類（しょるい）なんですが、<u>どうしたらいい</u>んですか。
Excuse me. About these papers, what should I do with them?
B: ああ、それは、部長のサインを<u>もらえばいい</u>んですよ。
Oh, those. Just get the division manager's signature on them.

2. A: 地下鉄（ちかてつ）のきっぷを買いたいんですが、<u>どうすればいい</u>ですか。
I would like to buy a subway ticket. What do I do?
B: ここにお金を入れて、このボタンを<u>おせばいい</u>ですよ。きっぷが出てきますから。
All you do is put your money in here and push this button. Out comes your ticket.

Note : As with「～たら」,「～えば」may also be left dangling (rising intonation) to make a suggestion equivalent to English "Why not do __?", "Why don't you __?", etc.

ex. A: こまったなあ。あしたの会議に出られなくなっちゃった。
What a bother! It seems I won't be able to attend tomorrow's meeting.
B: じゃあ、だれかに、かわってもらえば？（＝かわってもらったら？）
In that case, why not have someone take your place?

Directions not to do such and such are given by the negative form 「～なければいい」 "you don't have to __", "it's not necessary that you __ ". Notice how this differs from the form 「～ないほうがいい」 (see Lesson 16, p.206).

ex. A: 仕事がたくさん残(のこ)っていて、今日(きょう)も、また残業(ざんぎょう)なんですよ。

There's lots of work remaining. It's overtime again today too.

B: 1人(ひとり)で、何(なに)もかもしようと思わなければ、いいんですよ。少しは、部下(ぶか)にまかせたら？

It's not necessary that you try to do everything alone. Why not delegate a bit to the people under you?

B: 1人で、何もかもしようと思わないほうがいいですよ。

It's better you don't try to do everything alone.

Dialogues in English

Dialogue Ⅰ

B: Excuse me a moment, Mrs. Tanabe. There's something I would like to ask you, please.

T: Of course. What is it, I wonder?

B: This came in the mail. What can it be?

T: Oh, it's your electricity bill.

B: Electricity bill? Oh, you mean the service charge for electricity? Uh, where do I pay it?

T: You can pay it at a nearby bank. Any of the banks in front of the station will do.

B: I see. Well, what do I do at the bank then?

T: When you get to the bank, there will be a person to direct you. Ask him and he will tell you what to do.

B: I see. The banks are open until 3:00, right? Do I still have time, do you think?

T: Sure. If you go now, you will make it in time. However, you can pay the bill anytime before the eighth of next month, can't you? Why not go tomorrow when you have more time. I myself am going tomorrow.

B: Thank you for the advice. But, you see, I sort of have something else to do tomorrow.

Dialogue Ⅱ

B: Excuse me. I'd like to pay my electricity bill, please. What do I do?

Man: Your electricity bill? People with electricity bills go to this window over here. Please take a card from this box. When the number on your card appears here, it will be your turn.

B: There's quite a long wait, isn't there.

Man: That's so. The end of the month is always crowded, you see.

B: It will be awful if it's like this every month!

Man: True. Excuse me, but do you have an account with this bank?

B: Yes. It's my husband's though.

Man: In that case, it would be convenient to arrange for an automatic withdrawal from your account.

B: What is an automatic withdrawal?

Man: Your electricity bill for each month is paid automatically from your account.

B: What do I have to do?

Man: Fill in your name and address on this application form and apply your seal here, please.

B: I'm sorry, but we don't have a seal. Would a signature be alright?

Man: Yes, no problem. Please have your husband sign it and return it.

Dialogue Ⅲ

T: Why, Barbara! Have you finished at the bank already?

B: Yes.

T: How did it go? Easy, wasn't it?

B: Yes, the people at the bank were very kind and helpful. And so beginning next month we are going to have automatic withdrawal.

T: Oh, yes. Automatic withdrawal is very convenient, isn't it.

B: You certainly have a lot of things to carry, Mrs. Tanabe. Should I carry something?

T: Oh, my! Thank you.

Exercise 1: Make a suggestion, give advice or give directions for the following situations. Use the forms「～たらいい」,「といい」,「～えばいい」and「ほうがいい」as appropriate.

1) A: 東京駅から、ヒルトンホテルへ行く方法(ほうほう)が、わからないんですが…。

ex.（ホテルに、電話をしてみる）→ホテルに、電話をしてみればいいですよ。

① 東京駅から、タクシーに乗(の)る。 ② 地下鉄(ちかてつ)で、赤坂(あかさか)まで行く。

2) A: 日本語がじょうずになりたいんですが…。

① 日本語学校に行く。 ② 日本語のニュースを、毎日、聞く。 ③ Answer on your own.

3) A: 休みをとりたいんですが、仕事がいそがしくて、なかなか…。

① だれかに、てつだってもらう。 ② 休日出勤(きゅうじつしゅっきん)をして、仕事を、早くすませる。

4) A: この機械(きかい)の使(つか)い方(かた)を知(し)りたいんですけど…。

① 山本(やまもと)さんに聞く。 ② 機械の説明書(せつめいしょ)を読む。

5) A: 日本の大学に入りたいんです。どんな大学があるか、知りたいんですが。

① 日本の大使館(たいしかん)に行って、聞いてみる。 ② 図書館(としょかん)で、調(しら)べてみる。

Function II　Conditional (4) : "if it is" ; あしたなら、わたしも行きます

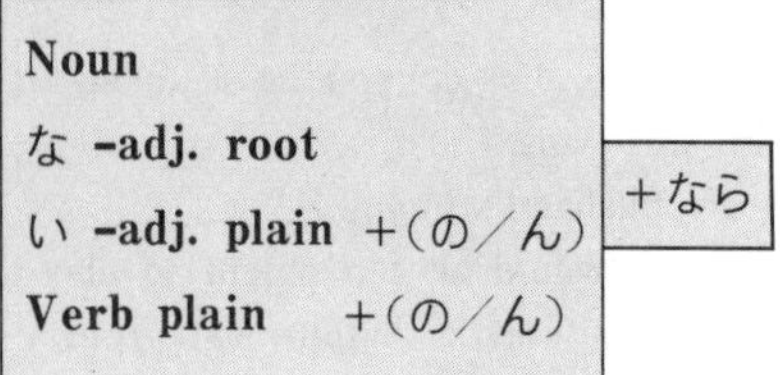

Noun	+なら
な -adj. root	
い -adj. plain +(の／ん)	
Verb plain +(の／ん)	

The be-verb has a fourth conditional form「なら」"if it is __".「なら」is often used to restate or clarify the item, thing, proposal, circumstances, etc. under discussion for the purpose of making some sort of comment, as shown in the examples.

ex.1. 客: このおさらは、結婚(けっこん)いわいのプレゼントに、どうでしょうか。

How would this plate be as a wedding gift?

店員(てんいん): このおさらなら、きっと、相手(あいて)の方(かた)も、気(き)にいってくださいますよ。

If (you give) this plate, I am certain the person you give it to will be pleased with it as well.

2. A: このへやは、少し、あついですね。 This room is a bit warm, isn't it.

B: あついんなら、そこの窓(まど)をあけてもいいですよ。

If it's too warm, then you can open the window.

3. A: 国に帰る前に、旅行(りょこう)がしたいんですが、どこへ行ったらいいでしょうね。

I'd like to travel around before returning to my country. Where do you suppose I should go?

B: 旅行に行くなら、北海道(ほっかいどう)は、どうですか。おんせんが、たくさんありますよ。

If you are going on a trip, then how about Hokkaido? It has many hot springs.

4. A: この仕事、来週の月曜日までにできますか。

Will it be possible to have this job completed by Monday of next week?

B: 月曜日ですか。月曜日は、むりですね。水曜日までなら、できますが。

Monday? Monday is impossible. But if (I have) until Wednesday, I can do it.

Note 1: The function of「なら」is not unlike the function of the topic marker「は」, except for a greater emphasis. Compare the following:

ex. A: お兄さんは、どこに、いらっしゃいますか。 Where is your brother?

B: 兄ですか。兄なら、公園に行っているはずですけど。

My brother? If it's my brother (you are looking for), he ought to be at the park.

B: 兄ですか。兄は、公園に行っているはずですけど。 My brother? He ought to be at the park.

Note 2: The conditional be-verb「だったら」can be used in place of「なら」.

ex. このおさらだったら、きっと、相手の方も、気にいってくださいますよ。

Exercise 2: Construct dialogues after the pattern below, using「なら」.

ex. A: 山に行きたいんだけど、どこが、いいでしょうかね。

B: 山に行くなら、富士山が、いいですよ。

山なら、富士山が、いいですよ。

1)
コーヒーでも飲みましょうか。
そうね。
ラ・メール
2)
おんせんに行きたいんだけど、どこかいいところを教えてくれませんか。
箱根
3)
寒いわね。
ストーブ
4)
ちょっと、スーパーに行って来るよ。
5)
家内のたんじょう日に、何をあげようかなあ。
アクセサリー
6)
あしたは、雨がふるそうですよ。
ゴルフ

Exercise 3: Construct dialogues after the pattern below.

ex. A: A社の株を買おうと思っているんですが、どうでしょうね。

B: (A社→上がらない, B社→上がる)

⇨A社は上がらないと思います。B社なら、上がると思いますけど。

1) A: 東京貿易の社長に会いたいんですが、会ってくださるでしょうか。

B: (社長→むり, 部長→会ってくださる)

2) A: 今、あなたが読んでいる本を買いたいんですが、駅前の本屋さんで、買えるでしょうか。

B: (駅前の本屋→ない, もっと大きい本屋→ある)

3) A: 新製品のカメラを、6万円で売りたいんですけど、どうでしょう。

B: (6万円→売れない, 4万円ぐらい→売れる)

Vocabulary

方法(ほうほう) method, way, manner
機械(きかい) machine
使い方(つかいかた) how to use
説明書(せつめいしょ) manual, instructions, explanatory pamphlet
大使館(たいしかん) embassy
株(かぶ) stock, share
新製品(しんせいひん) new product
アクセサリー accessories

Exercise 4: Complete the following conversations using「なら」 Use the word given.

1) Q: いつか、マイケルさんといっしょに、食事をしようと思っているんですけど、いつ、さそえばいいでしょうね。

You: そうですね。＿（金曜日）＿。

2) Q: ここに、住所（じゅうしょ）を、漢字（かんじ）で書いてください。

You: え、漢字でですか。こまったなあ。＿（ひらがな）＿。

3) Q: この時計（とけい）をなおしてほしいんですが、いつできますか。

You: そうですねえ、今、ちょっと、いそがしいから…。＿（３日後）＿。

4) Q: あの店で、食事をしませんか。

You: いやあ、さっき、食事をしたばかりなんですよ。＿（コーヒー）＿。

Function III　Showing respect (1): honorific and humble verb constructions

The use of honorific and humble terms was explained in Lesson 16 (p.204). The following are some commonly used verb constructions.

1 **お＋ Verb stem ＋ に なる／なります**　**honorific** — used when speaking of actions that other people do.

ex.1. 社長は、毎日（まいにち）、２時のニュースを<u>お聞（き）きになります</u>。

Everyday our boss listens to the 2:00 news.

2. けさは、何時に、<u>おでかけになりました</u>か。

What time did you leave home this morning?

Note: With honorific verbs such as「いらっしゃる」"to be, come, go" and「おっしゃる」"to say", it is not necessary to use this construction.

2 **お＋ Verb stem ＋ する／します**　**humble** —used in referring to actions you yourself perform.

ex.1. ちょっと、<u>おたずねします</u>が、ここから東京駅までは、どういけばいいでしょうか。

Excuse me, I'd like to ask you, how do I get to Tokyo station from here?

2. すみません。電話代（でんわだい）を<u>おはらいしたい</u>んですが、ここでよろしいでしょうか。

Excuse me, I'd like to pay my telephone bill. Is this the right place?

3. 辞書（じしょ）をかしてくださいね。あした、<u>おかえしします</u>から。

Let me use your dictionary, OK? I'll return it tomorrow.

Note: This construction is only used when the action directly affects someone else.
ex. やあ、つかれました。車に乗（の）りたいですね。（× お乗りしたい）
Wow, I'm worn out. I'd really like to ride in a car.

3 **お＋ Verb stem ＋ です**　**honorific** — used to tell what someone else is doing.

ex.1. A: それでは、しつれいいたします。　I'll be leaving then.

B: あら、もう、<u>お帰りですか</u>。　What! Are you leaving so soon?

2. 部長、お客様（きゃくさま）が、応接室（おうせつしつ）で<u>お待（ま）ちです</u>。

Mr. Division Manager, there's a visitor waiting in the meeting room.

Note: This construction is limited to a certain number of verbs, such as:

待ちます → お待ちです，　持ちます → お持ちです，　帰ります → お帰りです
聞きます → お聞きです，　読みます → お読みです，　使います → お使いです

Exercise 5: Complete the following conversations using honorific and humble verb constructions.

1) 先生：さいきん、田中君に会いましたか。
　学生：いいえ。先生は、（　　　　）。

2) 学生：重いでしょう。（　　　　）。
　老人：ありがとう。1人じゃ、とても持てなくて、
　　　　こまっていたところなんですよ。

3) 学生：　　　　　もしもし、先生は、（　　　　）。
　先生のおくさん：いいえ、おりません。
　学生：　　　　　何時ごろ、（　　　　）。
　先生のおくさん：今日は、8時ごろには帰ると言っていましたが。
　学生：　　　　　そうですか。じゃ、また、そのころ（　　　　）。

4) 社員：課長の話を、もう、（　　　　）。
　社長：いや、まだ、何も聞いていないよ。

Exercise 6: Looking at the picture, ask the guest if he would like to do such and such, or if you can do such and such for him.

Exercise 7: Tell what the people are saying in the pictures below using the「お～です」honorific construction.

1)
部長が、
＿＿＿＿＿。
ワープロ
あいてる?
2)
あなた、
お客様が
＿＿＿＿。
3) ○○駅
＿＿＿
＿＿＿。

Vocabulary

老人（ろうじん）elderly person

Function IV

Asking someone to do something (3): honorific request form; お書きください

		ください
お＋	**Verb stem** ＋	くださいませんか
		くださいませんでしょうか

The honorific request form is used in official or business situations to make requests or give instructions, while the various polite request forms we have learned are used in personal or social situations.

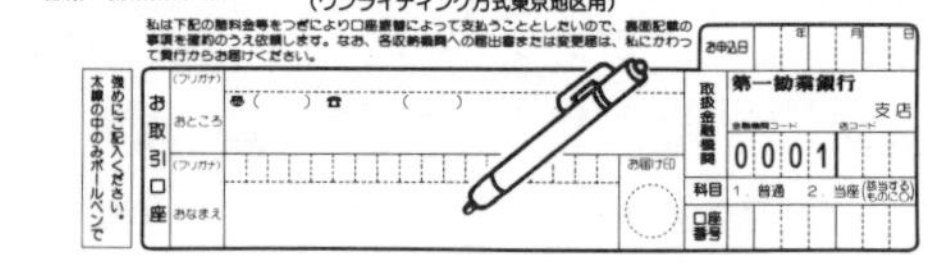

ex. 1. ここに、お名前と、ご住所をお書きください。

Write your name and address here, please.

2. お返事は、手紙で、お知らせくださいませんか。

Will you please inform us of your answer by mail?

Note: The irregular verbs「行く」,「来る」and「する」are not used in this construction. Instead use the honorific verb forms「おいでください」"please go, please come",「おこしください」"please come" and「なさってください」"please do".

Exercise 8: Choose which request form is most appropriate in the following situations.

1) あのかんばんが、よく読めないんです。すみませんが、

{a. 読んでくださいませんか　　b. お読みください}。

2) ごあんないします。コンサートは、６時半からです。あと30分ほど、ロビーで、

{a. 待ってくださいませんか　　b. お待ちください}。

3) ちょっと、その日は、つごうが悪いんです。日を

{a. かえてくださいませんか　　b. おかえください}。

4) (お客さんが店員に) ちょっと、寒いんです。エアコンを

{a. 止めてくださいませんか　　b. お止めください}。

5) (ホテルのボーイが、お客さんに) ご用のときは、こちらの電話を

{a. 使ってくださいませんか　　b. お使いください}。

Reading Comprehension Exercise

バーバラ・ウエッブ様

９月に入ったのに、毎日、あつい日がつづきますね。バーバラさん、お元気ですか。わたしは、あいかわらず、元気です。

先週、バーバラさんからのお手紙を、うけとりました。10月のはじめに、マイケルさんと、こちらに、いらっしゃるそうですね。たいへん、うれしく思います。ところで、こちらへは、何でいらっしゃいますか。長野に来るには、ＪＲ線で来る方法と、車で来る方法とがあります。ＪＲ線で来れば、速くてべんりです。特急に乗れば３時間、急行に乗れば、４時間と少しで着きます。特急のほうが、本数が多いので、べんりで

す。休日は、こむので、早めに指定席を予約しておいたほうがいいですよ。自由席じゃ、すわれないかもしれません。ＪＲ線で来るときは、わりびききっぷを、りようするといいですよ。くわしいことは、駅の「みどりの窓口」で聞けば、教えてくれるでしょう。車も、べんりですが、道路が、とてもこむので、やめておいたほうがいいでしょう。

宿の件ですが、わたしの家にとまれば、いいですよ。ホテルや、旅館は高いし、秋の旅行シーズンで、とてもこんでいますから。えんりょは、いりませんよ。

では、おふたりにお会いできる日を、楽しみにしております。

9月8日

坂本　洋子

◆Vocabulary◆

あいかわらず as always
はじめ beginning
うけとる (u-vt) to receive
ＪＲ線（ジェーアールせん）Japan Railways
特急（とっきゅう）special express
急行（きゅうこう）express
本数（ほんすう）number (of trains, etc.)
休日（きゅうじつ）holiday
早めに（はやめに）as early as possible
自由席（じゆうせき）non-reserved seat
わりびきする discount
りようする use
くわしい detailed
みどりの窓口（みどりのまどぐち）ticket window for reserved seats, etc.
宿（やど）place to stay, inn
旅館（りょかん）hotel, inn
シーズン season
えんりょする reluctance, hesitation

Exercise 9: Answer the following questions.

1) 坂本さんは、長野まで行くために、何を使えばいいと言っていますか。
   a. ＪＲ線の、特急の自由席　　b. ＪＲ線の、特急の指定席
   c. ＪＲ線の、急行の自由席　　d. ＪＲ線の、急行の指定席
2) わりびききっぷについて、どこで聞けばいいですか。
3) 坂本さんは、宿は、どうすればいいと、言っていますか。
4) 坂本さんは、いつ、バーバラさんたちに会えますか。

Listening Comprehension Exercise

Listen to the dialogue on the tape and answer the following questions.

1) ブラウンさんは、どうして、こまっていますか。
2) 鈴木さんは、どこに電話をすればいいと言いましたか。
3) 鈴木さんは、そこの電話番号を知っていましたか。
4) 電話番号がわからないときは、どうすればいいですか。

Vocabulary

かんばん sign board, sign
ロビー lobby
エアコン air-conditioning, air conditioner
ボーイ waiter, bellboy

第22課 かぜをひいたようですね

You Seem To Have Caught A Cold

Dialogue I

Michael goes with the people in his department on an overnight trip to Hakone. After hiking all day through the Hakone mountains, they arrive at the inn.

旅館(りょかん)の人：お茶(ちゃ)をどうぞ。何か、ご用(よう)がありましたら、こちらのお電話でどうぞ。

　　　　　では、どうぞ、ごゆっくり。

田辺(たなべ)　：はい、どうも。

マイケル：東京は、まだ暑(あつ)いけど、箱根(はこね)は、すずしいですね。

田辺　：ほんとうに、そうですねえ。ところで、食事をする

　　　　　前に、温泉(おんせん)に入りませんか。

マイケル：そうですね。山を歩(ある)いて、あせをかいたから、

　　　　　お湯(ゆ)をあびて、さっぱりしたいですね。

　　　　　温泉には、何か、持って行きますか。

田辺　：タオルと、ゆかた。そのはこの中に入っていますよ。

マイケル：ああ、これが、ゆかたですか。

田辺　：ええ、温泉に入ったあと、着(き)るんですよ。

Dialogue II

At the spa. Seeing the steaming tub.

マイケル：熱(あつ)そうですね。ぼくは、熱いおふろは、だめなんですよ。

田辺　：そんなに熱くないから、だいじょうぶですよ。

　　　　　じゃ、ぼくがお先(さき)に。ああ、いい気持(きも)ち。

マイケル：そうですか…。あ、熱い！

田辺　：熱いですか。

マイケル：ええ、ぼくには、ちょっと熱すぎますね。

田辺　　：そうですか。じゃ、少し水を入れましょう。(turning on the cold water) どうですか、このくらいで…。入れすぎると、ぬるくなるから…。

マイケル：そうですね。まだ、ちょっと熱いけど、このくらい熱いほうが、からだにいいような気(き)がします。

田辺　　：ええ。ここの温泉(おんせん)は、肩(かた)こりや、胃(い)の病気(びょうき)にいいらしいですよ。

マイケル：肩こり？　肩こりって、何ですか。

田辺　　：ああ、肩のきんにくが、かたくなって、いたくなることですよ。マイケルさんは、そういうこと、ありませんか。

マイケル：ええ、ないですねえ。

(outside, sounds of another group entering)

田辺　　：ほかの団体(だんたい)の人が、来たようですね。そろそろ、出ましょうか。

マイケル：ええ、そうしましょう。

Dialogue III

After dinner Michael and Mr. Tanabe step outside.

田辺　　：ああ、よく飲(の)んだ。やっぱり、温泉に入ったあとで飲むビールは、おいしいですねえ。

マイケル：ええ。みんな、楽(たの)しそうでしたね。

田辺　　：星(ほし)が、たくさん見えますね。あしたも、天気が、よさそうですね。

マイケル：そうですね。ハ、ハ、ハックション！

田辺　　：あ、ウエッブさん、かぜをひいたようですね。

マイケル：ええ。ちょっと、寒(さむ)けがします。それに、少し、熱(ねつ)もあるようです。

田辺　　：それは、いけないな。へやに帰りましょう。へやの中は、あたたかいから。

マイケル：そうですね。田辺さん、かぜ薬(ぐすり)を持(も)っていますか。

田辺　　：いや。でも、黒田さんが、持っていますよ。中国(ちゅうごく)の薬(くすり)で、かぜによくきくらしいですよ。

Vocabulary

Nouns:

7あせ sweat, perspiration
8お湯（おゆ）hot water
10タオル towel
10ゆかた *yukata*, summer *kimono*
23肩こり（かたこり）stiff shoulders
23胃（い）stomach
25きんにく muscle
28団体（だんたい）group, party
34星（ほし）star
37寒け（さむけ）chill
39かぜ薬（かぜぐすり）cold medicine

Adjectives:

4すずしい cool
13熱い（あつい）hot
20ぬるい tepid, lukewarm, not hot enough
25かたい hard, stiff

Adverbs:

8さっぱり（と）する refreshing

Verbs:

40きく (u-vi) to have effect, be good for

Grammatical words:

13～そう（な）seem, appear ☞Function Ⅱ
23＿らしい seem, appear, seem like ☞Function Ⅱ

Expressions:

1お電話でどうぞ By phone, if you please.
7あせをかく to sweat, perspire
22＿気がする to feel, think, have a feeling that ＿
35ハックション ah-choo! atchoo! kerchoo!
37寒けがする to feel a chill

Dialogue Comprehension Exercise

Mark T or F.

1) (　) 旅館の人に用があるときは、電話を使う。
2) (　) ゆかたは、温泉に入る前に着る。
3) (　) お湯には、マイケルさんが、先に入った。
4) (　) 温泉のお湯は、ぬるかった。
5) (　) マイケルさんたちは、ほかの団体の人といっしょに、温泉に入った。
6) (　) 田辺さんは、かぜ薬を持っている。
7) (　) へやの中のほうが、外より、すずしい。

Function Ⅰ　Describing temperature; 箱根は、すずしいですね

	liquids	solids	air, etc.
hot	熱い（コーヒー）	熱い（なべ）	暑い（日，夏）
warm	あたたかい（スープ）	あたたかい（手）	あたたかい（へや，春）
lukewarm	ぬるい（スープ）	——	——
cool chill cold	つめたい（水）	つめたい（手）	すずしい（風，秋） つめたい（風） 寒い（日，冬）

ex. 1. 寒いですねえ。そこの店で、熱いコーヒーを飲みましょう。

It's cold, isn't it. Should we have some hot coffee at that shop there?

2. A: あたたかいうちに、スープをどうぞ。　Please eat your soup while it's still warm.

B: ありがとう。あれ、少し、ぬるくなっていますね。

Thank you. Oh, oh. It has cooled off a bit, hasn't it.

C: あ、すみません。すぐ、あたためます。

Oh, I'm sorry. I'll heat it up in a jiffy.

3. 暑(あつ)い夏(なつ)が終(お)わって、すずしい秋(あき)になりました。

The hot summer is over and brisk autumn has come.

4. 今日(きょう)は、つめたい風(かぜ)がふいて、寒(さむ)い1日でした。

It was cold all day today with a chill wind.

Note 1: Hot water is called「お湯(ゆ)」, not「熱(あつ)い水(みず)」.

Note 2:「あたたかい」,「つめたい」may also be used to describe people, attitudes, etc.

ex. 1. お客様(きゃくさま)を、あたたかくむかえる。　Guests are given a warm reception.

2. 思(おも)いやりがなくて、つめたい人。　a cold, unsympathetic person

Dialogues in English

Dialogue Ⅰ

Inn Keeper: Please have some tea. If there is anything you need, please use the phone over here. Alright then, make yourselves at home, if you will.

T: We will. Thank you.

M: Tokyo is still hot, but Hakone is cool, isn't it.

T: That's for sure, huh? By the way, don't you want to take a bath in the spa before having dinner?

M: Yes, I do. I worked up a sweat walking in the mountains, and so I want to wash with hot water and freshen up. Do we bring something with us to the spa?

T: Your towel and *yukata*. They're inside the box there.

M: Oh, so this is a *yukata*.

T: Yes. You put it on after bathing in the spa.

Dialogue Ⅱ

M: It looks hot, doesn't it! I can't stand hot baths.

T: You'll be alright, it's not that hot. Me first then! Oh! Feels good!

M: Is that so? Yeow! It's hot!

T: Is it hot?

M: Yes. It's a little too hot for me.

T: I see. Let's add a little cold water then! About this much ought to do it, what do you think? Because if we add too much, it won't be hot enough.

M: Hmm, yes. It's still a little hot, but I would imagine that about this temperature would be better for the body.

T: Yes. They say that this spa is good for "*katakori*", stomach disorders and so forth.

M: "*Katakori*"? What's "*katakori*"?

T: Oh, that's when the shoulder muscles get stiff and become sore. Doesn't such a thing ever happen to you?

M: No, never.

T: It looks like another group of people has arrived. Should we start thinking about leaving?

M: Yes, let's.

Dialogue Ⅲ

T: Wow, I had plenty to drink! No matter what you say, beer drunk after bathing in a spa tastes good. Right?

M: You bet! Everyone seemed to be having a good time, huh?

T: Look at all the stars! It looks as if tomorrow is going to be nice as well.

M: Yes it does. Ah...ah...ah-choo!

T: My! You seem to have caught a cold, Mr. Webb!

M: Yes, I'm a little chilled. I also seem to have a slight fever.

T: That won't do! Let's go back to the room. Inside the room it's warm.

M: Yes, let's. Do you have any cold medicine, Mr. Tanabe?

T: No. But Miss Kuroda has some. It's Chinese medicine, and it seems to really work for colds.

Note 3: Words describing changes in temperature:

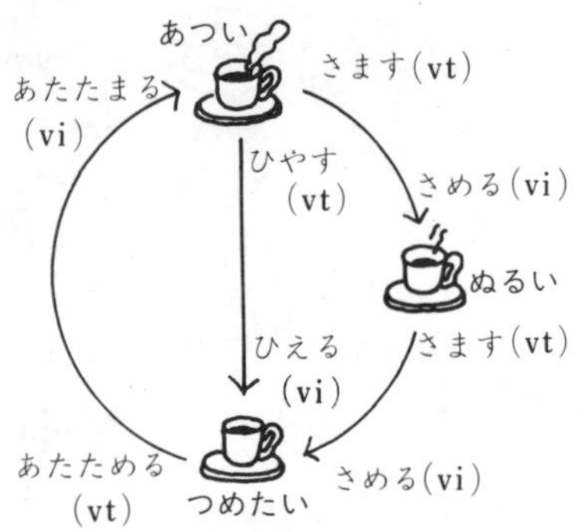

ex.1. そのお茶は、熱いですから、少しさまして、飲んでください。
The tea is hot, so please let it cool off and drink it.

2. A：つめたいビールを、どうぞ。 Have some cold beer!
B：ああ、おいしい。よく、ひえていますね。
Oh, it's good. It's well chilled, isn't it.
A：ええ、朝から、冷蔵庫で、ひやしておいたんです。
Yes. You see, I have been chilling it in the refrigerator since morning.

3. 寒いですねえ。温泉に入って、あたたまりましょう。
It's cold, isn't it. Let's go into the spa and get warm.

Exercise 1: Fill in the blanks with suitable adjectives describing temperature.

客　：今日は、外は、風が強くて（ ① ）ど、へやの中は、だんぼうが入っていて、（ ② ）ですね。もう少し、温度をひくくしてくれませんか。

ボーイ：はい、今、下げます。あのう、窓を、少しあけましょうか。（ ③ ）空気が入って来れば、すぐ、（ ④ ）なりますから。

客　：ありがとう。まず、温泉に入りたいんだけど、ここの温泉は、（ ⑤ ）ですか。

ボーイ：あまり（ ⑥ ）ありません。32度ぐらいで、（ ⑦ ）ので、ホテルで、少し、あたためています。

客　：そうですか。ふろから出て来たら、（ ⑧ ）ビールを、おねがいします。

ボーイ：かしこまりました。

ボーイ：お待たせしました。なべが、（ ⑨ ）ですから、気をつけてください。

客　：ああ、おいしそうな湯どうふですね。（ ⑩ ）うちに食べましょう。

Exercise 2: What sort of temperature is right in the following situations? Tell what you think using appropriate adjectives.

ex. コーヒーをいれるときの、お湯の温度は？ → 熱いほうがいいです。

1) 夏に飲むスープは？　2) 冬のプールの水は？　3) おふろのお湯は？
4) ビールは？　5) ワインは？　6) 夏、仕事をするへやは？
7) 海で泳ぐときの気温は？　8) 山登りをするときの気温は？

Function II

Talking about appearances: "looks, seems, supposedly";
かぜをひいたようですね。

1 「そう(な)」 is used when stating or exclaiming how something appears to you.

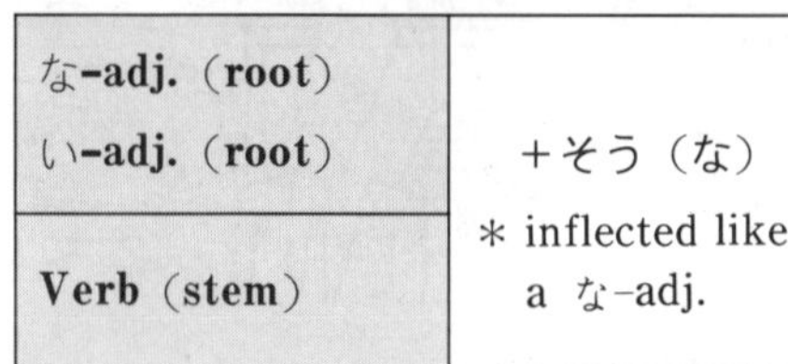

な-adj. (root) い-adj. (root)	+そう (な) ＊ inflected like a な-adj.	"looks"
Verb (stem)		"looks as if it's going to __" "looks as if it's about to __"

Note 1: 「そう(な)」 cannot be used after nouns with this meaning.

ex.1. 雨がふりそうです。 It looks like it's going to rain.

2. 黒田さんは、プレゼントをもらって、うれしそうでした。
Miss Kuroda received a gift and looked very pleased.

3. わあ、おいしそうなケーキ。3つぐらい、食べられそう。
Oh my, that cake looks good! It looks like I could eat about three pieces.

4. あの店(みせ)は、おおぜいの人で、にぎやかそうです。
That store is crowded with people and looks busy.

5. 急(いそ)いで、いなかに帰(かえ)らなくてはなりません。父(ちち)が、しにそうなんです。
I have to hurry and go back to my home town. It looks as if my father is going to die any time now.

6. あっ、たいへん! 子どもが、おぼれそうだ!
Oh, my goodness! That child looks like he's going to drown!

Note 2: The following negative forms are used.

① Adj. root ＋そう＋では（じゃ）ない	ex. おもしろそうではない
② Adj. adverbial form ＋なさそうです	ex. おもしろくなさそうです
③ Verb stem ＋そう＋にない／ Verb stem ＋そう＋もない	ex. 行きそうにない

ex. 1. あの本は、おもしろそうじゃありません。／あの本は、おもしろくなさそうです。
That book does not look interesting.

2. 人が少なくて、にぎやかそうじゃありません。／人が少なくて、にぎやかじゃなさそうです。
There are not many people and it does not appear lively.

3. 今日(きょう)は、雨は、ふりそうにありません。 It does not look as if it's going to rain today.

2 「よう(な)」 is used to state how things appear, based on certain pieces of evidence. Equivalent to English "seems __", "seems to be __", "must be __", "I guess it's __", etc.

Noun ＋ の／だった **な-adj.** plain non-past (-な), past **い-adj.** plain non-past (-い), past **Verb** plain non-past, past	＋よう (な) ＊ inflected like a な-adj.

Vocabulary

さめる (ru-vi) to get cold, cool down
だんぼう$_{する}$ heating, heater
温度 (おんど) temperature
空気 (くうき) air
気温 (きおん) air temperature
-度(ど) degrees (temperature, arc, etc.)
なべ pan, pot
湯どうふ (ゆどうふ) boiled *tofu* (eaten with soy sauce, chopped scallions, dried bonito shavings, etc.)

ex.1. 道がぬれています。雨がふったようです。

The streets are wet. I guess it must have rained.

2. 午後から、雨がふるようです。

I guess it's supposed to rain this afternoon.

3. この薬は、よくきくようです。熱が、下がってしまいました。

This medicine seems to work well. My fever went right down.

4. あの声は、マイケルさんのようですね。 That voice! It must be Michael.

5. マイケルさん ケーキがすきなようですね。3つも食べて。

You seem to like cake, don't you, Michael. You've eaten three whole pieces!

6. 今度の旅行には、マイケルさんは、行かないようですよ。

I guess Michael won't be going on the upcoming trip.

Note:「よう(な)」is often used when you want to avoid stating something with absolute certainty.

ex. A: 今、何時ですか。 What time is it now?

B: もう、3時のようですね。 It seems to be 3:00 already.

3「らしい」is used to state what appears to be true, but the evidence for which is slim, or else comes to you indirectly through some other source. Equivalent to such English expressions as "apparently __", "supposedly __", "it seems that __", "I believe that __", etc.

Noun +	―／だった	+らしい ＊ inflected like an い-adj.
な-adj.	root, past	
い-adj.	plain non-past, past	
Verb	plain non-past, past	

ex.1. A: 今日は、雨がふるようですね。

It seems as if it's going to rain today, doesn't it.

B: ええ、そうらしいですね。天気予報で、そう言っていましたよ。

Yes, I believe so. That's what they were saying on the weather report.

2. あの店には、行ったことはないんですが、おいしいらしいですよ。

I've never been there, but supposedly the food at that shop over there is very good.

3. たき火のあとがあるから、だれかが、ここで、キャンプをしていたらしい。

Apparently someone was camping here. There are traces of a fire.

Note: In many cases「らしい」and「よう(な)」are interchangeable, with「よう(な)」suggesting perhaps a bit more certainty. Be careful however. In situations where one's judgement is specifically required, use of「らしい」sounds as if you are irresponsibly avoiding making such judgement.

ex. 1. 寒けがします。かぜをひいたようです。 I feel a chill. Apparently I have caught a cold.

寒けがします。かぜをひいたらしいです。 I feel a chill. I seem to have caught a cold.

2. (doctor to patient)

× かぜらしいですね。 I guess you have a cold. (I couldn't say for sure.)

○ かぜのようですね。 Based on the evidence, I would conclude that you have a cold.

Vocabulary

あつまる (u-vi) to gather, come together

窓ガラス (まどガラス) window glass, windowpane

てぶくろ gloves, mittens

4 「みたい」(see Lesson 15, p.194) is used with the same meaning as「よう(な)」and「らしい」, and is popular especially among younger people.

ex.1. 今日は、雨がふるみたい。

Today it seems like it's going to rain.／Today it's supposed to rain.

2. あの薬が、きいたみたい。もう、すっかり、元気です。

That medicine seems to have worked. I feel really great now.

Note the differences between the following sentences.

①（見ただけで）熱が、ありそうだ。
It looks like you have a fever.

②（さわってみて）熱が、あるようだ。
You seem to have a fever.

③（だれかから聞いて）熱が、あるらしい。
It seems he has a fever.

Exercise 3: Tell how things appear to you in the following situation, using「そう(な)」.

1) ＿＿＿料理ですね。

2) へやは、＿＿＿。

3) 今度の魚は、＿＿＿。

4) ＿＿＿本ですね。

5) あっ！ 本が＿＿＿。

6) たいへん！ 会社に＿＿＿。

7) 人が、たくさんあつまって、＿＿＿ですね。

8) 何もすることがなくて、＿＿＿です。

Exercise 4: Tell what appears to have happened based on the evidence pictured on the right. Use「よう(な)」.

ex. はんにんは、ダイナマイトを使って、金庫をこわしたようだ。
It appears the burglar used dynamite to crack the safe.

Exercise 5: Tell what the people are saying in the following situations using「らしい」.

Exercise 6: Circle the letter of the more appropriate phrase.

1) まあ、あのケーキ、{a. おいしそう　　b. おいしいらしい}。

2) ガイドブックによると、あのホテルは、ながめが {a. いいらしい　　b. いいかもしれない}。

3) 医者：かぜをひいた {a. らしいですね　　b. ようですね}。

4) 山本：坂田さんは、今度の旅行に行きますか。

　中村：さあ、よくわかりません。{a. 行くかもしれませんね　　b. 行くようですね}。

5) （へやの中から、外を見て）外は、{a. 寒そうですね　　b. 寒いらしいですね}。

6) （車の止まる音を聞いて）あ、社長が {a. 着きそうですね　　b. 着いたようですね}。

Exercise 7: What are the people saying in the following situations? Make up something appropriate using「そう(な)」,「よう(な)」or「らしい」.

Exercise 8: Complete the following passage by adding「そう(な)」,「よう(な)」or「らしい」to the words in the brackets.

11月20日。今日は、社員旅行で、箱根に来た。朝、東京を出るときは、くもっていて、雨が［①ふる］だったが、午後からは、とてもよく晴れて、雨は、ぜんぜん［②ふる］ではなかった。天気予報では、ふると言っていたんだけれど。旅館に行く前に、みんなで、山に登った。みんな、元気に登っていたが、北村課長は、ずいぶん［③つかれる］だった。「土田部長に聞いたんだけど、さいきん、課長は、残業が［④多い］わよ。」と、黒田さんが言った。

旅館に着いて、温泉に入ったら、北村課長のつかれも［⑤とれる］。ビールを、［⑥おいしい］飲んでいた。食事をしながら、カラオケがはじまった。浜野さんは、うたが、とても［⑦すき（な）］。マイクをにぎって、何度もうたっていた。

食事のあと、旅館の外に出て、星を見ていたら、大きなくしゃみが出た。どうやら、かぜを［⑧ひく］。黒田さんに薬をもらって、早くねることにした。黒田さんにもらった薬は、中国の薬で、よく［⑨きく］。あしたは、また、元気に［⑩なれる］気がする。

Reading Comprehension Exercise

日曜日は、たいてい、恋人とデートをします。先週は、船で、浅草から浜離宮まで行きました。船に乗る前には、風が強くふいていたので、ずいぶん、ゆれそうだなと思いました。でも、船に乗ってみると、思っていたほどは、ゆれませんでした。船から、房総半島が、よく見えました。

船をおりたあと、銀座で食事をしました。行く前に、電話で予約をしておきました。レストランは、とてもこんでいたので、予約をしておいてよかったと思いました。食事のあと、有楽町で、映画を見ました。映画が始まる1時間前から、たくさんの人が、ならんでいました。新聞で、その映画をほめていたからだろうと思います。映画を見たあと、きっさ店で、お茶を飲みながら話をしました。彼女は、一日中、とても楽しそうで、今日のデートにまんぞくしているようでした。

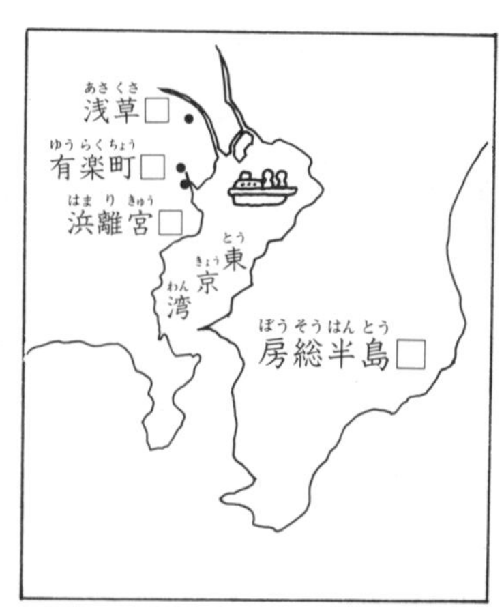

◆Vocabulary◆

たいてい usually, generally
ゆれる (ru-vi) to roll, pitch, rock, sway
船（ふね）boat, ship
きっさ店（きっさてん）tea shop
まんぞくする satisfaction, contentment

Exercise 9: Answer the following questions.

1) 船に乗る前、風は、どうでしたか。
2) レストランは、どうでしたか。すぐ、食事ができましたか。
3) なぜ、彼女は、今日のデートにまんぞくしたようだと思ったのですか。
4) Number the places on the map in the order visited.

Listening Comprehension Exercise

From the evidence contained in the dialogue and sounds on the tape, what do the people appear to be doing or arguing about?

① ② ③ ④ ⑤ ⑥

Vocabulary

◆Vocabulary◆

ながめ view
マイク microphone
にぎる (u-vt) to take hold, grasp
けんかする quarrel, fight
社員旅行（しゃいんりょこう）company trip
カラオケ *karaoke*, singing to taped background music
くしゃみ sneeze
ガイドブック guidebook
どうやら likely, seems

第23課 ゆっくり　休まなくては いけませんよ

You Must Get Lots of Rest

Dialogue I

Michael has a headache and fever, so he goes to a clinic nearby. At the reception desk.

マイケル：あのう、おねがいします。

受付(うけつけ)　：はい、どうなさいましたか。

マイケル：ちょっと、頭(あたま)がいたくて、それに、
少し熱(ねつ)があるようなんです。

受付　：そうですか。この病院(びょういん)は、はじめてですか。

マイケル：ええ。

受付　：ほけんしょうを、お持(も)ちですか。

マイケル：はい、これです。

受付　：はい。じゃ、名前をよばれるまで、そこのいすに、かけていてください。
それから、待(ま)っているあいだに、熱(ねつ)をはかっておいてくださいね。
はい、体温計(たいおんけい)。

(a while later)

かんごふ：ウエッブさん、マイケル・ウエッブさん。しんさつ室(しつ)に、お入りください。

Dialogue II

In the consultation room

医者(いしゃ)　：どうしました？

マイケル：ちょっと、頭(あたま)がいたくて、熱があるんです。それに、体(からだ)もだるいんです。

医者　：体温計を見せてください。

マイケル：はい。

医者　：うーん、なるほど。38度(ど)もある。
ちょっと、口(くち)をあけてください。

(Michael opens his mouth)

医者　：はい、けっこうです。それでは、上着(うわぎ)をぬいでください。

(examining Michael with a stethoscope)

はい、大きく、いきをすって。はい、はいて。

今(いま)までに、大きな病気(びょうき)をしたことがありますか。

マイケル：いいえ、べつに…。

医者　：うーん、かぜのようですね。2、3日、ゆっくり休まなくちゃいけませんね。

マイケル：そうですか。でも、ゆっくり休んでいられないんですよ。あさって、だいじな会議があるんで、その前に、会議の資料(しりょう)を、作らなくてはいけませんし…。

医者　：そうですか。じゃ、会社は休まなくてもいいけど、早くうちに帰って、ねるようにしてください。むりをしては、いけませんよ。

マイケル：はい。

医者　：それから、熱(ねつ)が下(さ)がるまで、おふろに入ってはいけませんよ。

マイケル：シャワーも、いけませんか。

医者　：ええ、シャワーもいけませんね。それから、しょくよくがなくても、きちんと食べなくちゃだめですよ。いいですね。

マイケル：はい、わかりました。

医者　：それじゃ、薬(くすり)を3日分(みっかぶん)、出しておきましょう。何か、アレルギーがありますか。

マイケル：いいえ、ありません。

医者　：じゃ、2、3日、ようすを見て、熱が下がらないようでしたら、また来てください。おだいじに。

マイケル：ありがとうございました。

Dialogue III

At the reception desk

受付(うけつけ)　：マイケル・ウエッブさん、はい、お薬です。1日に3回(かい)、食事のあとに、2じょうずつ、飲んでください。3日分、入っています。

マイケル：はい、わかりました。で、おいくらですか。

受付　：しょしん料(りょう)を入れて、合計(ごうけい)、2,300円です。

マイケル：はい、2,300円。どうもありがとうございました。

受付　：おだいじに。

Vocabulary

Nouns:

2受付（うけつけ）reception desk, receptionist
7ほけんしょう health insurance policy
11体温計（たいおんけい）clinical thermometer
9いす chair
12かんごふ nurse
12しんさつ室（しんさつしつ）consultation room
18口（くち）mouth
20いき breath
23 2、3日（にさんにち）a few days
32しょくよく appetite
35アレルギー allergy
35 3日分（みっかぶん）the amount for 3 days, 3 days worth
38ようす condition, state
44しょしん料（しょしんりょう）fee for the first visit to a hospital
44合計（ごうけい）する total, total amount

Counters:

42-じょう tablets, pills

Adjectives:

14だるい heavy, dull, listless, no energy
25だいじ(な) important

Adverbs:

33きちんと properly, exactly, the way it ought to be

Verbs:

20すう (u-vt) to breathe in, suck in
20 はく (u-vt) to exhale, expel, disgorge
30下がる（さがる）(u-vi) to go down

Expressions:

2どうなさいましたか What's wrong? What happened?
9 名前をよばれる your name will be called
23休まなくちゃいけません You must rest.
24 休んでいられない I don't have time to rest.
25作らなくてはいけません I have to make or prepare it.
28むりをする to overexert oneself, to try to do something that's hopeless or unfeasible
38ようすを見る to see how things go
41 1日に3回 3 times a day

Dialogue Comprehension Exercise

Answer the following questions.

Dialogue I : 1) マイケルさんは、受付(うけつけ)の人に、何をわたしましたか。

2) マイケルさんは、待(ま)っているあいだに、何をしましたか。

Dialogue II : 3) マイケルさんは、今(いま)までに、大きな病気(びょうき)をしたことがありますか。

4) マイケルさんは、なぜ、ゆっくり休めないのですか。

5) お医者(いしゃ)さんは、マイケルさんに、どんなことをしてはいけないと言いましたか。

6) マイケルさんは、アレルギーがありますか。

Dialogue III : 7) マイケルさんは、薬(くすり)を、何日分(なんにちぶん)もらいましたか。

8) 薬は、いつ、どのくらい、飲めばいいですか。

Function I

Expressing necessity: "have to", "must"; ～なければならない

Verb + [～なければ / ～なくては / ～ないと] + [ならない / いけない / だめ]

Imperative expressions of the type "have to" or "must" do such and such are formed by adding 「ならない」, 「いけない」or「だめ」after the negative conditionals「～なければ」(see Lesson 20, p.253) or「～ないと」(see Lesson15, p.195), or after the negative て-form＋ は,「～なくては」(see Lesson 13, p.173). Literally such expressions mean "It is no good if you do not do __".

ex. 1. どうしても、あしたまでに、このレポートを書かなければならないんです。

I have to write this report by tomorrow, no matter what.

2. 肉(にく)ばかりじゃなくて、野菜(やさい)も食べないといけませんよ。

You have to eat vegetables as well, not just meat!

3. たぶん、しんぱいしているだろうから、ニューヨークのご両親(りょうしん)には、もっと電話をしなくてはだめですよ。

You must telephone your parents in New York more often, because I imagine they are worrying about you.

Dialogues in English

Dialogue I

M : Excuse me. Could you help me please?

Rec. : Of course. What's the matter?

M : I have a headache. I also seem to have a bit of a fever.

Rec. : I see. Is this your first visit to this hospital?

M : That's right.

Rec. : Did you bring your health insurance policy?

M : Yes. Here you are.

Rec. : Fine. Alright then, please sit over there until your name is called. Also, while you are waiting, please take your temperature, Ok? Here's a thermometer.

Nurse : Mr. Webb. Mr. Michael Webb. Go into the consultation room please.

Dialogue II

Dr. : What's wrong with you?

M : I have a headache and a fever. Also I feel dull and listless.

Dr. : Let me see the thermometer please.

M : Here you are.

Dr. : Hmm. That explains it. You have a temperature of 100°F (38°C)! Open your mouth a moment please.
Alright. That's fine. Next, remove your upper garments please.
OK. Take a deep breath. Fine. Exhale! Have you ever had any severe illness previously?

M : No, not really...

Dr. : Hmm. I would say you have a cold. You'll have to get lots of rest for two or three days.

M : Is that so? But I don't have time to get lots of rest. You see, there's an important meeting the day after tomorrow, and before that, I have to prepare material for the meeting, and such like.

Dr. : I see. Well, you don't have to take off work, but please see to it that you go home early and go to bed. Don't over do things.

M : I see.

Dr. : Also you mustn't take a bath until your fever goes down.

M : I can't take a shower either?

Dr. : That's correct. No showers either. Also make sure you eat properly, even if you have no appetite. You understand, don't you?

M : Yes, I understand.

Dr. : Alright, I'll give you medicine for three days then. Do you have any allergies?

M : No, nothing.

Dr. : Well then, see how things go for two or three days, and come back if your fever doesn't seem to go down. Take care of yourself.

M : Thank you very much.

Dialogue III

Rec. : Mr. Michael Webb. Here's your medicine. Please take two tablets three times a day after meals. There's enough for three days.

M : I understand. And how much do I owe you?

Rec. : That will be 2,300 yen altogether, including the fee for a first visit.

M : Here you are, 2,300 yen. Thank you very much.

Rec. : Take care.

In everyday colloquial speech「～なければ」is often shortened to「～なきゃ」(or less frequently「～なけりゃ」), while「～なくては」often appears as「～なくちゃ」.

ex. 4. また、ちこくしたの？　もっと早く起(お)きなきゃだめでしょ。

You're late again? You have to get up earlier!

5. 10月の会議のじゅんびで、いそがしいので、毎日、残業をしなくちゃならないんです。

We're busy preparing for the meeting in October, so every day I have to work overtime.

6. むすこが、交通(こうつう)じこにあったので、これから、病院(びょういん)に行かなけりゃならないんです。

My son was in a traffic accident, and so I have to go to the hospital immediately.

Furthermore, it is very common to find the final「ならない」,「いけない」or「だめ」simply left off.

ex. 7. かぜのときは、ゆっくり休まなくては。(休まなくちゃ)

You have to get lots of rest when you have a cold!

8. あしたは、ゴルフだから、早くおきないと。

I'm playing golf tomorrow, so I have to get up early!

Note: Of the three forms「～なければならない」,「～なければいけない」and「～なければだめ」, the first is used when telling what you yourself must do, while the other two may be used to tell what someone else must do.

Exercise 1: Practice the following dialogue telling what you have to do using the sentences below.

山田(やまだ)：ウエッブさん、今度の土曜日に、うちに遊(あそ)びに来ませんか。

マイケル：ありがとうございます。でも、今度の土曜日は、仕事で、ゴルフに行かなくちゃならないんです。

山田：そうですか。ざんねんですね。じゃ、また今度。

1) レポートを書く。
2) 日本語のレッスンを受(う)ける。
3) 友達(ともだち)の子どもに、英語(えいご)を教(おし)える。
4) 新(あたら)しいコンピューターの使(つか)い方(かた)を習(なら)う。
5) 家内(かない)のてつだいをする。
6) 友達を、空港(くうこう)まで、むかえに行く。
7) べんごしに会(あ)う。
8) 入院(にゅういん)している友達の、おみまいに行く。

Exercise 2: Tell what has to be done in the following situations using any of the imperative expressions.

1) あす、福岡(ふくおか)に、出張(しゅっちょう)することになりました。

◆Vocabulary◆
レッスン lesson
旅費 (りょひ) traveling expenses
しゅじゅつ operation
むかえる (ru-vt) to meet, receive
係 (かかり) person in charge
とどけ notification
あく (u-vi) to become free
数 (かず) number
はんせい会 (はんせいかい) meeting to consider how to do something better next time

2) 社内運動会の、はんせい会をすることになりました。

①
10月
いつにしましょうか？
②
木曜日の午後、会議室はあいていますか？
③
かかりの人たちへのれんらくは？
今、やっていますよ。

④
出席する人の数をたしかめてください。
出 欠
広告部浜野○
営1課ウエッブ○
営2課

3) しゅじゅつを受けるために、入院することになりました。(hint: 会社に、休みのとどけを出す、etc.)
4) 結婚することになりました。
5) 外国にいる友達から、1週間後に、あなたのうちをたずねたいという電話がありました。

Function II　Saying such and such is not necessary; ～なくてもいい

1 **Verbal negative form（－なく）** ＋ ても / たって (colloquial) ＋ よい／いいです / かまわない／かまいません / だいじょうぶです

(lit.) It's alright even if not __. / You don't have to __.

2 **Verb plain non-past ＋ ことは　ない／ありません**　It's not necessary that __.

3 そんなひつようは、ありません。 Such a thing is not necessary.

ex.1. A: あしたは、8時までに来なければいけませんか。
Do I have to get here before 8:00 tomorrow?
B: むりだったら、8時までに来なくてもいいですよ。
If it's impossible, you don't have to come before 8:00.
B: むりに、8時までに来ることはありませんよ。
It's not necessary that you break your neck to get here by 8:00.

2. A: へやが、ちょっと、暗いようですが、もっと明るいほうが、よくありませんか。
The room is a bit dark. Wouldn't it be better a bit brighter?
B: いえ、そんなに明るくなくても、かまいませんよ。これで、だいじょうぶです。
No, I don't mind if it's not all that bright. It's fine the way it is.

3. A: すみません。今、青いシーツは、おいてないんです。
I'm sorry. We don't have any blue sheets in at present.
B: そうですか。じゃあ、青いのでなくてもいいですよ。
I see. Well then, it will be fine even if they are not blue.

Exercise 3: Complete the following dialogues.

1) A: あしたの会議には、どうしても出なくちゃならないんですよ。
B: かぜをひいているんでしょう？　むりに、(　　　　　)。
2) A: この報告書は、明日までに (　　　　　)。
B: いいえ、あさってまでに、作ってもらえばいいですよ。

3) A: すみません。いんかんを持ってないんです。いんかんでなくちゃ、いけませんか。
   B: それなら、(　　　　)。サインをしておいてください。

4) A: すみません。この仕事、今日中には、できないんですが。
   B: じゃ、今日中(　　　　)。あしたは、かならず、終わるようにしてくださいね。

5) A: 来年、ひっこしをするので、じゅんびを、はじめなくてはいけないと、思っているんですよ。
   B: まだ、(　　　　)。来年になってからでも、まにあいますよ。

Function III　Telling the frequency of an action; 1日に3回

How many times an action occurs within a given period of time is expressed by the following formula:

Period of time	に (optional)	Number of times (__回 or __度)	
1日　(日)	に	3回／3度	three times per day
1週間　(週)	に	1回／1度	one time per week
1月／1か月　(月)	に	2回／2度	two times per month
1年　(年)	に	4回／4度	four times per year

(1日に3回)
1日
0:00　24:00

ex.1. 食事は、1日に3度、きちんと食べてください。
Please eat regularly, 3 meals a day.

2. 会議は、1週間に1回、水曜日の午前中にあります。
We have a meeting once a week on Wednesday mornings.

3. サラリーマンですから、月1回しか、ゴルフに行けません。
Because I'm a working man, I can only go golfing once a month.

4. 弟は、デパートにつとめているので、年に4回ぐらい、ヨーロッパに出張します。
My younger brother works at a department store, and so he goes to Europe on business about four times a year.

5. お医者さんにもらった薬を、1日3回、ちゃんと飲みましたが、かぜは、ぜんぜんなおりません。
I took the medicine I got from the doctor three times a day like I was supposed to, but my cold hasn't gotten better at all!

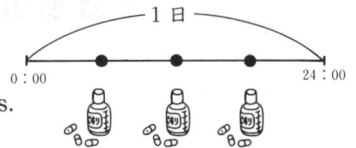

Another expression, used when telling how often something occurs, is「(period of time)＋おきに」"every __".

ex.1. この薬を、6時間おきに飲んでください。
Please take this medicine every six hours.

2. わたしの友達は、2年おきに、新しい車を買うんですよ。
My friend buys a new car every two years.

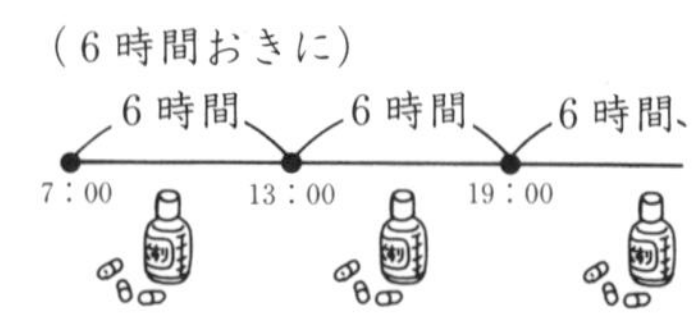

Vocabulary

食後(しょくご) after meals
いつものとおり as usual
昼食(ちゅうしょく) lunch
けっきょく after all, in the end
何回(なんかい) how many times?

Exercise 4: Read the following instructions and answer the questions.

1) この赤い薬は、1日に3回、食後に、2じょうずつ飲んでください。白い薬は、7時間おきに、1じょうずつ飲んでください。

〈**Question 1**〉 When is the red medicine to be taken? When is the white medicine to be taken? Indicate on the chart below.

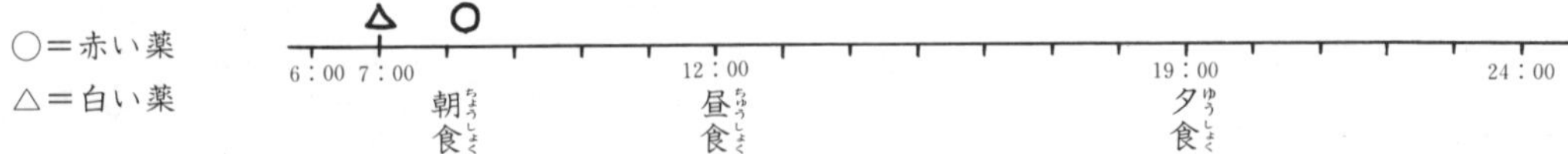

〈**Question 2**〉 6時から24時までのあいだに、ぜんぶで、何じょう、薬を飲みますか。

2) アメリカの本社には、週に1度、火曜日にレポートを送ることになっていますが、今週は、報告することが多かったので、月曜日から、1日おきに、送りました。来週からは、また、いつものとおりです。

〈**Question 1**〉 (A) いつものとおりなら、何日にレポートを送りますか。(B)また、今月は、何日にレポートを送りますか。Circle the days on which reports are sent.

A.

10月						
日	月	火	水	木	金	土
・	・	・	・	1	2	3
4	5	6	7	8	9	10
11	12	13	14	15	16	17
18	19	20	21	22	23	24
25	26	27	28	29	30	31

B.

今週 → (4–10)

10月						
日	月	火	水	木	金	土
・	・	・	・	1	2	3
4	5	6	7	8	9	10
11	12	13	14	15	16	17
18	19	20	21	22	23	24
25	26	27	28	29	30	31

〈**Question 2**〉 けっきょく、10月は、月に何回、レポートを送ることになりますか。

Function IV　**Illnesses and injuries;** 頭がいたいんです。

The following expressions are used when telling or inquiring about one's health.

ex.1. A: きぶんは、どうですか。　How are you feeling?
　B: ええ、とてもいいです。　I feel really fine.

2. A: お体のちょうしは、いかがですか。　How are you feeling?
　B: それが、あまりよくないんですよ。　Well as a matter of fact, not so good.
　A: それは、いけませんね。どうしました？　That's too bad. What's wrong?
　B: ええ、頭がいたくて、熱があるようなんです。　I seem to have a headache and a fever.
　　ええ、胃のぐあいが悪いんです。　My stomach is upset.

Useful expressions

1 病気 **illnesses**

頭がいたい　to have a headache (Don't confuse the expression「頭が悪い」"to be stupid")

　頭が、がんがんする　to have a splitting headache

　頭が、ずきずきする　to have a throbbing headache

歯が、いたい　to have a toothache　　歯が、ずきずきする　to have a throbbing toothache

おなかが、いたい　to have a stomach ache　　胃が、いたい　to have a stomach ache

　おなか／胃が、しくしくする　to have an upset stomach

　胃が、きりきりする　to have a painful stomach ache

むねが、苦(くる)しい to have a pain in one's chest

むねが、どきどきする

to have a pounding in one's chest

こしが、いたい to have a pain in the lower back

体(からだ)が、だるい to feel heavy, dull, listless

to have no energy

きぶんが悪(わる)い to not feel well, feel terrible

はきけがする to feel like throwing up

めまいがする to feel dizzy, head is spinning

さむけがする to feel a chill

耳(みみ)なりがする to have a buzzing in one's ears

げりをする to have diarrhea

熱(ねつ)がある to have a fever

しょくよくがない to have no appetite

せきが出る to have a cough

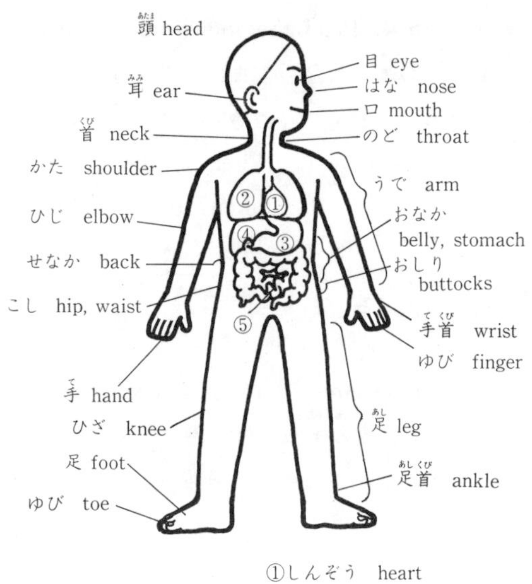

2 けが **injuries**

ほねをおる to break a bone
ねんざをする to sprain (wrist, ankle)
血(ち)が出る to bleed
やけどをする to burn oneself
すりむく to skin (knee, elbow, etc.)
かゆい to be itchy
あざができる to bruise
はれる to swell

Exercise 5: Tell the doctor what's wrong with you using the expressions above.

ex.
医者(いしゃ)：どうしましたか。
かんじゃ：ちょっと、頭(あたま)がいたいんです。

Exercise 6: Combining the above pictures describe more than one symptom, as in the example.

ex. 頭がいたい＋⑥ → 頭がいたくて、寒(さむ)けがするんです。

1) ①＋⑤ 2) ④＋⑦ 3) ②＋③ 4) ①＋③＋⑦

◆Vocabulary◆

かんじゃ patient
貝（かい） shellfish
色（いろ） color, complexion
よう (u-vi) to feel sick: 車に よう to get carsick
いたむ (u-vi) to be painful, hurt
もうちょう appendix, appendicitis
厚い（あつい） thick
虫歯（むしば） cavity
歯医者（はいしゃ） dentist
けんさする examination, test
ガス gas
はさむ (u-vt) to pinch
ぶつかる (u-vi) to bump against

Exercise 7: Fill in the blanks in the following conversations with descriptions of appropriate symptoms.

1) A: 元気がないですねえ。どうしたんですか。
　B: ええ、ちょっと、＿＿＿＿＿＿＿＿。
　A: それは、きっと、ゆうべ、貝を食べすぎたからですよ。

2) A: 顔の色が悪いですよ。
　B: ええ、車によったらしくて、＿＿＿＿＿＿＿＿。
　A: じゃ、車を止めて、外に出ましょう。

3) A: 苦しそうですねえ。だいじょうぶですか。
　B: ええ、さっきから、＿＿＿＿＿＿＿＿。
　A: おなかの、どのへんがいたみますか。
　B: ＿＿＿＿＿＿です。
　A: じゃあ、もうちょうかもしれませんね。すぐ、病院に行きましょう。

4) A: あっ、あぶない！　だいじょうぶですか。
　B: すみません、ちょっと＿＿＿＿＿＿＿＿ものですから。
　A: なんだか、顔も、青いようですよ。
　B: ええ、少し＿＿＿＿＿＿＿＿です。
　A: 早く帰って、休んだほうがいいですよ。

5) A: あ、いたた…。
　B: どうしました？
　A: きのう、重い荷物を運んだので、＿＿＿＿＿＿＿＿です。

6) A: 今日は、あたたかいのに、どうしたんですか。そんなに厚いセーターを着て？
　B: ええ、ちょっと＿＿＿＿＿＿ですよ。
　A: じゃ、かぜかもしれませんね。

7) 医者：どうしました？
　You: ＿＿＿＿＿＿＿＿＿＿。
　医者：そうですか。どうも、かぜのようですね。2、3日、ゆっくり休んでください。

8) A: しょくよくが、ないみたいですね。
　B: ＿＿＿＿＿＿＿＿＿＿。
　A: きっと、虫歯ですよ。歯医者さんに行ったほうがいいですよ。

9) 医者：どうしました？
　You: ＿＿＿＿＿＿＿＿＿＿。
　医者：目の使いすぎですね。しばらく、テレビを見ては、いけませんよ。

10) 医者：頭がいたいそうですが、どんなふうに、いたみますか。
　You: ＿＿＿＿＿。
　医者：そうですか。じゃ、ちょっと、けんさをしてみましょう。

Exercise 8: Combine pictures (①～⑤) with an appropriate picture (a～e) and describe what happened to you.

ex. A: あれ！　どうしたんですか。
　B: <u>ガスの上のなべにさわって、やけどをしたんです。</u>

Exercise 9: Tell about your medical history, using words from the list below.

医者：これまでに、何か、大きな病気をしたことがありますか。

You ：ex. 1. ええ、２年前、胃のしゅじゅつをしました。

Yes. Two years ago I had an stomach operation.

2. ええ、はいえんになったことがあります。 Yes. I once had pneumonia.

3. いいえ、べつにありません。 No, nothing in particular.

しんぞう病 heart trouble	けっかく tuberculosis	胃かいよう gastric ulcer
がん cancer	もうちょう appendicitis	はいえん pneumonia

Reading Comprehension Exercise

1) Read the following descriptions and try to guess the person's occupation.

① 

はじめてスキーをする人は、わたしのところに来てください。１日で、じょうずにすべれるようになりますよ。レッスンは、１日に３回、３時間ずつやっています。

② 

わたしは、いつも、社長と、いっしょにいます。社長のスケジュールは、ぜんぶ、わたしが決めるんですよ。社長のプライベートなスケジュール？　それは、ひみつです。社長のプライバシーを、まもらなければなりませんから。

③ 

わたしは、１日中、外で働いています。お客さんを乗せて、いろいろな所に行くので、道をよく知っていなければなりません。交通じこをおこさないように、気をつけて、運転しています。

④ 

わたしは、白い服を着て、働いています。どんなにつかれているときでも、えがおと、やさしさを、わすれないようにしています。相手は、体の弱い人たちですからね。

2) What sorts of things must the following people do? Answer on your own.

① スチュワーデス　② 日本語の先生　③ おまわりさん

◆Vocabulary◆

すべる (u-vi) to slide, ski, skate, slip　おこす (u-vt) to cause, bring about
運転（うんてん）する drive　プライベート（な）private, individual　スケジュール schedule
プライバシー privacy　まもる (u-vt) to defend, guard, keep, observe
えがお smiling face, smile　やさしさ gentleness　弱い（よわい）weak, feeble

Listening Comprehension Exercise

Listen to the dialogue on the tape and answer the following questions.

1) ジュリーさんの仕事は、何ですか。
2) ジュリーさんは、テレビ局に、週に何回、行かなくてはいけませんか。
3) ジュリーさんは、なぜ、６時半に、家を出なくてはならないのですか。
4) ジュリーさんは、なぜ、つかれるのですか。２つ、こたえなさい。

◆Vocabulary◆ テレビ局（テレビきょく）television station

Culture Note

Try reading the following comics, which depict the woes of the Japanese 'salary-man'. ('SANTARO FUJI' by Sanpei Sato, appearing in Asahi Newspaper)

第24課 おまわりさんに、しかられました

We Were Given A Scolding By A Policeman

Dialogue Ⅰ

Mr. and Mrs. Webb and Mr. and Mrs. Nakamura set out separately by car to spend their vacation at the foot of Mt. Fuji. Mr. and Mrs. Nakamura reach Shizuoka prefecture first.

中村氏（なかむらし）　：マイケル君たちは、おそいね。

中村夫人（ふじん）：きっと、東京の道が、こんでいるんですよ。

中村氏　：あそこに、いずみがあるらしいね。あそこで、マイケル君の車を待つことにしよう。（車をおりる）

中村夫人：あ、きれいな水！（水を飲む）
さすがに、富士山（ふじさん）の水ね。冷（つめ）たくて、おいしいわ。

中村氏　：(reading the information board) ここに、この水は、
日本の名水（めいすい）の１つに選（えら）ばれた、と書いてあるよ。
ぼくも、飲んでみようか。……あ、うまい！

中村夫人：こんなにおいしい水が、東京でも飲めたらいいのに！
帰りに、この水を持って帰りましょうね。

中村氏　：持って帰って、おとなりの鈴木（すずき）さんにもあげたら、いいね。
おふたりとも、茶（ちゃ）の湯（ゆ）の先生（せんせい）だから、きっと、喜（よろこ）んでもらえるよ。

中村夫人：それにしても、あの人たちは、おそいわね。
あ、あれは、マイケルさんの車かしら……。やはり、そうだわ。

Dialogue Ⅱ

Michael and Barbara's car stops and the two of them get out.

マイケル：おそくなって、すみません。うちを早く出たんですが、とちゅうで、じゅうたいにまきこまれて、ぜんぜん、動（うご）けなくなってしまったんです。

中村夫人：それは、たいへんでしたね。今日（きょう）は、月末（げつまつ）だから、よけいにこんだんでしょう。

バーバラ：それに、おまわりさんに車を止（と）められて、しかられたわねえ、マイケル。

マイケル：うん。中村さんの車においつこうと思って、少し、スピードを出しすぎたんです。

バーバラ：あんなしずかな所で、おまわりさんに見られているなんて、思いませんでしたわ。（マイケルに）あなたも、もっと気をつければよかったのに。

中村氏　：それで、どうしました？　はんそくきっぷを、切られましたか？

バーバラ：わたしたちが、まだ日本の交通じじょうを知らないから、しかたがないけれど、これからは、気をつけるように言われました。

中村夫人：とにかく、何もなくてよかったわ。ここには、おいしい水もあるし、おべんとうを食べるのに、ちょうどいいわね。

Dialogue III

Mrs. Nakamura spreads out the lunch beside the spring.

バーバラ：まあ、マイケル、見てごらんなさい。きれいなおべんとう！　ほら、いつか旅館で出された食事みたいだわ。おくさんが、お作りになったんですか。

中村夫人：ええ、そうなの。こちらは、あなた方の分ですよ。めしあがってみてください。

マイケル：わあ、ぼくたちの分もですか。どうもありがとうございます。食べるのが、もったいないみたいですね。どれから、食べようかな。（べんとうを食べながら）中村さんも、料理をすることがあるんですか。

中村氏　：ええ、たまにね。（夫人に）そうそう、このあいだ、ぼくが作った魚の料理ね、となりのねこに、食べられたようだね。さがしたけど、ないんだよ。

中村夫人：あなた、あんな、まっ黒になった魚は、ねこでも食べませんよ。わたしが、すてちゃいました。

中村氏　：えーっ！　それは、ひどいなあ。

Vocabulary

Nouns:

1～氏（し）Mr. __
3いずみ spring of water
8名水（めいすい）celebrated water
13茶の湯（ちゃのゆ）*chanoyu*, tea ceremony
17じゅうたいする traffic congestion, traffic jam
23スピード speed
28はんそくきっぷ violation ticket
29交通（こうつう）じじょう facts regarding driving
35あなた方（あなたがた）you (plural)

Adjectives:

9うまい ① delicious, tasty (same as「おいしい」) ② be good at, do something well (same as「じょうず（な）」(used only by men)

19よけい（な） excessive, more than needed

42まっ黒（まっくろ）（な） pitch-black

Adverbs:

31とにかく anyway, in any case, anyhow

40たまに occasionally, every once in a while

Verbs:

8選ばれる（えらばれる） passive form of u-vt「えらぶ」"to select"

17まきこまれる passive form of u-vt「まきこむ」"to involve in"

22おいつく (u-vi) to catch up with

21しかられる passive form of u-vt「しかる」"to scold"

35めしあがる (u-vt) honorific verb meaning "to eat"

Grammatical words:

8〜れる／〜られる passive inflection ☞Grammar Note

42Noun＋でも even __

Expressions:

6さすがに as to be expected, isn't that just like __

10〜たらいいのに if only (I) had done such and such

14それにしても even so, however that may be

25〜なんて such a thing as

32〜にちょうどいい just right for __

35〜の分（ぶん） a portion, share

33verb て-form＋ごらんなさい please do __ and see, please try doing __

Dialogue Comprehension Exercise

Answer the following questions.

1) マイケルさんたちは、どうして、おくれて来たのですか。
2) マイケルさんは、どうして、おまわりさんに、車を止（と）められたのですか。
3) マイケルさんは、ばっ金（きん）"fine" をはらいましたか。
4) 中村さんが作（つく）った魚の料理（りょうり）は、どうなりましたか。

Grammar Note

Passive form

Passive verb forms are made by adding the passive auxiliary. (see Appendix)

u-verb root ＋ areru	書く→書かれる
ru-verb root ＋ rareru	見る→見られる
Irregular: 行く→行かれる，来る→来られる，する→される	

In so-called passive sentences in Japanese, the subject is understood to be the person or object ultimately receiving the effect of the action. Most passive sentences in Japanese correspond to passive sentences in English, but in some cases "(subject) has such and such done to it" is a good equivalent.

	おいかける chase	読む read	なく cry
	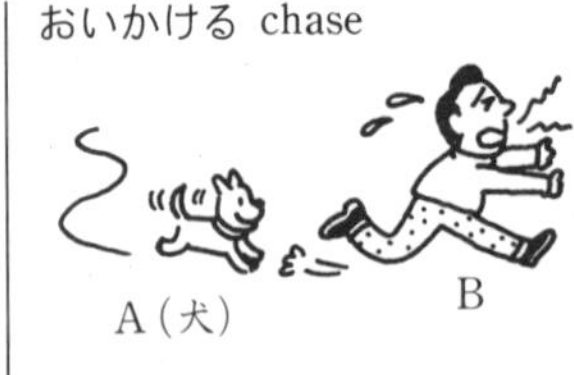	A B	
Active	Aが、Bを、おいかけた。 A chased B.	Aが、Bの手紙（てがみ）を、読んだ。 A read B's letter.	赤ちゃんが、ないた。 The baby cried.
Passive ①	Bが、Aに、おいかけられた。 B was chased by A.	Bの手紙が、Aに、読まれた。 B's letter was read by A.	
Passive ②		Bは、Aに、手紙を読まれた。 B had her letter read by A.	赤ちゃんに、なかれた。 We had the baby cry (on us).

Note 1: The doer of the action in passive sentences is indicated by「に」.

ex.1. この動物園（どうぶつえん）のぞうを、花子（はなこ）とよんでいます。 They call the elephant at this zoo "Hanako".

この動物園のぞうは、花子とよばれています。The elephant at this zoo is called "Hanako".

2. 写真（しゃしん）は、1839年に、フランスで、発明（はつめい）されました。

Photography was invented in 1839 in France.

3. マイケルさんは、おまわりさんに、車を止（と）められました。

Michael had his car stopped by the police.

4. みどりさんに花をプレゼントして、喜（よろこ）ばれました。

I gave Midori some flowers and she appreciated them.

Dialogues in English

Dialogue I

Mr. N : Michael and Barbara are late, aren't they!

Mrs. N : I would imagine the streets in Tokyo are crowded.

Mr. N : I believe there's a spring over there. What do you say we wait for Michael's car there? (they get out of the car)

Mrs. N : My! Such clear water! (drinks) And so cold and good. Isn't that just like water from Mt. Fuji!

Mr. N : It says here that this water was chosen as one of the finest waters in Japan. Let me try some too! Ah, what great tasting water!

Mrs. N : If only it was possible to drink such delicious water in Tokyo too! Let's take some of this water home with us on the way back!

Mr. N : We ought to bring some home and give it to the Suzukis nextdoor. I'm sure they'd appreciate it, seeing as both of them are tea ceremony teachers.

Mrs. N : Be that as it may, Michael and Barbara are certainly late. Goodness, I wonder if that's Michael's car? It is, just as I thought!

Dialogue II

M : I'm sorry we're late. We left home early, alright, but we got tied up in a traffic jam along the way and came to a complete standstill.

Mrs. N : That was too bad! I suppose it was all the more crowded, seeing that today is the end of the month, and all.

B : Besides that, we were stopped by a policeman and given a scolding. Isn't that right, Michael?

M : Yes. I went a little too fast, you see, thinking I'd try to catch up with your car.

B : I never imagined we would be watched by the police in such a quiet location. (to Michael) And if only you had been more careful yourself!

Mr. N : And what happened then? Did they write you out a violation ticket?

B : Seeing as Michael is not yet acquainted with the facts of driving in Japan, he couldn't be expected to know any better, but he was told to be more careful in the future.

Mrs. N : Well anyway, it's a good thing it was nothing serious. What a perfect spot for eating our lunch! There's good water and such...

Dialogue III

B : Oh my! Look, Michael! Such a lovely lunch! It's like the lunch we were served at the inn that time, remember? Did you fix it, Mrs. Nakamura?

Mrs. N : Yes, that's right. This over here is for the two of you. Please go ahead.

M : Wow! Some for us too? Thank you very much! It looks almost too good to eat. I wonder what I should begin with? (eating) Do you sometimes cook too, Mr. Nakamura?

Mr. N : Every once in a while, yes. Hey, that's right! (to his wife) You know that fish dish I cooked the other day? I have a hunch it was eaten by the neighbor's cat. I looked for it, but it wasn't anywhere.

Mrs. N : Oh you! Nobody could eat fish as burned as that, not even a cat! I threw it away.

Mr. N : What? That was mean!

Note 2: The correct interpretation of passive constructions depends on properly identifying the sentence subject. This is sometimes made difficult by the fact that sentence subjects are often omitted from Japanese sentences. Consider the following:

active：花をふんだ。 (He) trampled on the flowers.
passive ①：花<u>が</u>ふまれた。The flowers were trampled on (poor flowers!).
passive ②：花<u>を</u>ふまれた。I had my flowers trampled on (poor me!).

Note 3: A few verbs used in the passive in Japanese do not have a passive counterpart in English: 行く→行かれる，来る→来られる，なく→なかれる，死(し)ぬ "die" →死なれる.

Exercise 1: Change the following verbs in the picture below into the passive form.

Exercise 2: Make the following sentences passive, using the underlined words as sentence subject.

ex. デパートの前に、<u>クリスマスツリー</u>を、かざっ<u>ています</u>。
→ デパートの前に、<u>クリスマスツリーが</u>、<u>かざられています</u>。
→ <u>クリスマスツリーは</u>、デパートの前に、<u>かざられています</u>。

1) たくさんの人が、<u>この本</u>を読んでいます。→ この本は、＿＿＿＿＿＿。
2) 男の人が、<u>わたし</u>に、道をたずねました。→ わたしは、＿＿＿＿＿＿。
3) 来週、<u>斎藤(さいとう)さんの結婚式(けっこんしき)</u>を、おこないます。→ 斎藤さんの結婚式が、＿＿＿＿＿。
4) どこのオフィスでも、<u>ファックス</u>を使っています。 →＿＿＿＿＿＿＿。
5) <u>オリンピック</u>を、4年に1回(かい)、開(ひら)きます。 →＿＿＿＿＿＿＿。

Exercise 3: Look at the pictures below and complete the sentences using the passive form.

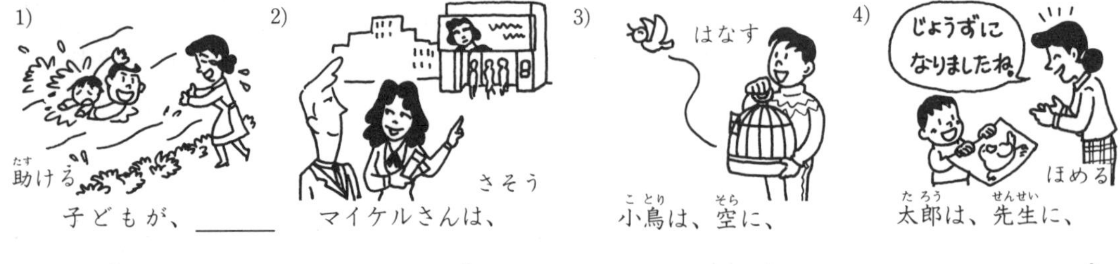

1) 子どもが、＿＿＿＿＿＿。
2) マイケルさんは、＿＿＿＿＿＿。
3) 小鳥(ことり)は、空(そら)に、＿＿＿＿＿＿。
4) 太郎(たろう)は、先生(せんせい)に、＿＿＿＿＿＿。

Vocabulary

ぶつける (ru-vt) to throw at, bump into
クリスマスツリー Christmas tree
ファックス facsimile　　オリンピック Olympic Games
開く（ひらく）(u-vi, vt) to open, hold (meeting, etc.)
わらう (u-vi, vt) to laugh, smile, sneer at ＿
おこなう (u-vt) to do, hold (meeting, etc.)
はなす (u-vt) to set free, let go off
小鳥（ことり）little bird

5)

花をあげて、

__________。

6)

マイケルさんに、

カップが、______。

7)

友達(ともだち)に、

__________。

8)

マイケルさんは、

__________。

Function I　Injurious or detrimental actions; use of the passive

One feature of the passive is that in certain situations it indicates that the action had an injurious or detrimental effect on the receiver. That the effect is beneficial or desirable is expressed using「〜てもらう」(see Lesson 16, p. 206).

ex. 1. 母に、友達から来た手紙(てがみ)を、<u>読まれてしまいました</u>。

I had the letter from my friend read by my mother (which was disastrous).

友達から来た手紙を、母に<u>読んでもらいました</u>。

I had my mother read the letter from my friend (which was helpful).

2. 夜(よる)おそく、友達に<u>来られて</u>、こまりました。

I had my friend come late last night and it was troublesome.

ひっこしのとき、友達に<u>来てもらって</u>、助(たす)かりました。

I had my friend come when we moved and it was a big help.

Exercise 4: Tell what the people in the pictures below had done or happen to them.

1) A：どうしたんですか。
B：家に帰るとちゅうで、雨に、________。
A：それは、たいへんでしたね。

2) A：ゆうべは、たいへんでしたね。
B：ええ、________、ねむれませんでした。

3) A：どうしたんですか。
B：となりの女の人に、________。
A：それは、いたかったでしょう。

4) A：洋服(ようふく)がよごれてますね。どうしたんですか。
B：きっさ店(てん)で、ウェーターに、________。
A：おやおや。

5) A：あ、ない！
B：どうしたんですか。
A：ここにおいておいたバッグを________。
B：えっ！たいへんだ！

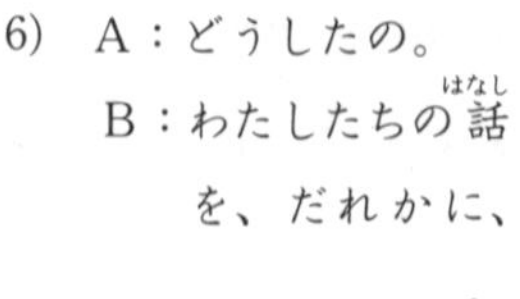

6) A：どうしたの。
B：わたしたちの話(はなし)を、だれかに、________。
A：えっ！いやねえ。

Vocabulary

カップ cup
よごれる (ru-vi) to get dirty, messy
はげます (u-vt) to encourage, cheer on
おやおや Well, I'll be!　Of all things!

Exercise 5: Form passive constructions as in the example.

ex.　おまわりさんが、わたしを　しかりました。(＋はずかしい)

→わたしは、おまわりさんにしかられて、はずかしかったです。

1) みんなが、わたしを、じろじろ見ました。(＋はずかしい) →わたしは、________。
2) 弟が、わたしのケーキを食べました。(＋おこる) →わたしは、________。
3) 母が、朝早く、弟を起こしました。(＋ねむい) →弟は、________。
4) 山田さんのひしょが、きゅうに、やめました。(＋こまる) →山田さんは、________。
5) せの高い人が、わたしの前にすわった。(＋映画が、よく見えない) →せの高い人に________。

Exercise 6: What do you think the people in the pictures below are saying? Use the passive form,「～てもらう」or「～てくれる」as appropriate.

Function II　**Reporting commands, requests, suggestions and warnings: use of「＿ように」**

「＿ように」(see Lesson 18, p.228) is also used to report a command, request, suggestion or warning that someone gives or was given.

ex. 1. 先生が、学生に、その本を読むように言いました。

The teacher told the students to read that book.

学生は、先生に、その本を読むように言われました。

The students were told by the teacher to read that book.

2. マイケルは、京都のおみやげを買って来るように、たのまれました。

Michael was asked to bring back a gift from Kyoto.

3. せきがひどいので、お医者さんに見てもらうように、すすめられました。

I have a terrible cough, so I was advised to have the doctor examine me.

Exercise 7: Tell what was commanded, requested, etc. in the following sentences using「＿ように」. Choose appropriate sentences from the box below.

1) お医者さんに、________言われて、がっかりしました。
2) 黒田さんに、________たのまれました。
3) 先生に、________注意されたので、練習しようと思います。
4) 母に、いつも、________言われるけど、なかなかできません。

5) 5時に区役所に行ったら、＿＿＿＿＿＿言われました。

6) 山田さんに、＿＿＿＿＿＿＿＿＿すすめられたので、さっそく、銀行に行きました。

a．京都のおかしを買って来てくれませんか。	b．もっと、字をきれいに書きなさい。
c．電気代を、自動ひきおとしにしたらどうですか。	d．あした、また来てください。
e．しばらく、お酒を飲んではいけませんよ。	f．へやを、きれいにしなさい。

Exercise 8: Complete the following dialogues by filling in some sort of command, request, etc.

1) 山田：もしもし。北村さんは、おるすですか。では、あとで電話をいただきたいんですが…。
黒田：はい、わかりました。帰りましたら、＿＿＿＿＿＿＿＿お伝えします。

2) 土田：郵便局に行くの？
マイケル：ええ、切手を30まい＿＿＿＿＿＿たのまれたんです。

3) 母　：となりのステレオが、うるさいわね。
子ども：そうだね。となりの子に、＿＿＿＿＿＿＿言って来る。

4) 母　：ごはんができたけど、お父さんは、まだ、おふろかしら。
子ども：じゃ、お父さんに、＿＿＿＿＿＿言って来るね。

5) 部長：マイケル君の報告書は、まだかな。今日中にほしいんだけど。
北村：じゃ、マイケル君に、＿＿＿＿＿＿＿言っておきます。

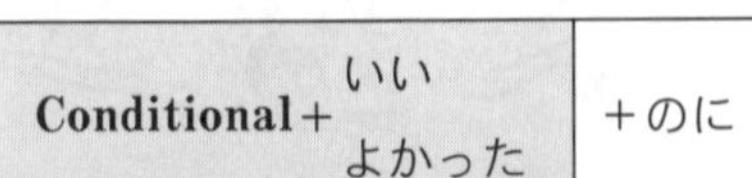

Function III　Expressing regret that things are not otherwise; 東京でも飲めたらいいのに

Conditional＋いい／よかった	＋のに

"(lit.) although it would be good if"
"(lit.) although it would have been good if"

「のに」"even though" (see Lesson 15, p.193) added after「conditional ＋いい」laments the fact that things are not otherwise, and is equivalent to English "if only such and such were", "too bad such and such is not", etc.

ex. 1. こんなにおいしい水が、東京でも飲めたらいいのに。（飲めると，飲めれば）
If only it were possible to drink such delicious water in Tokyo too.

2. 彼女が、もっと美人だといいのに。（だったら，なら）
Too bad my girl isn't a little better looking!

3. もっと早く、お医者さんに見てもらえばよかったのに。（見てもらったら，見てもらうと）
If only you'd had the doctor examine you sooner!

4. スピードを出さなければよかったのに。　If only you hadn't gone so fast!

Note 1:「のに」is not used with actions you yourself did.

ex. 1. おまわりさんに、車を止められてしまった。あーあ、もっと、ゆっくり走ればよかった。（×のに）
I was stopped by the police. Oh my! If only I had gone more slowly!

2. あんなに、スピードを出すんじゃなかった！　I shouldn't have gone so fast!

Vocabulary

じろじろ見る to stare
朝早く early in the morning
ひしょ secrétary
ステレオ stereo
はねる (ru-vt) to hit, knock down
注意（ちゅうい）する attention, caution, warning, advice
さっそく at once, right away
飛ばす（とばす）(u-vt) to send flying through the air, propel
子（こ）child
たんか stretcher

「のに」may be added after various other expressions as well to strengthen the meaning "too bad", "unfortunately!".

ex. 1. 太郎は、木から落ちて、うでの骨をおった。来週、ヨーロッパに行くはずだったのに。

Taro fell out of a tree and broke his arm. It's unfortunate because next week he was supposed to go to Europe.

2. あれ、雨が、ふってる。さっきまで、晴れそうだったのに。

Goodness, it's raining! Gee, up until a while ago it looked as though it would clear up. Too bad!

3. あしたは、雨がふるらしい。子どもたちを、ディズニーランドにつれて行くつもりだったのに。

It seems it's going to rain tomorrow. And here I was planning on taking the kids to Disneyland!

Note 2:「のに」is a rather forceful expression. A milder, somewhat more thoughtful manner of expressing disappointment or regret would be to use such expressions as「__のですが」,「__んですけど」, etc.

ex.　こんなにおいしい水が、東京でも飲めるといいんですけど。

It would be nice if we could get such delicious water as this in Tokyo.

Exercise 9: Tell what the people might be thinking in the situations pictured below using「conditional ＋いいのに」, etc.

Exercise 10: Looking at Michael's schedule and at the pictures below, tell what Michael is thinking using an appropriate expression plus「のに」.

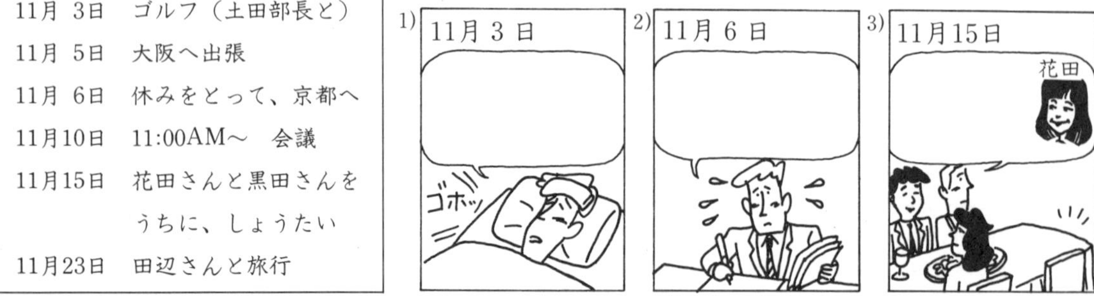

11月 3日	ゴルフ（土田部長と）
11月 5日	大阪へ出張
11月 6日	休みをとって、京都へ
11月10日	11:00AM～　会議
11月15日	花田さんと黒田さんを うちに、しょうたい
11月23日	田辺さんと旅行

Reading Comprehension Exercise

〔マイケルの日記〕

日本語学校から帰るとちゅう、雨にふられた。たいした雨ではないので、そのまま歩(ある)いていると、本屋のおばさんが、かさをかしてあげるから、さして行くように、と言ってくれた。ていねいにことわって、しばらく行くと、今度(こんど)は、男の人によびとめられた。いつも行く、パン屋のおじさんだった。まるで、ぬれねずみのようだ、とわらわれてしまった。

たしかに、わたしのように、雨にぬれて歩いている人はいない。そういえば、ずっと、まわりの人から、じろじろ見られていたような気(き)がする。そこで、パン屋のおじさんに、かさをかりて、歩(ある)き出(だ)した。もう、だれも、わたしを見る人はいない。どうも、日本人は、雨にぬれるのがきらいらしい。また、雨にぬれている人を見るのも、がまんできないらしい。

◆Vocabulary◆

そのまま that way, in that manner, as it is
かさをさす to put up an umbrella
おじさん uncle, or any man of that approximate age
ぬれねずみのよう to look like a soaked mouse
そこで then, at that point
歩き出す (あるきだす) to start walking
たいした雨ではない It's not a very heavy rain.
おばさん aunt, or any woman of that approximate age
ことわる (u-vt) to refuse
パン屋 (パンや) bakery
よびとめる (ru-vt) to call to a person to stop
＿ような気がする it seems as if ＿, I feel as if ＿
がまんできない I can't stand it

Exercise 11: Read the paragraph above and answer the following questions.

1) マイケルさんは、いつ、雨にふられましたか。
2) だれが、かさをかしてくれると言いましたか。
3) パン屋のおじさんは、マイケルさんの知っている人ですか。
4) パン屋のおじさんは、マイケルさんの、どんなようすを見て、ぬれねずみのようだと言ったのですか。
5) マイケルさんが歩いているとき、まわりの人は、どうしましたか。
6) マイケルさんは、日本人について、どんなことがわかったと書いていますか。

Listening Comprehension Exercise

Listen to the tape and do as directed.

1) Listen to Mario's story and answer the following questions.
   ① マリオさんは、英語で話しかけられましたか、イタリア語で話しかけられましたか。それとも、日本語で話しかけられましたか。
   ② マリオさんは、どうして、日本語で話してもいいかと言ったのですか。
   ③ そうしたら、女の人は、どうしましたか。
   ④ この話を、会社の人に話したら、会社の人は、何と言いましたか。
2) For each item Michael relates, mark ○ if he sounds pleased, and × if he sounds put out.
   ①（ ）　②（ ）　③（ ）　④（ ）　⑤（ ）

Vocabulary

ロボット robot
しょうたいする invitation
話しかける (はなしかける) (ru-vi) to speak to
イタリア語 Italian language
そうしたら and then
何と言った What did he say?

第25課 そちらに、おうかがいいたします

I Will Call At Your Office

Dialogue I

Michael makes a second telephone call to Mr. Matsushita of Yamakawa Trading.

松下　：もしもし、お待たせいたしました。松下でございます。

マイケル：先日、見本市でお目にかかった、阿部産業のウエッブでございます。

松下　：あ、あの時は、おせわになりました。先ほど、お電話をいただきましたそうで。会議中で、たいへん、失礼いたしました。

マイケル：いいえ、おいそがしいところを、もうしわけございません。さっそくですが、先日、ごらんいただいた、わが社の製品について、もう少し、ご説明したいと思いまして。ごつごうがよろしかったら、おうかがいしたいのですが…。

松下　：そうですね。じつは、あすから、九州に出張することになっております。木曜日には帰ってまいりますので、金曜日の午後なら、お会いできると思いますが、１時半では、いかがでしょう。

マイケル：はい、それで、けっこうです。では、１時半に、そちらにうかがいます。

松下　：あ、ちょっとお待ちください。１時半は、ほかの予定が入っておりました。わすれないように、メモをしておいたのに、うっかりしていました。もうしわけありませんが、３時にしていただけませんでしょうか。

マイケル：はい。では、３時に、おうかがいいたします。

Dialogue II

Michael visits Mr. Matsushita.

マイケル：先日は、お電話で、失礼いたしました。

松下　：いいえ。どういたしまして。お待ちしておりました。

マイケル：あの、部長の土田からも、よろしくとのことでございます。課長さんとは、むかしからのお知(し)り合(あ)いだそうですね。

松下　：ええ、大学のラグビー部のせんぱいなんですよ。おたがいに、どんなにいそがしくても、１年に１度は会おうと言っているんですが、なかなか、お目(め)にかかれないんですよ。

女性社員(じょせいしゃいん)：（お茶を持ってくる）失礼(しつれい)いたします。どうぞ。

マイケル：すみません。どうぞ、おかまいなく。ところで、れいの工業用ロボットの件(けん)ですが、わが社では、アメリカだけでなく、ヨーロッパの方(ほう)にも、進出(しんしゅつ)したいと考(かんが)えております。こちらでは、ヨーロッパの会社とのとりひきが多いと、うかがいましたので、ぜひ、わが社の製品(せいひん)も、輸出(ゆしゅつ)していただければ、と思いまして。

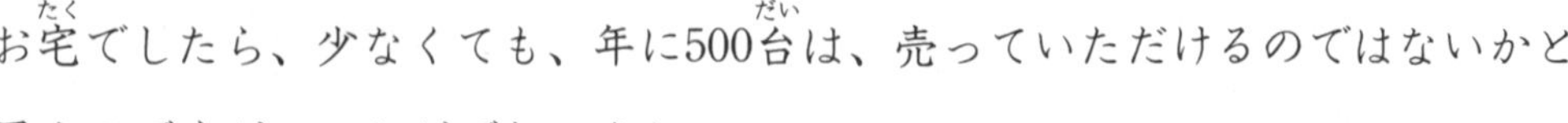

お宅(たく)でしたら、少なくても、年に500台(だい)は、売っていただけるのではないかと思うのですが、いかがでしょうか。

ヨーロッパに合わせて、モデルのチェンジもできますので、よろしくおねがいいたします。

松下　：よくわかりました。お宅のロボットがゆうしゅうなことは、さいきんでは、子どもでも知っていますからね。けっこうなお話だと思いますが、わたくしの考(かんが)えだけでは、すぐに、お返事(へんじ)できません。部長とも、よく話しまして、近(ちか)いうちに、ごれんらくいたします。

マイケル：よろしくおねがいいたします。おいそがしいところを、おじゃまいたしました。

Vocabulary

Nouns:

2先日（せんじつ）the other day
7わが社（わがしゃ）our company
21むかし long ago
22ラグビー部（ラグビーぶ）rugby club
27工業用（こうぎょうよう）industrial use
30とりひきする business deal
35チェンジする change, alteration
39考え（かんがえ）thinking, opinion
2見本市（みほんいち）sample show, fair
7製品（せいひん）product
13そちら there, you
21（お）知り合い（お-しりあい）acquaintance
22せんぱい senior member of the same group
29進出（しんしゅつ）する advance
32輸出（ゆしゅつ）する export
35モデル model, type
39わたくし I (formal)
25女性（じょせい）female

Adjectives:

37ゆうしゅう（な）excellent, superior　　38けっこう（な）fine

Adverbs:

15うっかりする carelessly (to be unheeding, careless)　　22おたがいに each other, one another

Verbs:

うかがう (u-vi,vt) 9① to visit ② to ask 31③ to hear (humble)

35合わせる（あわせる）(ru-vt) to fit to, do in accordance with

Grammatical words:

23〜ても（でも）even if, even though ☞ Function II

Expressions:

2お目にかかる to meet someone (humble)　3おせわになりました I am indebted to you for all you have done

7さっそくですが This is a bit sudden, but...　11お会いできる I am able to see you (humble)

20よろしくとのことです He told me to say hello.　26どうぞ、おかまいなく Please don't bother about me.

33少なくても at least　33〜のではないか I am sure __, in all likelihood

40近いうちに within the near future　41おいそがしいところを at such a busy time

Dialogues in English

Dialogue I

Mat : Hello. Sorry to have kept you waiting. This is Mr. Matsushita.

M : This is Mr. Webb of Abe Industries. We met the other day at the sample show.

Mat : Ah, thank you for your help at that time. It seems I received a call from you earlier. I'm terribly sorry about that. You see, I was in conference.

M : Not at all. I'm sorry to bother you at such a busy time. This is rather sudden, but I would like to explain a little more about some of our company's products which you so kindly looked at the other day. I would like to pay you a visit, if it's convenient for you.

Mat : I see. To tell the truth, I leave for Kyushu tomorrow on business. I'll be back by Thursday, so Friday afternoon I'll be able to meet with you, I believe. How would 1:30 be?

M : Yes. That would be fine. I'll call at your office then at 1:30.

Mat : Oh, wait a minute! I have another appointment for 1:30. Even though I wrote myself a memo so I wouldn't forget, it completely slipped my mind. I'm terribly sorry, but could you make that for 3:00?

M : Certainly. I'll be there at 3:00 then.

Dialogue II

M : Sorry to have troubled you on the phone the other day.

Mat : Not at all. I've been expecting you.

M : Uh, our division manager, Mr. Tsuchida, said to say hello as well. It seems he's an acquaintance of yours from long ago, right?

Mat : That's right. We were both members of the rugby club at the university. He was older than I. We keep saying we'll get together at least once a year no matter how busy we are, but we never seem to see each other.

Female employee: Excuse me. Here you are.

M : Thank you. Please don't bother about me. To come to the point then, in regards to the industrial robot we discussed previously, our company is thinking it would like to enter the market, not only in the U.S., but in Europe too. We heard your company does a lot of business with European companies, and so we were thinking how really nice it would be if you could export our products for us as well. I am sure your company could sell for us at the very least 500 units per year. What do you think? We would be able to make model changes as well in accordance with the European market, and so I would like to have you consider it please.

Mat : I understand you very well. I think you have an excellent proposal here, especially since recently even children are aware of the fact that your robots are superior. However I am not able to answer you immediately on just my opinion alone. I'll talk it over with my division manager as well, and contact you sometime within the near future.

M : I would appreciate that very much. I'm sorry for bothering you at such a busy time.

Dialogue Comprehension Exercise

Answer the following questions.

Dialogue I

1) マイケルさんは、なぜ、松下(まつした)さんに、2回目(かいめ)の電話をかけたのですか。

2) マイケルさんは、松下さんに、どんなことをたのみましたか。

3) マイケルさんは、いつ、松下さんと会うことになりましたか。

Dialogue II

4) マイケルさんの会社では、工業用(こうぎょうよう)ロボットを、どこに輸出(ゆしゅつ)したいと思っているのですか。

5) マイケルさんの会社は、なぜ、工業用ロボットを、松下さんの会社で輸出してもらいたいと思っているのですか。

6) マイケルさんの話を聞いて、松下さんは、何とこたえましたか。

Function I　Showing respect (2): further honorific and humble expressions

In addition to honorific「お＋ stem ＋になる」and humble「お＋ stem ＋する」introduced in Lesson 21, there is an assortment of commonly used honorific and humble words and expressions which you should become familiar with.

polite	honorific	humble	
行きます	いらっしゃいます（いらっしゃる）	まいります（まいる）	go
来ます	いらっしゃいます（いらっしゃる）	まいります（まいる）	come
います	いらっしゃいます（いらっしゃる）	おります　（おる）	be
言います	おっしゃいます　（おっしゃる）	もうします（もうす） もうしあげます（もうしあげる）	say
食べます	めしあがります　（めしあがる）	いただきます（いただく）	eat
飲みます	めしあがります　（めしあがる）	いただきます（いただく）	drink
します	なさいます　　　（なさる）	いたします　（いたす）	do
～ています	～ていらっしゃいます（～ていらっしゃる）	～ております	be doing
知っています	ごぞんじです	ぞんじております	know
会います	お会いになります	お目にかかります（お目にかかる）	see, meet
思います	お思いになります	ぞんじます	think
たずねます	おたずねになります	うかがいます（うかがう）	visit, ask
見ます	ごらんになります	はいけんします	look at, see

ex. 1. もう、あの映画(えいが)をごらんになりましたか。　Have you seen that movie already?

2. 月野様(つきのさま)とおっしゃる方(かた)が、いらっしゃいました。　A person named Mr. Tsukino is here.

3. A：毎晩(まいばん)、何時ごろ、お休みになりますか。　What time do you go to bed every night?

B：なるべく早く、休むようにいたしております。

I make an effort to get to bed as early as possible.

4. このケーキ、よろしかったら、もう1つ、めしあがりませんか。

If you would like, won't you have another piece of cake?

5. あの会社の山本(やまもと)さんを、ごぞんじですか。

Are you acquainted with Mr. Yamamoto of that company?

Expressions:

There is going to be a party at the company where Michael works on Friday of next week.
課長は、パーティーにいらっしゃるかしら。
課長、来週のパーティーにいらっしゃいますか。
ああ、行くよ。
部長は、パーティーにいらっしゃるかな。
いらっしゃると思うよ。
部長、パーティーにいらっしゃいますか。
わたしも、まいります。
ああ、行くよ。君は？
そう。社長もいらっしゃるそうだよ。
部長
課長

Note: The passive form 「～areru (rareru)」, introduced in Lesson 24, also functions as an honorific expression. This use is very common in daily speech, however the level of respect that the passive expresses is somewhat lower than that of other honorific forms.

ex. 田中さんが、来ましたか。	Did Mr. Tanaka come?	(polite)
田中さんが、来られましたか。		(passive used as honorific)
田中さんが、いらっしゃいましたか。		(honorific)

Exercise 1: Give polite, honorific and humble forms for the verbs below as in the example.

ex. いる → います／いらっしゃいます／おります

1) たずねる　2) 飲む　3) 見せる　4) 来る　5) 言う　6) する　7) 見る　8) 行く

Exercise 2: Re-express the sentences below using honorific or humble expressions appropriate to the situation.

1)

①A：アメリカには、いつ行きますか。

②A：どのくらい、アメリカにいますか。

③A：今夜は、どこで食事をしますか。

④A：このカタログを見ましたか。

⑤B：どうぞ、食べてください。　　A：はい、食べます。

⑥B：あのカタログを、持って来てください。　　A：はい、持って行きます。

2)

① 土田部長、クラーク会長が、日本に来たそうですね。知っていますか。

② クラーク会長には、お子さんは、何人いますか。

③ 部長は、クラーク会長が、お酒をたくさん飲むのを、知っていましたか。

④ 部長は、アメリカに出張したとき、クラーク会長と会ったそうですね。

⑤ クラーク会長が、来週、部長に会いたいと言っていましたよ。

⑥ クラーク会長は、部長に会えるかどうか、しんぱいしていましたよ。

3)

① 土田：クラーク会長に、電話をしてくれましたか。
マイケル：はい。外出中でいませんでした。また、あとで、電話をします。

② 土田：れいのカタログを、クラーク会長に見せましたか。
マイケル：はい。見せましたところ、たいへんいいものだと言いました。

③ 土田：クラーク会長に、うちの会社に、来てもらえそうですか。
マイケル：はい。来てもらえそうです。

Exercise 3: Express the underlined portions in the sentences below in appropriate honorific or humble forms.

1) マイケルさん、社長が、社長室に来るようにと言っていますよ。
2) これは、わたしが作ったクッキーなんですよ。食べてみてください。
3)〔お客さんに〕部長は、会議に出ているので、終わったら、すぐ来ます。こちらで待ってください。
4)〔土田部長が、社長の秘書に〕あしたの会議のことを、社長は知っていますか。
5) 社長に会いたいので、あした、そちらにたずねたいと、思います。
6)〔お客さんに〕部長は、となりのへやにいますから、そちらに行ってください。

Exercise 4: Kathy visits Takashi at his home. Takashi introduces the members of his family and they talk for a while trying to get to know one another better. Your task is to continue the dialogue below asking the suggested questions, and answering with information from the box below. Be sure to use appropriate honorific and polite expressions.

Personal Information

キャシー・スミス
アメリカ人
ニューヨークで生まれる
New York Times の新聞記者
日本語は、イリノイ大学で勉強
六本木のマンションに住んでいる
来年の3月まで、日本にいる
六本木のディスコで、孝と知り合う

Takashi's family

祖母：78さい
父：山川貿易営業部長
母：大学の英語の教師
兄：テレビ局のアナウンサー
ときどき、外国に出張する
孝：大学で、経済学を勉強している

Start 孝：(キャシーに) ごしょうかいします。こちらは、ぼくの、祖母です。
こちらが、父、母、それに兄です。
キャシー：はじめまして。どうぞよろしく。
みんな：こちらこそ。よくいらっしゃいました。　⇨ Continue the dialogue:

Suggested questions

① 祖母：キャシーの国を聞く。
② キャシー：祖母の年齢を聞く。
③ 母　：学生か、仕事をしているのか聞く。
④ キャシー：母が仕事をしているかどうか聞く。
⑤ 母　：今、どこに住んでいるか聞く。
孝と、どこで知り合ったか聞く。
⑥ キャシー：父の仕事を聞く。
⑦ 父　：アメリカのどこで生まれたか聞く。
⑧ キャシー：兄の仕事を聞く。
⑨ 兄　：日本語が、じょうずだとほめて、どこで勉強したか聞く。
⑩ キャシー：兄に、外国に行くことがあるかどうか聞く。
⑪ 父　：いつまで、日本にいるか聞く。
⑫ キャシー：兄に、アメリカへの出張の予定はないか聞く。
⑬ 兄　：来年の4月に、アメリカに出張するから、むこうで会えたらいいと言う。

◆Vocabulary◆

社長室（しゃちょうしつ）president's office
マンション apartment house where individual units are sold off rather than rented
知り合う（しりあう）(u-vi) to meet, become acquainted with
教師（きょうし）teacher
新聞記者（しんぶんきしゃ）newspaper reporter
アナウンサー announcer
年齢（ねんれい）age

Function II "Even if __", "even though __"; ～ても，～でも

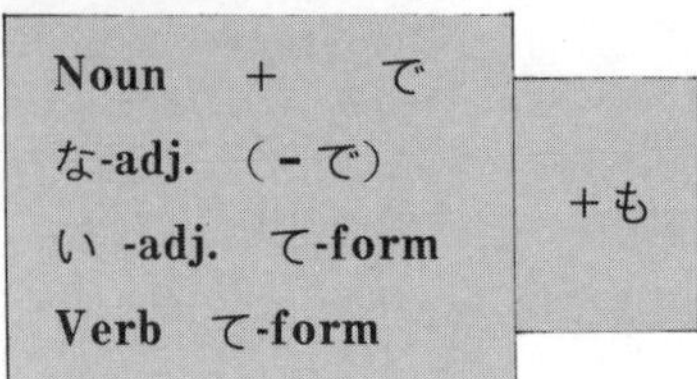

One use of the be-verb て-form plus「も」,「でも」"something like __" was introduced in Lesson 17 (p.216).「も」may also be added to the て-forms of other verbals as well to mean "even if __", "even though __", etc.

ex. 1. 日本では、土曜日でも、子どもたちは、学校に行きます。

In Japan children go to school even if it's Saturday.

2. 外国語を習(なら)うときは、へたでも、たくさん、しゃべったほうがいいんですよ。

When learning a foreign language it's better to speak a lot, even if you are no good at it.

3. 仕事がいそがしくても、月に1度は、映画(えいが)を見に行きます。

I go to see a movie at least once a month, even if I'm busy with work.

4. あの人に、ドイツ語で話(はな)しかけても、わからないでしょう。

That person probably won't understand you even if you speak to him in German.

Some words commonly used with the「～ても」construction include「たとえ」"supposing, for example",「いくら」"how much",「どんなに」"how much".

ex. 1. たとえ、雨がふっても、運動会(うんどうかい)は、おこないます。

We will hold the sports tournament even if it rains.

2. いくら強(つよ)い男でも、親(おや)が死(し)んだときには、なくでしょう。

No matter how strong he is, a man is bound to cry when his parents die.

3. どんなに寒(さむ)くても、わたしは、ストーブをつけません。

No matter how cold it is, I don't light the space heater.

With certain adjectives expressing amount, etc.,「～ても」indicates the extreme limit, and is equivalent to English "at the very __". Sometimes「～ても」is replaced by「～とも」, but this sounds somewhat bookish.

ex. 1. 仕事は、おそくても、午後(ごご)8時には、終わるでしょう。

I should finish up with work by 8 p.m. at the very latest.

2. 先日(せんじつ)のデモには、少なくとも、2,000人の人が、参加(さんか)したようです。

It seems 2,000 people at the very least took part in the demonstration the other day.

3. 冬(ふゆ)のボーナスは、多くても、3.5か月分(げつぶん)ぐらいじゃないかと思います。

I believe that the winter bonus will only equal about three and a half months salary at the very most.

Note: In a sense「～ても」resembles「のに」"in spite of the fact" (see Lesson 15, p.193).「～ても」however merely describes a situation, and does not express a strong emotional reaction on the part of the speaker in the way that「のに」does. Moreover, while「のに」comments on actions, etc. that happened in the past, always happen, or are scheduled to happen in the future,「～ても」may be used for describing hypothetical situations or actions that have not yet been decided upon.

ex. 1. マイケルさんは、お茶を出しても、飲まなかったんです。

Even though I offered Michael some tea, he didn't drink it.

マイケルさんは、お茶を出したのに、飲まなかったんです。
Even though I took the trouble to offer Michael some tea, he didn't drink it!

2. その辞書(じしょ)は、高くても、買ったほうがいいですよ。
It would be better to buy that dictionary, even if it is expensive.
× その辞書は、高いのに、買ったほうがいいですよ。

3. 今、道がこんでいるから、タクシーで行っても、まにあわないでしょう。
The streets are crowded now, so even if you went by cab, you probably wouldn't make it on time.
× 今、道がこんでいるから、タクシーで行くのに、まにあわないでしょう。

Exercise 5: Complete the following dialogues using「〜ても」.

ex. A：駅は近いですが、車で行きますか。
B：ええ、近くても、車で行きます。
A：そうですか。じゃ、タクシーをよびましょう。

1) A：あの店のピザは、安いから、おいしくないでしょう？
B：＿＿＿＿＿＿＿＿＿＿＿＿＿＿＿＿。
A：そうですか。じゃ、今度(こんど)、わたしも食べてみましょう。

2) A：おふろは、ちょっと熱(あつ)いかもしれません。熱かったら、水を入れてくださいね。
B：＿＿＿＿＿＿＿＿＿＿＿＿＿＿＿＿。
A：そうですか。外国の方(かた)は、熱いおふろは、にがてだと聞いていたものですから。

3) A：あしたは、雨がふるかもしれませんよ。雨がふったら、どうしますか。やはり、行きますか。
B：＿＿＿＿＿＿＿＿＿＿＿＿＿＿＿＿。
A：そうですか。じゃ、かぜをひかないように、気(き)をつけてくださいね。

4) A：今夜(こんや)は、帰りがおそくなるから、先にねてください。
B：＿＿＿＿＿＿＿＿＿＿＿＿＿＿＿＿。
A：そう。じゃ、できるだけ早く、帰るようにします。

5) A：あすは、日曜日だから、きっと、どうろがこんでいますよ。行くのをやめたらどう？
B：＿＿＿＿＿＿＿＿＿＿＿＿＿＿＿＿。
A：それなら、朝早く、でかけたほうがいいですよ。

Exercise 6: Construct dialogues patterned after the examples. Think up appropriate reasons on your own.

ex. ぐあいが悪(わる)い／明日(あす)は、休む
→A：ぐあいが悪いんでしょう？ 明日は、休んだらどうですか。
B：明日は、たいせつな会議があるから、どんなにぐあいが悪くても、休めないんです。

1) つかれている／ うちに帰る
2) いやな仕事だ／ ことわる
3) お金がない／ 両親(りょうしん)にかりる
4) 胃(い)のぐあいが悪(わる)い／お酒を飲むのをやめる

Vocabulary

ピザ pizza
にがて（な） not good at, weak point
できるだけ＿ as ＿ as possible
それなら well then, in that case

Exercise 7: What might B say in the following situations? Use the て-form plus「も」in your answer.

1)あしたは、雨らしいよ。行くのをやめたら？

2)この犬、どうしたの？元気がないですね。

3)あれ！子どもがビールを飲んでる！

4)ピカソの絵は、高いですよ。

5)駅までは、遠いですよ。タクシーで行けば？

6)この字、日本人なら読めるんでしょう？

7)おまわりさんに聞かなかったんですか。

8)ミッキーマウスは、ゆうめいなんですね。

Exercise 8: Circle the more appropriate of the choices in the brackets.

1) 外国にクリスマスカードを送るばあいは、{a. 早くても　　b. おそくても} 12月10日までに出してください。
2) ボーナスは、{a. 多くても　　b. 少なくても} 2か月分は、ほしいですね。
3) ボーナスは、{a. 多くても　　b. 少なくても} 2か月分しか、出ないでしょう。
4) 日本の会社では、お正月の休みは、{a. 長くても　　b. 短くても} 10日間ぐらいです。
5) あのくつなら、{a. 安くても　　b. 高くても} 5000円ぐらいで買えますよ。

Exercise 9: Complete the following sentences by putting the word in ( ) in an appropriate form, using「～ても」,「のに」or「～たら」.

1) この漢字は、きのう、(習う　　)、もうわすれてしまいました。
2) この漢字は、何回 (練習する　　)、じょうずに書けません。
3) この漢字を、何回ぐらい (書く　　)、じょうずに書けるようになりますか。
4) せっかく、マイケルさんの家に (行く　　)、かれは、でかけていて、会えなかった。
5) 遠いから、電車で行ったら？　電車で (行く　　)、1時間はかかると思いますよ。
6) その品物は、(安い　　)、買わないほうがいいですよ。よく、こしょうするらしいですよ。
7) わたしが、どんなに (注意する　　)、言うことをきかない。

Reading Comprehension Exercise

山川貿易　営業第2課　松下課長　様

前略

先日は、おいそがしいところを、お会いいただきまして、どうもありがとうございました。

さて、当日、おねがいいたしました件ですが、その後、ごけんとういただけましたでしょうか。当社では、ぜひとも、ヨーロッパへ市場を広げたいと考えておりますので、どうぞ、よろしくおねがいもうしあげます。当社の工業用ロボットは、アメリカでの売り上げもふえており、その性能と品質には、自信を持っております。ヨーロッパでも、かならず、まんぞくしていただけると、ぞんじます。

なお、先日、おとどけいたしました英文の資料のほかに、ドイツ語とフランス語の資料も作りましたので、お送りいたします。ヨーロッパの会社への説明のときに、お使いください。くわしいないようについて、ご質問がございましたら、また、ご説明にうかがいますので、ごれんらくいただければと、ぞんじます。

おいそがしいところ、おそれいりますが、ごけんとうを、よろしくおねがいもうしあげます。

12月10日

阿部産業　営業第１課

マイケル・ウエッブ

◆Vocabulary◆

前略（ぜんりゃく）"formal salutations are omitted"
さて now then, let's see
当日（とうじつ）that day
その後（そのご）after that, since then
けんとうする examine, discuss, talk over
当社（とうしゃ）our company, the company in question
市場（しじょう）market: 市場を広げる expand one's market
売り上げ（うりあげ）gross sales
ふえる (ru-vi) to increase in number or amount
性能（せいのう）efficiency, performance
品質（ひんしつ）product quality
自信（じしん）confidence
とどける (ru-vt) to deliver, send, submit
ないよう contents

Exercise 10: Answer the following questions.

1) これは、だれが、だれに出した手紙ですか。
2) この手紙では、どんなことを、たのんでいますか。
3) 何を送ると、書いてありますか。
4) マイケルさんは、どんなときに、また、松下さんの会社に行くつもりですか。
5) なぜ、ドイツ語とフランス語の資料も作ったのでしょうか。

Listening Comprehension Exercise

Listen to the dialogue on the tape and fill in the chart.

	名前	国	今、住んでいる所	働いている所
男の人				
女の人				

Vocabulary

えさ food, feed, bait
クリスマスカード Christmas card
こしょうする break down, out of order
言うことをきかない to never listen, never do as one is told

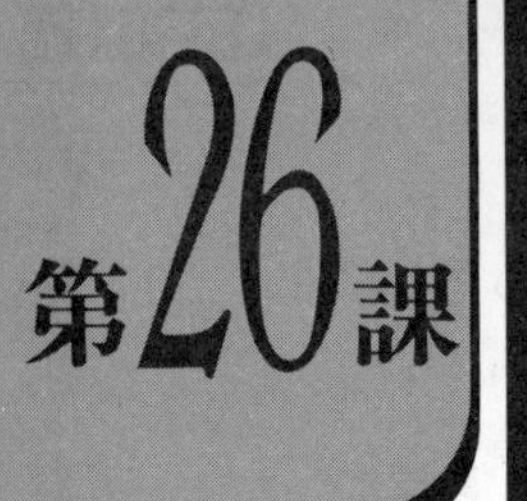

斎藤さんに選ばせたらいいんじゃないの

Wouldn't It Be Alright To Let Miss Saito Choose?

Dialogue I

Miss Saito is getting married and the people in her section talk about a wedding gift for her.

花田　　：もうすぐ、斎藤さんが、結婚されるでしょう？　わたしたちから、何か、結婚祝いをさしあげたら、いいんじゃないかと思うんですけど…。

マイケル：ああ、いいですね。どんな物がいいと思う？　黒田さん。

黒田　　：そうねえ。斎藤さんに聞かずに、決めてしまうのは…。

マイケル：じゃ、斎藤さんに、何がほしいか、聞いてみましょう。予算は、いくらぐらいにしますか。

花田　　：やっぱり、少なくても、５万円ぐらいは、必要なんじゃない？

田辺係長：じゃ、みんなに、お金をたくさん出させるのは、きのどくだから、ぼくが、少しよけいに出すよ。５、６万ぐらいの物を、斎藤さんに、てきとうに選ばせたらいいんじゃないの。

黒田　　：じゃ、わたしが、斎藤さんに言って、選んでもらいましょう。

Dialogue II

Discussing the gift chosen by Miss Saito

黒田　　：あの、斎藤さんの、結婚祝いのことですけど…。斎藤さんは、できたら、電気製品がほしいそうです。冷蔵庫と電子レンジは、もう買ってあって、あと、アイロンとトースターがないんですって。

マイケル：アイロンとトースターですか。ずいぶん、えんりょしていますね。色や形など、きぼうの物があるんでしょう？

黒田　　：ええ、お聞きしておきました。（カタログを見せる）

花田　　：あ、これがいい！　これが、気にいったわ。

黒田　　：（わらいながら）あなたが結婚するときには、これをあげましょうね。斎藤さんは、くださるなら、こちらがいいって、おっしゃってたわ。

田辺係長：じゃ、ぼくの友人に、電器屋をしているのがいるから、彼に持って来させよう。まず、電話をして、この品物があるかどうか、聞いてみなくてはね。品物によっては、ないこともあるそうだから。

Dialogue III

The wedding gift arrives from the store.

黒田　：この　のし紙(がみ)に、みんなの名前を書いておくりましょう。
係長さんから、どうぞ。

田辺係長：ぼくは、字(じ)がへただから、こまるな。
だれか、書いてくれないかな。
こういうときには、いつも、家内(かない)に書かせることにしているんだよ。

花田　：字なら、黒田さんにおねがいするのが、いちばんよ。
黒田さんは、字がきれいだから。

マイケル：ぼくの名前もおねがいします。ふでで、字を書いたことがないんです。

黒田　：いつも、わたしが書かされることになっちゃうわね。

（黒田さんが、みんなの名前を書いてしまう。）

花田　：さあ、できた。これ、だれが、斎藤さんのうちに持って行くの？

田辺係長：宅配便(たくはいびん)にたのもう。宅配便なら、おそくても、あさってまでには、とどくだろう？　会社の前の店で、あつかっているはずだよ。

黒田　：じゃ、わたしが、たのんで来ます。

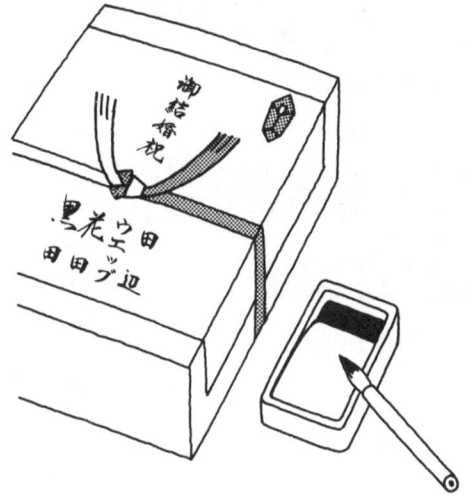

Vocabulary

Nouns:

2結婚祝い（けっこんいわい）wedding present
13電気製品（でんきせいひん）electric appliance
16きぼうする choice, preference
21電器屋（でんきや）electric appliance store
24のし紙（のしがみ）paper wrapper attached to the outside of a gift, used in place of a card
38宅配便（たくはいびん）home delivery service
6予算（よさん）estimated expense, budget
14トースター toaster
21友人（ゆうじん）friend
34ふで writing brush

Adjectives:

8きのどく（な）pitiable, regretful, too bad

Adverbs:

22まず first of all

Verbs:

39あつかう (u-vt) to handle, take care of, deal in

Grammatical words:

8verb+ aseru (saseru)　causative auxiliary ☞ Function I

Expressions:

12結婚祝いのこと regarding the wedding present
12できたら if possible, if it's not too much to ask
23品物によっては depending on the merchandise
23ないこともある sometimes they don't have

Dialogue Comprehension Exercise

Answer the following questions.

1) マイケルさんたちは、斎藤さんの結婚祝いの品物を決める前に、どうすることにしましたか。
2) 予算は、いくらぐらいにしましたか。
3) 結婚祝いのお金は、だれが、いちばん多く出すことになりましたか。
4) 斎藤さんは、何がほしいと言いましたか。
5) 結婚祝いの品物は、どこの店で買うことになりましたか。
6) どうして、黒田さんが、のし紙に、みんなの名前を書いたのですか。
7) 結婚祝いの品物は、どうやって、斎藤さんにとどけられますか。

Function I

To cause someone to do something; 黒田さんに選ばせる

Causative form:

u-verb root+aseru	書く →	書かせる
ru-verb root+saseru	食べる→	食べさせる
Irregular: 行く→行かせる，来る→来させる，する→させる		

The general meaning of the causative auxiliary「～aseru (saseru)」is "to cause someone to do such and such". Depending on the situation, causative「書かせる」might be rendered in English as (a) to have someone write, (b) to make someone write (using force), (c) to let someone write (permit or allow) (d) to get someone to write (using trickery, bribery or some other form of inducement).

Structure:

① (person causing) が、(person caused) に、(direct object) を	verb-aseru (saseru)
② (person causing) が、(person caused) に／を	verb-aseru (saseru)

ex.1. 課長が、マイケルさんに、報告書を作らせた。

The section manager made Michael write out a report.

2. A: 駅の前に、だれか、案内の人が立っているといいんですが。

It might be nice if we had someone standing in front of the station to give directions.

B: じゃ、マイケル君を立たせましょう。 Let's have Michael stand there then!

じゃ、マイケル君が、何か、てつだいたいと言っていたから、彼に立たせましょう。

Well then, let's let Michael stand there seeing as he was saying he wanted to help out in some way.

3. 学生たちに勉強させるための、静かな部屋があるといいんですが。

It would be nice if we had a quiet room for the purpose of getting students to study.

4. 子どもたちが、そんなに、その映画を見たがっているんなら、見に行かせたら？

If the kids are so anxious to see that movie, why not let them go?

5. A: おかずが多すぎて、ぜんぶは、とても食べられません。残してもいいですか。

There's too much food, and there's no way I can eat it all. Is it alright if I leave some?

B: 残ったら、犬に食べさせるから、かまいませんよ。

I don't mind. If there is anything left over, I'll feed it to the dog.

6. わたしは、1日に1回、犬を散歩させています。 I take the dog for a walk once a day.

Note 1: In colloquial speech「～aseru (saseru)」is sometimes shortened to「～asu (sasu)」.

ex. 子どもに薬を飲ましたんですが、なかなか、熱がさがらないんですよ。

I had the child take some medicine, but his fever took a long time to go down.

Note 2: The causative generally implies that the person you have do something is inferior to you. When the person is equal or superior, it might be more appropriate to use the forms「～てもらう」and「～ていただく」instead (see Lesson 16, p.206).

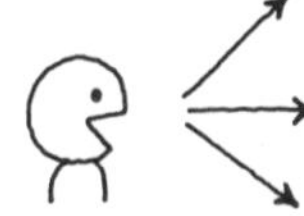

社長さんに、書いていただきましょう。 Let's have the company president write it.

黒田さんに、書いてもらいましょう。 Let's have Miss Kuroda write it.

うちの子どもに、書かせましょう。 Let's have my child write it.

Dialogues in English

Dialogue Ⅰ

H: Miss Saito will be getting married soon, you know. I think it would be nice if we gave her a wedding present of some sort from all us.

M: Yes, that's a good idea. What sort of thing would be good do you think, Miss Kuroda?

K: I don't know. To decide on something without asking Miss Saito ....

M: In that case let's try asking Miss Saito what she would like. About how much should we plan on spending?

H: When it comes right down to it, wouldn't you say we need about 50,000 yen at the very least?

T: Well then, seeing as it would be too much to have everyone put out a lot of money, I'll chip in a little extra. Wouldn't it be alright to just have Miss Saito go ahead and choose something for fifty or sixty thousand yen?

K: I'll speak to Miss Saito then and have her select something.

Dialogue Ⅱ

K: Uh, about the wedding gift for Miss Saito. She says she'd like an electric appliance, if it's not asking too much. She says they've already purchased a refrigerator and a microwave oven, but they don't have an iron or a toaster.

M: An iron and a toaster you say? She really seems to be holding back, doesn't she? She must have some preference though as to color, shape and so forth?

K: Yes, I asked her about that. (showing a catalogue)

H: Oh, let's get this! I really like this!

K: When you get married we'll get that for you. Miss Saito said, if we are giving her something then this over here is what she would like.

T: In that case, among my acquaintances is someone who operates an electric appliance store. I'll get him to bring us one. First of all I'll have to phone and ask if he has this merchandise or not, won't I. Sometimes they don't have certain things, depending on the item.

Dialogue Ⅲ

K: Let's each of us write his name on the paper wrapper before we send it. Beginning with you, Mr. Tanabe.

T: That's a bother, because my handwriting is very poor. I wonder if someone won't write my name for me? What I always do at times like this is make my wife write for me.

H: When it comes to handwriting, the best thing to do is ask Miss Kuroda. Her handwriting is beautiful.

M: Please write my name as well! I have never written with a brush.

K: You see! Every time I wind up being made to write! (Miss Kuroda writes all the names)

H: There, that's done! Who is going to take this to Miss Saito's house?

T: Let's send it by home delivery service! If we do, it should arrive by the day after tommorow at the very latest, right? They ought to take care of it at the store in front of the office.

K: I'll go and have them send it then!

Exercise 1: Hiroshi's and Yoko's weekly schedules are shown below. In the conversation between their mothers that follows, fill in the blanks using causative expressions.

ひろしの　1週間のスケジュール	
月：バイオリン	金：算数
火：水泳	土：書道
水：そろばん	日：野球
木：英会話	

洋子の　1週間のスケジュール	
月：食器をならべる	金：ごはんをたく
火：食器をあらう	土：庭のそうじをする
水：おつかいに行く	日：一日中、外で遊ぶ
木：犬の散歩	

ひろしの母：うちでは、ひろしに、たくさんのものを習わせています。
バイオリン、水泳、そろばん、英会話、算数、それに、書道を a.＿＿＿＿＿＿。
日曜日には、少年野球チームで、b.＿＿＿＿＿＿いますけれどね。

洋子の母：　まあ、すごいですね。うちは、何も c.＿＿＿＿＿＿が、毎日、1つずつ、
うちのてつだいを d.＿＿＿＿＿＿。
月曜は、食器を e.＿＿＿＿＿。　火曜は、f.＿＿＿＿＿。　水曜は、g.＿＿＿＿＿。
木曜は、h.＿＿＿＿＿。　金曜は、i.＿＿＿＿＿。　土曜は、j.＿＿＿＿＿。
日曜は、てつだいをさせないで、一日中、k.＿＿＿＿＿＿。

ひろしの母：まあ!?　うちも、少しは、てつだわせたほうがいいかしら…。

Exercise 2: For each of the pictures below, tell what one person is causing the other person to do.

1) 落語家が、客を＿＿＿＿＿＿。

2) お母さんが、＿＿＿＿＿＿。

3) バーバラさんが、＿＿＿＿＿＿。

4) ぼうを投げて、犬に＿＿＿＿＿＿。

5) 子どもに、りんごを＿＿＿＿＿＿。

6) 馬を＿＿＿＿＿＿。

7) 先生は、子どもたちに、話を＿＿＿＿＿＿。

Function II　Asking permission: "please let me __"; ～させてください

The causative て-form followed by「ください」means "please let me do such and such". Similar related expressions may be formed by using the other verbs of giving and receiving,「あげる」,「やる」,「くれる」,「いただく」and「もらう」.

ex.1. A: 部長、その仕事を、わたしにさせてください。

Mr. Division Manager, please let me do that work!

B: じゃ、君(きみ)に、やってもらうことにしよう。

Alright then, I'll have you do it.

2. 子ども：お母(かあ)さん、アイスクリームを食べさせて。

Mother, let me have some ice cream!

母(はは)　：いい子にしてたら、食べさせてあげますからね。

I'll let you have some if you're good (and so stop asking!).

3. あの店では、コーヒーを、自由(じゆう)に飲ませてくれるらしいよ。

At that store it seems they let you drink as much coffee as you want.

4. では、３時ごろに、また、お電話をさせていただきます。

Well then, I will have you permit me to call again around 3:00.

Note: The negative て-form (「～ないで」) plus「ください」means "please do not make me do such and such".

ex. あまり、残業をさせないでください。

Please don't make me work so much overtime!

Exercise 3: Complete the following conversations.

1) 社員(しゃいん)：カナダへ出張(しゅっちょう)ですか。いいですね。ぜひ、わたしに＿＿＿＿＿。

課長：君なら、英語もできるし、じゃ、君に、行ってもらうことにしようか。

2) 社員：家内(かない)が病気(びょうき)なので、早く＿＿＿＿＿＿＿＿＿んですが。

課長：それは、しんぱいだね。かまわないから、早く帰ってあげなさい。

3) 客　：すみません。うちの電話、こしょうして、使(つか)えないんです。おたくのを＿＿＿＿＿か。

店員：ええ、どうぞ、ごえんりょなく。

4) 子ども：お母さん、わたし、ピアノが習(なら)いたいの。おねがいだから、＿＿＿＿＿。

母　　：そんなに習いたいなら、しょうがないわね。習いに行ってもいいわ。

5) 今日の食事代(しょくじだい)は、わたしに＿＿＿＿＿＿。アルバイトのお金が入ったんですよ。

6) ぼくは、花子さんと、結婚(けっこん)したいんです。こんどの日曜日に、花子さんのお父さんに会(あ)って、花子さんと＿＿＿＿＿＿ように、おねがいするつもりです。

7) A: その件(けん)については、わたしにも考(かんが)えがあります。わたしに、意見(いけん)を＿＿＿＿＿＿。

B: どうぞ。言いたいことがあったら、何でも言ってください。

Vocabulary

バイオリン violin	そろばん abacus	英会話（えいかいわ）English conversation
算数（さんすう）mathematics	書道（しょどう）penmanship	食器（しょっき）dishes, eating utensils
おつかい errand	たく (u-vt) to cook, boil	ぼう stick

少年野球チーム（しょうねん やきゅう チーム）Little League baseball team

落語家（らくごか）comic storyteller　　馬（うま）horse

ごえんりょなく Do freely! Don't hesitate!　　食事代（しょくじだい）price of the meal

Exercise 4: The women in the office were asked if they had any complaints about their boss, and their answers are shown in the box. Your job is to rewrite each complaint as if it was spoken directly to boss, using「～させないで　ください」.

上司のいやなところ
コピーばかり取らせる。
お茶をいれさせる。
ことわりの電話をかけさせる。
おそくまで残業させる。
部屋のそうじをさせる。
たばこを買いに行かせる。
お酒を、むりに飲ませる。
男の社員の、てつだいばかりさせる。
やめてください
(8)
(2)
(7)
(5)
(3)
(1)
(4)
(6)
やめてください

Function III　Being forced to do something; ～させられる

Causative passive form:

u-verb root＋ ase＋rareru／as＋areru　　書く　→　書かせられる／書かされる*
ru-verb root＋ sase＋rareru　　食べる　→　食べさせられる
Irregular:　行く→行かされる*，来る→来させられる，する→させられる
The shortened form「～as＋areru」is commonly used with「行く」and u-verbs, except those ending in [s]：書く　→　書かされる，　話す　→　話させられる.

A combination of the causative auxiliary followed by the passive auxiliary means someone is caused to do such and such an action, which he does not really wish to do, and hence suffers discomfort, etc. The person caused to do the action appears as sentence subject「が」(or topic「は」), while the person doing the causing is marked by「に」.

ex.1.　生徒たちは、日本語の先生に、作文を書かされました。
　　The students were made to write a composition by the Japanese teacher.

2.　洋子さんは、いろいろなてつだいを、させられています。
　　Yoko is made to help out in various ways.

3.　おつかいに行かされたり、食器をならべさせられたりしています。
　　She's made to go out shopping, set the table, and so forth.

Vocabulary

上司（じょうし）superior　　ことわり declining, refusal　　セールスマン salesman

Exercise 5: For the pictures below, tell what the various people are causing other people to do or being caused to do.

1)

① お母さんは、子どもに野菜を________。

② 子どもは、お母さんに野菜を________。

2)

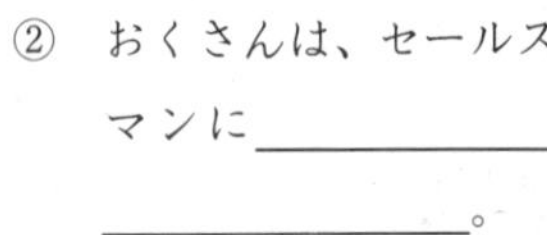

① セールスマンが、おくさんに________
________。

② おくさんは、セールスマンに________
________。

3)

① 課長は、花田さんに
________。

② 花田さんは、課長に
________。

4)

① お母さんが、子どもに
________。

② 子どもは、お母さんに
________。

Exercise 6: Using the information given in Exercise 4, have each person complain about what they are always being caused to do.

ex. (1) コピーばかり取らせる。 → コピーばかり取らせられるのは、いやです。

Function IV　Doing something without doing something else; 斎藤さんに聞かずに決める

Verb 1 (neg. stem)	+	ないで ずに	+	verb 2	"Doing verb 2, without doing verb 1"

Of these two forms,「〜ずに」is perhaps a bit more formal.

ex.1. さいふを 持たないで／持たずに でかけたので、何も買えなかった。
I was unable to buy anything because I left home without taking my wallet.

2. あしたは、胃のけんさをしますから，何も 食べないで／食べずに 来てください。
Tomorrow I'm going to give you a stomach examination, so please come without eating anything.

Note: The construction「**verb past tense** ＋まま ("state")」is used to form similar expressions of the type "to do (or not to do) something in such and such a state".

ex. 日本では、くつをぬがずに、部屋に入ってはいけません。
In Japan you must not enter a room without taking off your shoes.
日本では、くつをはいたまま、部屋に入ってはいけません。
In Japan you must not enter a room with your shoes on.

Exercise 7: Combine the two sentences into a single sentence using「～ないで」or「～ずに」.

ex. 朝ごはんを食べませんでした。学校に来ました。

→朝ごはんを　食べないで／食べずに、学校に来ました。

1) きのうは、会社に行きませんでした。家で、ねていました。
2) その電車は、駅に止まりませんでした。通りすぎました。
3) 父は、3日間、うちに帰りませんでした。会社で、仕事をしていました。
4) 今夜は、うちで、テレビを見ません。会議の報告書を書きます。
5) マイケルさんは、北村さんに、あいさつをしませんでした。家に帰ってしまいました。
6) マイケルさんの、つごうを聞きませんでした。マイケルさんのうちを、たずねました。
7) 店で、この服を着てみませんでした。買って帰ったら、小さすぎました。

Exercise 8: Complete the dialogues for the pictures below using「～ないで」or「～ずに」.

1)

A: ねむそうですね。
B: ええ、今日、テストがあるので、ゆうべ、________ 勉強したんですよ。

2)

A: 寒そうですね。
B: ええ、コートを ________ 来てしまったんです。

3)

A: あ、どうしよう。
B: どうしたの。
A: ガスの火を ________ 出てきたわ。
B: えーっ！

4)

A: そんなにあせかいて、どうしたんですか。
B: ええ、バスに ________ 走って来たんです。

5)

A: どうしたんですか。そんなにぬれて。
B: ええ、バーバラに、かさを持って行くように言われたのに、________ しまったんです。

6)

A: 部長のサインを ________ 来たんですか。だめですよ。もう1度行って、もらって来てください。
B: はい、すみません。

Vocabulary

どうしよう What should I do?

手入れ（ていれ）する care, trimming, repair, mending

Function V Indicating possibility or tendency: "sometimes such is the case"; 品物(しなもの)がないことがある

Verb non-past / negative ＋ こと が/も ある

"sometimes such and such is the case",
"there are times such and such occurs",
"sometimes I do such and such", etc.

ex.1. A: 社長は、昼休みには、社長室(しゃちょうしつ)にいらっしゃいますか。

Is the company president in his office during the lunch hour?

B: ええ。たいていは、いらっしゃいますが、たまに、散歩(さんぽ)にいらっしゃることがあるんですよ。今日は、天気もいいし、部屋(へや)には、いらっしゃらないかもしれませんね。

Yes, generally he is. But occasionally he goes for a walk. Today the weather is nice, so maybe he isn't in his office.

2. 急(きゅう)に、会議によびだされることがあるので、資料(しりょう)は、いつも用意(ようい)してあります。

At times I might suddenly be called to a meeting, so I always have materials on hand.

3. 朝、食事をしないで、でかけることがあります。

There are times I leave home mornings without eating.

Note 1: Equivalent expressions may be formed using「とき」"time" or「場合(ばあい)」"case" in place of「こと」.

ex.1. 品物が、ない場合もあります。 There are cases when the merchandise is not available.

2. 朝、食事をしないででかけるときも、ありますよ。

There are times I leave home mornings without eating.

Note 2: Not only verbs, but the non-past / negative forms of other verbals as well may be used in the above constructions.

ex.1. A: この店は、いつも、こんなにうるさいんですか。 Is this shop always so noisy?

B: いいえ、静(しず)かなときもあるんですけどねえ。 No. There are times when it is quiet as well.

2. 花田さんは、パーティーには、たいてい、ドレスを着(き)て出ますが、たまに、着物(きもの)の場合もあります。

Miss Hanada generally comes to parties wearing a dress, but occasionally she comes in a *kimono*.

Exercise 9: Complete the following sentences using「＿ことがある」「＿ときがある」or「＿場合がある」.

1) A: 日本語のニュースがわかりますか。

B: ときどき、＿＿＿＿＿＿が、だいたい、わかるようになりましたよ。

2) A: この店は、いつもすいていて、いいですね。

B: ええ。でも、たまに＿＿＿＿＿＿んですよ。給料日(きゅうりょうび)の後(あと)などにね。

3) A: 庭(にわ)の手入(てい)れは、いつも、マイケルさんがなさるんですか。

B: ええ、バーバラが＿＿＿＿＿＿が、たいていは、ぼくが１人でやります。

4) A: おいしい！ これ、おくさんが、お作りになったんですか。

B: いいえ、主人(しゅじん)なんですよ。主人も、たまには、料理(りょうり)を＿＿＿＿＿＿よ。

5) A: 朝ごはんには、いつもパンを食べていらっしゃるんですか。

B: パンの＿＿＿＿＿＿し、ごはんの＿＿＿＿＿＿。

Exercise 10: Complete the following sentences using「＿ことがある」, etc., together with「＿かもしれない」,「(たぶん) 〜だろう」and other such expressions.

1) A: 部長は、毎日、会社に車で来ていらっしゃるんですか。

 B: ①＿＿＿＿＿＿が、ふつうは、電車でいらっしゃいますよ。でも、今日は、大きな荷物を運ばなければならないって、おっしゃっていたから、②＿＿＿＿＿＿＿。

2) A: あの店へ行けば、その薬が買えますか。

 B: ええ、たぶん、①＿＿＿＿＿思いますが、ときどき、②＿＿＿＿＿＿そうですから、電話で、あるかどうか聞いてから、行ったほうがいいですよ。

3) A: バーバラさん、ご主人は、いつも帰りがおそいんですか。

 B: ええ。たまに、早く①＿＿＿＿＿＿んですけどね。今日は、急いでしなければならない仕事がないようでしたから、②＿＿＿＿＿＿。

4) A: 日本では、会社の人たちが、いっしょに旅行をするそうですね。

 1年に、何回ぐらいするんですか。

 B: そうですね。年に、2回する＿＿＿＿＿＿が、たいていは、1回ですね。

Reading Comprehension Exercise

お茶くみロボット

今年、40才になる田中氏は、会社で、工業用ロボットをたんとうしている、エンジニアである。彼は、お茶がだいすきで、いつも、お茶を飲まずにはいられない。いつも、会社の女性に、お茶を入れてもらっていたが、ある日、とうとう、「わたしたちに、お茶くみばかりさせないでください。」と言われてしまった。そこで、田中氏は、自分に、お茶を入れさせるロボットを作ることにした。言葉も話せたほうがいいと思って、言葉も話せるように作った。

2か月後、なかなかりっぱなロボットができあがった。まだ、言葉の使い方は、じょうずではない。とてもかわいい男の子の顔をしているので、「ロボちゃん」とよばれて、会社の人気者になった。

ロボちゃんが、おいしいコーヒーを飲ませてくれるので、女性たちは、もう、自分でコーヒーを入れずに、ロボちゃんに、まかせるようになってしまった。

女性A　：ロボちゃん、わたし、コーヒーのブラックがほしいわ。持って来てちょうだい。

ロボット：はい、ただいま、持たせます。

女性A　：え？　だれに？　持たせるって、まさか、田中さんに、持たせるんじゃないでしょうね。

ロボちゃん、そのときは、「はい、お持ちします」って言うのよ。

女性 B　：ロボちゃん、わたし、冷(つめ)たいジュースがいいわ。持って来てね。

ロボット：はい、お持ちします。

今度(こんど)は、正(ただ)しく言えた。そこに、外出(がいしゅつ)していた田中氏が帰って来た。

田中氏　：おーい、ロボちゃん、お茶。

ロボット：今、かわいいレディーたちに、コーヒーやジュースを飲ませているから、あとにしてください。

田中氏　：なに！　おまえの主人は、このぼくなんだぞ。何のために、おまえを作ったと思っているんだ。

田中氏は、かんかんにおこって、こう思った。

（やっぱり、あいつを、男に作るんじゃなかった。）

◆Vocabulary◆

お茶くみ（おちゃくみ）serving tea
飲まずにはいられない cannot stand not drinking
ある日（あるひ）one day
できあがる (u-vi) to be completed
人気者（にんきもの）popular person, celebrity
まさか by no means, on no account, I hardly think so
レディー lady
おまえ you (only used by men)
かんかんにおこる to be furious
エンジニア engineer
女性（じょせい）female
とうとう at last, after all
男の子の顔をしている has the face of a boy
ブラック black coffee
おーい Hey!　Hey you!
あとにしてください Please do it later.
主人（しゅじん）owner, proprietor, master, husband
あいつ him, that fellow (used only by men)

Exercise 11: Answer the following questions.

1) 田中氏は、なぜ、ロボットを作ったのですか。
2) 田中氏が作ったロボットは、どんなロボットでしたか。
3) ロボットの名前は、何といいますか。
4) 会社の女性たちは、どうして、自分でコーヒーをいれなくなったのですか。
5) 田中氏は、どうして、「あいつを男に作るんじゃなかった」と思ったのですか。
6) ロボットが、「はい、ただいま、持たせます」と答えたとき、女性 A は、「え？　だれに？」と言いました。それは、どうしてですか。

Listening Comprehension Exercise

Listen to the dialogue on the tape and answer the following questions.

1) 土田部長は、マイケルさんに、どんな仕事をさせたいと思っていますか。
2) 北村課長が、今度の仕事をマイケルさんにやらせてもいいんじゃないかと思ったのは、なぜですか。
3) マイケルさんは、今度の仕事をしたいと思っていますか。
4) マイケルさんは、今度の仕事のために、どんなことをしなければなりませんか。
5) マイケルさんは、今度の仕事を、１人でしますか。

第27課 ウエッブさん、お元気で

Farewell! Mr. And Mrs. Webb!

Dialogue Ⅰ

Michael is being transferred to the Osaka branch, so the people at the office give a farewell party for him in Roppongi. There is still time before the party begins, so everyone gathers around Michael and Barbara.

花田　：バーバラさん、もう、ひっこしのじゅんびは、できましたか。

バーバラ：ええ、やっと、すみました。それにしても、1年のあいだに、ずいぶん、いろいろな物がふえていて、おどろきました。

花田　：わたしも、部屋がせまいから、なるべく、物を買わないようにしているんですけど、いつのまにか、ふえてしまうんですよね。

バーバラ：わたしたちが、日本に来て、最初にこまったことは、かりた家に、家具がついていなかったことです。何から何まで、買わなければなりませんでした。

マルケル：ずいぶん、いろいろな物を買わされましたよ。今、買った物を見てみると、ほんとうに必要だった物は、少ないね。

田辺　：わたしも、転勤のたびに、古い物はすてて、ひっこし先で、新しく買うことにしているんですよ。そのほうが、安上がりなんです。

マルケル：それで、まだ使える物が、すてられてるんですね。わたしの知っている学生は、けっこういい物をひろって来て、べんりに使っていますよ。

田辺　：なるほどね。ところで、運送会社には、もう、たのみましたか。

バーバラ：ええ、来週の土曜日に、運んでくれることになっています。

マルケル：うんと、てつだわされるんじゃないかと思っていましたが、運送会社の人がぜんぶやってくれるんだそうで、安心しましたよ。

Dialogue II

Reminiscing about the past year

黒田　：ウエッブさん。1年、会社で仕事をしてみて、何が、いちばん、たいへんでした？

マイケル：そうですねえ。係長さんの、むずかしい字を読まされたことかな。黒田さんには、よく助(たす)けてもらいましたねえ。

花田　：そう。わたしも、係長の字には、なかされているわ。まったく、読めない字が、ならんでいるんだから。

田辺　：ぼくの字がへたなことは、みとめるけど、読めない字がならんでいるというのは、ちょっと、言いすぎじゃない？　そんなに、読めないって言われるんなら、ぼくも、これからは、ワープロを使うことにしようかなあ。

花田　：それがいいわ。わたしが、ワープロの使い方を、教(おし)えてさしあげますから。

マイケル：もっと早く、ワープロの練習(れんしゅう)をしてもらえたら、よかったなあ。

Dialogue III

The farewell party begins.

北村　：えー、みなさん、ごぞんじのように、ウエッブさんが、このたび、大阪支社(おおさかししゃ)に転勤(てんきん)されることになりました。この1年、ウエッブさんは、なれない日本で、わたしたちのなかまとして、よくがんばっていらっしゃったと思います。
大阪でも、ますます、かつやくされるよう、ねがっております。
それでは、ウエッブさん、おねがいします。

マイケル：はい。あの、本日(ほんじつ)は、わたしたちのために、このようなすばらしいパーティーを開(ひら)いていただきまして、どうもありがとうございます。
この1年、いろいろなことがありましたが、ぶじに、ここまで来られたのも、みなさまのおかげと、かんしゃしております。大阪にまいりましても、みなさまのご親切(しんせつ)は、けっして、わすれません。
どうぞ、これからも、よろしくおねがいいたします。

北村　：では、みなさん。おふたりの、大阪でのくらしが、楽(たの)しいものになることをねがって、かんぱいしましょう。

全員(ぜんいん)　：かんぱい！　マイケルさん、バーバラさん、お元気で！

Vocabulary

Nouns:

14運送会社(うんそうがいしゃ) shipping company, movers
17安心（あんしん）する relief, peace of mind
31なかま buddy, someone you hang around with
34本日（ほんじつ）today, this day
43くらし life, daily life
25言いすぎ（いいすぎ）exaggeration, overstatement
32かつやくする activity
39かんしゃする thanks, gratitude

Adverbs:

13けっこう quite, rather much
16うんと a lot, much, heavily
22まったく ① quite, entirely, completely (in affirmative sentences)
② not at all, not in the least (in negative sentences) ③ indeed, really
32ますます continue to increase, more and more
40けっして by no means, never

Verbs:

13ひろう (u-vt) to pick up
24みとめる (ru-vt) to recognize, admit, accept
32ねがう (u-vt) to wish for, desire, hope for, request

Expressions:

2それにしても even so, be that as it may
5いつのまにか before you realize it
7何から何まで anything and everything, from A to Z
10（の）たびに whenever, every time
11安上がり something is cheaper, more economical
29このたび on this occasion
39（の）おかげ thanks to __

Dialogue Comprehension Exercise

Answer the following questions.

1) マイケルさんたちが、日本にきて、最初にこまったことは、何でしたか。
2) 田辺さんは、転勤のたびに、古い物を、持って行きますか。
3) 運送会社は、いつ、バーバラさんたちの荷物を、運んでくれることになっていますか。
4) マイケルさんが、会社で、いちばんこまったことは、何でしたか。
5) 田辺さんは、これまで、ワープロを使っていましたか。
6) 田辺さんは、ワープロの使い方を、習いたがっていますか。

Consolidation

Exercise 1:

〔A〕Are the following sentences spoken by section manager, Kitamura, or by Michael? Indicate by writing K or M in the [ ]. Next number the sentences in proper order so they form a coherent dialogue.

a.（ ）［ ］ それが、急だけど、今月の末までに、行ってほしいんだ。
b.（13）［K］ 東京での仕事は、だいたい、おぼえてもらったし、サンフランシスコ支社の件で、大阪では、早く来てほしいそうなんだよ。
c.（ ）［ ］ いやいや、そんなことじゃないよ。じつはね、例の、大阪支社に転勤してもらう件なんだけど。
d.（ ）［ ］ 今晩ですか。今日は、家内に、早く帰ると言ってしまったんですが。
e.（1）［K］ ウエッブ君、ちょっと、話があるんだけど。今晩、1ぱい、どう？
f.（ ）［ ］ うん、そういうことになるねえ。

g．(6)［M］ はい。それが、どうかしたんですか。
h．(　)［　］ そうか。じゃ、会議室で話そうか。
i．(　)［　］ そうだね。予定より早くなってしまったけれど、これも仕事だから、しかたがないだろう？
j．(8)［M］ えっ！　それじゃ、あと２週間しかありませんね。
k．(12)［M］ はあ……。
l．(　)［　］ あの、何のお話でしょうか。何か、まちがいでもしたんでしょうか。
m．(　)［　］ でも、ずいぶん、急ですね。はじめの予定では、もう少し後になっていましたが。
n．(　)［　］ そうですか。よくわかりました。すぐ、転勤の用意をはじめます。

Dialogues in English

Dialogue I

H : Have you finished with your preparations for moving yet, Barbara?

B : Yes, we've finished at last. Even so, I was amazed at the great variety of things that have accumulated during the course of a year!

H : Me too. My room is small, so I'm trying as hard as I can not to buy things. But before you realize it, they pile up.

B : The first difficulty we encountered coming to Japan was that the house we rented had no furniture with it. We had to buy everything from A to Z.

M : I was made to buy all sorts of things. Now when I take a look at the things we bought, very few of them were really necessary.

T : What I do whenever I'm transferred is throw away old things, and buy new things at the place I move to. It's cheaper that way, you see.

M : Which means still usable items are being thrown away, right? A student I know has picked up and brought home some quite nice stuff, and is putting it to good use.

T : I see what you mean, yes. Have you asked the movers yet, by the way?

B : Yes, it's arranged for them to move our things Saturday of next week.

M : I was thinking I'd probably be forced to help out a lot, but I'm relieved because the movers say they will do everything for us.

Dialogue Ⅱ.

Ku : Michael. After working a year at the office, what was the most difficult thing for you?

M : Hmm, let me see. Perhaps being made to read Mr. Tanabe's difficult handwriting. I often received help from you, didn't I, Miss Kuroda?

H . Right. I too am forced to tears by Mr. Tanabe's handwriting. You see, it's nothing but a string of illegible characters.

T : I'll admit my handwriting is poor, but isn't it exaggerating a bit to call it a string of illegible characters? If it's all that illegible, I wonder, perhaps I too should start using a word processer.

H : That would be great! I'll teach you how to use one.

M : How nice it would have been if he had practiced the word processer sooner!

Dialogue Ⅲ

Ki : Uh, ladies and gentlemen. As you all know, Mr. Webb is scheduled to be transferred to the Osaka branch. It is my feeling that Mr. Webb has really made an effort this past year as a fellow employee, in a foreign land to which he is not accustomed. I am hoping he will continue to apply himself all the harder in Osaka. And now then, I'd like Mr. Webb to say a few words.

M : Sure. Uh, I want to thank you very much for having this wonderful party for us today. Many things happened this past year, but it is thanks to all of you that I was able to come this far without mishap, for which I am very grateful. Even though I go to Osaka, I will never forget your kindness.

Ki : Alright then, everyone. Here's hoping that Michael and Barbara's life in Osaka is an enjoyable one. Cheers!

All : Cheers! Farewell, Michael and Barbara!

〔**B**〕 Michael returns home with the news that his transfer to the Osaka branch has been moved up. At first Barbara is furious. She knew that he would be transferred to Osaka, but two weeks time is just too soon. Besides, with all the friends they have made in Tokyo, she doesn't really want to move. Michael has to do something to make Barbara understand. Actually Michael himself feels that things have moved too quickly, and a bit differently from what he had imagined they would, but there is nothing he can do, seeing as it's an order from the company. Moreover, he feels that's the way things are done in a Japanese business. You do as you are told even though it might be a bit difficult or inconvenient, because it will improve your capabilities as a worker. Pretending you are Michael, explain the situation to Barbara so that she will understand. (In the classroom, have different people play Barbara and Michael.)

〔**C**〕 Answer the following questions.

1) あなたは、いろいろな所に転勤させられるのは、いやですか、かまいませんか。
   ① 「いや」と言った人は、なぜ、いやなのですか。
   ② 「かまわない」と言った人は、なぜですか。
2) 会社から、転勤するように言われたときは、おくさんに、相談しますか。
   ①なぜ、おくさんに、相談するのですか。
   ②なぜ、おくさんに、相談しないのですか。
3) おくさんが、行きたくないと言ったら、どうしますか。
   （日本の会社では、転勤は、会社員にとって、とてもたいせつです。転勤をことわると、たいていの場合、昇進できません。）
4) あなたは、仕事と家庭と、どちらのほうが、たいせつですか。

Exercise 2: Complete the following dialogue.

バーバラさんと田辺夫人が、話しています。マイケルさんが、転勤で、大阪に行くことになりましたが、バーバラさんは、大阪へは、あまり行きたくありません。

田辺夫人：バーバラさん、今度、大阪へ（　①　）。
ひっこしのじゅんびで、たいへんでしょう？
何か、（　②　）。
バーバラ：ありがとうございます。でも、運送会社の人が、
（　③　）から、だいじょうぶです。
田辺夫人：そうですか。それは、（　④　）。
バーバラ：そうなんですけど…。
田辺夫人：あら、（　⑤　）。あまり、うれしそうじゃありませんね。
バーバラ：ええ。じつは、ほんとうは、あまり大阪へは（　⑥　）。
田辺夫人：まあ、それは、こまりましたねえ。でも、転勤だから…。
バーバラ：ええ、それは、わかっているんですが、東京へ来て、まだ（　⑦　）し、
せっかく、みなさんと、お友達になれたのに…。
田辺夫人：バーバラさん、そんなに、がっかりしないで。大阪も、いい所ですよ。それに、新幹線に乗れば、（　⑧　）から、いつでも、東京に、遊びに来られるじゃありませんか。

バーバラ：そうですね。大阪に行っても、ときどき、東京に（　⑨　）。

田辺夫人：ええ、お待ちしていますよ。また、２人で、買い物に行ったり、（　⑩　）ね。
それから、ときどき、お手紙を（　⑪　）ね。

バーバラ：ええ。まだ、日本語の手紙は、じょうずに書けないんですが、勉強だと思って、
月に１回は、（　⑫　）します。

田辺夫人：大阪での、くらしのようすなどを、知らせてくださいね。楽しみにしていますよ。

バーバラ：ええ、そうします。お話をしたら、少し、元気が出てきました。どうもありがとう
ございました。

田辺夫人：そう、それは、よかったわ。

Exercise 3: A person from the movers comes to the Webb's house to check things out and discuss details of the move. Compose a dialogue between the movers and Barbara, based on the information given below.

〔運送会社の人〕

1) いつ、ひっこしするのか。
（３月は、どこの会社でも、転勤が多いので、いそがしいから、早く、ひっこしの日を決めてもらいたい。）
2) どこへ？
3) 荷物は、どのくらい、あるのか。
4) ひっこしのタイプを説明して、どちらのタイプがいいか、決めてもらう。
＊タイプA：荷物を運ぶのも、パッキングをするのも、ぜんぶ、運送会社がする。料金は、高いが、安全で、べんり。
＊タイプB：荷物を運ぶだけで、パッキングは、お客がする。料金は、タイプAより安い。
5) せいかくな料金は、今すぐには言えないが、会社に帰って計算して、すぐ、手紙で知らせる。
パッキングは、ひっこしの前の日にする。そのときは、だれか、家にいてほしい。

〔バーバラ〕

1) ひっこしは、３月の月末の土曜日。
2) 大阪。くわしい住所は、マイケルに聞かないと、わからない。
3) 大阪に持って行きたい物を見せる。
（台所用品，洋服，マイケルのつくえ，たんす，パソコンなど）
4) 自分でパッキングするのは、たいへんだから、ぜんぶ、運送会社の人に、たのむ。いくら、かかるのか、会社に知らせなければならないので、たずねる。
5) パッキングの日には、自分が、家にいるつもり。

Vocabulary

昇進（しょうしん）する　advancement
パッキングする　packing
計算（けいさん）する　calculate, add up
家庭（かてい）　home, family
安全（あんぜん）（な）　safe, safety (used both as noun and な-adj.)

Exercise 4: Barbara makes the following speech at the farewell party. Put all the words in parentheses in their proper forms.

みなさま、今日は、わたしたちのために、送別会を（ ①開く ）くださって、どうもありがとうございます。この１年間、楽しいことや、こまったことが、いろいろ（ ②ある ）が、みなさまに、たいへん、親切にしていただいて、ほんとうに、（ ③しあわせ ）。

マイケルが、日本で（ ④働く ）ことに（ ⑤なる ）とき、わたしは、日本語は、ほとんど（ ⑥わかる ）し、日本のことは、少ししか（ ⑦知る ）ので、とても（ ⑧しんぱい ）。それで、日本に（ ⑨来る ）前に、日本語の本や、日本について書いてある本を（ ⑩買う ）（ ⑪勉強する ）。でも、本で勉強するのと、ほんとうに経験するのとは、ずいぶん、（ ⑫ちがう ）ね。ひらがなと、かたかなは、読んだり、（ ⑬書く ）たりできるように（ ⑭なる ）ので、日本に（ ⑮行く ）ても、だいじょうぶだろうと（ ⑯思う ）のですが、成田空港に（ ⑰着く ）みると、何も（ ⑱わかる ）ので、こまりました。わたしが、アメリカで（ ⑲勉強する ）日本語は、日本の人が話す日本語とは、ちがうのかしら、と思いました。でも、みなさまに（ ⑳教える ）いただいたり、日本語学校で勉強したりしたおかげで、１人で、買い物に行ったり、地下鉄に（ ㉑乗る ）たりすることが、できるようになりました。

今年の夏には、アメリカから、両親が（ ㉒来る ）ことになっています。そのときまでには、日本語がもっとじょうずに（ ㉓話す ）ように、がんばるつもりです。大阪へ（ ㉔行く ）からも、みなさまのご親切は、けっして、（ ㉕わすれる ）。大阪へ（ ㉖来る ）ときは、ぜひ、ごれんらくください。また、お目にかかれるのを、（ ㉗楽しみにする ）。そのときまで、どうぞ、お元気で。

ありがとうございました。

Exercise 5: Prepare a farewell speech including the following information, as well as anything you yourself might wish to include.

a. ３年間、日本の銀行で働いて、今度、ニューヨークの支店に転勤することになった。

b. はじめは、日本語がわからなくて、みんなに、めいわくをかけた。とくに、アシスタントの田中さんには、アパートをさがしてもらったり、いっしょに、買い物に行ってもらったりした。

c. 会社の旅行で、箱根の温泉にも行った。日本のふろの入りかたや、ゆかたの着かたも知らなかった。この旅行で、温泉が、とてもすきになった。

d. 日本にいるあいだ、週に３回、日本語学校で勉強した。もう、話すのは、ほとんどこまらないが、新聞は、まだ読めない。

e. いつか、また、日本に帰って来たいと、思っている。

Vocabulary

送別会（そうべつかい） farewell party
経験（けいけん）する experience
アシスタント assistant
ふろの入りかた how to take bath
着かた（きかた） how to wear clothing

Culture Note

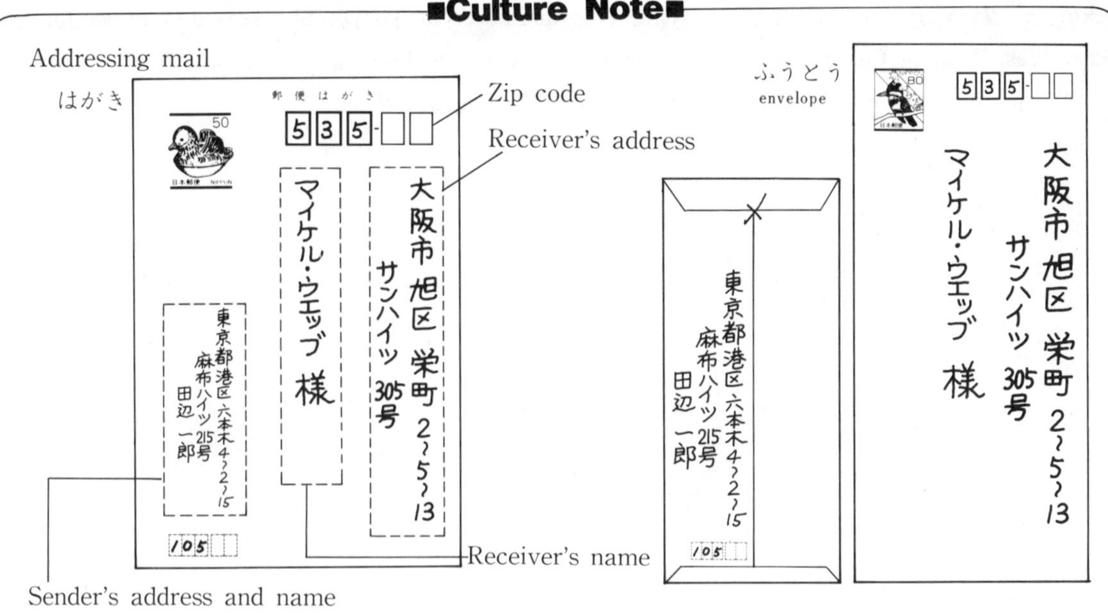

○ For postcards the names and addresses of both receiver and sender are written on the front. That of the receiver is large, that of the sender is small.

○ For letters, the receiver's name and address is written on the front of the envelope, while the sender's is written on the back.

○ The receiver's name is written in the center of the postcard or envelope in such a way that it stands out. Don't forget to add「様」after the receiver's name.

Exercise 6: Write a postcard from Barbara at their new address in Osaka to Mrs. Yoko Tanabe (田辺洋子). The contents of the postcard may be based on the dialogue in Exercise 2.

Exercise 7: Mary Suzuki comes to visit her grandfather in Tokyo. She sees a want ad for the East West Trading Co. looking for a foreigner to work at their main office in Tokyo. Below is Mary's personal history. Read it and answer the following questions.

1) メアリーさんは、今、何才(さい)ですか。
2) 最終学歴(さいしゅうがくれき)は、何ですか。
3) ミシガン大学では、何を勉強しましたか。
4) 前に、何か、仕事をしたことがありますか。
5) どうして、日本の会社に入りたいと思っているのですか。

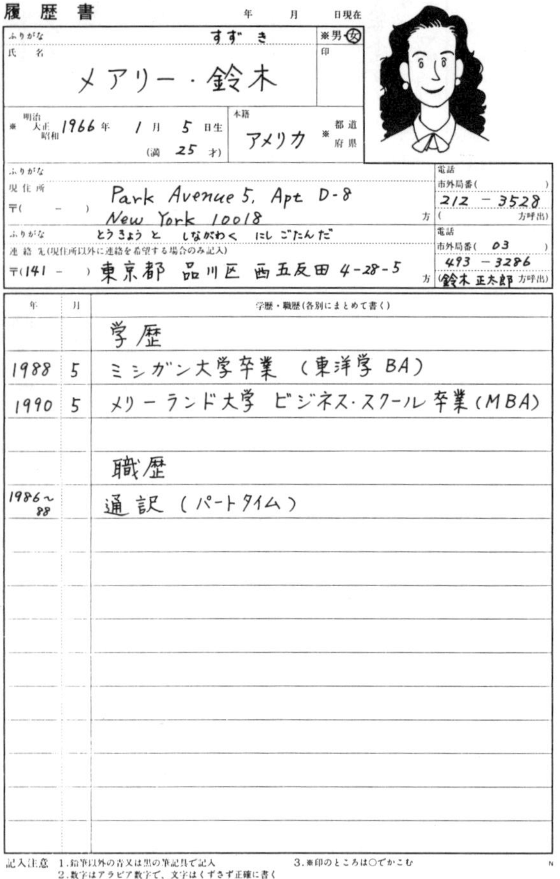

履 歴 書　　年　月　日現在

ふりがな　すずき　　※男・(女)
氏名　メアリー・鈴木　　印

※明治・大正・昭和 1966年 1月 5日生（満 25 才）
本籍　アメリカ　※都道府県

ふりがな
現住所 〒(　－　)　Park Avenue 5, Apt D-8 New York 10018　方
電話 市外局番(　) 212 － 3528 (　方呼出)

ふりがな　とうきょうと　しながわく　にしごたんだ
連絡先（現住所以外に連絡を希望する場合のみ記入）
〒(141 －　) 東京都 品川区 西五反田 4-28-5　方
電話 市外局番(03) 493 － 3286 (鈴木 正太郎 方呼出)

年	月	学歴・職歴（各別にまとめて書く）
		学歴
1988	5	ミシガン大学卒業　（東洋学 BA）
1990	5	メリーランド大学 ビジネス・スクール卒業（MBA）
		職歴
1986～88		通訳（パートタイム）

記入注意　1.鉛筆以外の青又は黒の筆記具で記入　2.数字はアラビア数字で、文字はくずさず正確に書く　3.※印のところは○でかこむ

年	月	免許・資格
1990	12	日本語検定試験 1級

得意な学科　東洋学，日本語
健康状態　たいへん よい
趣味　音楽を聞くこと
スポーツ　テニス
志望の動機　◦東京で働きたい。◦日本の会社のシステムにきょうみがある。

本人希望記入欄（特に給料・職種・勤務時間・勤務地・その他についての希望などがあれば記入）
給料は、年3万ドルぐらい、ほしい。社宅を使わせてもらえるのなら、もう少し安くてもいい。

家族氏名	性別	年令	家族氏名	性別	年令
鈴木 正夫	男	51			
スーザン	女	48			
ナンシー	女	18			
ジャック	男	15			

通勤時間 約　時間　分　｜扶養家族数（配偶者を除く）　人　｜配偶者 ※有・(無)　｜配偶者の扶養義務 ※有・無

保護者（本人が未成年者の場合のみ記入）　ふりがな　氏名　住所 〒(　－　)　電話 市外局番(　) －　(　方呼出)

コクヨ

Vocabulary

履歴書（りれきしょ）personal history, curriculum vitae
本籍（ほんせき）permanent address
現住所（げんじゅうしょ）present address
学歴（がくれき）educational background ; 最終学歴（さいしゅうがくれき）last attended school, dates and degree earned
職歴（しょくれき）work experience
通訳（つうやく）する interpretation, interpreter
パートタイム part time
資格（しかく）qualifications, status
－級（きゅう）grade,class, rank
卒業（そつぎょう）する graduation
東洋学（とうようがく）Oriental studies
免許（めんきょ）license, permit
検定試験（けんていしけん）licensing examination
配偶者（はいぐうしゃ）spouse

Listening Comprehension Exercise

Listen to the tape and do as directed.

1) Mark the following statements ○ or × depending on whether they concur with or differ from the information given in Mr. Kitamura's report. For sentences marked ×, underline the portion that is mistaken and supply the correct information, as in the example.

ex. (×) 安部産業(あべさんぎょう)は、ヨーロッパに、工場(こうじょう)を作ろうとしている。
アメリカ

Part 1 会社が買おうとしている土地について

① ( ) サンフランシスコの近くにある。

② ( ) サンフランシスコから、北に、50キロぐらいの所にある。

③ ( ) 広さは、5エーカー。

④ ( ) 土地(とち)を売りたがっている人は、スミスさん。

⑤ ( ) サンフランシスコから遠(とお)すぎると思うアメリカ人は多いが、ほかに、てきとうな土地がない。

Part 2 アメリカに作る工場(こうじょう)について

① ( ) 工場で働(はたら)く人は、最初(さいしょ)は、80人。そのうちの、60人は、日本人。

② ( ) 工場のそばに、プールと、テニスコートを作るつもりだ。

③ ( ) 最初の工場長(こうじょうちょう)は、アメリカ人にするつもりだ。

2) Draw a line graph representing the projected number of employees at the San Francisco plant for the first five years. The plant opens in 1991.

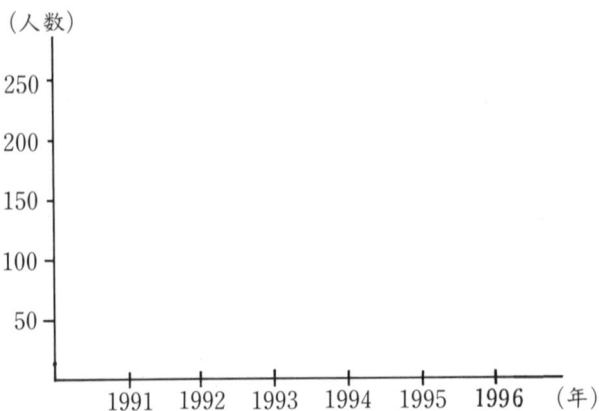

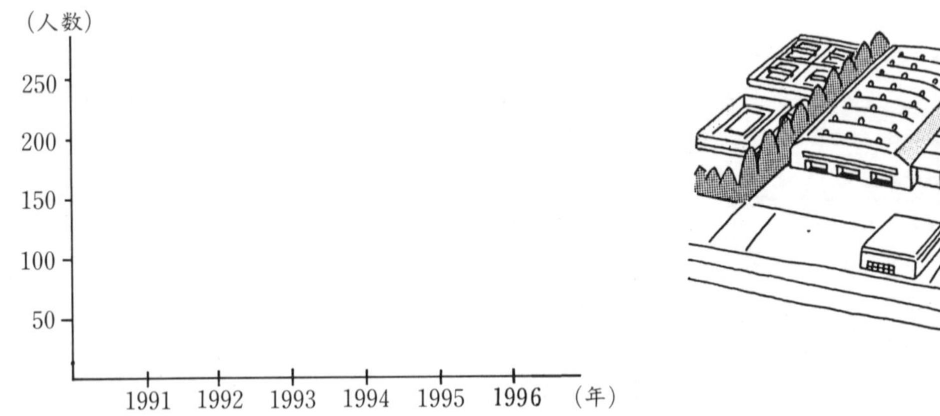

Vocabulary

工場(こうじょう) factory, plant
広さ(ひろさ) area, extent, width, breadth
テニスコート tennis court
土地(とち) ground, land
エーカー acre
工場長(こうじょうちょう) plant manager

Quiz　Lesson 1 ～ Lesson 27

1 Circle the correct form given in the (　). × indicates that nothing should be added.

A：ウエッブさん。1度、晩ごはん ①（を・が）ごちそうしたいんですが、土曜日 ②（が・で）かまいませんか。

B：それは、どうも。でも、土曜日③（に・は）バーバラと買い物に行かなくてはならないので、できたら、金曜日④（が・で）いいんですが。

A：そうですか。じゃ、金曜日⑤（に・で・を）しましょう。

B：何時 ⑥（に・×）しましょうか。

A：そうですね。5時半 ⑦（ぐらい・ごろ）は、どうですか。

B：いいですね。

A：じゃ、「とりせん」の店の前 ⑧（に・で）会いましょう。

B：あの、「とりせん」 ⑨（が・って・なら）、どこにあるんですか。

A：ああ、場所 ⑩（を・が）わからないんですか。じゃあ、地図(ちず)をかきますからね。ほら、駅 ⑪（が・を・で）出てから、このかど ⑫（を・から）、右 ⑬（に・で・を）まがれば、いいんですよ。

B：ああ、わかりました。そこなら、前に、行ったこと ⑭（も・が）ありますよ。「やきとり」 ⑮（も・は・の）おいしい店でしょう？

A：ええ、そうです。じゃ、そこ ⑯（に・が・で）、5時半までに来てくださいね。

2 Choose the most appropriate of the items appearing in the {　}.

1) マイケルさんは、けんこうのために、もう少し、やせる {a. ことにしました　b. ことになりました}。

2) 日本語の新聞は、むずかしくて、なかなか読めませんでしたが、さいきんは、少し読める {a. ようにしました　b. ようになりました}。

3) 日本語 {a. だけ　b. しか} わからなかったら、外国に行ったとき、こまりませんか。

4) あしたは、朝早く {a. おきなきゃ　b. おきちゃ} ならないから、今晩は、もうねます。

5) すみません。こんなアイロンは、どこで {a. 売っているかどうか　b. 売っているか}、{c. 教えてもらえませんか　d. 教えてあげませんか}。

6) お客さんが来るので、ビールが {a. 冷(ひ)やしています　b. 冷(ひ)やしてあります}。

7) A：　何か、{a. 冷(つめ)たい　b. 寒(さむ)い} 飲み物 {c. なら　d. でも} いただけませんか。

　B：　ビール {e. なら　f. でも} ありますが、それで、いいですか。

8) A：　会議は、{a. もう　b. まだ} 終わりましたか。

　B：　いいえ、{c. もう　d. まだ} なんですよ。

9) A：　空(そら)が、暗(くら)く {a. なっていきました　b. なってきました} ね。

　B：　ええ、今(いま)にも、雨が {c. ふるようです　d. ふりそうです} ね。

10) 声(こえ)が、聞(き)こえませんね。{a. だれも　b. だれか} いない {c. ようです　d. そうです}。

11) これから、会議が {a. はじまっている　b. はじまる　c. はじまった} ところです。

12) えっ、子ども {a. なら　b. でも} 知っているんですか。ゆうめいなんですねえ。

13) わたしは、あしたの会議に、出席(しゅっせき)する {a. はず　b. つもり} です。

3 Complete the following sentences using the item from the list that makes the most sense. The portion in parentheses will also have to be changed to an appropriate form.

1) (おふろに入ろうとする)、電話が、かかってきました。
2) かれは、(学生だ)、勉強をしないで、アルバイトばかりしています。
3) (わかい)、いろいろなことを、経験しておきたいと思っています。
4) サンフランシスコに支社を作る(じゅんびをする)、アメリカに出張することになりました。
5) 課長は、いつも、部下の人たちに、(もんくを言う) しっかり働くようにと言っています。
6) ヨーロッパでも、この製品が、よく(売れる)、モデルチェンジをしました。
7) ごはんを(食べる) テレビを見るのは、よくないですよ。

ように	うちに	ところに	ために	のに	ないで	ながら

4 Fill in the blanks with the most appropriate adverbs from the list below.

1) 熱があると言っていたから、マイケルさんは、(　　)、今日のゴルフには来ないでしょう。
2) この仕事は、あさってまでには、(　　) しあげますから、安心してください。
3) (　　) よく働くロボットは、作れないんですか。
4) 今度の日曜日、うちで、パーティーをするんですよ。あなたも、(　　) いらしてくださいね。
5) 銀行の前に、人が (　　) あつまっていますね。どうしたんでしょう。
6) あら、もう終わったんですか。(　　) 早いですね。
7) 心配したとおりですね。田中さんは、(　　) 来ませんでした。

おおぜい	きっと	ずいぶん	もっと	やっぱり	ぜひ	たぶん

5 Complete the following sentences putting the items in (　　) in appropriate forms.

1) こんなにおいしい水が、東京でも (飲む, いい) ね。
2) すみません。おそくなって。ちょっと、スピードを出しすぎて、おまわりさんに車を (止める)。
3) 頭がいたいんですか。それなら、病院に (行く)。
4) A： 毎日、何時ごろ、シャワーをあびるんですか。
   B： わたしは、朝、(起きる) から、シャワーをあびるんですよ。
5) おもしろい話をして、みんなを (わらう)。
6) おそくなったので、友達に、車で (送る)。
7) 今日、病院に行ったら、お医者さんに、酒やたばこを飲みすぎないように (言う)。
8) 部長に (会う) したいんですが、(いる) か。
9) どんなに (働く)、生活は、楽になりません。
10) よく練習したおかげで、やっと (できる)。

Vocabulary

今にも (いまにも) any minute now, any moment now
楽 (らく) (な) comfortable, easy
生活 (せいかつ) life, living

APPENDIX 1: Inflectional Endings

The following lists all inflections and auxiliaries included in this text, categorized according to the pattern in which they are attached to the verb root.

(1) **Plain Non-Past Pattern**— endings attached directly to the verb root. The first form is used with u-verbs (roots ending in a consonant), the form in ( ) is used with ru-verbs (roots ending in a vowel).

	~u (ru) Plain non-past	~e (ro) Imperative	~oo (yoo) Let's form/Probability	~eba (reba) Conditional	~eru (rareru) Potential	~areru (rareru) Passive	~aseru (saseru) Causative
u-verb	書く [kak-u]	kak-e	kak-oo	kak-eba	kak-eru	kak-areru	kak-aseru (asu)
ru-verb	食べる [tabe-ru]	tabe-ro	tabe-yoo	tabe-reba	tabe-rareru	tabe-rareru	tabe-saseru (sasu)
be-verb			daroo	de ar-eba			
い-adj.	高い [taka-i]		takai daroo	taka-kereba			
negative	ない [nai]		nai daroo	na-kereba			

Note: Potential, passive and causative auxiliaries are inflected in the same manner as ru-verbs.

(2) **Negative Pattern**— an [a] is inserted between u-verb roots and the inflectional ending.

~ない	**Negative;**	書かない [kak-a-nai],	食べない [tabe-nai]
~ずに	**"without doing";**	書かずに [kak-a-zu ni],	食べずに [tabe-zu ni]

(3) **I-stem Pattern**— endings attached to the i-stem. The i-stem is formed by adding [i] to u-verb roots (ru-verb roots are unchanged), and functions as the noun form for certain verbs.

	~ます Polite non-past	~たい "I want to"	~たがる "Appears to want to __"	~なさい Polite command	~ながら "While doing"	~すぎる "too much"	~出す/~はじめる "start doing __"
u-verb	kak-i-masu	kak-i-tai	kak-i-tagaru	kak-i-nasai	kak-i-nagara	kak-i-sugiru	kak-i-dasu/kak-i-hajimeru
ru-verb	tabe-masu	tabe-tai	tabe-tagaru	tabe-nasai	tabe-nagara	tabe-sugiru	tabe-dasu/tabe-hajimeru

(4) て-**form Pattern**— root shape of u-verb is altered, initial [t] is sometimes pronounced [d] (see p. 18).

~て　　て-**form;** 書いて [kai-te], 食べて [tabe-te] (see p. 18 for て-forms of other verbals)
~た　　**Past;** 書いた [kai-ta], 食べた [tabe-ta] (see p. 18 for past forms of other verbals)
~たら　　**Conditional;** 書いたら [kai-tara], 食べたら [tabe-tara], Be-verb plain だったら [dat-tara], Adjectives 高かったら [taka-kattara]
~たり　　**"and so forth";** 書いたり [kai-tari], 食べたり [tabe-tari]. Be verb だったり [dat-tari], Adjectives 高かったり [taka-kattari]

(5) Various verbs, adjectives and particles may be added to the て-form to function as auxiliaries.

~て いる　　**Progressive;** 書いている (sometimes shortened to「書いてる」) "I am writing", "I have written", "I wrote (and the result is still in effect)."
~て ある　　**"Has been done";** 書いてある "it has been written", "it is written"
~て ほしい　　**"I want you to __";** 書いてほしい "I want you to write", "I would like to have you write"
~て みる　　**"Try doing";** 書いてみる "I will try writing", "I will write and see"
~て おく　　**"Do in preparation";** 書いておく "I will write and have ready"
~て しまう　　**"Do completely";** 書いてしまう "I wrote it completely", "I finished writing", etc.
~て ください　　**Polite request;** 書いてください "Please write!"
~て あげる　　**"Do for someone";** 書いてあげる "I (will) write for you"
~て さしあげる　　**"Do for someone";** more polite than「~てあげる」
~て やる　　**"Do for or to you";** 書いてやる "I will write for you", "I'll write, and thereby cause you grief!"
~て くれる　　**"Do for me";** 書いてくれる "He writes for me", "He is going to write for me"
~て くださる　　**"Do for me";** more polite than「~てくれる」

～て　もらう	**"Have do for me";** 書いてもらう "I have him write for me", "I am going to have him write for me"
～て　いただく	**"Have do for me";** more polite than「～てもらう」
～て　も	**"Even if do __";** 書いても Used in constructions like 書いてもいい "it's alright if you write"
～て　は	**Conditional;** 書いては "if I write". Used in constructions like 書いてはいけない "you must not write!"

APPENDIX 2: Demonstratives

Demonstrative words are used to indicate objects, people, places, directions, times, etc. in reference to the position of the speaker and listener. In Japanese they follow a very convenient pattern. (Note: Demonstratives may be interpreted as singular or plural, as the case may be.)

Relative location / Grammatical function	(こ～) near speaker	(そ～) near listener	(あ～) distant from both	(ど～) question word
pronoun (Lesson 1)	これ this one (these)	それ that one (those)	あれ that one (those) over there	どれ which one (ones)?
noun modifier (Lesson 2)	この this __	その that __	あの that __ over there	どの which __?
location pronoun	ここ here	そこ there	あそこ over there, yonder	どこ where?
pronoun	こっち this direction, this one (of several)	そっち that direction, that one (of several)	あっち that direction, that one (of several)	どっち which direction? which one (of several)?
same as こっち but politer	こちら this direction, this one (of several) this person	そちら that direction, that one (of several) that person	あちら that direction, that one (of several) that person (3rd person)	どちら which direction? which one (of several)? which person? who?
adverb	こう this way	そう that way	ああ that way	どう which way? how?
noun modifier	こんな this sort of __	そんな that sort of __	あんな that sort of __	どんな what sort of __?
adjective and adverb modifier (amount or degree)	こんなに this (much)	そんなに that (much)	あんなに that (much)	どんなに how (much)?
な-adjective 〔この＋よう(な)〕	このような this sort of __ このように in this manner	そのような that sort of __ そのように in that manner	あのような that sort of __ あのように in that manner	どのような what sort of __? どのように in what manner?
noun modifier 〔こう＋いう〕	こういう__ this sort of __	そういう__ that sort of __	ああいう__ that sort of __	どういう__ what sort of __?

Scripts for Listening Comprehension Exercise

Lesson 1

1) A：これは　なんですか。
　B：あのう、じつは…
2) A：それは　ビールですか、ウイスキーですか。
　B：ウイスキーです。
3) A：パスポートを　みせてください。
　B：はい、どうぞ。
4) A：これは　なんですか。
　B：くすりです。
5) A：あのう、ゆうびんきょくは、どれですか。
　B：あの　たてものです。
6) A：すみません。ちょっと　かさを　みせてください。
　B：はい、どうぞ。

Lesson 2

1)はなやは、ぎんこうの　となりに　あります。
2)デパートの　まえに、えきが　あります。
3)本やは、ホテルの　となりです。
4)えきの　まえに、ぎんこうが　あります。
5)ホテルの　となりに、えきが　あります。
6)デパートの　うしろに、ぎんこうが　あります。
7)レストランの　まえに、ぎんこうが　あります。

Lesson 3

1)Mr. Tsuchida is on his way to Narita to meet Mr. & Mrs. Webb. He is listening to the radio to get traffic information.

　みなさん、こんにちは。11時のニュースです。東京から成田(なりた)までのみちは、とてもこんでいます。いま、東京から成田まで、くるまで4時間ぐらいかかります。成田くうこうへは、でんしゃでいってください。でんしゃでは、東京から成田まで、1時間はんぐらいです。もういちど、いいます。いま、みちは、とてもこんでいます。成田くうこうへは、でんしゃでいってください。

2) ① 5時40分　② 8時5分すぎ
　③ 10時10分まえ　④ ちょうど7時
　⑤ 3時はん　⑥ 1時20分

Lesson 4

Mr. Tanaka and Mr. Nakamura are talking.

田中：中村さん、たいへんです。こまりました。
中村：田中さん、どうしましたか。
田中：テキストをわすれました。かしてください。
中村：いいですよ。はい、どうぞ。
田中：あのう…
中村：なんですか。
田中：ペンもわすれました。
中村：はい、これをつかってください。
田中：それから…
中村：まだ? なにを　わすれましたか。
田中：ノートと、じしょと、けしゴムを、わすれました。
中村：ぜんぶ、わすれたんですか。
田中：すみません。それから、しゅくだいもわすれました。しゅくだいのノートを見せてください。
中村：しゅくだいは、だめですよ。田中さん、どうしましたか。びょうきですか。うちへ、かえったほうがいいですよ。

Lesson 5

1) The following is Michael's schedule for April.

　きょうは、4月15日、水よう日です。きのうの夜、土田さんと、しょくじをしました。今週の土よう日はバーバラとテニスをします。来週の土よう日には、土田さんと、ゴルフにいきます。さ来週の水よう日は、「みどりの日」です。会社は、やすみですから、土田さんといっしょに、ディズニーランドにいきます。

2) Indicate the correct number.
　① 03-238-5006　② 0471-59-8252
　③ 0478-52-1489

3) Television shopping announcement：

　きょうは、とても　おかいどくな、でんしレンジです。いま、おかいあげのかたには、すてきなペンダントを、プレゼント。さあ、いますぐ、でんわをしてください。でんわばんごうは、東京 03-277-9612、東京03-277-9612 です。おまちがえのないよう、おねがいします。

Lesson 6

1) ① 3240円　② 1690円　③ 6980円
　④ 1680円　⑤ 2740円

2)

てんいん：いらっしゃいませ。
きゃく　：そのネクタイを　見せてください。
てんいん：青いのですか、赤いのですか。
きゃく　：青いの。
てんいん：かしこまりました。はい、どうぞ。
きゃく　：これは、日本のネクタイですか。
てんいん：いいえ、フランス製(せい)でして、ピエール・カルダンのでございます。
きゃく　：おいくら？
てんいん：10,000円でございます。
きゃく　：うーん、ちょっと、高いねえ。もう少しやすいのは、ありませんか。
てんいん：こちらは、7,000円でして、イタリーのです。おにあいですよ。
きゃく　：そうですね。じゃ、これを　ください。

はい、10,000円。

てんいん：しょうしょう、おまちください。3,000円のおつりです。まいどありがとうございました。また、どうぞ。

Lesson 7

1) The weather report：

それでは、全国のお天気です。おきなわと鹿児島は、はれ。朝から、よくはれるでしょう。福岡はくもり。すこしさむいでしょう。高知は、はれ。あたたかい1日でしょう。広島と松江は、くもり。ときどき、雨がふるかもしれません。京都は、はれ、金沢はくもりです。東京は、はれ。ごごからは、くもるかもしれません。仙台はくもり。雲のおおい1日でしょう。青森は、雨。朝から夕方まで、ふるでしょう。札幌も、雨。山のほうでは、ゆきがふるかもしれません。

2)

土田：やあ、田中さん。よく日にやけましたね。

田中：ええ、このまえの日よう日に、つりをしてきたんですよ。

土田：魚は、たくさんつれましたか。

田中：ええ、よくつれましたよ。来週の土よう日に、また行くんですが、土田さんも、ごいっしょにどうですか。

土田：ええ。つりは、まだ、したことがないから、ぜひ行きたいですねえ。でも、ざんねんですが、来週の土よう日には、テニスをするつもりなんですよ。

田中：ほう、テニスですか。いいですねえ。わたしは、テニスは、したことがないから、こんど、おしえてください。

土田：ええ、いいですよ。ところで、ゴルフにも、また行きたいですねえ。

田中：ええ、このまえは、たのしかったですねえ。また行きましょう。

Lesson 8

1) Dialogue I

土田　：マイケルさん、音楽は、ジャズとクラシックと、どちらがすきですか。

マイケル：わたしは、ジャズのほうが、すきですが、土田さんは?

土田　：わたしは、ジャズもすきですが、クラシックほどじゃありません。

マイケル：そうですか。かないも、クラシックが、とてもすきなんですよ。

2) Dialogue II

マイケル：土田さん、来週は、今週よりいそがしいですか。

土田　：今週ほど、いそがしくないでしょう。

Lesson 9

Dialogue I

Mrs. Hayakawa and Barbara are talking.

Mrs. 早川：バーバラさん、これ、むすめが作ったクッキーですけど、すこし、どうぞ。

バーバラ：まあ、どうもありがとうございます。おじょうずですね。

Dialogue II　Ichiro is speaking to his uncle.

たんじょう日に、父から、イギリスの切手をもらいました。それから、山田先生に、英語のじしょを、いただきました。ぼくは、京子さんに、ボールペンを、あげました。京子さんは、ハンカチをくれました。妹も、京子さんから、ブローチをもらいました。

Dialogue III　Mrs. Yamada and Mrs. Hayakawa are talking.

Mrs. 早川：山田さん、お子さんは？

Mrs. 山田：3人です。上の2人が女の子で、下は、男の子です。

Mrs. 早川：おいくつ？

Mrs. 山田：上のむすめは、25になりました。中学校で、英語をおしえています。

Mrs. 早川：まあ、そう。で、下のおじょうさんは？

Mrs. 山田：下のむすめは、もうすぐ、22になるんですよ。デザイナーになりたいといって、デザインの学校で、べんきょうしているんですよ。

Mrs. 早川：それは、いいですねえ。で、ぼっちゃんは？

Mrs. 山田：むすこは、18才。高校3年生です。

Mrs. 早川：あら、3年生？それは、たいへんねえ。

Lesson 10

1) Dialogue I

男 1：もう、そろそろ、しつれいします。

男 2：まだ、いいじゃありませんか。

男 1：もう、おそくなりましたし、うちの近くは、10時ごろ、バスがなくなってしまいますので。

男 2：そうですか。じゃ、また、ぜひ来てください。

2) Dialogue II

子ども：何か、くだもの、ある？

母：れいぞうこに、入れてありますよ。りんごが、3つ、入っているでしょ。

子ども：もう食べてしまったから、ないよ。

母：えっ、3つも？おなかが、いたくなるわよ。

3) Dialogue III

女 1：日本語の手紙、書いたことある？

女 2：まだ、書いたことない。でも、もらったことは、あるわよ。読むのがむずかしくて、こまったわ。

Lesson 11

1) Dialogue I

島田：こちら、安田産業の島田ですが、営業の田中さん、いらっしゃいますか。

Op.　：ただいま、でかけておりますが、1 時までには、かえります。こちらから、お電話しましょうか。

島田：ええ、おねがいします。電話番号は、03-726-8111です。安田産業の島田ともうします。

Op.　：03-726-8111 ですね。

島田：はい。

Op.　：わかりました。おつたえします。

2) Dialogue II

あしたは、しけんだから、日本語と英語を1 時間ずつ、べんきょうしましょう。日本語は、漢字と会話を、30分ずつ、やりましょう。

3) Dialogue III

女 1：ウエッブさんのたんじょう日に、プレゼントをあげましょう。みんなで、1,000円ずつ、出しましょう。

女 2：10,000 円になりますね。何を買いましょうか。

4) Dialogue IV

70円と100円の切手を、5 まいずつください。

Lesson 12

1)

Dialogue A：「林さん、こんどの日曜日に、みんなで、山へ行きませんか。」「そうですねえ。このごろ、いそがしいし、日曜日は、ちょっと、したいこともあるし…」

Dialogue B：「林さん、こんどの日曜日に、みんなで、山へ行きませんか。」「そうですねえ。このごろ、ずっと、いそがしかったし、まあ、いいかな。」

2) みなさん、こんにちは。わたしは、フランク・グーディッシュともうします。どうぞよろしく。アメリカのサン・アントニオから来ました。ウエスト・テキサス大学をそつぎょうしてから、しばらく新聞社につとめていましたが、今は、スポーツ・ジムのけいえいをしています。こんど、日本にも、ジムを作るために来ました。日本に来るのは、こんどで、2かいめです。つまと、子どもが1人います。

Lesson 13

1) A：ここで、たばこをすいたいんですが。
B：そりゃ、ちょっと、こまりますよ。

2) A：あのう、たばこをすいたいんですが。
B：ああ、今、禁煙時間なんです。

3) A：ちょっと、たばこをすいたいんですけど。
B：さあ、よくわからないけど、まあ、はいざらもありますしね、いいんじゃないんですか。

4) A：あのう、たばこをすいたいんですが。
B：いやあ、それはですね、ほかのお客さんも、いらっしゃることですし…。

5) A：すみません。ちょっと、たばこをすいたいんですけど。
B：えーっと、ちょっとまってくださいよ。ああ、まだ3 時ですね。どうぞ。

Lesson 14

1) Dialogue I

「渋谷、渋谷。東横線、井の頭線、地下鉄銀座線、新玉川線、ごりようの方は、こちらで、おのりかえください。」

A：今のアナウンス、何て言ったんですか。

B：私鉄や、地下鉄にのる人は、渋谷でおりてくださいって、言ったんですよ。

A：わたし、六本木へ行きたいんですが、渋谷で、のりかえるんですか。

B：いいえ、六本木は日比谷線だから、渋谷じゃありません。恵比寿でのりかえるんです。

2) Dialogue II

A：日本で、いちばん、おおぜいの人がするスポーツは、何だと思いますか。

B：それは、もちろん、野球でしょう。

A：そうですね。野球や、ソフトボールをする人がいちばん多いそうですよ。

B：それから、テニスも多いでしょう？

A：ええ。でも、2 ばんめは、ピンポンです。3 ばんめは、バレーボールで870万人、テニスは4 ばんめで、802万人です。

B：へえ、そうですか。

3) Dialogue III

日本人のいちばんすきな仕事は、エンジニアだそうです。そのつぎは、パイロット。おいしゃさんはパイロットほどの人気はありません。のうぎょうもすきな人が、わりあい多くて、先生のつぎ、5ばんめになっています。

Lesson 15

1) at point A：

A：すみません。道をおしえてください。

B：ああ、それなら、この道を左にまっすぐ行ってください。「しゅとこうそく」をくぐると、すぐありますよ。

2) at point B：

A：すみません。道をおしえてください。

B：そうねえ。どう行くとわかるかなあ。それじゃあね、こう行ってください。この道をまっすぐ行くと、「はるみどおり」に出ます。かどに、「かぶきざ」があるから、すぐわかりますよ。そのかどを右にまがってしばらく行くと、「みつこしデパート」があります。そのデパートの前の「にっさんギャラリー」のとなりですよ。

3) at point E

A：すみません。道をおしえてくださいませんか。

B：えーっとね、この道をまっすぐ行って、2つ目のかどを、左にまがってください。「まつざかや」があるかどを左ね。それから、まっすぐ「はるみどおり」をわたって、「みつこし」と「わこう」のあいだを、まっすぐ行ってください。「はるみどおり」から1つめのかどにあります。「まつやデパート」の前です。「みつこし」のよこの、「さんわ銀行」とまちがえないでね。

Lesson 16

佐藤：こんにちは。四谷商事の佐藤ですが、課長の北村さんは、いらっしゃいますか。

黒田：もうしわけございません。北村は、今、ちょっと席をはずしておりますが。四谷商事の佐藤さんですね。少し、待っていただけますか。

佐藤：はい。

黒田：では、こちらの応接室へどうぞ。こちらのいすにかけて、お待ちください。

佐藤：はい。あのう、北村さんは、どのくらいで帰っていらっしゃいますか。

黒田：そうですねえ。あと15分ぐらいで、もどると思いますが。では、しつれいいたします。

ああ、花田さん、すみませんけど、お客様に、お茶をおねがいします。

Lesson 17

北村：ウエッブ君、あした、新宿の東京貿易に行ってほしいんだけど。

マイケル：あした、新橋の東京貿易ですね。

北村：いや、新橋じゃなくて、新宿だ。

マイケル：あ、新宿ですか。それで、何時までに行ったらいいでしょうか。

北村：10時までに行ってほしいんだ。

マイケル：10時ですね。わかりました。で、用件は？

北村：サンプルとカタログを持って行って、くわしくせつめいして来てほしいんだ。山田課長には、会ったことがあるだろう？

マイケル：ええ、1度。ちょっとふとった方ですね。

北村：いや、やせた人だよ。ああ、ふとった人は山本さんだよ。山本さんは部長だよ。

マイケル：ああ、わかりました。

Lesson 18

人事課：Your name?

マリー：Mary Smith.

人事課：You are an American, right?

マリー：Yes, that's correct.

人事課：Can you speak Japanese?

マリー：Yes, I can, though I'm not very good at it.

人事課：じゃ、日本語で話しましょう。スミスさんは、日本語、読めますか。

マリー：ひらがなとカタカナは、ぜんぶ読めます。漢字も、800字ぐらい、読めます。

人事課：漢字を書くほうは、どうですか。

マリー：100字ぐらい、書けますが、あまりじょうずに書けません。

人事課：そうですか。ほかに、外国語は？

マリー：フランス語が、少しできます。

人事課：英文タイプは、うてますか。

マリー：タイプですか。ええ、うてます。

人事課：コンピューターは、つかえますか。

マリー：いいえ、コンピューターは、つかえません。

人事課：うちは、朝、早い日がありますが、来られますか。

マリー：ええ、だいじょうぶです。

人事課：そうですか。で、何か、ごしつもんは？

マリー：お金は、いくら、もらえますか。

人事課：1時間、2,000円です。

マリー：2,000円ですか…。

人事課：ええ。それよりたくさんは、ちょっと、はらえません。ほかには？

マリー：いいえ、べつに…。

人事課：ありがとうございました。けっかは、1週間後に、手紙でお知らせします。

Lesson 19

バーバラ：ゆみ子さん、何を見てるんですか。

ゆみ子：あ、バーバラさん、このパンフレットですか。これは、札幌の「雪まつり」のパンフレットですよ。どうぞ。

バーバラ：「雪まつり」？「雪まつり」って、何ですか。

ゆみ子：雪で、大きなたてものなどを作って、おおぜいの人に見せる、おまつりのことですよ。

バーバラ：ああ、このたてものは、雪で作ってあるんですか。

ゆみ子：そうなんですよ。

バーバラ：ところで、この札幌って、どこにあるんですか。

ゆみ子：北海道にありますよ。

バーバラ：へえ、北海道ですか。で、札幌の「雪まつり」って、いつですか。

ゆみ子：2月のはじめですよ。

バーバラ：え、2月のはじめなのに、もう予約をするんですか。

ゆみ子：ええ、札幌の「雪まつり」はこみますから、早くから予約しておくんです。

バーバラ：ふうん、そうですか。たいへんなんですねえ。

Lesson 20

ケニアチーム、速（はや）いですね。今、橋をわたったところです。トップを走っています。そのあとに、4人ぐらい、続いています。えー、オーストラリア、中国、アメリカ、カナダのじゅんです。日本チームは、どうでしょうか。あ、今、橋をわたるところです。

Lesson 21

ブラウン：こまったなあ。
鈴木　：おや、ブラウンさん、どうしました？
ブラウン：ええ、じつは、だいじな書類を、タクシーにわすれたんです。
鈴木　：そうですか。じゃ、タクシーの会社に電話すればいいですよ。
ブラウン：それが、タクシー会社の名前を、おぼえてないんですよ。
鈴木　：それは、こまりましたねえ。どうすれば、いいかなあ……。あ、そうだ。
「タクシー近代化センター」に電話すればいいですよ。
ブラウン：タクシーきん……
鈴木　：「タクシーきんだいかセンター」ですよ。
ブラウン：「タクシー近代化センター」ですね。
鈴木　：ええ、タクシーでのトラブルをあつかう所です。
ブラウン：あ、そうですか。じゃ、そこに、電話をかければいいんですね。
鈴木　：ええ、たぶん。
ブラウン：ところで、鈴木さん、そこの電話番号、わかりますか。
鈴木　：うーん、ちょっと、わからないなあ。ああ、NTTの104に聞けばいいですよ。教えてくれますから。
ブラウン：114ですか。
鈴木　：いいえ、104です。
ブラウン：104ですね。すぐ、かけてみます。どうもありがとうございました。

Lesson 22 (omitted)

Lesson 23

洋子　：ジュリーさん、さいきん、テレビに出ているそうですね。
ジュリー：ええ、そうなんです。
洋子　：どんなばんぐみに出ているんですか。
ジュリー：朝の英語ニュースで、アナウンサーをしているんですよ。
洋子　：え、アナウンサーですか。それは、すごいですねえ。毎日、出ているんですか。
ジュリー：いいえ、週に3回。えーっと、月曜日と水曜日、それに木曜日です。
洋子　：じゃ、テレビ局には、週に3回、行けばいいんですね。
ジュリー：いえ、金曜日には会議があるので、金曜日にも行かなくちゃいけないんですよ。
洋子　：ふーん。朝は、早いんですか。
ジュリー：ええ。ほうそうは、9時からなんですが、うち合わせがあるので、家を6時に出なくちゃいけないんです。
洋子　：へえ、じゃ、ずいぶんはやく起きるんでしょう？
ジュリー：ええ、じゅんびがあるから、4時半には、起きなきゃいけないんですよ。
洋子　：4時半ですか。ずいぶん早いんですね。
ジュリー：ええ、朝が早いのは、ちょっと、つらいですね。
洋子　：アナウンサーって、たいへんなんですねえ。
ジュリー：そうですね。それに、ほうそう中は、まちがえないようにしないといけませんから、つかれますよ。
洋子　：そう。がんばってくださいね。
ジュリー：ええ。ありがとうございます。

Lesson 24

1)Mario is speaking.

きのう、電車の中で、わかい女の人に、英語で話しかけられてね。それで、ぼくが、イタリア人だから、英語ができない、と日本語で言ったら、その人は、イタリア語で話すんだよ。ほんとうに、おどろいちゃった。しかたがないから、ぼくは、今、日本語を勉強しているので、ほかのことばじゃなくて、日本語で話したいんだけど、いいかと言ったんだ。そうしたら、彼女は、英語で、つぎでおりますからしつれいしますって！きれいな人だったのに、ざんねんだったなあと、会社の人に言ったらね、イタリア語で話せばよかったのに、と言われたんだよ。ほんとうに、そうすればよかった。

2)

① きのうは、ぼくのたんじょう日だったでしょう。黒田さんから、花をプレセントされてね。みんなの前だったから、ちょっと、はずかしかったよ。
② ゆうべおそく、友達に、うちに来られてねえ。
③ 会社の野球チームのメンバーに選ばれてね。毎週、土曜日は、練習があるんですよ。
④ 今日は、残業をするように言われたんですよ。バーバラと買い物に行くやくそくをしなければよかった。
⑤ あの映画を見たいと思っていたら、ちょうど、浜田さんにさそわれたんですよ。

Lesson 25

男　：はじめまして。わたしは、住友銀行の山下ともうします。しつれいですが、イギリスの方でいらっしゃいますか。
スミス：ええ、スミスともうします。どうぞよろしく。
男　：こちらこそ。それで、イギリスの、どちらから、いらっしゃいましたか。
スミス：ワトフォードから来ました。ロンドンの北にある町です。
男　：日本では、どちらに住んでいらっしゃるんですか。
スミス：今は、六本木におりますが、来月には、中野のほうにひっこしたいと思っております。
男　：そうですか。わたしも、中野なんですよ。
で、おつとめは、どちらでいらっしゃいますか。
スミス：銀座のデパートにつとめております。
男　：銀座ですか。じゃ、少し、遠くなりますね。
スミス：ええ、でも、中野のほうが、へやを安くかりられますから。

Lesson 26

土田　：北村君、今度の三井産業とのとりひきの件ね。あれ、マイケル君にまかせようかと思っているんだけど、どうかね。
北村　：この前の、山川貿易とのとりひきの件も、うまくやったようですし、マイケル君にやらせてもいいんじゃないかと思いますが。ただ、今、ほかの仕事もやっていますので、そちらのほうのようすも聞いてみませんと。
土田　：そうだね。じゃ、マイケル君に、今度の仕事もやれるかどうか、聞いてみてください。やれるようだったら、マイケル君にまかせることにしよう。
北村　：はい。マイケル君１人じゃ、たいへんでしょうから、野村君にも、てつだわせることにします。
土田　：ああ、それは、いいね。
マイケル：およびだそうですが、何か。
北村　：ああ、じつはね、今度、三井産業ととりひきをすることになったんだけど、土田部長が、この仕事をマイケル君にやってもらったらどうかと、おっしゃっているんだよ。
マイケル：ええ。
北村　：君は、今、例の件でいそがしいんじゃないかと思うんだけど、どうかね。
マイケル：ええ、今の仕事は、もうすぐ終わりますから、だいじょうぶです。ぜひ、わたしにやらせてください。
北村　：今度の仕事は、いそいでいるから、たいへんだよ。残業も、これまでよりたくさんしなくちゃいけないだろうし、出張も、何度かしなくちゃいけないと思うよ。
マイケル：ええ、だいじょうぶです。
北村　：じゃ、野村君にもてつだってもらって、しっかりやってください。
マイケル：はい、がんばります。

Lesson 27

えー、では、報告させていただきます。
えー、ごぞんじのように、わが社では、アメリカへの進出を計画中でございますが、この件につきまして、大阪支社から、げんざいまでのじょうきょうが、ファックスで送られてまいりました。さきほど、おくばりした資料を、ごらんください。まず、だいいちに、土地の件ですが、やはり、サンフランシスコの中は、むずかしいということでして、えーげんざい、こうほにあがっておりますのは、サンフランシスコから、南に50キロほど行った所にありまして、土地を持っている人も、売りたがっているそうです。じつは、前回の会議に出ました、スミスさんの土地なんですが、こちらのほうが、場所はいいんですが、……えー、その後、何度かこうしょうしましたが、５エーカーだけでは、売りたくないそうでして。うちのほうとしましても、それいじょうの土地を買うための予算は、ちょっと、出せませんので、残念ですが、あきらめなければならないような、じょうきょうになってまいりました。
えー、それでですね、今、新しく、けんとうしている土地なんですが、サンフランシスコから、50キロということで、ちょっと、遠いとお思いになるかもしれませんが、あちらには、フリーウェイがありますし、それほどでもないそうです。もっと近いほうがいいんでしょうが、なかなか、てきとうな土地がなくて…。つぎに、工場について、もう少し、くわしくもうしあげますと、…
まず、社員についてですが、まあ、さいしょは、80人ぐらいで、はじめたらいいのではないかと思います。80人のうち、20人を、こちらの本社から行かせて、あとは、アメリカ人の社員をやとおうと考えております。最初の２年は、そのままで、その後、少しずつ、アメリカ人の社員をふやしていって、５年後には、200人にする計画です。工場長につきましては、現地のアメリカ人がいいという意見もありましたが、いろいろと、けんとうしましたけっか、やはり、日本人でスタートしたほうがいいのではないか、ということになりました。しかし、これも、５年後には、アメリカ人にしたいと考えております。また、工場で働く人のために、工場のそばに、プールと、テニスコートを作る予定です。
えー、いじょうでございますが……。

ANSWERS

Answers have been provided for the exercises in this text to aid the student′s understanding. Wherever composition type answers are required, more than one answer may be possible. The sentence or expression given here should be used as a guide in forming various other expressions.

Lesson 1

Exce. 1 1)はい、バーバラさんです。/ はい、そうです。 2)はい、パスポートです。/ はい、そうです。 3)いいえ、本 じゃ/ では ありません。/ いいえ、ちがいます。(メニューです。) 4)いいえ、ラジオ じゃ/ では ありません。/ いいえ、ちがいます。(テレビです。) 5)いいえ、スーツケース じゃ/ では ありません。/ いいえ、ちがいます。(バッグです。)

Exce. 2 1)かさです。(わかりません。) 2)バッグです。 3)スーツケースです。 4)でんわです。 5)ラジオです。 6)ビールです。

Exce. 3 1)A：これは、ビールですか。 B：いいえ、ビールじゃ ありません。 A：じゃ、なんですか。 B：ウイスキーです。

2)A：これは、ちずですか。 B：いいえ、ちずじゃ ありません。 A：じゃ、なんですか。 B：えです。

(3～6, same as the above)

Exce. 4 ①あれ ②どれ ③あれ ④これ ⑤それ ⑥どれ ⑦あれ ⑧それ ⑨どれ ⑩これ ⑪これ ⑫それ

Exce. 5 1)マイケルさんです。 2)かんこうです。 3)ワインですか，ワインです。 4)ゆうびんきょくですか，びょういんですか。

Exce. 6 1)A：すみません。それは、しんぶんですか、ざっしですか。 B：これですか。これは、ざっしです。 A：そうですか。どうも…。

2)A：すみません。それは、ラジオですか、テレビですか。 B：これですか。これは、ラジオです。 A：そうですか。どうも…。

(3, 4 are same as the above)

Exce. 7 1)A：すみません。 B：はい。 なんですか。 A：なまえをかいてください。B：はい (ええ)、いいですよ。/ あの、ちょっと…。/ わるいけど…。/ もうしわけないんですが…。/いいえ、いやです。/ いいえ、だめです。

2)ちょっと、まってください。 3)しんぶんを とってください。 4)本を よんでください。 5)かさを かしてください。 6)パスポートを みせてください。 7)スーツケースを あけてください。 8) おかねを かしてください。

Exce. 8 ①スーツケースを あけてください。 ②くすりをのんで。 ③すみませんが、てがみをよんでくださいませんか。 ④ちょっと、まってください。/ ちょっと、まって。

L. C. E. 1)C 2)D 3)A 4)F 5)B 6)E

Lesson 2

Exce. 1 ①日本語の本です。 ②バーバラさんのパスポートです。 ③スペインのワインです。 ④マイケルさんのスーツケースです。

Exce. 2 ①これは、だれのかさですか。(バーバラさんのかさです。)/ これは、どこの かさですか。(イタリアのかさです。) ②これは、だれのコンピューターですか。(マイケルさんのコンピューターです。)/ これは、どこのコンピューターですか。(日本のコンピューターです。) ③これは どこのビールですか。(ドイツのビールです。)/ これは、だれのビールですか。(土田さんのビールです。) ④これは、どこのスーツケースですか。(アメリカのスーツケースです。)/ これは、だれのスーツケースですか。(マイケルさんのスーツケースです。) ⑤ これは、どこのテレビですか。(ソニーのテレビです。)/ これは、だれのテレビですか。(土田さんのテレビです。) ⑥これは、なんの本ですか。(えい語の本です。)/ これは、だれの本ですか。(せんせいの本です。) ⑦これは、どこのカメラですか。(日本のカメラです。)/ これは、だれのカメラですか。(マイケルさんのカメラです。) ⑧これは、どこのラジオですか。(東芝のラジオです。)/ これは、だれのラジオですか。(土田さんのラジオです)

Exce. 3 1)A：どれが、マイケルさんのかさですか。 B：このかさです。 2)A：どれが、つちださんのつくえですか。 B：あのつくえです。 3)A：どれが、バーバラさんのバッグですか。B：そのバッグです。 4)A：どれが、フランスのワインですか。 B：このワインです。

Exce. 4 B この本は、ふるいです。/ これは、ふるい本です。/ この本は、あたらしくありません。 **C** このりんごは、大きいです。/ これは、大きいりんごです。/ このりんごは、小さくありません。 **D** このへやは、ひろいです。/ これは、ひろいへやです。/ このへやは、せまくありません。 **E** このくつは、たかいです。/ これは、たかいくつです。/ このくつは、やすくありません。 **F** このかわは、きたないです。/ これは、きたないかわです。/ このかわは、きれいじゃありません。 **G** このへやは、せまいです。/ これは、せまいへやです。/ このへやは、ひろくありません。 **H** このテープレコーダーは、やすいです。/ これは、やすいテープレコーダーです。/ このテープレコーダーは、たかくありません。 **I** このテストは、やさしいです。/ これは、やさしいテストです。/ このテストは、むずかしくありません。 **J** このりんごは、おいしいです。/ これは、おいしいりんごです。/ このりんごは、まずくありません。or このりんごは、小さいです。/ これは、小さいりんごです。/ このりんごは、大きくありません。

Exce. 5 1)A：どれが、土田さんの本ですか。 B：そのふるい本です。 2)A：どれが、マイケルさんのへやですか。 B：あのきれいなへやです。 3)A：どれが、ゆうびんきょくのたてものですか。 B：あのひくいたてものです。 4)A：どれが、バーバラさんのコートですか。 B：このあかいコートです。 5)A：どれが、田中さんのへやですか。 B：あのうるさいへやです。6)A：どれが、マイケルさんのかさですか。B：このあたらしいかさです。/ この大きいかさです。

Exce. 6 1)はい、ひろいです。/ いいえ、ひろくありません。せまいです。 2)はい、しずかです。/ いいえ、しずかじゃありません。うるさいです。 3)はい、やさしいです。/ いいえ、やさしくありません。むずかしいです。 4)はい、やすいです。/ いいえ、やすくありません。たかいです。 5)はい、むずかしいです。/ いいえ、むずかしくありません。やさしいです。 6)はい、あたらしいです。/ いいえ、あたらしくありません。ふるいです。

Exce. 7 1)B：このへやは、どうですか。 C：そうですね。ちょっと<u>ふるい</u>ですね。 B：そうですか。じゃ、これはどうですか。これは、<u>ふるくありません</u>よ。 C：そうですね。<u>あたらしい</u>ですが、ちょっと<u>せまい</u>ですね。

2) たかい/ たかくありません/ やすい/ うるさい

3) とおい/ とおくありません/ ちかい/ たかい

4) きたない/ きたなくありません/ きれい/ ふべん

5) うるさい/ うるさくありません/ しずか/ とおい

6) ふべん/ ふべんじゃありません/ べんり/ たかい

Exce. 8 1) ex. アメリカのワインは、どうですか。/ おいしいですよ。 2) ex. 東京のみちは、どうですか。/ せまいですね。/ ひろくありませんね。 3) ex. かんじは、どうですか。/ むずかしいです。/ むずかしくありません。やさしいです。 4) ex. 日本のぶっかは、どうですか。/ たかいですね。/ やすくありませんね。 5) ex. あたらしいコンピューターは、どうですか。/ べんりですよ。 6) ex. 日本語のべんきょうは、どうですか。/ むずかしいです。/むずかしくありません。やさしいですよ。 7) ex. やすいウイスキーは、どうですか。/ おいしいですよ。/ おいしくありません。/ まずいです。 8) ex. あなたのへやは、どうですか。/ しずかです。/ せまいです。/ きれいです。 9) ex. きょうのてんきは、どうですか。/ いいですよ。/ よくありません。わるいです。

Exce. 9 ① ex. 田中 ②よろしくおねがいします。 ③, ④ ex. 山田 ⑤はじめまして

Exce. 10 1. はじめまして。ジョー・アトキンソンです。どうぞよろしくおねがいします。あの、こちらは、ともだちのマイケルさんです。 2. はじめまして。ジョー・アトキンソンです。どうぞよろしく。こちらは、ともだちのスティーブンです。 3. はじめまして。ジョー・アトキンソンです。どうぞよろしくおねがいします。あの、こちらは、かないのエリーゼです。 4. ジョー・アトキンソンです。はじめまして。どうぞよろしくおねがいします。こちらは、ウエッブさんのおくさんのバーバラ

さんです。

Exce. 11 1) あります 2)います 3)あります 4)います 5)あります 6)います 7)あります

Exce. 12 1)A：ねこは、どこにいますか。 B：ねこですか。ねこは、つくえのしたにいますよ。／ねこですか。ねこはつくえのしたです。2)A：いぬは、どこにいますか。 B：いぬですか。いぬは、はこのなかにいますよ。／いぬですか。いぬは、はこのなかです。 3)A：めがねは、どこにありますか。 B：めがねですか。めがねは、テレビのうえにありますよ。／めがねですか。めがねは、テレビのうえです。 4)A：ゆうびんきょくは、どこにありますか。 B：ゆうびんきょくですか。ゆうびんきょくは、びょういんのうしろ／ むこうにあります。／ゆうびんきょくですか。ゆうびんきょくは、びょういんの うしろ／むこう です。 6)A：ベンチは、どこにありますか。 B：ベンチですか。ベンチは、ふんすいのまわりにあります。 ／ベンチですか。ベンチは、ふんすいのまわりです。

Exce. 13 1)ほうせきやの となりにあります。／はなやの まえにあります。／びょういんの むこうにあります。 2)はなやのまえに います。東京ぎんこうの まえにいます。 3)レストランのなかにいます。4)マイケルさんがいます。 5)本やがあります。 6)こうえんがあります。／ ゆうびんきょくがあります。／東京ぎんこうがあります。／ほうせきやがあります。 7)いぬがいます。

Exce. 14 ex A：あのう、すみませんが。 B：はい、なんですか。 A：びょういんは、どこにありますか。 B：びょういんですか。びょういんは、ゆうびんきょくの となりにあります。 A：どうもありがとうございます。 B：どういたしまして。

Exce. 15

L. C. E. 1)T 2)T 3)F 4)F 5)T 6)T 7)F

Lesson 3

D. C. E. 1)くるまで、2時間ぐらいかかります。 2)いいえ、ちかくありません。とおいです。 3)タクシーでいきます。4)いいえ、あまり こんでいません。すいています。5)いいえ、小さくありません。大きいです。

Exce. 1 1)すしは、おいしいですが、たかいです。 2)日本は、せまいですが、人が、たくさんいます。 3)日本語は、むずかしいですが、おもしろいです。 4)このざっしは、ふるいですが、あのざっしは、あたらしいです。 5)タクシーは、べんりですが、たかいです。 6)ここは、しずかですが、あそこは、うるさいです。 7)きょうは、つごうがいいですが、あしたは、だめです。 8)このレストランは、たかいですが、あのレストランは、やすいです。

Exce. 2 ex. 1)ええ、おいしいですが、たかいです。 2)ええ、よみますが、むずかしいです。 3)ええ、べんりですが、たかいです。 4)ええ、みますが、おもしろくありません。

Exce. 3 1)はい。とてもたかいです。／いいえ。あまりたかくありません。 2)ええ。とてもあたらしいです。／いいえ。あまりあたらしくありません。 3)はい。とてもおいしいです。／いいえ。あまりおいしくありません。 4)はい。とてもむずかしいです。／いいえ。あまりむずかしくありません。 5)はい。とてもおもしろいです。／いいえ。あまりおもしろくありません。 6)はい。とてもきれいです。／いいえ。あまりきれいじゃありません。 7)はい。とてもとおいです。／いいえ。あまりとおくありません。 8)はい。とてもいいです。／いいえ。あまりよくありません。

Exce. 4 1)まいにち、ビールをのみますが、きょうは、のみません。 2)まいにち、てがみをかきますが、きょうは、かきません。 3)まいにち、テニスをしますが、きょうは、しません。 4)まいにち、りんごをたべますが、きょうは、たべません。 5)まいにち、しごとをしますが、きょうは、しません。 6)まいにち、テレビをみますが、きょうはみません。 7)まいにち、しんぶんをよみますが、きょうはよみません。 8)まいにち、かいしゃにいきますが、きょうは、いきません。

Exce. 5 1)よく、日本のえいがをみますか。／ex. はい、よくみます。2)あなたのとなりに、だれがいますか。／ex. 田中さんがいます。 3)いつも、なにをべんきょうしますか。／ex. 日本語をべんきょうします。4)きょうは、どこにいきますか。／ex. 本やにいきます。5)いつも、なんの本をかいますか。／ex. 日本のざっしをかいます。6)きょう、なにをたべますか。／ex. すきやきをたべます。

Exce. 6 1)から，まで，で 2)が 3)の，に，が，が 4)で，の

Exce. 7 1) juu−go 2) hachi 3) nijuu−go 4) hyaku go−juu 5) yon−hyaku nana−juu−san 6) roku−juu− san 7) ni−sen rop−phaku 8) sen kyuu−hyaku hachi−juu−kyu 9) ichi−man san−zen san−byaku ni−juu 10) juu−man 11) juu−nana−man yon−sen nana−hyaku hachi−juu−kyu 12) hyaku−man

Exce. 8 1) 2時5分(すぎ)です。 2) 3時はんです。／ 3時30分です。 3) 4時25分です。 4) 5時55分です。／ 6時5分まえです。 5) 9時45分です。10時15分まえです。 6) 8時15分(すぎ)です。 7) 4時40分です。／ 5時20分まえです。 8)ごぜん8時16分です。 9)ごご11時28分です。 10) 2時40分(ごろ)です。 11)ちょうど12時です。

Exce. 9 1)(ごご)11 時にねます。 2)(ごぜん) 6時におきます。 3) 7時間ねます。4) 7時間します。5)(ごぜん)12時から(ごご) 1時までです。 6) 1時間です。 7)(ごぜん) 7時はんにでます。 8)(ごご) 8時です。 9) 1時間みます。 10) 1時間します。 11) 1時間はん、かかります。 12) 6時はんごろ／ 7時ごろ、たべます。

Exce. 10 1)あなたのいえからがっこうまで、でんしゃで、どのくらいかかりますか。／ex. 1時間40分くらいです。 2)あなたのいえからかいしゃまで、でんしゃで、どのくらいかかりますか。／ex. 1時間はんぐらい、かかります。 3)成田からあなたのくにまで、ひこうきで、どのくらいかかりますか。／ex. 15時間ぐらい、かかります。 4)東京から京都まで、しんかんせんで、どのくらいかかりますか。／ 3時間10分、かかります。 5)東京えきからディズニーランドまで、バスで、どのくらいかかりますか。／30分です。

Exce. 11 1)A：すみません。東京から おかやままで、しんかんせんで、どのくらいかかりますか。 B：4時間ぐらいです。 2)A：すみません。なごやから はかたまで、しんかんせんで、どのくらいかかりますか。 B：4時間ぐらいです。 3)A：すみません。東京から ひろしままで しんかんせんで、どのくらいかかりますか。 B：4時間はんぐらいです。 4)A：すみません。東京から はかたまで、しんかんせんで どのくらいかかりますか。 B：6時間ぐらいです。

Exce. 12 1)A：ビールをのみましょうか。 B：ええ、のみましょう。 2)A：テニスをしませんか。 B：ざんねんですが、ちょっとようがあって…。 3)A：えいがをみましょうか。 B：ざんねんですが、ちょっとようがあって…。 4)A：ワインをかいましょうか。 B：ええ、かいましょう。

Exce. 13 1)A：12時ですね。ごはんをたべましょうか。 B：① ええ、たべましょう。 2)A：むずかしいですね。せんせいにききましょうか。 B：①ええ、ききましょう。 3)A：雨ですね。タクシーでいきましょうか。 B：①ええ、いきましょう。 4)A：田中さんのたんじょう日ですね。パーティーをしましょうか。 B：①ええ、しましょう。 5)A：あしたはテストですね。いっしょにべんきょうしましょうか。 B：①ええ、しましょう。

Exce. 14 (omitted)

Exce. 15 羽田：こくないせん／ちかい／東京のみなみ／モノレールで30分／べんり
成田：こくさいせん／とおい／東京のひがし／くるまで、2時間ぐらい／（すこし）ふべん

L. C. E 1)① a ② a. F b. T c. T d. F

2) 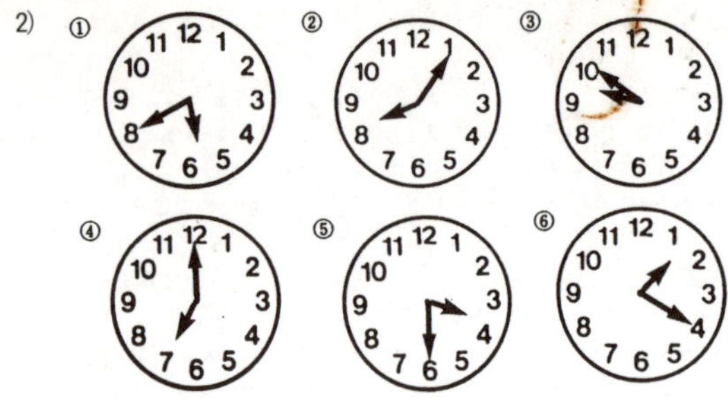

Lesson 4

D. C. E. 1)バーバラさんです。2)マイケルさんです。3)シャワーをあびています。4)ホテルのバーでまっています。5)にくとやさいでした。6)おすしをたべます。7)すきです。8)すきです。

Exce. 1 1)まえは、しずかでしたが、いまは、しずかじゃありません。うるさいです。2)まえは、あたらしかったですが、いまは、あたらしくありません。ふるいです。3)まえは、きたなかったですが、いまは、きたなくありません。きれいです。4)まえは、たかかったですが、いまは、たかくありません。やすいです。5)まえは、せまかったですが、いまは、せまくありません。ひろいです。6)まえは、ふべんでしたが、いまは、ふべんじゃありません。べんりです。

Exce. 2 1)ええ、日よう日でした。/ いいえ、日よう日じゃありませんでした。2)はい、いそがしかったです。/ いいえ、いそがしくありませんでした。3)はい、いい天気でした。/ いいえ、いい天気じゃありませんでした。4)はい、雨でした。/ いいえ、雨じゃありませんでした。5)はい、おもしろかったです。/ いいえ、おもしろくありませんでした。6)はい、さむかったです。/ いいえ、さむくありませんでした。

Exce. 3 1)はい、みました。/ いいえ、みませんでした。2)はい、しました。/ いいえ、しませんでした。3)はい、のみました。/ いいえ、のみませんでした。4)はい、こんでいました。/ いいえ、こんでいませんでした。5)はい、よくねました。/ いいえ、よくねませんでした。6)はい、よみました。/ いいえ、よみませんでした。

Exce. 4 1)B：こうえんへ　いきましょう。A：こうえんですか。きのう、いきましたよ。きょうは、うちで本をよみましょうよ。2)B：えいがをみましょう。A：えいがですか。きのう、みましたよ。きょうは、ドライブをしましょうよ。3)B：レコードをききましょうよ。A：レコードですか。きのう、ききましたよ。きょうは、プールでおよぎましょうよ。

Exce. 5 1)しごとをしました。2)はなをかいました。3)成田くうこうへいきました。4)マイケルさんとバーバラさんにあいました。5)マイケルさんとバーバラさんと、しょくじをしました / おすしをたべました。

Exce. 6 ①うまれました ②いました ③いきました ④はいりました / いきました ⑤すきでした ⑥いました ⑦べんきょうしました

Exce. 7 a. しんぶんをよんでいます。b. てがみをかいています。c. コーヒーをのんでいます。d. ビールをのんでいます。e. えをみています。f. チェック・インをしています。g. ねています。h. 本をよんでいます。

Exce. 8 1)てがみをかいています。2)おきゃくさんと　はなしています。3)でんわをしています。4)コーヒーをいれています。5)かいぎをしています。6)ex. となりのへやに、いっています。

Exce. 9 1)レストランのなかにもあります。/ 本やのよこにもあります。/ ぎんこうのなかにもあります。/ たばこやのまえにもあります。2)それも、日本語のじしょです。/ あれも、日本語のじしょです。3)本やのなかにもいます。/ レストランのなかにもいます。/ ぎんこうのなかにもいます。4)本だなのうえにもあります。/ でんわのよこにもあります。5)すいえいもします。/ やきゅうもします。/ ジョギングもします。6)アイスクリームもたべました。/ サラダもたべました。/ メロンもたべました。/ うどんもたべました。

Exce. 10 1) マイケルさんとバーバラさんがいます。/ マイケルさんがいます。それから、バーバラさんもいます。2)黒田さんとおくさんにかけました。/ 黒田さんにかけました。それから、おくさんにもかけました。3)本だなのまえと、つくえのしたと、バーバラさんのそばにあります。/ 本だなのまえにあります。それから、つくえのしたと、バーバラさんのそばにもあります。4)日本のワインと、フランスのワインと、ドイツのワインがおいしいです。/ 日本のワインがおいしいです。それから、フランスと、ドイツのワインもおいしいです。

Exce. 11 ①マイケルさんは、てんぷらがきらいですが、バーバラさんは、てんぷらはきらいじゃありません。/ マイケルさんは、てんぷらがきらいです。バーバラさんはてんぷらがすきです。②マイケルさんは、ゴルフがすきですが、バーバラさんは、ゴルフはすきじゃありません。/ マイケルさんは、ゴルフがすきです。バーバラさんは、ゴルフがきらいです。③マイケルさんも、バーバラさんも、えいががすきです。/ マイケルさんは、えいががすきです。バーバラさんも、えいががすきです。④マイケルさんは、かぶきがきらいですが、バーバラさんは、かぶきはきらいじゃありません。/ マイケルさんは、かぶきがきらいです。バーバラさんは、かぶきがすきです。⑤マイケルさんも、バーバラさんも、テニスがすきです。/ マイケルさんは、テニスがすきです。バーバラさんもテニスがすきです

Exce. 12 (omitted)

Exce. 13 1)e 2)d 3)b 4)c 5)a

Exce. 14 1)はやくうちへかえったほうが、いいんじゃありませんか。2)すこしやすんだほうがいいですよ。/ はやくねたほうが、いいんじゃありませんか。3)電車でいったほうがいいですよ。4)くすりをのんだほうがいいですよ。/ びょういんにいったほうが、いいんじゃありませんか。5)すぐべんきょうしたほうがいいんじゃありませんか。

R. C. E. Part 1 (1) 3, 6, 2, 4, 5

Part 2 (1) 3, 5, 2, 6, 7, 4, 8

L. C. E. 1) b, c, d, e, h 2)しゅくだいのノート 3)③

Lesson 5

D. C. E. 1) T 2)F 3)F 4)F 5)T 6)F

Exce. 1 1)ぜろさん(の)さんさんななきゅう(の)よんきゅういちいち 2)ぜろさん(の)さんよんきゅうさん(の)さんいちごうぜろ 3)ぜろさん(の)さんななにいろく(の)はちさんごうなな 4)ぜろななよんにい(の)さんよん(の)ろくななにいにい 5)ぜろにいきゅうにい(の)ごうよん(の)ろくいちよんいち 6)ぜろよんごう(の)ごうはちにい(の)ごうぜろいちにい

Exce. 2 (omitted)

Exce. 3 1)ビールを3本、おねがいします。2)ビールを6本、おねがいします。3)ケーキを3つ、おねがいします。4)ワインを1本と、パンを1つ、おねがいします。5)ケーキを2つと、コーヒーを2つ、おねがいします。6)えんぴつを3本と、けしごむを2つ、おねがいします。

Exce. 4 1)△ 2)○ 3)△ 4)△ 5)△ 6)○ 7)○ 8)○ 9)△ 10)○

Exce. 5 1)3月6日(さんがつ むいか)、火よう日です。2)土よう日でした。3)おととい、しました。/ このまえの日よう日にしました。4)やまのぼりをします。5)いいえ、来週の土よう日にいきます。6)いいえ、さ来週の火よう日です。7)17日です。8)ex. あさって、いきましょう。

Exce. 6 (omitted)

Exce. 7 1)ほっかいどうへいきたいです。2)サンドイッチがたべたいです。3)コーラがのみたいです。4)ビリヤードがしたいです。5)ロックをききたいです。6)やまのぼりにいきたいです。/ ハイキングにいきたいです。7)りょうしんにあいたいです。

Exce. 8 ex. 1) やまのぼりがしたいです。2)てんぷらがたべたいです。3)やきゅうがしたいです。4)京都にりょこうしたいです。5)りょこうの本がよみたいです。

Exce. 9 1)みずをのみたいです。2)しんじゅくにいきたいです。/ しんじゅくまでのきっぷを、かいたいです。3)あのシャツをかいたいです。

Exce. 10 1) ①はなす, はなさない, はなした, はなさなかった ②いう, いわない, いった, いわなかった ③まつ, またない, まった, またなかった ④のむ, のまない, のんだ, のまなかった ⑤うたう, うたわない, うたった, うたわなかった ⑥わかる, わからない, わかった, わからなかった

2)①たべる, たべない, たべた, たべなかった ②いれる, いれない, いれた, いれなかった ③うまれる, うまれない, うまれた, うまれな

かった
3)①する, しない, した, しなかった ②いく, いかない, いった, いかなかった ③くる, こない, きた, こなかった
Exce. 11 1)あした、はやくおきる ので / から、きょうは、はやくかえります。 2)チェックインをします ので / から、ちょっとまってください。 3)ゆうべ、あまりねなかった ので / から、きょうは、ねむいです。 4)テレビをかいたい ので、秋葉原へいきます。 5)いい天気 だから、銀座まであるきましょう。 6)日本人じゃない ので / から、かんじは、あまりしりません。 7)あのセーターは、たかかった から / ので、かいませんでした。
Exce. 12 ex. 1)少しやすみましょう 2)はやく、かえります 3)0 3ですね。 4)とてもやすかったので 5)かいません 6)そうじをしてください 7)つかれたので 8)パーティーをしますから、
Exce. 13 1)10時ごろ、ニューヨークへかけました。 2)りょうしんに、でんわをしました。 3)りょうしゅうしょをわすれたからです。
L. C. E.
1)

4月						
日	月	火	水	木	金	土
			1	2	3	4
5	6	7	8	9	10	11
12	13	14	15	16	17	18
19	20	21	22	23	24	25
26	27	28	29	30		

2)① c ② a ③ a 3) 03-277-9612

Lesson 6
D. C. E. 1)ちょっとつかれましたが、おもしろかったです。 2)みんな、しんせつで、あかるい人たちでした。 3)わかくてきれいな女の人が(たくさん)いました。 4)銀座のデパートへいきます。 5)バーバラさんといきます。 6)かいませんでした。 7)11,000円のアイロンをかいました。 8)かるくて、じょうぶなアイロンをかいました。
Exce. 1 1)あした、テストがあるんです。 2)じしょをひいたんです。 3)みちが、こんでいたんです。 4)くにから、ちちが、来るんです。 5)高かったんです。
Exce. 2 1)コンタクトレンズをおとしたんです。 2)ええ、コートをかいたいんです。 3)ええ、ははに、でんわをしたんですよ。 4)ええ、パーティーをするんですよ。 5)こどもが、びょうきだったんです。 6)(さかなは、)あまりすきじゃないんです。
Exce. 3 1)ええ、たべました が / けど、おいしくなかったです。 ええ。でも、おいしくなかったです。 2)ええ、かけました が / けど、りょうきんが高かったです。 ええ。でも、りょうきんが高かったです。 3)ええ、べんりです が / けど、あさは、こんでいます。 ええ。でも、あさは、こんでいます。 4)ええ、見えます が / けど、雨の日は見えません。 ええ。でも、雨の日は見えません。 5)ええ、おもしろいです が / けど、とてもいそがしいです。 ええ。でも、とてもいそがしいです。6)ええ、よみます が / けど、むずかしいです。 ええ。でも、むずかしいです。
Exce. 4 1)日本語はわかりますが、スペイン語はわかりません。 2)ステーキは高いですが、ハンバーグは安いです。 3)なつはあついですが、ふゆはさむいです。 4)ハワイはあたたかいですが、アラスカはさむいです。 5)アメリカはひろいですが、日本はせまいです。
Exce. 5 ex. 1)白くてあたらしいです / 大きくてひろいです 2)せまくてにぎやかです / ひろくてしずかです / 安くておいしいです 3)つめたくておいしいです 4)小さくてかるいです / あたらしくておもいです 5) 大きくておもいです / 白くて大きいです 6)やさしくてしんせつです 7) ふるくてしずかです / 大きくてにぎやかです
Exce. 6 1)マイケルさんのおくさんで、カナダ人です 2)男の人で、阿部産業のしゃいんです 3)ふるい町で、ゆうめいなてらが、たくさんあります 4)わかくて、きれいです 5)ひろいにわがあって、犬が2ひきいます
Exce. 7 1)このボールペンは、田中さんのです。 2)このテレビは、ソニーのですか。 3)このかばんは、バーバラさんのですか。 4)このかさは、だれのですか。 5)土田さんの車は、あの白いのですか。 6)このワインは、どこのですか。
Exce. 8 1)A:すみません。セーターを見せてください。 B:はい、どうぞ。 A:赤いのは、ありませんか。 B:黒いのはありますが、赤いのはありません。
(2, 4, 5 are same as 1)
3)A:すみません。カメラを見せてください。 B:はい、どうぞ。 A:ドイツのは、ありませんか。 B:日本のはありますが、ドイツのはありません。
6)A:すみません。マフラーを見せてください。 B:はい、どうぞ。 A:じみなのは、ありませんか。 B:はでなのはありますが、じみなのはありません。
Exce. 9 ex. 1)そうですか。じゃ、青いのをください。/ そうですか。じゃあ、けっこうです。 2)ええ、それでけっこうです。/ 10日は、ちょっと、つごうがわるいんですが…。 3)①ワインをください。 ②ええ、それでけっこうです。
Exce. 10 1)で 2)が 3)が, で
Exce. 11 ex. 1)A:このスカーフはいくらですか。 B:1まい、10,000円です。 A:ちょっと高いですね。こっちのは? B:それは、1まい7,000円です。 A:じゃあ、それを1まいください。それから、ハンカチを2まいください。 B:ありがとうございます。ぜんぶで、8,000円です。
2)A:このえんぴつはいくらですか。 B:1本200円です。 A:ちょっと高いですね。こっちのは? B:それは、1本120円です。 A:じゃあ、それを2本ください。それから、けしゴムを3つください。 B:ありがとうございます。ぜんぶで440円です。
3)A:このラジカセはいくらですか。 B:30,000円です。 A:ちょっと高いですね。こっちのは? B:それは、23,000円です。 A:じゃあ、それをください。それから、でんちを3つください。 B: ありがとうございます。ぜんぶで 23,240円です。
R. C. E. ①大きくて、きれい。てんいんもしんせつ。 ②ねだんが高い。 ③ねだんがやすい。 ④こんでいる。てんいんは、あまりしんせつではない。
L. C. E. 1) ① c ② × ③ b ④ a ⑤ ×
2) ①青いネクタイを見ました。 ②見ませんでした / 見なかった。 ③10,000円でした。 ④7,000円のイタリー(イタリア)のネクタイをかいました。 ⑤3,000円でした。

Lesson 7
D. C. E. 1)港区の区役所に、(外国人とうろくに)行くつもりです。 2)行ったことがありません。 3)すこしふべんだからです。 4)しませんでした。 5)11時すぎにつきました。 6)土よう日で、とてもこんでいたからです。 7)あしたの朝。/ 火よう日の朝。
Exce. 1 1)びょうきがなおるまで休みます。 2)あしたの朝までふります。 3)大学をそつぎょうするまでいます。 4)こどもがうまれるまで、はたらきます。 5)漢字をたくさんおぼえるまで、べんきょうします。
Exce. 2 1)ともだちが来るまで、べんきょうします。2)雨がやむまで、まちます。 3)しょくじができるまで、キャッチボールをします。/ おかあさんがよぶまで、あそんでいます。 4)いや、えいがが、おわるまで見るよ。 5)京都につくまでねます。 6)マイケルがかえってくるまで、レコードをきいています。 7)バーバラが来るまで、ゴルフ用品を見ています。/ バーバラのかいものがおわるまで、ゴルフ用品を見ています。
Exce. 3 1)A:日本のおさけをのんだことがありますか。 B:はい、のんだことがあります。/ いいえ、まだのんだことがありません。 2)A:ゴルフをしたことがありますか。 B:はい、まえに、したことがあります。/ いいえ、まだ、したことがありません。 3)A:きゅうしゅうに行ったことがありますか。 B:はい、きょねん行きました。/ いいえ、まだです。 4)A:かぶきをみたことがありますか。 B:はい、先週、みました。/ いいえ、まだ、見たことがありません。 5)A:やきとりをたべたことがありますか。 B:はい、きのう、たべました。/ いいえ、まだです。 6)A:日本のまんがをよんだことがありますか。 B:はい、よ

んだことがあります。/ いいえ、まだ、よんだことがありません。

Exce. 4 1)よんだことがありますか 2)行ったことがありますか 3)見たことがありません 4)たべたことがありますか，いいえ、まだです 5)あったことがありますよ

Exce. 5 (omitted)

Exce. 6 1) ex. おちゃをのむつもりです 2)みるつもりです 3)のぼるつもりです 4)行くつもりはありません 5)はたらくつもりです

Exce. 7 1)A：こんばんは、どうするつもりですか。 B：ひとりでテレビをみるつもりですが、あなたは? A：わたしは、ともだちとコンサートに行くつもりです。 B：それは、いいですね。

(2～4, are same as the above)

Exce. 8 1)とこやに行って、かみを切ります。 2)学校に行って、日本語をべんきょうします。3)ホテルへかえって、すこし休みます。 4)銀行へ行って、ドルをかえます。

Exce. 9 1)えいがを見てから、しょくじをします。 2)まどをあけてから、そうじをします。 3)駅を出てから、10分あるきます。 4)大学にはいってから、アルバイトをします。 5)にくをたべてから、やさいをたべます。 6)チェックインしてから、へやにはいります。

Exce. 10 6時におきて、はをみがきます。それからジョギングをします。あさごはんをたべてから、家を出ます。電車にのって、9時ごろ、会社につきます。

Exce. 11 1)東京は、きっとはれるでしょう。 2)きっとゴルフをしたんでしょう。 3)(ビデオやカメラをもっているから)、たぶん日本人でしょう。 4)(人が、たくさんならんでいるから)、きっとおいしいんでしょう。

Exce. 12 1)びょうきだから、きっと来ないでしょう。 2)くもがおおいから、ふるかもしれません。 3)土よう日だから、たぶん、こむでしょう。 4)スポーツマンだから、きっと、テニスもするでしょう。 5)しごとがたくさんあるから、きっと行かないでしょう。

Exce. 13 1) 行ったことがあります。 2)外国人とうろくをするためです。 3)区役所が、こんでいるかもしれないからです。 4)バスで行きました。地下鉄は、ふべんだからです。 5)10時まで、まちました。

L. C. E. 1)

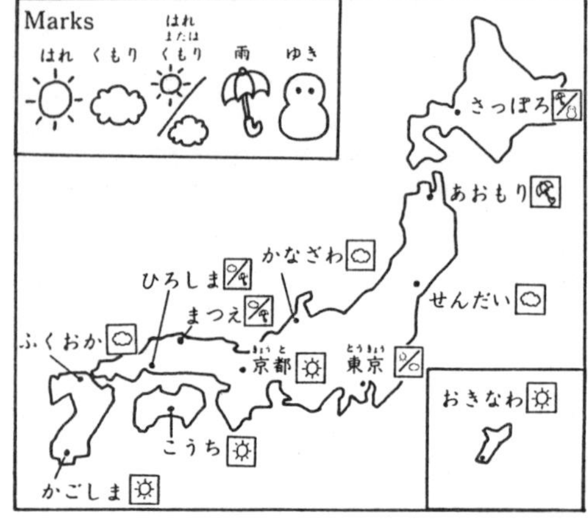

2) 田中： × ○ ○
土田： ○ ○ ×

Lesson 8

D. C. E. 1)六本木にあります。 2)しずかじゃありません。うるさいです。 3)近くありません。遠いです。 4)2時間ちかくかかります。 5)電車のなかで、大学生やサラリーマンが、まんがを読んでいるからです。 6)こうこくを見ながら、漢字やカタカナのべんきょうをしています。

Exce. 1 1)はなしている 2)しゃしんをとっている 3)スケードボードであそんでいる，たろうくん 4) (ふんすいのそばで)えをかいている 5)およいでいる 6)なわとびをしている 7)はなしている / たっている

Exce. 2 1)わたしのつとめている会社は、日比谷にあります。 2)ともだちがかったじしょは、小さくてべんりです。 3)じゅうしょと電話ばんごうを書いた紙は、つくえの上にあります。4)みちがわからない人は、こうばんに行ってたずねます。 5)野村さんが、きのう行ったレストランは、安くておいしかったです。

Exce. 3 1)うるさくて 2)あつくて 3)すきで 4)わからなくて 5)こんでいて 6)高くて

Exce. 4 1)いいえ、遠くて、ふべんです。 2)ええ、あまくて、おいしいですね。 3)ええ、にぎやかで、すきですよ。 4)いいえ、雨がおおくて、きらいです。 5)ええ、絵がたくさんあって、いいですね。 6)いいえ、漢字がおおくて、わかりません。

Exce. 5 1)ギターをひきながら、うたをうたっています。 2)アイスクリームをたべながら、あるいています。 3)ちずを見ながら、ともだちのいえをさがしています。 4)じしょをひきながら、本をよんでいます。

Exce. 6 1) 3年(間)います。2) 4日(間)いました。 3) 5か月まえに、かいました。 4) 2時間まえに、出ました。 5) 8週間です。 6)30分まえに、おきました。 7) 1か月後に行きます。 (8, 9 are omitted)

Exce. 7 1)A：ビールを、5本のみました。 B：えっ、5本も。そんなにのんだんですか。 2)A：日本のけっこんしきは、300万円かかります。B：えっ、300万円も。そんなにかかるんですか。 3)A：ざっしを4さつかいました。 B：えっ：4さつも。そんなにかったんですか。 4)A：ヨーロッパへ2か月りょこうします。 B：えっ、2か月も。そんなにりょこうするんですか。 5)A：車を、3だいもっています。 B：えっ、3だいも。そんなにもっているんですか。 6)A：石川さんは、こどもが6人います。 B：えっ、6人も。そんなにいるんですか。

Exce. 8 ex. 1)せんざいや、トイレットペーパーや、けしょうひんなどが、あります。 2)レタスや、たまねぎを、かいました。 3)やきゅうや、ラグビーが、すきです。 4)つくえや、本だななどが、あります。 5)コーヒーとか、ジュースをのみます。

Exce. 9 1)A：日本とアメリカと、どちらが広いですか。 B：アメリカのほうが、ずっと広いです。/ 日本は、アメリカほど、広くありません。2)A：6月と8月と、どちらのほうが、あついですか。 B：ex. 8月のほうが、ずっとあついです。/ 6月は、8月ほどあつくありません。 3)A：月曜日と金曜日と、どちらのほうが、つかれますか。 B：ex. 金曜日のほうが、ずっとつかれますね。/ 月曜日は、金曜日ほどつかれせん。 4)A：レコードとCDと、どちらのほうが高いですか。 B：CDのほうが、少し高いですね。/ レコードは、CDほど高くありません。 5)A：行きの電車と、かえりの電車と、どちらのほうが、こんでいますか。 B：行きのほうが、ずっとこんでいます。/ かえりの電車は、行きの電車ほど、こんでいません。 6)A：日本のワインと、フランスのワインと、どちらのほうがおいしいですか。 B：ex. フランスのワインのほうが、ずっとおいしいですよ。/ 日本のワインは、フランスのワインほど、おいしくありません。 7)A：和食と洋食と、どちらのほうが、すきですか。 B：ex. 洋食のほうがすきです。/ 和食は、洋食ほど、すきじゃありません。 8)A：しんかんせんと、ひこうきと、どちらのほうが、はやいですか。 B：ひこうきのほうが、ずっとはやいですよ。/ しんかんせんは、ひこうきほど、はやくありません。

Exce. 10 1)和食のすきな人のほうが、(少し)おおいです。 2)いいえ。山へ行った人より、海へ行った人のほうが、おおいです。 3)たばこをすわない人のほうが、2人おおいです。 4)たばこをすう女の人は、すわない人より、22人少ないです。

Exce. 11 1)えい語の先生のほうが、ながいです / モデルのほうが、みじかいです 2)えい語の先生のほうが、1万円おおいです 3)六本木より、千葉のほうが、遠いです 4)ex. モデルのほうが、おもしろいです。/ えい語の先生のほうが、むずかしいです。 5) (omitted)

Exce. 12 1)日本の車のほうが安いと思います。 2)はやく、びょういんへ行ったほうがいいと思いますよ。 3)ワープロは、べんりだと思います。 4)マイケルさんは、べんきょう家だと思います。 5)あのレストランは、安いけれど、あまりおいしくないと思います。

Exce. 13 ex 1)ええ、たくさんしたほうがいいと思いますよ。 2)そうですね、あまりよくないと思います。 3)ええ、とてもむずかしいと思います。 4)絵や、しゃしんがおおくて、おもしろいと思いますよ。 5)みちがこむから、電車で行ったほうがいいと思いますよ。 6)あまりよくないと思いますね。

Exce. 14 1) テニスをした 2)おたんじょう日おめでとう(と) 書きました 3)電車のほうがはやい(と) 思います 4)じこがあった(と) きき

ました
Exce. 15 1)どこへ行った人が、おおいですか 2)どちらのほうが安い 3)いつ、ヨーロッパへ行きたいと思っていますか 4)どのくらい(何週間ぐらい) ヨーロッパへ行きたいと思っていますか。
L. C. E. 1)① T ② F ③ F ④ T 2)今週のほうがいそがしい。

Lesson 9
D. C. E. 1)①(コアラと、パンダと、魚の)切手をあげました。②いいえ、ともだちにもらいました。③むすこが、切手をあつめているからです。④バーバラさんの妹さんのご主人です。⑤いいえ、妹さんのご主人です。⑥いいえ、おそいです。2)①静岡 ②静岡 ③大阪 ④ドイツ
Exce. 1 1)べんりになりますね 2)そう。きれいになったわね 3)すきになりました 4)お兄さんになるんですね 5)いそがしくなりました 6)遠くなりました
Exce. 2 ①まんが家になりたい ②スチュワーデスになりたい ③先生になりたい ④ (omitted)
Exce. 3 1)住んで 2)つとめて 3)あつめて 4)けっこんして 5)もって 6)そつぎょうして
Exce. 4 1)先週から、りょうりの本をかりています。2) 3年前から、大阪に住んでいます。3)よしこさんは、2時からでかけています。4) 5年前から、テニスクラブにはいっています。
Exce. 5 1)買った 2)買った 3)つくった 4)つくった
Exce. 6 1)えいがを見るの，音楽をきくの 2)テレビですもうを見るの 3)おかしをつくるの 4)切手をあつめるの
Exce. 7 1)車で来たのは、山田さんです。2)銀行につとめているのは、田中さんです。3)テニスがすきなのは、マイケルさんです。4)電車にのっているのは、土田さんです。5)買いものをしているのは、バーバラさんです。
Exce. 8 1)テニスもゴルフもします 2)テニスもゴルフもしません 3)テニスはしますが、ゴルフはしません。
Exce. 9 1)ナイフもフォークも 2)バナナもりんごもありません 3)上にも下にも 4)ワインはあります(が、)ビールはありません 5)ひだりにあるのも
Exce. 10 1)②むすこ(の)太郎，むすこさん / ぼっちゃん ③むすめ(の) 花子，むすめさん / おじょうさん 4 兄(の)たかし，お兄さん 5 弟(の)ゆきお，弟さん ⑥妹(の)はるみ，妹さん 2)①いいえ、いません。②いいえ、お姉さんじゃありません。妹です。③2人います。④いいえ、けっこんしていません。⑤いいえ、おい / おいごさんです。
Exce. 11 1)①本をくださいました。②マフラーをもらいました。③花をもらいました。④チョコレートをくれました。2)①山田先生にいただいた / 山田先生がくださった ②太郎にもらった / 太郎がくれた ③母にもらった / 母がくれた
Exce. 12 (omitted)
Exce. 13 1) 36(さい)になりました。2)田中さんのかおをかいた絵をもらいました。3)奥さんにもらいました。4) 1時間ぐらい前から、とまっています。5)いいえ。かぞくといっしょに来ています。6)いいえ、お兄さんじゃありません。弟さんです。7)田中さんのおくさんです。
L. C. E. 1)①バーバラさん，クッキー，あげ ②早川さん，クッキー，もらい③早川さん，おじょうさん / むすめさん
2)

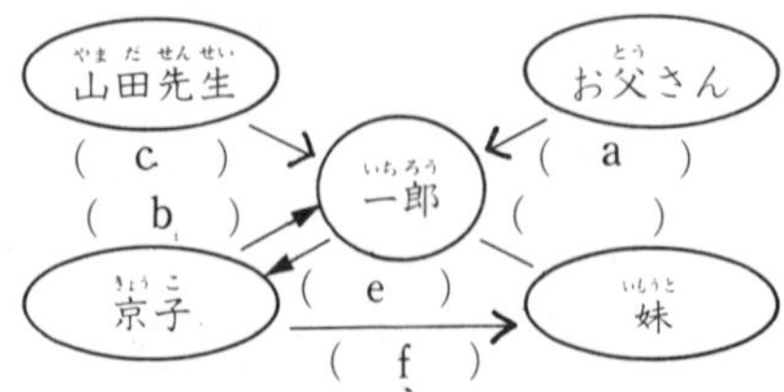

3) 1st： 女 / 25(さい)/ 中学校の英語の先生
2nd： 女 / 21(さい)/ デザイン学校の学生
3rd： 男 / 18(さい)/ 高校3年生

Lesson 10
D. C. E. 1)F 2)T 3)F 4)F 5)F 6)T
Exce. 1 1)あく，あける 2)しまる，しめる 3)出る，出す 4)きえる，けす
Exce. 2 1)きえています，つけています，つけてあります 2)しまっています，あけています，あけてあります 3)あいています，しめています，しめてあります
Exce. 3 1)ついています，つけてある，ついています 2)あいています，あけてある 3)ならべてある，ならんでいる 4)入れてあり
Exce. 4 Q：Bさんは、もうアイスクリームを食べましたか。A：いいえ、まだ食べていません。/ Q：Cさんは、もうコーヒーをのみましたか。A：はい、もうのみました。/ Q：Dさんは、もうケーキを食べましたか。A：いいえ、まだ食べていません。/ Q：Eさんは、もうおよぎましたか。A：はい、もうおよぎました。/ Q：Fさんは、もうおよぎましたか。A：いいえ、まだおよいでいません。/ Q：Gさんは、もうシャワーをあびましたか。A：いいえ、まだあびていません。/ Q：Hさんは、もうシャワーをあびましたか。A：ええ、もうあびました。/ Q：もう、2時になりましたか。A：いいえ、まだですよ。
Exce. 5 1)もう、かぶきを見ましたか。→はい、もう見ました。 いいえ、まだ見ていません。/ もう、しんかんせんにのりましたか。→はい、もうのりました。 いいえ、まだのっていません。2)もう、しゅくだいはおわりましたか。→はい、もうおわりました。 いいえ、まだおわっていません。/ もう、本は読みましたか。→はい、もう読みました。 いいえ、まだ読んでいません。3)もうあのえいが見た？ええ、もう見たわ。 ううん、まだ見てないわ。/ もう、この新聞よんだ？→うん、もう読んだよ。 ううん、まだ読んでない。4)もう、かおをあらった？→うん、もうあらったよ。 ううん、まだあらってない。/ もう手をあらったの？→うん、もうあらったよ。 ううん、まだ。
Exce. 6 ex. 1)Q：もう、ケーキを食べてしまいましたか。A：はい、もう食べてしまいました。/ いいえ、まだです。2)Q：もう、本を読んじゃった？ A：うん、読んじゃった。/ ううん、まだ。3)Q：もう、ビールをのんでしまいましたか。A：はい、のんでしまいました。/ いいえ、まだです。4)Q：もう手紙を書いちゃった？ A：うん、もう書いちゃった。/ ううん、まだ。5)Q：もう、しごとをしてしまいましたか。A：はい、してしまいました。/ いいえ、まだです。6)Q：もう、しゅくだいをしちゃった？ A：うん、もうしちゃった。/ ううん、まだ。
Exce. 7 1)この本、読んでしまうから 2)コーヒーをのんでしまうから 3)コピーをとってしまうから 4)あらっちゃうから
Exce. 8 1)小さくして 2)みじかくし 3)安くして 4)あたたかくし 5)きれいにして 6)じょうぶにした 7)あかるくした 8)ジュースにして
Exce. 9 1)せつめいしましょうか 2)もってきましょうか 3)つけましょうか 4)てつだいましょうか 5)ごちそうしましょうか
Exce. 10 ① ex. (your name) です ②おじゃまします ③どうぞ ④しつれいします ⑤いただきます ⑥いいえ、もうけっこうです / ありがとうございます。では、もう1ぱい、いただきます。⑦そろそろしつれいします
Exce. 11

L. C. E. 1) b 2) d 3) a

Lesson 11

D. C. E. 1)(山川貿易の)月野さんが、(阿部産業の)課長の北村さんに、電話をかけました。2)しりょうのコピーをたのみました。3)電話のよこにおいてありました。4)北村さんのつくえの上においておきます。5)いいえ、あったことがありません。6)ひろしです。

Exce. 1 1)むすめ(と)むすこ(が)ふたりずつ 2)エビ(と)トロ(を)みっつずつ, むっつ 3)ビール(と)ジュース(を)4本ずつ, 8本、おねがいします 4)しりょう(を)10部ずつ, 20部おねがいします 5)魚の切手と花の切手を、5まいずつもらったんです / 62円の切手と、41円の切手を、5まいずつもらいました

Exce. 2 b. お母さんは、りょうりを作っておきます c. お父さんは、ビールをれいぞうこに入れておきます d. 一郎は、げんかんを、そうじしておきます e. ゆりえは、テーブルをふいておきます

Exce. 3 1)①ホテルを、よやくしておきます。②きっぷを買っておきます。③ちずを見ておきます。2)①へやを、かりておきます。②家具を買っておきます。③けっこん式のしょうたいじょうを、出しておきます。3)①テキストを、ふくしゅうしておきます。②テープをきいておきます。③漢字をべんきょうしておきます。

Exce. 4 1)たって 2)つかって 3)のって 4)あるいて 5)かけて / つかって 6)いそいで / はしって

Exce. 5 1)電車にのってかえります 2)きいておぼえます 3)見てべんきょうします

Exce. 6 1)課長：ウエッブさん、このほうこくしょ、あしたまでにできますか。 ウエッブ：あしたですね。はい、できます。/ あしたまでにはちょっと… 2)母：ゆうがたまでに、そうじがおわる？ 子：ゆうがたね。うん、おわるよ。/ ゆうがたまでには、おわらないよ。3)客：すみません。いそいでいるんですが、りょうりは、11時までにできますか。ウェーター：11時ですね。はい、できますよ。/ 11時までには、ちょっと… 4)ウエッブ：黒田さん。このしごと、4時までにおわりますか。黒田：4時ですね。ええおわりますよ。/ そうねえ、4時までにはちょっと… 5)男：このセーター、たんじょう日までにできる？ 女：たんじょう日ね。ええ、できるわよ。/ たんじょう日までには、ちょっと…

Exce. 7 ①までに ②まで ③までに ④までに ⑤までに ⑥まで ⑦まで ⑧までに ⑨まで ⑩までに

Exce. 8 1)①ウエッブですが ②おねがいします ③でかけておりますが ④6時 ⑤おことづけがありますか ⑥けっこうです ⑦お電話します

2)①林さんをおねがいします ②外出中ですが ③ウエッブに電話をしてしてください ④電話番号 ⑤567-8910

3)you：もしもし(山田さんのおたくですか。)一郎さん (your friend's name) をおねがいします。お母さん：一郎は、いま、るすですが。you：あ、そうですか。では、またのちほど、お電話します。 お母さん：(そちらさまの) お名前は？ you：(your name) です。

4)A：もしもし、Cさんをおねがいします。B：Cは、いま、でかけておりますが。A：そうですか。では、すみませんが、やくそくの時間がかわったとおつたえください。B：はい、やくそくの時間がかわったんですね。おつたえします。

R. C. E. 1) e 2) b 3) d 4) c 5) f 6) g

L. C. E. 1)①島田(しまだ)さん ②いません ③1 ④03-726-8111 2) 2時間 3)10人 4) 850円

Lesson 12

D. C. E. 1)T 2)F 3)F 4)F 5)F 6)T 7)T 8)F 9)F

Exce. 1 1)いるはずです / でかけていないはずです 2)わかるはずです 3)きれいなはずです 4)中国人のはずです 5)来るはずです

Exce. 2 1)ちずをわたした 2)びょうきでねている / びょうきだから 3)土よう日だ 4)電気がついている 5)1940年にうまれた 6)バーゲンだ

Exce. 3 ex. 1)ええ、たぶんあるだろうと思います。2)ええ、たぶん、するだろうと思います。3)ええ、たぶんおわるだろうと思います。4)会社にいるはずです。5)そうですね。たぶんつづくだろうと思います。/ つづくかもしれません。6)くれるはずです。/ たぶん、くれると思います。

Exce. 4 ①行くことにします ②食べることにしています ③かえることにします ④にしましょう ⑤行くことになっている / 行くことにしている ⑥ことにしています ⑦行くことにします

Exce. 5 ex. 田中さんは、10時はんに、Y新聞社の人にあうことになっています。1時に、B社に行って、4時はんに、会社にもどることになっています。/ ウエッブさんは、ごご1時に、課長と大手町の銀行に、行くことになっています。3時から会議があって、7時に、A社のカークさんとあうことになっています。

Exce. 6 ex. ①コーヒー ②こうちゃ ③アイスコーヒー ④Aランチ ⑤スパゲッティ ⑥アイスコーヒー ⑦Aランチ ⑧スパゲッティ ⑨2,300

Exce. 7 1)あつすぎます 2)高すぎます 3)あますぎます 4)大きすぎます 5)たべすぎました 6)のみすぎました

Exce. 8 1)それじゃ、はやすぎますよ 2)はたらきすぎ 3)やさしすぎましたね 4)ひろすぎる 5)入れすぎた 6)おそすぎます 7)あつすぎます 8)むずかしすぎて / おおすぎて

Exce. 9 1)もし、道がこんでいたら、電車で行きます。2)もしも、100万円あったら、ダイヤを買います。3)もし、あした雨がふったら、家で本を読みます。4)もし、へやがさむかったら、ストーブをつけてください。5)12時になったら、サンドイッチを食べます。6)日本語がじょうずになったら、ガイドになりたいです。7)もし、安くていいアパートだったら、けいやくします / かります。

Exce. 10 1)はやい, べんりだ 2)おいしい, 安い / おいしい, きれい etc. 3)せまい, 高い 4)近い, ゆうめいだ / きれいだ, ゆうめいだ 5)かるい, 大きい

Exce. 11 1)きれいに / ていねいに 2)大きく 3)しずかに 4)みじかく 5)おそく 6)にぎやかに / たのしく

Exce. 12 (omitted)

Exce. 13 1)F 2)F 3)F 4)T

L. C. E. 1)A…× B…○ 2)① T ② F ③ F ④ F ⑤T

Lesson 13

D. C. E. 1) F 2)T 3)F 4)F 5)F 6)T 7)F 8)T

Exce. 1 1)かりに行きます 2)見物しに行きます 3)食べに行きます 4)およぎに行きます 5)買いに行きます

Exce. 2 1)本屋に行って、ざっしを買って来てください。2)びょういんへ行って、くすりをもらってきてください。3)銀行へ行って、お金をおろして来てください。4)としょかんへ行って、本をかえして来てください。5)区役所に行って、外国人とうろくをして来てください。

Exce. 3 1)きのうは、どうぶつえんで、パンダの赤ちゃんを見て来ました。2)さっき、新聞屋さんが、お金をとりに来ました。3)きのう、ともだちが、わたしに会いに来ました。4)きのう、わたしは、ともだちに会って来ました。5)あした、としょかんで、本をかりて来ます。6)あさって、駅で、しんかんせんのざせきを、よやくして来ます。7)来週、いなかの両親が、わたしの新しい家を見に来ます。

Exce. 4 1)だれか, だれも 2)いつも 3)どれも 4)どこでも 5)いつか 6)いつでも 7)何も, 何か, 何でも 8)どれか, どれでも 9)どこか 10)どれでも, どれも 11)どこか, どこにも / どこへも, どこも

Exce. 5 1)日本のしょうせつを読んだことがありますか。/ おもしろいですよ。ぜひ、いちど読んでみてください。2)伊豆に行ったことがありますか。/ きれいなところですよ。ぜひ、いちど行ってみてください。3)日本のきものを着たことがありますか。/ きれいですよ。ぜひ、いちど着てみてください。4)ファクシミリをつかったことがありますか。/ べんりですよ。ぜひ、いちどつかってみてください。

Exce. 6 1)行ってみたいです 2)見てみます 3)(食べに)行ってみましょう 4)着てみます 5)きいてみます

Exce. 7 1)入っているかどうかわからないから、あけてみます。2)つごうがいいかどうかわからないから、きいてみます。3)(へやに)いるかどうかわからないから、見てみます。4)(アフリカに)すんでいるかどうかわからないから、本でしらべてみます。5)新しいかどうかわからないから、不動産屋にきいてみます。

Exce. 8 1)むずかしいかどうかわからないけれど、読んでみます。2)(せつめいが)できるかどうかわからないけれど、してみます。3)あいているかどうかわからないけれど、行ってみます。4)おいしいかどうかわからないけれど、食べてみます。5)くれるかどうかわからないけれど、たのんでみます。

Exce. 9 ex. A：さるに、エサをやらないでください。 B：花をおっちゃだめよ。 C：しばふに入っちゃだめだよ。 D：ふんすいの中であそんじゃいけないよ。 E：ごみを、こんなところにすてちゃだめよ。 F：赤ちゃんがいるので、たばこをすわないでいただけませんか。 G：ここでサッカーをしちゃだめだよ。
Exce. 10 1) b 2) d 3) a 4) e 5) c
Exce. 11 1)とちゅうで、食事をしてこなかったからです。2)おべんとうやビールを売っています。3)おすもうさんが、大きくてふとっているからだと思います。
L. C. E. ①N ②N ③P ④N ⑤P

Lesson 14
D. C. E. 1) ①F ②T ③F ④F ⑤T 2)①土田さんのおくさんです。②(事務の)鈴木さんです。③まだ会社で仕事をしているからです。④おすしが、いちばんすきです。⑤いいえ。(でも、いつか行くでしょう。)
Exce. 1 1. h 2. g 3. b 4. f 5. d 6. c 7. i 8. e
Exce. 2 ex. 1)びょうきで休むとき、会社に電話をします。2)ことばがわからないとき、じしょでしらべます。3)お客さんが来るとき、ごちそうを作っておきます。4)コーヒーを飲むとき、おさとうを入れます。5)さむいとき、まどをしめます。6)かぜをひいたとき、くすりを飲みます。
Exce. 3 1)一年中 2)一晩中 3)一日中 4)一晩中 5)一日中 6)夏じゅう 7)一年中
Exce. 4 1)今日中に 2)今週中に 3)今年中に 4)今月中に
Exce. 5 1)①ぼうしと、くつしたが、おなじです。②とけいと、ハンドバッグと、洋服と、くつが、ちがいます。 2)①とけいと、ハンドバッグと、くつが、おなじです。②ぼうしと、洋服と、くつしたが、ちがいます。 3)①ぼうしと、くつしたが、おなじです。②とけいと、ハンドバッグと、洋服と、くつが、ちがいます。 4)①洋服がおなじです。②ぼうしと、とけいと、ハンドバッグと、くつしたと、くつが、ちがいます。5)洋服がおなじです。②ぼうしと、とけいと、ハンドバッグと、くつしたと、くつが、ちがいます。
Exce. 6 1)①おなじ洋服を着ています。②ちがうぼうしをかぶっています。etc. 2)①おなじくつしたをはいています。②ちがうとけいをしています。etc. 3)①おなじくつをはいています。②ちがうぼうしをかぶっています。etc. 4)①おなじくつしたをはいています。②ちがうハンドバッグをもっています。etc. 5)①おなじ洋服を着ています。②ちがうとけいをしています。etc.
Exce. 7 1)A：銀行は、まだあいていますか。 B：いいえ、もうあいていません。 2)A：まだ、雨がふっていますか。 B：いいえ、もうふっていません。 3)A：まだ、いたいですか。 B：いいえ、もういたくありません。 4)A：ケーキは、まだありますか。 B：いいえ、もうありません。(売れてしまいました。) 5)A：まだ、食べたいですか。 B：いいえ、もう食べたくありません。(おなかが、いっぱいです。)
Exce. 8 1)A：田中くん、てんきんするんだって。 B：うん。ぼくも聞いた。それで、ニューヨークに行くんだって。 2)A：田中くん、びょうきなんだって。 B：ええ。わたしもききました。それで、にゅういんするんだそうです。 3)A：田中さん、アルバイトがいそがしいんだって。 B：うん。わたしも聞いた。それで、勉強をする時間がないんですって。4)A：田中さん、仕事がおわらないんですって。 B：ええ。わたしも聞いたわ。それで、パーティーに行かないんですって。
Exce. 9 1)かぜをひいたので、今日は休むそうです 2)会議でおそくなるから、ばんごはんは、うちで食べないって 3)雨がふる だろう / かもしれない って言っていましたよ 4)やさしいって言ってた
Exce. 10 1)8月が、いちばんあついです。2)1月が、いちばんさむいです。3)9月です。4)1月です。5)10月が、いちばん雨が多いです。
Exce. 11 1)これほどおもしろい本は、読んだことがありません。 2)今日ほど、うれしい日は、ありません。3)これほどおいしい物は、食べたことがありません。4)エベレストほど高い山は、ありません。5)8月ほどあつい月はありません。6)あなたほどしんせつな人は、いません。
Exce. 12 ex. 10さいの男の子が、いちばん、まんがをおおく読んでいます。/ 男の子と女の子では、男の子のほうが、よくまんがを読んでいます。/ 大きくなると、まんがを読まなくなっています。etc.

R. C. E. 5, 3, 6, 2, 4
L. C. E. 1) 六本木, ひびやせん 2)やきゅう, ピンポン, バレーボール 3)エンジニア, パイロット, おいしゃさん, 先生, のうぎょう

Lesson 15
D. C. E. 1)F 2)F 3)F 4)F 5)F 6)F
Exce. 1 1)①テレビばかり見ている。テレビを見てばかりいる。②ジュースばかり飲んでいる。ジュースを飲んでばかりいる。③まんがばかり読んでいる。まんがを読んでばかりいる。④ひらがなばかりで書いている。⑤お酒ばかり飲んでいる。お酒を飲んでばかりいる。⑥遊んでばかりいる。⑦ねてばかりいる。⑧食べてばかりいる。
2)①テレビばかり見ていてはいけません。しょくじもしてください。/ しょくじもしなさい。②ジュースばかり飲んでいてはいけません。おかずも食べてください。/ おかずも食べなさい。③まんがばかり読んでいてはいけません。しょうせつも読んでください。/ しょうせつも読みなさい。④ひらがなばかりで書いていてはいけません。漢字もつかって、書いてください。⑤お酒ばかり飲んでいてはいけません。仕事もしてください。⑥遊んでばかりいてはいけません。べんきょうもしてください。/ べんきょうもしなさい。⑦ねてばかりいてはいけません。うんどうもしてください。/ うんどうもしなさい。 ⑧食べてばかりいてはいけません。うんどうもしてください。/ うんどうもしなさい。
Exce. 2 ①ばかり ②だけ ③だけ ④ばかり ⑤だけ ⑥ばかり ⑦ばかり
Exce. 3 1)c 2)d 3)f 4)a 5)b 6)a, e
Exce. 4 1)45分もまったのに、バスは、まだ来ません。2)電話で、行くと言っておいたのに、マイケルさんは、るすでした。3)走ったのに、電車にまにあいませんでした。4)雨がふっているのに、マイケルさんは、ゴルフに行きました。
Exce. 5 1)こおり 2)公園 3)日本人 4)子ども 5)春 6)サンダル 7)ようちえん 8)夜
Exce. 6 1)おす, ひが、きえます 2)あきます 3)テレホンカードを入れる 4)おす, 大きくなります 5)右にまがる 6)①およぎたくなります ② ex. ビールが飲みたくなります 7)まっていました / いました
Exce. 7 1)マイケルさんに電話をしたら、るすでした。2)げんかんのドアをあけると、にもつを持った男の人が立っていました。3)へやをかたづけたら、つくえの下に1,000円がおちていました。4)夕方、魚屋へ行ったら、さんまを安く売っていました。5)うちのそばまで来ると、ピアノの音が聞こえました。6)山の上までのぼったら、遠くの海が見えました。
Exce. 8 1) 1つめの交差点を左にまがって、50m行くと、右がわにあります。 2)この先のはしをわたって行くと、左がわに銀行があります。その前にあります。 3)この先の交差点を左にまがって行くと、2つめのかどに、ゆうびんきょくがあります。そのかどをまがるとあります。ゆうびんきょくのとなりです。 4)この先の交差点を左にまがって 100m行くと、かどにガソリンスタンドがあります。そのかどを右にまがって、つきあたりを右にまがって4けんめです。 5)この道をまっすぐに行って、つぎのしんごうのてまえにあります。
Exce. 9 ex. 1)この道をまっすぐ行ってください。この道のつきあたりにありますよ 2)①この通りをわたって、まっすぐ行ってください。 5つめのかどに、さんわ銀行があります。そのかどを左にまがって行くと、左がわにありますよ ②「わこう」は、「みつこしデパート」の前にあります。3)「はるみどおり」をまっすぐ行くと、3つめのかどに、「さんあい」があります。「みつこしデパートもありますから、すぐ、わかりますよ。そのかどを右にまがって、1つめのかどに、「まつざかやデパート」があります。そこを左にまがって行くと、右がわにありますよ
Exce. 10 1) ① 2) F1+F3+1
L. C. E. 1) c 2) b 3) c

Lesson 16
D. C. E. 1)四谷商事の山下さんと話しました。2)いませんでした。3)北村と言いました。北村さんが、自分の会社の人だからです。4)仕事のあと、日本語学校にかよってみたらいいと言いました。5)レポートを今日中にしあげることをたのみました。6)四谷商事の山下さんで、応接

室にいます。7)だいたい10人ぐらいです。8)曜日や授業料について書いてあります。9)いいえ。家に帰って、かんがえてみることにしました。

Exce. 1 1)すみませんが、つぎのバスは何分に来るでしょうか。/ ex. あと5分ぐらいで、来るとおもいますよ。 2)あのう、すみません。ここに、さいふがおちていませんでしたか。/ ex. さあ、見ませんでしたけど。 3)お仕事中、もうしわけありませんが、駅に行く道を教えてくださいませんか。/ ex. ええ、いいですよ。この先のかどを、右にまがると、駅ですよ。 4)あのう、すみません。お金を小さくしてください。/ ex. ああ、すみません。いま、小さいお金がないんですよ。 5)すみません。こんどの日曜日は何日ですか。/ ex. 28日だよ。 6)あのう、すみません。きっぷを買いたいんですけど。/ ex. お金を入れてボタンをおすと、きっぷが出てきますよ。(どこまで行くんですか。)

Exce. 2 1)さきに会社に帰ったらどうですか。/ さきに会社に帰ったほうがいいですよ。/ さきに会社に帰らないほうがいいですよ。 2)山田さんに、この仕事をたのんだらどうですか。/ 山田さんに、この仕事をたのんだほうがいいですよ。/ 山田さんに、この仕事をたのまないほうがいいですよ。 3)あの本を読んだらどうですか。/ あの本を読んだほうがいいですよ。/ あの本を読まないほうがいいですよ。 4)けいやくをキャンセルしたらどうですか。/ けいやくをキャンセルしたほうがいいですよ。/ けいやくをキャンセルしないほうがいいですよ。 5)マイケルさんに会いに行ったらどうですか。/ マイケルさんに会いに行ったほうがいいですよ。/ マイケルさんに会いに行かないほうがいいですよ。 6)ホテルを予約しておいたらどうですか。/ ホテルを予約しておいたほうがいいですよ。/ ホテルを予約しておかないほうがいいですよ。

Exce. 3 1) c 2) f 3) e 4) a 5) b 6) d

Exce. 4 1)① a. いいかばん b. アメリカの母が送ってくれた c. お母さん ② a. しゃれたネクタイ b. 妹がプレゼントしてくれた c. 妹さん 2)①a. 新幹線に、まにあいました b. 友達が、車で送ってくれました。 ② a. 駅までの道は、わかりました b. おまわりさんが、教えてくれました。 ③ a. 仕事は終わりました b. 田辺さんが、てつだってくれました。 3)① a. れいの書類 b. 部長にサインしていただきました。 ② a. 来週のきゅうか b. 課長にきょかしていただきました。 ③ a. このあいだの企画 b. 社長にほめていただきました。 4)① a. 買い物をして来てくれました。 b. 食事も作ってあげたよ。 ② a. お医者さんに電話をしてくれました。b. くすりももらって来てあげたよ。 ③ a. こおりで、あたまをひやしてくれました。 b. ねつも、はかってあげたよ。 5)①漢字のまちがいも、なおしてくださいました。②書類の書き方も教えてくださいました。

Exce. 5 1)この本を買って,(むすこに) 本を買ってやった。(父に)本を買ってもらった 2)散歩につれていってください,(犬を)散歩につれて行ってやりました,(太郎さんに)散歩につれて行ってもらいました 3)サインしていただけませんでしょうか,でんぴょうに、サインをしてあげました,(部長に)でんぴょうに、サインをしていただきました 4)10円玉をかしてくれませんか,(ウエッブさんに)テレホンカードをかしてあげました,(花田さんに)テレホンカードをかしてもらいました

Exce. 6 (父は) ぼくの顔をかいてくれました,(母は) ごちそうを作ってくれました,(妹は) ケーキを作って / 買ってくれました,(ガーフレンドは) セーターをあんでくれました

Exce. 7 1. F 2.F 3. T 4. T 5. F 6. T 7. T

L. C. E. 1) 北村 2)C 3)15分

Lesson 17

D. C. E. 1) ①大阪です。②大阪の第一貿易でします。③アメリカに支社を出す件についての会議です。④何も持って 行きません。⑤いいえ、おくさんもいっしょに行きます。 2)① T ② F ③ F ④ F ⑤ F

Exce. 1 1)しないでほしい 2)使いすぎないでもらいたい 3)たいせつにしてほしい 4)してもらいたい 5)きれいに書いてもらいたい

Exce. 2 1)いただきたいんですが 2)ほしいんだけど 3)ほしいんだけど,買って来てよ

Exce. 3 1)黒田さん、この書類をコピーしてもらいたいんだけど。2)あした、朝8時に、駅のまえに来てもらいたいんだけど。3)そのサンプルを、見せていただきたいんですが。4)あの、わたしたちのけっこんしきに、出席していただきたいんですが。5)時間がありましたら、このレポートを見ていただきたいんですが。6)すみません、電話をかけるので、お金をこまかくしてもらいたいんですけど。

Exce. 4 1)みきもとという店を知っていますか。/ どんな店ですか。/ しんじゅを売っている店で、(とてもゆうめいなんですよ。) 2) バーバラさんと言う人を知っていますか。/ どんな人ですか。/ マイケルさんのおくさんで、(あかるくて、とてもいい人ですよ。) 3)きんたろうと言う人を知っていますか。/ どんな人ですか。/ 日本のむかし話に出てくる男の子で、(とてもつよい男の子なんですよ。) 4)サンシャインビルというビルを知っていますか。/ どんなビルですか。/ 東京で、2ばんめに高いビルですよ。 5)カーネーションという花を知っていますか。/ どんな花ですか。/ 母の日に、お母さんにプレゼントする花で、(赤や白のものがありますよ。)

Exce. 5 1)つめたいジュースでもいかがですか 2)テレビでも見ましょうか 3)テニスでもしませんか 4)ハンバーガーでも食べませんか 5)トランプでもしていましょう 6)箱根にでも行きませんか

Exce. 6 1)おさとうを入れてもよろしいですか。/ ex. いいえ、おさとうはけっこうです。 2)このかさをかりてもいいですか。/ ex. ええ、どうぞ。 3)先生、いけんを言ってもいいですか。/ はい、どうぞ。 4)テレビの音を小さくしてもいい?/ ex. ああ、いいよ。 5)カードではらってもいいでしょうか。/ ex. はい、けっこうですよ。/ カードは、ちょっと…。 6) 5時前に帰ってもよろしいでしょうか。/ ex. ああ、かまいませんよ。どうぞ。

Exce. 7 1)A:あつくなったから、まどをあけてもいい? B:ええ、いいわよ。 2)A:くらくなってきたから、でんきをつけてもいいかしら。 B:ええ、いいわよ。 3)A:ほかに席があいてないので、ここにすわってもいいですか。 B:あのすみません。友達が来ることになっていますので…。

Exce. 8 1)仕事が終わったら、ホテルに電話をすることをたのみました。2)これからもずっと、きょうりょくしてもらいたいとたのみました。3)電話をしなかったので、バーバラさんがちょっとおこっていたからです。4)会議のあと、えんかいがあったからです。

L. C. E. 1) ①6, 6, 10 ②新宿の東京貿易 ③山田課長 ④サンプルとカタログを持って行って、くわしくせつめいする 2)① a, c ② b, b

Lesson 18

L. C. E. 1)F 2)T 3)F 4)T 5)F 6)T

Exce. 1 2)ex. もうしわけないんですが、パーティーに行けなくなってしまいました。きゅうに、大阪に出張することになったものですから。〔d〕 3)ex. 会議が、ながくなってしまったものですから。〔b〕 4)ex. もうしわけございません。書類に、コーヒーをこぼしてしまいました。〔e〕 5)ex. かえすのがおそくなってすみません。いそがしくて、読む時間がなかったものですから…。〔c〕

Exce. 2 1)ex. うたをうたったり、おどったり、ゲームをしたりします。/ めいしをこうかんしたり、人をしょうかいしたりします。 2)ex. せんたくをしたり、そうじをしたり、本を読んだり、デパートに買い物に行ったりします。/ 洋服を作ったり、犬をつれて散歩に行ったりします。

Exce. 3 ex. 1) 散歩をし,ジョギングをし 2)食べすぎ,飲みすぎ 3)ホテルを予約し,洋服をバッグに入れ 4)テレビを見,テープを聞い 5) 映画を見,食事をし

Exce. 4 1)行ったり行かなかったりです / 仕事がいそがしいときには行きません 2)見たり見なかったりです / おもしろいばんぐみがあるときだけ見ます 3)かぶったりかぶらなかったりです / 夏のあついときだけ、かぶっています 4)高かったり安かったりです / 夏は、だいたい、安いですよ

Exce. 5 1)Aホテル:①ゴルフができます,プールで泳げます,テニスができます ②日本料理が食べられます,ちゅうか料理が食べられます ③テレビが見られます,れいぞうこが使えます,バス・トイレが使えます ④ボートにのれます,つりができます Bホテル:①ボウリングができます,テニスができます,山のぼりができます ②日本料理が食べられます,フランス料理が食べられます ③テレビが見られます,バス・トイレが使えます ④バードウォッチングができます,おんせんに入れます。

2)①泳げます，泳げません ②テニスです ③使えます，使えません ④Aホテル，Bホテルでも食べられます ⑤食べられます，ちゅうか料理が食べられます ⑥つりをしたり、ボートにのったりすることができます ⑦おんせんに入れます(入ることができます)

Exce. 6 1)ニュースを 聞き取れるように / 聞き取ることができるようになりました 2)500m 泳げるように / 泳ぐことができるように なりました 3)のれるように / のることができるように なりました 4)書けるようになりました 5)うたえるようになりました

Exce. 7 1)聞くようにします 2)すわないようにします，のまないようにします 3)電話をかけるようにするよ 4)おくれないようにします 5)わすれないようにします

Exce. 8 1)T 2)F 3)F 4)F 5)T 6)T 7)F 8)T

Exce. 9 1)①課長になってから、前より残業がふえたり、休みの日も、仕事のことをいろいろ考えて、ゆっくり休めないからです。②課長の仕事が、ちゃんとできるだろうか、部下をうまくコントロールできるだろうかなどとかんがえています。③夜ねむれなかったり、朝早く起きれなかったり、朝食もあまり食べられなかったり、新聞を読むと、頭がいたくなったりするようになりました。

2)①1人で何もかもしないで、部下に仕事をまかせることを、すすめています。②スポーツをしたり、散歩をしたり、いい音楽を聞いたりすることを、すすめています。③せんもんのお医者さんにそうだんすることを、すすめています。

L. C. E. 1)①○ ②○ ③○ ④× ⑤× ⑥○ ⑦× ⑧○ 2)① b ② a ③ c ④ b ⑤ c

Lesson 19

D. C. E. 1)休みでもらいたいと言っています。2)0.8 か月分ぐらい、もらえます。3)少ないと言っています。4) 1か月ぐらいです。5)鹿児島です。6)お盆だからです。7)「盆おどり」というダンスをすると言っています。8)ほんものの桜島を見てみたいと言っています。

Exce. 1 ex. 1)えっ、こまったなあ 2)さびしくなる 3)あー、おどろいた 4)ざんねんだなあ 5)0.7%しかないんですか。(がっかりだなあ) 6)えっ、(ほんとうですか?)うれしいなあ 7)いやだなあ

Exce. 2 1)①こまっています ②がっかりしています ③うらやましそうです ④よろこんでいます ⑤さびしそうです / かなしそうです 2)こまっているようです / いやがっています /いやそうです 3)うれしそうです 4)(女の子は)くやしがっています，(男の子は)よろこんでいます 5)おどろいています

Exce. 3 ①うれしそう ②うらやましい ③ほしがっ ④しあわせ ⑤うれしい ⑥ざんねん

Exce. 4 1) 2時間45分しか、かからないんですよ 2) 2万円しか、かかりません 3)20分しかないんですか 4) 2、3人しかいないんですよ 5)1,000円しか持っていない 6) 3つしか買ってないの 7)買いに行くしかないわね 8)見に行くしかないですね

Exce. 5 1)A：鹿児島というのは、どこにあるんですか。 B：九州の、いちばん南にありますよ。2)A：A社の社長ってだれですか。 B：中山さんです。3)A：かきって、なんですか。 B：あきの、くだものですよ。4)A：夏休みっていつですか。 B：7月20日から9月5日までですよ。5)A：山のぼりに行けないって、なぜですか。 B：びょうきで、ねているんです。6)A：京都って、どんな所ですか。 B：ふるいおてらや、じんじゃが、たくさんある所ですよ。

Exce. 6 1)って，は 2)は，って 3)は，というのは，は

Exce. 7 1)斎藤さんの結婚式はいつか、聞いていますか。2)駅で何時間ならんだか、もうわすれてしまいました。3)だれが来ないか、早く調べておいたほうがいいですよ。4)大阪はどこにあるか、この地図で教えてください。5)あしたのパーティーに、だれが来るか、知りません。6)ホテルを予約できたか、黒田さんに聞いてみます。7)田中さんが何をしているか、木村さんだったら、知っているでしょう。8)会議をいつするか、マイケルさんと、そうだんしておいてください。

Exce. 8 2)A社の社長はだれか、知っていますか。3)かきって、何か知っていますか。4)夏休みはいつか、知っていますか。5)なぜ山のぼりに行けないのか、知っていますか。6)京都がどんな所か、知っていますか。

Exce. 9 1)ことばのいみを調べるために、辞書をひく。2)新幹線にのるために、東京駅に行く。3)マイケルさんのかんげい会をするために、レストランを予約する。4)わからないところを教えてもらうために、先生のへやに行く。5)ガソリンを入れるために、車のエンジンを止める。6)書類を、速くきれいに書くために、ワープロを使う。7)家族旅行に行くために、休みを取る。

Exce. 10 1)とどくように 2)聞こえるように 3)会うために 4)おくれないように 5)まちがえないように 6)読めるように 7)よろこぶように 8)なおるように 9)なおすために

Exce. 11 (omitted)

L. C. E. 1) d 2) 1 3) b 4) a

Lesson 20

D. C. E. 1) 自転車にのって、うちの近くのかどをまがろうとしたときです。2)リレーに出ます。3)えんきになります。4)黒田さんです。5)黒田さんです。6)はい。足を強くうちました。7) 3位になりました。8)ビールを飲みに行きます。

Exce. 1 1)あしたは、学校に行こうと思っています。2)もっと勉強しようと思います。3)この本を、今日中に読もうと思っています。4)あのベンチにすわろうと思います。5)10時に、会議を始めようと思います。6)あの店で、コーヒーを飲もうと思っています。

Exce. 2 ①毎日、会社に歩いて行こうと思っているんですよ。②体重をへらそうと思っています。③両親に電話をかけようと思っています。④たばこをやめようと思っているんですよ。⑤ヨーロッパに旅行しようと思っています。⑥おれいの手紙を書こうと思っています。

Exce. 3 1)プールにとびこもうとしている。2)電話をかけようとしている。3)電車に、のろうとしている。4)買い物にでかけようとしている。5)レコードをかけようとしている。6)タイプをうとうとしている。7)魚をきろうとしている。8)車が、左にまがろうとしている。

Exce. 4 1)起きるようにします 2)起きようとして 3)起きてみます 4)わたろうとし 5)わたるようにします 6)泳いでみます

Exce. 5 1)打つところ，打っているところ，打ったところ 2)火をつけるところ，火をつけているところ，火をつけたところ 3)わたすところ，わたしているところ，わたしたところ 4)食事をするところ，食事をしているところ，食事をしたところ

Exce. 6 1)くつをはいているところです。/ でかけようとしているところです。2)電車にのるところです。/ 電車にのろうとしているところです。3)これから、山にのぼるところです。4)川のそばで休んでいるところです。/ 川の水を飲んでいるところです。/ かおを、あらっているところです。5)マイケルさんが、ころんだところです。

Exce. 7 1)打った / 打ちました 2)走った / 走りました 3)来た / 来ました 4)いた、いた / 見えた

Exce. 8 1)安けれ 2)よけれ 3)車で行け 4)ひけ 5)高けれ 6)ほしけれ 7)ふれ 8)すいていれ / すいてれ

Exce. 9 1)○ 2)× 3)○ 4)× 5)○ 6)○

Exce. 10 1)がんばってね。2)早くよくなってくださいね。3)あらえば、きれいになりますから、だいじょうぶですよ。気にしないでください。4)ゆうしょう、おめでとう。5)お仕事、がんばってね。6)そんなにがっかりしないで。

R. C. E. 1) ①運動会のじゅんび ②日曜日 ③代休をとりたい ④家 2)ex. 運動会のじゅんびでは、よくやってくれましたね。ごくろうさまでした。

L. C. E. 1)

Lesson 21

D. C. E. 1)電気代のせいきゅうです。2)近くの銀行ではらえばいいと言いました。3)いいえ。1人で行くことにしました。4)自動ひきおとしにすればべんりだと言いました。5)いいえ。(自動ひきおとしにすることにしました。) 6)荷物を持ってあげました。

Exce. 1 1)①東京駅からタクシーに乗ったらいいですよ。②地下鉄で、赤坂まで行くといいですよ。 2)①日本語学校に行くといいですよ。②日本語のニュースを、毎日聞いたらいいですよ。③ (omitted) 3)①だれかにてつだってもらうといいですよ。②休日出勤をして、仕事を早くすませたほうがいいですよ。 4)①山本さんに聞くといいですよ。②機械の説明書を読むといいですよ。 5)①日本の大使館に行って、聞いてみ

るといいですよ。②図書館で、調べてみたらいいですよ。

Exce. 2 1)コーヒーを飲むなら / コーヒーなら、ラ・メールがいいわ 2)おんせんに行くなら / おんせんなら、箱根がいいですよ 3)寒いんなら、ストーブをつければ? 4)スーパーに行く(ん)なら、くだものを買って来てね 5)おくさんのたんじょう日のプレゼントなら、アクセサリーがいいんじゃない? 6)雨なら / 雨がふるんなら、ゴルフに行くのは、やめようかな。

Exce. 3 1)社長はむりだと思います。部長なら会ってくださると思いますけど。2)駅前の本屋にはないと思いますよ。もっと大きい本屋ならあると思いますが…。3) 6万円では売れないと思います。4万円ぐらいなら売れるかもしれませんね。

Exce. 4 1)金曜日ならいいんじゃないですか 2)ひらがななら書けるんですが 3) 3日後ならできますよ 4)コーヒーなら飲めますけど…

Exce. 5 1)お会いになりましたか 2)お持ちしましょう 3)いらっしゃいますか / おいでになりますか, お帰りになりますか, お電話します 4)お聞きになりましたでしょうか

Exce. 6 コートをおあずかりしましょうか。/ コーヒーはいかがですか。/ さとうを、お入れしましょうか。/ レコードをおかけしましょうか。/ 車の本を、お見せしましょうか。etc.

Exce. 7 1)お使いです 2)お帰りですよ 3)かさをおわすれですか / お持ちじゃないんですか

Exce. 8 1)a 2)b 3)a 4)a 5)b

Exce. 9 1)b 2)駅の「みどりのまどぐち」です。3)坂本さんの家にとまればいいと言っています。4)10月のはじめに会えます。

L. C. E. 1)タクシーに、だいじな書類をわすれてしまったからです。2)「タクシー近代化センター」に電話すればいいと言いました。3)いいえ、知っていませんでした。4)NTTの104 で聞けばいいです。

Lesson 22

D. C. E. 1)T 2)F 3)F 4)F 5)F 6)F 7)F

Exce. 1 ①寒いけ(れ) ②暑い ③つめたい ④すずしく ⑤熱い ⑥熱く ⑦ぬるい ⑧つめたい ⑨熱い ⑩ 熱い / あたたかい

Exce. 2 1)つめたいほうがいいです。2)あたたかいほうがいいです。3)熱いほうがいいです。/ あまり熱くないほうがいいです。4)つめたいほうがいいです。5)つめたいほうがいいです。/ あまりつめたくないほうがいいです。6)すずしいほうがいいです。7)暑いほうがいいです。8)すずしいほうがいいです。

Exce. 3 1)おいしそうな 2)あたたかそうです / あつそうです 3)大きそうです 4)むずかしそうな 5)おちそう! 6)おくれそう! 7)にぎやかそう 8)ひまそう / たいくつそう

Exce. 4 ①はんにんは、まどガラスをわって、中に入ったようだ。②はんにんは、せが高いようだ。③はんにんは、てぶくろをしていたようだ。④はんにんは、1人のようだ。

Exce. 5 1)北村さんは、病気らしいわ 2)あしたは、雨らしいですよ 3)バーバラは、どこかに、でかけているらしいな 4)じこがあったらしい 5)おなかがすいたらしいわ 6)パーティーには、出ないらしいな 7)あのねこが、魚を食べたらしい 8)あの2人、けんかをしたらしいな

Exce. 6 1)a 2)a 3)b 4)a 5)a 6)b

Exce. 7 1)小さいようです 2)田中さんらしい 3)出そうなんです 4)するらしい

Exce. 8 ①ふりそう ②ふりそう ③つかれているよう / つかれたよう ④多いらしい ⑤とれたらしい / とれたようだ ⑥おいしそうに ⑦すきなようだ ⑧ひいたらしい ⑨きくらしい ⑩なれそうな

Exce. 9 1)強くふいていました。2)とてもこんでいました。でも、予約をしておいたので、すぐ食事ができました。3)一日中、とても楽しそうにしていたからです。4)浅草…1, 有楽町…3, 浜離宮…2

L. C. E. ex. 1)けんかをしているらしい。2)料理を作っているらしい。3)やきゅうをしているらしい。4)テニスをしているらしい。5)シャワーをあびているらしい。6)プールで、およいでいるらしい。

Lesson 23

D. C. E. 1)ほけんしょうを、わたしました。2)熱をはかりました。3)ありません。4)会議の資料を作らなくてはいけないからです。5)おふろに入ったり、シャワーをあびたりしてはいけないと言いました。6)ありません。7) 3日分、もらいました。8) 1日に3回、食事のあとに、2じょうずつです。

Exce. 1 1)レポートを書かなくちゃいけない 2)日本語のレッスンを受けなくちゃならない 3)友達の子どもに、英語を教えなくてはならない 4)新しいコンピューターの使い方を習わなくてはいけない 5)家内のてつだいをしなくちゃいけない 6)友達を、空港までむかえに行かなくてはならない 7)べんごしに会わなければならない 8)入院している友達の、おみまいに行かなくちゃいけない

Exce. 2 1)①仕事のせつめいを聞いておかなくてはなりません。②ひこうきや、ホテルの予約をしておかなくてはいけません。③旅費をもらっておかなくてはなりません。④会議の資料をよういしておかなくてはいけません。2)①日にちをきめなくてはいけません。/ いつにするか、きめなくてはなりません。②会議室を予約しておかなくてはいけません。③かかりの人たちに、(日にちと場所を)れんらくしなくてはなりません。④出席する人の数をたしかめておかなければなりません。3)ex. 会社に休みのとどけを出しておかなくてはなりません。/ 仕事をすませておかなければなりません。4)ex. 住む家をさがさなくてはいけません。5)ex. 友達に、成田からうちに来るほうほうを知らせなければなりません。

Exce. 3 1)出なくてもいいんじゃないですか 2)作らなくてはいけませんか 3)いんかんでなくてもかまいませんよ 4)でなくてもいいです 5)はじめなくてもいいんじゃありませんか

Exce. 4 1) Q 1:

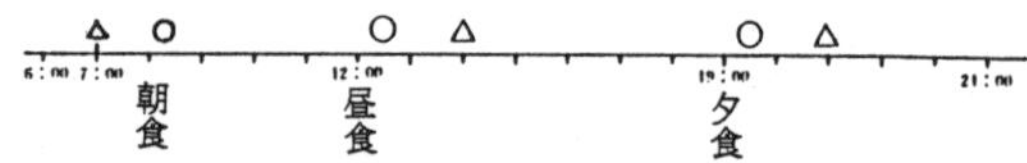

Q 2: 9じょう、飲みます。

2) Q 1:

A

10月						
日	月	火	水	木	金	土
・	・	・	・	1	2	3
4	5	⑥	7	8	9	10
11	12	⑬	14	15	16	17
18	19	⑳	21	22	23	24
25	26	㉗	28	29	30	31

B. (今週 →)

10月						
日	月	火	水	木	金	土
・	・	・	・	1	2	3
4	5	⑥	7	8	9	10
11	⑫	13	⑭	15	⑯	17
18	19	⑳	21	22	23	24
25	26	㉗	28	29	30	31

Q 2: 6回です。

Exce. 5 ①胃がきりきりするんです。/ 胃がいたいんです。②歯がいたいんです。/ 歯が、ずきずきするんです。③しょくよくがないんです。④熱があるんです。⑤はきけがするんです。⑥さむけがするんです。⑦めまいがするんです。

Exce. 6 1)胃がいたくて、はきけがするんです。2)熱があって、めまいがするんです。3)歯がいたくて、しょくよくがないんです。4)胃がいたくて、しょくよくがないんです。それに、めまいもするんです。

Exce. 7 1)胃がいたいんです / おなかがいたいんです 2)気分がわるいんです / はきけがするんです 3)おなかがいたいんです, 右のほう 4)めまいがした, ねつがあるみたいなん / きぶんが悪いん 5)こしがいたいん 6)さむけがするん 7)熱があって、体がだるいんです 8)ええ、歯がずきずきするんです 9)目がいたいんです 10) ずきずきします / がんがんします

Exce. 8 ①かいだんからおちて、ねんざしたんです。②手をドアにはさんで、ゆびのほねを、おったんです。③かべにぶつかって、あざができたんです。④ころんで、手と足をすりむいたんです。⑤ナイフで切って、血が出たんです。

Exce. 9 ex. はい、胃かいようのしゅじゅつをしたことがあります。/ ええ、3年前、もうちょうのしゅじゅつをしました。etc.

R. C. E. 1)①スキーの先生 ②タクシーの運転手 ③ひしょ ④かんごふ 2) (omitted)

L. C. E. 1)テレビの英語ニュースのアナウンサーです。2)週に4回、行かなくてはいけません。3) (ほうそうの前に)うちあわせがあるからです。4)朝早くおきなくてはならないし、ほうそう中は、まちがえないようにしなくてはいけないからです。

Lesson 24

D. C. E. 1)じゅうたいにまきこまれたからです。2)スピードを出しすぎたからです。3)はらいませんでした。4)おくさんが、すててしまいました。

Exce. 1 ①ぶつけられる ②おいかけられる ③とられる ④わらわれる ⑤見られる

Exce. 2 1)たくさんの人に読まれています 2)男の人に、道をたずねられました 3)来週、おこなわれます 4)ファックスは、どこのオフィスでも使われています 5)オリンピックは、4年に1回、開かれます

Exce. 3 1)助けられました 2)映画にさそわれました 3)はなされました 4)ほめられました 5)よろこばれました 6)わたされました 7)はげまされました 8)山田さんに、しょうかいされました

Exce. 4 1)ふられたんです 2)赤ちゃんになかれて 3)足をふまれたんです 4)コーヒーをこぼされたんです 5)とられたようなんです 6)聞かれたみたいです / 聞かれたようなんです

Exce. 5 1)みんなにじろじろ見られて、はずかしかったです 2)弟にケーキを食べられて、おこりました 3)母に朝早くおこされて、ねむいようです 4)きゅうに、ひしょにやめられて、こまっています 5)前にすわられて、映画がよく見えませんでした

Exce. 6 1)お母さんに、本を読んでもらっています 2)車にはねられました 3)じゅうたいにまきこまれています 4)a.たんかで、運んでもらいました b.男の人が、たんかで、運ばれています 5)風に、ぼうしをとばされました 6)子どもが、ピアノをひいてくれました 7)子どもが、料理をてつだってくれています 8)コンピューターの使い方を、おしえてもらっています

Exce. 7 1)しばらく、お酒を飲まないように 2)京都のおかしを買って来るように 3)もっと字をきれいに書くように 4)へやをきれいにするように 5)あした、また来るように 6)電気代を、自動ひきおとしにするように

Exce. 8 1)電話をするように / 電話をさしあげるように 2)買って来るように 3)音を小さくするように 4)早くおふろから出るように / あがるように 5)早くしあげるように

Exce. 9 1)しんごうを、よく見ればいいのに / もう少し待てばいいのに 2)a. 車で来ればよかった / タクシーが来ればいいのに b. かさを持って来ればよかったのに 3)バーバラは、電話をしてくれればいいのに 4)子どももつれて行けばいいのに 5)しゅくだいをしてくれるロボットがいればいいのに 6)もっと大きな魚がつれればよかったのに / もっと大きい魚だったらよかったのに 7)おまわりさんに聞けばいいのに 8)あんなに食べなければいいのに

Exce. 10 1)土田部長とゴルフに行くはずだったのに 2)休みをとって、京都に行くはずだったのに 3)花田さんも来るはずだったのに

Exce. 11 1)日本語学校から帰るとちゅうです。2)本屋のおばさんです。3)はい、そうです。4)雨にぬれて歩いているようすを見て、言いました。5)じろじろ見ていました。6)日本人は、雨にぬれるのがきらいだし、雨にぬれている人を見るのもがまんできないらしいということ。

L. C. E. 1)①英語で話しかけられました。②今、日本語を勉強しているので、日本語で話したいから。③英語で、つぎでおりますと言って、電車をおりてしまいました。④イタリア語で話せばよかったのにと言いました。2) ①○ ②× ③○ ④× ⑤○

Lesson 25

D. C. E. 1)1回目は、松下さんが会議中で、話せなかったからです。2)じぶんの会社の製品について説明するために、会ってもらうことです。3) 金曜日の3時です。4)ヨーロッパに輸出したいと思っています。6)松下さんの会社では、ヨーロッパの会社とのとりひきが多いからです。7)部長とよく話してから、返事をするとこたえました。

Exce. 1 1)たずねます / おたずねになります / うかがいます 2)飲みます / めしあがります / いただきます 3)見せます / お見せになります / お見せします 4)来ます / いらっしゃいます / まいります 5)言います / おっしゃいます / もうします 6)します / なさいます / いたします 7)見ます / ごらんになります / はいけんします 8)行きます / いらっしゃいます / まいります

Exce. 2 1)①いらっしゃいます ②いらっしゃいます ③なさいます ④ごらんになりました ⑤いただきます ⑥持ってまいります 2)①いらっしゃった，ごぞんじです ②いらっしゃいます ③めしあがる，ごぞんじでした ④お会いになった ⑤おっしゃっていました ⑥いらっしゃいました 3)①いらっしゃいませんでした，電話をいたします ②お見せしました，お見せしました，おっしゃいました ③来ていただけそう，いらしていただけそう

Exce. 3 1)おっしゃっていますよ 2)めしあがってみてください 3)出ております，まいります，お待ちください 4)ごぞんじですか 5)お会いしたい，おうかがいしたい，ぞんじます 6)おります，いらっしゃって

Exce. 4 祖母：お国はどちらですか。/ キャシー：アメリカです。おばあさんは、おいくつですか。/ 祖母：78さいです。/（キャシー：お元気そうですね。）/ 母：学生さんですか、それとも、何か仕事をしていらっしゃるんですか。/ キャシー：ニューヨーク・タイムスの新聞記者をしています。お母さんは、何かお仕事をなさっているんですか。/ 母：大学で、英語を教えているんですよ。キャシーさんは、今、どこに住んでいらっしゃるんですか。/ キャシー：六本木にすんでいます。/ 母：孝とは、どこで、知り合ったんですか。/ キャシー：六本木のディスコです。ところで、お父さんは、どんなお仕事をなさっているんですか。/ 父：山川貿易につとめているんですよ。キャシーさんは、アメリカのどこで、お生まれになったんですか。/ キャシー：ニューヨークで生まれました。お兄さんは、お仕事は、何をなさっているんですか。/ 兄：テレビ局のアナウンサーをしているんですよ。キャシーさんは、日本語がじょうずですね。どこで、勉強なさったんですか。/ キャシー：イリノイ大学で勉強しました。お兄さんは、お仕事で、外国にいらっしゃることがあるんですか。/ 兄：ええ、ときどき、ありますよ。/ 父：キャシーさんは、いつまで、日本にいらっしゃるんですか。/ キャシー：来年の3月まで、います。お兄さんは、アメリカへ出張する予定はないんですか。/ 兄：ありますよ。来年の4月に行く予定です。むこうでお会いできるといいですね。

Exce. 5 1)いいえ、安くてもおいしいですよ 2)熱くてもだいじょうぶですよ 3)ええ、雨がふっても行きます 4)いいえ、おそくても、おきてまっていますよ 5)いいえ、こんでいても行きます

Exce. 6 1)A：つかれているんでしょう？ うちに帰ったらどうですか。 B：ex. 今から、だいじな会議があるので、いくらつかれていても、帰れないんですよ。2)A：いやな仕事なんでしょう？ ことわったらどうですか。 B：ほかにする人がいないから、いくらいやな仕事でもことわれないんですよ。3)A：お金がないんでしょう？ ご両親にかりたらどうですか。 B：両親は、今、旅行中なので、お金をかりたくても、かりられないんですよ。4)A：胃のぐあいがわるいんでしょう？お酒を飲むのをやめたらどうですか。 B：すきだから、いくら胃のぐあいが悪くても、なかなかやめられないんですよ。

Exce. 7 1)雨がふっても行くよ 2)やっても食べないんです 3)子どもでもビールを飲むんですよ 4)高くてもほしいんです 5)遠くても歩いて行きます 6)（こんな字は、）日本人でも読めませんよ 7)おまわりさんに聞いてもわからなかったんです 8)子どもでも知っていますよ

Exce. 8 1) b 2) 3) a 4) a 5) b

Exce. 9 1)習ったのに 2)練習しても 3)書いたら 4)行ったのに 5)行っても 6)安くても 7)注意しても

Exce. 10 1)マイケルさんが、山川貿易の松下さんに出したものです。2)先日たのんだ、（阿部産業の工業用ロボットをヨーロッパに輸出する）件についてのけんとうをしてくれるようにたのんでいます。3)ドイツ語とフランス語の資料を送ると書いてあります。4)くわしいないようについて質問があるときに、また行くつもりです。5)ヨーロッパの会社への説明に使ってもらうためです。

L. C. E. 男の人：山下（やました），日本，中野（なかの），住友（すみとも）銀行 / 女の人：スミス，イギリス，六本木（ろっぽんぎ），銀座（ぎんざ）のデパート

Lesson 26

D. C. E. 1)斎藤さんに、何がほしいか、聞いてみることにしました。2)5、6万円です。3)田辺係長です。4)電気製品（アイロンとトースター）です。5)田辺係長の友達の店で買うことになりました。6)黒田さんは、字がきれいだからです。7)宅配便で、斎藤さんのうちにとどけられます。

Exce. 1 a. 習わせています b. 野球をさせて c. 習わせていません d. させています e. ならべさせます f. 食器をあらわせます g. おつかいに行かせます h. 犬の散歩をさせます i. ごはんをたかせます j. 庭のそうじをさせます k. 外で遊ばせます

Exce. 2 1)わらわせています 2)赤ちゃんにミルクを飲ませています 3)マイケルさんを待たせています 4)取って来させています 5)取らせています 6)走らせています 7)(読んで) 聞かせています

Exce. 3 1)行かせてください 2)帰らせていただきたい 3)使わせていただけませんでしょう 4)習わせて 5)はらわせてください 6)結婚させてくださる 7)言わせてください

Exce. 4 1)コピーばかり取らせないでください。2)お茶をいれさせないでください。3)ことわりの電話をかけさせないでください。

(4 ～ 8 are same as the above.)

Exce. 5 1)①食べさせています ②食べさせられています 2)①(けしょうひんを)買わせています ②(けしょうひんを)買わされています 3)①お茶をいれさせています ②お茶をいれさせられています 4)①買い物に行かせています ②買い物に行かされています

Exce. 6 (2) お茶をいれさせられるのは、いやです。3)ことわりの電話をかけさせられるのは、いやです。4)おそくまで残業させられるのは、いやです。

(5 ～ 8 are the same as above)

Exce. 7 1)きのうは、会社に 行かないで / 行かずに、家でねていました。2)その電車は、駅に 止まらないで / 止まらずに、通りすぎました。3)父は、3日間、うちに 帰らないで / 帰らずに、会社で仕事をしていました。4)今夜は、うちで、テレビを 見ないで / 見ずに、会議の報告書を書きます。5)マイケルさんは、北村さんにあいさつをせずに、家に帰ってしまいました。6)マイケルさんのつごうを聞かずに、マイケルさんのうちをたずねました。7)店で、この服を着てみないで買って帰ったら、小さすぎました。

Exce. 8 1)ねないで / ねずに 2)着ないで / 着ずに 3)けさずに 4)のらないで / のらずに 5)持たずに来て 6)もらわずに

Exce. 9 1)わからないときもあります 2)こんでいることもある 3)するときもあります 4)することがあるんです 5)場合もあります，場合もあります / ときもありますし，ときもあります

Exce. 10 1)①車でいらっしゃることもあります / 車のときもあります ②たぶん車で来ていらっしゃるでしょう / 車でいらっしゃっているかもしれません 2)①買えるだろうと ②ないことがある 3)①帰って来ることもある ②たぶん、早く帰って来るでしょう 4)こともあります

Exce. 11 1)会社の女性に、お茶をいれてもらえなくなったからです。)お茶をいれてくれるロボットで、言葉も話せます。3)ロボちゃんです。4)ロボちゃんが、おいしいコーヒーを飲ませてくれるからです。5)田中氏にお茶をいれないで、女性にコーヒーや、ジュースを飲ませているからです。6)「持たせます」というのは、ほかの人に、何かをさせるときに使う言い方だからです。

L. C. E. 1)三井産業 (みついさんぎょう) とのとりひきの仕事をさせたいと思っています。2)マイケルさんが、山川貿易とのとりひきを、うまくやったからです。3)したいと思っています。4)今までよりも多くの残業や出張をしなければなりません。5)いいえ、野村さんといっしょにします。

Lesson 27

D. C. E. 1)かりた家に、家具がついていなかったことです。2)いいえ、持って行きません。(ひっこし先で、新しく買うことにしています。) 3)来週の土曜日に、はこんでくれることになっています。4)田辺さんの(へたな)字を読まされたことです。5)使っていませんでした。6)あまり、習いたがっていないようです。

Exce. 1 〔A〕 **a.** 7，K **c.** 5，K **d.** 2，M **f.** 9，K **h.** 3，K **i.** 11，K **l.** 4，M **m.** 10，M **n.** 14，M (〔B〕，〔C〕 are omitted)

Exce. 2 ex. ①転勤するんですって ②おてつだいしましょうか ③ぜんぶやってくれる ④よかったですね ⑤どうしたんですか ⑥行きたくないんです ⑦1年しかたっていないし ⑧3時間ぐらいです ⑨遊びに来ますね ⑨映画を見に行ったりしましょう ⑪ください ⑫書くように

Exce. 3 (omitted)

Exce. 4 ①開いて ②ありました ③しあわせでした ④働く ⑤なった ⑥わからない ⑦知らなかった ⑧しんぱいでした ⑨来る ⑩買って ⑪勉強しました ⑫ちがいます ⑬書い ⑭なった ⑮行っ ⑯思っていた ⑰着いて ⑱わからない ⑲勉強した ⑳教えて ㉑乗っ ㉒来る ㉓話せる ㉔行って ㉕わすれません ㉖いらっしゃる / おいでになる ㉗楽しみにしております

Exce. 5 (omitted)

Exce. 6

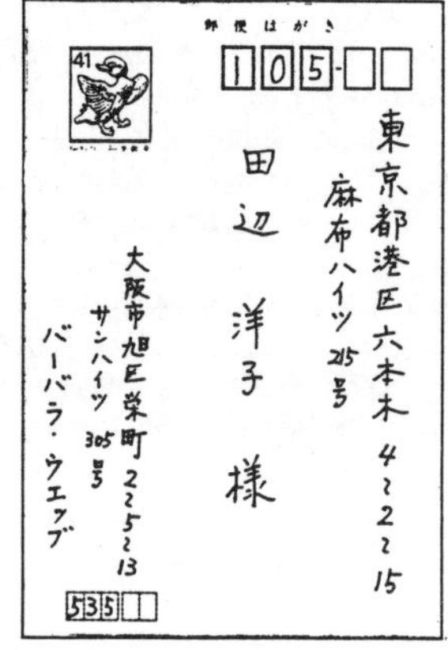

(letter is omitted)

Exce. 7：1)25 才 2)メリーランド大学 ビジネススクール卒業 (MBA) 3)東洋学 4)パートタイムで、通訳(つうやく)をしたことがあります。5)東京で働きたいし、日本の会社のシステムにきょうみがあるから。

L. C. E. 1)**Part 1**：① × (近くにある→近くにない) ② × (北→みなみ) ③ ○ ④ × (売りたがっている→売りたがっていない) ⑤ × (アメリカ人→日本人) **Part 2**：① × (60人→20人 / 日本人→アメリカ人) ② ○ ③ ×(アメリカ人→日本人)

2)

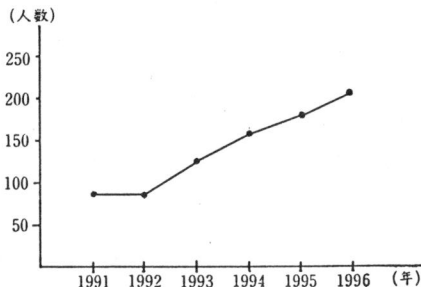

(人数)
250
200
150
100
50
1991 1992 1993 1994 1995 1996 (年)

Quiz

1 ①を ②で ③は ④が ⑤に ⑥に ⑦ごろ ⑧で ⑨って ⑩が ⑪を ⑫を ⑬に ⑭が ⑮の ⑯に

2 1) a 2) b 3) b 4) a 5) b, c 6) b 7) a, d, e 8) a, d 9) b, d 10) a, c 11) b 12) b 13) b

3 1)おふろに入ろうとしたところに 2) 学生なのに 3) わかいうちに 4) じゅんびをするために 5) もんくを言わないで 6) 売れるように 7) 食べながら

4 1)たぶん / きっと 2)きっと 3) もっと 4) ぜひ 5) おおぜい / ずいぶん 6) ずいぶん 7) やっぱり

5 1)飲めたら / 飲めると 2)止められたんです 3)行ったほうがいいですよ 4)起きて 5) わらわせる 6) 送ってもらった 7) 言われました 8) お会いしたい / お目にかかりたい，いらっしゃいます 9) 働いても 10)できるようになりました

INDEX

photo by Dave TELKE

1. This index lists all the words and many of the expressions used in this text. Each entry includes romanized spelling, Kanji or Kana, the meaning in English and the page on which the word first appears. More detailed explanations are found on pages listed in boldface type. Consult the text for example of actual usage.
2. Verbs and other words which change with use are given in their dictionary form.
3. Due to matters of space, several words borrowed from English and closely resembling English in pronunciation have been omitted.

A

‘Sudden shower on Nihonbashi’ *Ukiyoe* by Hiroshige ANDO

PARTICLES AND OTHER GRAMMATICAL MARKERS

は[wa]	sentence topic
が	subject ("doer" or "undergoer" of the action, state, etc.)
を[o]	direct object (thing acted upon)
に	(1) indirect object ("receiver" of the action)
	(2) location or target toward which the action or motion progresses (to)
	(3) location in/at which something exists, resides, etc.
	(4) time (at, in)
	(5) purpose (to)
で	(1) implement or means (by, with)
	(2) location in/at which the action occurs or is done
	(3) cause, reason or purpose
へ[e]	direction (to, toward)
から	from (beginning point in time or place, origin)
まで	until (up to and including)
の	"possessive" marker
と	(1) __ and __ (2) together with (3) quotation marker
か	(1) question marker (2) __ or __
や	__, __, etc.
とか	for example, __, __, etc.
も	also, too, as well as, even
が	(1) but (2) softening
けれども	but
でも	however, but
しかし	however, but
ところが	but in fact
から	because
ので	because
のに	even though, in spite of the fact that
とき	when
ところで	by the way, to change the subject …
そして	then
そうしたら	and then
そうなら	if so, if that's the case
それから	and then, next …
それに	besides, moreover
それで	and then, consequently, for that reason
それとも	or else
それでも	even so, in spite of that
ね	tag question marker
よ	emphasis
わ	emphasis (women)
かな	I wonder __
かしら	I wonder __ (women)